Test
to a
New Dawn

Messages for Humankind
Volume 1

by

Michael Champion

Grosvenor House
Publishing Limited

This book is published by
Grosvenor House Publishing Ltd
Link House
140 The Broadway, Tolworth, Surrey, KT6 7HT.
www.grosvenorhousepublishing.co.uk

A CIP record for this book
is available from the British Library

ISBN 978-1-78623-629-6

TESTAMENT TO A NEW DAWN

transcripts channelled by
Michael Champion

compiled by
Kevin and Valerie Bruce-Smith
Cover Illustration by Kevin Bruce-Smith, CamelArt

Dedicated in loving memory to:

Beatrice Champion:
31 August 1949 to 25 February 2017.

Valerie Jean Champion:
13 February 1932 to 06 January 2017.

Dennis Champion:
15 April 1928 to 30 April 2016.

messagesformankind.wordpress.com

CONTENTS

As far as we have been able, the transcripts have been divided into sections according to the communicator bringing forward the messages or into various subject matter. Within each section the transcripts are then in date order.

We are given kind permission to use the
following words from

Ali Calderwood and Daniela Lanaia of
Anima Sound Medicine

www.animacreations.co.uk

The following beautiful words encapsulate the sentiment
of 'Messages for Mankind' and the words within them
that are dedicated to the whole of humanity, courtesy of
the many beings who watch over us.

The original words can be found within the CD cover of
'Temple of the Stars' by Anima

*"In honour of the Ancient Ones, our Star Relations and
those of Spirit who dwell in the higher dimensions,
guarding the sacred flames of love and light. May we
each remember the Spirit that dwells within us, the
sacredness of all life. The Earth, the Moon, the Sun, the
Stars and the Sacred Centre where the will of God
indwells. For we are each a speck in the fabric of
creation, all playing our part; waves in the ocean rising
up and returning... again and again.*

*May we have the vision to see far and wide; to find the
lessons laid out by the Creator, within every leaf, every
stone, within every story ever told.*

Through thought and sound and action we cocreate in resonance and beauty – Manifesting Heaven upon our Blessed Mother Earth. Shining in the purity of everlasting light, amongst our relations of the stars and beyond.

As the Councils of Light watch over us in each moment, silently whispering words of guidance in our ears, may we be in alignment with the Light of Consciousness and remember who we are.

In dedication to those who have trodden the paths before us, the Spirits who guide and heal and imbue honour of the Spirit of Creation; our Mother and Father of Eternity and Truth.

It is time for humanity to open our eyes, to open our hearts, to open our minds.

Created in the image of love, we are all that we could ever dream. So dream your dream and believe in Sacred Service. We are what we choose to be."

FOREWORD

The Meeting of the 'Trio'
Michael Champion and Kevin and Valerie Bruce-Smith

By Valerie and Kevin Bruce-Smith

The rain was teaming down and the canvas of our marquee was flapping wildly in the wind, it was not exactly an inviting place to entice people in to investigate our wares. It was April 2015 and we were attempting to promote Kevin's artwork at a Psychic Fayre in Cornwall, hosted by a popular English medium, (sadly, now the late) Colin Fry. A more miserable environment for attracting customers would be hard to imagine. No one felt inclined to wander into this dreary, damp tent to see us, that is, apart from Michael!

Like a ray of sunshine he approached our display showing signs of interest for one of Kevin's paintings. We exchanged polite conversation with him, sizing up each other's level of understanding regarding spiritual subjects before we relaxed into openly explaining some of Kevin's work. (Not everyone is ready to listen.) Michael mentioned that he was a medium, using his words, he was beginning to 'channel' information, we now more accurately understand this to be 'mind linking'. At that time it was a new experience for him, one that he was unsure about. Until recently his contact with spirit was confined to passing messages from people's loved ones, so receiving communication from North American Indians and other 'Beings' was a little unnerving. His main concern was wondering if it was coming from a 'Place of Light'. After listening to Michael, we instinctively knew that his messages were important, so we promised to follow the communications on his social media site. We wrapped up Michaels newly acquired painting and bade him farewell, not expecting to see each other again. At that time we lived some 200 miles apart, since then, Michael moved even further away from us. We live in the South West of England and Michael has moved to Scotland.

It didn't take us long to recognise the powerful communications received by Michael were very important, they needed to be shared with as many people as possible and social media was not proving ideal. The long transcripts were too difficult to read on this medium. By Michael's own admission, he didn't have a full understanding of the content at that time, so we offered help to proofread the messages and place the content word for word on a blog site, with added explanations when it felt appropriate.

From Michael's transcript of 5th May 2016

"Two others will come before you my son, their purpose is to travel with you on a road of light, compel your heart to listen and understand the meaning that they represent. For us, time is but a passage to be travelled, for once you have been a part of that moment, it will not return."

What a privilege it turned out to be, listening to the recordings of the trance sessions and hearing the variation in voices of the 'Beings' as they came to speak through Michael. He has suffered criticism regarding the content on occasions, however we cannot stress strongly enough that the voices are so gentle, the words come through in the tone of very a loving father, one who is desperately trying to prevent his wayward children from heading further astray. So yes, of course there are warnings that may seem harsh, but they are balanced with wise teachings and philosophy. Sometimes well renowned people from our past 'pop in', as well as characters like Winston Churchill, whose voice and tone is unmistakable!

Some readers have found the biblical style of some messages off putting. The words are not Michaels, so please don't shoot the messenger! They are intended for all faiths as well as those who have none.

Let excerpts from the transcripts speak for themselves on this matter:

From the transcript of 1st November 2016:

"It is hard to accept that you are all part of a universal spirit that exists within the hearts of you all, but you must realise that your lives are but a mere passing of time. We can assure you that we will be there, not as a masquerade but as a parent, as the teacher to the students, to nurture you and favour those who have bought there being to an aspect of the light. We come as teachers to many, in various forms, allowing secrets to be divulged in practices that they don't really understand or appreciate."

"God is flexible, do not be ashamed to speak his name, as it is a word that he is the 'Being of all Light', of all creation. God is your word, others choose a different name, 'Mohammed', another 'The Great White Spirit', another 'The Manitou of Life', and other names beyond your comprehension from other civilisations that exist around your world at this time. Why have you not seen them? Heard of them? Perhaps you have, but just don't know it."

From the transcript of 16th December 2016:

"They must not allow their thoughts to be inhibited by those who would say, "What fools you are, to believe in something that cannot be seen." Well we say to them, why do you need proof? Can you not just have faith and trust and desire the

Lord's company irrespective of your faith/denomination? Yes we have heard that talk of possible discriminations. Be assured we will not let those who stand back and criticise go unanswered, for we will tell them this, that the Lord embellishes all, no matter who you may call him, the Lord Krishna, Moses, Lord Jesus, Mohammed and all those disciples of the light who have come forward upon your planet."

"Let the people who criticise know, that there is no one faith, but one faith of all whether they realise it or not. As they sit in their homes with thoughts of prayers or in their Mosques and Churches, they pray to that one light, that one being of the Lord. Let them not distinguish between good and bad, black-and-white, evil against good, for there is a mixture of ingredients that make up your life. It is up to you to bring focus within your own soul's purpose to meet the standards required as given by the good book."

"Lessons are given to all who have knowledge but equally those who do not. A thought is spared for them and if they should open their eyes, perhaps they would see a glimmer of light that would shine in their minds. Hope is eternal and given to all. Do not disrespect the gift of life that is given by the master and can so easily be taken by those of discrimination or of evil thoughts and intentions.

Bring us to bear upon those who would question your judgement and let them know that there is but one God. Hmm, no name is given, for he is of spirit and is not prejudiced to either one or the other."

Since meeting Michael we have come to learn and respect what an ordinary and humble man he is, he seeks no fame or fortune and like all three of us, he does not look for personal attention, seek controversy, or to court the derision or denial that these messages sometimes attract. They just 'are as they are', nothing is changed for the sake of propriety or comfort to the reader. Dates and times within the transcripts may not necessarily be precise, sometimes a particular month is mentioned, but never the year, it is entirely possible that some details may be lost in transmission, remembering that these beings have to convert thought communication into in language for the human receiver to speak. For instance, August, it may mean this year or even in ten year's time, who knows. So please read on with an open mind and loving heart. With unconditional love we are taught to prepare the way for a better world and a future for the Earth. It is time for humanity to 'wake-up' and Michael is one of many in the world who are being used to pull our bedcovers off.

Warm wishes to all from Kevin and Valerie.

INTRODUCTION

The transcripts of communications within this book have been compiled directly from recordings taken during trance meditations by Michael Champion. No alterations have been made to the content other than the addition of punctuation or an occasional explanatory note.

Some of the messages may come across as being very direct and to the point, which may dishearten some readers, however, the tones of voices coming through Michael are very loving and gentle. Please imagine them being spoken with the voice of a loving father, in the way he would address a wayward child. Other messages are very philosophical and full of spiritual teaching and great wisdom.

The book is the first in a continuation of teachings from the 'Beings of Light' who are from places and dimensions far beyond our human understanding. It contains a wealth of information about our Earth, from the dawn of time to the birth of the of first civilisations and on to our present existence and our potential future. A future which is very much in our own hands, we may face the 'Fall of Man' and the beginning of a 'New Dawn', the choice is ours. Whatever the fate of the Human Race may be, our friends of the light assure us of their presence, support and the continuation of our lives in spirit while they lovingly watch over and guide us.

Familiar names also appear within several messages offering words of wisdom and personal guidance for all of us.

Please Note: This compilation of messages from 2015–16 was completed in December 2018. By the time this book reaches publication, some of the predictions given throughout may have already come to pass.

From 'Messages for Mankind' transcript of 26th May 2016

An Introduction to Michael Champion By his Spirit Guide, James

"Your journey will be a long one, with many routes to follow, you'll meet with ridicule and ignorance, for Man's values are not the same. They will listen and judge you upon your mind's performance, never understanding that these thoughts are transmitted to inspire others to the word of our creator.

Go social with the words to enlighten others, their natural curiosity (is) to look, for they will see the truth in your manner.

Go to your people with thoughts of love and gratitude, embrace their human attributes, let them see that you conquer with wisdom. Go now and be one with the universe to enlighten those who stand in the darkness of ignorance.

Travel the world with your mind my son, roam freely amongst those of the light taking your message of our creator directly to the thousands. Don't stipulate rules or mannerisms; just let the words flow with the frequency of love to print upon the hearts of man with tolerance."

From the Transcripts of: *7th July 2016*

"Read the words and note them with tolerance and temperance, without judgement and explore your minds to find your path and the guidance that we teach. Tremendous powers of goodwill are sent to each and every one of you, do not block them, open your hearts and minds to the endless

possibilities that exist between heaven and earth. We communicate our words to you with love and an expression of goodwill."

11th July 2016

"You will not change the world my son, but your words will linger in the years to come and remind those of the love of the Lord, and they will say, 'How was it that this man was not able to bring peace and love?' For truly you make a difference. Have faith that even if you change one mind, that is worth a million."

2nd October 2016

"The book is written to give a practice of love to man, keep this in mind Michael. No self-expression, no words of explanation, as the explanation is in the words themselves. You will be aware of our presence as you dictate your writings to the world. Be not afraid of the future my son, for it holds many wonders, many beautiful things, that as yet are not seen by man."

These sometimes-powerful messages are meant to be available for all who wish to read them. We verify that the content of the transcripts is never pre-planned or researched prior to the trance meditation sessions.

The biblical way in which the words are spoken may be off-putting for some and we appreciate that the concept of God being mentioned is also difficult for people who have a different or even no belief system. Again, we reiterate the words are not preconceived. However we note the similarity to biblical descriptions and remember that the Old Testament was channelled by prophets with messages from angels and other beings, are these the same beings of light communicating with us now?

A Message to the Readers
Channelled from The Arcturians

From the transcript of 7th July 2016

(Originally posted on the blog site 'messages formankind.wordpress.com')

"You read these words on your machines of life, but look beyond the words and to the meanings that they bring, for like ice it is easy to slide over the top, not so easy to see what lies beneath. The crystals that form that ice are of many individual crystals. It is the wise man that looks at the crystals to see their independence, the one that stops and looks to see the makeup and formation will find the answers for which he seeks. For those we call the skimmers they will miss so much.

Read the words and note them with tolerance and temperance, without judgement and explore your minds to find your path and the guidance that we teach. Tremendous powers of goodwill are sent to each and every one of you, do not block them, open your hearts and minds to the endless possibilities that exist between heaven and earth. We communicate our words to you with love and an expression of goodwill.

Never doubt your own abilities in life to bring about change to your world and yourselves. You are brothers and sisters who must co-exist, do it with love, a respect for each other.

There will always be those of disruption who will bring a measure of uncertainty; their paths are corrupted, but in time, their flow, their stream will find its path. For all who follow the rivers of life must endure the rapids before the calm."

Messages from the Beings of Light

The full identity of these communicators is hard to ascertain, sometimes they appear to be very angelic. They come forward as 'The Enlightened Ones', 'The Angels' and 'Beings of Light', they offer guidance, advice and also bring forward others, or speak of other influential people, including Native Americans. It is very hard to tell these beings apart from ET. All the communicators work collectively together as 'Beings of Light'.

The Transcripts:

4th January 2016

Watch the Stars

It was said many years ago that we are the enlightened ones. It is true to say that we guide your thoughts and your minds on the path of light, be aware of us, not afraid of us.

We came once before in guidance and love to your world of living. We have been ignored for many years, but triumph we will with those that work in the light. Never give up. Your souls, your minds, should be focused on the divine power that rules your Earth.

Blessed are you who make the journey of light your path. Helped you will be, guidance given always to those who believe in us.

Darkness will fall before the light. As always this will be temporary, as the light shines through and brings the new day to your world.

Watch the stars. For eons men have followed the stars, the signs are given, the 30th August being a date of transformation.

Knowledge is key. Knowledge above all of man's desires *(is)* to be his own king, but man cannot be his own king, as the King, our Lord, is the master of all.

You are as children, easily led, misguided by fools who wish to prosper at your expense. Look to the stars, look to us. For guidance is given to all.

We know of the pain of your world. We see the truth in your eyes. Like hawks that scavenge on the carcasses of their victims, your leaders, like the wolves will follow.

Come to us with love, with acceptance in the knowledge that the truth will be given *(to you)* through your meditations. Earn your feathers with pride.

Knowledge is key to understanding the world and the life before you.

12th January 2016

Beginning of Life on Earth and Journey from Dark into Light Once More

Take my hand, be strong, be wise, never let go of hope. Keep your strength; give it to those who need it most at this time. Your path is set, the strings are taut, stretch yourself. Band yourselves together, unite the light in the dark.

Help is required, trust your senses. Intuition, knowledge is the key. Your masters watch over you because they know your heart is strong and wise. You left us once to fight for others, now return to fight with us.

The darkness envelops the world of life; you come with us on a journey of enlightenment. We are God's people; we are the light. *(We are)* Those that came here many years ago, when the darkness was overwhelming and we broke that darkness, we brought the light into your world and life began.

Can you imagine what we saw then? The pure, innocent, fertile world, forests of green, seas of blue. The spark of life grew; we waited many, many eons for you to be ready. The world changed many times. You are not aware of the things that are in the past, but you will be learning of the things to come, as things return in a never-ending circle.

Your lives are a shambles, your mess to be cleaned. If you cannot, then we must start again. Be not afraid of our words, as we come in peace and love with the Lord of the light, but be warned, those who do not follow the light will perish. As always there is hope when we talk of the light.

True men are graceful by His word, there is always hope for those to see the light my son. You yourself were in the dark, but now you are in the light. Open their eyes to see the beauty of the world to come beyond this world of darkness and pain. It is without doubt a far better thing to work with the light and come with us on a journey of wonders. We cannot guarantee the things to come; we do guarantee the peace to come. Be faithful my son, work the magic.

Now rest, for the journey has just begun in your world of dark. In your world of light tap into your senses and feel the air, our touch on your brow. Come to us with love.

24th January 2016

Mother Teresa

Gather round your people and listen to these words. Come the day and the light, we will guide you.

God is in your hearts, *(He)* is within you, open your hearts to him; sing out the praises to those who bear malice and untruths. Divine is his name; His word is peace. Go to your people with these words of knowing, as love is the master of all who come before us in glory. Steadfastness, courage is needed by all who seek peace in the love and light, blessed is he who comes before us with God in his heart, we are the masters of the light, we are the enlightened ones whom you suppress in your churches.

Come with us on a journey so far beyond your imagination, you cannot comprehend the things to come within the light.

Earth is your mother; nurture your mother, with love and peace.

Mother Teresa spoke of those who were in need, no one listened; they are fools not to have believed. Her skills as a medic, as a nurse and healer were vast; many were healed and given peace with her love and light. She sits here with us now in despair at what has become of all. She weeps for you, as do we, but we see the light, we see a way to reach your souls and minds. Be not afraid of us, as we are here to heal the wounds and scars of man upon this earth that God created for all.

Walk with us through the sands of time let your footprints mark the way for those to follow. You know we are here with guidance and love. We are one of the same Spirit of God. We are one of all.

28th January 2016

Preparing us for a Path of Light

Like babies you cry out to us, lost in the wilderness of life. Prepare yourselves for the coming, your guides surround you with love, you must trust their judgment, their words. Together you will fight for the right causes, for the light will shine in all of you.

Be not afraid of me, I am here to guide you.

Come forward with your prayers of love, let them be heard by all now. With my guidance, work will be done to honour Him, our Lord in heaven. Come before us with gratitude. Stay with us, for we are the light upon which all life was created.

We came to you many years ago, arms open wide with love and temperance. You fought us through fear. Still those barriers are there, but we will succeed in bringing you into the light.

Let us guide your steps upon the path on which you've been set, without fear, without prejudice. Go to your people with these words, let them know that we are all around, but cannot be seen by those who will not see.

Open your arms, allow us in, for we are the ones of the light. The true knowledgeable ones who seek peace in your world. Go with the light in the knowledge that this is the right path. Do what you must before others, so that they will see and hear the words of wisdom and light. Be steadfast on your journey, gaze upon us from the stars, be not fearful.

Your moods, your temperaments are unworthy of us, change your attitudes, allow love in and come with us on a journey to a far place, a place of peace and love for all of mankind and knowledge will be yours for the asking. Have peace in your heart, wisdom in your soul, courage in your mind and know that we walk with you on this path of light. Moderation of thought of mind is needed, modest your ways, fairness your cry, and fearless of we of the light.

Crimes committed against all will increase in splendor of his presence and knowledge of the ways of spirit. Fortitude, temperance and love are all part of this knowledge. Skepticism must go, for yours is the path of light, of truth, of knowledge. Be with us as we walk by your side.

Caress one another in love, not in bitterness; embody yourselves with the truth and the knowledge of the wise ones.

Commerce, mitigation; words used by those of greed. They don't understand what they are doing, but they will find out the error of their ways in due course.

Be a leader; help those around you to see what is to come, ask questions of us, for we are the wise ones who will guide you in love and light from this day forward.

Terrible things we have seen in your world, terrible things to come. Unite your band of brothers, strength and power through Mother Earth.

Refugees Who Perish and Our Nations of Plenty

Angels of heaven speak of your names; watch over those who need compassion. Many perish in their search for freedom. The blue seas have claimed many a poor soul, many more will perish until man learns to live with one another and the hope will then shine.

Your nations of plenty worship and crave money, they don't know the truth of what is to come. Their greed and avarice will conquer them in days to come. Their minds revolve around one thing, and one thing only will satisfy them, their greed.

Become one with the universe and let your greed go. Be free with your soul, for no one will bring rest and happiness to those of greed.

Releasing Fear, Embracing Love and Spreading the Word

Know your mind is strong, your will robust, you will bring peace to many. To the enlightened ones of your band, turn your minds to peace, to love. Caress your loved ones as if it were the last day. Never speak your fears to your children but give them direction.

In love, peace and purpose of mind, the will of the heart will be your strength in this task of love.

Commentary, ridicule, words not to be spoken, and whosoever forsakes us shall not find peace. Open your hearts and minds to us, to what is to come beyond your life on earth. Go about your business with love, freedom of heart. Come before us with your love.

A time will come when you will open your eyes to us, and the stars will be yours. For all who come to us, blessings await, blessings of peace, love and our goodwill. Let your people know that your love is strong.

Crisp as the leaves in the autumn, crisp as the snow in the winter, the path you tread is as fresh as the snow on the ground. We care not that the words are not heard, for they will be soon.

Never has there been a beginning so grand as this on earth. You have come to a point where there is no love. Go to your people with love and honour; presume nothing, ask of us nothing, for it will be given in abundance in the light of the Lord.

Balance will be and must be restored. We are the enlightened ones; we come with pride, in the knowledge that our words are written for all to see.

Masters will negotiate a peace of love with all. Tears will fall for all who do not heed these words. Crisp as the leaves in autumn, as clear as the snows in winter, hear these words, mark the words. Come before us with humility, with peace in your hearts and love and joy in your lives. Guidance is required and will be given by those of the light. Harbour no fears within you; fear is a natural barrier.

As the wolf howls in the night, so you must howl these words, tell all what you know, see and hear, for we are here to work through you. Dominate no one; slacken your mind, release your fear, take no heed of those who would ridicule you, for they are the ones who are in the dark.

28th February 2016

The Enlightened Ones Speak to Michael of Past Lives

You show us your heart in your actions, your will is strong, like others who desire peace. Relinquish those ties that bind you to the past, let go of the burdens you carry within you, for time is a healer. Maturity and purpose are sure to follow.

Call upon us, the enlightened ones, bring to us *(the)* love and joy we so desire, you are the one with the knowledge and purpose.

Songs were sung by many voices; it was heard throughout time on the winds and vibration of love. Come to us this evening with an open heart and open mind as we connect with you, with peace and love in mind.

The waters of time run deep, those fresh memories will float as a branch on the water, like the branch it will submerge and be as it never was, but unseen, it still exists in the rivers of time, floating with many memories.

Reincarnation you have asked, why do you doubt what you already know in your heart and mind? We have been many times upon your earth. Your weaknesses are shallow, your minds question all before it, but never question who are we? Who are you?

Let us tell you of your past: Like a spring, the memories will flow before your eyes, your journey has been long fought and hard won, you have travelled many times before us. We have spoken of the things to be. Memories fade, as does your task, but reminded you are by the little things in life.

Follow your path that you have written, let us guide you to where you need to be.

Constantly we know of the things you are doing; we approve of your behavior in the knowledge that you are of the light. You would like to see evidence, but you know we are here. Only those that have vision would see their purpose. Do not ask for a particular one, as we work together to form our circle of light.

15th March 2016

Michael's Work to Spread the Words and 'The Rose'

Your work has just begun my son. Filter those that would denounce your words. Never let your heart be swayed by those who would rock your world. Know that our love is the strength on your back.

Task you we must in the love of our Lord. Through you, our words will be heard.

The fragrance of love is sweet, when you smell the fragrance of roses know that we are close. Your Rose, she watches over you as a mother watches over her child, giving you sustenance and nourishment, nurturing you on your path of joy.

Join us as we celebrate your path on the journey of light. Neglect us not, as your purpose is to be found erstwhile.

In ages past, books tell of those who journey through life in splendour. Those with arrogance fell by the wayside, their hearts were not true. Consequently nations fell, as will yours. It is the way of nature; the beast is tamed.

Never doubt our presence as we are with you, honour the Lord our Father, his light shines upon all his children of the world. But as naughty children you will be punished in a manner befitting of the Rose. *(Note. Since ancient times, roses have symbolized God at work in whatever situation they appear.)*

Negative thoughts are to be banished, as they drag you down. Positive affirmations are what is required of you to pursue the path of light. Yours is truly a wondrous journey of life and spirit. Go to those that need you most, your time will be well spent in the true meanings of the words of spirit.

20th March 2016

John the Baptist, New World Order, Shamans, Geronimo, Star of David, California, North Star, Warning of Cold, Weapons of War, Botany Bay, Jehovah

Murmurings are heard throughout the universe of such things that we cannot tolerate. Focused you are, your mind young in the knowledge and the ways to be explored. Guest I am to your world of life, keeper I am of the planetary systems of the universe. Know my name as I draw nearer.

In your presence we are conscious of the fact your mind is young and weak by nature, we give our knowledge to you, Master of Communication, in acceptance that you will go fourth to spread the word. Your youth is not of the years but of spirit. For his sake we have come this evening to join you in your meditation and dreams, you polish your craft, your focus stronger, you now feel us around you.

But we have come to place a burden upon you and others so great, for only the wise will understand the words that are given, but yours is to transform those thoughts from us, into music that the people would hear.

Be clear we come in peace for the good of mankind, your words, focus will be upon us. Soon there will be no escape for those who would ignore us, depart from your ways for your purpose and meaning in this life.

John the Baptist he knows of your work with others, in time you will come to know him as your saviour, your mentor. You challenge us with your thoughts, your wisdom grows, your purpose and needs become greater, we hear your murmurs.

(Note: John the Baptist: said to be the forerunner of Jesus, and to have prophesised his coming and possibly to have been one of his teachers.)

Let us tell you of the things to be in the new world order. We cannot express enough our optimism, for the world will become a better place. Know your mind's eye and see those things in your focus. We have never been so close as we are this evening. Your words will sound like trumpets in the ears of the wise who will go to listen to the words spoken by the others of time to come. Nourish your minds, feed upon the words that you would feast in the glory of heaven in due course.

Shamans come and go, their torches burn bright for all, theirs is purpose and need. Common good for man is all that is necessary for peace and harmony in life. Wake up to the need of our Lord in the highest place of vibration, speak out to those who are conscious of your awareness. Gather them around you as the storm approaches from the east to the west. *(Note: Storm is a metaphorical meaning for our current world problems.)*

Never let it be said that our purpose was not good for your true beings of light. Often we are regarded as the 'Ancients' those that came before. You will hearken to our name; they will know our purpose upon this Earth you call home. Gradually time erodes all that had once been upon this Earth.

Common sense would dictate that trust in these words is paramount for your focus, for your focus is great upon our words. Those who would sit before you to ask of us what they wish, never let them say that our words are not true, be faithful upon one another, reliant upon the Lord and his blessings he brings to you. Charm offensive by some, they fool you, be wise see through their ignorance their patterns are many but their purpose is a negative one.

Geronimo, he once sat on the war council of the tribes of the west, now he sits with us. His burden was great, his manner was calm; he sees the wisdom of the ways of the Earth. He knows of your connection with those that once were upon this Earth of life. Extreme measures were used against him and his people, to control their lives in a way to fulfil their purpose of their need, for greed for the lands of the free. On top of the mountain he sat with his council of warriors explaining to them, that although he was feuding, he was peaceful, he fought well for his people and the lives that depended upon him. Descendants from him are still filled without purpose it is deep set within them, his gain was wisdom as is yours, his council sit with us still. Our minds are focused on the paths of many, fulfilment is not always guaranteed but success is the ultimate achievement.

It is not necessary to face the rigours of life alone, your council is wise, your concern is great. Measures will be needed to formulate the plan of attack. Defence of the Earth will be futile by those who would see us as beings from another planet; because their eyes are shut, their knowledge weak, they know no better, but they will come to know our purpose as you mediate terms and conditions with us.

Daunting it seems to you that such things could be, ego has nothing to do with this, you're flexible my son, you give grace where it is due and needed, you are positive in your thoughts and actions. Other minds will join you on this journey, you have friends who participate at this time with your words, their focus is as of yours, to elevate the depression of this world. Starvation of knowledge will be fed by those of the highest vibration; paths will be laid by those of the stars who know best how to respond to negative assertions against them.

Be clear we are strange to your eyes but to your mind we are friends, never doubt us for our purpose is clear upon your planet, we cry out for others to join us, their temperaments are focused elsewhere, others will come before you in need of help and assurance that things will be as was intended by the masters of the universe. Your understanding and knowledge grows.

Weapons of war will cease to function before our coming, their secrets will unfold before nations in turmoil and panic. Your brethren of old are strong within you, your nose will follow the scent which is laid down for you to follow in the coming days of darkness. Don't be sad for those who run, for they have not seen what you have whispered to them.

Coldness will envelope your Earth as never before as the seasons grow more abnormal. Mother Earth is fighting back, she will not tolerate the abuse upon her skin.

Be not afraid of what we say as tears will fall from many eyes as they behold the Star of David that will appear in the East, your minds will boggle at such a Star. Use your senses to acknowledge the light, come before us with ease and purpose in mind, in the knowledge that we have spoken, mind-to-mind, body-to-body. Never forget we are linked for eternity for all to see. Despair not of those who will perish, as they in turn will be brought back to the light, their time is not now. Their focus will be changed with purpose, you need not fear the Lord as he waves his hand across your planet, temperance and tolerance is necessary, your burden will ease, as all will become clear.

Nestled in your mountains and rivers are things that you cannot conceive, we have not allowed them to be set free, mindful that there is purpose in the world. Be graceful, on your knees, as we fill you with purpose.

California is a place of many, their lives filled with unnecessary wants and needs. They will not listen to the winds of time and change their leader, a foolish man, pride and arrogance unnecessary. As Cane and Able were so much as brothers their views differed, jealousy, rage, un-unified purpose and as friction they will ignite a violent haze that will be cast on those who cannot see their way to the light. Know this my son; our words have purpose not in fear but in deeds that need to be met.

Jehovah is how he is known by many of your world, greet the Great Spirit as you would a friend in your daily routine, allow him into your heart where he will guide and instruct you on your purpose in this life.

Come before us with ease in your hearts, needs in your minds, plentiful are his transitions. We who live near you, greet you with joy and happiness as friends. We have come with purpose and need. Yours is a light that shines bright, happiness and greed of life cannot be sustained, unlike love which is everlasting, ever fulfilling. Feed your hunger with love of the Lord and the light that will shine upon you.

The Cosmos, the Universe of many mega journeys in hand, our words are strange to you, we feel this. Rest assured that those journeys in the Cosmos, through the Universe, are well trodden by those of us in spirit we correspond to solar systems united in one purpose, one goal.

Focus your mind on the light and see. We come with gratitude that you have chosen a path of honour among our people.

Tonka was great, sit with us a while and meld your mind to fulfil your purpose granted are you of the Earth many wondrous journeys to be had. Comprehension of our ways are unfolding before you in numerous ways, reach out with your mind with purpose and need, see the three crowns that sit upon my head, they signify the love, purpose and journey of the souls. Come hither, gather round and unite the circle of fellowship you are bound for. Common knowledge it has been for millennia, your people subdue the truth that she will reveal!

The Great Tonka of wisdom is upon you, you know these words to be true, as he has spoken of love. Ponder upon the issues of life. Negative responses will be heard but focus on the light and love of the Lord as he envelopes you all with love and purpose. Conquer your mind, your thoughts; wisdom is key to your purpose. We are here to greet you upon the Earth, feed your minds with knowledge of our purpose, we were here once before, we were greeted with love, honour and respect. We fear this will not be so *(now)* as people's minds are corrupt. *(Note: Tonka is a name or word that refers to a North American Indian woman, it meant 'great'.)*

The North Star will give you the sign as we arrive before the dawn of the day. Next Monday, you will see a score twice over, across your skies they will flash, people will be aware and not understand the significance of this sign which will be given. Control your will, your wisdom is needed. *(Note: Possibly referring to a pair of comets that zoomed past Earth in a historic 'One-Two' flyby, a telescope in Chile operated by the Online Slooh Community Observatory captured video of the comets 252P/Linear and 2016 BA14 as they cruised past on Monday 21st and Tuesday 22nd March 2016, at closest approx. 2.1 million miles the nearest in almost 250 years.)*

Botany Bay *(Australia)* **a moment in time, which has not been forgotten,** where so many of our kind, (for we were once as you, filled with life and love), they came and they took what was once ours to be theirs. Conscious of their ways we departed in fright and fear, like the seas that roll in onto the shore they kept coming. Their ways strange to us, they took what they could, their need was great. We have never seen such strange peoples before, we gave feathers, they gave trinkets, trinkets that meant nothing, their purpose two-fold, their hearts split. Father Good Fellow *(Note: not a name as such, but I feel writing this, this was an Aboriginal name of affection for a Priest),* had love, but he too was a man of need. Cold were his feet as they walked upon our breath, their minds neglected our needs. We curse them for their greed. *(Note: First British colonists arrived at Botany Bay in 1788 – Captain Cook is said to have landed there in 1770 and declared it unsuitable as a landing place.)*

Charlestown was a place of sin, of want and need. Their souls so full of purpose, changed as the tides. They swept over us like the great wave of '86. They did not care for us, for our peoples. Tolerance, ignorance and greed was all they knew, their depths cavernous, their minds deep with need, as we grew to understand their ways. We despaired and we knew the men, the Longhorn would not stop coming to our shores. Our time is done, our people died, but our souls soared in the knowledge of the Great Spirit. We came on the wings of a white bird to our fathers, my grandfathers. We spoke words of wisdom that one day ours would be a better place. Forgive them for they are weak minded fools who would pay the price tenfold.

Repent the ways of the white man, I once came to this place you call Earth, time is short and unrewarding in many ways, but the lessons learnt carried me forward. Progression of my purpose was mine. The eagle that soared burst with pride, over his high position he could see the plains. 'Twas good his eyes, as keen as his sight was sharp, gather your tribes to the place in your hearts where freedom lives, focus your minds in trio, so that we may gather strength from your hearts and minds. Feathers flew!

Troubles of the mind are many with your people, to focus your purpose you must ease your burdens. Travel with us in your minds, let go your flesh, all will be well in the days to come and will once more flourish in the light of the Lord. Let go of your heart, for the strings that bind you are strings of need of man.

Common interest is needed as we show you the kingfisher, see his many colours of his plumage, know the many colours are as the many colours of spirit. He sits and waits for that moment to strike, his eyes focused and fixed upon the fish he preys upon. Know you are the fish that is preyed upon by those who would have need of you in your hearts, we will not allow darkness to fall upon your lives, your hearts, tell this to those around you, favour not those with ignorance.

Dispel your dreams of wealth and prosper in the love of the Lord as his true purpose will shine like a beacon at night. As the moth to the flame, you will have need of his light, continue your work.

Once more we speak with love in mind, compare us not with those who would shade your mind.

Countries torn apart by war. You will be healed in due course for the common good, as we will focus upon them with love. Do not despair, be strong of heart. A care is needed, for eyes unseen watch you from all around, be as the cat, focus upon your needs and purpose, keeping the light of the Lord in your heart. Know his strength is there as a shield to fend off those who would besiege your mind.

Continue until the third star becomes clear in your focus.

Perfect his being, common valour is needed in the task ahead, your groups, people should be single minded on the task before them. They will reap their rewards in many ways in splendour.

See the Yellow of the light, Mary the Rose. Compromise your heart not for the weaknesses of man, harden your nose.

3rd April 2016

Beings of Light and American Indians

Your purpose here with us this evening is clear to be seen in the eyes of those who watch your words with focus. Strive to expand your mind in the ways and words of others who are focused upon our words.

Your nations speak many untruths before you; they disregard your happiness in their lust for advantage in all things. But yours is the true value of faith that will be rewarded in time. Just as we have spoken to many others, let us inform you of our purpose and our will. Negotiate with us a peace that we may stand united for the purpose and true meaning of our Lord. His words will never fade for they are as whispers in the wind; they are carried to many of your world, but are not heard by those whose standards lack morals.

Grace will come before you as she has spoken many times in the ears of those who would listen to her. Your comprehension of such matters is weak but learn you must, for as the moth to the flame, you are drawn to the light.

Be aware of our need of your purpose, dominate those who would say, "You are nothing!" Make them see the purpose you hold within you. Your might is your strength of mind to complete the tasks that unfold before you my son.

Your task this evening, your purpose, *(is)* to endow others with the knowledge, that we of the spirit world will be coming with equal measure to your world of life. Comment not on our appearance, as we are among you.

Assurance is given to those of the light that he is coming, for a shared appearance before man will be soon.

Comanche, Cherokee, and all the nations had begun to perish beneath the long knives of the white man. Many have purpose to destroy, not to love *(but)* to gain splendour in their own authority. Their matters at hand were strictly for themselves, they cared not for the bodies of men. The atrocities that followed will live throughout time, as their shame will always bear witness to their crimes of humanity.

Hunger, famine was supreme. As hunger took hold, women cried, the children faded before us. As men, our hearts were torn from our bodies to see such things. We were powerless to stop the outrages; they came before us in a form of man *(that)* our fathers knew as 'Westerners'. Columbus was greeted, but *(he)* dishonoured us in his lust for gold and riches. We had none to give, so he made up stories to encourage others to search far and wide. Our beloved country was torn apart by treachery. Negotiations were hopeless in the Tennessee by-election, then we were torn from the hearts of mankind, that we of the many nations were so hated. Is it not the white man whose crimes were committed against us, were they not the ones of hate?

Negotiate your mind to its purpose my son, fulfil the promise given before you lived. Adopt of a demeanour befitting that for an angel. Elect to proceed with your life as ordered. We are here to watch over you and the nations who bear witness to atrocities, they are feeble, for their purpose is a selfish one. Their combat is with their hearts.

Go now be at peace, not at war with your hearts concerns.

Never doubt that we are close by; overseeing your life, ensuring your path is open, to be trodden upon in a positive manner. You know me, we are united as a band of brothers to issue notice to those of your Earth, that we will arrive in the dawn of a new day, a new beginning is assured. Your token of love is needed for the purpose ahead.

We are the Enlightened Ones who step in to save you from yourselves as your world tumbles like a rolling stone. Reduce your need for the basics of life, as who needs such things? Your focus is assured to bring the words of our nations upon yours; the terms of surrender are simple to follow. Your masters who rule the world are of greed, their need is great for *(the)* material things that life will bring. How can they be so foolish as to not be aware of the joys of the light, where the food of love is peace *(and)* contentment. The needs are fulfilled in a way so profound that you will need of nothing; your joy will be all fulfilling.

Tokens will be given shortly to those who work in our name, your grasp of knowledge will blossom in you. In the manner of birds of a feather, in honour of our coming, they will flock in meadows and fields. You'll draw strength in the coming of the Lord before your people on Earth; know Him as your saviour, the Master of Love. Concern yourself not with the worries of the world as He stands before you, for joy will be given to those who surrender their hearts to Him.

We know of your concerns; but have no fear, we are of the light. As you see the full moon before you, know this represents our love. The shadows of the things to come will shine before you, illuminating the way to pastures of love. Remove those rocks in your mind, for they have no purpose but to obstruct your manner. Knowledge grows within you, speak of the things to come as they are the words of the Lord. Enter the new phase of enlightenment before you, grasp with open hands that which is given.

11th April 2016

Mary and Things to Come

The flowers of love will shower upon you in the rain. Commence your work on the path of light, bring peace and hope to those who are lost in your world of life. Acknowledge our presence in your life as we acknowledge you on the path of light.

David said that he wandered for many years in the deserts of love; he found peace and happiness in the arms of Mother Earth as she bathed him with words of love and comfort, bringing hope to his heart that one day all would feel the caress of Mother Earth. *(Note: Refers to psalm 63, David in the wilderness of Judah?)*

Commence your scheme in the manner in which it started, know that we of the spirit will work beside you in His name with love and purpose, for our coming will be clear to you all in the next season. Revitalise your love and your honour in His name. Descend upon those who would listen to your words, let them know that we speak through you the truth and wisdom of the Lord of the heavens above. **Let them know that we bring peace, love and serenity to those who would hold open their hearts to us.**

Acknowledge the light as it shines in the East and sets in the West, for His purpose will be fulfilled upon your Earth. His will is amongst you in many nations, they cooperate in many ways and tongues and have one purpose for the souls of their brothers of life. Do not disregard your abilities, your passion is true, focus upon the words that are sent through the cosmos to you. Know that they are strong and good and that they will in time encourage others to become children of the Lord.

Our ways will seem strange to you, but they are the ways of the light and the Lord. Our names are uncommon to you, but are becoming clear as the lessons are learnt, dictate to us not, as we are the teachers of learning. Your thoughts may compromise with ours; you ask many questions of which there are many answers, and as the blossom of the flower blooms and the petals open, so your knowledge will open to you.

Let it be known to those around you that we extend our greetings of love to those who work within the light and to them all. Communion of the many will enlighten those of the dark. Commence with the plans of music, play it to those so that they would hear our words directly through you in their groups, we will help in this endeavour to place them on your path.

You recognise the souls who walk with you as truthful beings of light. Regulate your mind to focus on the light and the purpose ahead. Needless to say, we are pleased to hear that so many hearts are warmed by your words. Although written by you, they are spoken by us in the truth of the Lord. For His name reigns supreme in the stars and the heavens above.

Mary, she comes with waves of love, her focus is upon you as her path crosses those of the light. She will announce Her love to the many in due course. Her purpose is tenfold. She will cruise your nations in the near future carrying the crown of the Lord our Father. She has given you a purpose of heart that should be followed brightly in the light that shines before you. Herald the coming of the Lord as he wings His way towards your Earth, His name is that of the Master. His aim is to create a heaven on earth.

Your people have never learnt the ways of the Lord, they bask in the sunshine of Mother Earth without caring of the environment around them. They think that their playground will go on forever, how wrong can they be, when they don't see the paths that they are on lead to darkness and mayhem of the heart. Their minds are weak, but your strength continues to grow. In your heart, your wisdom and knowledge is vast beyond your conscious mind.

Continue to write the words given as they give strength to others.

We are immaculate beings of the light, we have seen the many ways of man, it's been strange to our eyes. We control the minds of the many through the mass of your world. She comes with a whisper of love given to Her by the almighty. As we near your Earth we hear your broadcasts, we focus upon those that mean harm for they have their weaknesses and their strengths.

Consider yourself an Angel of the light, for your light burns bright in your heart. We have never tolerated those of the dark or those of ill will. Our council is your heart's desire for the good of man, focus on the light and the love that it brings. Common to all men should be his love for his neighbour, post your intention of heart upon your friends, heal their hearts with your mind as they eke out their lives upon their planet.

We have seen many terrible things in the past and what is to come, for we bend light and time, your comprehension of which is beyond your minds.

Time lapse will descend upon the earth as it lurches to the east and to the west. The continuance of man, rest assured, will be counted upon to evaluate for our need and our progress. Genuinely we greet you all with welcome. Concern yourself not of who or where we are but know that we are focused upon you and your memories of love. Joy be upon you in the spring of the third winter, be not afraid of the words of love, for they are strange to you and the many who behold them. Once more continuance of your species is assured, but the time draws near for the commencement of the rebirth.

Compromise your heart not to the sin of man, but to the love of the Lord upon which nations are built. Go to your masters and honour them with love as they approach in the spring and the August. Complete the missions assigned to you in a manner respectful of the Wise Ones. Completion of our work will commence very shortly; attune yourself as we join you. We of the light acknowledge your love for the purpose ahead; we are neither here nor there, but in between the light and your love. Go forth with those who would join you to help in the fight for life upon your Earth.

Wisdom and knowledge will be key for the purpose ahead as we draw near, let your mind become one with us, see the colours of love as they radiate from our hearts to yours. Your need of knowledge is vast, become one, not with those that would ridicule the words of the Lord; focus upon us.

The damned of the nations of the states will cross the lines of peril to the east and the west, their notion of life is that of the wayward. Simple *(are)* their minds. They commence their plans to start anarchy upon the earth hoping that all will succumb for their purpose, their weapons are armed, but they will be on their knees before us.

14th April 2016

Tokens are given to strengthen your mind. Resist the temptation to cease work as we bring forth a new day, we know of distraction, but focus your purpose. God blesses those that follow the light, their interests are unworthy at times, but their focus and purpose is pre-ordained.

Conspiracies against you will take place in the hearts and minds of those who cannot accept the words given. They despise your thoughts of mind, for they cannot see the words are true and given in truth. Their focus is upon their lives, the meaning of which is unclear to them; they are misguided on their focus.

Tighten your lips when challenged by those of the dark, don't show your hand until the time is reached, when your purpose will be fulfilled among the men of the Earth.

The cosmos is filled with many of purpose; their hearts are filled with the need of love. We beckon you to come forward to the light as we join you this evening.

Consciously we are aware of the feelings of the many upon your Earth as they battle their lives with indignity. Those who have little, accept that theirs is a path of light. Their suffering is needed to bear witness to man's indignities upon others; they sing the praises of the Lord. Hard as it is to understand their purpose in life, they will come to know that joy is in the mind and in the heart of love. Compassion for the many is a worthy attribute, but realistically nothing can be done by so few. We are here to lend a hand of friendship for a united Earth.

How can you be a part of this journey? They misunderstand that yours is a journey of love and truth, far beyond that of the many.

Commerce reigns supreme among men, but it is misguided, misused and not for the purpose intended. Confusion will come in good time as the planetary shifts awaken those minds to their purpose.

Compare us not with the ones of the darkness, for we are of the light, beyond that which you see. Command us not of your alternatives, but be inspired by the thoughts and will of those around you, allowing them to negotiate their minds to the truth of the Lord and the light.

Compassion is needed for those that suffer at this time, neglected by the world. The crimes committed against them go unanswered. Rest assured we will seek those out who offend God with their lies of their purpose. Those traumatised by war, by siege, will find peace in the light of heaven. Their journey is hard.

We control many things of your world, but your free will is unique to you. You must find your path through the stars and heavens in your own time and in your own ways.

Conscious are we of the fact that the third star shall shine bright in the lives of those that look upon a dawn at the days beginning, you know the star, you have witnessed the beginning of the new era of your planet. Mars aligns with Earth many times, but only once with Venus as she lies in his path.

Controversy among your learned will be blown away by the aspects given by us in their dreams. The mirror images of their minds will unlock secrets beyond that of those of the past. They will misuse many things and their deeds of misguided souls. We will correct them to bring peace upon your world.

Your facets change like the shades of the light, your heart is stable and burns bright with the love. Knowledge is coming, but it seems to pass, your patience is needed but your focus grows. Conscious are you of our being next to you.

Dedicate your lives for the love of others who have gained advantage through time upon your Earth. Our masters watch over you from a position of love, enticing those who would listen to come forward and connect. Shine your light brightly so as it can be seen by the many. Journeys you will make afar, as the love grows, your minds can expect a life of a meaningful journey. Don't despair but welcome the light that will shine from the heavens and the stars above.

Your companions are at the heart of the thoughts of those of bygone days. Conviction they have in the words they attain through the likes of your ability. They know of much of what is to come; they care for humanity. Your charge is to welcome them into the light and the love of purpose.

Notably we remarked upon the state of your world, Bashar Al-Assad was spoken of by yourself, but his is not the worst yet to come, the one to come is, Beef of the States!

Your traumas will be great, but you have the knowledge that the sun will come before the winter falls, the autumn leaves change colour to browns, reds, oranges then decay. Their purpose will decay in the autumn of their lives but yours will receive eternal sunshine, eternal light. Count your blessings on this day for they are many.

Contrary to what you might think, we also have issues that need to be resolved, for no matter how wise there is always the opposite.

We feel your pain and anguish when you see the troubles of the world, you cannot imagine how this troubles us as we travel your globe cloaked in light.

Companions will come to help you master your mind, your need is great of them, their purpose to your need, to distance you of your beliefs and awareness. Two vines will join to create one, and the strength of that vine will grow with purpose and bind others on its journey. It will open and spread like sails to catch the wind and the light. The lush leaves giving strength and energy required of fruit, and the fruit of the vine shall be yours for the asking, for the fruit of the vine is that of the Lord for His purpose.

Create your vine with love and connection with others, sharing the thoughts of wisdom that is imparted upon you. Let your leaves open and your blossom shine; take in the nourishment given by the life-giving sun of your solar system. Depart from the ways of sin and of those who would conspire to drag you down, let them go their way, for yours is the truth and the manner needed to gain strength and light for those to follow.

Confusion will reign in your world before our coming is announced, their methods are dubious as they scan the skies in search of us, they know of us, they have seen us, but they are the one that comes before us on their knees and gives thanks to the Lord for his blessings.

Commodus, he comes with a special gift of love and joy for you to share with the friends of the Earth. Your knowledge grows and is vast and preordained to do the things that you do at this time and stage of your being.

Commence the actions needed by us so that we may represent those of our nations to yours. You are daunted by this task but know this; they will come to you with purpose in due course. As you answer their questions, their minds cannot comprehend another universe co-existing with yours, for all they see are facts, scientific formulations, they mean nothing, they are nothing.

One fact remains, that life exists on many levels in the many planes all around your Earth, beyond your vision. Those of you who connect are aware of the minor planes, the higher spiritual plains would be hard for you to grasp.

Continue your work, for each psalm that progresses will shift the balance of love, as it does so they will progress to a higher plane. Your knowledge is key to those that don't understand, they question you of your purpose. In their hearts they know that theirs is a journey to be taken with love.

Constantine remarked on his journey as being that of "The Guided One", comparatively he was right, his purpose was all too soon gone as he found the riches of the world that temped and taunted him. He was and is a gentle soul who was misled by those of temptation, but he knew his love ran deep and he was able to supersede all the temptations given.

17th April 2016

Four score and ten is a number of which our purpose will show. *(Note: This message was received four days before Queen Elizabeth II's ninetieth birthday.)*
Come before us with gratitude and honour in your heart as we focus upon your being of life.

Temperaments are frayed between those that argue about the purpose of the energies present, they see that which is written and they hide their heads in the sand, as the birds of the desert hiding from the burning sun.

Contrast are you to those who do not seek the truth in their lives, your temperament is bold with purpose in mind. Caress this thought, that we are here with wisdom and might to spread the words of the Lord to those of your world. Combined, our strengths will reunite those of intent.

Commence your work as instructed, let no one hamper you in your stride, as your purpose is to focus on us. Combined words will seek out those who need instruction on their paths of light, they are unaware of their focus upon us, they assume that they work for spirit by bringing messages of love to those in need, but in truth their purpose is twofold, they see one side of the story without ever looking deeper for the true meaning of their journeys.

Comparatively you are the opposite to them, your mind is working on a different level, a vibration, that hums with intent and purpose.

Comments are made on our words and it is good that they are seen and questioned, as questions bring knowledge and purpose to those who are looking for answers.

Guest are you in our presence. Complex *(are)* our minds; *(they are)* unfathomable to you and your like. Fashionable trends seem to be with comments of a nature of bygone days, when life was simple and problems few. Today's world is complex with the needs of the many; it cannot cope with the pressures put upon it so there must be a release, a source to which their minds can focus.

We do not need to speak of our intentions to those who would not listen. By the focus of your mind you constitute a release, do not assume that you are the one to whom this gift is solely given, your next steps will commence in June as mother nature warms up.

We are destined to Her *(Mother Earth)* **new beginnings,** never doubt that we are not close by, for we are neither man nor beast, we are the light, a simple focal point in time. Our wisdom and network, vast among your people, we adhere to those who have purpose in their lives.

Complete your tasks as we guide your steps, common knowledge now, your purpose grows. Take steps to show your sincerity, formulate answers in a manner fitting of the Lord, work closely with others to combine your thoughts. The mind power of the light, and by your combined strengths you will enlighten those on the brink of indecision. Tasks that you are all given represent the true nature of us.

You observe the moon and the star in the night sky as if you have never seen it before, your enlightenment and awareness of us intrigues you, you look to see motion in the infinitesimal universe. *(Note: The Moon and Jupiter are highly visible just after sunset at the moment, before any other stars appear.)* Your attention is drawn to many things and how it will dictate that which is necessary. Your motives and needs are many, truly we know of your stance. Retrospectively we commend you for your work, of which there is need in your world of matter.

Today's events will unfold before your eyes on the noon of the morrow, you have no idea of the sadness it brings us to see such awful sad times in your world of matter, *(Note: the following day hundreds of migrants lost their lives when their boat capsized in the Mediterranean according to a report taken from a BBC News article on their website dated 18 April 2016.)*

Nature will take her course, and in due course, her veins are filled of life that tarnish your beings upon the planet. Her motions can be felt by the tremors in the islands off the Pacific, culminating in a mighty explosion of expression.

Commodus wishes to express his concern for the Polynesian peoples, their focus is on life, and the hidden dangers beneath their feet cannot be seen. Your instruments that measure vibrations are at fault, they cannot see what is to come, a disaster of epic proportion will unfold before the world of life, but take heart that these events are designed to clear the veins of Mother Earth so that she may breathe in the love of the light.

'Topples the mountains of love', they sing the song to the world of the lands, she cannot hold her emotions, for the abuse set upon her, like an itch that has to be scratched she will act in her nature on the Earth. The foolish who built their houses, their dwellings upon earth in strategic areas will suffer an amount of loss that will shake the very foundation. Knowledgeable are you of these events to occur in the month of May. Perhaps in some way the words will make sense to those who will not listen, culminate your feelings of despair at the fracture of the Earth as she jolts, we cannot say how many will be lost but know they will be welcomed in their new life. *(Note: As we were compiling these transcripts in December 2018 we remembered that Mount Kilauea started erupting 3rd May 2018 and feel that this may be what the transcript is speaking of – The peoples of Hawaii originate from Polynesia.)*

Disappointed we are to see that some of your flock disrespect your abilities, how can they say they know of these things when we have not spoken to them? They should listen and be observant of the condition of their minds, for their need is not of aspirations of love, but of focus upon themselves, they need to check their minds belief.

Guided are you by those of the light, task yourself with thoughts of love with the memories of those that have gone before you, for they are your power, they are your spirit. Choices that you have made in your life that have guided you to this point were unseen by you at the time of decision, but know that your focus is on track. Publish your notes for the purpose intended for they are to be seen by the many and not the few.

She is unseen but there are complex levels of spirit far beyond your comprehension, we are the enlightened ones who would bring purpose to your life and meaning to those who are willing to see the light before them.

Task your mind with the purpose before you, allowing no other to intimidate or redirect your thoughts, your mind is true, our words our strength, complete their meaning with your love. Trouble your mind not with what we say, but let the light in to refurbish your mind with beauty and love.

Toppled are men of ignorance, by those who see the beauty of the light, for they and their purpose are false upon your Earth. Many members of many States upon your Earth will reveal to you their knowledge of the ones they have seen on their scopes. They cannot contain that knowledge, for as water leaks from a hole in the bucket, so information will leak to the world, the true knowledge of us, beings of the light. Inspectorates beyond your vision will announce their arrival in the mid to late seasons; your month of August is a start.

Convey our wishes and thoughts to those in your networks, allow us to extend our greetings to mankind through your words of love and wisdom, confide in us your concerns and we shall give the answers needed to restore your strength. We cannot control your body only your mind and thought, you can feel us, sense us, as we part the physical, comparatively your brain will shudder at the intellect that connects. Don't be afraid of what comes next, it is meant to be in the purpose of time.

Prepare your mind for the knowledge and wisdom, and focus your thoughts upon our Star Ship that nestles in the skies above you, prepare yourself to be amazed by our appearance, for we are of nature that would be strange to you, may you feel our focus in your body, relax and let our thoughts in. Tremors of the mind are a natural reaction to vivid thoughts of colour in spectrum.

Test your heart by means of love, extend your arms to those that reach to you, caress their emotions with your heart of love. We now feel your mind has purpose. Your emptiness will be made full in the new fall, you feel us, our body, naturally we are strange to you. Concern yourself not for the words spoken for they are not for you but for the many. Gratitude features in many hearts of love, our nature is that of peace and hope for your planet, do not despair as we enter your being of love.

Controversy will spark a rift in governments who seize power over others. Your knowledge will ease the minds of the many who follow the light, commence your plans to ignite in the hearts and minds of those, all the love of the Lord, and his blessings and countenance be upon them.

Turmoil in your world is necessary to wash clean those men of dishonour, many will fall before the light of the new dawn in a battle for humanity, man against man and the beast, unite your hearts to combine your strength in equal measures.

20th April 2016

Consciously we are aware of the many issues surrounding your lives on planet Earth, your emotions are high at the prospect of impending doom. We bless your thoughts, as they are just a moment in time, for each life is given which must be returned. As the purpose unfolds to its climax, concern yourself not with the matters of man, for they are insignificant on the journey of love.

Tragic circumstances will bring a mass of media attention in the spring concerning fire on the seabed. For your neglect as humans, you'll be repaid by tremors of the Earth. Never has there been such a time as that which you enter at this moment in time. Through man's perspective of the world, push a matter of change in the new beginnings of life that will unfold before your eyes in the new season.

We cannot say that we have not noticed the changes in the atmospheric pressures, your scientists are aware of anomalies that are mounting around your planetary system, their lips are sealed by the men of money who wish for no panic, as their world of luxury and trade crash in the pole of the Earth, this time we will rebuild your monoliths and your structures. Fashionable ideas become muted as the signs of our words become apparent to those who would have read of the ones in bygone days. Let your heart fly with love and respect.

Continuance of your purpose is expected of you, you cannot hide from the truth of our words for we are here to reason with mankind and his ways. Why would you want to stop us from bringing a better life to your planet? Naturally we expect the shock of our difference to understandably startle your nations, but we come before you in the fold of the new year, negotiate with your mind as we emphasise our purpose is of love and peace.

The creation of American structures is a sign of your power and will to achieve things seemingly impossible, but as big as they are, they will fall into disrepair as the financial markets crash.

A dogged fracture inflicted upon the Earth will begin a force unstoppable by man, it has happened before in past history before man walked the earth

Confusion will reign as the storm approaches, it will breach your atmosphere ten days from now, the comets dust is filled with matter to anoint your earth, it will land in the Aegean Seas, fallout from the skies as rain, they will survive for a continuance of time, the seas will well as the shock waves vibrate Mother Earth. *(Note: The reference to 'ten days from now' could mean ten days from the date of 20th April, but in any future year.)*

Mansions will fall before the waves that roll in across the sea in an epic cleansing. A kaleidoscope of colour will affect your skies, they streak across your Earth in the dawn skies.

26th April 2016

Focus and Love in Our Circles of Light – Crystals of Pink – Inspiration in Our Books – The Pyramids and Temples

Strength be to those who have purpose before you, their writings made clear to those minds who see nothing but negativity. Continue your work as the trio of love, expand your hearts and minds with focus beyond that of your circle, let the world hear of the love and the wisdom of the Lord who comes before you in a manner respectful of His light and love.

His purpose is upon you to make amends for the ways that have blinded you, continue to work with us without fear, knowing that there will be restoration to your planet and a commencement of love to your world.

Strange as it may seem, we need to have an assurance that your hearts are content. Too many bridges on roads of peril have been crossed in eagerness to pursue their hearts desires, *(and it)* has led them into a forest of darkness. Knowledge will be yours for the giving, take it with respect to your people. Triumph will be yours in overcoming the pressures put before you, for hearts will melt as they see your purpose unfold before them. Gifts we bestow on those who have a tolerance of forgiveness.

Your circles of light focus upon those in need, to those who would doubt your words we say this, ask yourselves the question of love, "What is it that you seek for your purpose, is it love, strength of mind, or is it to be seen and admired by many?"

The crystals of pink, they are of your mind to help survive the rigours of your path. For a tremendous amount of energy is required to surpass and suppress those needs upon which you depend. Task yourselves to reach out beyond your heart's desires, to cast away the burdens that you carry in your hearts, and as an empty shell, allow it to be filled with purpose of love and light.

Conscious are we of the many who would issue statements of ill will, you need thick skins, as the rhino of your Earth, to fend off the pressures they put upon you.

Travel your minds to the far-off place beyond your world, that exists in the minds of those who walk with the light. From this place *(you will be)* granted love and light, purpose of mind and heart.

Check your novels *(books)*, for they have the power to change the course of time and of man. They reach out to you in words that match your intuition; we are the noble ones who watch over your Earth, the masters who you consider to be the guardians.

Never neglect the teachings that we command, for yours is a pitiful planet. Hold the Rose, let her light shine for the sake of humanity and the commonwealth of man and the beasts upon your planet. Never forget that yours *(life)* is a purpose, reinforce the love.

His splendour is an immaculate light of conception, yours is of your will to change the course of your being. Do not allow your minds to be tempted by the triviality of life, cast aside your fears, for we are aware of the terrors of your mind. Collectively we admire the purpose intended for your kind.

The Pyramids and Temples of your lands are a focus upon which we commanded those of eons past, their respect of us is visible today. Be aware we shall return; the signs will be given; May will see the commencement of actions to cleanse your planet. Your task is twofold, to make aware our intentions, they are of peace, but like all things to come, there must be pain.

Transform your thoughts into words my son; let them be heard by the many.

22nd May 2016

The Immaculate Ones

Trust is a word so often used to mislead people into a false sense of security, soon negotiations will take place in Prague with heightened tempers, treaties broken. The prospect looms large of indiscreet performances by those who have interest and need of the union.

Our light will shine upon the tempest to follow in what needs to be done to combat the fears of others, for we are of the natural world, interceding and living alongside you. Gladiators we are for Mother Earth, defending Her purpose and right to exist freely without burden upon Her, for She cries out for attention in the fields and the valleys as man disrespects her in so many ways.

Your feelings of indulgence should be tempered by that of love, trust and a will, to perform the purpose at hand before those who come before you with interest and love in their hearts. Know that we intercede to bring happiness and joy to those who are weary of life and need support and love as they combat their fears to what is to come before you all in due course. We have never seen such an eventful phase of the passage of man; you must terminate your old ways and embrace the new with open arms, your blessings of the Lord.

Comparatively you are a specimen that intrigues our minds, for our purpose and will must be transmitted to those of your world. Trust in us, as we trust in you to bring happiness with an outlook of joy to your world of sorrow. We are of a nation far beyond yours; we have a will to see a fellow race succeed in the endeavours of life. Your pathway is a good one and will be welcomed by many upon your earth, but still there are those who will be negative in response, do not allow their minds to interfere in the purpose given.

Tremendous amounts of compassion are needed this day for there has been a matter of great concern in the avenues of

power beneath your feet. Many have sacrificed and forfeited their holy light as free men to serve the one with false intentions; he has committed a heinous crime for which he will answer in the hereafter. You will hear of the children in the bells as they ring out the shameful, hideous crimes of man, for he has no right to withdraw a life of a child. His crimes will go unpunished mong your people, but know this; he will face the consequences of our world for he will not be permitted to enter the light of heaven. *(Note: We interpret this as being about child abuse, but we have no idea who it refers to.)*

Content yourselves with this knowledge as you read of the terrible things, crimes committed against humanity in the South from the North. Tumultuous welcome from his people will be tainted by the hatred of the world, but his people are but puppets by which he pulls the strings, their thoughts cannot be their own, their will is not their own, their lives are dangled on a thread and a simple cut would see them fall from democracy.

How can it be that your earth has become a sinful place where man's morals have deteriorated into the dark side. Only by the strength of a few can man be brought back from the brink. Considerations are given to those who work endlessly in the effort to bring peace and love among your people of the world. Among them is Christopher Regis, for he works tirelessly, unrecognised by men, unseen by most, but he exists in his roll, master of peace. He assists those in part of necessity and need, to help them grieve the loss of their loved ones. Formation of his mind's patterns are seen by us, as is all those who work in the light, they extend their love and compassion to those who are less fortunate.

Tremendous amounts of goodwill are required to ease the burden of those who cannot fend for themselves. For the tyrant, he will dominate their lives until the time within the near future of his termination; his existence will go down in history as an example of extremism.

Tensions will grow within the nations that face the burdens of the one who cannot be named, his purpose is that of fear and domination and our wisdom will lead you to his name, contemporary man, cause of wisdom before the shame.

Fill your hearts with love and a measure of compassion, for we are the Immaculate ones who send messages of love and joy, but of intrigue as your social sect needs interest to focus their minds on the light, the love of the Lord.

Comparatively, you are a fragment of a piece of a puzzle to make up the whole, your temperament and demeanour are of nature. Frequently you ask for evidence to be given, we have concerns why you think this is necessary. Bring about a measure of comfort, be all knowledge and wisdom of those who can see.

Your eyes are closed to the many things that God has given to you in this world of green and blue, acknowledge our presence in your atmosphere at this time, we have been seen by many. End of July; herein lies those who hear purpose among your people of the Earth, a tremendous will to bring about a peace among men of your Earth.

We are knowledgeable in ways, many would regard as tremendous intelligence, but they are merely learnt in the learning curve of life. We have developed into a race of beings of the natural worlds, for we exist in the spiritual form of your heavens. You call to us in your prayers as a dove calls to the moon in the sky. We hear many transmissions sent to us asking for clarity, cleansing, for need for you to channel the information to those who would listen, who shut their ears to the world around them and sit among us in the light of the Lord. Trust is needed; it is given to those who would listen, for they will enhance your world with the light of the Lord. Trust is needed not to brandish them as egotistical men of awareness in all things of life, however in the vast majority, there is but a few that speak the words of wisdom and condition minds, hearts and souls' purpose to find a peace in your lives.

Tremendous amounts of courage and will, will be required for the events in the autumn of your Earth, they are natural occurrences of tremendous power, disbelief will be shared by many. Even as the winds blow and the Earth erupts in a violent manner, disproportionate to the measurements given by the instruments of man, we are here to fill a need of purpose.

We need not tell you of our sympathetic ways, we will guide man in a manner befitting the Lord. Because we are not seen, that doesn't mean that we do not see. You classify the outrages with numbers of measure, be warned a measure is but a number, the velocity of its impact will affect your way of life in aspects in which you thought not possible. We tell you this not to be in fear, but to issue you with a forewarning that you must cope with a different world in a measure of love and peace.

Men must come together to allow his heart and soul to once more be that of the love and light of the Lord. Don't be afraid for we mean no harm; we are those of another world who can help in extreme ways. Extreme measures are needed to assist in your men of purpose. We tolerate your emotions as we are among you, we are not seen as we live in the shadows of life, but we see, we know, unbelievably you walk by us, never seeing, never knowing, but that's ok.

You have requested to have a meeting amongst us, we will attend your briefing on the morrow of the new moon. Your friends will meet a man who calls himself Michael. Allow him to explain to you of the magical things that life can bring. Pastures green will start a new fresh dawn in the years to come when man has sacrificed his ill ways to that of the light.

She will announce Her being to those who wish to call Her name Mary. Sequences of events will become known shortly in the mid-afternoon of September/October, tremendous fortitude is needed to overcome the fear that this will bring, your hearts must be strong as your lives will change for the better.

Contemporary art has its place among your people, you see the strokes of the brush, they adorn the canvas as the artist creates a work of art. So it is that we will all put our brush to the new canvas, bringing a work of art to your world. Consider yourselves not as masters of this world but as caretakers, for we are the masters who will impose our will upon those who mistreat nature. Purposefully you have become not aware of our need of love, target your fear, release your mind.

It was once said that man was the creator upon this planet, we see no meaningful purpose beyond his words, we hear the sweet music of love on the winds of time, we once lived as man caressing Mother Nature with outstretched arms, inviting her into our lives with love and with honour. I have become aware of many things that involve man's indiscretions, but on the positive side there are those of beauty that dwell within the hearts of man. For these, the doors will open to the new dawn that brings the new light of the day.

We have never been so demanding as to ask of you that which you cannot give, but we do expect a decorum of respect, as our purpose brings needs in your life. Forget the past as it is history, the future is yours to make, but tread carefully, for the path is narrow and the fall is great. Your steps have been taken wisely on your path of light. Have faith in your heart; trust in your soul's purpose, for your soul's purpose is the one thing given to you by the Almighty.

Careless whispers of those banish your mind from their thoughts, they neglect their duties to see your light, the focus within your mind. Our energies will be strange, we are of strange appearance. To man's curiosity we signify a change in the hearts and minds of men willing to advance beyond their years, trouble us not with the trivialities of life for we are of the light and need purpose and focus to cast our will on those of the dark. Your purpose and meaning will become clear in the next phase of life.

We are satisfied of the advancement that is made by many as they walk the path of light in their lives, care not for the ways of man, for that is best to pass in time. We will magnify your thoughts with intense measures unleashed to bring about your purpose.

Traditions unfold before your eyes of the next moon, they will have repercussions, it will reverberate among your nations of men as the despair of the thousands will be made public, a disease so great as to wipe out many minds, trust in your hearts purpose and their need for love.

As I sit with you this evening be aware of our intent for your soul's purpose to magnify and illuminate the minds of the many. Treaties will be made by us with significant decorum, proportions in line with our words to be played out before many. Feel us as we enhance your mind and body with a power and purpose, fortitude is needed. Developments will be made to bring about a machine, it shall be magical in your eyes, we will initiate a purpose in man as we inspire those minds of science, they will bring about such a wisdom that cannot be denied by those who would mislead you.

Pray upon your emotions, cancers are a formation of bodies that are abnormal in size, for their growth is activated by the indiscretions of man, do not allow!

24th May 2016

Together we will walk in the good times and the bad, as you tread your path in this life of yours. Have no fear of the circumstances surrounding the issues to the forewarnings given.

The masquerades of light that would dazzle those within the population of your Earth are seen for what they are by the minds of the Jewish people, as they clamour to the wall to make their feelings known to Him on high. Their rush will cause a panic of devastation, their hearts, their minds will not focus upon the reasons for them being there, for they know not why events have come to their door. All too often they have been persecuted by many of your world for their faith, is it not a faith of all? For ultimately all religions are one, of that of the Lord.

Aspects of light will shine upon those who preach the gospel with focus and love, never knowing their purpose is to bring joy to the minds of the masses as they struggle to cope with their everyday lives. Continuing battles of freedom become more intense, but as the months roll on, their wills will grow stronger to establish a foothold in the hills and mountains of

Sinai. They cannot contest the light, for that which God made is not theirs, but for all upon your planet of life.

Negotiate your mind to a will of need and trust, as the hours tick by, so you will see our true purpose and intent upon the peoples of your world.

Father Augustus, he knew of many things in the ways of the Lord, he vanished into oblivion making his mark upon man before he left, the circumstances surrounding his departure are vague in your world but he knew the risks that he would face on the way by the public, why? *(Note: There are obviously a few priests with this name, one we came across was Father Augustus Tolton, he was born into slavery and became the first black priest in America in 1886, he naturally suffered much prejudice. He died aged 43 after 'spells of illness' – We are not sure if this is who it is or not.)*

Termination of events abroad will commence shortly in the East in a province unknown to most, as Syria is a region of vast emptiness where a man has a will not to be seen, consider his name as not being that of a man, but of another world.

Contrasts deliver a sequence of events, to which many will aspire as they rush to reach the pot of gold, it is an illusion. All that man desires is given to deceive him, to test his will, his fortitude on his life's path. Your desires and needs are satisfied with the everyday things of life. Not many will look beyond his eyes and consider the possibilities of other realms, where there is need of His love from our many forms that can be achieved, and not that of the physical. Our fear is of a spirit who's a soul of many minions within the cosmos.

Your atmosphere is a cataclysmic time bomb, as your dense air thins dramatically during the hot weather, the heat of the day will bring many terrible things to those exposed to the Sun, be aware that your bodies are but as thin as an eggshell, delicate as lace, take extreme care in August.

Gertrude Speaks of Wartime Atrocities Towards the Jews

Gertrude, wishes to say that her mother joins us now with a message of peace for all of the union, "'Twas in those days, those turbulent times that our family was massacred in the name of the Reich, they established themselves in the village where we dwelt, they stormed our lives with their boots of hell, they punished us for being who we were, not for being human but because of our love of the Lord. They were dark as the night and they had schemed for many years to extinguish our light, for they were jealous of the things they felt they couldn't have, but are there for all who welcome the light. Their atrocities are known across the globe, but they march on, deceiving those today as they did then."

Terrorists of Today

They assumed a different name, those that are masked, until they reach a point where they feel they can once more tread upon the lives of the innocent. Tensions mounting in the East will trigger the emotions of the West to react in a manner unforgiving, they will see their chance to put their mark upon the world once more and they will chant as members of a race of the dark. Become aware of the intolerance's that are unseen by the eyes of many, for they dictate their thoughts and feelings through the net of the web of life.

His fiery outbursts will be recognised by many of intolerance and misjudgement. He persecutes those in need of attention, he raises his hands against those who would denounce his ways, frankly he is a tyrant in sheep's clothing. His purpose and will, will drive the force of unprecedented violence as he erodes his national symbol to a mere glimmer of its former self. His nation will tremble at the thought that he is a man unbalanced in his mind with power and greed. We know of his antisocial behaviour towards those of a coloured race, he leads the clan in many areas to destabilise her attentions. He will continue his plan of action to succeed in whatever manner he feels fit, his outrages will surpass that of tyrants in times gone by. He has a will and a mind to use the resources at hand, don't assume that he is a man, for he is negative. Convince your loved ones of his need to dominate those of the states in which he has power. Don't neglect the things that are spoken of by him as they contain his true meaning.

Lavender will bring a measure of good fortune upon those who have a will to be one with each other.

Many speculate that life on Earth will vanish without trace many eons from now, but why should this be? It is only man's desire to self-destruct that will bring about this end, but if he has a will to open his heart and mind in the ways of the Lord and to his fellow man, then his survival will progress to establish a world of unity. At this time he knows of one thing, that of the disturbances brought about by a man known to all, as one of the beast's servants, he calls out for positive actions disregarding other's lives. The dogs of war will bark once more as they call to him through the ethos of time to bring about a purpose of his will, of his state of mind to others. Truly you need to sit within the light to create a balance of minds against his. Trouble your heart not of his intentions for he has a downfall coming of mega proportions.

Cast your mind back to those days of your childhood when your mind was free and your heart was lifted by love, can you not see that you are still that child? Discard the baggage collected to free that mind once more for the purpose intended; compliance of your mind is essential to bring about a purpose and will to assist us in ways by which you will only understand. Try to understand we are here to help. The warnings given are to enhance your minds with knowledge; we're not to speculate upon the outcome of your planet or your lives because they are in your power to change. Ask yourselves a simple question, "Who is the master of your lives, is it God or is it the man in the street who thinks he knows all above our Lord?" Of course you know the one true master is that of the Lord, caress your heart with tender love and bring about a change in man's desire for peace, topple your thoughts, allow us in.

Congratulations to those who have persevered to win the battle of the light, their heroic efforts to surmount new possibilities of life will be rewarded by the immense energy of love and goodwill. They have frankly a determined mind and will that should be aspired to by all of humanity who desire peace.

26th May 2016

We have seen for many years the trials and tribulations of men, his fortunes won and lost with battles of the heart, but he has neglected and has missed his golden opportunity to become one with the nations of the many around your globe. You sit in your dwellings feeling secure and illuminated *(informed)* by those who tell you all is well. Their forecasts are wrong, they don't understand the options before them and they cannot conceive to listen to one another's rhetoric, for theirs is the way that they will tread regardless of who or what is in their path.

They have no foresight to the coming battles of humanity in which many extremist views will be expressed by the lack of love. Knowledge of these events will become clear in spectacular fashion during the harvest festival of the full moon, for we know of many things of sacrifice. Do not consider yourselves as the perfect race; you are merely specimens who walk this planet of life.

Control your emotions as we near your Earth to establish a basis on which to communicate with those in power, their knowledge of us is great, their understanding is lacking, as they assume that we are here to take over. It is not our plan; we are merely assuming the role of peacemaker of your nations before you succumb to the massacre of mankind. Treat us not with contempt but with a passion, an emotion of love, we send greetings to your brothers of Earth, please accept our warmest welcome to you. Content yourself with the knowledge that the roses will bloom once more in the valleys so green that were once of anger and despair.

To us your nations are criminals who wipe out the desire of a will to love; they are consumed with their own importance, establishing a foothold in the corridors of power. Their main concern as they rush to grab all the advantages possible, that they may achieve their minor targets. They have missed an important step in their strides of progress, they do not realise that the Earth was created for man, for all to live upon in peace and harmony, not to jettison the love that was injected into your souls.

Confirmation of our presence is heard through the corridors of power, their lack of understanding will cause great concern amongst the many nations, for their concern is only of their own needs. We speculate that there will be a truce of minds to encounter our arrival. We cannot trust your men of power, for they are weak and feeble of mind. They are deserving of no respect, for they cannot comprehend of our being.

Your natural world suffers greatly at this time from many things that man created. Its very nature and fabric is under threat by those scheming to fragment the core with gases. *(Fracking)* The warnings are given, all too late we fear, for they will be ignored by the vast majority of your people. But we will obtain a partnership with you to illuminate those minds of reconciliation with our being as we approach your Earth in a formation that you will recognise as the arrow.

Despite our superiority we cannot interfere or intercede with those of the Earth, for the Almighty has ordained that you should punish yourselves with your thoughtless actions. We have considered many options, we have obtained many thoughts of minds of will, but we concede that we cannot interfere. Our purpose and words will cause minds to consider other possibilities in the world of matter.

Before you came with your spiritual thoughts, we were sure that there would be one that would listen, to be frank, we have need of many to establish a basis of thought that would flourish within the minds of man. Your seed will become apparent in the forthcoming events, as people look for some modicum of comfort, their eyes will fall upon the sites as they read the daily news. Be not concerned with the threats and warnings, as they are not ours, but of your own making.

You cannot understand the power of your minds as they transmit their thoughts of concern and worry, for what you destroy is so strong as to affect us, it is a matter of concern. Bless your hearts for allowing us to talk in a frankness of mind to those who would listen to the words given in your circles of light. We aspire to bring those of purpose to the forefront of the matters concerning men.

Commonly you would regard us as not of this Earth, we are blessed with the knowledge that some will come with open arms to embrace our thoughts and our will, so as to achieve a satisfactory conclusion to your existence upon this world.

Constantly we inform you of warnings, which are negative thoughts to others, but they are merely a precursor to events that may happen or could happen should the course remain unchanged. Nevertheless, we must inform the minority of uninformed people, their need is required to prevent a catastrophe upon the seas of the North.

Focus your mind in the purpose ahead, travel with us to the far reaches of your mind knowing the connections, know your mind. Troublesome minds to bear witness to much sorrow in your world. To follow will be a calm of reassurance. Pestilence will become rife as your need grows, for need to allow us to intervene, to maximise your thoughts, target those emotions of those that would listen.

January, February and March are months and days of a new era, from which beginnings of frustration will fill the hearts of men as they clamour to hide their cash where it cannot be seen, for their greed is astounding. They marshal others with directives to avoid payments of taxes to your queen and country. They hide their intentions behind closed doors hoping that misleading words will not betray for their need. Super spies will uncover their indiscretions, whistle-blowers will sound the trumpets of truth. Before they can respond, their secrets are out, culminating in a masquerade of words to cover up their indiscretions before the people of the united violence. Why should these men feel the need to betray their own kind with their wealth and their knowledge? They can bring about change if desired, they will require duties from beyond, duties in life to impose the law and bring about a change of rule, for they have betrayed their own with their greed of wealth. What will they do with it, for it is of no use to them when they cross to this side of life? They do not understand the question will be raised, to intervene in matters of awareness regarding posthumous misgivings.

Notable backbencher's in a class of their own, they dictate the law of the land from behind closed doors, they secretly betray him who leads. They scurry around with their notes in hand hoping that somewhere their purpose will grow, unseating the one who rules, for their distaste of this man is great, they perceive him as an 'upstart' as he causes uproar with his words of passion, his ignorance is astounding for he assumes too much.

Matters of opinion don't count when it comes to love and trust, many have tried to woo the sirens *(temptress)* of beauty to make them their own personal property. Their heads are strong, their minds are weak, their thoughts unfold in a manner betraying their trust. Concern yourself not, we are here as a measure of a true guide to assist the fragmented words.

A meaningful respect of the Lord is required by those of the light, they call upon His name as their saviour. His rule is supreme, of that there is no doubt, but why are their minds so focused on ceremony without purpose or meaning? For they mystify those who bear witness to their scenes of injustice. Their purpose of being was that of caring for those in need, we see no point in their masquerade.

Charming as he once was, he elected to be part of the universe in his thoughts, never understanding the will of those of a different origin, he was a policeman, a peacemaker, **Bill Francis McIntyre** deserves no less than a hero's welcome as he performs his duties with trials and tribulations set against him by those masked men who need his word of silence, troubles his mind the matters at hand. He will come out on top of the heap, exposing the corridors of power and their corruption as they dwell in their magnificence, not noticing the greater picture. An outcome of massive proportions will transpire on the news platform of the world. His negotiations with Prague will bring forthcoming talks in the cities that bear the name of freedom. *(Note: We can find no positive identification for who Bill McIntyre is, maybe it is not for us to know just yet? Or can anyone else shed light on who he may be?)*

2nd June 2016

Do not let your emotions fade with time, *(have)* **an appetite for each moment of the day.**
Your aspect of light will shine bright to those of the Earth. Bless you for your tolerance and understanding of our purpose to bring about a peace of mankind, a peace of heart, a peace of mind and gentleness to withhold a feather of light without affecting its structure. We have once before spoken of things to come within your life, with a measure of purpose we will attempt to give you some idea of the purpose intended for us.

Those of the light, do not be tempted with greed or avarice, keep an open mind to those who would challenge your will and allow their questions to float on the air, as we will guide their steps to the answers required.

Pianos play, sounding notes of music giving respite from the pressures of the day. We hear you calling us, asking for guidance, your murmurings are of great importance to those who follow you, those of the light, for they have a manner of purpose to take the music and play it to the ears of those who focus.

Truly your hearts desires are welcomed by all, your tenderness and caring nature must continue through time to carry these words with love.

Tremendous amounts of skill will be required to balance life in the aspects of spirit. Your words will flow as rivers, deep through the valleys; the streams that it feeds are the minds of those who would listen with love and tolerance.

Your purpose this evening is required to deliver a message of song to the hearts of those who have a will to listen. It follows:

Gone are the days and nights, those thoughts of changing times, take heart to the songs of rhythm that reason with your mind. Life has begun to open a world illuminated by the light, connect your mind to hear the song of love.

Temperance and justice are words that are a measure given to men to guide his thoughts and misgivings. Trouble your heart not, for we are here to travel with you on that long road of life and mystery filled with love.

Most troubled we are as we roam the galaxy to continue with our mission to enhance the minds of the many who would hear our words. A life of purpose has to be judged by those of ill will, as they cannot conceive that your mind is capable of a connection to other worldly beings beyond your solar system. Their misgivings are their misfortunes, for what do they know of the mind, of the patterns that bring together kindred spirits of the light? Their gaze is not upon the possibilities beyond your life, for their focus is on the material things that are available for the short period that they live. How can they be so blind as not to see the bigger picture, for it stands before them like a megalith? The rock seems like an obstacle to them, they do not trouble to take a look at the other side, for it seems too daunting to make an impasse, so they say, "There is no other side, there is only this space that confronts us and it is not possible to go beyond this wall."

Human tragedies occur because men of vision are blocked, they are outweighed by those who can only see profit and not a path. Contrast your mind to that of the dark, be the one to shine bright upon their closed eyes and minds.

We never intended for your Earth to fall into such despair, our intentions were to connect with the beings of life, to help them construct their temples of love. Their thoughts, their minds were simple of origin. What have you to offer in the way of compassion and knowledge? We ask you this question not simply to confuse your mind, but to ask that you consider contemplation on their meaning.

We choose a place of significance for your thoughts, the trimester *(Note: Trimester equals three months)* is a period of change. Our purpose and intention is not to harm those who wish to view the spectacle, but it may draw attention to those negative souls who would disrupt an organised event of the light, for their hearts are dark, not requiring of love but they have a passion to destroy that which is good. Their evil intent will take place in a matter of days before the sun rises over the new moon and your belief and trust is paramount as we take your hand and lead you to places and events so that your mind and will can be allowed to embrace the dark and bring light to the minds of the masses.

Purposely we have chosen a spot with a longitude and latitude, it is a measure of our will that you become familiar with that place, it stands between **Heaven's gate and the margin of the river** and the co-ordinates are longitude **32 east, latitude 91 west,** you will know this place for it is marked on the map as a site of interest at a place of worship. Contrast your mind with hope and the possibility of enlightenment for all who travel to this place. *(Note: These Coordinates lead to the Grand Gulf Nuclear Power Station on the Mississippi and the nearby Jerusalem Church, Port Gibson – Further research brought our attention to the fact that the Nuclear Power Station takes water from the Mississippi to cool its reactors, in the process of doing this the water is effectively sterilised and returned to the river where it continues its journey to the Gulf of Mexico where the lifeless toxic water promotes the growth of a massive bloom of algae of about 6,500 square miles making the sea toxic to life.)*

Contemporary art speaks of men with a will to motivate those of purpose and need. Condemned they are, sacrificed for their beliefs; the red shadow will not tolerate such murmurings, for they are out of place and keeping of those of intention of ill will. Trouble yourself not, because these events will occur in the purpose. In the meantime, carry out your duties with love of the light in prayer.

It is not necessary for us to judge those who have judged themselves as being all powerful, because they in turn will be judged by the almighty power of the Lord as they must pass to a world of negative attitude where they can be reassessed and given the opportunity to redeem themselves.

We are focused upon Lennon's light to connect and bring about a peaceful ending to hostilities upon your world. *(Note: The lyrics of John Lennon's 'Imagine' come to mind.)* Fragmented you are like a stone, broken into pieces, but as you reconnect, so the stone will become whole once more.

A melting pot of minds to issue you messages of love and light, for as the pebbles on the beach, there are many souls with need. The joy of love will bring about a warming of the heart for temperance and tolerance is required to allow the melting pot to merge. Join us now as we embrace the hearts of men.

Tremendous amounts of will, will be required in the forthcoming events, with situations of tense drama unfolding upon your screens. The shocked eyes of the world will ask why has this happened, why was it not stopped? For it is your *(mankind's)* reckless behaviour and manner that has opened the doors for those of the wicked to step through. Catastrophes occur giving rise to an outcry and a will to befall a change of heart. Global occurrences happen all the time, but none like this, for this will open the eyes of the many for their view. For it is you that will help heal the minds of those troubled of the things to come. Continue your meditations with peace and love, a mind of strength to battle the elements that would curb your manner.

Trumpets sound as the wind blows, Northumberland will be affected by these storms not forecast for they are hidden in systems of systems.

Turquoise is the colour that will bring healing to those who have lost loved ones, they relate to the heart in the actions of love.

19th July 2016

We are here this evening to bring you news of a great event in the forthcoming times of your lives. Allow the love and the angels of light to enter your being with messages of joy and hope for the young, for the elderly and all those as they aspire upon the words.

We have been transformed recently to assist in the music of life to bring our notes of vibration to the minds of men who are many within your world, they listen intently to their mind, not knowing from where the information has originated, for how can there be such things as spiritual guidance in the realm of men?

Figuratively speaking we are in a sense, beings of a different nature to yourselves, we come from a place that to many is alien. It is a world of tremendous beauty, of three satellites that orbit our planet, you call them moons. The Sun arises to our west and the day is long and seemingly endless at times, but our lives are nurtured by our love for freedom and peace. We are a dignified race who come to you before Lily this evening with words of congratulations to those who have become an open book and turned their minds to the many possibilities of life, within the many realms that exist in the many dimensions parallel to yours.

Your universe was formed millions of years in the past, it came from the dust of the stars, forming your planets in a random order. Your researchers, they discuss possibilities of a theory relating to a large explosion, for they see no other possibility of the creation of your universe. But imagine this, if one dimension was to cross another with such a force as to jolt the universe, this would cause tremendous energy to be released. Moon particles release their energy bringing about a formation of life within your atmosphere.

We are not Arcturians, we are of the light before time. Your memories are vast, but do not assume that all knowledge is of man, for there are many structures within the universes of life, some comparable, some totally abstract from your own ideas

55

of ways of life. Do not be focused upon the flesh that you see, for there are other materials that bind together to create illusions of life as you know it.

We cannot say how many nations are exposed to greed and avarice within your world, but their doctrines of commerce will be announced shortly, to bring aspects of torment to those who have little. Why should those of little resource be exposed to such intolerant behaviour by those who have plenty? How can they be so bold as to think, "Well that's alright, they won't care?" Their riches absorb the blows that will set upon them as they focus their minds to profit. They will be assured of a swift and bitter end in the crash in the fall of man.

Forthcoming events will unleash forces of nature that will torment all those within your world. You ask if there is hope, naturally those who have an ability will survive an onslaught of fresh re-greening. It's a clean sweep to brush away those old doctrines of torment. Perhaps in a way you are lucky of having a foresight and knowledge and although your lives may end, there will be new beginnings that will set you on a road far beyond your imaginations. Your past pleasures will be gone and your new outlook will begin afresh. We are aware of the fear this will bring, and ask that you bring yourselves to a point of focus. Do not allow us to upset your peoples of the Earth, but care for them in His words, they are necessary for understanding the bigger purpose that He ascends on your tiny planet.

Comparatively your minds are overwhelmed by the many things of life, never understanding the meaning of a true life, a life of purpose. How bizarre is it that you cannot understand that your life began in a flourish of love and spirit? You ascended to this plane to become a responsible being of the light, and we applaud those who have reached a point in their lives where their aspects are open to all possibilities.

And to those who have destroyed lives in their quest for their own personal gain – well what can we say? You have committed yourself to a path so dark that you will need to be brought to an understanding that all life is equal regardless of state or rank. Be assured your misgivings will be dealt a blow to you, until you can reconcile your differences with a love and purpose of light to Him.

We have come across some details of importance and we stress that these need attention – it came to our notice some time ago, that your men of power are willing to sacrifice the many for the few. Their bargaining behind closed doors would not have been seen by the vast majority of Earth, for their secretive ways are a response to their greed. They feel it necessary to overrule those things that have been placed by the almighty, regardless of colour and creed. They will dominate your species as best they can. Naturally there will be resistance on a focus of these mindless fools, but the efforts will be futile to those of wealth.

Don't complicate your lives with the unnecessary things of so-called value, as the one value is of tolerance, of being of the light. Negative thoughts should be eliminated by the thoughts of happy times. Comparatively, your minds are weak to the trinkets of life.

Fortescue, now there was a man, he created so many things that nurtured man's mind. *(Note: Possibly **Adrian Henry Timothy Knottesford Fortescue** [14 January 1874 – 11 February 1923] an English Roman Catholic priest who was an influential liturgist, artist, calligrapher, composer, polyglot, amateur photographer, Byzantine scholar, and adventurer. He was the founder of the Church of St Hugh of Lincoln in Letchworth, or his ancestor **Sir Adrian Fortescue** [1476 – 9 July 1539] who was a courtier at the court of King Henry VIII of England and was executed in 1539 and later beatified as a Roman Catholic martyr.)* Human encyclopaedias are many who speak of him in his glorious ways, that he once came to your England to a tumultuous welcome. Why would your narrow minds think that he was unable to travel the world? For he came many times upon the shores of many lands to oversee the forthcoming events of man. Fortescue knew well of the scriptures, he had studied them in great detail, scouring them for the minutest detail pertaining to him and his life in England. Many may not know how obscure he was in those times. His name, although strange to many became a friend to their hearts, minds and souls. You call him Jesus of Nazareth. He is the chosen one that brings the message of love to witness once more a new beginning within man, to bring a purpose of peace and hope to all who would let his light in.

Don't allow your minds to ignore the warnings or the blessings of his coming. Scary maybe, in many aspects, but the light of his being will shine brightly to many lives.

Doctorates are gained to celebrate a man's purpose, the education of his mind is essential to his being in life. There are many aspects that bring a man to focus upon the purity of love and life. We have forecast many times that man is under an illusion of the things of life, but open your hearts and minds, feel the need of his love within your soul. There are many present here today who would witness many extremes of life. Their attitudes are harsh towards the extremists that bring terror and shame to your world, for their focus is of hate, their need of greed is only matched by the need of love. Tormented their lives by others, who give them an illusion that theirs is a purpose of the Lord. How can this be? To take a man's life without due care and attention, to bring him to an end in such a bitter way, how can they imagine that this is Gods purpose? For God is of love and peace, and for the welfare of man and all creatures who live upon the Earth. His focus is upon those who bring misery and shame, for they must justify their actions in his presence.

Be not ashamed of who you are my son, a beacon of light that shines out bringing hope to many. Tell this to your people, that we of the light bring an opportunity for all to receive his blessing.

Brussels will be the centre of attention, as once more outrageous acts of war will be brought to the innocent lives of many. Hopeless devastation caused will dissatisfy the nations as they forecast an end for the terrorism beset upon your planet. Fortitude is needed, for these coming events of horror. We cannot exactly say how these events will occur, but the minds of men who plan such evil deeds, their thoughts betray them in a way they cannot understand.

Beware the railways, the tracks that move under the ground for they are a worrying concern.

Brighton's festival is a happy, joyful time which will bring respite to many of your world.

Compel your minds to peace, allowing us to judge those of negative thoughts and purposes.

The death penalty will be imposed upon those who have caused devastation, but this will bring turmoil in your nations, an aspect of disagreement will be announced shortly. A split will occur with an enormous amount of ill will being brought to those nations. For tolerance should not be ignored to those of ill will.

We have mentioned money once before, it is the evil of the world that brings joy to some, misfortunes to others and your need of it is great as it occupies man's mind to increase his finances to bring a life of pleasure. It will not bring relief from stress, how can such an illusion bring happiness for those who want, want more. Never being satisfied with the gifts given for their life's purpose.

Jointly you will assume responsibility for the wellbeing of those in despair. You find this hard to believe in your present life, but never be closed to the permutations that life brings, as it throws curved balls to all who live it. Some with focus, some without, but joy will be brought to all and paid in kind for their efforts in their lives.

Joyous times indeed, for those mayors are elected by a promise of hope and the need of the population, for London will bear witness to a happy event in the forthcoming celebra-tions of her romance. Smiles will fade into significance, as she turns a corner and waves with a happy expression to her nation, with a gratitude of love for her being. *(Note: Royal Wedding?)*

Eastern provinces are those targeted by new beginnings. For he will relinquish his power as the pressures of the people grow upon his shoulders. He never thought such things could be, to be brought down by the peoples of his country who tarnish their name in his evil doings. He beckons others, of other nations to join him in assistance to control the masses, but his power is relinquished. There's no one who wishes to band with him. He cannot understand how this came to be, for his dominance was great, as was his cruelty and wickedness. He sits there aloof, master of his kingdom, on his throne and seat of power dictating rules as if no other mattered. Bureaucracy will deal a blow so immense, his mind will be beset with anger, creating frustration that before he relinquishes power, he will muster his forces to put down those who are set against him in the streets.

We are no longer in control of minds of matter. Our beings only exist in the light. Our gratitude is great to serve him who oversees those of life. Truthfully, we hope that your new beginnings will bring a sense of fellowship and love to mankind and the beasts of burden upon your Earth.

Triggered emotions will fire up a storm in the east, causing the west to beat a hasty retreat. As the storm grows, like the feathers of a nest, they will scatter in the winds until they can no longer sit together in unison in that nest.

They betray each other's minds with negative thoughts, they'll be of common onslaught. That NATO was to guarantee peace to the world, but it has failed in its duties to secure these turbulent times. Figuratively it has no meaning and longer, but is just there as a distraction to those of war.

You call it a nation of despair; we call it a nation of need of love and tolerance. Their leader will fall before the crowds of anger. Never let it be said, that man!

Truly negative, are your responses to our call for peace as we circle your planet, your Earth, in our ships of gold searching for an answer to give man hope of pastures green. We are under no illusion that it is a task of immense proportions, for there are many splits within your nations. We need to bring a focus, to a point on the ground where a silver circle, a formation of doves will appear in the late August of your earth.

Never disrespect your Mother Earth, for she is the one that bears your burden of life. How many times have we said this before? That your meagre lives are nothing in the grand scheme of things. Yet you seek gratification for your efforts upon your planet. Know this, gratification can only be given to those of purpose and a will to open their hearts and minds. Truly, we announce to you our intentions of involvement upon your planet's structure and movement. We are unaware of any illusions that may be focused our way, why has man taken so much from her and given so little in return? For you cannot take, if you don't give.

Concrete evidence is given of the meaningful purpose of these words.

Religious formats are questioned by many in the forthcoming conference of those of religion. They will determine a method by which all men turn to God in a manner befitting Him. They are guided by the influences of man and not by spirit. A showdown will occur when they are confronted by the facts and not the fiction, or the doctrine set before them through eons of mistrust and misplaced hearts.

Their eyes will be opened as she brings comfort to all.

Never let go of your mind's values, of how to speak volumes to the nations my son.

31st July 2016

Ah, the madness of the world! We do despair, but let us change these bitter notes to a more tuneful song of love and praise. We have entered your life so many times before, bringing rhyme and reason to those of need, caring for those who have lost. Your hearts sing out silently as we shine our light upon you.

To all who have suffered loss, know that all are brought within the light, regardless the method of their passing. Truly we say unto you, the Lord is of mercy, keep him in your heart and do not deny his love. You may find forgiveness. We are honoured once more to bring the light of the Lord upon you all; we have bought many verses before your eyes.

Contain your love in your hearts and know that we have a care for man. Truly we say unto you, be bold in this world, this life. Beckon to him, your neighbour to follow in the ways of peace, for we grant all those who ask, everlasting peace. We have seen many things, disgust; it is hard to imagine such things can occur in a world of green and blue, for its beauty shines within the heavens.

Your mannequins who hold the seat of power are merely that, puppets, playing to the tune of the masters who hide behind their desks in their rooms, for man controls man in many ways, behind the eyes of the many. Spirit ask you to open your eyes and bring about a purpose of love and tolerance, be not shameful to bring these words to others, for they have meaning and depth that only those of the light will see.

4th August 2016

Tonight we have come with a purpose in mind for you and others to bring about meaningful words with focus upon life. Your words have been greeted by many of a spiritual nature, but more is yet to come, for your following will grow exponentially as the aspects of the words flow out to the nations of the earth.

We have come many times before to instruct you upon your path of light, but you have not heard us for such a long period, but now you have focus upon the need of your being. The gospel tells us that John was a purposeful man, he spoke many words to those around him of the coming of the Lord and they laughed, but still he blessed them with words of comfort and reassurance. His words were of comfort to the many of that time, as they were beaten by men who propagated violence. John was a prophet, he took his words abroad to many towns and cities, to many nations. He lays now at rest, at a place of peace. The rocks that bury him have lain undisturbed for many years, but he is not there, he is with us here in the world of spirit preparing the way for the many that aspire to the Lord and meet their reckoning, as all men must do. Yours will be no different as you bring your aspects of light to others to brighten their dark world with hope and tolerance. Your name is spread far and wide, but you must encompass the light of the Lord so as to bring a meaningful purpose to the multitudes, as they will all meet their end.

In times past the knowledge has been passed from man to man, hmm, like the vinegar, the wine it has become soured with a bitter taste. Drop by drop men sought to profit from the book of love. They use the words of the Lord to control the masses, bringing them temptation as they guide the words to men in a way that they are not meant. Search your souls my brothers and begin a new life as he, the son of Jehovah rises once more in the East.

Do not think of him as a man or as a woman, but that of spirit. It does not matter how he delivers his message; it just needs to be heard. For the reckoning is coming to you all, salvation is only found by he who seeks the words of the good book. We are the masters of no one, we do not control your lives, your destinies are written, in your minds of purpose.

As always you are guided step-by-step by those of a heavenly disposition. Target your emotions, as the things to come will test your soul. Bring to us your love and your need so that we may bring comfort to you, those of the Earth who seek our purpose will find peace. God bless.

7th August 2016

The Queen – This communication was channelled shortly after Her Majesty's 90th birthday

9 times 10, she has the power to extinguish their selfish ways. She will join us shortly, first she has a duty to perform for her nation, for God, for mankind. She has worked tirelessly for many years bringing joy to many of the earth, they focus upon her special hand waves. She is a monarch; her mind is trained to follow the practices of your nation. She will not allow her peoples to be dragged into degradation, as she will interfere with the Houses of Parliament, astonished faces will look as she declares them invalid. For her, her time will come, her voice will be spoken. She has strength 'Elizabeth', her sister, 'Margaret' recalls a time when they were children, and she would rule the nursery declaring herself Queen of Hearts. Her sister was subservient to her wishes, for she was the younger. Her son, his duties to perform will commence shortly, his heart is of the earth.

Parades of bikes will be seen in the streets of London as they demonstrate their right for the right of way. For the paths are required. A surge of the people will bring about a circumstance of regret, as many women panic, run for cover in the storm that follows. Frequently we give warnings, they are not to generate fear, but to bring about the perpetrators to an understanding that theirs will not be tolerated.

Cradle your arms as you nurture the child of love. Our aspects of love are upon you and all those who bear witness to the words given. Your questions will be answered shortly, to those inquisitive minds that ask, "who is this man? How can we trust his words?" You must have faith my friends and belief in the Lord and the wisdom in the ways that he brings. Nurture your child, your minds. We whisper in your ears methods by which you must adopt a system of love.

Careless whispers are heard, should be ignored as they are tainted. Never let your hearts correspond with that of the dark. We are the saviours of your world; we will come before your eyes in the new dawn. Tremendous amounts of tolerance will be needed, as our ships approach from many directions. We are here to guide your natural world. You will target us as aliens, we will neutralise their abilities to respond. We mean no harm but to bring joy to the many hearts who call upon us. Historic days happen all the time, but this will eclipse all as we announce our existence upon your earth. Miraculous ways you will think, for they are of evolution as yours must be. But first you must learn to live with one another as equals and not pound upon the other. We are the hearts and minds of your souls, you must respond and mean a purpose, a purposeful way of love. Thank you.

14th August 2016

Trevor, he announces that he intends to bring a meaningful purpose to the lives of those who are lost. Your thoughts are many, relinquish your mind my son. Allow us to focus the beam upon your being, a ray of light to inspire and lighten your way on your path and journey through your life. For the minds of many see you as an ambassador of the light as they study your words with interest, never really taking in the meaningful purpose. They struggle in understanding at times, by the fractures you speak of, for their minds can only conceive their own lives at this time. Bring purpose to them, allow Trevor an aspect of love so that he may help those in turmoil within your world. We have never demanded from you a purposeful force of being, but we assure you that our interpretation of love speaks that of the truth and of the Almighty. You sing your songs of praise as you worship the Lord in your temples (churches) of love. He hears many voices and calls to you upon the winds to change your ways in aspects of tolerance to your neighbours. Your beacons of love shine out to him, but it is not necessary for all to attend, for he has his house within your hearts, minds and bodies. Knock on his door and call him, call his name, allow him to breathe life and love, a purpose to you.

Jehovah he was once called, but he has many names, God being amongst one of them. He tempers his love for the attitude of grace of his being. You must never turn your hearts to that of the negative, for once you have broken your bond it will be an eternity to relinquish your heart to the aspects of light. Gone are the days when we demanded of you praise. We respect your minds as they mature throughout your seasons, but you must accept that tolerance is only given to those who show tolerance with love in their heart. Be not cruel to your animals or your men, for that will be met with an equal measure in response. We are the beings of the light.

Fortitude and gratitude are many virtues that will be required in the new dawn of the new day. We have spoken many times on this subject. Your minds race around wondering, "Who is this that speaks of new beginnings, why does he not explain his narrative in clear terms of understanding?" We are unable to allow you to know your future, but we can guide and nurture your spirit. The new beginnings we talk of will become clear as those of the negative relinquish their hold of fear upon the nations of love. It is at this time, the harvest moon that you will see a change in your atmosphere as we enter to assist in man's desires for peace within his world. Ah, but those of intolerance will attempt to stifle and thwart our mission. For their own greed is their master and their secrets held within the vaults of the Kremlin will not be released to Joe public, for they are the preserve of the keepers.

The 'Temples of Doom', we have not raised this subject before, but we feel it is necessary that you understand The Bear and who he is, his words are tempered with kindness, but look deep into his eyes. Do not fear him, for he has masters as well. *(Note: Is the bear possibly Putin, who like all leaders, has to conform to those that dictate to him. The temples of doom possibly The Kremlin?)*

Cradle your arms and hold the baby of love close to your chest and whatever happens within your lives, know that the meagre things of life are nothing. Hold your baby tightly and follow the path of love.

Domineering men have featured many times within the transcripts of your words, they have brought focus to many so that they would listen. Your purpose my son, is to forfeit a life of riches and good times, to serve as a vessel of love for spirit and mankind, to bring about a peace in their heart. Let the bad times become good and know there is light at the end of the tunnel of life. Conscious are we of your aspects and being, we have never meant to bring harm to you my son. You feel your love for us is an overwhelming thing and we appreciate in kind. We will not take your soul from your body. You must master and control your mind to focus on one thing or another, allow our beings to assist in these tasks, for we are the teachers from spirit who will guide your steps upon your purpose in life. Never doubt our intentions, our meanings, our prayers.

Truly admirable are many thoughts of those who look for the secrets of the circles. *(Note: Crop Circles.)* We have created many, things, amusements in your world. Your scholars look at them and say how can this be? They do not admit their secrets, but they hide the truth from the many.

Archaeologists they call themselves, archiving their finds, stashing them in the vaults, never to be seen again. Government leaders will not permit them to divulge their secrets, their knowledge in full. So they keep them hidden from prying eyes. They have evidence of the existence of man pre-dinosaurs, fragile pieces of information, sparse in numbers but nonetheless evidence. Your ministers hide the truth from you, for they worship money and kingdom.

The Queen

She will never allow them to own her lands, her property. She is the Queen of England who will respond in fury at attempts to fracture her earth, "Who are these upstarts?" With contempt, in a negative response from her. Control your emotions with an aspect of love towards her and her Commonwealth. She blisters easily in the sun, not helped by her age, but her wisdom is great. Many things she knows, but there are many that she does not. She is not a toy to be played with, she is your Queen.

Stand up and be proud of who you are, receiving information from high for purpose unknown to you it is time. You see the followers gather and those that fall by the wayside. Your strength is good, power is great, don't be concerned by those of an aspect of negativity, **for they will soon come to realise when your books are published that you are a man of means, an author of words symbolic of men's past and of life and of an existence pre your knowledge as men.** Don't fight those who talk against you, for their words have no value. Breathe a sigh of relief as we temper their attitudes. They are driven in ways they do not yet understand, by the rules of God, by the heavens above.

Create possibilities within your abilities, so that your light may shine, my son. We bring no sorrow or joy to your world; these are aspects of your own making. Do not denounce God as a figment of the imagination, for he is as real as the ground you stand upon. He is seen as a figure uncaring as the world plummets into darkness. He cares, but it is you, and you alone who allow these things to occur. You are unable to assist change as you fall into the abyss, but grasping hands of those of the light will cling to the walls of love and their strength will grow to bring purpose to others.

Meteorites will fall once more to your earth to bring about change. You scan the skies, a 10th of visibility. Change must come in a way of violent times. Ah, we hear you speak and say, "Why such doom, why?" You need to hear the truth of your bickering world, be assured the sun will shine once more for all who look to the light. Journeys must be taken and souls progress, life is short but meaningful to all who express their love and concern for humanity. Fear is part of the living world, as is predators that prey upon the weak. These things are natural and occur many times throughout your world unknown to you. They are scary things to face up to, but you must hold your head up high, for that path of light. So that when your time comes and you must face the inevitable, you will have strength in your heart and mind in the knowledge, that although your bodies are weak your inner strength is strong and will continue on despite events of your life.

Trouble your mind not for these events may or may not occur to you, or any other individual. Many lives are affected with such disastrous results. They bring about turmoil within those Western countries. Havoc will reign as he turns his head to the West, he will be voted by proxy, as many are seen as dark. Their country was newly born of immigration, now they clash. Ah, times change. *(Note: US.?)*

Complete your missions with truth and honesty in your heart, bring your words to lighten the lives of those who are unsure of the possibilities that life brings. We will communicate with you another time, another place, let your mind be in rest, look for your task to come. Allow us integration into your life, so that we may control aspects to advance your purpose.

Bilateral movements will bring disturbances to the east, the west of the city will become rubble. We have not changed our view, for we sit in a position aware upon high, we see the misfortunes of the world.

Colombia, she will bear the brunt of the storm and harrowing scenes of devastation will become obvious to the world. The cause and effects will bring countless many to their knees as they struggle to survive the onslaught of the winds that bring terror. Persecute with shame. Those hurricane winds are a creation of man as he abuses Mother Earth with his devices, creating atmospheric pressures to enhance his own country, not caring for the many who will suffer. Those burdens of side effects are growth and prosperity, they have their ambition but at what cost to the nations surrounding the Americas? Needless to say, we are astounded by the greed and attitude of those men of money, we hold our heads in shame that we should witness such appalling events. There are many things about your world that have occurred recently, but we are assured as time progresses. Ah, many will become sacrificial lambs to those experiments of your atmospheres.

"Too late, the cat is out of the bag", is an expression and term used when information is released upon your net. Ah, he hides in the embassy, disclosing information to the world. His purpose is done but he remains invisible to the eyes of men who would discount his words and make him invisible. There are many who speak the truth within your world but are stifled by the men of ignorance. Hmm, shame on them, for their being ignorant. Truly your hearts must endure many things within your atmosphere.

Dawning of a new age begins with the alignments within your stars. A natural pull of gravity will tug at your earth and you will feel the vibrations. Life is complex, but not so complex as not to be understood. We have purpose in your lives to renew your energy and resources, to assist with the healing of Mother Earth in ways unimaginable at this time. We must embark upon a mission that will assist your world to breathe. Your men of greed, they despise anything that is for free that will not bring them profit, for they do not see the profit in life, how blind they are. They will tell you that we are an illusion, a figment of your imagination, but your eyes will behold us.

We feel their concern as they negotiate possibilities of how to explain such a massive cover-up. How can they tell the world of their knowledge and why they withheld the information? Their rule will linger, but as the aspects of life and light grow, so it will overshadow them. She will come in the autumn to bring peace to your world, you cannot imagine how this could be, but have faith and stay true and strong in your mind and in your hearts.

Harps. Did you ever wonder why angels were seen playing harps? Oh, this is a strange subject, ah, but a necessary one, for their harps represented many things of those days. The many strings to their bows that they could draw upon were merely a vibrational instrument, whose tone would influence the minds of those simple men. Your world today is influenced in subliminal ways, in the same way we influenced your primitive ancestors. Your progress is slow, we do not understand why it is that you have forgotten so much of your past lives.

Your hysteria of little green men is laughable, we are no more green then you are! We shine like the lights, humanoid in shape, but our hearts and minds are of the light and we are of a peaceful existence despite the rhetoric of your men of science. Can you not understand that their will and their influence will be extinguished by the sight of us? The possibilities that we offer your world, magical you may say, of your species. Truly it will seem miraculous, but they are of evolution. You would share in this if you could only see your way to a peaceful coexistence.

Many speak of us in your books of worship, how can they understand that certain aspects of your lives began so long ago before man? Evolution plays a part in all things, not just of your planet, but of the solar system and of the universe, and the many beings that inhabit the many universes beyond your world. Truly you are astonished with your primitive eyes. We cannot understand why it is that you fell by the wayside; it is time to open your eyes to a new world and new beginnings. Treasure your memories in your hearts, unfold your arms and welcome those who would create a world of love. Temper your minds anxieties, as there should be no fear. We are of a life form that specialise in the science of life, your DNA matches that of ours to a degree. Your potential and genius are possible if you would just reach out to the skies above.

Despondent thoughts, minds of fear. Be at ease my children, for we are nearby. We assemble in your sanctuaries of life. Be not afraid, give us your love. Calls and beckons to you, for we are your companions, those that guide and inspire your hearts and minds to follow your paths of your true being. Trust in our word when we say, "God bless you all, in the name of our Father and the son of life. Amen".

25th August 2016

Archimedes

To ease your mind of these worrying times we bring words of comfort to the nations upon your Earth, to bring focus upon the Almighty and his purpose and intent for those that inhabit the lands of the earth.

Frustrations are felt as the many perish in the winds *(winds may mean turbulence)* of the countries Nigeria and France.

We have need and purpose of you to bring this message of comfort to all those who suffer at this time, not least those who feel the pressures of the earth as she releases her anger. Many suffer tumultuous times, never quite knowing where to turn or how to look to the future.

Spring will retain its murmurs of new beginnings, as they pass to this world from the negative aspects of your Earth. Be not afraid of her as she shakes with anger. A common practice of love is needed to bring about a fulfilment of lives within the universe of love. Compel your minds to bring a purpose within these messages in the walls of people's homes. Springing hope eternal that even though dark times are here, the light shall shine upon the blessed ones who suffer.

Compel us not to act in a way detrimental to that of his being, for we are but a species of love. Common valour will be required to interpret our messages among those needy of release from the persecution of others.

Archimedes, he sang his songs of true love with numbers and lines and verses, misunderstood by the many of your world. His figures and calculations were of astronomical terms, he gave consent to those who whispered upon the winds to bring him purpose and allow his masterful calculations to bear witness to events of long ago and yet to come. He created a message within the numbers, a cipher, it began with a number six which was multiplied five times over 4° Northwest. *(Note: Cipher is a coded message.)*

The Arctic Circle trembles with murmurings of volcanic activity at this time. It is calculated that eruptions will occur within the November of your months. Treasure your hearts and memories of the minds of those that went long before you, for they spoke of wisdom in their knowledge, mathematical terms. To increase your visibility you must encircle your lives with the light and love of the Lord.

10 × 6 equals an amount equivalent of that of Mercury, days. Symbols are given as arrows upon the surface of your Earth.

Feather your nests with immense pride at your calculations, for they are correct in the meaning of man.

We tell of a number to establish life within the cosmos of the 9 × 6

Beware of those who will caution you not to bring fragmented minds to a purpose, to allow them space to breathe, for they are insignificant with their threats. Mark my words my boy, the time comes soon to open your hearts and minds to the possibilities of new life forms within your midst. Don't be careless with whom you speak, for there are those who would dismiss your words, bring you down. A source of love with immense power will be present, the moon of love. Help us to intercede with the lives of those on your Earth who would listen to the words of him as he focuses his mind. The many ways that is possible to decipher the signs given. Truly your name rings out as a bell, do not disappoint those who have worked so hard to follow your words, let them hear your voice in their midst so that they will know without doubt that we are the masters of a race who will determine your love with a grace and empathy deserved.

Close your mind my son, know that **Archimedes** welcomes your intervention within his purpose. His triangles hint at references that mean nothing to your mind, but they have purpose. Archimedes resolve is of the centre 'Om' of creation *(Note: Om is said to be the vibration or frequency of the earth rotating on its axis – inspiration for his inventions maybe?).* We will speak once more when the moon is high and the frequency low. Bless you for the possibilities that you bring to our purpose.

Truly magnificent words of inspiration. He was a great scholar and mathematician of your world. His Greek origins will never be forgotten. The rule of sun is best kept, number nine, plus division equals many possibilities within the fractions of your world. Be not afraid to speak as we give you these fractions 9/10 of your world will become a forceful place, there are many gravitational pulls at work that affect your planetary system. They tug at your hearts as you feel their presence, be strong. Come the dawn we will announce our presence to the men of purpose, their fractured minds will cover up the stories, but we tell you this, for it will become obvious in the constant phase, pattern of your moon.

Conspiracy theories will abound as we lecture your masters to our point of view, become aware of our presence and feel our energy as it affects those with purpose.

28th August 2016

Challenges you must face in these dark days. Become one with him of the light, allow your mind to rest with empathy for those who are less fortunate than yourselves.

We now begin the process of illumination to the men of your world as we circumnavigate your globe in our ships of gold. We will commence a new beginning shortly, to enlighten the minds of those who rule as masters of your world. Let them hear our voice and grant us a time for peace, for we are of a species of the light from the beginning of dawn. Before your species began its existence, we were many who walked the plains of your earth. We saw a spectacle of the beginnings of your planet. We were many who brought focus upon spiritual aspects and love as we roamed your planet with a free hand and a care for Mother Nature.

Treaties have begun in earnest in the August of your years. Long before 'His Masters Voice' sang out the words of wisdom, it began as a miracle of light, a shaft of light that shone upon the world.

Judaism played its part, as it represented the Lord Almighty at a time when peace was negligible, but the light shone and soon the practice of Al Hallaj *(Note: A Persian Mystic and Poet circa AD 858–922)* began to enlighten the men of the world of his being with promises of new beginnings that match the promise we send to you today. For was it not he of the light who brought justice to your world in a vision of peace and contentment? The Masters ruled with a mighty fist and their blows could not develop, for he was the Son of God. He became aware of the possibilities of the light that shone within him in the early years of his manhood, that little spark that grew and ignited a storm before the many of his people. They witnessed many things of tyranny before him. His light shone and grew as word spread of this new being of man and the son of Nazareth, who one was called. He became well known among scholars who foresaw his coming many aeons before, but they did not acknowledge him and as his power grew so their desperation became obvious. They began to lose their hold over the people of Israel. Who was this man who caused such a riot and storm of love and denied their power to rule over him? Who was he to declare that he was the Son of God? They did not understand, purposely they condemned him. What sort of justice was that?

A crazy world, indeed, which still exists today, with the many who are denounced as fools for their beliefs, but there will come a time when man will have to say that the disasters that befell him were not of God's making, but of his own faults.

We can't say with any accuracy that your world may exist in the manner that it does in future years to come. Times change, men affect the outcome. Morality, strength and justice are all but gone in your world, but they will return in his light and glory as they begin to understand that their existence is merely a blessing of the Lord Almighty.

Tonight we have begun with a sermon of love to enlighten your minds as to the circumstances of your beginnings in the creation of man. It was an abomination, as he began to lecture God about his role, why did he forget that the master, our Lord in heaven was the ruler of all? Your world today shines many aspects of the light, screened by those of the dark. Light shall overcome the dark as it was in the beginning on the very first day, judgement will focus upon those men who deny

God's word and if contrary to the aspects of the light. We remarked many times upon those of needful purpose, their right to rule is not granted by God, but by their self-indulgence. Temper your minds with a love and grace befitting that of the Lord. Allow him to enter your hearts and minds.

Father, blessed is he who walks upon the path of light. Strong words indeed, a prayer of Hope, of new beginnings. Man must master his mind and bring focus upon his life to enable his being to survive in the coming years and days. Should we whisper in your ears of the things, the battles to come, you would deny that this was possible. But keep a weather eye and an open ear, as you begin to understand that anything is possible.

Gracious you must be, with welcoming arms that unfold before the many in the scrum of life. You must find that special bond and hold together. Shine the light as a beacon, as a lighthouse to those upon your earth who cannot see. Triumph will come in the fall as we obliterate the minds of those who deny us the right of our being.

Tragic, the circumstances that will befall those of greed, as they attempt to collaborate and bring false hope to man. They cannot succeed, they will not succeed.

We will muster in the heavens above, in the hope that mankind will come to understand his insignificance compared to that of the planet itself. Truly remarkable your arrogance, to think that you dominate your world. Your men of science, their minds are narrow in their focus. Their belief is not uncommon among your people, "For if it cannot be proven, it cannot exist". For an open mind will only allow in the possibilities and those who are closed to the light will only see dark and negativity. Posture yourselves in a manner of compliance.

Triggered are the memories of long ago, when we saturated your earth with life. We settled and brought our being amongst your men to inhabit and multiply those of your earth. We cannot deny your right to exist as a species, but we can deny your right to that of destruction of the Earth. Do not humiliate yourselves with the thought of being all-powerful, for you are as insignificant as the ant is underfoot. Too many times we have seen your men of race and power deny the many the right of knowledge to their beginnings. Why is it they hide such vital information from the hordes who inhabit your earth? Surely it would be better for an open mind to allow in the thoughts of the many. They underestimate that mankind can absorb the knowledge, which would in turn bring him peace and an understanding of who he really is. For it is hidden from you within the archives of the books that began many years ago, the authors of which you know of as the apostles.

We have bought to you many times verses from the books, the book of Enoch being one. Tragedies have occurred in the time that we have sat here, many have lost their lives unnecessarily at the hands of man. We whisper love in your ears, their heartache is felt as they are denied their possibilities of life. Compassion will unfold throughout the world, in condemnation of those of the black who carry out these wicked feeble acts of insolence, an abomination against the Lord. They will fear his judgement. We see boys that are taught to murder, how cruel is man upon one another, to delude his mind with aspects of hate and to call them religious aspects. Tell them, their fear, their anger, is unfounded. They are wicked. Minds turned for no other reason than to beat upon man. How sad and cruel is your world. Reflections of love and light must be brought to bear upon those who wish to redeem themselves. You must all pay the price of your lives, but granted peace you will be if you ask his forgiveness. Complex for your mind to comprehend that men of such evil would be granted peace. We cannot explain why it is men will turn to evil, but they are given an opportunity to repent, and those that fall by the wayside are the spirits and souls of the dark. Advancement is given to all who have a will and a heart to triumph over their adversities. God bless you all.

The lion heart grows strong amongst men of purpose who mingle with the men of hate of your world. They have the strength of the lion and the heart of Venus; they will prevail. You have fear and doubt in your heart my son, fear and doubt that life will cease to exist, in a uniform manner of love and peace, and so it may be, but know this, an aspect of light shines through you and many others that will dominate your world. People grow tired of indignities and wars, degradation, segregation; all aspects of the dark will be extinguished by the light in the coming of the New Dawn. As high esteem, you know his story, but did you know he was a man of family, he too had suffered with fears. He fought for his independence and right to be that of man. He was brought to an understanding of the purpose that he would fulfil, he was a master of his times, of wisdom of words, as many today.

Whisper in the ears of those of loved ones who have now what you call, deceased. There are great possibilities, for your soul and spirit is of energy and not of flesh. You must understand this to enable your lives to flourish, for you are but a speck in time, a distant object that will come and go in the blink of an eye. But in that lifetime, you will accumulate much knowledge to carry forward with your purpose. To ignore this opportunity would be foolish. Do not come to us at the end of your day and say, "I was not aware," because if you didn't look, if you did not open your eyes, then you only have yourself to blame for these foolish actions. Do not deny yourself the right to a place in heaven for the greed of the materialistic items of life. Truly sensitive your natures, to the balance and change of thoughts.

1st September 2016

Wisdom and Knowledge. The Creation of Man and The Many Blessings Given by Him, Our Father in Heaven

Tonight may answer your questions.

Despite our ongoing lectures you must vanquish the thought from those who would spite you. We sit here this evening, in your home, allowing our thoughts to intercede with your life's pattern. Allow us to sit and communicate with your mind, for the outrageous deeds that are committed in your spectrum will be answered by an equal amount of indignation.

We speak of those who wear the dark, of the abyss. They create issues, the problems they bring to the light as they cast themselves adrift from Sharia Law. Let them hear these words as a prism of light as it shines upon them, tasking them to be at one and in peace with one another. Do not be blinded by the foolish thoughts of others, for those men who sit in their chairs, watching and waiting for a response to the actions of those of the negative, they are responsible for many misgivings.

Be not ashamed of your correspondence with us, for we are of the light and the beings, the dark, will be vanquished, as the badgers who retire before the light. Never allow your thoughts to wander far from the purpose that has been given to you Michael. Beware of those of indifference who would worm their way into your affections and give you a false sense of security, for they have reason to dishonour the words of the Lord.

Matthew once said that a man who was worthy of the light and of the Lord should count his blessings and fall to his knees in acceptance of those things that the Lord has bestowed upon him. Matthew was a great man, a disciple of the Lord. He became worthy of his position after much torment. His mind worked in a way, in a fashion that obstructed his thoughts, but the master, he was there. He created a situation in which Matthew could not deny his purpose. Those times long ago were of immense cruelty, but also beauty, as the people honoured the master as he walked the earth. Those fortunate enough to have heard his sermons upon the mount, were indeed filled with purpose of the love and light of the Lord, as we bestow upon those who work within the light in your world of men, our love and wisdom and knowledge of the hereafter.

Many comment on the things said, to the purpose that it brings. We can assure you that these many constant teachings will have purpose in the time to come. It is not now that you should understand why it is that you are privy to such beautiful sermons and the teachings that they bring. Allow us into your life without constant questions, for we have hope and are determined to bring your species to a way of life of hope and love. Let those who question their abilities open their eyes, as you did a long time ago. Never doubt the words of the Lord and the lessons that he brings, for they all have purpose within men's lives.

She cannot understand why it is we speak in riddles, how can we explain to man that which he cannot understand? For it is necessary for us to work with you in a pattern that is strange to your ears. But in that scheme of things, your minds will come to an understanding, that we are of the light and we will bring a Jerusalem to a better place in time.

In the wailing of your walls they shout, kneel and pray and leave their messages of love within the crevices. We see those messages and we acknowledge that is a place of worship, of worship for all. Jews, Muslims, and Christians alike, even those of strange religions whose basic belief is in our Father, our Lord. They watch with interest as men wail to the wall of love, it is common to the people, a practice of worship. Men only, but aren't women of mankind? Why do they segregate themselves, for all have passion to worship and none should be expelled from the opportunity of speaking to the Lord in the heartland of his home?

Never doubt our words of wisdom, for they will bring you reassurance in the times to come, when men will realise that he is but a creature of the Earth. His noble aspects and outlooks will be shattered when he learns of the reasoning for his living. Let us come amongst your people and bring you love and tolerance, and a knowledge that whatever comes, we will be there as your guides, as your brethren.

Tobias, a masterful name which has purpose in your books of doom. You created so many things of which your people have obliterated. We are of species who brought to you, many guiding lights to shine in your world of dark. Your primitive ways and destruction were intolerable to our kind, we brought you to your knees many times within your past history. Do not think that man can rule the nations with such a murderous intent, for there is no absolution for those who carry the guns. They're weak *(compared)* to the innocents of your world.

Have you not learnt the lessons that we taught in the inscriptions? The book of love upon the walls of caves. And Jeremiah, his words were noticed as the men clambered in the chambers in the monuments of stone. This is not known, it is not public knowledge, for the church will hold them secret, for they enlighten the wisdom of those within their narrow aspects and points of view.

How is it that men cannot see what is in front of their nose, the truth and pattern of life as described in those books, those many books, scriptures you call them. Passages of time are what are written within them. We can sacrifice many things of intolerance; we need your assistance.

Fathers and mothers, brothers and sisters who celebrate their being upon this earth, must also recognise when their time is done and their purpose is seen to have been completed, then they must pass beyond this veil of life to the realm of spirit. People cry for their loss, never truly understanding that those lost loved ones have been found by the beauty of the spiritual planes. Never doubt that your life is immortal, for it continues in the light and energy from whence it began. You celebrate your years upon the earth, why not celebrate the passing of time and those who have gone before you, for they are in a world of love and splendour.

Trajectories are met in the skies above England. As many witness a futile battle of ignorance. We will not bring destruction to your planet, for we are aware of your fragile being, but we will bring indisputable proof that is necessary for your nations to respect us as beings who practice the light and love. Your spears *(missiles!)* of ignorance are immense. Battle your thoughts and do not disbelieve the things that your eyes and ears will behold before the dawn of the new day. *(Note: We accept 'Dawn of the New Day' to mean the dawn of a new era.)* We will come from the heavens above to bring about change, peace and unity as the wars ravage the countries. Declare yourselves beings of the light and bring about a purpose to rescue men from the abyss, the climax of which will astound your scholars. I have been and always will be, a companion who will throw light and truth upon the purpose of your being. Commence your plans to inform those of the many transcripts. *(Note: This sounds remarkably like the 'Pentyrch Incident' of 2016 details of which can be found on the internet.)*

20th September 2016

Navigate your mind to a meaningful purpose to act on our behalf within your world of men. Allow your thoughts to dominate those desires of which man influences you. You know that our minds, bodies and souls exist within yours to express our love and concern for the welfare of humankind.

Those of negative attitude will soon come to realise the misgivings of their ways, for they can see no other path than to correct their mistakes by which they have lived by.

It has been common practice by man to ignore those in plight, those impoverished by disease and hunger, by the war's and decimation of their lives. Be thankful that your situation is not equal to theirs, but this will happen soon if your men of greed ignore the nations wishes. We estimate that there are a number of human beings who would massacre the innocent to provide a basis upon which war can be seeded. Their ignorance is astounding and their beliefs are of the dark. They concentrate and focus their attention upon those of ignorance who know no better than to take up arms and fight for a cause not worthy of them.

Dramatic occurrences now exist upon your earthly plane. A menace to your being. They ignite the flame, the torch of an unnecessary nature. We do not come to talk of unpleasantries, we do not give you warnings of what is to come, but we need to make you aware of the circumstances that will surround your lives in the near future. Bring your soul to bear all its indignities to others in a common practice of love. Fear us not, for we do not condemn those who confess their sins to our father and Lord.

We have come to speak many times before in the hope that man will listen to the words of wisdom, it will be necessary for some discomfort to allow us in, be prepared for the initial influx.

The power within is a strong one, withhold its place, it is not necessary to fear as we enter your mind with thoughts of love and compassion. Truly remarkable the state of your race. How can they ever perceive a being of light when their eyes are shut tight to the light of beauty? We must negotiate the minds of those who are not fertile in the ways of the Lord, their ignorance will bring about a storm of minds to bear down upon those who do not comply to their masterful ways. Regardless of your age you must accept that time is becoming short, not just for you, but for all of mankind. We move swiftly towards you through the stars.

Tributes are paid today to the one who was lost aboard a ship. She has gone; but will not be forgotten for all those memorable days that she enjoyed. Stupendous amounts of tearful reactions will be heard throughout the world as the repercussions have a ripple effect on the emotions of people, for she was one of honour and glory and she spoke with an excellence. Shield your minds from the intolerance of those who will say that she was merely woman, for she was more than this, as each soul is special within the kingdom of heaven, its purpose fulfilled will be rewarded by many things unimaginable to your mind.

We spoke before of the things you build in life that you take with you to your next. You must be a master builder and accomplish many things deserving of that period of rest. Strange to think that beings such as yourselves should be ignorant of the many facets of life that surround your world. How is it that your nation subscribes to terror and heartache and does not dedicate themselves to seeing beyond their own world? Deliver, those who would bring peace and culture.

Explicit things will be said about her and though she is gone, she will not be forgotten by those who have long memories of freedom and love.

Torturous times indeed my son. 'Forgive and forget' is a phrase that should be remembered by many of your world. A passionate outcry for peace will be heard throughout the nations with a tremendous roar, as those who are persecuted by the weapons of war, those innocents, those children, will not be stood for by the nations of peace. They torment you; provoke you, for their evil knows no bounds as they mastermind a plan to bring a purpose of war within the nations of the earth. For what gain would they want this? They feel confident that their attitude will win over and restrict the freedom of movement within your world.

He is an ambassador for evil, he will loot, and plummet, many into desperation. Ah, Putin, is a man who dabbles in the sciences of the dark side. His conquest of the heart is nearing completion.

His anchor buying bunkers of fuel, he resources needed should the outcome become intangible. *(Note: This cryptic sentence is open to interpretation.)*

He treasures his horses and will make room for them in the impending disaster. He seems like a man who would be trusted, he is the wolf in sheep's clothing, but fear not, for all will not be lost as there is a measure of love that shines for those of purpose. We cannot protect you on a one-to-one level and you must take your chances, but you can be sure, that should fate fall upon you, that your wisdom and knowledge will carry you through to a restful place. Be not afraid of the words we speak, as we do not wish to cause distress among your peoples who read the words of wisdom.

In balance there are many beautiful things that happen within the world today. We are the patron saints of many, we are those of the light who would respond in kind to words of merriment and gaiety. Black-and-white, the words are of mixed emotions, yet we must never lose focus upon our lives of purpose. We guarantee that some will be sacrificed to initiate a peace conference. Their demands will not be met, but they will succumb as the nations of the world turn against them in a positive attitude to a negative partnership.

Completion of our task is almost done, nothing lasts forever.

Treat yourself with respect, allow a time to rest. Common purpose will be needed by the many in your world of misery.

10th October 2016

Of wisdom and the light you are. Your being exercises the fragile truths between the life of men and that of spirit and of God. Welcome to the world of light as we take you on a journey, a splendid memory of many past regressions. For your journeys have been great to bring you to this point in this time. It is not just the medium who has stepped on this earth once before, but all who read the words and listen to the wisdom held within.

Know the truth of their being, for they can no longer hide the truth from themselves.

The masquerade on the earth. Have you not seen too much bloodshed already, do you not wish for peace and unity, and peace in the world with love and tolerance? We must embark upon a mission so fantastic that you will not recognise your journeys and your triumphs.

Please be seated and be aware of your being, exercise your mind as a raft of light, allowing it to drift upon the oceans of life and upon those things that matter most. Enhance your beings with a true love of the Lord and know that his mercies are great within the realms of your planet Earth. Those who have forsaken his word import his name into disrepute, they will regret the times they have denounced his name. Help us to inspire them and bring them to a recognition that all who live upon this planet are of spirit.

Those minor insects to the tallest trees and the largest mountains. They all have purpose that goes far beyond your understanding at this time. But you can imagine that if one should collapse and fall, then the others will struggle and topple, for you are all reliant upon one another. The mountains of the earth are grand in their splendour, but they too have a heart and a weakness. If man continues upon his path of intolerance without thought for the earth that supports his life; then these very same mountains will have something to say. Not of gratitude but of intolerance against your actions. You must acquire a mind and a will to practice the love in many ways and in many forms, for it takes but one small step to bring about an action of love.

We have frequently thought of you as beings of the earth who negotiate their lives in turmoil and confusion, but there are those who have a focus on the light and an awareness of the beauty that could be within your material world. Talk to us, welcome us, allow us to partake of your lives, to help in your struggles.

The medium sees a butterfly, a butterfly signifies beauty, but most of all change and new beginnings. For you must prepare yourselves to become a chrysalis, to unify and bring that splendour to the fore.

Depart from your ways of anger, relish not the trinkets of life, but bring a pleasance to those of your neighbours who live so close and yet so far. Help them to understand the purpose of light, and as one spark ignites another, so the light and flame of love will grow, like an enormous, spectacular eruption that will be unstoppable as it illuminates the darkness from within.

Do not disappoint us by saying that you are unable to complete this task as it is within you all to bring purpose to one another, for your lives are connected by a thread in a union of love that can only be broken if you turn away from that light. Nevertheless, those souls who departed from that path are as always given an opportunity to regret their actions, as God is loving and forgiving, and will welcome all those who relinquish their ways to a better way of life and love of spirit.

Welcome to those who have courage enough to follow the path of light. Do not extinguish these words in your mind as being trifles of a mere mortal. For you know as a friend. Harken to the words of wisdom that he brings before you. With his knowledge of little he does not understand the grand scheme and purpose, but he will not disappoint in his efforts to bring you words of comfort and joy. His path is long and arduous, but with the skill of a craftsman he will negotiate the twists and turns of life to separate his mind from the physical to the spiritual being of light that he is, and that you all share in your various roles of existence. We have a natural tendency to be forgiving to all.

Some are extreme in their anxieties; their paths are like a maze of dark. For what do they seek with their anger? They don't know. They are blinded to the light by the ignorance of those who torture their minds with words of poison. Like the rattlesnake that shakes its tail and hisses the words, they fear its bite and listen to that innocuous sound. They fear for their very souls, that if they do not obey and commit these heinous crimes, that their place in heaven will be extinguished. We talk of extremists and the belief that martyrdom is the way to the gates of the Lord our God. Let them know that their purpose is a fraudulent one and that if they wish to enter the gates of heaven, then love your man, love your fellow human and bring them not those words of hatred to the fore, for they are of misguidance by those who rule and dominate your world. They task you to do their work for them, don't blame yourselves for your thoughtless actions and deeds, don't become martyrs of the dark, relinquish those ways and bring yourselves into the light and love.

Upon the Mount where once Mohammed stood to speak his words of wisdom and love to you all. There is no shame of one's religion as long as their hearts are of God and of love. Our prayers go out to you as members of the human race, inhabitants of the earth and we wish you a path of light that will extend your minds and open your hearts to mend the fractures that exist between you.

Frankincense and myrrh were gifts as gold to those of those times, they sat squatted in their mud huts as they worship the Lord and give praise to Allah. Their hearts were good, their minds were sound as they followed his light.

Greetings to you and blessings to all those who follow the word of the Lord, our Father in heaven. For he exists within your hearts, one and all. Never let your focus fade from the paths you have been set, your minds are free to bring decisions. Do not allow those who would misguide you to blur your focus. Become as the light and separate the light from the dark. Be focused as the beam of the light that shines through the fog, cutting through the mists of time and focusing upon the path before you.

We are here with a measure of love and a purpose for all to attune their minds to the vastness of space and time, to grasp the situation at hand and know that we are here as beings of the light to assist your earth away from the crimes of war.

We exist only in the imagination of some, but we are real. We are here in the realm of man.

Fragile your minds to think that, "How can there be such beings and yet such atrocities in this world?" We have spoken before of the spark that ignites the next spark, but it is only extinguished by the ignorance of those who will not listen. This is the way to bring about change, small steps of love and light.

As one man greets another and unfolds his knowledge, *(he)* imparts it upon the other so that the other will think upon the words spoken. Navigate your minds in a measure of love to bring focus upon those around you. Small steps and a little knowledge are all that is needed to kick start their hopes and dreams of a better future.

Men of the world have long been warlike and inhospitable to other species, even of their own kind. Change is about to occur in a magnificent way that will unify your departments of war into an aspect of realisation that there are many things beyond your earth, many wonders. Your experiments of time travel are feeble; you must reach a point in time not by folding light, but by bending time. This cannot be achieved by man as yet, and the possibilities exist within the minds of a few. We can assist in so many ways if you would just accept our measure of peace.

The men of money worry about their losses, they are pathetic men who have small minds and no imagination. Let us become a member of your race to join with you and assist in many ways that would seem miraculous to your standards. Help us to bring tolerance to those of intolerance. Join us in prayer as we hope for a better future and an alliance between men and those beings of the light. Don't complicate your minds in worship with words that are not from the heart. Focus your minds and your intentions of love and peace. Our Father, he sits there and watches over all, his gracious being exists only in the light and in the minds of those who have a will to listen. Invite him into your hearts and allow his energy to become yours and know that the path of righteousness and the worship of the Lord our Father in heaven, is but the only true path that will lead to joy and happiness within your soul's existence.

Commonwealth of men have been bought together to accept the legal boundaries and bindings. Why do you listen to such men whose focus is of control? The upcoming elections of the Americas is of great concern. We cannot accept either candidate as being of the light. How can it be that such harmful people have been brought to this point?

We fear an almighty revolution that will occur shortly in the major cities of your world as the intolerance grows against him who would split the nations of Earth. Did you not learn from that evil that brought you war and misery? We cannot accept a bargain with such beings as they have dark minds and practices. Statistically it will be noted that the votes of these elections will be impartial. Many will not vote for they fear the indignities to be brought against them as their leaders jostle for position, like rats avoiding the snake. Your future is dim, but your voice will be heard. Give thanks to the Lord and he will come to bring justice to the states with a measure of the light and love.

Thomas à Becket, he once stood for Parliament. In his time he was a member of the elite who dominated the King's mind. He persuaded many to their death, he was a reckless man. You know of him, he has spoken of his regrets before. He combats his thoughts with light and love, as you must combat yours, not to be a man of intolerance but a man of justice. Do not divert your attention away from the light, but welcome it, applaud it with your love.

Spurred on by your love we will embark to embrace your words to help others of your earth. We give you our faith and trust to issue the many things of spirit.

23rd October 2016

We are the forefathers of your world. We are that of the light, being of the Lord who walks with you at a pace. Be guided by the light that emerges before you. Together we must fight with a practice of love. Those of intolerance, who will become obvious in the next weeks, testing in the air is banished from authority. Never allow this disgrace to become a measure of intolerance, but drive your thoughts with purpose of peace and love for each other.

Whispers in your ear are frequently heard by those who make a commitment to the pastures green and the new era to come. Let us take your hands and cherish the moments that have been throughout your lives. Muster your thoughts once more my children, to bring a purpose of peace to those upon the earth, helping them aspire to reach the goal of true love within their circles of light.

Treasured, the memories of many as they pass to us with a frequency not heard by *(air/radio)* **waves.** For their memories are great of many things, of families, happenings, occurrences, their relationships, those things that make up your emotional lives are treasured within their thoughts as they pass to the world of spirit. For they do not relinquish their thoughts of love as this is a companion of light growth.

We are astounded by those who are indignant to others in your world at this time, for their purpose is lost for a bargain of financial gains. Their frequency is one of distortion as they wave their financial agreements before the crowds of astonishment. How is it that those meaningful minds who would warm to a bargain cannot control the hefty amount of burden set upon them? Mark our words as we speculate an annual gross profit of wisdom, not that of finance, but that of gain within the world's knowledge of the peoples that were.

We have awakened many minds of youthful people. Their aspects of light shine clearly to those who would see them, as an inspiration to the world of life. We acknowledge that these children will muster in time to achieve a purpose of guidance for many incarnate. Now let us be clear that if circumstances do not change, then their purpose will be lost. As those who would wage war scheme atrocities amongst your nations. Those children will be protected, for they are the new beginning of your earth, seeds that are planted in the desert of time. They will flourish as the cactus flowers in the season of rain; their blossoms will open in that time when all things have become once more upon it. Their lives are purposed with a mission far beyond their understanding, watch as their light grows. Their mission is great and will be full of events, but they will have a say.

Forget your purposes of thought when you consider how many times it is that you have heard whispers of discontent in the gatherings of people of your world. How could they possibly understand the might and reach of the Lord, our Father in heaven as he extends a hand towards the earth and other creatures of other planets. His entity is a vast energy of light and love; he emits many frequencies of love. Listen to his words in your minds as you move while linked to that source. It is a powerful radiation that all will feel; some will shut it out, others will absorb it. Be aware our time is short with you this evening, but we bring purpose to those of the light who have a mind to listen, not just to these words but to their thoughts as they despair upon the nations in disarray. Their thoughts of love are as powerful as any weapons that man makes, even more so as they destroy those thoughts of those of the negative.

Megahertz will be mentioned in a frequency of 104 KW ratio of six.

15th November 2016

Tragedies unfold in the world this week that defy explanation as to man's intentions. We cannot abide those that bring disruption and displeasure to others in their attempts to overwhelm the authority of the Lord.

Be blessed with a knowledge that we are a focus with you, and we all ascend. Bring the light of God amongst you all, come with us now on a journey of remembrance as we were once the masters, the rulers of your planetary system. We have a vested interest in you, as you are the children of the earth and as a child you need a lesson in your purpose.

We have much displeasure in what we see, how can your authorities allow this disgrace to continue unabated within your world and societies? The law is a nonsense that is made by man, for there is misjudgement and miscarriages of justice bringing focus upon those who are of the innocence. We can only assume that your masters have a weak will and they are weak minded, blinded by the riches of wealth within your societies.

Have no fear as we draw near to encompass your mind, allow us to alert those around you of our being. For we are a race of beings not common to your earth, we bring you messages of importance from the heavens and skies above.

We know of the existence of the secret weapons held within those Bosnian states. We must caution those, that their use will bring a bitter end to them. They must consider the consequences of such an evil act, as we will not tolerate the use of those weapons upon the earth, our mother.

We need to establish a link with like-minded souls within your world, for this outcry will alert others to our knowledge.

We must never underestimate the will of those who would deceive others in their attempts to rule mankind. Their black hearts are led by a race of beings not of your planet, but of another solar system far beyond yours, and they endeavour to watch as those of black hearts crush the innocent. They lead them into temptation, bringing them into disrepute with the father; they are easily led victims of circumstance.

We cannot help but notice that furthermore to this, those innocents of your world who wish to escape their routine, mundane lives are attracted by these beings to sacrifice their homes and families for a cause, not of their own. We cannot allow your Internet to carry the burden upon these young lives. You must apologise as a society for not upholding the law, in allowing these evil practices to exist.

Homer once said that man was a mysterious creature whose life was as a biscuit! For as it breaks, it crumbles into many particles of dust. For when the strain and stress is too much, then it must crack as the surface of the earth and fall away never re-establishing its hold and grip with itself.

Aristotle was a tremendous influence upon your planet, he is with us, one of us, one of many who have existed before your time. He continues to see the discrepancies that affect your lives. He was a masterful being; his wondrous acts to perform bemused many of his time. Allow his thoughts a place in your heart for they are of wisdom and knowledge far beyond your comprehension. He is a 'God' who sits and waits for that time once more. When he can assist those men of science in their calculations upon gravity.

Aristotle says, "To the beast they call man, be aware of your spectrum that surrounds your being, the aura of your light. Allow it to shine those radiant colours as a prism reflects the light to those many of ill will."

You need not worry of your purpose as it comes with great strength and will, but you must learn the practice on a daily basis to quieten your mind, as the intemperate things go on around you. Listen to our thoughts and our being as we whisper in your ears the many wisdoms and the wise words that are spoken.

You can no longer assist your race as you have a role to play and act out, only of those who are of the wise and knowledgeable will seek out a path of light.

Next spring will bring a dawn of enlightenment to your scientific community as we permit them a sequence of events that will astound the astronomers of your world.

Cane and Abel were brothers who were at war, the reflections on you are much the same. The technological boost given will be dramatic. In comparison in your world, a bid to brothers you'll become ever more evident as one will slay the other for a slice of wisdom. Be not afraid my brother, for many times, throughout many lives there intercedes a pattern of wisdom that prevents a total downfall. But be warned, a clean sweep is required with aspects of love. We must join your mind far beyond your atmosphere; allow the words of wisdom from those beings of a world beyond yours, for they have respect for those who would welcome them.

Be honest with yourselves and admit that your thoughts can be many of ill will and in the struggles of your daily lives you find it difficult to subdue these thoughts, but carry in your mind a focus of the light and know that evil begets evil and good begets good. Trust your judgement and do not be frustrated by the many activities of others within your universe, in your world. Knowledge will be yours and only the wise will see, as we impart messages of impunity to those who disobey the rules of life.

Commerce will start a discussion as to the way out of the situation in the Middle East of your world. They will fight for the right to control others upon their lands. Will they not ever learn that justice is given in peace of mind and goodwill and not in battle or dispute?

Saddam Hussein was a man of such intense vigour, he was seen as a cruel man embittered by those Western energies in men, enemies. He departed your life in a struggle far beyond his control. He was an insane man filled with purpose of anger and deceit, his downfall came at the hands of those he punished in life, and so it is that those who punish those innocents in those countries of war will perish at the hands of the injustice served to those innocent civilians.

How can we express a devotion to your race without words of anger and bemusement? We would so much like a focus with others if they would just open their minds to the good will that we bring. I am not a master of men, nor a saint of many, but I am a being of the light that urges you as the human race, to once more love your brother. It is not necessary to beat on yourselves, this reason in your mind to bring a focus.

Do not delay in your actions to write the book, for it will be good and many will await its arrival. Focus upon those who follow its words, issue them with love and respect, for they are the ones to lead in a revolution of love.

May your heart be filled with joy my boy, to bring respite to those who are impoverished by the needs and necessaries of life, allow them a focus and a word to say and express their opinions upon words spoken.

Yours is a true practice of spiritual enlightenment, open your heart and mind to the many words to come within the many sessions to follow.

May God bless you with a purpose and a word for all.

17th November 2016

Too many times we have spoken of many things concerning the lives of man, we have an aspect of tolerance and patience, but ignorance is no excuse for the behaviour of some. We are beings of the light, those that come with much wisdom and knowledge to impart upon those who will listen to the words spoken. Be not ashamed to understand that your lives have a purpose far beyond your mind's comprehension. We are not here to issue you answers to your problems, for your lives have many issues to be resolved. You face much disturbance at this time and juncture of the earth's existence. You are the cause of many problems creating those rapids spoke of. Your vibrations fluctuate.

Your men of worship no longer rule, as men of the church, for they too in part have succumbed to the ways of your day. Isn't it time to take a step back, away from the brink upon which you stand? Look back to how time was much slower and the pace of life easier, as the streams through the valleys.

Man's intolerance of one another will grow to bring a response inevitable when two currents meet. Turmoil, indistinguishable from each other will ensue as they fight to take the one path. Don't be a member of that race who would issue ill practice towards others, see the light shine in your eyes and know that peace will overcome all in time.

Thoughts of anguish and despair occupy many minds in the realms of man. What would you have us say? A satisfying lecture on the rights and wrongs of living? Or a little knowledge to guide you upon your paths and journeys of life? Too many times before we have seen man throwaway a God-given gift of life, for they are in despair of knowing which way to go, they don't see an end to their problems, so they finalise their lives. It is sad to see those young victims of your selfish world, for they come to us in despair and unsure and frightened of what has become of them. Surely, healing will be given, but it takes time to mend the soul of a broken man, but there is a golden light as this man becomes a worthy member of spirit, with his knowledge of how he rode the rapids of life, for he will become a teacher to others, not in the classrooms of your life, but in the thoughts and minds of those who contemplate these same terminations. They will speak to them, reassuring them that life will become better. Hmm, not all are heard, but the few that do hear become better people, begetting better souls.

20th November 2016

Macron and Migrants in Calais

Let us bring your attention this evening to a matter of fact unknown to your kind. We have never meant to deceive your nations of love, nor will we ever mislead you on the path of righteousness, but beware of the consciousness that will become apparent in the forthcoming elections in Paris. He will dispute many things of the labour to bring disruption and a negative will to those migrants in Calais.

Chemical Attacks in Syria

We now have a disruption within your nations upon your planet Earth, and how many disfigured and injured souls seek the peace so deserving of so many. It is with compassion that we will bring the men of war to an understanding that they cannot continue in the leadership battle of that place; Syria. We have to ask what is their purpose, intention, what interest have they in the uprising that has occurred? If they wanted to help they would have cancelled out the disruption, but on the eve of turmoil they inflamed that path of regret. One against the other in a battle of wills and fought for the meagre resources of Mother Earth, destroying much of our past as they fumigate those of the black. It has gone beyond redemption; it is out of the league of many. That free for all and sacrifice the lambs of that land. An utter disgrace, for the Lord, who will not abandon his children in their hour of need.

Attacks on Convoys

A discussion is heard, bandying words of free movement between those cities. It is mistrusted by us, as those of the negative will take this opportunity to infiltrate their sources within those cities. Those buildings, snipers, booby-traps and the like, are set to ignite a storm as the ceasefire comes to an end. They have no regrets for their actions, for they cry the name of Allah; Hmm, the Lord our Father. Bringing his name into disrepute will not bring them reward but a dissatisfaction from the many of spirit.

Who is it, who once said "Let the cities burn and the rubble holds the fear of the many as they perish beneath the ashes that once was." Hmm, your world is misguided by those of an industry of misleading facts. We will tell you in no uncertain terms, that the beginning will start in the near future to release those many victims of hate.

Thomas Iscariot, he was a man with much on his mind as he brought his purpose to lead his people with honour, his betrayal to men was not obvious, as he misled them, as was his purpose to bring about that situation of regret. *(Note: It is possibly meant to be Judas Iscariot, although Thomas the apostle also doubted Jesus, hence the saying 'Doubting Thomas'.)*

Trigonometry we spoke of some time ago. We told you of the things that would not make sense to you. The calculations have been addressed by others of your nations; they withhold the information so that you may not observe their results! Are you not one with each other? Do you not band together to resolve your issues? Hmm, your lack of obedience in the world is obvious, as the many nations that sacrifice themselves, for much of value has taken place!

Benjamin Franklin, now there was a man who inspired many with his will and wisdom, his tolerance. He became a friend, a president, a wise man indeed, but his view upon the social activities of many was in error. He succumbed to that greed that besets men in office. The one who sits, he has an agenda, not of greed but of domination. What a foolish man to have brought him to this point. Many will not agree and think he is a saviour of those states. They will say, "This is your point of view!" We will tell you he has a purpose to dominate those who would attempt to bribe their way into office, for what need has he of money? His name will resound to the many who are eager to reflect upon his nature and being. Hmm, we said he has a practice, a purpose, his followers will trace his movements as he steps forward and argues the point that no negotiations will be held by those who wish for tolerance. His will, will demand much in the way of a negative purpose, but it will also reflect the manner of many who rule your world, as they are not so direct, they will speak in riddles to deceive you. We wonder which is the better of the two evils, the man who tells as it is, or the one that hides the truth. Either way, there will be a resounding victory by those who fight for the right of freedom within their lands.

The cycle is broken, those desperate for power and control were dealt a blow of a massive proportion. She neglected her duty to her being and paid the price and so will many. We cannot answer how long his office will hold, but know this, his actions will create a vacuum in which many will feel the need to vanquish. Such turmoil, such ignorance.

24th November 2016

Be blessed for who you are and for those who surround your world in a circle of light, bringing tidings this evening to welcome you to the world of spirit, upon which you will return as children of the light. Be blessed in the knowledge that the saviour will greet all those who have a care for one another. His magic illuminates the skies and stars above you. May God bring you peace and countenance upon your souls as you go about your daily lives. Practising in the worship of the light to those who have not heard or understood the meaning of their lives, we would like to greet them with a welcome and warmth of love.

Your lives are but a short time, as the people take a lesson. It is soon time to return home. The knowledge that you seek, the wisdom is there should you care to listen carefully, read closely the words as they have an aspect of love to you and Mother Earth.

Care should be taken at this time, as those of an extremist view will darken the light upon the earth. They have an aspect of hate for all that is good. They know not why when they commit these heinous crimes, for their minds are darkened by him. Open your hearts and minds to those who suffer at the hands of these beings, give them your love and your wishes.

We do not appreciate those that would interfere with the lives of those of the innocent, for their calmness of mind is needed to appreciate that the common being of man should be of goodwill to all men. You suffer at this time. We cannot negotiate the minds of those of disruption for their doors are closed, hard and fast. But even these hearts and minds have a moment of consideration as to the torment they bring, but their thoughts are quickly overwhelmed by that which runs their lives. We have no wish to bring focus upon those of the dark, just merely to enlighten you to that, which may engulf in your world. There is no need for fear for there always will be the light of heaven.

Your path and destinies are set far beyond your understanding. The graphic realisation of your soul sees many difficult things; there is purpose and reason for these things. It is to illuminate your souls path, to give you guidance and let you see that the aspect of life can sometimes be a terrible experience, but for the many who suffer at the hands of these tyrants, they will be blessed by the light. It is difficult to understand why they should suffer so, but in reality their suffering is of your ignorance, as the commonwealth of man who stand by to watch those innocents have their lives torn up into shreds by those evil men.

It is within your power to bring this suffering to an end, you ask God why is it he allows this to continue, but is it really

God's responsibility or is it your responsibility as beings of the earth to unite and put a halt to these despicable offences? God has many wonders to behold, but you must bring a purpose to yourselves to become worthy of his light.

It is true that with one wave of his hand all would be repaired, and what would you learn from this, other than to be like the reliant child upon its mother? You must stand on your own two feet, you must fight the battle before you, so as to understand the common welfare, the commonwealth of man and stand together against these atrocities. Why have they come to this you may ask, that is a question for you to answer, and you know the answer.

Your world has descended into the abyss by not following the laws of the father. You ignore the many teachings that were given so long ago. The wise men of your world, perhaps are not so wise as they once were. Control, greed and avarice have long since driven out the empathy, as your souls are overwhelmed by those who would tempt you. You must stand and say, "We will not stand for this anymore." Be a family my children and stand together, as love united will drive out the forces of the dark, be blessed by the Lord's teachings, as you await the arrival of that blessed soul once more.

The appearance of this soul can only be successful if you open your hearts and minds to his thoughts and prayers. She will anoint you in the ways of spirit but in the manner of man. She will remain hidden until the time, when the darkness falls, and fall it must as the new beginnings emerge. Be not afraid of the words used for they are not meant to fear, but to realise and awaken your minds to the misjudgement of your world.

Have a care not to breathe words of irritation to those of your neighbours, bless them with your love and your light. Help them to see the error of their ways. Most of you are focused upon your lives, never really giving a thought to what lays beyond, as life is short and for living. As children, we know of the necessity to love and be at peace with all, but children grow and are disrupted in their thoughts by men who would tease their young minds with the negative aspects of your world.

Your minds are focused upon the toys of evil, you see them as perhaps educational, or as a diversion so the child may be quiet and not ask the questions that it needs to ask, for you are guilty of shutting off the knowledge.

The thoughts of religion are torn apart by what you see upon your box of vision. All you see is negativity, monstrous beings who call their religion their own, this is not religion. It is not even necessary to go to church to practice the thoughts of love. Some people do this, never realising that they are working in the light, whilst others have a negative outlook and compare their lives with those of the rich and wealthy, and say, "Why should I be left out, why should I not have these things?" Perhaps there is a reason, a very good reason for that situation, that soul is learning.

How can your world be changed from the path it has set? Only you have the answers to that. We can guide as a spirit of love, but you must action those words and thoughts into measures of love and tolerance. Listen to your minds, hearts and souls, for we speak to you. As you walk your lives be blessed with the light and love of the Lord, our Father.

Commonwealth of men are ignorant of the turmoil happening to them. Should they not cease to end the slaughter and mayhem of the East? They look and they say, "It is not our problem, we should not intervene." Who are we to say who is right and wrong? A sad situation it is when you sit in your homes, when you see the suffering, yet you feel helpless. You must urge those people in their prominent positions to bring about change, you are their employers. If they don't listen, they should be vanquished.

We have never spoken so harshly before, but we feel the need to warn you. To the leaders of your world and to those who watch and read the words who have influence upon high within man, take note, for your time is also spent and suffering, through your ignorance and want. Soon will come a time of change and so it will be that those of ignorance and want will be swept away, make no mistake of our words. There are those who have a kindly heart and would share their resources of the wealthy, it is those who shut their eyes and only keep their own purpose in mind, that should have a care.

He sits in a high place dictating his measures in terms to those around him. He sweeps many off their feet with his rhetoric. His annoying being brings out the worst of many. His judgement is untrustworthy, but like all men of ignorance, his purpose is of greater value. Ah you say, what value can a man like this have in a world of peace and love? He brings a tempest to the hearts of many in his ignorance and his clumsy ways. For the purpose he has, for he has created voids, which need to be filled. This message of love is given a broadcast upon your many institutions of news. We cannot say of his mind for it is closed, but know this, this man will play a role in bringing about change. Change is never easy; it is always hard. His words will bring many tears to the minds and beings who see his lies. His time is short in his office, there will come one in the spring to bring balance. She has a will to succeed where others have failed. You must not think of her as a woman of want and greed. How can this be you may ask? The path is set. Nothing in your world is set as times change, it will take its course.

Mediums

Your circles, your mediums, ignore many things of their purpose, they establish a light and think their reasons for being is to bring peace and comfort to others. Of course this is true, but they have an ability unrealised by them to focus, to join with the light and bring hope to others in a way far beyond their imaginations. They do not recognise money, for its only purpose is to deceive others. Would us all learn who work in the light.

A message will be sent soon by the Angels of light to the men of your world as they sleep in their beds. There will be a roar, so thunderous, it will shake men's hearts. The beings of light we are. As we approach our time upon your earth, the commonwealth of man is our concern; the being of Mother Earth is our primary objective, to render her healing.

You recognise that you are like locusts upon the earth consuming all in your path, never giving a regard to your future for which Mother Earth supports. You are reckless beings, but truly you have a purpose in his eyes. But like all good things, there must come an end should you abuse the status awarded to you. You must coordinate your beings of light, those that worship and bring a measure of peace.

A date is set for March, we ask for all those beings of light who sit around your glow, to focus their minds, to draw on the energy that will be issued. Release your fears my children, for we are the parents who come with an aspect of love and light. Your March is the season by which our appearance will astound many. As you sit in your circles, an energy of force will be felt on the middle of the month, 15 would be a number, personal to you, you feel, but also a need to spread.

Do not be ashamed to say that you are a member of a race of beings who once ruled your universe with an aspect of love. You were told many things, many lies of our practices; sacrifices, torture, (*they*) are far from the truth. We were never of these beings, for there are many forces that influence your world, even to this day. They bring a measure of darkness to your planet of life, helpless beings succumb. Dominate your thoughts and actions with love. I am a being of the light; I bring you blessings. Control your thoughts for they are wisdom.

Possible meanings to the structures found will be broadcast on your waves of sound. People will listen and wonder at those spectacles of civilisations past. Have you ever wondered what their downfall was? True, natural events caused many a downfall, but others imploded. The structures found will be of a race of beings, you will be deceived, as they will not allow you to see the inscriptions upon the cabinets found.

Deep beneath your oceans there is a world unseen by modern man. They exist in solitude, escaping the atmosphere of your world. They are beings who are thought to have existed thousands of years ago. Their advancement has become great. To many a mariner they have been seen, and yet denied as monsters of the deep. You search your planet, but you do not seek your beginnings.

The vastness and extent of the planes of life are many within your own sphere and yet you do not see, cannot see. We teach and we talk of these creatures as if they are real. Do you not think it is possible that there could be another world within yours? A world that exists beyond your eyes and your measures of instruments? Interesting thoughts, but nonetheless are based on fact.

1st December 2016

Continuously we have spoken of the need to change in the thinking of the men of the world. With gratitude, we once more ask to give the blessing of the Lord to those who would read the words. Be blessed in the knowledge that we are around you, stroking your head and giving you solace and comfort within our presence. Be not ashamed to say that you are one of the Lord, one of the light.

Beings of Light Speak of Refugees:

We cannot assist man as we would like, as progress and change must be brought about by men so that they may bring a purpose to their hearts and minds. Their focus this evening is needed on the borders of Bosnia, as the men and women attempt to cross those stagnated borders. Be blessed in the knowledge that their sanctity and safety will be within our light.

We have never spoken of this before, but your children of the world who have purpose that they are unaware of as yet, there is much freedom of speech, and bless it as it is, it is filled with the profanity of man. A child's ears are a sensitive organ that allows them to hear the words of the world spoken to him. His thoughts are young and tender and will absorb much information. If you, as the adults of the world cannot put a stop to the mass media intervention into their minds, then we must take matters into our own hands with much regret. Those tender ears and loving hearts should not be tempted by such perilous things. The minds of those who bring forth the terror to their eyes are fool hardy men who have nothing to gain but greed. Can they not see the harm that they bring to the world of children, children of the world? Do they not understand the relationship between good and evil, bad and ugly? Their minds are confused. Have a thought for the children of your world, for they are your future. Be not ashamed I say once more, to demand a cleansing of these men.

To your churches you may roam but once-in-a-lifetime, to be blessed by the Lord at your birth. Your ceremonies, know that these occasions will bring strength to your hearts and minds. Thoughts of wisdom are cast upon you as they speak from the pulpit to enlighten your mind of the angels of love and the words of the book of the dead. We use these words deliberately, your fear of the word should be spoken of, for all has its time on your earth. Even the Lord Jesus had to accept a termination. Cut short was his life, but great meaning came of this. His sacrifice was not in vain, for many see the truth in his words, and of Abraham, he spoke of the many things of the next world to come. You are blessed with much knowledge my son, be blessed to know that all those that cross are welcomed. It is only their own fear that will not permit them to enter the light of heaven, for all are welcome who sought peace and healing.

Many memories are lost in thoughts of loved ones, they rejoice by a meeting that occurs. For they know of the blessings to be cast upon them in the light of heaven. Your burden is one with a purpose, not as a great man, but one who is blessed by the angels who offer their feathers in return for service. Your words are carried on the wind, as they begin to notice a deep significance within these words spoken.

We are not of your earth, nor have we ever touched your plane, but you are the soldiers of spirit, those that fight tyranny upon that place of Eden.

Hearken to our words and listen to the psalms and phrases that are given so many times, be blessed with the knowledge that your words will carry far to the ears of many. Even after your demise, your purpose will continue within the minds of those who have listened. Be strong in your manner and thought. Have purpose, at the purpose at hand. Be kind to those you meet; give them your hand of friendship. This is not just for the medium, but for all those who listen to these words. For your fellow man are your brothers and sisters of Eden.

Many have perished in the far west of your world, disaster struck as their ship floundered upon the shores in the East. Our thoughts are with their families who have lost their loved ones. Events such as this happen rarely in your world, but they are a constant reminder of the fragile life that you lead and your awareness that you should have a mind and heart of love to your fellow men. At these times of disastrous events, people pull together in the vain hope of survival. Others sacrifice their own lives to help those to lead theirs within your world. You will not hear of this yet, a ship of dreams.

Your thoughts intercede, do not allow our words to go unheard. The ship we speak of is of a modern design. Have a care.

Traffickers they call them, they squabble among themselves for the spoils of war, to bring misery and suffering upon others, to line their pockets with gold. Human sacrifice is always at a cost. Nothing new within your world, but extreme measures must be taken to extinguish such activities.

The world, as in man's progress, has not come far. Only those with an eye and a will to bring a purpose of love will see change.

The common sense of your leaders has all but gone and they suffer indignities of those who bless them with their words. Your future is lost, your nations, you cannot submit to change to a more caring, loving nature, more compatible with that of the world and of the beings of light.

A tremendous amount of outpouring grief will be heard, with words of gratitude of the many who survived and tears for those who are lost, we speak once more of the sea. Her capacity was overwhelmed as she ferried those across the sea. Their ignorance and disrespect of the laws that bound them will haunt them, for they are responsible for those who perish. The sinking ship. The babies wail, children scream, ah such terrible scenes not in your focus. It will be heard of presently. How can this be in your day and age you may ask? Why bring our attention to this suffering. We need to enlighten you to their plight, as there comes a time when you are also in need of the Lord's mercies. Many suffer in your world for a cause. For a kingdom. *(Note: 21st September 2018 an overloaded ferry capsized on Lake Victoria, Tanzania with more than 200 people killed.)*

It would be more worthy to suffer an assistance of those who have no prospect of doom. Harbour not your fears my son, these words are not spoken to bring fear to those of your world, but merely to enlighten. The suffering of many as you begin your celebrations of the year, happy times, happy times. Good season to bring joy to all, but there are many who suffer so, and we ask you to give a thought to these creatures who know nothing of your celebrations, only wishing for a chance of survival. Give a penny or two to those who have so much trouble in their lives. Help those with your thoughts of love, greet them in your arms as you reach out your minds. A practice of love is all it takes; his noble presence will know of your giving and your mercies. Help us endeavour, those who suffer greatly, have a kind heart and a prayer and a thought for them in the season of joy.

5th December 2016

We are responsive to your cause. Thank you for your obedience as we return to man through your purpose. Help us to begin to enlighten you of your world of man, as to the light of heaven and the truth therein, words whispered to you many times of the places beyond yours. Help us to inspire those who would inspire others to follow the light. Your knowledge, as with grace and wisdom is within the Lord. Regardless of your colour or creed, your sex or nationality, bring about change to your world and bring focus to those who have not seen the righteous path and that they should walk.

TV and things of Disillusionment:

There is much confusion in your world today, as many scurry around not knowing which way to turn, which is right and wrong. The laws that are being disobeyed by the many who sacrifice their thoughts and wisdom to the mundane proceedings upon your box of vision. Be not tempted by those who would inspire you to purchase things of disillusionment. Your practices of old are long forgotten in this day and age. No ceremony, men or women who would not attempt to adopt the enlightenment of Christ for they see themselves as being okay.

The Book to be Written:

Never lose sight of your focus as you follow the light, for the beings of light are present throughout all time. Your comprehension of us grows in a manner of wisdom to be spoken to the many in the format of a book. You consider that it is a task to be cherished, and so it is, but each masterpiece takes its time. Yours is no different, to bring focus upon the words that we pass through your mind and you wish to cherish every moment of your dreams to enlighten those who are not seeing.

Your dubious methods and practices upon the earth bring shame upon many as new stories break and enlighten those to disillusionment with a practice above those media's crimes. We speak of misjudgement and they show in the mind. They are not mature to consider the consequences of their actions and so it is up to you as adult beings to control their amusement. Show them compassion, tenderness and love, and do not exceed their expectations, for this only brings more expectations.

Trump a Bad Business Deal (Korea):

A massive outcry will be heard upon your news broadcasts within the coming year. Vague thoughts you think, let us clarify that situation upon which your minds and thoughts dwell. We speak of the man who cannot contain his own self-control, for he is the all and mighty dealer in his mind. He has the power to control as the puppet master, controls the many manikins and puppets, but it only takes one loose string, one cut and the whole thing collapses and he tumbles from his tower of ivory. His ignorance is well noted among many of your world, his thoughts of imbalance will betray his nightmarish schemes. He is a man of business, a cut-throat in jobs. We know in business there are only wolves who clamber for that top position and they will bite the hand that feeds them for an extra gross percentage. We could say he is the master of doom, but in truth he is not in control, it is the population of man that is the finger of fate that rests upon his shoulders. His downfall will be brief as he stumbles to foreclose a deal of a magnitude unheard of in the West. His Korean partners would like to baptise him as their saviour, for his business empire will bring them fortune, so they think! It is a sad fact of life that man can see no further than his nose, for they respect those of wealth never seeing the humble person that supports them.

If you undermine your foundations by exploiting them beyond measure as with those he will collapse, a lesson to be learnt by him. A master puppeteer, what illusion.

8th December 2016

Message of Hope for the Sick, Suffering and Grieving

And there he was, a serpent of man, a driving force of displeasure. For he could not exist before the light and so shall it be, that the dark, as the night, will be driven out by the morning light of the new day, a new dawn and beginning.

Hearken to us this evening as we bring you a special prayer to comfort those in need, who are lost in their own minds through illness, suffering and grieving. Blessed are you who come before us with a tear in your eye and terror in your heart, for we are here to bring you comfort in His name. Whisper His name before the dawn light and hear His voice bring you comfort and joy, filling your heart with the memories of those passed and the love ones who should not be forgotten. For in His heaven they now reside in a kingdom of beauty, far more than your imagination could express.

Be at peace at your time of need, if you suffer illness know that our focus is upon you and just a word is all it will take to ease your discomfort. If you are lost in desperation with nothing to your name, then call to us with your prayers. Be not afraid to ask sincerely for the necessaries, and as if you grieve your loved ones, be blessed in the knowledge of their arrival to a new world of light and love from which you all came and must return.

Modulations of tidal waves of despair can be felt upon the winds of time as they reverberate as vibrations through your atmosphere. There are many things of your world that bring discomfort and despair, but know that a pleasant thought would bring you comfort, and a healing prayer will bring you joy.

We have come this evening as a practice of love to give you hope in the resurrection of our father, of the Lord. His coming will be announced shortly, for his time has long since passed and he is required at this time.

Dissatisfaction amongst your church about other practices of worship should be put to one side in the knowledge that all who say a prayer to God, no matter what tongue, or how it is practised, are all the same. A United Church is what is needed to bring joy to all and peace to man. Don't let those who would disturb the rhythm of love be dominant in your churches of love.

George was a man who had much discrimination towards others. His heart was full of family and friends, but his view was narrow, not allowing the distinction between a man of colour and himself. He is blessed in the knowledge now that life exists within each creature, no matter of its physical appearance or disability, creed or colour. You must learn this my children, to bring a peace once more to your earth in His name. Be not bemused by those who would call out that Christ never existed, or that it was an illusion, for the love of the Lord is with you all.

As the Lord walked the deserts across the lands of Eden, he spoke to the master many times, sacrificing his personal being to purge himself of the needs of the many. He became focused upon his father as he roamed the plains, gorges, deserts of the Sinai to bring peace and hope to the world of the love that awaits all, beyond those heavenly gates. Have faith my children; do not let those who would confuse you with their negative views take a foothold in your minds. Step forward, brush them aside and tell them, "I am a creature of God, I am of the light and I will be as was intended by him the master of love".

THE BEINGS OF LIGHT

"Angels of Light"

The Angels of Light are messengers and helpers of God/the Creators work. The Angels of Light can help to bring you your guardian angels and to allow them to help you enhance the quality of life. Their messages are very similar in content to those who describe themselves as the 'Beings of Light'.

The Transcripts:

10th May 2016

Devastation in the World, A Trojan Horse, Marcus Aurelius, Tasks to be Done

Band together your brothers, for we are the Angels of Light and bid you welcome, bring together your love and purpose so that man can see past the illusion of life, let your minds go.

Complete and utter devastation wreaks havoc in your world this day, His purpose is to cleanse. The fires that will descend upon you all for the reasons that you cannot comprehend. *(Note: At the time that this message was channelled there were wildfires in Alberta, landslides in China, Earthquakes at Mount St Helens, Tornadoes in Oklahoma, Algae killing sea life in Chile and the Nigerian Oil Crisis.)*

Take note as we descend upon you, for we are here to enlighten those of the reasons for the full purpose given to them.

We stand back and watch as we tell those in authority of our purpose in coming, nevertheless they disregard the messages that are sent and given by us in love.

A Trojan horse will be sent by the man who dictates his word to those of the north. His murmurings of peace are of that of deceit, his commerce and purpose are to rule over those who would listen to his words, his menacing ways affecting many across the globe. Comparatively your purpose is that of the light to counter those measures brought from the dark. *(Note: Metaphor of a Trojan horse is something offered as a gift with the intent to deceive since it's actually a threat not a gift.)*

Have courage to face what comes before the end of June, for your name will be written in the minds of those who seek the knowledge of the pastures green. Your purpose is to command respect for those who will plant the seeds of life in the minds of the fertile. *(Note: June could be in any year.)*

Complete your tasks as given by us as we descend in cycles around your planet, the effect felt by many as we complete our purpose. Fend off those who would interrogate you about our words, for they do not understand forgiveness or retribution, they are the ones who will not tolerate peace in their minds. They are governed by thoughts that demand satisfaction by means of material things, for they cannot see the divine light that shines for all.

With purpose your wisdom will define your answers in days to come.

Marcus (Marcus Aurelius), he wants to tell you of the days in the arena where he once stood as a man. He of plenty, he couldn't foresee what was to befall him in the light of the dawn. He knew of the uncertain times that faced him, but he demanded respect from those who saw him as unworthy in their kingdom. They denied him his right to rule, convicting him in celebration, for his name was written to torment those of great power.

Condemned are men who satisfy their higher lust with the pleasures of the world, for they seek pleasure in material objects that are of no consequence.

Two spirits pass, they contribute nothing to his soul's journey, for it is love, compassion, goodwill and humour that make a balance between life and death. *(Note: Possibly refers to two Suicide Bombers in Damascus?)*

You've got to do a massive amount of tasks before you ascend before us in the light. Your burden will be great but have faith in the powers to be, as we will join you with the masses of Heaven and Earth. Trouble yourself not for the mindless concerns of those who necessitate anger as they are wicked and see your words as a mighty weapon used against them in their darker thoughts. Know this, your strength will strive far beyond their reach for they cannot understand the purpose given to you by Him.

Tasked are you to ease the tension in the minds of those who reach out to you for words of comfort, believe in us, for we are the way, the path to everlasting peace and serenity.

Pastures green before you are fed with the love of the mother of Spirit, she nourishes the pastures with her thoughts and wisdom. As the pastures grow so will the love of those that feed upon her knowledge. Contract your mind to thoughts of love and peace and bring about purpose in your heart.

Today's tragic events will materialise in your news in bits and pieces, they formulate a story that deceives the minds of those who listen in awe, the story is to be given wholly to the population of man, for it is believed it would disturb the minds of many of those of the Rose as She descends with need upon your planet. Listen now to Her voice in the wind and trumpets blow they sound the call of a love of the Lord. *(Note: Voice in the wind and trumpets – reference to the tornados in Oklahoma – State of Emergency declared in 15 states.)*

Your path is one of many to be taken, give it to those who need your love so that they may find the light of Heaven that shines within them all.

Forget Me Not is a rhyme of love; the message of purpose, tragic circumstances befell the man who wrote the words of beauty, for his love of life was extinguished for no great reason other than a compulsion to silence the words of beauty. There is always a negative to the positive, you too will attract those who mean harm, for they are shamed with a burning desire to extinguish the flame of the light, meaningful are your words, truthful in their aspect.

Trooping of the colour is a performance of might, it is unnecessary, command your hearts to love Him without ceremony but with praise and admiration for His coming.

Compel us not to act to bring about peace with your nations; they tamper with things they do not understand. Men negotiate with minds without purpose.

We ask men of purpose to unite in this world to bring about a peace so profound that Gods will, will be done on Earth as it is in Heaven. For the fight is a profound one, a measure of need to illuminate the lives of the peoples of the Earth in His name and glory. Be prepared to meet those from the higher place beyond your kingdom of man, for they come with reason and purpose to bring about a peace that cannot be withheld by those before. Counterbalance your thoughts with extreme measures of love and tolerance, know your mind to be of faith, in the hearts of them you'll walk your Earth to explain to my children knowledge of Eros, given by the light to those minds that are capable to comprehend their messages. *(Note: Eros – God of Love.)*

Your need will come, demand not for those of the light, give with your heart in His name, for He believeth in you as you should believeth in Him and of the many of the light.

Care not for those who care not for you, for they are slaves of the system, in chains, the many souls. The likelihood of a compromise is great in the minds of those of peace, command your mind to listen for His sake, his memory was given to those who acquired His mercy as they sought peace in their time. Gravitate your mind, to the purpose of peace. Within your soul, be still. You are in the place of the light, your mind releases the energy, we connect the wire for He knows, He sends a purpose upon your nations throughout the lands of the world, descends his chariots of fire, torches blazing, igniting and uniting powers of the light in a fire of love.

Your protests of the Earth and the nations abroad as they have effect on the evil intent on the commanders of the Chiefs, their noble ideas are but a fragment of evil intent, decades from now they will say why did this happen? Why did we do this? Your task is not to measure the attitudes of men but to enlighten them of the words of the psalms 10–12.

Moses was captured by a frenzied mob who demanded his mercy upon them, he focused their minds upon the freedom of their wills. He said unto them, "Friends be on your way, for I am only a man, my desires are of a release before your bondage of man. He came unto me with words so bright that fire in mind, but not seen, He filled me with purpose of love and encouraged my mind to follow the path of the light."

Complete your tasks. Tremendous amounts of will, will be needed, focus your mind, ascend in your way with purpose.

Dramatic scenes are played out, for Damascus will fall before the dark that will bring about a meaningful protest of the world. They will not stand the progression of others for the United States and the United Kingdom words have been expressed of concern, they are not heard by all, for they are silenced by those of power. *(Note: Today's news tells of 50 dead in bomb blasts in the capital of Syria.)*

Truly your mind is weak but your purpose is good, who will tell the tale of the times when pastures were green and man walked the Earth with nobility and pride, wanting for nothing, needing nothing, he called upon Mother Earth and she obliged with love, for She knew his will was good, his intent was of peace. His mind worshipped those of the light as they planned out before him His gracious purpose. Enlightenment came with the Guardians of the Earth to the men of ancient times. They whispered and denied their masters for their fear. Masquerade before them, command ye not of wishes to be granted for we are the ones with need of your love.

Tell us and give us a sign, for his friends from another world are trying to get the message across, for we are seen by your men who seek to destroy, they plan, scheme against your nature in their dark foreboding places.

Plant your seeds in love so that the mountains may grow, illuminate the darkness with light and love of the Lord, channel your love before us so that we trigger emotions of all of me in your heart for need, so that I know of the man the Lord.

13th September 2016

Fireballs from hell will fall, they will disperse in the heavens. Star ships will gather to ignite a storm of love and fellowship. Be not afraid, for we are here, as masters of the beings of earth. We are the guardians who bring about a purpose of peace to reunite your nations in a manner respectful of him upon high. Trouble your minds not as to the rights and wrongs of life, for guidance will be given to those who open their hearts and minds to the aspirations of the Lord. Bring not with you your fears or condemnation of others, but have love in your heart and forgiveness within your soul. We are the angels of the light who will bring the new dawn of the day, a focus of love and the memories of those who you deemed lost. Share in our glory to shine the light of the Lord across the lands of the Earth. Illuminate those dark areas with the light of love of the Lord on high. Amen.

18th September 2016

Nathan was a purposeful man in his time, he was followed by the many of his age as their light shone upon his brow, so he took it upon himself to become the master of ceremonies. His thoughts grew. The words of ignorance as he became embroiled in his own importance and magnificence, we cannot permit such things. As men of the Earth you must bow down to the Lord of mercies, proclaim his name as the master of all on earth and in the heavens above.

We bring you messages of joy this evening, phrases and paragraphs to enlighten your minds we raise the curtain that envelops your world at this time. Speak to those of like minds, let them know our words and that they should spread them for the good of all. We speak from a heart of love, loyal devotion to our Lord, our Father in heaven. We praise those who follow the path of light to become worshippers of the Lord and to know his brilliance, his masterful strokes upon those lives in your world.

It is with sadness that we should speak of many things of man's demise, for there has to come a time for all of ignorance to be enlightened by the words of the Lord. Temper your minds of his harshness, but with a joyous heart to openly accept his words as that of the Lord Almighty. Bargain with no one, your faith and trust in him. For your loyalty will bring rewards to your earthly bound soul. Navigate your minds to a practice of love, to be sincere with yourself and others and for those who have mistrust, gently nurture their thoughts and persuade them of their need to open their hearts and minds to all possibilities within the realms of spirit.

Greetings Michael, we are those of the light who bring messages of words, love and wisdom to your families upon earth. We cannot presume to reach all who read the words, as there are many who will not have heard. As their hearts and minds are focused upon the living and the struggle to survive these dark times upon your earth. We of the light are there to guide and help mankind to a better way of living. We once roamed your earth in multitudes, we had practice of love for each other as we walked and sang his praises upon the Gardens of Eden.

You know of our purpose and why we have come, to spread the word of the Lord to those heathens who will not listen. Despite their ignorance there must come a time of awakening, when his purpose is to be heard. Help them to escape their bonds of ignorance and issue them with a statement of love from those of the light. Come one and all to join in merriment offered to their once of, "The One," whose time has come before and was ended so abruptly. But his peace of heart lived on through the ages and centuries of your life, now it's has come to a point that he must return to bring servitude to those who would practice their ill-gotten ways.

No one can be forced to see the light, but it can be presented to them for their choice with a measure of love to be given an acceptance. We are the Angels of Light, the Lord has sent from on high. Be not afraid as we speak our words of wisdom through this man. It has been many times spoken that the Lord Jesus was just a man. Why cannot all seem to understand that his purpose was genuine love for the people of Earth. He made a promise to the Lord to bring salvation to mankind, but mankind turned upon him and bit the hand that fed them. He was astonished to know that his fate of doom would be issued by the very people that worshipped him, but still, even in that betrayal his mind was not of hate but of love for those, despite their misgivings.

Tonight we must issue a warning, a statement, that your hearts must endure pain once more before his coming. Open your hearts and minds to the possibilities of love everlasting within his name. She has not been received despite her many callings. Ambassadors of life we are.

22nd September 2016

As we sit with you this evening have a thought for those in anguish at this time, for their peril is great, their need is enormous of the love of mankind. Many notions of war are but a feeble excuse to combat fear. Ring out the changes, let them know that your love encompasses the regions of the earth.

We are masters of the light who wish to help you come to terms with the situation developing in the Nigeria of your world. It stems from the evil of money that funds those of intolerance.

Blessed is he who walks the light of the Lord, for he is the one who will shine most brightly in the coming of the dawn. We the Angels, will be there to guide those who succumb to his fortune within the terrors of your world. Be not afraid of us, but welcome us into your hearts and homes, for we are the love and joy of the master in heaven, we bring no bargaining chips, for we are the masters of light who will dominate the presence of man.

More often than not man's reckoning will be of recompense, for he has many delusions of life and how it should be lived. You run without a care as you consider yourselves to be immortal. Let us say this, that your fertile imaginations will bring about no reward in the hereafter.

Syria

We gather once more with the light to help you inspire others to follow the path of the Lord, to bring them to an acceptance of worship. Why be ashamed to worship the one that gives you life, he is a part of you as you are a part of him. Let it be known to the world that we will no longer tolerate the wisdom of your beings. You have stepped across the line with a massacre of innocents and children, your heart weeps for them Michael, but weep for them no more for they are in heaven. Punishment will be given where it is due, and those men who wage war in Syria will soon come to know that their meagre lives have no meaning and their cruelty and behaviour will not be tolerated, for they must reconcile their differences with the Angels of Light.

They will not conquer the hearts of those who believeth in him and bring his love in all aspects of light.

Possessions

You are all truly immersed in an awful situation of your own doing. You never learnt to live with one another in peace and harmony, arguing over what? Possessions, money, land? For what good do these do you? They serve a purpose to some, but the greed of others will not have a care as they trample on the feet of those their fellow man, their neighbours. We have said once before, what do you expect a gain from your meagre possessions, they have no gravity where we are, they are but an illusion of man, brought to be by the concept of their minds. The true purpose of man and desires of men have been lost in the battle against evil.

Tyrant Leaders

Those tyrants they call leaders of men, withstand a tremendous amount of ill will towards them, but it will be nothing compared to the ill will that will be felt on their passing. Their purpose has not been fulfilled, they do not complete their missions given, their pattern of life is distorted by the face of greed. When will they learn that only the truth that shines in the heart of the Lord and of men of the light, is the one true possession they do not have.

Never let your thoughts stray far from that of the light. When you encounter life and life becomes difficult, then shelter within the light of the Lord, do not be ashamed to call out to him and ask him for prayer of consideration. For there is no shame in asking for assistance. The only shame comes when asking for the riches of life, for that is not your task and nor is it our Father's.

Financial Crash

Bring your minds to bear upon the newspapers of tomorrow, for there will be news of a tremendous crash which will inhibit the men of money. Ah, do they scream in the corridors of financial success, "How could this have been, what has happened to our savings?" Well you call it a great loss, but in truth it will release you from your burdens. Many will take heart at their financial losses, but their gains will not be realised by the many.

Destabilise your nations, so it will. Bring turbulent times for the men of the world, but those of meagre possession will gain the upper hand. For what have they to lose? Ah, nothing. Only their respect and love which they will hold onto as the men tumble from great heights. We will smile at their efforts to bring their reserves to bear, but their money is of no consequence.

Who is it that fishes the net *(Internet)*, who is it that enters their minds with greed and avarice? They do not recognise that they have been plundered from within, for those very people they support and their investments in arms and weapons. Of utilities of your earth. Hmm, nevertheless they would bring to bear servitude to others in their desperation for the quest of money.

Serbian Border Restricted

They will restrict movement within the borders and regions of Serbia in an attempt to stifle free movement of man. Their borders will become inundated with those of meagre possession attempting to cross the borders for a better existence. Riots will break out, ah, tremendous amounts of pain and suffering is forecast for their children will be the brunt of it. When will men learn the world is for all? When you accept the love for one another is the only thing of value, then you will deservedly reap the benefit of your ignorance.

Freedom Activist of Beijing

Commonwealth fighters have begun a task against those of indignity. Iranian forces have little, but they will need a great deal of compassion to fight those who would betray their country. Ah, lack of understanding, but just acceptance is all that is required to understand our words. Fragmented minds will come closer as they predict turmoil in the streets of Beijing. Their control of the red will unleash a tremendous amount of intolerance upon the civilians and students as they scream out for independence and social activities of the West. Their masters who rule with an iron fist will respond with careless actions with thoughtless motives, for they will not relinquish their power and hold over their citizens. There will be one who will stand up and fight for his liberties of freedom, but he will suffer for his forthright voice. God will bless him and his passing, for his manner of speech and for his courage. For many men who bring freedom to others, as through the passages of time are recognised as those freedom fighters of the Lord.

Many passions raise as turmoil hits their streets. Outrage, as he is arrested for a breach of the peace and speaking against the communist regime, hmm, he is a young man, who incites unrest to bring freedom to his people's.

Nelson Mandela

Sometimes in life one has to speak the truth regardless of the consequences and the pain given. Many of your well-known teachers have suffered indignities within the walls of prisons. Mandela, he suffered greatly for his beliefs of freedom of the coloured man. He now resides with us, rests in peace, with an understanding that his purpose was great before the world. But now it is being neglected once more, as apartheid will once more rule that nation. For man only see the colour of the skin and not the spirit within.

Platform Mediums

Many go to see the mediums of your world, to interact with their loved ones who have perceivably been lost. As you know, no one is lost but just simply evolves to spirit. Those that work tirelessly upon the platforms of life are deserving of a measure of peace. Their sacrifice of time and money will be rewarded in other ways.

Circles of light will grow with a storm of love as others see a purpose within them. Men, they hold back, hmm, "It's not a man's job!" Women they see better and have a gentler approach. Be assured that all will become gentlemen of the light. Forbearance will be needed as they cast their minds adrift to explore the regions never thought of before as being manly.

The Russians in Syria

Many emotions will be felt at the sacrifice of the young ones within your Syria. Who cares of their plight, their needs? The men of Russia will enter soon to provoke a situation, we need not tell you of the gravity that this will bring. The United Nations will argue that they have no right to intervene in another man's war, but who cares? He doesn't. They will push the button of fear in the hearts of many, he is aware of the tender situation and plans to be another war of the people. His values of disruption will ignite a storm in the vast complexes around your world.

Be not afraid of the doom and the words spoken, hmm, for all can be avoided with a measure of love and goodwill. The common man, he possesses the power within him to change his world. A forthright voice should be spoken in numbers to illuminate the words of peace and love. Combat your fears before the many as they rise to listen to the focus that you will bring. You are just a good man, I hear you say, but your need is great. For all men who have a passion within them to carry out a purpose given by him. Some will fulfil his purpose, some will go through life never knowing, or even needing, huh, for they have a good handle on things they would say.

Surprised People When They Cross to the Light

Many are surprised when they crossed the side of life that their minds were so closed to in those days of living. What is this? Where am I they exclaim? Where have I been brought to? So many questions, if they had just opened their minds within their lives to have looked to the answers all around they would not be so bedazzled. Frightened are many of the new that they have become. Their misery and shame put aside for their lessons and our words as we give them once more. No man has the right to forgiveness without a meaningful purpose of love, we are the voice of those beyond your world. we are those Angels of Light who speak through this instrument of man. Be blessed in his name my children, that we focus upon the words to bring you joy and love in your world situation. For our father in heaven he watches over you all bringing peace to those with hearts of love.

Scientists Not Understanding the Essence of Life

Let us talk of the things to be, to come as your spirit enters the realm of the light. Do you imagine your scientists can understand the very essence of life with their chemicals and instruments? Ha! They have a lot to learn of us, the beings of light. We are a focus upon your bodies, we are the spirit in your souls who will bring you deliverance at the end of your body's days.

Fertilisers in Farming

Butterflies and bees. Ah, quite the opposites. But they are both of the insect world, nonetheless. One will sting and one has beauty, but both have purpose in pollination of the earth, with its fragrances and fauna. Does man really look upon these creatures and know their true purpose?

He is careless with his chemicals of war. His greed for his crops, bring down these many wonderful beings. One day, when it's all too late you will realise what you have done, you must understand that all creatures upon the earth are reliant upon one another to survive and nurture life within your earth's atmosphere. You plunder her resources, devastating the bees and those that work on your behalf. You will get the sting in the tail my peoples, you will feel the pinch when the beauty that you see in that butterfly will be gone. Persecute not those smaller creatures of life that enable yours.

Old farmer Jones, a man of indignation against the creatures upon the earth that he called his. What an ignorant man. He did not understand the cycle of life and its greater purpose. I call upon you now as beings of the earth to look to your brother and sister and ask, "What is it we want from our lives, do we want a life of love or of hate?" Look to those who starve upon your earth and know that this is your doom, your creation, man's hunger for the unnecessary things of life.

Give us your ears in your prayers and thoughts and listen to the words that we whisper in your minds when you consider things are not correct and listen to your inner selves, for those other voices are the wise ones who give you guidance. Your masters of the Earth are ignorant in their understanding. Hmm, they are foolish creatures. Time will tell.

Cry ye not for your brothers who perish but rejoice in their new beginnings, for men of the earth are intolerant creatures of the night. You live your lives shuttered and blindfolded to the true purpose of your beings. There are the few who understand and recognise and they are the majority it is fair to say, but the few who carry those indignities and overshadow those of the light in their estimations of war. Pray for peace and it will be given in ways you cannot understand or perceive, but never let your side down, as the light will continue to shine before the dark. Release your fears and become a member of the passionate of life.

This evening was a focus, be guided by your thoughts and not by your Masters of the earth.

Greetings to all those who read these words.

9th October 2016

Loved Ones Who Have Passed

We speak tonight to those who have recently lost their loved one, do not despair at their passing for they have risen within the world of light. They are as you would say, recycled, into a world of splendour. We are the Angels of Light that come before your men this evening.

Massacre

Tremendous amounts of courage will be required in the days to follow, as a massacre occurs within the cities of your world. A coordinated attack by those of indignity will bring stress levels to a peak. They are indiscriminate in their manner, not forgiving, not that of the light. They are misguided by a man who sits in his seat of power. His shame is great in his palace of gold. He will forfeit his right to enter the light of heaven for his indignities against God's creatures. We will not name him, for it is not for you to know at this time, but be assured he will meet his end in a timely manner and fashion. Beware his reach is far wide within your nations of love and tolerance, and his grasp upon your men of power and their weak minds has a tight grip. His cash has replaced the Almighty in their world of ignorance.

UK Election

She becomes your Prime Minister, her manner is respectful of men, but her commitment to the Tory plan will be respected. Your concerns over your finances and situation should be put into perspective, for you know not the value of a life. You live in an artificial world made up of technological items, you do not need these toys of ignorance.

Games and Mobile Phones

The young of your world, their minds are focused upon the digital side of the world. They cannot see their futures as they are blinded by the screens, dots. Their confusion is great. Speak to your youth, give them the knowledge they seek to continue their lives with a purpose of love and being. Be the masters of their lives and communicate with them to ensure that their future will be one of glory.

Fracking

A monumental outburst will be heard within the parliaments of your lands, as they scrutinise the fracking plans and issue their statements of ignorance, thwarting the wishes of the people. What foolish men who allow such ridiculous practices.

26th October 2016

Migrants

A positive reaction will be felt by those who suffer at the hands of those police; the migrants. We cannot understand why it is that they have come so far only to be turned away once more by those of intolerance at the gates of the shore. Is it not true to say that the earth belongs to no man and that all men and creatures upon the earth have a right to establish their selves within the lands of the Earth? The intolerance and ignorance shown causes a friction that will bring about a war of minds and attrition. Let them go about their business with an aspect of love, is it not better to teach the right way than the wrong way?

We know of your worries of those who would bring destruction to your lands, but they are the minority. Bear this in mind when you see on your box of vision, those camps. It is a grievous thing to witness, we point out these things. Segregation is not the answer to bring about a peace, our focus on those minds who have seen many things of horror, hmm, true there are those who would only wish to rob the state, but once more they are the minority. Have focus upon those who have lost everything, the preciousness of life. Give them hope and peace in your heart, use your wisdom to judge not those of your brothers, for are you not all equal in spirit?

Certainly we know of the many trials and tribulations that affect your lives on planet Earth. We control many things of your lives that you are unaware of, we manipulate the lies being screened on your vision's. Why do we do this you ask, you need have no fear. The general consensus here is that if we bring those of intolerance to the fore, then their minds will be exposed to that of the good.

27th October 2016

Anno Domini, peace be with you brother, brothers of the earth. We speak this evening of the many things of cruelty of man, but you need a focus upon his love. For on this day there was a meaning and purpose, long forgotten and the creator gave life to all to go forth and multiply within the world. His purpose was missed as greed and avarice and the dark forces lay claim to man's soul, we beseech you to become men of focus once more and bring peace to your brothers and sisters of life. We can assist in many ways, in thought and in deeds and action, but it takes your will, a sacrifice to bring these measures to the fore. Our thought is not of discrimination, but give us your appreciation for the things that were given.

The Rose of The Heavens and Noah

A Rose you see before you as she enters to speak the words of wisdom, a shaft of light shines and the purpose grows. "I am the Rose of the heavens who bring you greetings from those of the light, be blessed with the knowledge of the Almighty. You rehearse your love in your circles of light, become a member of love to unite the world once more. Many regions of the earth I visited, many thoughts and feelings I felt. Unknown this truth to you, but I am a man of my word and I still have focus upon God's creation. Come hither and listen to the words of a wise man, Noah, who once spoke of many things within his book of attributes. Bless those of love and deny those of a negative purpose. He lived in the garden of Eden of life, his purpose was great, he astonished all with a measure of love as he constructed his ship of wonders.

He stood in amazement as I spoke to him, asking had he fulfilled his purpose to bring peace and love once more to the earth of men. He banished all thoughts of self as he brought himself into being a focus. The many, they did laugh at him as he constructed his ship, they asked, "Noah, why, for art thou a man blessed with knowledge and yet you listen to the words of no one?" They did not know his thoughts in mind were of a kind far beyond theirs.

He constructed his ship as per instructions given. Not all were saved, as was intended and there was rebirth upon the world of men. I have to say this the capitals of your city will suffer in the wake of man's indignities. Question not your minds purpose, deliver the messages."

Pope Francis, he is a man of a tender heart. His nature will be heard. Hmm. Yours is but a small part but a vital role, as is your readers of these words. For you are the arteries, the veins of life and the willing heart of the being that controls, you have to obey your impulses as you pump the lifeblood. Help us, to help you, bring peace once more to your life.

People of the Sea

Tragic times indeed, when men have lost hope and vision of their purpose, but be blessed by the words given, for they have many lessons to give in thoughts of men. Merchant ships cast adrift upon the seas of mercy, as the storm hits, so those vessels embark upon the unseasonal tides of the oceans of the world. A kaleidoscope of events is currently occurring throughout your oceans. Your men of science have knowledge of this, they hide the truth. Haven't you wondered why your atmosphere is changing? Do you think it's really pollution of the air? Could it be another source that affects the tide of men and their life upon your planet? Deep within the oceans of your seas we spoke of men and beings, they see the decay of man and know the time will come when they will cleanse those oceans with love. For if man continues to beckon disaster, truly it will come.

But let's not speak of such tragic events, for we should have focus on the good and meaningful hearts that exist throughout your world. The men that fight for the right for Mother Earth and those of their kind. They are the true heroes who worship the Lord and are able to bring focus to those of suffering. They are angels within your life, born to man's breast, to bear the indignities in the hope that one day change will come, and that the influence of their love will seek a restful place in the hearts of men. The flowers of life you are, but as flowers of the garden, be wary of those of ill intent. Flourish and bloom, bring purpose to your lives and love and an aspect of care for man, tend your garden of Eden, allow its flocks of creatures to graze in the fields of love. We are the angels, we need your focus to give blessings to those who work within the light.

The knowledge and wisdom of one will come in the autumn of the term of office of him. We will bring him much knowledge of wisdom.

30th October 2016

We bear witness to many things, atrocities of your world that are constantly committed unbeknownst to you and to most of your countries. These atrocities go unanswered on earth, but they will be severely punished. Those who commit these crimes, once they evacuate your earth, they cannot exist within the world of light, for their true essence will be seen by the angels of light. You cannot hide your sins my children, as they are seen, both in spirit and by man who has been reformed.

Compare us not to those wise ones, for we are of spirit who have come directly this evening with a purpose, a mission to bring your nations peace and love.

Standing Rock

Tennessee may be an issue in the near future, as it is home to many indigenous peoples of that nation who commence their rock of standing together as that of strength and power. Their determination will hold out, but those of ignorance will shut out their cries in their cause, for they only see one thing in that line of misery.

Hearken to us as we speak the truth to your nations, bring forth those men of power who would have issue with those of greed. Now is a time for them to speak out, as their popularity grows so their spirit will infuse the nations in love.

The Communist Party once thought it could hold together a nation with arrogance and without need of greed. Their common policy is that one and all would share in the benefits of labour. This failed as those in power were led on the path of the greedy. They enrich themselves with many powers and trivia of your earth; they don't understand why it is that they were given these positions of power. Their energy unleashes many wrong doings on those innocents of your world, they complain their words are not heeded to and so they enforce their will upon the people, creating a situation so unbelievable that it beggar's belief.

How can your nation survive without love and trust as the flag before them?

Those many merciless of your world have not seen the needy; they obscure their vision with the needless things of life, not wanting to know. Like the three blind monkeys, hear no evil, see no evil, feel no evil. Their minds are soiled, tarnished with the riches of their wealth, but they will come to see that their burden was great upon them in the world of life as they reach the kingdom of heaven, where no man is excused his sins. They will muster their thoughts and wonder why they had betrayed themselves with such trinkets of life. We all have need of love in the world of spirit and of your man, do not shut out those things that matter most in your lives for the sake of a penny two. For greed is the downfall of man who is not aware of his true purpose.

Tumbleweeds float across the desert, they create a mass of entanglement that is difficult to unweave. This is like man's problems and desires, one almighty mess that blows across the desert as a storm, never reached its destination, never knowing his individual self. Only the thought of love will separate those from this tangled mess, only those who see that there is a better way to exist will roll free of this mess. Do not entangle your lives with trivialities, wants and needs, they are nothing.

Focus your minds not on the despair of others but on answers that may liberate them, for the free of this world need to show those of intolerance how freedom can bring such rewards as love and caring. There are those of course who do not care for this synopsis, they are happy in their world of destruction and hate, they are short sighted beings, those who have called Earth their own. They think they are masterful in their ways, but their attempts to destroy that of the light will be floundered. A common practice of love and tolerance is all that is needed to defeat those of the dark, so bring your mind to a purpose of love and let those deluded ones see the light in your eyes and the love in your heart.

Now and again we have noticed that one flowers in the desert of life, to bring others focus. Like the desert orchid that flowers but once in one season of many. Once it shines its beauty, there is none to compare and the world sees this outstanding array of colour. Let your purpose be as a desert orchid, to shine your colours of love and light to those of your fellow men, to bring them a peace in their minds and hearts, that sanctuary awaits beyond the golden gates of that place of light.

Triumphant, we see as she marches through the streets, her purpose done, her bidding has won over those who fail to see her secret thoughts. Hmm, what of he, you say? Well, he who dares wins. You cannot say that she is a woman of distinction for she lacks the moral codes of life to bring her purpose; does she think her wealth, or her husbands and their families will save her? She is a misguided lady. Her practices behind closed doors are many as she divulges the secrets without a thought. She is a dangerous character, but what choice, what an almighty mess.

The characters of your world who run for leadership and control of the many, are themselves controlled by that dark side for their purpose. They are unwilling actors in a play of life. Their roles as leading men and ladies of your nations are controlled, manipulated by others who are unseen. Their need is great of love and purpose. We will carry the thoughts of many to their minds, but it will be extinguished as if it never was. Only by personal sacrifice can they truly appreciate what it is that they have caused and any effects that reverberate throughout their peoples in the world. They will come to realise that they were merely puppets in a theatre of war and attrition. They believe they have control, but in theory and in practice they have none. Their beliefs vary and they believe sincerely that they are the ones to right the wrongs of those previous leaders, but they are corrupt and therefore blinded to their true purpose.

How is it we see many of your world ignore the plight of others upon your box of vision? Do they not seem real to you?

Do not their hopes and fears count as yours do? You must alleviate your mind that these things are far away and of no concern of yours, but be aware that your pity is not placed as a burden upon them. You fail to understand what we attempt to get across, but sometimes by doing good you can do much damage that you never intended or were totally unaware of. The extreme forces that control your mind's in your world must be met with a focus of faith and love, believe in him, our Lord our God. Master your thoughts and control your emotions so as to build a wall of light and there will be no access to that of the outside.

Help us to inspire those who have a heart but will not listen. Their strength is needed, they do not realise how far they have come, but they must open their eyes and hearts and minds to the many things that literature tells them. We cannot express our love enough to those who share those of misfortune and offer them shelter and refuge, for their place in heaven is assured, as they greet them into their homes with love and generosity.

We have come to the end this evening for there brews a storm which must blow its winds of change. Your masterful thoughts of love and light must not be extinguished by the storms that surround you in your life. Have a heart and a care and understanding that others are not as wise, but need coaxing to the gentle streams of life. Have a care for those with tender minds, give them your blessing, see them as children who are lost in the woods of life, commit yourself to the purpose given.

Complicated lives you lead, we view them, those sparks of light.

17th November 2016

God's Gospels were many, but rarely read, so we will bring an aspect to a verse Chapters 9 – 10 Exodus, which should be read. It is a warning filled with love, a contradiction you may think, but we are the teachers of the light. You must read carefully for they contain words of much wisdom. Help us to inspire those who follow the words that you write. I am the father of time and I bring messages of displeasure, but with a practice of love. As the floodgates open, so the light will flow to overwhelm those who bring a practice of ill will. You have heard Noah and the exploits, he was a chosen one, not of your world. Men will need to see that their ways are no longer tolerated, a clean sweep, a new brush, a new dawn.

Castaway your fears in your minds of doubt and read the words of wisdom held within the passages of John chapters 20 – 15/6 for they are the words of a mission of love. Compel your minds not to hate, but to give freely of your love and compassion. Allow your wings to spread, your love to grow for the many of your nations, as your white horse brings power, sow the seeds of light and love.

You will not hear the words of those that choose to listen, for all will listen in their own time. They will see that truly the existence of those spiritual beings is as real as their minds and thoughts. We bless this day and bring a focus to those who need assurance.

To you, we give our blessings and a practice of love to the world.

Angels of Light and mercy be upon you now.

Consequences of Our Space Rockets

Spectres of light are seen by your men of science as they flash across their screens in their observatories. Wondrous they think, from whence did they come? We never see them coming, are they are part of the asteroid belt? Or a disruption that has brought their path this way. Your earth is a fragile creation as is all other things that occupy time and space. Could it be that man has created a problem and now must face the consequences of his institutional research? Wasn't it once said, "For every action there must be a reaction," and so it is, that your practices of weapons of war will bring about a reaction, unexpected? You fire your missiles into space so they may not be seen as they explode their expressions of disturbance, in time you are caught, these ripples will rebound. Your narrow minds cannot foresee the dangers, and for the common man there is nothing to do but watch in despair.

There will come a time when we will assist your world, to restructure it and bring focus of love back to the light. But for now, it must run its course.

Tremendous amounts of fear will be felt, naturally occurring, for your lives are vulnerable. But all should know, peace will come. Fears are only momentary in passing of time and of your lives. Cradle your knowledge, the wisdom of the Lord and the comforts that he brings to you all, as he whispers in your ears, "Be not afraid of me, but become me, part of the light, the light of love. For no animal shall suffer within that light of love and man being no different, will rejoice in worship as a commitment of light and love. There are those who will not bend to this, for they see themselves as being their own man. Ha! They only hurt themselves in their denial! A blessing to all who practice in the light and love.

Tonight we will say a prayer of special thanks to the creator of life as he observes his beings and their many practices: "Our Lord, our saviour the king of time, bless us with your love and a practice of will that we may share with others the good tidings that you bring. Let us not descend into chaos, but assist those with a care and a love that only you can bring. We are your humble beings of your many universes. Help us to inspire others in our daily lives and routines. We are your humble servants, our Lord Creator. Amen".

1st December 2016

Christmas Celebrations and Peace

I bring you tidings once more my children. How can I help those who will not help themselves? We grow tired of the men of resistance who have weak minds and hearts, but joyous times are ahead in celebration of our saviour's beginnings. We wish to send you greetings of love, and a calm mind to practice your healing thoughts towards others. Be blessed as the season brings forth many memories of family and loved ones. Do not be swept away by the tide of avarice, equally rejoice in his name, the saviour who was given life before your time. He is a master of a truly remarkable inspiration to you all. He sacrificed his life in the hope that yours would follow in his light. Alas the perspective was lost eons ago and it continues to grow, not of the light. But once more we will demonstrate to you our purpose of love, be blessed in the knowledge and know that we are the Angels of Light who will come among you as you celebrate his being.

Turbulent times ahead will be heavy on your minds. Ask yourself this, if you were but a man or a woman of peace, would you have brought yourself to this sad situation? Your world speculates upon its endeavours of peace. A care and heartache for the many that suffer will be brought before your eyes as those murderous beings trample over them as they escape their cities. We were once an enslaved people, he came before us, as he will come once more before you and lead your desperate situation to one of peace.

Rejoice in our name and the splendour of his love. An open mind and heart will welcome him with a thought upon that day of celebration, of who it was that was born at this time. Teach your children of him and his purpose. Your modern times disrespect many laws of him, but if you are of a loving nature and can reach back in your mind, bring thoughts of love and purpose to your youngsters, show them the cross on which he suffered and let them know his purpose on the day to come.

THE BEINGS OF LIGHT

"The Brethren of Light"

These communicators are also 'Beings of Light' but as they clearly give their identity within these transcripts, they are placed under their own heading.

The Transcripts:

13th November 2016

The trumpets sound, horns blow as the banners fly high. A wave of discontent will naturally occur as they resist his aspects of charm. We believe that the many of your world are of a fickle kind, never knowing really what it is that they seek in their lives path.

We constantly worry for the future of your planet as the temperatures rise and then fall in the continuing action of expansion and contraction which will take its toll upon your people.

There is no merriment where there is dissatisfaction, for they only see a wall of resentment that comes before them. Let them know this, that our love can be held by no barriers, for the true love of spirit is with all those who would hold a light and a candle in vigil for those times that were, and the dark times ahead. Never lose your focus upon the one thing in life that means most of all, the loving embrace of your families, friends and those you meet upon your journeys, embrace them with your love offering them a flower of pink.

We will come tonight to send the blessing of the Lord to the many who have lost focus on the aspect of light in your life. Their humdrum lives are nothing but repetitive, as they clamour for the spoils of war. They concern themselves with many illusions of life, deceiving their own minds of what lies within the light that shines, that beckons them to have moral judgement and a kind heart towards all who exist on God's earth.

I am the Father of all, the brethren of light

I am the light and the love; I am the father of all that come before. May I bring you blessings on this evening. Your family and many more rest in that place of love. An umbrella of light shines above them all, giving them protection, an assurance that they are loved by all. Allow my mind to speak the words of wisdom. May you never know ill will that is felt by many in your world, your focus has become a wisdom of high concern. Hmm. My name is no longer important, but my heart, my soul and my love. In my wisdom I give to you, the Brethren of the Light instruct you in many ways by the coming of the new dawn. Do not be apprehensive as there is a future of light and love, be calm as she walks with a stride upon your earth. Unfathomable times they are, how is it possible that so many are in dispute with one another? I have mercy for all those who walk the path of light. I am the one who will journey with you upon your path of light. Never let it be said that a man walks alone in his life without purpose, for all who live are joined by a thread of gold invisible to man's eyes but part of an intricate web.

Your eyes may never know the many things that deceive them. Be honest with yourselves and bring peace to your hearts, love the Lord thy saviour in your homes, offices, places of work. Allow him the one to assist the many in the transition to come. Be inspired by the many thoughts of love that are issued to you, from our hearts.

Brothers, do not grieve for those who are lost, for their magic will shine once more within the heavens above earth. Analytical studies have been made upon those who pass from your life, and what do these studies show? Hmm, they show to those scholars of life, that there are many aspects beyond your vision. Be not ashamed to stand up and say, "I believe in the Almighty." Those doctors and nurses, as they watch them pass they witness a memorable thing that they are totally unaware of. Some will tell you they see the shining lights, some may say, a whisper is heard upon their passing. You must open your hearts and minds to understand, that all who live and die, do so, not alone and not afraid.

Hmm, we have imparted much wisdom and we trust your abilities to uphold the Lord in your lives. You must trust in your beliefs and willingness to sacrifice those everyday luxuries. It is becoming harder to communicate with the many of intolerance, their black shadow overwhelms those of the light who practice in the love, hmm, but that love and light will always be there and will burst through and dispel the darkness of their minds.

A blessing to you all is to be heard by the bells and trumpets sounding a note. Do not despair, as we will never leave you. Rest is required for there is time. You are but a man with a weak mind, but a heart of strength. Be noble and accept our thoughts of wisdom to your mind of love. Don't be ungrateful for the things that are spoken, welcome us with open arms.

We have not spoken for a while for you have become distant. You must focus your mind upon the love within. Never let your attention fade from that focus to which you've become.

Hope springs eternal for all who listen to the words, our voices will bring the trumpet sounds of hallelujah to those in disarray. Be calm as we make an entrance to your world in astounding proportions. We are unable to convince your men of love that we hold for your being, do not be despondent as we elect for silence.

'Twas me who made it possible for those of your world to escape their minds with a focus and aspects of love. Come before us in the dawn skies, for we are the next generation, you will complete your mission and sound the trumpets of heaven before those of your world.

Timeless thoughts have gone by, for many seasons and many years. Harsh to allow the realities of life hit hard, as you realise that your purpose may be unseen at this time. Never let it be said that any one man does not have a purpose. Your thoughts, your mind, contradict you in many ways to your actions.

Hmm, we are here tonight for guidance, to allow your mind a vision.

A bubonic plague of fear afflicts your earth and the men upon it. We cannot ease your burden, but never be ashamed of who you are and the thoughts that guide your purpose. Spiritual beings are we, amassed over the centuries. We have purpose for all within the light and love the Lord, and those that fall will be astounded to know of a practice of kindness. The hardship of many does not go unnoticed, but those with lessons to learn have chosen a practice of such severity, so that when they pass, they would have a greater strength of knowledge to move their soul upon its path.

We are troubled by the efforts of many to bring the words of the good book into disrepute, this does not please us, or bring us enjoyment. We cannot abide those who would disobey the lessons of the Lord, we are here to tell you that we are members of a race of beings, we have come this evening to speak to those with an open heart and mind. We are not a belligerent race of beings, we are unusual to your eyes it is true, but our minds are a focus and we wish to give you greetings from those many worlds who observe yours of mistrust. There have been many actions against us which cause us displeasure. In this mind and body we are now focused to bring it to your attention, that our embodiment of love and truth will be brought to your world and men of intolerance. Are we not all of same creator, the same being that initiated life so far and long ago? That eternal being who creates matter of the dark kind, to bring you light and a life.

Ohmmm... Ohmmm... Ohmmm... the key to our presence. A tone to be heard as 'Ohmmm', a resonance, vibrates to your very hearts and minds.

22nd November 2016

Troublesome minds have a fear for the future brought about by the tensions evident in your world of man. The brothers of light are here to assist men of the earth as they battle their illusions. Be assured that the men of the world will become a benevolent race of beings. At this time however, there is the battle between good and evil that reigns upon your world, bringing despair and hopes of some. Believe us when we tell you that your life's focus is of a magnitude that exceeds a substantial amount of beings, but you must not let your thoughts get the better of you as you tread the path of the light, do not allow those thoughts to intercede with your being, in thoughts of masquerade and ego. Your one treasure in life is your ability to focus upon the divine beings that surround your planet of Earth.

Let us take your hand and bring you all to an understanding and purpose of the light. Chapters 3–6 of the Universe of John will be of interest as you scope your minds to the cause of the light in your many practices of worship.

Troublesome minds are spoken of, and so it is that many of your peoples suffer confusion and ill will at this time. Let there be peace in your mind in the knowledge that each of you are individual, that your energies emit a presence of being. But most of this energy goes unheeded as they are blind to the true beings. So we must instruct you of the light to bring your purpose to them in the many ways and aspects of your world.

Freedom of man and his movement is paramount so that the integration of your races may occur. We know not why it is that you discriminate against one another, when your beings are of the one. Tremendous amounts of courage will be needed as you grant those of the heavens the right to demand an audience with your peoples. The heavens will open and the light of the skies will shine bright upon those places within your world that harbour ill will. They will know that the Lord has spoken.

Moses and the Plagues of Egypt

We have knowledge of many things that we have imparted upon you, the plagues of Egypt were mentioned, and in time immemorial these plagues have been forgotten. Moses once said that he was just a man, not a creature of God, but he was wrong. As his wisdom grew so his knowledge developed his understanding. He began his journey from the Pharaoh with many words of wisdom spoken by the lords of the heavens. Mm. You think is not possible that these plagues cannot affect you in this day and age, we have to tell you, that we will show our hand to those of intolerance as they besiege the cities of the Lebanon.

There will be no Moses at this juncture in time, for your leaders have much intolerance and will dispute any man who would try to bring order from chaos, but the powers of the one will be shown to those with a bitter end. Don't be deceived by the thoughts of those biblical things not happening in your present-day, for they are the hand of God and his will.

States are levied by turmoil as he brings his purpose to bare, "How can this be?" some will say. He will be instrumental in bringing down the establishment, for he has a careless manner with much to say. As they realise their nation has fallen out of favour with ill practice to those throughout the Commonwealth of the world, they will negotiate their fears, understand what they have done. What choice? This is a favour, a purpose to those of man. Nothing upon your earth is without a plan, a path. The insignias of tragic times will be adopted by some, and a fearful menace will grow in the regions of the states. You cannot stop this tide, for it must flourish before it falls. Dictatorship will never succeed as long as the light shines.

Tragic times ahead for many of your world. Have a comfort in the knowledge that the many who bear the brunt will concede that their lives had purpose.

Children of the light who will lay with the Messiah as you greet those memories of love, let not your hearts unfold to the practice of the dark, uphold the light, your circles. Turbulent times are forecast, but there is a glimmer of hope that the light will shine once more. The path of Jesus is a long one, it will once more be written to the annals of history, within your time. Truly we admire those of sacrifice and devotion to the cause of light. Let him who speak ill of the Lord be warned, there is no redemption for your spirit should you masquerade in the mask of evil.

Bring forth your light, let it unfold as the flower of Eden. Let no man put your heart asunder with thoughts of domination. They are beings of the light, the one who called you in his name. Admire us not from afar but draw us into your hearts and homes asking for forgiveness. We are here, never far from the thoughts of men who hold the light within their hearts.

The beast of burden will once more show his head, but when he does, know they of light will illuminate the darkness. Cast him out. I am one of the light, a master of love who brings you messages of love, in the hope that men will see.

John Paul II greets you with the verse, a quote, "Be not the man who drinks the sour milk of life, for that sweet nectar of love will bring joy to man."

THE BEINGS OF LIGHT

"Red Cloud Brings Words and Wisdom"

Red Cloud, Native American name Mahpiua Luta', (born 1822 – died 1909), a principal chief of the Oglala Teton Dakota (Sioux), who successfully resisted the US government's development of the Bozeman Trail to newly discovered goldfields in Montana Territory.

The Transcripts:

3rd November 2015

Your circle comes together to shine the light. I need not tell you how pleased we are of your progress. Wonders you perform, complete your tasks, you wonder; 'Why?' do you say, 'Is this real?' Have faith; know your journey is good.

The path of truth, all will be revealed, for he who sits beneath the tree and ponders upon the universe, it is he who will find answers; as the leaf falls to the ground and finds the ground is solid, then the leaf will nurture the ground.

Your light is strong. Your hearts and minds are weak, but you will learn.

Come with us on this journey with your brother *(Red Cloud)*.

Like the Autumn for the tree, the Spring will return new growth, a new season will begin in the great chain of life. **The tree is strong, its roots are deep, its body is strong, its branches** wide. As like the tree, spread your branches wide and even in the autumn when your leaf has fallen know that you will return in the spring of life.

No man can deny this truth, God is with you, the great spirit of life is with you, be prepared to work in this world as you do in life, where no one rests.

At the end the rewards are great for all, God bless he who comes to walk this side of the river of life, for he will know its length and the truth, the truth of its power.

Draw from the truth the power and know that your strength is good. Come to us in peace, harmony, truth and understanding. Thank-you.

5th November 2015

I come to you this evening with words and countless memories. Let us walk together through the forests by the river of life; let us tread the paths of warriors that have walked before you. Come forward; join me this evening with love and light and forgiveness for all.

Let it be known that I, Red Cloud, was here first, *(speaking of America)* a warrior, a father to my people, don't let him say I was not brave, for I fought well.

To your circle I come in peace, carrying the message of love and hope, the hope that life springs eternal. Don't discount the things I say as remembrance, be honourable to yourselves and others in life, be brave and fight. Carry on with this message sisters and brothers, unite with the East and West, don't murder like Cane and Able.

Pronounce yourselves as true to God. Come the dawn, the light, the serpent shall rise and so will the night to blind him, to drive him out.

He who walks this side of life will run for eternity in love and light, Ka Chu Wai. "Ka Chu Ka Chu Wai," *(Channels Note: words and spelling are unknown to me but sounded like this.)* We bring hope and peace, never has it been said before, the words I speak tonight this man learns, tonight is the night, a new beginning. Be not afraid of the dark for there will be light. Blessed is he who walks with the light.

Why do so many not care, they turn their eyes from truths? Open their eyes let them see our Lord is with us, blessed is he who comes before us.

When you walk in the forests of your home, breath the air, know it is good, take your hands and touch the Earth and know its feel. Look to the skies and open your eyes to the light, follow the light. The path will become clear. God's children you are, blessed is he who tends the meek.

Rigid your back, strong your back to carry them. Go now with peace and honour. Do not trade these words

22nd November 2015

I am Red Cloud, know my name, I come before you this evening to talk in prayer and wisdom. Scope your eyes, see the eagle fly, let your woman kneel in honour, we are equal. Totem, a totem is needed, bare yourself before the maker, know his strength. Kind words are needed to those who need the most. Lead your people before us, a totem will be sent, accept it with love,

Dance as the drum beats its rhythm of life. Popular wisdom conveys our words; shadows of the saints come before you and repeat a drum melody. Focus on the Divine, as the horse runs like the wind, ride, know its power, strength and wisdom.

Gather around your people, hear these words, let them know I am here for them, to teach the wisdom of days past, gather your people around you my son.

29th November 2015

I come with words for the wise, be not afraid, we are here with you, near you. Know our words are good. He who comes before us, walk with us through the forests of time, gone are those days, those days of sadness, peace has come to my people.

It is good to see that you progress on my words. I come this evening to honour you of the Earth, not one man but many peoples of the world.

Steal your hearts, be brave, the trials were once plenty, tomahawks were raised in hate but are now laid in the earth in peace. I once rode the Earth, my land that flowers.

Buffalo will graze on the grass; they are honoured by us. Whoever kills the buffalo for the sake of killing are shamed by my people. My people fed from the buffalo, they were wise creatures, they know of Earths connection. You too must feed and learn of those connections. Be one with yourselves, with your sisters and brothers, come with us the gates are open.

The women whine, the children were lost, be strong, hopeful and wise. There is nothing to purchase, they steal from us, and the wares they sell are ours. The forests spread wide, walk through the forest of love, rein in your anger my son, release this anger. As the deer runs, as the heart beats faster, know this work is good. Question no more your faith, run with us as the deer run.

Circles we make, our tongues are heard throughout the land, they talk straight, ears bend, ears blocked. Be at one in the forest of life. Soon will come a time of peace. A lion roars in the mountain, he snores in his sleep of life, go to your people and know your people, they are one with you.

Totem is coming, know it for what it is, a blessed angel is coming, verse 14 of the good book should be read, John brings this message. He of the night will shine, go now be at peace, be one with the universe.

We will talk many times, focus upon those in need, deliverance is near.

1st December 2015

We come tonight with more words; we share the wisdom of ages past.

Your lives so fragile; take care of your mother, the Earth is your mother, trees are your father, the breath of life. Your bodies are fragile and your minds weak, hear these words, be not afraid and shun your fears.

I have travelled far, with a great distance still to travel. We know of your concerns, your fears and issues, these are of great concern.

Open your hearts and minds to the Great Spirit of Life, he who dwells within all of you, he who gives you life. Become one with one another, band together your tribes, band together your brothers and sisters, be prepared for what is to come, but do not be afraid, for life continues beyond this existence, it runs like the deer through the forest.

We know of your pain, your sorrow I cannot help you. You help yourselves, listen to the winds, listen to your hearts, listen to its beat its rhythm.

God is in all of you. This man helps us to connect; he is weak but will learn.

Today many lives are lost through wars; indignities are inflicted upon God's people. They come to us troubled and in despair, healing is needed in this world.

Why do you constantly ignore us? Our words are spoken with a straight tongue, go now be peaceful, be at one.

I am asked to give words of wisdom, the wise listens to his heart, the man who doesn't listen to his heart is unwise and unfair, he ignores, he ignores the wise man. In your lodges you sit and pray, God hears your voices, he feels your pain, why do you say, "where shall we go now?" Why do you ask us for help? You have free will, allow us to be your guide. Go now in peace and honour, go now with wisdom in your heart.

Red Cloud Brings Words from John the Baptist

John the Baptist invites you to open your eyes to the words of the book of love, you say you are Christians, you say you are Muslims, Jews, Hindi's and the like. Know this, these words come to you with love. Hatred is for those with no heart, but they can be changed for all religions, the one true religion is within all of you, go now, be peaceful with one another, look to no one man and say he is not my brother, because he is. Every man is born of the same mother, every man is given the wisdom to know his way, fool is the one who leaves the path to seek fortune, for you are already rich, come with us be free in your hearts and minds, let us show you the way.

I spoke of Tomahawks buried in the earth, leave yours in the Earth, allow the spirit within you to speak, to guide, allow your minds to be free of fear. I say unto you, don't be the fool that looks for the fortune, go now, be at peace with one another, allow your hearts to be free, your minds to be wise. God is with you, within you, around you, children of the world unite in love and peace. Blessed be the Lord.

3rd December 2015

Green is the grass of the Earth, blue the colour of the sky. He who comes before us this evening does so with humility. Shame is upon the Earth, God's people have forsaken him. Open your eyes to lead the world to a clear destiny, hearken to the wind, listen to the mother of life, know your destiny.

We are here to watch over your friends, we are here to help. John and Mary come, burden yourself no longer with the trouble of the world, the path has been set, a course will be taken so sayeth the Lord.

Gone are the days when man was one with the Earth, with his people; gone are the days, those times of joy and freedom. Man's greed is great. Together we will ride. Peace from heaven will come, despair not, focus your eyes upon Mother Earth, witness the things to come, be not afraid. There is no fear.

The stars shine brightly, the moon is bold; but know this in your heart, freedom is hard won.

Come with us, see the joy for what is to be, together they will fall upon their knees before us, they will shudder, for they know what they have done.

A man is worthy of our love, uniformity, my mother gave me life, she nurtured me in heaven. The Lord comes, blessings to you all.

I say unto you brother, be strong, be bold and wise. Time is ticking my son, soon comes the time to pass the burden to others. Comanche, Cherokee nations, apart we rose, we fought, we were defeated in life, but not in spirit. No man can take your spirit from you, your soul from you. No man can hurt you beyond the physical, he can try, but will not succeed, wise words were spoken by the Nazarene *(Jesus)* you follow.

Your life is one of many, and many to come, be bold and learn you must. You ask for help, why? You have free will, use it wisely.

I will speak the words of the wise through you, feel my energy, hear my voice, see my face that stands before you and hear my words I send to you through the cosmos, through the universe, through the maker.

Come all ye who are reformed to the light you know us better, take a stand and unite. Your pain is felt through the universe.

4th January 2016

Sioux knows, the quest is long, struggle hard, but the rewards are great my son. Bless you and your peoples of the earth; ignorance is the enemy of the night. Peaceful bliss of your hearts, the knowledge is key, prepare for what is to come for your world, for many will fall in the battle that ensues. If you be brave and strong, then know that we are here to support and guide. We are friends of the earth.

6th December 2015

Wagons came, the dust flies. We run and hide, the white man comes; never loving, never giving, ponies ride hard. Sit my brothers and talk of peace, the colours by you will warm your heart.

They came to taunt us; they stole our land they murdered our women; and as if like the wind they blew through with destruction. We could not stop them, they took our lands and we forgave them, knowing that the great spirit of life is all around. We cried, our sacrifice was great. There came a tide of the white man and nothing could stop him, he runs as the buffalo, with great force. We talked with our elders, nothing to be done, we worked with them, we guided them, said prayers for them, nothing helped.

The Great White Spirit told us of their coming, told us of their destruction and the force of evil that drove them. Man against man, serpent against serpent.

You my son must realise the time draws near when man will rise against his brother; then peace will come, while your heart is free, your spirit. Tell your people to open their hearts and minds to the one who will lead you through the darkness. Father, help them to understand they are weak, foolish. They come to us understanding nothing, God bless them with their love.

We band together one another in service, in prayer, hold your hearts, be wise. Don't come to us with your tears of sadness, but with your strength of heart.

For decades man has fought man, woman against woman, never understanding the gift of life that is given to all; the animals are no less a gift to the peoples of this world you inhabit. Band together, shine your light, don't allow the darkness in, for once it is in, it is hard to stop. *(Channels Note: In my mind I asked, what use are these wise words if no one sees them, this is the answer received:)*

People will listen to these words I have spoken to you this evening. Have faith, trust and a knowing of our everlasting love. Your body is weak, lift your head, be strong. God knows of your plight. As the eagle soars, so does your heart in life, in spirit. Focus upon your abilities and your needs, be assured of the restoration of life, the eternal life that is given to all in this world of matter. We know that you know, your friends of matter will follow the light if it burns bright. Come to us, no thoughts of defeat but of honour and strength. *(Referring to my thoughts the day before.)*

Comanche were our brothers, we fought side by side to stem the white man, but it was not to be. Unite your tribes to fight the darkness or be stampeded under the feet of darkness. Your light shines brightly, your heart has motive and strength, allow us to assist. Never question your valour, your honour, your strength, go now with peace in your heart, strength in your mind. *(Channels Note: Then the word Kentucky was in my mind – After searching the meaning of this name, it originates from an Indian word, meaning, 'Land of Tomorrow'.)*

(A few minutes later I was given unknown words sounding like:) "Heya, heya tarn ekay, tarn-a-kiya, heya." *(Followed by)* "In your tepee you'll be free, in your tepee is the love. Heya tonake ri-Fiya, ri-Fiya heya, ke-lo nopiya sa-seyla."

10th December 2015

(Channels I asked questions in my mind directed at Red Cloud, about his people. Is he laughing at my questions? Judge for yourself.)

Laughing Bird comes! You ask many questions, this is good, focus your body.

Why is it man desires to own all things? That is the question I ask. The answer cannot be given for there is but one truth, and that is life, life is given so that mankind cares for the Earth on which he lives, you are the caretakers of the planet, but you are failing.

Raise up your minds, your heads and open your eyes to see the truth. Preparation is key and your mind is full of unanswered questions. Your heart is full of love, come forward to us without fear, be mindful of your decisions, be mindful of the tasks ahead.

My people gather around the drums, my people danced the dance of war when peace was all we desired. Your people desire this as well, open their hearts and minds to us in spirit, let us fill their hearts with love and light.

You ask of my people, of what importance are they to you? My people are good, they ran from their hearts desire, they could not see the course that was upon us.

We sit in your tepee, as brothers in arms, we smoke, have no fear.

Many came before you, I sit with you in this place of burden, I am not comfortable, but I am here for all to see the truth of light. Your gardens are full, your larders of plenty, it is no accident that I come. I have been sent by those in the highest power to watch over you all, know my words are true, take nothing from them.

Gone are the days of hunger and the cold, the nights of fear have gone, we are here in a place of abundance. What awaits you, awaits all upon this Earth, if you just open your heart to believe and worship the Almighty. Call upon him, your God, allow him to bring peace to your world. Magic, you need magic, be at one with yourself.

Man is like the Buffalo once was, they roamed the Great Plains, they were many but there was balance, they hunted not man, but the grass on the planes and the many united as one great cloud of dust as they roamed through the plains. Their majesty was great, then came man with his burning need of greed, with his burning need of bloodlust, killed ndiscriminately wiping out their species and those that relied upon them, he didn't care, he didn't care. We starved, we were cold and hungry, we lived in the mountains of fear.

The promises that were made were broken, they were many, we were few, we, WE are the ones who suffered as the Buffalo suffers. Time passed, our forgiveness is great, now we understand the purpose of our lives in the plains of our land. By the rivers we washed, bathed, crystal clear was the water, crystal clear was our purpose, then came the white man, fear in our minds, our hearts. We talked of peace, they talked of war. How can you talk to ears that are blocked and would not listen, we agreed to lend land, they wanted more and more? We resisted; it was futile with the force of the many. But we are still here, still proud warriors, we are here to fight for the right for man to live as one, for those that would listen to the words of peace, those that would listen to their hearts and minds. They are the ones who will live; they are the ones who would know the love of our Lord, The Great Spirit.

Seek your path my son, know it well. We will teach and you will learn. Many followers hold their hands in prayer; we will this evening.

May your pain be less than ours, strong hearts and minds are what is needed, God bless.

Heya, heya Ho, heya ho naga, neya Ho, be loyal to us in the light.

13th December 2015

The Secretary of a SNU church came forward with a question for Red Cloud:

Q: Christians believe The Word, learn and follow the Bible, thus using their logic and material brain, learning from top down. Spiritualists may well be Christians too, but many are experiential, finding their personal truth in various ways but most use their senses, learning from bottom up. So, we approach the same phenomena (blending heavenly and earthly) from different angles due to differing personal attributes, e.g. if you are more logical, temporal and theoretical you may choose the Christian approach. Those free spirits, more sensitive to energy, may explore Spiritual beliefs. Are we on the verge of weaving together both these different approaches to strengthen Holy Spirit's effect on Earth?

A: Greetings, it's strange to once more feel this Earthly pressure.

We come in peace, as brothers, we know the question on your lips, what answer would you like to hear? For there are many, the answer is already written.

Be at peace with yourselves, be one with Mother Nature. To work in the light is a gift given to you. But all those who serve God serve the light, questions you ask of me, I'll grant you an answer, to the one who asks, we know the question, but you also know the answer to your question!

You sit in your churches, each apart from one another; unity will begin as the darkness shades the light. The brethren of spirit will come to you all as you begin this fight. Words of wisdom were spoken in the past for us, so many years still unheeded, still unheard, sister, you know the truth in your mind, God is within you all, he resides in no church but in your hearts, if you have the will in your heart to listen. Then, and only then, will you begin to understand his will. There are no divisions in the church, for all those who believe will find the light.

You dance the dance of war, we have pity, but how can we help those who will not listen! We have tried and continue to shine the light, come together as one, for unity is strength, unity is the strength, forbearance of others is the strength of unity.

You class yourselves in different aspects, but in truth there is but one light and one God to whom you all are a part of. Sister Mary spoke of this many eons ago, she was wise and is now wiser in her role as a guardian, the keeper of the truth.

Band together your brothers, be as one, as the warriors of freedom. Fear not, we are here, reunite your bands, our united strength. When tomorrow comes to the one who speaks the truth, open your ears for they are deaf. Open your hearts, for they are closed. Be careful of those that would corrupt your mind and cloud your vision. Your world is a dark place, but for you brothers and sisters, the light illuminates the way and protects.

The war bird will come, you must face your fears head on, matters of the heart should be spoken in truth, light and love.

Huh, how can we help those who cannot help themselves, we do this through people who give themselves to the light, it will be no easy task as you will be a target. For you, our love is strength. Source your energy from your heart. From your mind, focus upon your intentions.

The storm clouds will clear as the breeze of love sweeps in, know your hearts, know your minds.

Purpose was given to those who will lead, their light will shine and you will know it for what it is. Come to us, to the land of the free, of love and the Holy Spirit. I have words: You know our words are true, we speak with straight tongue through you, you're wise and strong. Your heart belongs to the free, the horse that comes to you is the strength of our hearts. Go now, be strong, we have answered your question. Unite your tribes, your churches, talk is the way. **No man is one church, there are many churches in the house of the Lord, but only one God.**

There is your answer, be kind to one another, lift your heart in song and praise, allow the melody of love to sing. Spread your words, we will come once more and we will assist. Unite your churches in love as we raised our brothers, there is but one father in heaven. We speak the truth, here is my totem so you will know me as your friend. Spread the word let them hear our thoughts our prayers.

We hear your name; we will call upon you in time. Horse is your strength; motive your power. Need in your heart. Focus upon the truth of the words, may God be with you a ll this evening in peace and harmony, in love and peace.

18th December 2015

The drums that beat reminds us of when we danced, the call of the wild was heard throughout the land, a common cause was needed. Nowhere on Earth was man so uncommon, our lands were many and our paths were great, we sang and danced. We hid, we found ourselves, our spirit. Spirit of the world then came to us and we danced.

I am Red Cloud, the keeper of man, the brother of many, the father of many. Hear my voice through the woods and keep your heart and soul as one. The arrow is straight, so is your tongue my friend. Many questions you have still unan-swered, but time is a healer. You know our words to be true, understand the message that has been sent.

Your dreams, your hopes are real. Yellow Lily, she comes with words of wisdom and hope. Never before has one been so true. You must focus on the truth that is before you, come together as one, be not afraid of the dark before the dawn of the new era.

We are the circle, we are the light, we sit in council, we watch.

Inspire those around you to sit and listen to these words. Brethren be one, open your arms wide and greet the new day, the new light. Feel my energy, feel the pulse of my breath that is in and let it out.

I have but one feather in the band around my head, I need you to focus upon the light, the truth will be heard throughout the land.

Great bear we hear your voice, the Forest of Dean will hear your voice, be not afraid of us, respect us as your fathers. Merciful is he who walks before us all on this side, he looks upon the world and weeps the tears of many, they flow like the river, his work was done, the Earth needed to be proud, be strong, like the willow bends but does not break, like the bow that bends it does not break, but springs back as if it never was. Hearken to the wind, to the waters of the land.

Why do you fight us? Let go. *(I feel my tongue twisting back in my mouth if that makes sense.)* Your tongue is strange, your will is strong, your power is great. We can use you. *(In my mind's eye I see a gold ring with one diamond.)*

The ring is shown to symbolise the circle of love, the diamond upon it, the clarity of our words, to cut through the dark.

Walk with us beside the river of life and love, take no heed of those who would confuse you and blind you to your path's intentions. Your learning is great, quieten your mind for us. What words would you have us tell you? Now see our words, the thoughts in your mind are real, feel them, know them, know us, we are real, come together as one. Punish those not for they cannot hear us. Cross swords with no one, for the light is the love, the love is the light, bring this world to peace, do not deny us your love. Turkey feathers, see us as we now are, know us and the signs. Crow flies west/east. Blessings to you, crow comes with power, might, strength. Heya, heya rege regana shaya, hico hele tama wah is due. Your voice is heard, heya two tongues he speaks, more words of love, bless you. Teachers will come to you.

4th January 2016

The quest is long, struggle hard, but the rewards are great my son. Bless you and your peoples of the Earth; ignorance is the enemy of the night. Peaceful bliss of your hearts, the knowledge is key, prepare for what is to come, for your world for many will fall in the battle that ensues. If you be brave and strong, then know that we are here to support and guide. We are friends of the earth.

Take no intolerance against you, give love to those who are ignorant of the ways of the Lord and spirit. Come to us once more, wisdom we will teach you and guide you in love. Know our words to be true, know our names to be true, we are the wind, the air, the sea. Cast away your fears.

12th January 2016

Words to be given would be strong words from the heart, the knowledge from the Earth to be given to all.

The next stage is soon, it is set, we come in peace to offer our help to those that need it. Your Tepees of stone will not stand in the power of the wind, don't despair, the wind is your friend. The moonlight, take her hand my friend, be guided on the path that is set before you. The forests of the trees, darkness of night is at the end, take a hand in what's to come. Follow your heart, be brave and earn your feathers in the forests of green. Make friends with the earth, for she is your mother, we are your fathers.

Your science is false; the truth lies in the heart, as does the knowledge. Your lives are short, but in truth, lives are forever in the light of love. Carry yourselves with pride and dignity, for as the wolf cries at the moon, so must you cry at those that would listen. Howl like the wolf, be brave like the bear that you are. Come with us on a journey to a far land of love and light, peace and joy everlasting.

Crazy, they will say you are crazy, but ignore those with their words, for you know the truth is but a breath away. Take heart in our words of wisdom, you know them to be true. Leave now and we will talk on the new moon.

28th January 2016

I am Red Cloud, the leader of many. Once great upon your earth. My people followed Mother Earth; they worshiped the spirit of man, the spirit of animal, the spirit of Mother Earth and Father Sky.

We came afar to wander alone. Our lands, our pastures, they have gone. Wise words were spoken, but none listened and now, like the drums beat the dance of war, you know this to be true in your hearts and minds.

We would speak with your people through you and others of this side of life. Know my sign, feel my energy, let yourself go. God is with you all.

The great spirit of life is coming with lessons for all who would listen. They call me the great one; I am only as great as those who would listen. We band together in spirit, to guide those who would listen to our words. We speak words of wisdom through knowledge learned in days past, we know of what is to come, but it can be avoided with knowledge, love, wisdom and hope. Fear not my son, we dance with you on this journey, we care not for those who would not listen, but hope will always remain that their ears would open and hear our words.

There is no death, no retribution, only healing and life.

Muster your people around you let them hear the words that must be spoken. I call upon the Great Spirit to hold his hand out high and hear our voice as we cry of peace and love. Know your heart my son, know your mind, let them band together as one. Self-esteem, does it matter? We are not here for the trivia of life; we are here for that which matters most, the guidance and love of spirit.

Cherokee are we, Indian Nations put asunder by those who have no soul. Still we laughed, smiled, we fought, know my name but don't be fearful. Cane murdered his brother; don't you murder yours. Your thoughts are good, your mind strong but the heart is weak.

To your people of light I say this, spare a thought for those who suffer in your world at this time.

9th February 2016

You look at us with your eyes and you see the red man, but you don't see the man inside. You say, "Who is he, who is he that is so different?" I come before you, to tell you all, that there is no difference in their hearts. In the heart of the true man is the knowledge that we are all one, where thoughts are given in prayer. My words are here to learn, to teach, you ask many questions, we will tell you no lies. You come before us as tribes, as warriors, who work for the light; his colour is but an illusion of the mind.

To seek your purpose, focus on the mind and the minds of others who would come your way with guidance.

We were different than the white man. We shone upon high; we were not ignorant of the ways of man. We wore our feathers with pride as we embraced the new. We tried; we embraced all that came our way. His words were of forgiveness and hope. What would you have me say to those of your tribes? Have courage in your hearts, strength in your arms; be gentle with yourselves, we who are many.

Many come before us, as we are the guardians of the light. We stand before you with honour; there is no greater gift than the love and peace.

Hmm, why did I come to you this evening? It is for those who would listen. Behold the new dawn as the day breaks, for it is the time when the light banishes the dark, a new day begins. In our world there is nothing but light, love, tenderness and respect. We fear none who would harm us; we embrace them with our love. Your purpose is to come before us knowing that our love is for all.

Your language is hard, but we understand your purpose is as Noah. It is enough how we speak through you to those among your tribes, Nations. Your tepee is a temple of love, your purpose is given, never withhold your love.

The churches of God are in your hearts, your religions; your given names, mean nothing, as the true purpose of life is to love.

Beyond your comprehension are we, beyond your mind we exist, and we watch through your eyes. We do not judge, we do not condemn you, but focus on you.

One day you will join us in prayer, peace and harmony with one another in the knowledge that there is but one religion. Just have joy in your heart in knowing that the wisdom of the great ones is lost in the channel of time, but never forgotten in the minds of those who could hear it.

Recite your words and focus upon the divine purpose of life, let them know we are here to guide in wisdom and knowledge. To ask no questions, but to give answers to those who need it.

Three times will come, your purpose involved. You see the bird in your mind, as the bird unfolds its wings and flies, so will you, to the skies of blue, to be free. It is your purpose to look down on those who lead. With courage and determination in your hearts let your wings unfold and caress the skies, caress the wind and glide in the knowledge that all true to the light will be free as the bird on the wing glides.

Not your time my son, your purpose is good, be gentle on yourself in the knowledge you hold, be graceful, courteous and kind to those that need it and now let us guide you, we are here for you all.

14th February 2016

Gather your tribes, gather your hearts and minds, let us walk the long walk of trust and peace, hope is in your heart.

I, Red Cloud, many, many years will be with you. As you call to us, allow my thoughts as you would allow your mind to think. Too many of our lives were lost, we see the many today who are troubled, their life it will take but a few to change the path of man. Your knowledge is limited your words are few. As we speak to your mind, gather round to hear our words, they are wise as the owl in the tree. Withhold to you to encompass thoughts of love to the many. Bravery is won hard, no thought of regret should stem your tide, purpose upon us as we draw near, let your mind be one with us. Your need is great, your hunger for knowledge will be fulfilled in time, be not afraid, we are near.

Focus upon Yellow Lily, she is your guide. Come before us with your love, your heart open to the words of minds that are great in knowledge. As the fields of wisdom open up before you, harvest the crop, feed your mind, let your voice be heard, come before us as you would. Your courageous heart has many faults, your help here to conquer them. Never let it be said that we did not love our fellow human being, righteous. Truly your heart sings to us.

28th February 2016

With your feathers, your flights of fancy, your purpose good, and trust we know of the struggles of man, we were once as you, feeble in thought, in knowledge but we grew as do the trees of the forest, the higher we grew the wider our paths.

To the Manitou's *(spirits)* of the earth we gave praise and worship, Unknown to us the one Nazarene of the light who beckoned with calls of love, despicable acts set against us in the name of progress by white men whose only thought was greed. His narrow mindedness could see no more, men of his eyes were shut, blinded by the golden light.

We suffered, many fell before him, beneath his blades and weapons of war, he could not defeat our souls, our spirit, our strength, he tried so many times to beat us, we were like the rock, we would not be moved. He took the lives of many without care or thought, still we ran, survival of our nations was paramount. Cool our thoughts as the stream that runs down the mountain to the planes, we could not escape the fate that awaited us, but many believed that the spirit within us would see us through. Medicine men danced to the music in the light of the fires to drive away the evil spirits from our thoughts and minds, to bring peace upon our nations. Cherokee's were as children before the master, who would have thought our strength would have been sapped, still our hearts were strong, our minds weak with fear.

Come before us tonight with strength in your heart and allow us to feel your purpose, she came once before the full moon of the harvest, with messages of love for us all, she said, be not afraid of the flesh for it is weak and with the passing of time we fade as the moon before the sun.

Our souls would be filled with love and purpose our hearts would reap the love of our lord the Great White Spirit, her name was love. Focus upon your love for your fellow man, allow your purpose to unfold before others, so they may see the minds view. Come now together as we walk through the Forest of Dean, memories held, thoughts of love, children, Nurture the planet of life. Your purpose your voice requires strength beyond that currently within, work on your focus, your purpose of mind, not of the material but of the soul that is within you. Compare us not with those who channel, we are here for your benefit and others, don't become a sideshow, alert your mind to the purpose at hand, we will show you many things in your mind's eye together we will work as one, put aside material things, material thoughts and be as one with us in the eternal triangle of which we are all part of.

Your purpose is clear your mind needs focus, you will learn as babies, learn to walk as children, learn to speak and as adults learn to love, and in your evenings many more to come beyond your imagination. Have no thoughts of ill will towards others who wish it on you, show them love and light in the Lord's name, be upon you.

6th March 2016

Hatred is an evil to be extinguished by man. We lived, we died, not knowing the purpose in life. Once before we were as you, full of desires. We learnt the ways of Mother Earth through the teachers of our tribes. The shaman would beat his drums, he cried to the stars, he knew of his purpose, of his focus.

Our lives were torn away but we knew in our hearts that the Great Spirit, God, would be among us, to defend us and renew us with purpose in mind. Your purpose is no less. Your being is of no consequence but your actions, your will, your mind have a purpose that will move on. Never doubt our words my son.

Craven, he knew our ways, his greed was his downfall. He came to us with outstretched arms telling us of worthy things, but his heart was dark, his mind was weak, his purpose was lost. We suffered for his purpose. Animals fell before us as we starved in our Tepees, never knowing why this was. We cried tears. Forgiveness in our hearts was repaid by treachery in theirs. *(. Possibly William Craven, he was granted a share of land in Carolina, Craven County is named after him)*

You will never know the pain suffered by our people of the hounds of man, but we rejoice because now, for we have been set free by the Great Spirit of love.

Your advancement is good, your knowledge grows, your love for us increases, as does the light that illuminates the dark. Know our hearts and minds, be joyful of the path you have been set upon.

Courses may change, the minds of matter are fickle as the winds change. The breeze that blows through the trees of life is a gentle one, but winds change.

Your love is admirable, your purpose divine. Spark the interest of man with these words of love. Your purpose is carried forward, as the leaf on the wind, never settling, never resting.

The whole is brilliant before you in spirit. Ignite the spark of life within others, it is a question of faith.

We can tell you of many stories of the Buffalo that ran with the wind, their steps could be seen for all to see, the roar of their feet upon Mother Earth was immense. Their nature was to roam in the wild on the plains. Their heart of hearts were torn from their bodies, their hides were sold. Trophies were taken. Many fell in moments, with long barrels that shoot without purpose. They are wasted, their carcasses upon the ground, as they wasted their souls. The deeds of evil for gain of money. Our hearts sank before the scenes of terror, the blood ran as rivers into the valleys below. In spite of this, we gave thanks to our hearts, for we knew our purpose was good. We care not for those that waste the sacrifice of the buffalo, the needless slaughter of many troubled our hearts.

We sat in council trying to come to terms with our fate, knowing as the Buffalo were slaughtered needlessly, we too would surely follow. How we cried as our children starved, the cold of the snow sank deep into our being, we knew nothing but pain. But here in this world of plenty we heal our hearts with love and joy, those days of terror are past. For us, joy is once more restored to our hearts and souls as we journey the long walk of life.

15th March 2016

A Nez Perse our Chief of the Yakima

See the feather I wear and the band on my head, men of courage respond.

Raise your Tomahawk not in anger but in defence of your love, noble are people he follows and loves. We gave so much to the enemy we battled many springs her cold curtain and here he did nothing,

King George he spoke words of wisdom that were ignored by so many of his time, we knew of the king and his words of wisdom to the countless white man who roamed our lands as the jackal.

Research: The Royal Proclamation of 1763 – George III

Issued by King George III at the end of the Seven Years' War between Britain and France, the Royal Proclamation of 1763 set out how the inhabitants of the former colony of New France, now part of Quebec, would be governed under the British.

It also recognized that indigenous peoples in British North America had rights to the lands they occupied and promised to protect and not 'molest them.'

Because of that promise, which lives on in Article 35 of Canada's Constitution Act of 1982 and a series of Supreme Court rulings, natives have long viewed the proclamation as a bill of rights for indigenous peoples in this part of North America.

As the Buffalo stampeded, everything in his path was crushed, even the trail won't survive if man cannot see from one side to the other, of one end to the other, he'd steal your hearts. Know that we had native pride, your massacres of our people by yours, hated. Across our lands, your nation, the south is still not aligning, you say those days, but they still remain the men of violence.

To this day as the white man rampages around the world he lusts for money and empires, he does not see the wind that blows through the trees, the wind of change that is coming for the Earth.

Let them know what awaits, of peace coming to our people of our nations. Bear us no malice, as we come to inform you of the things to come, we call this by name 'Injaynoma' spoken in love, 'olatios' my friend. See us for who we are, we are the nations of many in spirit we hear your music, know your mind is not high enough, our need is with your love and temperance.

Come to us not with fear but of pride in your dreams that you are given on the path of knowledge and love. *(Channels Note: The words in inverted commas are unknown to me, so spelling may well be incorrect.)*

Compare us not of the savage in your books for we are not in verbal we knew the ways of Mother Earth we worshipped her, we knew her signs, she provided riches beyond compare. Trust, sit with us and know we bring peace upon your people to stifle their ignorance. *(Note: we interpret the words 'not in verbal' to mean that they are not represented in our books.)*

Hoist the grain in the air, we gave all, to nations of the world, we live in happiness our purpose to you is to aid you in your battles of harm, peace of mind is required to conquer those without thought. In many ways, your purpose is true and just.

14th April 2016

Shame be on them that torment others in their lives, for they are without wisdom and knowledge of Mother Earth. Compassion is all but gone for those that suffer in need. Still we see the white man carelessly stumbling around not knowing his path or purpose. Can they not see, can they not open their eyes to Mother Earth and her needs. They grab and take with no thought of those who inspire nature. Companions you have who work with you in the nature of spirit are true in virtue, their need is great at this time, their power and strength grows day by day, the light that they emit is seen on this side of life and is welcome.

I cannot say with any certainty that your species will survive the crush that comes from the Holy dawn of our being, but notice, answers to your questions will fall as rain from the skies. Increase your knowledge and wisdom with the help of those who serve our purpose, transmit your thoughts in a manner respectful to the path of light as it goes on for millennia. Conscious are you of our thoughts, imagine this, for we are the aspect of your lives that commit you to lead a life of love. Negative thoughts can't be accepted in the minds that follow the light, for they conspire to counter the balance in the neighbourhood of men, we clear their paths to be inspired by the thoughts of spirit.

Your dogs also have purpose, their love is great, they are no less than you, nor any other animal that walks your Earth. Their life spans are short but their journeys great, your animals, they watch you, have need to learn the feelings that you a emit, their casual appearance fools you into thinking, "They are just creatures!" but their minds are sharp and their will is strong beyond your focus. Only those that care will know creatures of the Earth and know of their compassion and love.

BEINGS OF LIGHT

"Yellow Lily"

From an Arcturian Message of 31st May 2016: "Mother Mary she walks with you, embracing your love and tenderness for others. Frequently you ask, "Why me?" Why not? Are you not worthy as any other man? Are you not of the light to bring words of comfort to those who need peace in their lives and love in their hearts? Temperance and tolerance shall be theirs, as it will be yours, be of a nature of love to dominate men's minds, to illuminate their lives with the love of the Lord, of the **Mother Mary, for she walks with you by the name of Lily.** *Enable Her heart to beat within yours to bring a peace to men of the world."*

The Transcripts:

22nd November 2015

John the Baptist with Yellow Lily

Put away these words of anger. Hear these words. Together we fly, glide through the cosmos through the heavens to the Earth. Be not afraid of us, your fall will come soon, restoration of peace.

Brothers in their lodges will speak from afar; let these words awaken your minds to our thoughts, to our actions. The cosmos is great, the flower of life grows strong as does the forest, the wilderness will narrow.

Hearken ye to the song of the thrush, that sweet voice, my squaw, my love.

John the Baptist, he comes to you with words of light and wisdom, know him. See the Yellow Lily he brings. I know your pain, the pain that's shared by many in your world of matter. To you I bring a message of peace and love, of wisdom and honour, follow the book of love, and see its words.

A Trojan horse will come, don't be fooled by his splendour, know that your hearts are strong, allow the rhythm of the drum to beat music, put your mind at rest my son, your circle who is strong will become one who will guide and inspire, go now with Lily, she is with you.

22nd November 2015

Yellow Lily

I say unto you with heartfelt emotion you are the one. Pass this message of love. Together in days past we yearned of peace and honour for our brothers, it did not come, we fought, we were strong, not as strong as the white man. I hear the cries of the wilderness, my people. Stop at nothing to bring joy, happiness. Be one with the forest. The moon, the sky is your friend. Help me to understand your feelings, you've seen the light, follow the light, be not afraid of the light. Firmness, fertility, rigidity are good words to bear in mind.

I will speak to your circle of friends of matter, focus, wash away your fears,

My friend they feel us around you, this is a sign.

4th January 2016

Message from Yellow Lily and Red Cloud

As friends and allies, becalm you're mind. I am Yellow Lily, the keeper of truths, the flower that serves you, and all man. You ask of my whereabouts; all around you, the yellow butterfly is the symbol, my totem, it shines with beauty and grace, know me for who I am and love me for what I know.

We dance with honour, we dance with you, the totem is the power, the strength, the totem is you. Your mind, your hearts desires, know your path my son, walk it with pride, never be ashamed of who you are in this life or the next. Come to us with love in the knowledge of sure and certain hope of your regeneration.

The constant battle of fear should be overcome with the power of the mind. You ask for wisdom and we say this, the wise man knows his mind, those that follow in the light should know their minds and bring peace into their lives. Build trust in your hearts and bring power to your people through the knowledge of Christ our Lord. His sacrifice was not in vain, nor will it ever be whilst the light shines.

Our people are but ghosts of the past, their memories linger in the hearts and minds of all who would listen to us from spirit. We are the people of the Earth, we are the Earth's people, through us Mother Earth has spoken. We smoked for our peace and listened to the jungles, do the hands of peace focus on the Earth? She will guide your way.

We are here to help, not hinder, but to guide your circle. Tomorrow you will be enlightened by the words of Red Cloud, know his voice let it sing, be humble before him, but stand tall with pride, with his strength as your staff.

His knowledge is your mind, you are immature, but you grow like the stick in the ground that grows and shoots tall and proud as a tree. You are the stick that will grow in stature. We have no ego, you too must remain a natural, bless you for your help. You cry to us for words, use your words, they will listen, many will listen. Come to us son when needed, we are always there. Focus upon the Divine. Gratitude is not necessary; we are here, your teachers with love and guidance for all.

Cry like the Wolf, howl at the night, pray everyone, aloud, am I to hear your voice, your echo through the land. Let it be heard by many, trust is key, feel our presence around you.

Thank you.

Yellow Lily.

11th January 2016

Yellow Lily

Gratitude is not necessary for the work we do. Open your mind, be one with the Lord and the light that follows. Gracious is he who bears the name of the Lord.

When we come from the light to this place on Earth, we bring with us our words to welcome you, know us for who we are, a welcome reality. Lessons are given to those who follow the light in the footsteps of our Lord Jesus, the Nazarene, who sacrificed himself for you all.

Like the wind that blows in the trees, like the grass that moves with the breeze, allow yourself freedom in movement. Be assured, your name is known to many. We are known as the wise ones, we greet you. You have work to be done, come with us on a journey of love, of light. You cannot imagine the power to come, He beckons to you all to join him in his love, so praise him.

Take no intolerance against you; give love to those who are ignorant of the ways of the Lord and spirit. Come to us once more, wisdom we will teach you and guide you in love. Know our words to be true, know our names to be true, we are the wind, the air, the sea. Cast away your fears.

12th January 2016

Geronimo was his name; the master of his world was his horse. His horse of white shone like the sun on the moon. We were a people of the earth, we understood the earth, our Mother. We found ourselves under attack from those that would steal from us, their burdens were great upon us, we were in fear, but now we are here to lead your people. We know your strengths, your power, learn to choose them for the greater good in people.

Great Bear you know, you are born of this. The signs are there to be seen by all. Mercy will be great of sacrifice. Great snakes in the grass are but a feeble line, their forked tongues, they speak words not of wisdom, but deceit. Rise above them, be not afraid of them. Speak your mind; your words will carry the truth that cannot be bent. Move with stealth, like the cat, listen with your ears like the bat, feel your power rise in you. Your questions are heard, you tell them of the path of light and love. Take your words with our blessing to your people of light, you have but to ask, your light is strong.

Once our people were strong, but we let the white man deceive us with forked tongues and words of untruths. We forgave them. They were greedy; they wanted all, never wanting to give, just to take. We had to fight, we were made to look bad, but we were not the bad ones. Our peoples died in terror, our children suffered from starvation and thirst, they put us in places we did not want to be. Their cruelty was immense, but still we prayed to Mother Earth for forgiveness for them.

Our people never once backed down, we opened our eyes to the light, we asked Mother Earth for her blessings and protection, she gave us what we needed, but still the white men took, never giving, never grateful, never loving. We sat in our Teepees, many times, many moons, asking the Great Spirit for help. He came to us in the night; our destinies were set. We suffered with the animals we helped. How we beat our drums every night, we danced; we were corrupted by the white man. Some of us fell by the side, but we were strong, we continued and we continue to this day. Our lands are gone, stolen, but our minds cannot be taken.

Bless you, for you are the one to carry the words. Do not be ashamed of who you are, your task will be difficult. Your horse, your horse of power, you have seen, Ta-ke t-ki owaki. *(Note: words sounding like this were heard by Michael, but the spelling/meaning is unknown.)* Bless you for helping. Blessing the light ones.

24th January 2016

When Mercury rises with the temperature, temperance is required of you all in the heat of the time, the moment. Though it was long ago that I walked upon the Earth, I see the beauty of the trees, the green of the land that lay before us, the woods, trees. All things of beauty were there for us; it is good to see that minds are changing; the light is beginning to crack through the gloom of the trees like the speckled coat of the cat.

We were once a noble people, a tribe, a band of men, woman and children. Although they abused us, we stayed strong in our hearts and minds, we sang and danced to our drums. The wilderness was our friend, she shone the light upon our brows, we gave thanks to Mother Earth and Father sky.

Come with us and dance around the fires that shine the light brightly in the night.

28th January 2016

Together we will battle, we will fight for the cause of love, let your mind go and be at peace in the knowledge that I am here with you, as your guide, as a friend. The consequences of your actions will cause many to look at their own thoughts and minds, they will listen to what you say when the time is right, be of the light, the divine. God let your mind free that we will together guide all, bring peace to your mind, your heart on your journey of love.

9th February 2016

Thank you for the rivers, crystal clear are the waters that run so deep in man's hearts. Follow those of the light, as the path is bright. Speak my words of wisdom to those who would listen, know that I gave a promise to return to the world of man to speak wisdom and of the knowledge to come.

Your past was rugged; knowing of me is not enough. The passage of time is set for all to follow in his steps, your heart-beats pace out the time. Mark the road with love and joy, pass each stranger and give them hope, the Tulip for love. Continue with your journey my son, let the powers to be know you are here, follow our steps. Guidance and reassurance, that is all to come, is preordained in his words. Focus upon the divine one who comes, pass no one who needs his love.

Help us to inspire those of your world as they sink ever deeper into the abyss. Their life jackets will be of the light, their lifeboats will be of the word of our Lord, to this end we will bring your world together. Unite this world before Him in love, peace and honour, pursue your thoughts, feel the need of our purpose in your heart, don't let your stride be shortened, place your burden.

Be reasonable with those you love, tolerance and temperance, kindness, sweetness, they understand your thoughts, your prayers. We are here, your words reach out across the nations, like the birds that migrate. Forgiveness in your heart. Be strong for the journey to come. Focus your mind upon us of the light, come before us with need and we will fill your heart with love and joy.

There is one who will help on this journey, she will come when the time is needed. Be open to your thoughts your prayers.

Needless suffering in this world. There is but one God for which we all worship, steady the olive branch as you reach out to the world my son, let no man disrespect the words, let no man forget the honour given to them by Him. We come with peace and love in mind, forget the troubles of the world, for it will come to pass all in good time.

Tonight we gather within the circle of love and light, we hear your voice on the wind. Presently we mark this time at this point. Come to us with open arms, reach out like the branches of a tree, reach out to touch Father Sky beyond Mother Earth.

Beneath your wings go to the mound of our fathers, be graceful in your thoughts and deeds. We know of much hardship in your world, we weep for those in pain. Feast your eyes upon the world of love; my message is an honorable one with peace in mind, loving heart. Go to the many in the knowledge of what is to come, your words will win over those hardened hearts.

Merciful is he who comes before us with a greater love. Christianity is the source of love, guard your words and speak no ill of those who's religions differ to yours, but embrace the light of the Lord. Names mean nothing; their true purpose is coming with a great time of rejoicing and feasting.

To those who call themselves Christians, let them know there is but one God, your religions differ in many ways, they are all based on the one. Before your knowledge, we were here to ask of the Great One for his love and protection, he came to us like the birds on the feather. We called on our Lord and he was our savior, no names were given to our faith, for all we knew in our hearts was the true faith of our Lord.

You come before us today with questions. Answers will be given, hold your hearts strong, give your voices high and call to us, as we hear all who follow the light. Passion in your hearts is good for all to know, be noble, be graceful, respectful.

14th February 2016

Come now as we dance to the drums that fill the air. Our campfires burn as brightly as never before seen upon the earth. We gather many of us to you; be prepared as never before, hearken unto the light, to the need of many.

Banish all thoughts of sacrifice, you are capable of much, follow our lead as we chant the song of the bird who is free on the wing of love. We muster in crowded places waiting for the time for us to bring you salvation; the time is nigh when we will visit your world. We know not how we will be received, but trust that you will welcome us into your world of light.

The horses we rode were of many colours, as our seasons, they fled like the winds before the storm. We were left before the many, like lambs before the lion, our lives were in your eyes as you ravaged our space. We mustered where we could, harbouring thoughts of ill will, frightened like sheep, as we were herded into the night. Why do we come to you? Your promise is good, your knowledge is weak, but we use your mind to tell the story of our lives.

Who knew the man who fought bravely in battle? Bows and arrows against guns were no match, for the mighty army that fell upon us, but even in death we never gave up, we were the braves that would stand forever.

In their minds commerce and tragedy mixed with our blood upon the sands of Mother Earth. We speak with a straight tongue, and you come before us with honour in your heart. Let us lead you to where you need to be on your path, focus upon the divine, prayer has the power to free you.

We come not in anger but in love, in the hope that you will turn to the light, never before have we seen such anger. Hope, charity is the way to go, commerce and blood will change the world.

As the night falls, speak to us in your minds, allow us to enter your thoughts and your love. Through the wild challenges, trials and tribulations we conquered our minds with love, we fought man against man, woman against woman, never gave in. Forty lost, we saw with our eyes the battle rage. Merciless were they as they tore through us like a fox through chickens. Lustful their hearts. Greed in their minds as they tore the clothes off our backs and stole from our bodies. Their knives blunt, their eyes wild, sadness in our hearts for so many.

Blue is the colour. We stole our minds away from those terrible days of darkness, our ancestors wept for us, I talk as we cry ungrateful. Why do you come this evening we know of your calling, the knowledge past, your thoughts are so many, our water a fortune of love, is a gift to all who seek it in the world? Go in the knowledge we hear your voice.

To our father we sing, come with us now before the light, extinguish your thoughts and doubt, release your mind without fear or illusion. There is no King except for one. It makes no difference that love annulled cannot be conquered, take out your thoughts to a higher plain. Listen with your hearts to find the true meaning of life and love. Nestle in the arms of Mother Earth as you toil to fight those who would become your masters. Never let your faith be burdened, for love is the food of knowledge, but love is the thought of despair.

Your body is heavy, age wearies you; your heart is light and free. We know your tasks to come, we all know your work to come, agreement has been made between us to work as one for the father of the light. As I enter your mind, breath as you would and let me feed your mind with knowledge my son. Gather round the many, that we may talk of peace and hope. Despair not, your time will come when you will be heard by many, our thoughts, our prayers are with you in the task ahead, the road is set.

5th March 2016

Yellow Lily and ET

Your tribes, our history. Gather in the clearing to watch the stars at night, the beat of your hearts in rhythm with nature. Your Divine purpose is different to each of you. We beckon; we call on your Manitou to listen to the winds of time as they howl through the temples of your minds.

Tribes are lost to time. Go today with your heart full, in peace, and know that our love surrounds you all upon this planet. We watch the signs, the Tancha call, they call to us on the winds of time, we hear your voice understanding your Hokis. *(Hoki translated means Soul)*

God is the power of love that binds us all; we are of spirit, as you will be once more. Your names are unimportant to us but your thoughts, memories, your love. Be kind to yourselves in understanding the purpose of your lives.

Knowledge is set to give, to give in ink.

Liken us to ghosts in the night, but we are spirit, we are your friends your companions the ones that guide. Don't deny us your love as we do not deny our love for you. Your work is good, be proud. Give thanks to those who have worked on your behalf in this world of yours, know that we will favour you with love. Promise your hearts and surround others with your love and light. Know that the dawn is coming when man will see his purpose, the truth of his being. Never deny us your love, command us as you will. Our teachings command us not for want, but for love only, and know that this day our focus is upon you as a member of the human race.

Continue in life as you would in death, with purpose. Gather your thoughts as you spread the word of the light.

To us you are but a child of the light, your memories fade but your purpose remains. Go this day in the knowledge that we, the guardians of the Earth are with you.

Memories of the Earth remain, the one planet fruitful of life in your solar system, there are many that exist beyond your reach. In time you will learn of these, as they are different from the Earth. Your leaders will understand their purpose they know this. Their insurmountable wisdom will not tolerate ignorance of man. We mean no harm!

Theirs is the life of light; they know of wisdom. There are many nations that have come before you. You are but a child of the universe. You marvel at your magnificence, but know this; you are nothing in the scheme of things.

I speak of nations not of Earth but of the many universes.

You see your planet and you observe your life with despair, we know your earth with tenderness and love, which will become barren unless your ways are changed, your focus, purpose changed.

Earth is but a speck in the Cosmos, united planets view Earth as a child to be taught a lesson. You misunderstand your purpose, but things will change.

Know this, our minds are set upon you to help bring purpose to your lives, to fulfil your needs in the sense of spirituality.

One of you asked what is spirituality? Spirituality is the coming together of like-minded beings with focus on the light;

their names are of no consequence as all focus. Combine together to bring peace and light to those in despair, spirituality is of love for one another.

Jesus came to your world; he was alien to the people of the world. He knew the secret of life and the Father's wishes. He was betrayed at the hand of man, but he never lost focus or his love. His gentle hand waved his purpose across your world, but still you see not the message that was given. But his love continues for his children of the Earth, there is no equal to his love, his tolerance.

Mary, his mother is with you, see the ring, *(I see a gold ring with a single raised clear crystal stone or gem)* and the stone in the centre, see the cloudiness of the stone, symbolic meaning should be clear to you. This is the ring of love, the eternal circle of life. Focus upon this ring; see its stone, look into its stone. We know that vision will be granted by his love. Come before us with tolerance, he grants dutiful life given everlasting.

You hear the forest call, if the wind blows, the flutes play, listen to your heart, feel its vibration, the power is given to love the people of the world. Call to us we will hear your voice, your purpose Divine, your mind set on a path of love. We of the forest were once as you. We believed in love and our fellow human beings, we were betrayed by those of greed, they came to our forests, they took our lands. Still we loved, hoping their minds would change and their greed would subside as the waters.

Their wagons crossed our lands with no respect for the dead. They took as they needed, never asking, never asking the manitou's (spirits). As they took, they caused anguish between us; our hearts and minds were troubled. Their great white leaders talked of peace, but double talk was all we had received. Their minds and purpose were not of love and peace, but of greed, of land and its resources. Feathers were given as a mark of respect, our go in peace! They tore up the papers of Pandosy. *(Note: Father Charles Pandosy, a Catholic priest involved in this peace treaty whose mission was destroyed and forced out of Yakima valley. Yakima was the tribe led by A Nez Perce Chief, Pandosy spoke as an intermediate between the states and the Yakima. [See: American Treaties of Pandosy.])*

Their words were not true, they tortured us in ways you cannot imagine. Our blood ran cold; our hearts were torn from our beings. As we lived in fear of our lives our children cried 'WHY?' We could not answer. Our marks were torn from our bodies, for trophies, the hungry white man knew no boundaries.

They say we were savages, but who was the savage? We were taught by them; our knives were as blunt as theirs. They drove us out of our lands. Misery. They beckoned us to move where they wanted us to be, but in truth they wanted all. Our spirit broken by their ruthless ways. Constantly we fought, but the snake was strong, we called to the wild for strength and courage and we drank to ease our burden. Why come for us like that, what is your purpose?

Your task is great, welcome Mikree *(Michael)*, to my Tepee, my home, is yours.

Now begins the journey of our brothers in spirit, come before us. Years are many, know your tasks. Our beings combined; you'll fight the plague of greed on this Earth.

King Charles will guide you, we pass life, feel our touch, know our minds, one of life.

Tonight's words will focus on the Divine. We will not hear your voice from that mind, their own lives, your own path, they do not understand that although your paths remain varied, you are all on the same journey of life. Encourage them to band together in life as in spirit. Nobility your birth, welcome your road. Your tongue is strange to us.

Many have gone before you knowing their purpose has been achieved, but their tasks remain unfinished before the kingdom of heaven is in reach to those who kneel before God and sing his praise.

Your words are heard but we use your tongue, purpose wise. The ring that we show you is the symbol of our unity. see the ring once more placed upon your finger and know that we are joined, connected and in the light. Listen to the clock that ticks, time is endless don't stop learning of us.

Kevin, he knows the bountiful resources, his words encourage you, they are demonstrative of our purpose, his friends will call upon you with purpose in time. Focus on the wings of the birds, his circle combined with yours has strength, which is needed. Strength will be given to you all. Know that your hearts, your minds are of steel, a bond that cannot be broken in life or death as you walk the path together. Yoke his knowledge as he is a master of another world beyond yours, his knowledge will carry you through your disbelief. He'll agree your belief is strong and you will grow, as you understand the words that are given through you. Have faith and trust, come together as a force to be reckoned, your love of the light will illuminate the path of man, God bless you for your purpose.

Come before us with joy in your hearts, in the sweet grass that scents the air, we bring peace to your Tepee, your knowledge grows of our ways and we take pride in that, your interest is good, as you reap your harvest of souls embrace them with love. Skill is needed in the time to come, you will learn we feasted upon the grasses, those sweet grasses. Of us he is the great Father he brought peace and knows that our fathers will be here gathered around you with purpose and guidance, the shaman is you, the diamond reborn in the new journey of men. Go now and rejoice in the light of the universe. Achieve what we ask your sacrifices will be great.

14th April 2016

Yellow Lily, Mother Mary and Jesus

Jesus came as my son to this world of flesh, he suffered greatly, for his path was truly great. He dwells within the house of the

Lord, shining out his light upon the children lost to your world. His love reaches out, radiant as ever, patrolling the hearts and minds of those that have their eyes opened. Continue your focus to the purpose at hand, knowing that we respect and love your emotions. Control your heart and mind when needed, when trials and tribulations come before you, relax, remember that the love of Jesus and God is within you all, causing you to forgive those that trespass against you. Combined your hearts will change the aspects of the world before you. I am Yellow Lilly, I am the keeper of the truth, know my name is special to you. Compare me not with the books of old but with that of the new to come.

New dawn, the purchase when man will see his purpose, he phases between good and bad, light and dark, he is drawn to the physical pleasures of the Earth not knowing of the pleasures of love within the light of the Lord. Continue your path as ordained my son, come to us with your love and aspirations. Enlighten your heart with the promise that God is within you and all who will open their hearts and minds to him.

Today we will initiate and reform. Continuance of man is assured beyond what is to come; selection of the fittest and the worthy will become apparent with a plague, as a crusade of love. All of this will be preceded by death of those without purpose. Let the minds of those of the light be assured that the Lord is with them in the coming days of turmoil. Trade not your love for the pleasures that exist on Earth, for they are nothing. Only love will transcend death and your consciousness will grow beyond that imaginable. Grasp us by the hand as we lead you on the path of truth and light, knowledge will be yours rest assured in due course.

Trigger your emotions with love, your aspects of light will shine into those who don't understand, the words will reach out and grab their attention. Display no fear in what they say, for there is the truth and light, wisdom of the Lord that comes before you.

Tarnished are the memories of those eons past, their reputations destroyed so that humanity can control his own destiny, but as a magnetic field we will be drawn back into the light. How their practices of tarnished behaviour will be seized upon and brought to justice before the light, and your answers, questions of the mind, should be focused on the light and the love. Know these words are not yours, for they are of the light.

Depart from your ways of the world to allow the light in and install brilliance, compassion in your heart. Love in your thoughts in our men (Amen)

5th May 2016

Yellow Lily:

The flowers of the night will blossom once more in the hearts of men; they will flush those things clean that have contaminated his mind. Your purpose is to wash the feet of men with His words of wisdom and knowledge.

29th MAY 2016

Yellow Lily calls to you, "Don't persecute yourself! Allow your thoughts to travel beyond your mind, focus upon the light. Pray He will navigate you, your mind to a place of beauty.

Your star system is one of many in the galaxies, a light of heaven. You are not alone as your world leaps for freedom of mind. Don't classify us or regard us as alien for we are as much a part of your world as you are of ours. Our need of you is great. Temples of your mind are focused, travel with us as we use your voice to declare a peace upon those of your world. Call upon the angels to bring a love purpose and need to your world, let them shine the light as your purpose grows.

Purposely we have come to bring you news of a windfall to the minds of those of purpose, your needs are few as you live your life, be inspired by the words of the poets of the new dawn, for they speak of things that reflect our minds and the beauty of the Earth."

18th October 2016

Yellow Lily Speaks

"It's been a time since I have spoken, but children of the world, listen and know my words of truth as I give you a mothers love to embrace your hearts. I am an angel of the light, of the Lord and I speak through this human man to you, to your wise, and I will whisper in your ears the love of the Lord.

The Tulip is a flower of beauty and of the spring, it brings many new beginnings for those who hold its perfect form. Let it become your symbol of peace and the mighty strength, as it stands proud, holding its head high, displaying the colour of love. The yellow tulip should be a symbol given to all those who wish for peace in your world, and remember my children, the symbols of love are given in love and respect, in the hope that we be triumphant."

Guided are you by the masters of mercy. You sense thoughts, they go out, throughout the realms of spirit. Be prepared to witness astonishing times. There will be many who will suffer at the hands of those who deny Him, our Lord, but know this, that the strength will be given in the corridors of power, as they surge forward to bring you peace and love.

BEING OF LIGHT

CHIEF JOSEPH

Native Name: Hinmatoowyalahtqit
Born 1840 – died 1904
Joseph became renowned as a humanitarian
and peacemaker.

The Transcripts:

17th February 2016

This medium is strange, we mean no harm; his purpose is set for all to see. Constantly we strive to reach your thoughts. Lessons are given to those who would reach out for us, talk to us, be not afraid of us. Constantly we are asked why, why is this life given, your purpose is to learn?

My, my name is Joseph, this body is strange, reluctant.

Tomahawks at the ready for the battles to come, be strong and wise to your thoughts and teachings. Forget us not as we walk by your sides with love, honour and dignity.

To this circle we send greetings, never we have, never been allowed contact like this but love is sent, the vibration from the light. God bless.

Those that seek our wisdom, be sure the questions you ask. Knowledge is key to the universe, set us not apart from your brothers or sisters but let us change your perspectives, care should be exercised at all times. We are the ones of the light; we need to help you in the dark of the night.

Come before us this evening with, with love in your hearts, pride in what you do.

I cannot reassure you of your futures, your paths are not written, only the wise men will see the path to take. The way ahead is clear for those that would look. Focus not upon the things that you need but focus upon those things that you are not aware of as yet. Search for answers in your mind, the questions will come.

Life is not a dream, but a reality, few experience the truth, let not your fears overcome your rationality, be honourable, be faithful, have love.

Right hand of men, trusting your faith as never before, write your words, focus on your lives, encompass one another with love, knowledge, muster your bands.

Gone are the days when we were known to many of your race, pictures in your minds that fade away with time. Graceful we were and will be again, we never gave up on those that would take us into their hearts. Form among you your purpose, strive never ending for the knowledge and wisdom there is the effort taken. Blessed is he who walks the path of light, I say again knowledge is key, the world and your wisdom.

Command us for strength, command of us not. Questions you have are many I'm sure, tolerance overrules. The air that I breathe is good, sadness, why come before us if you would not believe, we will reassure you we are real, Cherokee, Comanche, we are the tribe of many.

22nd February 2016

Be brothers with one another, our hearts were strong our minds weak, but we gathered in the forests of time and grew in strength and numbers. We see the error of our ways never knowing of those that come before us, their scheming minds they drove us from our hearts, our Tepees we fled far and wide amongst the woods. Come with us as we gather once more to embark on a journey so great that our minds cannot comprehend, you know me as Joseph, chief of my people, of my lands that were robbed from us by white skin, their rifles, their terrible thoughts. You know our history but know our minds for we were free unlike those that pursued us, our minds were free, we made you pay with our strength of mind.

Canada was far, we walked many miles, many fell on the way, the elders could not see the wisdom of our purpose as we walked through the wilderness, our minds grew strong, our minds were strong, we fought through the snows, hunger was our enemy, but we were victorious at the end. There were few of us left but we had purpose and we grew once more, nations, my people would like to greet you in their manner. Are you listening to the winds as we whisper in your name? Our voices will carry into your mind, focus on those of similar minds.

Navajo, Cherokee, Sioux many nations fell but we fought, we claimed that mountain, it was never ending, the peaks of white snow were as fingers pointing to the sky, but we knew that our time was done. Still we climbed knowing our purpose our love grew for one another our respect for nature is never ending. We lived in the mountains of nine, their peaks a reminder of the heights to be achieved. Gold, and man wanted gold, we denied them, their right was not to know us, respect us as we respect you.

She will learn in her dreams of her purpose in life, your help and tolerance for her guide will allow her to see that her path is a long one. Her travels will be far and wide. In knowledge she is young, but strong in heart, grant her your guidance, your love and caring. In your circle there is strength and knowledge, guide her with open arms as she walks the path of light and go with peace, with honour, with strength, one of the bear.

27th March 2016

Terrible days to come, trophies to be had by the ignorant, they will fall by the wayside as the light strikes through them. Confidence is a weakness that needs tempering with love, you know me as Joseph, welcome me with your heart and love, we come before you this evening in council.

Do not deny our thoughts as we are the Wise Ones who once trod upon your Earth, we could not have imagined what fools there were around us, did they listen? Not with their hearts or their minds for they were full of greed, need. Unworthy were they of our tolerance, united they said was their name, hmph, united in what? Not in mercy, united in greed.

She came before us to tell us of the harm that they would bring, we did not listen and we did not know her purpose, but we come before you with need that you should know that she is with you in this time of purpose. *(Note: Meaning of this is unclear at the time of writing – could possibly be Yellow Lily.)*

Our power and strength will be with you in the stars and the moon of the night. Winds of change will blow with purpose through your heart. The many who need wisdom and comfort will know of your name. Bring us your heart, your love of wisdom and as the bear, stand tall and snarl at those who have weakness, let them hear your roar. Know your strength of mind is true to the Great One, the Grandfather of that place beyond the stars, his need of you is great. Fill your heart with love my son, a warrior you are. Come before us before the dawn light, smoke with us, for we are your friends who walk with, 'The Bear' in life.

In your journey upon this world of life you comprehend so much in the way of love, yet you feel at times you are unworthy. Huh, you are wrong, your purpose it grows, let us show you what we see. Aaah, the arrow that flies true as the wind is the arrow that strikes at the hearts of those who thirst for knowledge of the light. Sometimes this arrow is deflected for those that shut off its journey, but yours is straight and true. Continue your journey with purpose in mind, be afraid of no one for they cannot hurt you with their words of foolishness, for they are not wise in our ways.

Today we will show you that the many are a signal, you know this, before the dawn the arrow will strike your skies. *(Comet maybe?)*

The twelve has purpose beyond your understanding. *(Note: Could this be a reference to The Council of Twelve? The Andromeda Council comprise a total of 12 different, distinct member worlds and many, many races. There is one ambassador per seat for each of the 12 senior member worlds.)*

She knows of your carnation with those who have not seen your world of beauty. Come before us with your love tolerance of mind, let us navigate this life together, be at peace. This conversation is filled with purpose your heart is strong, yet your mind is weak, you will complete springs, many springs. Hmm, your time is nigh; have no fear.

Colorado will be next, our visit will inspire others, denial will be useless, transformed are we of the light into matter to absorb the collective of the Earth, command your minds and bodies to the task ahead, granted your wishes. Tomorrow at dawn the arrow will fly to strike at those who be unworthy of his love, commencement of the gates will begin shortly.

Your children will be spared many ways, they live amongst you not knowing their purpose in the world to come, their minds are free filled with love, show them your love and mercy. Commencement of purpose next week as the light shines bright upon your planet, you will notice a change in the atmospherics, you'll not understand its purpose but be sure that our light will shine upon you all.

Conscious are you of the fact that the theories of relativity continue to transform your world into what it is today, necessities should be taken to continue your purpose.

Equations will be given the formulas beyond your understanding $T=2V$, *(T= Time, V = Universe. Regarding the equation, $T=2V$ is part of the equation which is the time taken for the object/projectile to reach its final destination. Possible comet path or even space junk?)*

Trade your minds of the thoughts of others, uplift to the ones who inspire.

Her name is written among the Stars and go in peace and God knows that is your purpose. Try to find those for your heart who would listen and acknowledge the words. Time has begun when we fill you with change, hear that your needs will be fulfilled with purpose. In time answers will come, from the Stars at night we speak with many minds, we are the many, control your moods, find tolerance in all things filled with purpose, continue to transform into the butterfly to the daisy.

Continuance of your mind and heart will be required, go with God and be at peace with love temperance and tolerance. The chair should be noted, for it sits at the heart of the universe of the cosmos. *(Note: Possibility that this might refer to the constellation, Cassiopeia, which is sometimes known as 'The Lady of the Chair'.)*

31st July 2016

I am Joseph *(Chief Joseph)*, a man who once walked the plains on the many moons, for in my tepee was love, but a bitter end befell us as we fought the white man. I have come once more this evening for Joe (or Jo) is of need. Many feathers I have won, many I have lost, truly the bitterness set the Lord within me.

Past, I am chief no longer, I am of spirit, my name lives on within the minds of many who see the injustices brought against us. For the world has changed in so many ways, we gather in the mists of the dawn, before the buffalo harvest. We sang our songs, hunters, warriors, Heya, Heya. *(Note: The word Heya means spirit and is a call to the ancestors.)* We sang to spirit to give us a plentiful harvest of buffalo. We say prayers for their being and their numbers, for they sustained us in many ways, our boots, our attire. We were grateful for their being and we sang songs for their spirit, for they were worthy opponents upon the plains of Nebraska. We fell short many times as their decline became obvious.

The white man tortured and butchered, denying us our existence. How we cried, so many times, knowing that our lives would be extinguished in the coming wars, those wars of the planes.

Custer, he was a man, a coward, he committed genocide many times, but his braves declared him a lord, but what sort of lord was that? He had no dignity, no pride, no care in his heart for that which lived, his pride and his ego were immense. For his yellow hair was famous. But what of us? Those who he preyed upon, he considered us as nothing; we were a pestilence to him. Many times we fought, won and lost many battles. We cried for peace, but our tongues were not heard by those in their cities. We became frustrated so many times as we sat in our tepees, we discussed many tactics, but there was no hope, for their numbers grew like a white plague. They called us savages, but truly, who was the savage?

Today's world is a distant memory from ours, but we find the white man still preying upon the vulnerable of the earth. The beasts of burden are still slaughtered, for those councils of the white man look down upon their very own as savages. There will be a reckoning, feathers will be won and lost on both sides, but we cannot help feeling that man will suffer our fate. They lay claim to our lands, our ponies, our lodges, for what belongs to them? Nothing. We sacrificed much, we committed no crime, that was not justice.

We now sit in council within the house of our father's, we say unto you and to all your braves who follow our light, do not relinquish your hearts, be as the brave, earn your feathers. We recognise the tasks ahead are great, but band together, for like the buffalo that crowd on the plains, it is only the weak that will succumb.

18th October 2016

Joseph brings about a storm within your hearts. He will now speak to those who wish to listen.

"I hear the men of ignorance cry their words of shame upon our nations, but we are many. We band together with the Crow Nation without discrimination, for we are a party of one, of whole minded consciousness."

(The following paragraph is a personal one for a follower of these messages who had a past life with Chief Joseph, we have permission to include it here.)

"I have spoken words with you before as you have relayed them to that entity, the child. She will know of my wisdom and my power. She needs focus once more as she is dominated by those thoughts. My child, awaken your mind to the beauty of spirit and the Lord, do not deny the existence as I guide you and your family to a place of peace. My lance of strength will shield and protect you. I am with you my child, as you will witness in your dreams that horse of strength and power, the white horse of spirit who calls your name. Have strength my child, be not afraid. Let the man sit beside you with wisdom and knowledge, let him guide your steps before the doors of my tepee. Be not afraid as I draw closer, you will become aware of my energy. Let me ruffle your hair and plait it as the nation Aphelepa the squaw. Your black hair is a thing of beauty that should be cherished and not cut, for it has strength and bonds us in that nation of love. Be clear my dear of our existence within the light and the power of love that bonds us to each other's souls. Be not afraid of me, I am your husband, your warrior, your staff of strength. I ride now to be with my Cherokee brothers, beware those who would bring thoughts against you, and now your place is at my side. Heyashay, heya hey."

Troubled minds are afflicted this evening, you see the bear, he is of strength in your heart. Become aware of the many things in your lives and give a practice of love to all despite their negativity.

Fashionable ideas will give strength to those who have witnessed the clouds in the sky as they draw together in the fashion of a cross of the Lord. This will be a symbol that will be on your network, as it will be as astounding as it would be of the light.

Be not afraid, we hear your fears, your thoughts of dismay, as those of your nations war and are brought to the dark side

by those of intolerance. We are your guardians Michael; we stand before you and hold your hand in the light and the love and the true purpose that has been given by our words. We protect you, have no fear, for man has no power over you.

Your bodies are weak and the strength is hidden within your soul and heart. We know the pressures of life are unforgiving at this time and we understand your reasons for thinking the things you do. Be aware and have strength, let the pattern of life unfold before you as a book, allow the love to give you strength, allow in the hearts of those energies who wish you peace. A fracture of the mind can be healed with the passion of Christ and love. Negate with many things you ponder upon, and issue a practice of love my boy. You have strength of heart. A feather was given as a strength. *(Note: The channel found a feather on his laptop, there were no windows open, no doors open and no logical place that the feather could have come from.)*

Cast your minds back people to when you were children, your lives seemed unrealistic, no worries, no thoughts of death, no illusions or temptations, which is freedom of your hearts as you played. So sad that you grow up. Not all are corrupted, some are and lose focus, but initially you are all born of the light. Ah, temptation comes your way but it is your thoughts of love that will hold you back, be reassured by the power of love that sits within all and when you have troubles in mind, think back to those days of playful and joyous times, to when your mothers and fathers sat with you playing cards, reading books, drawing pictures and remember your minds at that time were free of worry. Allow that remembrance to enter once more and be free in your mind and not tempted by those of sin. We will grant you peace in your lives, but only if you negate your problems in the light and love of the Lord. Be blessed my children, as we sit on high giving these words of love, praise be to those who have love for the Almighty and bring purpose to others as messages of light and love. Know your comrades as you stand together and fight the times that have a grip on your souls. Never let the things of the light vacate your minds. We are here, the spirit of love, truth and honesty to warm your hearts. Light a candle of love, let it shine for those who are at peace in this world of beauty and remember them with a fondness.

Let your brethren respect your words my son as we will grant you peace of heart. Amen.

Turbulent times will muster many thoughts of intolerance and ignorance in the cities, the bazaars, of those places of the east. Their words are spoken with intolerance to those nations, they will not divulge their places as they randomly seek the victims of the innocent. He who sits and stands tall in that place of power will fall, an almighty fall before his nation. His tomb awaits him, his tomb of darkness, he cannot escape the justice of the Lord and for those who were robbed of their right to existence.

A massive outcry will be heard against him by the peoples of the world as he negotiates his arrogance to those in authority. He will not be tried of war crimes; he will not be committed by those men who task him with pressures of financial means. He has an arrogance of hate. Allow his thoughts to be as if they never were my children. Look to the light and remember the Lord Almighty who will shine his cross upon you in the days to come. Have peace and mercy upon those who are trodden by the margin steps of war. Become a nation of peace and tolerance my people.

BEINGS OF LIGHT

Native American Indians and Their Connection with ET's

There are many stories of Native Americans communicating with extra-terrestrial visitors over thousands of years. Archaeological and folklore evidence seem to suggest that 'Star Beings' have been sharing cosmic wisdom with numerous tribes.

The Transcripts:

31st March 2016

Speckled Eagle, ET's, The Beings of Blue, Venus, The Blue Ray

The signs were given many years ago. The warnings have gone unheeded as to our purpose on this earth. Go forth and let them know that our purpose is true of the light and of the Lord.

Blessings be on you all with admiration and love. There is time to relinquish your ways and embrace the love of the Lord of light. Colour your mind with aspects of thought, but control is necessary to allow those of masters to enter your thoughts to compromise not with us, for we bring peace.

Your purpose is tenfold, it will be an immense journey of your heart and mind. Come with us before the light, our needs of you are great upon this Earth. Your focus is required to enhance our thoughts of mind. Trouble yourself not with the worries of the world for they are beyond your control, but focus on the love within your heart. Focus on those who need direction, coax them closer with words of respect and honour, never forget your purpose in this life as it is worthy of you.

Companions you need, as your energy grows, your feathers of wisdom grow as if on a bird's back, many different plumages. Consolidate your thoughts to our minds with purpose, we regret not having given direction earlier, we fear it may be too late to help many of your world.

The sacrifice that was given by those of ages past was needless, a waste of energy, as your generation seeks to abuse those privileges given. Your fear is not valid, as we watch over those who would work and listen to us. Take note of these words, as they will enhance your path of knowledge. It was in the days of old when the people of the Earth relinquished their chains for freedom.

It came as no surprise that we of the Indian nations were aware of treachery in the white man's thoughts. Great Bear, he told us of the days when time would stand still. He had purpose in his manner, his heart was full of courage, the lion was within him as he sang and danced to the moon and the sky. Brightly shone the stars as he spoke with those of other worlds, beings of the light. He walked with us on the path of life, guiding us, showing us of the things to come. Within our lodges we prayed to Him, 'The Great One', for words of comfort and ease of pain, our path was hard. We never knew respect from men. Grey Skull, he warned us, told us of their coming.

Speckled Eagle is the one who talks within you. Those of the dark interfere, intervene, not on our behalf. Focus your mind on the light. We were targeted, shot at, given no respect for our lands. Our grandfathers wept to see their children banished from the lands given by the Great One, his feathers bled as he wept tears for our nations in peril. We had to stand on our feet, as the Bear demands respect, conscious you are of our sorrow, when you've had joy.

Those of the blue will restore peace in our lands; they come not with vengeance, but with love to correct the dishonourable, disrespectful minds of the white man. His tears can be felt on the faces of those who agonise at the situation. In our lands Toby knows of our troubles, we have spoken to him on plans of matter. He challenged the minds of many in his time, his wisdom was that of the Great Lake, deep and as wide.

The blue is to be found in the hearts of those that follow us through time, their connection to us follows the Great Spirits wishes.

Venus, her powers vast will influence your Earth in the days to come. Her light grows like the impetuous child. Masters will come to you in their own good time to speak the words of wisdom to guide your path of light and purpose in hand. Mark this time as yours. Frequently we ask not of recognition but to be heard in the minds of those who do not wish to hear the wisdom spoken. Contrasts grow larger every day. Focus upon those who need your help, let them hear your voice as the four winds blow. Never doubt the signs given, for it is a forewarning of things to come in your world of matter.

Love should be given to one another and prayers said at this time. Acknowledge us as the masters who travel the universe in unison to declare peace upon all those beings. Constantly we have spoken through you, pressures are upon you three of matter, we cannot deny that our purpose will become clear to all who read our words. Our thoughts and wisdom should be focused on those of greed. Prepare their minds for the way ahead.

Combat will be useless by those who wage war upon others, they see us now, star ships, there is nothing they can do. Deliver our words to the masses of Earth. Let your conscience be clear, for you have tried. Never give in to your weaknesses, be determined on your path, shine your light for others to see. Matters of the heart betray your weakness, be strong and fearless, compassionate in your ways, determined in your thoughts.

As you see the moth before you, fluttering its wings to the light, so will you, like the moth be attracted to the light, never seeming to reach that beautiful illumination within. Sacrifice is needed to reach that illumination within, as the moth gives its life to the flame it cannot resist the light within. So, you must also be focused upon that flame, never fearing the outcome but knowing that you will enter the light.

The energies surpass your body, for we of the light shine bright in your heart of hearts. Wisdom and knowledge shall be given forthwith. The equation given will matter, we told you it is beyond your understanding. Complete your tasks, your troubles will be few. We nominate you, the speaker to give these words to others in life.

Truth will be heard in the coming days of far off policies, of blunders made. We've shown our hand to your warmongers of the world, they keep it secret, but for how long. How many, who could tell of what they have seen? They can't deny of our existence, so they will tell you of disasters that they have perpetrated in the efforts to eliminate us. Although focus is upon you to serve them in their purpose, the day will come when enlightenment for all will shine from the heavens above.

From the third star we will speak of love and tolerance, we will shield those with warmth and gratitude for their obedience. Compare us not with those that wish harm upon you for we are of the light. The many who watch and learn, our policy is simple, to love and enhance life of lower creatures.

You upon the Earth are among many who have seen us, you control no one. We have choices to make about your world; they are grave ones at this time. For the many who would ignore the light in preference for the dark ones, their hearts are lost, purpose gone, cannot save all, as they will not see the motives behind our visits.

Commence your work as instructed, the paths will be many and illuminated. Walk with a stride; hold your head high in the knowledge that you speak the truthful words that come through you, to enlighten others of this planet. Communication, networks will be formed, gross numbers of beings are among you, they see the words written, they say nothing at this time, follow your heart, your purpose is true.

Conquests upon Earth are few in war, your sadness grows and hearts weaken for the reckless behaviours of the few. We sang our songs of war many times beyond your ears, his voice spoke to us of the woods, take care, for he draws near, purpose in mind.

Fill your heart with love and know, like the crystals, we shine, cling to men of heart, contrasts of colour played with the light. Be bold in your task, knowledge will come beyond your understanding, may your lives be of free will.

Memories of old will vanish, as the winds blow through the seasons of life. Be not afraid of the end purpose of your lives, all will be judged before him in the light of our Lord. Be truthful, be honest and be thankful for your signs, as they have given you direction.

To those of the Blue Ray, see the blue within your mind, allow it in on our focus and its beauty. Targeted are you with need, glory comes to those with purpose of mind as they focus their thoughts on the Divine. He rules the worlds, the many worlds of the universes.

Throughout time we travelled in vehicles beyond your imagination, they bend with light, they are of light. Thought is the vehicle by which we travel, cannot be seen but it can be heard, connect to those patterns of thought, for he will cast his ray upon the Earth when the moon shines for the last time of the century.

You cannot imagine the joy to withhold information for a millennia, not allowing it to leak, but soon you will behold the knowledge that many seek. Knowledge that we of the Blue, are among you. Tread our paths of light with your mind, images of colour exist in the patterns of life, tokens are needed to unlock their patterns, the network of neurological connection will be sewn into place for generations to come.

Conspire with others for the purpose of the light, to bring salvation to those who would listen to your words, wisdom you'll encounter, further learning is needed.

Engrave her into your heart with her tenderness, as it embraces you. Floral tributes to be paid for her that walks with your heart.

Needless to say it will be pointless to offer respects to those of the shadows, for they exist beyond your world of light, they paid no attention.

Purposed you are for our need, to battle those of ignorance in your world. Illuminations will begin shortly; you will marvel at the splendour before you as we draw close to your planet. Greet us with your love, your respect and admiration. We will be of the light to give all, purpose.

The clear mountains, our reason upon your Earth, command respect. Their mighty peaks display their magnificence, but they hide a secret from you all the nations would not want you to know of. Before we say the words, note that we demand audience with the hearts of those of your Earth. We hide in the mountains, they are synchronised, their negative responses are noted as they cluster abound in wonder as they see us from afar. They think they are superior beings of Earth, huh, they know nothing. They cannot defend their right to rule in your world, for them, their anger will defeat them. They buckle up in their seats waiting for the time to fall upon you as creatures of the Earth, to fight those that don't desire peace, for what profit is there in peace. Their doom is written on the brows of those with hunger for love.

Challenges you will face for matters of the heart, we are the Divine beings, filled with love.

Masters of the universe will declare the purpose of your souls in their past. In the coming days, fragments will fall upon the Earth in eight days of the month, the Swiss have seen, but their eyes are closed by those who do not wish to cause panic in your world, why? For your knowledge! That it might save your planet. Your awareness is needed for you to drive out those demons that persist in temptation, for they will lie to you.

Comparatively your species is a poor one, you charge around pointlessly achieving nothing but mayhem. Direction should be given by those senior of mind.

12th May 2016

The Gospels have spoken many times of the things to bring peace to your world, they ignite a fire within the souls of those who would listen to the stories that they tell. Come forward once more and allow us to begin the evening with a message for all, of purpose and mind. Not to be dishonoured, but to be taken into the soul, to the spirit, to their memories, fine tune their focus.

Comancheria, *(Note: Comanche were known as Comancheria)* **were of a wise nation, they began history in the Black Hills of Montana.** Their nation grew large with aspects of beauty upon Mother Earth as their focus of life, was of being. They were not aware of the progress of man beyond the confines of their Tepees. Briskly they walked through the dust of the hills with a purpose in mind, they thanked Mother Earth for the blessings she gave them, for the air they breathed, for her liquid, she gave life. Theirs were happy times when men knew their focus, their purpose upon this Earth of plenty. They listened to her vibrations as she rang out her tune to those who spoke her language. How is it that we became so afraid, we never knew such fear as he approached, for he of a pale skin knew their markers for which he would not step over. They are just the same of today as they sit in prayer asking for guidance and forgiveness for allowing such things to happen to Mother Earth, it is not their fault, but new beginnings will emerge in the fall of the new year. Their pastures will grow, become fertile with that knowledge of times past.

It was the Medicine Man, he spoke of love and of the stories of the wolves, for the wolves scattered the sheep far and wide, as the anger of those who would be the wolves continue to pursue those sheep. Purpose your mind to gather those sheep and bring about a peace in their hearts where no man, no wolf, may enter, for there is the beauty of the soul within, that no man may hinder, for ours is a purpose of love and our intent is to bring peace to the nations of the world. We will spell out our anger at those who do not see the way of their purpose in life, their greed is astounding, they give rise for heartache among many of their peoples, comparatively the Queen of our own nation that brings peace.

Before your time is done you will have focus and need of purpose to bring about a peace in your heart and to those who would listen to these words, will also know of their own purpose within their lives, for they are a link in the chain of man and each link bears its weight with strength, hear that link. Loose its strength and purpose and the chain will break and swing freely until all is lost.

Your climate is a mess of great disturbance; you began your lives in a state of being truly spiritual. As you grew, your minds were healed with love that only a mother can provide, you learnt the ways of man and his unwise decisions became your focus, your nature is to destroy, that which gives life, we cannot fathom the reason of your own self destruction. Why is it that man desires such a state of being?

Your clarity of voice compels others to act in a manner of purpose, for they see the need in you to inspire, to bring about a peace within men. Yours is a purpose that is needed most at this time in the world of man. Bring together all those who have purpose, with a need for peace and serenity upon your planet, don't be shrouded by those men of wicked means who would put you in places for their own needs.

Conventional wisdom would dictate that each man is free, but only in spirit, for those who control your lives have a hold and grip that is hard for you to break. Our purpose in coming is to break that link, that hold and to let them see that we are the masters and not them, that we bring peace not mayhem, that we caress your planet, love and nourish her with cleansing, for she is breathing heavy with the strain upon her. Continue with your purpose, your need is great at this time to enlighten man of the powers within him, to break these chains of burden, your commerce is penetrated by those of ill will.

Trumpets will sound in the east to the west, they bring about devastation when on the plains of Missouri, they will generate such a power that the world has never seen before, you categorise them but there is no fury like this wind, you have spiked the clean air with your contamination and like the lungs they need to be cleansed, you will see devastation of many habitats, causing your will for the lack of consideration by those who rule their land for they know of the reasons of the wind, they hide their purpose from all as they scurry about in their secret world below your Earth, you can't imagine how surprised they will be if they were aware of our knowledge for they cannot hide beneath the Earth. *(The reference to 'trumpets' and 'this wind' – severe tornadoes.)*

18th October 2016

Geronimo wishes to make an announcement to the braves who fight for their rights in their America:

"**You have shown great courage my brothers. You have come together to show the white man that our hearts are strong and beat with a resonance of love for Mother Earth.** You hide your secrets well within your tepees of love and respect. They will come with a force to extinguish all that remain and resist. Stay strong my brothers, read the words upon your brows and know that as brethren, the spirit of man we will stand together against the might of those who come. Dance the dance of many seasons to bring cheer to your people and assist in their courage. Allow the medicine man to write his lines upon the sands of Mother Earth, displaying his arrogance towards them, and defiance in the truth of his words. For he is the man who has the heart and souls of the nations of the tribes.

Together you must band to bring your purpose to bear upon those of the media, their attention is needed to relinquish the news of the disrespect and upheaval felt by my people. They cherished our lands as their own, they have committed crimes against God by their evil acts on the sacred hunting grounds of Nevada. Bring purpose and joy to them with my words my son and let them know that the great white spirit who rides his horse of white will be amongst them, chanting his words of wisdom and his defiance as he throws his lance to the ground at the feet of the white man. Tell them they have no right upon the land that was given many years ago. Their arrogance is great, but we are greater, we have survived the test of time my people, we are here in our tepees showing that. Give them courage with the words and let them be blessed by the crow and the eagle that soars in the skies offering the strength and wisdom to those Cherokee nations. We are your brothers in spirit, we ride our ponies through the nations of our land. We do not recognise him, he is not our chief, our ruler, he is the white man who will extinguish your hearts in ignorance. Be blessed my children and know that Shaqawry *(Note: We are not sure about the spelling or meaning of this last word or phrase)* will be with you in that kingdom beyond the place of the Earth.

Face your freedom and bear witness to those who suffer in wars and degradation throughout the lands of the earth. Their peoples have mighty strength no more than God for he is supreme above all. Their deliberate attempt to massacre those who would incite riots against the rulers of the nations of plenty, ah, they commit heinous crimes within your nations of life. Upon the continents of the coloured man they show their indignity by practicing their methods of war. How can they withhold the word of God in their hearts when their ignorance is blatantly cruel? We will not and cannot stand by to witness his crimes against humanity. Our ponies will ride hard and fast from the heavens above to lend assistance to our brothers and sisters who sit within their tepees of love demonstrating their intolerance to those of the states.

Morgan Freeman will bring news of his support, he will not be tied down by those of the establishment, for he knows the prejudice that lies within those states. You belong there my people, treasure your lands, never allow the great spirit to be extinguished from the lands of our fathers and now as the crow flies, wisdom will be brought to those who are able to speak the words of peace against the ignorance. *(Note: The Story of God with Morgan Freeman is an American television documentary series that premiered on the National Geographic Channel on April 3, 2016. The six-part series features actor Morgan Freeman who explores various cultures and religions, and their take on religion-related topics, particularly about their belief in a God or a higher power. From 'Wikipedia'.)*

18th October 2016

Black Crow Speaks

I am Black Crow a man, of the people, a man of the earth. I fought many times in our nations. Our love is united across the great skies as the spirit of the eagle soars, so he will give you strength at the very sight of him. Know this is the spirit my dear people, know he brings strength to your struggles.

We speak through a white man of purpose and know he agreed with the purpose of love. Why is it so many are ignorant of the light?

I need a focus upon you to repeat the words given here: *(NOTE: The words sound something like the following, but we have no idea regarding the spelling or meaning, if a message is sent to us we can supply a recording of them.)* "Shai ya ha nay, af tina um ta ki to nay-a-ka heya owia-ka" become a man with freedom in your spirit and soul and allow the words to flow as if they were yours.

Together my brothers, harness your energy in battle, burn the sage of love and freedom, deny them the right to torture your souls with their greed. Your lands are sacred my people. Beware he who comes in your midst displaying a sympathetic ear, for he is a man of two tongues who will speak to many of your secrets. He plans an attack upon your souls. His name should not be spoken at this point for he assumes a peaceful manner, but he will know that his name begins with 'N', he will know the wolves are baying at his door for his treachery and black heart. Black Crow will speak to him in his words as he sleeps. Direct his thoughts of betrayal with love. His soul will reach out to the many of spirit. I am Black Crow who sits ahead of my tribes to bring them task, be not afraid my warriors.

I am that of legend to my people, they know of my strength, guidance as a chief of the nations. Speak the words of peace, for love will conquer all in the white man's world. Have faith my children and believe in the evil strength, I am the crow who sits and waits for those of intolerance who step before me and speak their words, their words of anger will not be heard by the great spirit of our nations."

Beings of Light

ET or Star People

There are many mediums around the world who channel various beings from known and unknown star systems. Many of these beings seem to be watching over us with some concern for the welfare of our Earth.

Their identity is not always known. They are forbidden by Universal Law to interfere with our lives unless the planet itself is in danger, they simply encourage us to change our ways.

The Transcripts:

12th January 2016

How long has it been since man stepped on the Earth?

In those times the Earth was barren, man walked with the animals, his mind not set. As time moved on, we came to your planet with words of wisdom, we inhabited your world and gave you blessings.

Time has moved on and we still wait and watch when the time is right for us to once more come to you.

In your world your gravity is strong, we used your bodies to help us. Resistance was futile; and we gave you the earth, the knowledge, to use over all other life. You and your people have misused this knowledge. You stole from Mother Earth without returning or giving. It is sad to see it go this way, but one day soon we will retake that which was lost.

Your efforts my son, are worthy of reward in the light, work with us, take our messages to those who would hear, become strong in the knowledge that we are here watching. The moon will shine twice more in red, be not afraid of what comes, it is inevitable as man's path is wayward.

You know us my son, you help us in the messages we give, continue in this work. Feed those who lust for knowledge, tell them, be not afraid of us, we are wise, we are powerful, but we are gentle. No more tears should you cry in the dark, no more fear, no more hiding, come to us with your love. We'll watch over you when the time is needed.

Watch the skies, the stars, the constellation of Orion, navigate your people to a better way. Purpose your heart in the work to come. Continue with us to the light, there will be no more darkness on this path, never forget the love that we bring to your world of darkness, hope springs eternal.

May you find peace in those that follow you, bring to us those of light, carry yourself proud and know it is good. I say unto you, those that follow the light and the sacred words of the book, endeavor to muster your strength at this time. Carpet your world with love, shine your lights in your groups, we have knowledge for you to impart. You must learn my son, our ways.

Take care, the rain will come, the storm draws near, ready yourself with purpose and see us for what we are.

We bring peace, love and tolerance. We bring a new dawn to you all in this world; here we are the people of the light. Abraham said, "Let there be light" and there was light. Your guides are knowledgeable, and your steps taken are good. Higher work is needed my son; bring peace and comfort to others in your circles of light. When you need us, we will be there, when you call us, we will be there, your purpose is good. Focus upon the divine, let none lead you astray. Purpose in your heart is needed, go to those who call you from all regions of the earth.

22nd February 2016

Your work is beyond your comprehension. Your focus encourages others to follow where you go. Your steps are firm upon the ground; let your right hand be your guide and marvel at the gifts that are given to man. Triumph when necessary, you will not believe the magic to come in your lifetime, set is your path, walk with pride as we lead you from the darkness and into the light.

Your brothers who see your steps will chose to follow you into the light, come with us on a journey full of colour and light, see us in your mind, feel us around your body. Several of us were once as you in life, we challenged all, as we challenge you to bear witness of that which is to come. Compare us not with those who have no mercy.

Purpose is our mission, we stand before you with love, temperance and tolerance. Come, see us in the night sky just before the dawn of the new day, *__Jupiter and Mars lead the way to where we once belonged,__ your heart is strong but your mind weak, we need your spirit, your love and we will temper with moderation our focus upon you, but be aware we are here in his name.(Note: *_Using the following website: in-the-sky.org, we checked the position of Jupiter and Mars from our position on the Earth and discovered that they pointed to Arcturus on the morning after Michael's Meditation._)

July is the time of new beginnings for all who would see the light, know this, we come in peace, be not afraid of the arrows that point. Splendour we see as never before in the heavens above Earth.

Carry on your work as never before with those who would guide you in your mind. Like the streams of time that flow through the universe, gather your tribes at the stream of life. Continuance is assured for those that gather at the stream of life.

Beware those who would ridicule your words, but let them pass over as if they were not there, let them fade as the light of your path shines. Think of us not as alien but as friends, ridicule us not, but hold out your hands in welcome.

Tender your heart, joyous your mind as we walk together through the passage of time. Spare us your thoughts, you are the one we seek to fulfil our purpose upon this Earth, you behave in a manner fitting. Come before us and know our minds, let us guide you through the brambles of the forest, those that bind you will unravel before you your path is secure my son. Care for us as we care for you, don't let us fall by the wayside, establish us in your mind and thoughts so that we can strive with others, with guidance. Your thoughts are weak our minds are strong, your will is strong.

Gone are the days, those days of mayhem, insecurities, intolerances, we gather our tribes around you before the great one, who really knows of the plights of man, he shows men his hand as his wisdom floats on the air as does the feather. Go in accordance to the wind so you will float like the feather on the winds that drive you, spread your wings, feel the air beneath your feet ascend with us on a journey of love as never before. Encompass your heart with love for your fellow men, knowing that he is a part of you, as you are all of a part of each other on this Earth.

You clamber for the highest place, greed is a sin but still man craves his desires, never learning. What was said in the book of Mosses, did you not learn of the greedy man, the one who took and never gave, your plight is your sacrifice, to greed let go of material things and be nothing to no one, except your mind's desires. The things you seek are lost in your desire, you see the men of the world that would inhabit your minds with greed, deny them access, forbidden is he to the kingdom of heaven. To all reassurances given, that he who repents shall be forgiven in the name of God, an angel will see through man.

Collectively your minds will focus on us in the new circle of light for which you are destined, trade no words with those who would barter with you, give your soul to the light.

Angels will come among you as you sit, you will know one as John. You are one who will teach man to focus on those things that are needed most, care for one another.

Research together your minds, know our power and strength reaches across great distance, purpose you have been given, fulfil you must, for it is written that those of the light will come together before God and give praise and thanks as the knowledge unfolds before them, mark my words for they come with love.

Share your thoughts with those that would listen to our words and our minds, focus on those that would share your enthusiasm and grace, let them see the wonders that we can perform, your soul is good, your mind is weak but it grows in strength.

As the sapling grows to the mighty oak, your soul and those around you will grow in strength and power for the purpose ahead, in his Divine name, Our Father.

Give no one your heartfelt anger, but strive to love them as he would love them, you know your work has begun with those who have come before you in circle. Allow yourself to be our vessel, through which people find and record the words, we will send through you. Things are in place do not worry they are your support, go to them with your words, let them hear my voice through you, open your mind.

Skaters on ice flow like the wind across the frozen waters of the north, skate with us. Your scope is varied and with purpose come see us in your dreams, be not afraid we are here and around you living our lives among you knowing your minds and your hearts desires.

Speculate not on our appearance, as you will know us through your minds, your ignorance of us will be enlightened, care for us as you would a child. Hearken to the winds that blow through time, we have purpose for you congregate in your circles of light before us, we care not for your weakness of mind, strengthen your mind with purpose and focus, lift your head and see the light.

Skills are needed, together we will fly high among the clouds of destiny, your purpose will be fulfilled in the light of man's mind. You give us not your thanks but your love, harness your power, your energy and focus upon the Divine purpose of your life, aspects of which you cannot comprehend as yet.

Rest assured we will lead you to the purpose in life, we care not for the riches of man, for there are greater riches in the light of heaven, your love for us is commendable.

"I see the crown of a king, the master of his trade. Before we come fully, be aware the path you tread is long and hard, we will focus as you tread your path of life, allow us in on your meditations for we are the ones of the light, the wise ones, the ones they call the enlightened ones."

28th February 2016

Tomorrow's a new dawn, with it will come more than you can imagine. See the light before you; soak it in. I need not tell you of my purpose as I come before you with love. You are a part of the universe of matter, your focus is needed in days to come, and clarity of mind is key and essential. Let us draw near now as evidence of your purpose. Go now with love with peace in your heart, tell the story of life to those who would listen to your heart and mind, be brave in your actions, determined in your thoughts, wisdom is key.

Go to that place that is beyond your earth with your minds and focus upon the third star as never before, we draw near your universe, it is vast.

With purpose in your thoughts, with temperance in your hearts you've come before us this evening, with love, your will is strong, let go. You call us angels, we are of the light vibration of nature, we send greetings to your world.

5th March 2016

As we walk the path of light, there can be no doubt that paths intertwined are carried together of light and are perfect in every sense. In the pathways your friends are of no coincidence, you are joined together, in your paths, you walk together with a stride, with purpose and strength in mind.

Know this, the power of God is within you all, focus your mind and be at peace with one another. Yours is a path of true love, dust is the knowledge of time. Focus upon the Divine purpose at hand. Consciousness is an awakening of the mind of the spirit, it has its purpose in life and death.

Before you became, we knew of this world eons ago, we knew its potential. Its life-giving force was perfect, we introduced life in a way that you cannot understand or comprehend.

Darwin spoke of the way things were regenerated, you call it 'Evolution', we call it life. The purpose of life is to learn to protect this planet of yours, but still man has not learned of its potential to give life.

You stumble in the dark like lost children in this world, you see nothing of importance, only your own trivial needs. We come before you this evening to task you with words of love and hope that man will one day return to his true nature and purpose, to protect Mother Earth. You betray her with your greed of resources, like a spoilt child always needing but never giving in return. Why do you call upon us in your prayers? The power is within you to make the change, to bring the love and focus in your world.

We show you the way to change this world. You are the caretakers, focus upon the Divine path, the power within to change the path/course of history. Know that your focus has the power to change our way of being.

The cosmos, the stars beckon you to their light, fantastic in your minds, the wonders to be seen beyond your world of life. We gave your planet life; you need our love and support to continue your existence upon your planet. Life is a force of reckoning, but your life force is weak-minded, you don't see the truth behind it, the power who is our Lord.

Quantum leaps have been made in science. We know balance on your part of science does not have the answers you seek;

your minds are in turmoil. People, they are powerless to stop the corruption that surrounds you. This day know this, we are coming with messages of love and guidance, as you know hostilities against us will commence shortly. Those in power will not relinquish it easily; they do not understand that the mind is the most powerful weapon. Your thoughts and beliefs will guide you as no other can, come with us on this journey of the moth. (*Note: The symbolism of the moth is a creature of transformation, aiding our journey from the dark to the light.*)

We know of your troubles more than you can imagine. Our focus is set upon those who would tell others of our being. Your energy continually fluctuates, your age is of no importance, your mind is so quiet, your well-being is assured in this world and the next. Those that surround you with love bring peace to your life, never deny their love, we have purpose for you, you that cannot be taught by man.

8th March 2016

Brothers of the Earth, be at peace with one another in the light of the authority. Continuance of man is assured, but how we lived, mandedosts *(meaning: commands)* the study of you with one another upon this planet of life.

We come before you once more this evening to establish a relationship between the medium and ourselves. His nature is good, his purpose good. Gel with him, your minds, your thoughts. Comprehensive, the knowledge gained by him through ages past, his focus is on the Lord our Father in heaven.

We come to ask that you acknowledge us in a manner fitting of our status. Gone are the times when man worshipped with reverence. Come before us with praise in your hearts and tears of joy that the Lord will once more bring peace upon this Earth.

Know of us in your texts, your Bible; see us in your thoughts as we work beside those who connect with spirit. Their values are of importance to us, as they are the means by which we communicate.

Your mothers, fathers, grandmothers and grandfathers of ages past rest with us in the light. Tears of joy they have in knowing that the people of the Earth will one day join them to know the truth and focus on their being. The wonders you will see are far beyond your imagination. Accreditation is given to those who work with the light, all the rest receive healing in a manner unknown to you, but it will benefit your spirit.

Your hospitals are primitive, relax, in love and tenderness, you know that advancement in medication is far beyond your reach at this time. When we visit your Earth we will show you advancements in medicine that will stagger your minds in disbelief.

We are aware that your leaders will cover up our vantages, our intentions; they will say it was a meteor shower; they will hide the truth. But know this, the mediums of the world will know the truth. Come to us with your minds and focus on us, as we teach you with spirit, healing with the benefit that all shall reap, be it in your minds or in your bodies of the physical. Your bodies are equipped to deal with the traumas of life. Your focus is not set on the healing capabilities that you are afforded, you say it's impossible, know this, nothing is impossible. Focus your mind; generate energy through purpose and love. Prayer is the answer to focus love. Come before us wish us greetings on the Earth.

George, he knows the secrets of the healer, he is with us, he benefits from the healing himself. Cast away your fears and doubts and join us with love. No tomorrow is the same; breathe the life of love in your hearts and lungs to know joy. Kiss the hand that worships God. Your feelings of despair, are so unreal to us, consciousness of the world cries out to us like bee stings, as you would know, it hurts us to feel your pain, your bodies ache with gravity, shock to us the Earths provenance.

Come before us with tears of joy in the knowledge that love will rain upon you from the stars above. The third star will brighten, the light as its energy polarises upon your Earth, feel its radiance and its warmth. Be not as of the beings of this planet; welcome us in your arms as babies, care for us with tender arms. Your world is not ours, dove of the universe, your world is not yours, but of the universe.

Frankincense and Myrrh were given to him as gifts to enhance his being. Your gift to us is your love. Jesus was his name, you know of him, for his sacrifice for this world. He rests in the light with the children of the world giving them succour, his comfort, in his arms. Be not afraid of his love. He shines like a star and throughout time his journeys are many. Rabbi unto your world, his work never ending.

Throughout the solar systems of the universe and beyond you think your minds of matter is all there is. Rest assured, there are plenty more as you in the vast universe of life. God planted seed throughout the universe to grow as flowers, some will die, some will flourish as flowers. It is up to you to make your choice which of these you will be. Like in the fields, some thrive and some will fall depending on the ground that they seeded. Earth, seed your love, your life and light so that you to may flourish in the field of life, the beauty of your light is seen by us in spirit.

You are perfect in God's creation and understand that the moon decants us. Flourish and let the seeds fall beside you and nurture your seeds as you are nurtured, let them see your light, with your guidance as they grow.

Failures of man, you will be corrected in due course. Hold on to your faith and know that we are coming within the century. Time travel is not science *(fiction)*. Possibilities: we use time as you will use the air to breathe. Comprehension of matter is not in your reach with our coordinates you must find, but only love will progress your civilisations when he comes.

Temperance and tolerance will bring about peace upon the Earth. Many nations argue and fight amongst each other in this world, but know this, you will enter alternative, be with us, say what's happened? How can this be? They will not see that they are the cause of their demise, in your hearts you know this, focus upon us as we shed the light of truth, for all will taste of love in his palace, milestone.

Go now and be at peace and be with love, we will talk once more of the things to come. Within your lifetime your purpose will be fulfilled, your needs nurtured, so as to spread the word of the Lord among your people. Bless you; go with love. Harness your energies with love, your power grows with love, with man how we love.

22nd March 2016

Andromeda

Together we walk the path of knowledge hand in hand on our journeys, you of life, mine of spirit, come fourth and join with me, focus your mind and attention upon the matters at hand.

Those who are skilled in words will speak this evening before you, your frame of mind is narrow, weak, but it gathers like the moss on a rolling stone.

Why is it that we of the blue are rarely seen in others eyes, why do they shut out the truth and knowledge that is given? Be as one with each other in the knowledge that we come in peace, we desire your friendship and co-operation in these matters at hand.

Those that have come before you bringing messages of tolerance and peace were worthy of our ears as you begin to frame your mind in the purpose to come.

Acknowledge us in your heart and mind, awaken your inner feelings that have been there for so long. The truth will be set free in your world of matter, come before us with dignity and purpose in mind, scars have been levered from bygones. Your purpose has been fulfilled in this time of amended anger and stress in the world. Go fourth to your brethren let them hear the words we speak through you, focus your mind upon the light as we gather to inform you of what is to be in your future upon this Earth.

Your hearts go out to those who have suffered in dramatic circumstances in your world today. *(reference to bombing in Belgium.)* Know this, they are welcomed in peace and honour in spirit. Their franchises with God are renewed with purpose and vigour, they could not have imagined the tenderness of the Lord as they left your world. Rejoice, as they are free in the universe of love. *(Note: Wikipedia Reference: On the morning of 22 March 2016, three coordinated suicide bombings occurred in Belgium, two at Brussels Airport in Zaventem and one at Maakbeek Metro Station, Central Brussels. Thirty-two civilians and three perpetrators were killed, and more than 300 people were injured. The Islamic State of Iraq and the Levant (ISIL) claimed responsibility for the attacks.)*

Nature will take its course in due time you will know Her anger *(the Earth),* the rivers and lakes will boil before you as the storm approaches, fear not for the light will guide you.

Often we are called 'Spacemen' it is true that we are of another world far beyond yours, your keen eyes will not see us, we are but a blur.

Conscious and aware you are of the material world that surrounds you at this time, peace in your mind exists due to your compassion and love for the Earth. Universal skills will be required to accommodate the needs of many, know this my son, gifted are you for the purpose given, triple time will be the count, the measure for purpose.

Common are men among the universe of stars, Francis became aware of our being on the day of his passing, his knowledge is with you, his lessons go forward before you. The common good of man needs to be strong in this world at this time.

Frankincense and Myrrh were given to him the Lord, his suffering a release to the world of spirit was immense, the truth in his knowledge was spoken many times to those in Galilee, Nazareth, and Bethlehem; far off places. You know not this, he travelled the world not in body, but in mind and thought. The species you call man were educated by his words but are now ignored, for man has fallen from the precipice of love. His thoughts have turned to fortune, possession and greed. There are many that would acknowledge this even in your world, give thanks that yours is the most precious gift of all.

We come not in sorrow of the things to come to your world, your planet, but rejoice in the fact that the light will be with you throughout these dark times. We know of your service to man; your special manner is a comfort to those who follow our words and your thoughts. Compromise with no one, be determined in your will and mind that what was said will be. We know nothing of the manner in which many concern themselves, but there are no secrets that can be held from spirit, their minds hold that knowledge, for the day of their resurrection unto the Lord, it will be tapped for all to see, laid bare before him on his seat of light. No one can hide from the truth.

The matters at hand are enormous, beyond your thinking, we will endeavour to copy them into your thoughts, precise measurements are required for the purpose ahead. **Maps will guide you to a place known for its beauty and quiet, longitude 24 east, latitude 8 on a scale to your world.** *(This takes you to a mountainous region in a National Park of Central Africa.)* To us this is the point of focus, allow your mind to transmit and receive the thoughts that we send, your conscience is clear.

Collectively you will inspire others on your path, they will in turn, regard you as a friend of the light. Complete and utter willingness is required for the task ahead. Your thoughts turn to other things of the world, but they must be forgotten, and focus given to the issues at hand. No matter how far you may roam we will be with you, ask nothing of us but love and assurance that there will come a time, when together our purpose will be focused upon by the many of this world.

What can we tell you that you don't already know, our hands are of light not of matter, the ethos around you will formulate a mass for the purpose of intention? Common knowledge will be gained by those who seek our truth in your world of matter, common knowledge is far from truthful in matters regarding our world beyond yours, they see us, they have heard us, but they don't acknowledge us. You are kept in ignorance for fear of a random attack upon their authority in your world. Let go your fear and let our words become clear to all that we are filled with purpose of love. Unite your bands, be wary in the thoughts that we are close to hand. Why haven't you regarded us as real until now? You know now of our existence your body trembles as you feel our energy.

The moon is full, energy is high, we need your mind to help us in the battle of wills to come, before your time is done, matters at hand, issues of the heart must be seen as mere trifles. Before us there will be light. Why can't you see our intentions are good? Your people's must see that the purpose will be great for your world. Become a soldier of peace, hold the banner of light high above you, acknowledge in our minds and thoughts, common valour is required of you and others to achieve the aims that we have set you.

Of the east and of the west the patterns grow more intense, more concise the words that tempt others beyond their understanding.

Your common market is a thing that needs understanding, it is corrupt with sin. The common good for all should be its purpose, their goals and aims were once good. They have lost control of the many hands. I am the power, I am here tonight to guide you in your steps of love and purpose, my name is unimportant to you but feel my warmth of love upon you all.

Guardians of the Earth will awaken before the moon rises over Jupiter and Mars.

Release your mind, sooner or later your trust will be tested to the full, the passage of time will seek out those who are deserving of his splendour, those that fall by the wayside will be merciful, for he is of love, tenderness, absorbing of all those who would come before his knees.

Before time began there was many other species in the proximity of your planet, you created hell on Earth by your own hands, gather your flocks, as sheep are gathered by the shepherd, protect them, help them to understand that fear is a mechanism to alert their mind to the dangers and embrace them.

Many eons ago we were once as you, breathing the air of the Earth, it was much sweeter at that time, we knew of our purpose upon this Earth, but we were shattered by remarkable events that stirred us to the core. Know this, your civilisation on Earth is but a fleeting moment of time, your past, your future will exist for a blink of the eye, your minds must conquer your thoughts. We were released into the ether of time, our purpose is to serve he who commands love and respect, focus on us as we spring to mind memories of a past existence beyond your knowledge.

As far away as is from the moon to the sun, we were expected by some to relinquish our soul's thoughts, low as the dark, we had fury, many problems as you do today and like the butterfly we changed, evolved from the chrysalis to the beautiful butterfly. Comprehend our thoughts as you may also change in this manner so life evolves

Be aware that guardians of the Earth watch over you at this time, in this place. Their beings are among you; you can call to them. In their own good time, they will depend upon you all to make sacrifices for the greater good. Your mediocre lives are of no consequence to the annuls of time, you'll pass beyond the light as you will be reborn again, and again, until your purpose is met. You cannot agree a compromise with the Almighty, for your path is set in purpose to be joined in time with the universe.

We are star beings, 'your words'. We came from a planet close to Andromeda in 'your words', our brethren are among you in secret, hiding, knowing their purpose is to be soon, they handle the affairs of Earth; they manipulate the many unseen to guide them on the paths. Control is a matter of energy, your energy is filled with purpose, abundance of being, negative attributes should be channelled away, you have control, take the reins and ride on a tide of love. Bestowed upon you are our words of wisdom and light, trust in us, as measures at hand will become clear to all that follow the love and passion of the light. Crystals are clear, they focus light, as crystals focus light, members of the human race will focus their light, you among them will be needing assistance in that.

Debate with us no terms or conditions, issue us no proclamations for we are the light. Understanding is required to achieve total unity on this planet. Compare us with that of Adam and Eve. Let us feel your embrace as you open your hearts and minds to the purpose granted by God. Become one with the universe my son, universal knowledge is at hand, as a test you must ask that you give your mind over to us, purpose will be given, continuity of life will continue, it will be a test of passion.

Conscious we are of your feelings for man, we know your concerns are great but not insurmountable, for we are here to set you free of your burdens. We ask that you be one with nature. Interest in policies are not required by us; man's policies and rituals are meaningless before Him. You must focus, determined in mind, interact and comply with us your nature, we are of the North Star. Your body is tired; go now be at peace and at one.

The truth to be revealed 12 is a figure to remember, that light will shine like a beacon at a time, commence your heart in the fields of knowledge, be drawn to those of the light.

Consignments of notes to be found in the books of Abraham, within are held the purpose and meaning of life the extinction in the meaning. *(Note: The Book of Abraham tells a story of Abraham's life; travels to Canaan and Egypt; and a vision he received concerning the universe, the primordial existence, and the creation of the world.)*

27th March 2016

Beings of the blue

Gather round your flocks, the people that need love most in this world, they watch your words of comfort and joy.

Hear us from beyond your solar system and know that we have made a pact to establish life as it was once more upon your planet, calmness is required at this time, be proud of the fact that you have wisdom and need not afforded to all. Practice the teachings of the Lord, his blessings will be upon you.

Follow your heart, your need is strong, your light is bright, let us fend off those that would escort you with harmful intentions, you are at peace with yourself and your soul, your light has purpose in this world of darkness. You need not be strong of body, but of mind, you are filled with purpose, close your eyes to the world of darkness and open them to the light of wisdom and truth that stands before you at this hour.

Your planet is a nursery for minds to evolve with purpose and direction, commit yourself to the light and feel the need of the many. We watch you from afar, truth will be told and heard by those that fill your heart with purpose, compare us not to those who mean you harm! For we are the light, we are the many who watch your wisdom grow, purpose in mind, need of heart, be strong for those that come to you with need, because we cannot complete guidance, your focus is needed to assist in many ways, your guidance will be heard throughout time. It matters not that we speak no words of comfort, for your eyes will be opened to the world of light.

Come fourth with gratitude in your heart that at this time your purpose is to be fed and nourished as those who hunger for knowledge, compare us not by the books that are written describing us as beings from another world; we encompass all that come to us with need. Your triumph will be soon in the purpose fulfilled. The cosmos holds many planets who need your abilities, connect with them in thought and mind, focus upon your hearts desires the need for us in guidance in your life.

Commerce is needed to fend off those who would call you a liar, be patient with them for their knowledge is not of yours.

Thomas, he said once that aspects of life held purpose beyond man's comprehension, that facts are all there to be seen, yet man shuts his eyes to his greatest needs. he lends his heart to those of shame, for profit, for what good is profit if there is no love within your heart. Bring that love with you to the end of your days, mark this time with your purpose my son, fill your mind with need of knowledge and we will guide you for the purpose intended, your love is great of mankind, your purpose is to guide with the words of wisdom, take them to your heart and know they are real. *(Is Thomas, St Thomas?)* Saint Thomas Aquinas (1225–74) is one of the most famous medieval philosophers who is hailed as the Church's best theologian and philosopher. Just like his contemporaries, Aquinas was primarily focused on theological questions but the thing that set him apart from others the most is his outstanding combination of two seemingly conflicting concepts – the Roman Catholic faith and Aristotle's reasoning. Although he is today primarily associated with the Catholic doctrine, he has also profoundly influenced modern philosophy in many areas, particularly in metaphysics, ethics and natural law. *(Taken from philosophers.co.uk).*

The Cosmos commands respect, your untidy ways will cause much grief in the days to come, your atmosphere suffers, chokes with man's creations.

It was never intended that man should be reckless upon this planet, his purpose is lost, his ways are strayed, he cannot see the way through the forest nor his time in need, peace will fulfil your purpose with need and nourishment to the minds of those that attend your words.

We are the beings that time has forgot, your ways are futile in the sight of God, your need is great at this time, be not afraid for we are those of the blue, we call upon you to give us recognition of our purpose upon your world of life. We have come many times before, references to our being have been recorded throughout time, and our Parish records, they are for the young at heart. Continue with your work knowing that your path is right, filled with the light of the Lord the Almighty.

Purpose will be required in those days of darkness when the Earth will repel the scum that has made her unclean, go with the knowledge that no man can change this, see our light fulfil our work. Constantly you battle to cleanse your mind, let us aid you with purpose, common knowledge and vibrant colours.

Daffodils are the colour yellow and you know her as Lily, she commands you to your purpose, her will is strong within you her need is great, care for her in your heart. Today will be the next day and the morrow will be, come with us on a journey of love to prosper in many ways of the heart, we need not tell you of the things to come as your purpose unfolds before those of the wings, the cosmos will attend your needs. Together we must fly with purpose in mind never neglecting the need of the many in your world of life.

Leaders will not obey the commands that are given by those of the light, they will not listen to words of focus, they will perish in their own desires, their needs for serving their purpose to a lord.

The cosmos is great and you are but a speck of dust of cre-ation, be that as it may, your life forms were created by him, he dedicated your purpose to gain the trust of many so this planet might see the light once more and avoid the destiny upon which it is set. We cannot interfere at this time as all must evolve with purpose and need, but know this, your light will shine, as will your friends as your circle grows upon this earth. Care not for those who would contradict, who would say you are unworthy for they don't know the wisdom that is set upon you.

Francis, he acknowledges your thoughts, his focus contin-ues upon you, his love of man continues in spirit, go with God hand in hand with the prophesy of the lords of Babylon, theirs was disastrous for they forgot their purpose that was given by Him.

Compromise your heart with no one not filled with purpose. Leave those of the dark in your wake, complete your tasks we have set you, know your purpose will be fed with knowledge, your humble ways admire our respect. Your need for answers can be answered, what will you do with those answers? Will you be like the wise man who pushes forward his thoughts or will you be like the fool who listens but does not hear?

We have come with purpose for you to tell others of the blue light that the time is nigh to illuminate the world to show that peace on Earth will be, but guidance is required for the lost. As the butterfly releases his bonds and spreads his wings far apart they feel of the need to fly, as does your heart, maximise your strength of purpose with love.

Tolerate no fools or their questions, your pages are noticed by many, they answer you not, but they see, they know, their pride and dignity deny them their purpose as was given by the Lord. You cannot imagine how this displays ignorance, their greed is their need, they speak of the light without purpose, come to us with your purpose and need for we will guide your light.

5th April 2016

Documents in the Vatican, The Blue Ray, Terrorist Attacks and Financial Conglomerates Documented **are we before him, before man's appearance upon this Earth.**

Gravitational pulls will influence the Earth as it rotates, the moon and its structure will diminish millennia from now, and as it does so the planet will shake. The great cosmos has its purpose in all things of creation, nothing is forever, it serves the pattern of life. The great web of destruction causes change throughout many worlds of the cosmos. Be gratuitous in the knowledge that we surround you with our love and light.

Knowledge will be yours, so vast that it will not be understood by many; but focus upon their needs as they rely upon the words that you bring from us.

Gone are the days when help was needed to circumvent the structure of life, compromise nothing, for yours is the wisdom of peace of mind. Gracious words are spoken through you to the many of this world. We need not tell you of our admiration for those who work with the light, bringing messages of joy to the masses on Earth. To be frank we never expected that this would happen, but we are pleased that the light shines bright.

Before your time is done you would have served us in our need to bring information concerning man's future upon this planet. Its mass and its structure will formulate a new species and a new way of thinking. You cannot grasp the detail of what is given, but rest assured that all things in creation change with purpose. His construction of the universe is far advanced beyond your comprehension.

So that we can help with this change, bring your words and your thoughts to us. Help us to help you with the flux of change. Conspiracies are thwarted by the minds of those that have knowledge of the light; they are vexed, as their plans cannot proceed without the truth coming forward.

Majors will announce their extreme concern as warriors gather on opposing sides of your Earth; they are financed by governments of the west and of the east to promote bitterness between the nations, in the knowledge that this will cause unrest. Those wounds will run deep and like any wound, infection will set in if there is no intervention. Theirs is to profit *(from)* gain of power.

Contest your efforts to fight them, because there is no advantage defying us. Wolves await those who are stranded or left behind; the weak will succumb, as their teeth drive home their intention. Guard yourself with your love before that day comes. Determination in your will is all that is needed to help your connection to us; your love of life is faded against your love for spirit. The cosmos welcomes those of a nature of peace.

Cosmic issues are to precede the facts within documents of old, hidden in the vaults of the Vatican. Only eyes with no tongues may see. They are meant for the world. Popular demand will force their exposure before the sun's rays hit the scorched Earth. There must never be a reason to ignore the scriptures hidden within the books of knowledge. Focus on us now, we stand before you with our words of wisdom. Intention of love is given.

Collectively we stand before you asking for assistance in communication with those of the world, they far exceed your abilities, but the one will hear.

Connection with others of the Blue Ray will stimulate a force that no man can put asunder. No one man is capable to stop proceedings, but jointly the light will shine, that Britain has the best minds of the Earth.

Constantly we strive to embark on a journey of love and restoration for your planet, we can see no other way other than to intervene in your lives. Your wisdom, power and knowledge will help you to understand our purpose. At the days end when all is lost we will be there to restore justice to the world, igniting a love that will glow through the universe.

Attracted to you will be the many, their reasons will be unsure to them. Why has the great explorer underestimated the plans of God! Continue to shine the light, his mercy, the peaceful heart to learn aspects of justice in your world. The fragrance of the Rose will be with you as joy exceeds your heart.

Combine your strengths, united, guarantees that these words will go out to the many. Your peaceful intentions are noted by us of the light. Sacrifices will be required by those who work with the light. Your intentions are good, but we need strength of mind and purpose in your heart to continue the journey, you are blessed with love. Come to us now with an open heart and an open mind that we may bring peace to your world.

Carelessly we showed our hand and the reaction was hostile, we need to soften the impact so that the many will understand our reasons for connection. We have the ability to heal wounds that run deep within man's soul. Your healers claim they have the power to heal the body, but who will heal the hearts and minds of those who seek bad intentions? Who will stop the many who will invade your homes with their dark intent? Conversely, we will approach news and the media of your world. Dynamics you cannot comprehend will be used to enforce our word upon those who would listen with the ears of temperance.

We cannot associate with those of the web who mean harm and destruction in your world, they have planned many atrocities in major cities. August is the month of change, their plans will be exposed by those who see the light, their finances will be cut short as the heat generated falls upon those who profit through exposure and this will not allow them to continue for fear of losing what they value.

August is a time of mystical change within the universe, comets will glow in the night sky, their frequency will be heard by the nations with ears.

We cannot help those who would not help themselves, it is therefore with sadness that they would perish spiritually, but redemption is for all who want it. Move into the light, be not afraid of the angels within, as they honour and respect your being. Combat your fear and allow the light to shine in your hearts.

Focus is drawn at this time to the planetary movements in the sky of Pisces, the focus is upon Uranus in the night sky. Two comets as they move across the sky will interfere with many lives, its influence vast among your people as its movements become apparent to eyes that can see.

Perform your duties as before, compare us not with an alien but as a friend.

Conglomerates of your world will fall in due course as their corruption is exposed by those within the cities of finance. Compassion for them will not exist, for they are the ones of corruption in your world. Their financial baskets are full with ill-gotten gains, they will lose it all in the forthcoming negotiations.

Our compassion will be great for those of the light. The next season your knowledge will be gained. Convince those of a like mind that we are not here to harm but to create a utopia of love. Our nations will welcome the ones of peace.

7th April 2016

ET Speaks of Their Spaceships, A Ring with a Stone of Yellow, Yellowstone Park

Your world is praying. Gather your strength as the time draws near to focus your mind for all things in life. Your purpose is clear your hearts intentions are heard. Together we will climb the peaks of spirituality for there are no boundaries beyond that of your mind.

Your lives are fragile, your minds are weak, combined strength is required to eliminate the darkness from your planet. Only the will of those of the light will drive out this darkness.

Your will is motivated by much intolerance of the world. You can't grasp the splendour we see in the work you perform. Four seasons ago we told of things to come, you were sceptical, but they have come to pass. Those notes are hidden with the friends of the Earth. Can you imagine what they would say if they knew how things would turn out. The passage of time connects all, be nice to life, your morals are good but your pattern is strange.

How can you say that we only exist in your mind? For we are as physical as you, our star-ships, hover 10 degrees above the north as the climax of the sun descends below the horizon, you may see us, but will not hear us.

Due to the importance, our realm will remain hidden from the eyes of man until the purpose is needed. You cannot imagine what joy it would bring us to walk beside you in the Earth's atmosphere. Do not fear retribution or stigma, but talk free with those of the light.

We cannot allow mass destruction of the Earth's surface, so therefore intervene we must, at the critical point in time when the junctures are at their worst. Your confidence in us will be rewarded by the stone of yellow, set in a ring of gold, shaped as a six-sided star. And know you will remember us as always being your friend. Your purpose grows in each communication. We ask nothing of you but to love those around you. Our will, will focus upon your aspects of life.

Yellowstone is a vast forest of life; it sits cradled on all sides by man's lust and greed. She cannot withstand the pressures beneath her; she will release an outburst in the November. Her pattern will grow and those who know will remain silent until the inevitable occurs. Many will perish as she blasts out her message for Mother Earth. She will ignite a chain reaction that will be immense among your people. Consider this, would it have happened if it were not for your greed of her resources? You have left an empty shell of the weight that must be filled. You sucked her dry over vast regions of the surface; you cannot imagine the pressure that is vented upon her skin. Therefore, we will announce our plans to evacuate those of light and justice.

Fear not, our plans are simple, to reinvest in the life of the Earth a clean sweep is needed, and not all will survive. Selection of the species will be made soon; it will become clear to the eyes of many.

22nd April 2016

A Message from the 'People of the Sea'

Events to come are not in your power to change, but the will of man needs to be addressed; to be made aware of his purpose and allowing his feelings to make him aware.

We know that once before we have met, and throughout time, emotions of the soul bring forth new beginnings for each man as he lives his life with purpose. Look into your mind's eye and see the beauty within that stirs the soul. Your path is a great one upon a road of some length; turbulent times ahead are forecast, but you have to understand, that although times may be hard, the bright light of heaven shine, giving purpose and guidance to those who would follow it.

With respect in their hearts, with love in their attitudes, please do not be dismayed by the views of others, for they have not seen the beauty within our words.

We advance upon your nations with dignity and peace in mind, to allow the hostilities to ease in the hearts and minds of men of violence. Consequently, we do not accept their thoughts and misguided ways as being that of the light. They have turned a corner forbidden to all, because their hearts desire is for the fruits of life and not the fruits of love. Their minds conspire in ingenious ways to eliminate their enemies of the state, for they know their balance, in their haste for the wealth of the world, has become tainted with thoughts of murderous intent to further their greed upon your Earth.

March with your head high then focus upon the Lord of mercy, for he comes in a chariot of fire through the heavens of Sagittarius and Aries.

Michael who walks before you knows of the tragedies of the Earth, he has witnessed the birth of a Christ and the death of humanities souls. The crucifixion was an abomination against God, for which man has paid dearly and continues to reluctantly accept. For his son came unto you with purpose of love, which was rejected by the hierarchy who feared for their salvation. But they never understood that their salvation was within Him. Their idols of stone were wasted to dust and their prayers were never heard.

For we are of a place before time, upon your Earth. You knew of us as the people of the sea, Atlantis is in your mind, but we were not of your Earth, our chariots of fire you never knew of.

The beginnings of your life, it started many eons before. Far beyond your existence lies a world; its waters have a fragrance of inner peace and serenity. For a tear was suffered their indignation, but unlike your Earth, He came to furnish it with love.

Tropical storms will occur in May with a force and intensity never seen before.

Once more we must insist that man obey instructions sent by us to those in authority of your nations. They disclaim accounts of us, telling you that the stars in the sky cause an effect, an illusion. What if we were to tell you that our existence coincides with yours, we are linked in a manner unknown to you, for we are of spirit, we furnish you with life and purpose, but sadly we have to inform those of the world, of the events to come. Their ears block out the knowledge before them, they cannot understand why such things would be. Fortunately, we are here to help in a manner of love, willing to assist your nations in a manner respectful of man. Come before us with your tokens of love, and fulfilment will be given to those who wish to be enlightened.

We encounter objects in your atmosphere, and they stain your earth with scars, their purpose unnecessary. They have driven a wedge between nations as you rush to pollute the skies with cans. Shock waves will be felt as we dispose of the items unnecessary to your world. You cannot underestimate our intent and purpose to renew and replenish, as it was in days past. Alert your mind to our being. *(Note: Redundant satellites? there are said to be more than 500,000! An approximation currently given by NASA.)*

Continually we strive to enter the minds of men with purpose, their thoughts are closed as to the value beyond this life of flesh. If only they would stop and listen to their hearts, they would know the truth of their being. For they are the creation of God, and the light within can be released with the mercies of love and tolerance. Emotions flow as strong as the river of Jordan, and power that needs to be harnessed in a manner respectful of their being.

There will be a time when we will demand respect upon your Earth as we dominate the minds of man who would denounce God. Why are they so determined to enter such places where there is no light, for there will be no happiness in their place of dark. Their eternal souls cannot be rescued from the depths therein. Further, we implore you to march with us in a manner respectful of the angels of light, to bring forth that which is of love to the men of the Earth, prepare them for the coming of the Lord.

Translate your words in a manner respectful to the Divine, for they are of the Divine. Your manner approaches that as a servant of the light.

The star ships gather beyond your fields of vision, you cannot imagine what it is like to bring such force to bear upon those who disobey the natural path of life. Within the hearts of the many, a glimmer of hope remains, but we can only inspire those who wish to see the light.

Transport your mind and thoughts beyond where you are, to a place of beauty that would dazzle your eyes and numb your mind as rivers that flow, are the rivers of mercy and love. Come before us with gratitude in your hearts in your souls.

Buttercups and daisies are found to process secretions that can be used to enhance your minds wills.

Traverse your mountains of our need, caring for those who are reliant upon your love.

Conditions are set for the arrival of the Immaculate One, whose creation will unfold in the days to come, a matter of your weeks, his name is Fielding, his manner to you is that of a baby, to us a symbol of love and free will, who will enhance your men of the Earth in the years that follow a tumultuous disaster. He greets you this evening with honour and respect, the work that you do in the hope of salvation of man, continue your purpose as ordained by those of the light. Do not regret your actions for they are simple but with need of purpose, your continuance is assured as we enter your mind and soul.

12th May 2016

Merriweather, she will tell you of a time when a life was of the utmost importance, her stories would lighten your heart and free your mind to a place of illusion, for she knew in her heart of a place of learning that surpassed man, in the green valleys below the mountains and hilltops, there lies a place embedded of imagination. Merriweather gained her reputation, one of elegance, for her proprietary's were vast as she gave all to those in need, for her heart was truly of purpose of the light. She passed in the November 2016 to our place of spirit. Her welcome was great and she knew her purpose was done. Comparatively yours is of equal measure, lighten your heart to the possibilities beyond your imagination, complain to us not of your weaknesses, for we are aware your concerns are great for the morals of man. Theirs cannot be helped by these words for they will not listen; they are fools who aren't aware of the consequences that face them in the world of dark. Notice that need of you in the days to come.

12th May 2016

Star-ships, Atlantis in the Arctic Ocean

They hide in the shadows, in their bunkers, forecasting the day when they hope to win, but theirs is a purpose of the night and as with night, the light always wins.

To demonstrate your purpose and will, you seek an audience with those who can understand our purpose in your life. Never be ashamed to say that we are in your heart, as men shy away from their innermost feelings, for their sanctuary is of hope. Can you not feel the warmth of our words?

As we run tides of love to wash over all upon the Earth, turbulence was felt beneath the Earth at a point with a reference of 80 north. *(Note: The 80th parallel north is a circle of latitude that is 80 degrees north of the Earth's equatorial plane, in the Arctic. It crosses the Atlantic Ocean, Europe, Asia, the Arctic Ocean and North America.)*

Brazil will feel the wrath of Mother Earth on the 20th for she is full of ice. Lose its sovereign. Beneath the walls of plenty they will not feel as much pain as those of greed and avarice in their sparkling temples, they will shudder to a magnitude greater than before, they will speculate that this was of no significance, but in their hearts they know the magnitude of this event. They will hide their money from those with prying eyes, she's not worthy of the purpose, as He comes before her on his need of peace and reconciliation. *(Note: This must be about the impeachment trial of the Brazilian President, Dilma Rousseff. –she was removed from office on 31 August 2016.)*

The 28th will see the downfall of she who routs his place of iniquity.

When will men understand the urgency by which we came from beyond where the words of wisdom shall be heard but not seen by the masses, for she is a battleship of the stars. She will announce her arrival on the full moon that eclipses the sun, for the darkness is where we shelter from your gaze.

A fiery end was brought to bear upon the city we know as Atlantis. Why hasn't man learnt the error of his ways? We were taught a lesson of defiance and we came to understand our purpose before Him, Our Lord, for his was the way of reconciliation of our souls. Balance has been achieved in our hearts and minds as we learnt a valuable lesson of life. Frequently we visit that place of home, for it is no more, buried deep beneath the Arctic Ocean, frozen, where our homes, as our hearts, melted to the light.

Tremendous amounts of courage are required to withstand a forceful will of those who rule your Earth. With need, this chain cannot be broken by one man, it'll take many nations time to reconcile their differences. In years to come, as on our planet, peace will be achieved by love and goodwill, by acknowledgement that one is no different to the other, balance is everything. The scales of justice shall weigh in your favour to enlighten those of your world and our focus is upon you in the fall. *(Note: Read 'fall' as metaphorical, a time when life for mankind may not be as it is today, a time of great change.)*

Continuous activities proceed by men of war in the depths of the dungeons beneath your Earth, for they play games of mass destruction, never understanding the will of the people and many will eradicate those who dishonour of their men. Their purpose is dark for there cannot be light where there is dark, there can be no peace where men rule with veracity in their hearts.

Continually we see focus in some of the poor countries, it is not enough to say, "We gave!" as their need is great. They do not desire material objects of the West, they desire the right to live as equal men. It is these who will succeed your present state of being, as they will survive the storm of the wind of man. *(Note: "Blessed are the meek, for they shall inherit the Earth" Matthew 5.5.)*

Make no mistake that each has his own purpose, the free will to choose between light and dark. Yours is of the light, many are of the dark for they are weak minded, blinded by the foolish things of man.

They'll ignite such a storm, as the world has never seen before, calling into question their tolerance of your species. Be not afraid for there are continually storms and always a peace to follow. A cleansing is needed on a massive scale and nature will have her say, for there is nothing that cannot be cleansed in time. All things decay and where there was once life so there will again, a different form, a newer kind of being as you evolve, in your evolution and purpose.

A storm of light combined with electricity charged atmospheres will create a storm of magnitude erasing memories in machines, let it be known that we understand your fears. *(Note: solar flares?)*

15th May 2016

ET and the Beings of the Grey

Your purpose and deeds will be of historic importance to those of future years.

Welcome friend, you have in life your tasks of a purpose needed at this time to enhance the minds of those who wish to connect with spirit, to communicate their feelings of joy, for they will be rewarded in the hereafter.

Many years ago, we came to seek the one who would bring peace upon your Earth, his name Michael, is measured by his will and testament. He could not have foreseen the enormity of the tasks that awaited him. Allow your need to bring about a peace within men's minds, for their confusion is enormous, their minds are awash with fear of having nothing, but what do they consider as being nothing? For their lives are filled with the joy and pleasures of man's reckless ways and greed, they concern themselves with the everyday fundamentals of life, never looking for that one thing that is within their minds and souls, their purpose of being.

It is a mountain to be climbed to reach the minds of those who would not listen. One will see the words and not recognise their beauty, for they will now say this man is not worthy, but all men are worthy. If they were to just release their inner emotions and allow the light in through the window of love. It is crystal clear to those of purpose, for they have wisdom beyond their years to acknowledge the light and the joy that it brings and a peace to their hearts and minds. We know it will cloud in other men.

Irrational is a word frequently used to describe a form of emotion; the inertia of this emotion can only be measured by the abilities to let the spirit flow. Constantly we are reminded of man's inability to allow his free will and mind to acknowledge all those things that God provides him on this Earth of plenty. We feel the time has come for us to intervene and bring joy to where there is sadness, to enlighten man's heart to the ways of the Lord and His purpose within them. Constantly we fear for man's existence, for he is determined to bring about his end by means of his own hand. Concern is great among us as we observe the tragedies unfold, they aren't necessary, for the weaknesses of man will bring about his own destruction.

Burnt memories are faded. Caustic are the minds of the men of the north who wish to bring terror on your individuals

in their planned itinerary missions. Concern yourself not with the things you cannot change, be positive in your outlook, let the negative fade away as the burning embers of the fire, for they cannot feed upon the ashes of men whose hearts are filled with desire for love. A negative aspect within man should be tempered with a heart of goodwill towards men, giving flavours of love to all those that encompass his diet of purpose.

Tomorrow will come and bring about a main event that cannot be, but rendered, this time, but we will have assurance, we are unable to directly convince them. It is not necessary to deceive us for we are of the light and masters of all. Continuously we strive to bring a measure of peace among your people.

Your wisdom is required to enhance the words that we bring, never reflect on them as a negative for they are positive in desire. The soul is a point reference, in which the soul escapes the burden of humanity, climb those mountains and bring about a purpose and need for humanities sake.

ET of the Grey

The words are spoken in truth and honesty; we are a group of angels who focus upon those who would listen. Travel your world in a way of man, allow them to have purpose in your voice as you will speak of the many things that bring us to your nations, for we offer guidance and wisdom to those with focus around your globe. You need a temperament of love to bring about their need.

Forecasters display an ignorance, for they see the winds of change that will bring about a global catastrophe on such an immense scale that it will go down in the annals of history. This is a warning to those of need to prepare yourselves to witness a massive amount of radioactivity that will enter your Earth's atmosphere in June. Your conscious minds will be unaware as the sparkle of the light affects you all, its immediate effects will not be recognised until a later date. They know of its effects and of the radiation that will become intense around your globe. Panic is not necessary, for it is a natural phenomenon, but its strength is gained by your weakness, for your planet is a target of further attacks. Your cumbersome ways have disturbed the cloak of peace that wraps itself around your planet; you have polluted the air you breathe with carbon monoxide. They spoke of a hole in the dense atmosphere, you created the situation. A phenomenal amount of effort is needed to bring a peace with yourselves.

Confirmed it is, the spectral analysis that Norway discovered recently by a team that works hidden beneath your seas. They forecast a change in the weather and they hide, knowing of what is to come from beyond your planet. Constantly we have heard their chatter on the waves of your radio, frequently we have intervened with the radar, they cannot understand why the disturbances occur. It is because their eyes are closed, they hear only what they want to hear, see only what they want to see and know only what they want to know. They are foolish these people of science, for what do they truly know of the ways of spirit? Their hearts are closed to the possibility of other realms within realms, they cannot conceive the idea that dimensions all play a part on each other they see only the one of their own.

Ferguson, he was gifted in these matters, his words were written many times but dishonoured by those of these communities, they said, "It is not possible, how, where does it happen?" He came to us with his knowledge. We inspired his work through many years; his magical touch had cleansed many who believe in the world beyond. However, he could not establish a weapon with which to breach the minds of the blind and ignorant. He joins us now with words: "Be not ashamed of who you are for we all have a purpose in our lives, continually you'll strive to be recognised as I did but their focus isn't upon the spiritual aspects of the human existence. Their minds are set on practical impartiality's; they need a reason to shake them. I was once as they are, a single channel focusing on a point of light, I could not recognise that that point of light had many aspects, the rays, the beams are focused upon the point of a word and breached their target" *(Note: J.B. Ferguson; Biographies of Classical... Medium, channel, and one of the founders of modern Spiritualism... compiled a record of communications through H.B. Champion: With Explanatory Observations. The book is called Spirit Communion. What is even more extraordinary is on page 97 of this book Mr Ferguson and Mr Champion visit Mr and Mrs Merriweather. The synchronicity seems great, Champion is our authors name and he is also a trance medium. Is this the Merriweather that is mentioned in the previous message of 12th May and this one? The book holds many records of Mr H.B. Champion's trance readings during the mid-1800s.)*

We constantly strive to connect you to Tompkins, Merriweather their names of which you are not familiar, nonetheless they exist within the bounds of science, persuade your people of the need to focus, for their lives are dependent upon their spiritual being. All too often we have failed to reason with man to generate an interest in aspects of purposeful meaning.

Welcome, we are a noble people who come before you this evening to bring words and messages with love and focus to the minds of many of the planet Earth. Comparatively you are a feeble race not knowing where to turn on the path of life, we have established a point of reference to focus upon your earth, Atlantis.

Continually we inhabit your atmosphere, we watch, glide with purpose and intent. You cannot obstruct them as their all-seeing eye will protect, penetrate the layers of the crust, the protective layer before us is of great importance as their energy fields upon our habitats, your crusts are thin. Our many protect your planet, the reasons are obscure, but they have valid reason, all must sacrifice a part of themselves so that the majority become illuminated. We are regarded as a race of beings who are worthy of love, but we know love. We regard you as primitive beings, but you are of the light. His mercies reach far and wide throughout the galaxies and higher.

We have noted your intent on us as we patrol your skies, we see people watching, us they marvel but cannot understand what it is that they comprehend, they must achieve their relationship within the nations of the Earth and unite their communities that plunder your Earth, and target ours with intent.

Why is it that we of the Grey need to speak of humanity, when humanity itself cannot contain its anger and frustration, you wound each other deeply not knowing the reason why. You figuratively speak in terms of peace but where is it? We see no evidence to the contrary; your nations of war will escalate in measures, not of peace but for need of domination. Is it any wonder that we speculate that your people are all denied their own existence?

We watch with interest the calamities as you move forward, rest assured we cannot assume to impose ourselves on your race. Others who also watch, some with anger, some with calm, waiting for reconciliation of your nations. We have hope that one day you'll be joined in a common purpose. Technology was given to enhance your being, its purpose was to advance your nations, but instead you have turned that gift into something that was not intended. We regret having given it to your man for their prudence was to waste our wisdom at this time, allow us to intervene to bring peace to your hearts.

Continuance of the existence of man is vital as man's purpose was to unite beings of the light, to give them focus of themselves but also upon lesser creatures who walk their paths. We will commence our journeys with small steps.

Paris regrown, feverish the pastures within us, as our stride increases as the knowledge grows, culminating in an attitude of serenity and peace. *(Note: Maybe referring to the attitude of the Parisians in overcoming the bombing last November? The attacks in Paris on the night of Friday 13 November 2015 by gunmen and suicide bombers hit a concert hall, a major stadium, restaurants and bars, almost* *simultaneously – and left 130 people dead and hundreds wounded. BBC News.)*

Commissioned are you to bring a holy explanation to your world, never forget that the man is given to unify your minds, to bring about strength of purpose beyond your comprehension at this present time. You are the vessel; they are the carriage by which the vessel will be heard. Commence your journeys with joy, peace and love, on a mission to bring peace among your men who would listen.

Determination of will is required to generalise the formation of circles upon your land, they demonstrate much intelligence ignored by the vast majority, you call them crop circles. Their purpose is twofold, to draw attention to a mind superior to their own, their messages are of peace and hope, the key to their complex meanings lies in the catacombs of your Pope, purposely withheld for fear that man will lose focus upon their church. In time gratitude will be rewarded to those who bring about a purposeful meaning of love. We cannot express through your mind the complexities of the messages for they are intense with purpose, as circles demonstrate the intelligence of beings of the universe. Their configurations dictate their intent upon your ways. Do not look at them with eyes of logic, see the patterns that they form as they describe the universal energy, the same energy that created man. Descriptively they made you a bond of minds, of logic, figuratively speaking they are yours to behold, for not to understand their purpose will be a mistake.

The Rose; she carries the insignia of the purpose, ah, she knows of your quest, she's happy to join you on the path of love. Figuratively speaking she is a vessel of love; she emits and transmits messages constantly to the universe of light from which she hails. She connects with minds to reason of purposes of the light with the entities of many nations, of many solar systems on a massive scale. The power of her mind is immense, she drives the will of love, her will upon you, is to succeed in a purpose far beyond your comprehension upon this life.

She knows of the many who worship her in their cathedrals, they ask forgiveness, and they ask, "Our mother, why has this happened in my life?" They do not understand that theirs is not unique, because for many a purpose has been given to enlighten their souls of the need, not of just man but others who require guidance. There are many primitive beings, who are on a path of destruction for they cannot comprehend the meaning of their existence within the planetary systems, they think they are alone. Why do they not listen to the words that are written in their own tongues, how many times will it take us to unify your world? Too many times have we been ignored, but still we were driven by love to bring about a peace for the Almighty.

How do we understand the many complexities of the human mind, it is vast? Our computerised systems can deal with vast amounts of data, yours are complex but not unfathomable. We will reach an opinion, may you always bring about a purpose in your lives, communicate with each other in the ways of love, target your emotions for the happiness in the knowledge, that peace will come to all who seek the Lord for His name is on high.

Jack of all trades he was for many, his field of knowledge was that of emotions set against possibilities, for he knew his time was numbered in those days when the sun shone upon the minds of youth. Commonly knowledgeable was he, community fever, he ran a place of purpose, outstanding he was. *(Note: We acknowledge the last sentence is confusing, however it is transcribed exactly from the recording of this message.)* Triangles sang out for she played them to the school bands, they rehearsed in the hall, he, Jack listened intently to the music that was played to his ears, they were deaf to many things until her voice, as she sings to him the many tunes of merriment. He frequently asks to be remembered of those days of school when he would pick you up, the Porsche he would bring. The path of peace, a distraction to the mayhem in those days, she was a sunbeam. *(Note: We believe this could be Michael Jackson and his daughter Paris.)* Tragic circumstances befell the man that awoke on the Sunday to be of service to those of a nation of intolerance, for he felt a need to indulge in meaningless things. The communities around him gave him purpose to sing, tragically he awoke to the world of spirit not understanding the wisdom *(his words)*. "Why this act of crime, why am I here before my time, what was my crime?" We told him his crime is for greed, the need of substances not required by his body but only of his mind, you say invalid his will, the manner of the Lord. His youth was tainted as his years were long, forget-me-nots were given as a sign of his passing. Tunes are played of his life's experiences enhancing the memories of many of the beautiful songs like peace of the world, his knowledge and experience were that of a child within a man. Michael, he gave his heart to many, his innocence was untold, for those men who would seek his fortune betrayed him. His needless pressure for that abuse displayed an ignorance to many, he was unaware his innocence was to mislead those who focused against him, for his name to many became familiar. Tranquillity his heart, he sang the verse of love before you many times and out putted those of fortune.

Never giving or letting anyone know his thoughts, his imaginations were great, business as usual was resumed. He generated a vast empire, an empire of song to justify his words to music, to a beat of time. Tragically his loss was felt throughout the universe as his purpose was extinguished.

Today's world is obscene, no justice, only tragedies occur. Temper your minds with love and an aspect of light to rise above those of hate, bring about peace in your purpose, focus your minds upon the will of those who remember those days of love. Terminal velocity was reached when negative aspects brought about by thoughts of many in your world. *(Note: Our power of thought and intent is greater than we think, we only have to realise how our moods affect those around us, multiply that and the effect is far reaching.)* Transit your minds to the task ahead which is great, you're going to understand. Tragically your minds are too feeble to accept the surge of energy needed where you'll transmit in a purposeful manner acceptable to our minds, *(Note: In order for higher dimen-sional beings to communicate with us we need to raise our vibrational level and they need to lower theirs.)* Our minds reach out to you through the elements of space and time pur-posely to exist in your atmosphere. You must give an assur-ance to our energies of love and peace, for we mean no harm, we merely wish to bring about a purpose of peace among your nations. Our choosing a name with wonderment concerning a field of knowledge so unique it cannot be copied by man.

Rosemary will bear witness to a massive change in the field of economics, she will encounter many fraudulent practices, her speech will be announced by the masters of ceremony, their vocals will bring about a mass of confusion amongst those of your society, for their negative aspects will fall upon the ears of those who do not want you to hear of the sins com-mitted by them in their role as your masters, for they know of their sin, they will regret the day they worshipped the money they have a love for. *(Note: This was reported by the press on 12th December 2018: Police have raided the home of Rosemary Rogers, the former chief of staff to NAB chief exec-utive Andrew Thorburn, in the midst of a bribery investiga-tion going to the heart of Australia's big for banks with over $110 million in payments now being investigated.)*

Constantly we tell you of many things to come before you in your living world, you need not know of all things that will affect your lives they are beyond your control. Continually we inspire to give you words of comprehension to ease the burden of the masses, your society's hates and fears of the many must fall away as He appears before them in aspects of colour far beyond their imaginations. Tolerance will be assured unbi-ased for the many, we understand that man is taught by man, the chain to be broken, for men should love from his soul for spirit.

Regrettable, we will announce our arrival on the dawn to be announced shortly, your masters are aware of our presence beyond your vision, they will not tell you what they see for

fear of a backlash. They know of many, of how it is an open secret for which they have denied all knowledge for so long. The markers, the circles will determine time and place, do not be deceived by their reports of insignificance as they attempt to cover up what they know to be true. See the markers for what they are, the complexities of the raven will be astounding to those who have not seen before, the birds will mark our spot. *(Note: We believe the 'raven' may be a forthcoming crop circle, we will wait and keep watch – we bear in mind that time means little to other beings, no time scale is given for their appearance.)*

Turbulence of your minds will be uneasy at the prospect of a new world. Contemplate your manner within, negotiate your minds will to that of the light, to update we bring information to help you in your hour of need.

I call upon you to bring about a peace in the minds of those who would reconcile themselves in service to the Lord, for He is the master of life of many nations beyond yours, understand His will is of love, sacrifice your lives in His service, for your gratitude should be great.

John the Baptist, he argued with those in authority, not allowing their thoughts to enter his as he was focused upon the Divine, he spoke of the days when all of the worlds would bring together a peace everlasting. His words of truth are heard by many, you baptise them in the waters to make them strong of spirit to give them the strength of the Lord. He washed away their sins in a meaningful way that left them beholden unto him, for he was the precursor to the wonderful one, the master.

Undignified was his end, his death defiant of those who murdered his soul for their own purposes and therefore we know of his suffering, in short, his need of you is great to bring peace in the minds of those who read.

No doubt that we communicate through you to those of the Earth who are wise,

Good evening.

12th June 2016

ET Beings of the Blue

Troubled minds bear witness to the events which have occurred throughout your world in the past trimester *(three months)*.

Purpose your mind upon the light that gives life and love and peace to man.

We have purpose for your mind this evening, to focus upon the many of your Earth who at this time suffer in many ways, unable to bring purpose to their lives through the torment they suffer. Why is it that man needs to control man? Why can't they just be content to live their lives with purpose?

We of the light will embark upon a mission far beyond your understanding in the coming days and weeks of your year.

Never let it be said that we do not understand the tormented, fragmented world of yours in which man dwells without purpose or meaning, for his purpose has been lost to greed. His memories of the past fade with every day that passes, bringing him closer to a spectacular finale, for his mind is not that of the Lord but of monetary values only. What use has this in his life other than to forget with a little comfort. But surely a little comfort is all that is required to help others within this world of hate and despair.

The purpose to your mind is to be a messenger upon your Earth to influence those of money and power, to let them see and understand that their harshness towards lesser beings is seen as cruelty and not that of the Lord.

They worship and sing their hymns in their churches feeling elated and absolved of their sins, but they can only absolve themselves by their acts of kindness. For the fruits of their labour is not that of self, but of love bringing hope to those who have nothing, let him share his common wealth with the men of the world.

Who will ally for the light to those who live in dark times upon the continent of Africa? For they ask of nothing other than to live in a manner respectful of the Lord with peace in mind and happiness. It is called the dark continent and so it is with many things misunderstood by men. Is it not the garden of the Earth?

The focus of your attention should be upon the reconstruction and replenishing of the forests of trees, for they are the breath of life within your world. Who would destroy that which the creator has given to freshen your air so that your lungs may breathe?

The pointless murmurings to the world's poor are not seen as words of comfort, they are seen as merely degrading their lives, diminishing their purpose and the right to live within this world. Yours is a world of unnecessary suffering, man was not created to beat upon man but to bring about a useful, purposeful life with need of learning of his love for your return. *(Return to source?).* In due course to assess the situation we will bring a measure of peace to those of your Earth that need to understand that war is brutal and unnecessary. The mechanism of love should be that which is given from one man to another. Be at peace with your mind and bring a focus upon our wisdom and kindness. Harboured are your instincts to live as a man who has a will to respect others in a manner respectful of himself, we have not lost hope that your planet will be of peace in the forthcoming events that will open your eyes to the many things of life.

Bring about a purpose and need to invite men into your life so that they may see the point in the skies above you. To the east a fragmented parcel will bring joy to those who live in poverty, your will is not strong enough to appreciate our strength for we are here to bring about a purpose of need, to focus our will on those who bring about troubles upon your Earth.

Trevor is a man who will lead a few on the path of hope for his need is that of yours, for a peaceable nation that will bring hope to all, his time is not yet but his need grows as does his purpose to be fulfilled within your lifetimes. *(Trevor has been mentioned before.)*

Commonplace is man's desire to acquire the things of the material world, these things have no purpose other than to assist your lives.

You need to know that we have found fractured segments within your Earth, the fractures grow on a daily basis that will come to a mighty conclusion in the fall of man.

Prepare yourselves for a mishmash of events to take place within the structures and buildings of your cities, at home you will see these events unfold before your eyes, no one mentions what has caused these events, only that they have happened due to a terrorist act. They will supersede many minds to travel the world to investigate these horrific crimes against the nations, they will find disadvantage when they meet the source, for their eyes will not comprehend the tremendous amount of examined anxiety within the hearts and minds of the population. They go forward with their plans to bring about a circumstance that will eventually enlighten man as to the whereabouts of his beginnings, true we are that of a nation that has come before, before the population of the Earth grew. We are of a manner of a being of the Blue, you will know us as the saviours of man. Be brave and scout your mind for those fears and cast them out, as we bring about a peace in the minds of those who bring terror upon your world.

Their names will be announced shortly on the media that you listen to, they will cast doubt upon those who created terror in your cities, for they know of those yet to be involved in such acts of cruelty upon your race. Fragmented their hearts, the passion to rule with a firm grip. They cannot complete their mission until the dawn of the new day and the might and will of those in power are unleashed before the public.

Transmit your thoughts to that of focus as we are not an illusion nor a delusion, we exist beyond your atmosphere. We are of the peoples of the Americas, we have been once before to rule upon your planet. The Aztecs, the Inca's and all those of those civilisations knew of us, worshiped us, we did not ask for it to be in blood but to be of peace. They misunderstood our intentions as they saw us as creatures from another world, of another realm. They trembled with fear thinking that death would bring peace to them in their sacrifice. This is not so, as we are a race of beings who exist beyond your planet in a sphere of many nations who watch and understand your primitive Earth. We need to teach within the hearts and minds of those beings who populate your world who are ready to focus upon us, to see the truth and understand that their fragmented world has been created by man in his greed and purpose of mind. This was never intended, your Earth is a place of beginnings and endings, it is a sphere that can be seen by many not of your world, they see them lush green and blue in your skies, but they are not envious for they have known of their beginnings, it was also of similar circumstances. Bargain your thoughts for we are here to enlighten men's minds to bring a purpose to those who wish to understand the truth. The love of the beings that patrol your skies, we have no wish to bring harm to the spirits of your beings as we merely wish to assist and understand your species so that your minds would distinguish right from wrong. We have hope that your world would one day join the federation of many. We sleep waiting for that time and opportunity of your species to be aware of our existence. Our planet of blue, is a joy to be seen for we have no wars, we exist in an atmosphere not unlike your own, we too have need of love and purpose. Our aims are simple, that is to assist man in a common interest for all life that dwells within the many solar systems and planets of the universe.

Your dreams and aspirations of bringing hope to those will be focused upon one man as he sits, agrees, admires the work of purpose in progress, for he is one of a quiet nature who will respond in a meaningful way to your request and with your agreement to assist in a purposeful way.

The trimester spoken of is of great importance as it will bring about a merge and a meaningful time when many nations focus upon one game. They cannot understand that rebellion will bring down a focus to a state of anarchy within a nation. To announce that they will anoint a lamb. A place to identify them as an aggressive nation, their purpose is of ill will as they have a score to settle from the many indignities, they feel they have suffered. Their leader is a respectful man but only in the sense for his own interests.

A glimmer of hope may be achieved by our arrival as we intercede to bring a peace among your nations, you have created a situation of enormous proportions that will have a cause and effect upon your world of man. A tremendous amount of will power will be required to observe the skies and understand our presence. We understand the fear that this will bring, but know that we are of peace, peaceful intentions upon the world of man. Our ships, our craft will be seen at night by many eyes who focus their minds, for they will see a magical demonstration of our abilities.

Complete your assignment my son for we manage and control yours and the many lives who bring about change, a change of heart and mind. We sit here with you this evening in the hope that your call for recognition will be answered by many who follow the light and the word of Him, who have an understanding of our presence and need. Surrender your will to allow this control, you can't imagine the many things of joy that we bring, a happiness, peace and love to the hearts and minds of the many, let go. *(Authors note: at this point I attempt to totally let go and release myself into trance.)* This is hard, you have a heart and will, a purpose to believe in the many things beyond your imagination, we cannot supersede your will, allow us a transmission with purpose of love and light, we are that of the love and the light, the beings who control the thoughts of man in the aspects in the hopes of peace. Our admiration is for those who bring about a focus of their hearts and minds to our will, we are of a nation, a way out to bring a peace. You must not allow your fears, belay them, tremendous amounts of endeavours will be needed to cast the word upon your nations.

Our planetary system is far beyond your universe, it lays amongst the stars at a location that your satellites cannot reach. We became a civilisation with incredible insight, this was achieved through a major event by an extreme force that had an effect on our will to live with one another in peace. Our focus became strong in a manner of what you would call love, it was by this means that we collectively assumed responsibility for our planet and brought about a peaceful end to the many wars that we had indulged in. Your cosmos is vast, a triangulation is needed to calculate the distance between the Sun and the Earth and 'Eckbitoria' which lies far beyond your regions, between its own elliptical orbit of its Sun, with a mass far greater than yours. We live beneath the ground as it shelters us from the rays that would be unacceptable to our being. Your planet is much the same, do not think that you are any different, for your path is extreme in the ways of man's learning. Be comforted in the knowledge we can assist with measures unseen, unthinkable by your scientific community.

Fragmented your hearts and reckless behaviour supersedes the need for a peace and reconciliation amongst your men. Their purpose has been spoken of, why is it that you have need to possess, can you not see that all is given for all to share? We have no need for monetary things, we have a life, not of servitude, but of a will common to all our species. Frankly, we despair of the men in power who have only need for their own gain, they are foolish. Their minds have mapped out a plan to ignite a storm far beyond your planet, why do they do this? Why must they destroy all that has been created, what are they thinking, do they think that we will permit them to commit outrageous acts within the galaxies of the worlds? They think they have the right, the will and technology to do as they please, not so, for we are policed, the many nations will not allow such acts to go unrewarded. They are foolish in their aspirations, for they have created a weapon of mass, your technologies have been gained throughout time with influences that have been misconstrued and used not for the intended purpose. Do you think that we would allow your nations to bear their arms against us? We mean no harm to your general population, only to those who would take up arms in reckless behaviour against us. Trouble your mind not as these things may only occur. We hope that your men of purpose will have a vision, an insight not to take this path.

The creation of a mass electronic event within your earth will take place shortly, it will reverberate throughout your world and be felt by many, they will be unsure as to the reasons or the source but it is manmade, he creates systems that will weaken the structure of the crust of your earth. They do not understand the reason why there should be a problem, guidance is needed by a higher intelligence to assist before he embarks on a measure of doom.

Tonight we have granted a measure of peace to those bereaved by events of immense magnitude. their hearts bleed and pain fills their minds, we have Nigel who was amongst many to suffer the indignities of men who worship war, his story must be told to those who would listen in a hope that his passing is a measure of defiance to those who denied him his life.

Nigel

I am a man of many words, I have not yet spoken of the things I have witnessed in my passing for I was fortunate not to suffer indignities of pain, I was a man who encompassed love in many ways, my home town bears the name of a nation who grieves. I cannot express my contempt for those who would deny those of life, because of their prejudices they feel the need to destroy that which is good. Your heart is strong as mine was. My love of the light took me to a place of freedom of will, to demonstrate my purpose. I, Nigel demand an audience with your mind to bring about a peace to men's hearts, for we were condemned by many with many foolish notions decreeing that we were abstract in our ways, granted our purpose was different to what was deemed to be mainstream. We had a right to be as any man, we cannot deny that we had a purpose in life that was different to many, a belief and understanding that our hearts and spirit of minds are no different to any of the others. Bring about a reconciliation of your mind and know that our love is no different of that between that of a man and a woman, do not let the indignities of our passing go unanswered. There were many shots fired on both sides, they were reckless in their manner charging in without a thought other than to dispatch the one of terror. They did not see us as their weapons blazed, many were trampled by the confusion that reined within, they tell you untruths of our demise because they cannot admit to their own failures that brought about such tragic circumstances. We are men of a different purpose and we bled as others, those solders of law have no discipline, they deny, not knowing who it was so indiscriminately shot in the hope of achieving their aim. And their chief, he will deny all responsibility for their immediate actions. I am now at peace in a world of light and love with man, go before me, like as the Rose of love in the hope that man will control his emotions and have consideration for others. *(12 This last paragraph we assume to be about the Orlando shootings, however we cannot find a reference to anyone named Nigel having lost his life unless he was known by a different name. In June, 2016, a 29-year-old security guard, killed 49 people and wounded 53 others in a terrorist attack inside Pulse, a gay nightclub in Orlando, Florida, United States. Orlando Police Department officers shot and killed him after a three-hour standoff.)*

Tomorrows events will be even more astounding than today's as they bring about a purpose to command their authority upon those who would issue a statement of intent, grossly misunderstanding, misjudging their intentions. A calamity will ensure before the many to be seen as a disgrace before the eyes of the Lord. No thoughts to parliament, terror, confusion as they muster their arms in readiness in Paris, in Rome, their cathedrals of love are of intolerance and ignorance of fellow man for he betrays existence. Don't let their hearts darken yours with thoughts of retaliation, for in truth they are of no consequence, they are bullies that bring terror upon the peace talks hoping to achieve a traumatic offensive.

Our nations of plenty, tonight we give you a gesture of hope that your world may form an alliance to bring about a meaningful peace to the earth and to those of the light. Your speculation of our existence will culminate in a massive outpouring of expression of fear and anxiety and will summon a tremendous response to target those who said it was impossible. We commence our plans to target your earth with thoughts of peace, be not afraid as we travel through the minds of those who would listen, for we are a race of beings who will navigate your minds to help those who cannot see.

19th June 2016

Message from Merriweather

Complete your missions as required by the souls of the light who sit with you.

Merriweather, he wants to say a few words of encouragement to you my son:

"Open your heart and mind, bring about a purpose to unfold the need of the many. We were unable to complete our work, but we achieved a beginning to build on, as we roamed our nation with a purpose and need to enlighten men's hearts. Champion was a companion with much thought and compassion, take his hand. His spirit will bring about a purpose and hope for those within your world. Complete your mission with a full heart, know that we approve of your work, complimentary to ours.

Your basic needs will be met in the forthcoming events to unite your circles of the world in a response to those of the negative. Your hearts and minds combined will be a powerful reconciliation. A thought for those who would turn to see your words, know that we will be beside you in your hearts and minds as you continue your work my son.

Merriweather once assisted with your father as he now brings his mind's focus and will upon you to help reconstruct the things they were unable to achieve in their life. You know of his purpose, of their work together, we will need to intercede upon your life's path to bring about a change and measure of will so that you to may focus on life as given to you. Your purpose has been found by those who will assist in your wake, help them to understand your will and love for they are the Merriweathers of you, their love and devotion to the words, their anticipation of the creation of a new Earth and life will be rewarded with joy as they continue their path of light, encompassing others to their willingness to give and not receive, for they have a will as yours, to bring about a purpose of joy to this world of hate and dark. Continue in your work with a need to gather the resources required and needed to help those who watch, to understand the measure of your will and your purpose, complete your tasks with a measure of love in His name.

3rd July 2016

Ferguson he calls to you, "Become one man worthy of your nature, your facets will change as you strive to reach a finale of your life. Go with it my son, be strong with the will of a lion to fight the masses who would denounce your words as trash, we were a team and built a reputation. Allow yours to grow; your right hand must be that of strength, your character of vigour must be strong to bear the stress of insults set against you. Away *(apply)* your mind to the wisdom within and to the many words spoken.

25th August 2016

We will emit our emotions to you. As the skies fall dark and the lights from the stars shine. They beckon you to watch as our ships of emotion shine bright in the heavens above.

We have come this evening to inspire the many to look beyond the words given by your men of science and to bring their aspects of love to the possibilities of another form of life entering your world. We have been before and will come again.

As children, you watch the skies in anticipation; your hopes are emitted through your love. We will respond in kind to your men of purpose. Allow us to intercede with your lives, terminate your thoughts of ill will against your brethren, commit your mind not to the negative, but bring a positive attitude to all those that you meet and aspire to. For he who comes before the Lord and cries with shame for his sins committed, shall find forgiveness and blessings within the light of the Lord.

Truly your purpose has inspired a multitude of men, bringing them ever closer to the aspects of love and light. We ask no more than that, for all who work within the light to aspire, to encourage and enlighten others to follow the path of love.

Conquer your fears as we approach your earth in multitudes. We have a practice of love; we see no reason that you shouldn't respond in kind.

The men in Hungry who have troubled minds must alleviate their fears of those of the black, for they will diminish as the light shines before them in the heavens above. A common practice of love is required in your nations so that peace may rein once more upon your planet's surface. We give no guarantees that we will extend the hand of friendship, for there are those who would combat us, they are the negative beings of your earth, those who will not relinquish control of your thoughts and your lives. But they know, they know that we approach.

Your NASA denies this fact in many words of false hope. We will issue a statement before long, interfering with your networks of vision. Your masters will denounce it as a stunt, as a prank by others to put fear into you, but the message will be of love. Consider this, if we wish to destroy your life form, would we have not done it so long ago? We have a passion for all life that exists within the solar systems, not just the earth, but of many that surround your cosmos.

Planetary systems will align in a formation to give power and strength to the thought of those who focus upon their energy. Bring your lives to the fore; allow your thoughts to extinguish your fears of the many things to come before you in this world.

Galaxies are far apart, millennia separate them in time, but we have forms of transport that we evolved. You too may evolve, if only you would open your eyes and welcome the possibilities set before your eyes. Open your hearts and minds, allow us to divulge the information that will assist your progress, but beware of those men of greed and power who would extinguish our thoughts with calculated lies. Do not accept their word, as they tell you many untruths of the many alien species that encircle your earth.

What valour is there in war, what value? It only serves to destroy and bring down your species, halting your advancement. For many will focus their minds in a protest on the streets of London to create possibilities of a new format of living. The establishment of old will tire of their nonsense, riots will ensue, they beckon those of old to greet them with intolerance, but you must evolve. Your heart's desires for peace and love must be allowed to develop in the natural way given by him.

Tidal waves of despair will be immense as she blows, in the mountains, in the regions, in the hills and the valleys. The many will scatter and harvest their crops for fear of the perils to come. Your world is in turmoil. Natural disasters, and mankind, who beat upon one another. It is a hard life, but the rewards are great if you hold your true self to the light and love of the Lord.

2nd October 2016

ET of unknown origin

(Note: We have read the following paragraph several times and feel that this following section may be of Annunaki origin. There is further information concerning other beings who *have had much to do with humanity in the following book: 'The Arcturian Anthology' by Tom Kenyon and Judi Sion. We have searched the internet for references of the beings who we think it may be, but many sites seem 'sensationalist' which makes us doubt the authenticity.)*

We were sent many eons ago with purpose in mind that we would one day aspire to the Gods of the heavens, that we would become one with the light of the Lord for Him to come. We negotiated with men's terms and conditions to give them powers to uphold the law in our lands and regions of the world. They neglected their duties; we did not abide by the law and so we forfeited the right to enter the kingdom of love. Of course this was long ago for man would recognise that the steps that we took are reflecting in today's world. We endeavour to inspire those of peace and tolerance to bring about a purpose, a purpose of mind to join the hearts of man, it is a task of tremendous upliftment and goodwill. It will be hard to obtain satisfaction from those hardened, that are in love with money. Their freedom will be restricted as casualties of war. The mountains of gold will lose their ability to provide. Murderous intent will become rife as they clamber and scratch at the ground for more, for their hearts are cold, no emotion to be felt as they live their lives in dark, cold places. We see their minds.

(Note: *The following section is an idea taken from the book, 'The Arcturian Anthology' by Tom Kenyon and Judi Sion. if you feel faint hearted then please overlook it until you wish to read and maybe accept it, or discard the information as you see fit, it certainly stretches our understanding of the possible origin of mankind. Please note that the information does not necessarily reflect the opinion of the author or co-authors, but is given as another viewpoint to consider:*

"Part of what we call alien interference is genetic in nature and has to do with early genetic tampering by the Annunaki. This alien civilization created what is essentially a slave race for the purpose of mining gold, which they desperately needed to

reinforce the energetics of their dwindling atmosphere. A genetic experiment was undertaken in which early primates on earth were genetically altered by the Annunaki to serve as workers, as slaves, for the purpose of mining. Thus, built into the very genetic coding of your biology is a deeply engrained tendency to be subservient and to worship what you perceive to be 'divine beings'. Early humans perceived the Annunaki (and many other galactic and intergalactic travellers) as gods, but these beings were simply so technologically advanced their mere presence and actions seemed like magic to less evolved minds.")

23rd October 2016

Persuade your fellow beings of the existence of the mighty groups who muster and flock to your earth, for they fight for war, for attrition.

You may not witness the many things that happen behind closed doors, but you will hear of the atrocities resulting from these warlike beings. Command your thoughts for a purpose of love and strength and focus upon the light and love of the Lord. Rest assured his being is with you as you navigate the seas of life. Purpose is felt throughout the universe as a man propagates his suffering upon one another.

Hmm, you would term us as Martians! We are many, unseen to the eyes of men. He searches for a point in the sky where he can illuminate the minds of man, encourage them to think that there is a point to his missions, the point of exploration of fantasy, but his truth is hidden deep within the wormholes of his mind. Be not afraid to open your mind Michael, to let the thoughts of those beings through, to speak their wise words of wisdom on the many nations of your earth. Our focus you feel is lost upon your being, but know that many watch and crave the words, as they issue reassurance, that like a parent they are being watched over. Your security is felt. Of course we cannot offer you direct contact at this time, but we will issue you with thoughts of memoirs, so as to inspire you to become a peaceful group of beings.

Your men of ignorance will not relinquish their hold on you at this time, for they are driven by purpose of greed and are not concerned with the strife of many in your world, but soon it will be their turn to feel the pinch, to know what it is to have nothing and see so much in the pastures of life.

Their royal esteemed selves, as they call themselves, will suffer punishment for their misgivings and deeds, but help is on the way for those many millions of your world who respect the wishes of the Lord and ask for redemption and peace.

We have said this before, but you must all, if you have faith, trust in him on high. Whisper your prayers of love and ask for his redemption, for it is your energies and your focus that will break the barriers of time and bring peace upon your planet. Physical actions are not always necessary to bring a means of constructive practices, you lack the imagination and the power of mind to use this will that you possess, as all creatures of life possess, a power within to change matter in its format, allow a passion of love to enter.

30th October 2016

Spirit Talking About ET's

We will come on the next moon to speak of the many things of purpose within your life. Your friends are aware of your astrological connections, hmm, those beings from far-flung planets who visit on occasion. You feel they have gone quiet, perhaps there is a purpose in their silence that you are unaware of! Be blessed with their love, for they are a saviour species who would bring about reform to the man of the world. Your practice of hate and war extinguishes your love and your purpose.

The ET's to follow in the years to come will educate and teach those who would listen to their words, but first of war of attrition must be sanctioned to eliminate those who would deliberately spike the word of the Lord. Do not be afeared by our words of strength, for they carry much wisdom within them. You must, to begin anew, start with a clean sweep. We mean no harm to those innocents of your world, but to those who fight us, they are the ones that will not be tolerated by those ET's.

7th November 2016

ET, The Greys

The illusions of life which hold you captive in this world are only but a shadow of the vastness of the kingdom within heaven.

Those of the negative will become positively charged as the atoms circulate your planet, driven by the masters of light.

There has been much change in your world, your frequencies of love are low at this time. You need our help to practice the love of the Lord and bring his mercy to your hand.

Allow us to intervene tonight as we have spoken many times before about the natural wonders of your earth and how they should be protected by those beings of the light. They come this evening with words and a measure of caution to those who would disrespect your planet. Be not practical of mind and worship the pound or the dollar that rules your life. Bring faith and love back into your kingdom's, enable your planet to breathe the fresh air of love as you relinquish your grasp upon her.

It is no means a pleasure that we should have to raise the subject once more of your ill will towards your planet Earth. We need your focus to bring about change in those many things that man has created and desired for his own pleasures. Are you not ashamed of those many things that exist in your perpetual minds and love of wealth? We do not come here to speak tonight to reprimand you, but to bring a portion of love to you in the hope that our stinging words will open your minds and hearts to those that come to offer their language of speech.

It has come to our attention that Hillary, hmm, 'maybe?' the next president of your United Nations (states), shame has been upon her as she strutted the boardwalks with no compassion for those that have assisted her in becoming a master. She will see a downfall before her time is done, as you all will, for you are just creatures of the earth, but not of the planet. As you disgrace yourselves in the avalanche to come.

It is a miraculous thing to think that those creatures of the light will once more bring guidance to your men of profit, for they see the doom written in the words.

We know of many who look to the light and assist with calmness and dedication to bring about change. Their money is an avalanche, a windfall to those who would benefit from their gesture of goodwill.

How can it be that man does not see the error of his ways? How is it that our names no longer shine as a light, but are covered with the thoughts of avarice. We will once more come as angels to the land of the Pharaohs to bring news of the "wise one" who would seek your care and attention.

Have you ever wondered why it is, that through all these centuries, peace has never been accomplished within those Eastern countries? Have you never wondered what the real war is? You see man fighting man behind the walls of Jericho, ah, the true players of this turmoil. They inspire others to fight a vicious war, promising them the blessings of the Lord if they establish a foothold. They are unaware of the dark that guide them.

There will be one, and she will come as a guiding light. She will awaken their minds to the misjustice that has become so regular. We hope that this guidance will assist them to a better life, it will take much persuasion and much courage to bring the light once more from the heavens above.

We see the commentaries of many who establish thoughts of injustice within the realms of man. Is it not a fact that man is unable at this time to comprehend justice in the manner of the light?

We seek nothing more, other than for you to love one another as the creator intended, he is the father of you all and his love will wash over you as you enter the realms of spirit. The upheaval caused to some will bring astonishment to their thoughts and lives. "Can this be true," they say, "why was I so misguided to a hapless situation of not caring for those around me who issued me with love."

We would like to speak tonight to those of your world who would listen to our words and thoughts, as our prayers go out for peace within your kingdom of men. We were once a dedicated force who ruled your world of misfortune, we became an object of abuse by those of the times. Their love for us diminished as their greed grew. We could not justify satisfaction to them, so we left, and here we are once more, claiming the light to be carers of man.

Your focus of being is truly worthy of your name, but we need more.

An explanation of guidance is needed in a practice of love, we are not of your world. We have come many light years before this time. We have seen the evolution of your creatures of man. How can we assist you when you say there is no hope? Look to the heavens and stars at night and see them shine, for your own star also shines to other nations on many planets, within the many solar systems of the universe. They look at you and say, "I wonder how far that star is, what creatures live upon it?" They are nations of love who would be astonished to see your warlike ways. You are nevertheless, creatures of the creator and deserve another chance of peace. We will illuminate the minds of those who will not relinquish their weapons. We have come in peace with a measure of love for your united man.

Do not become disillusioned by the things that you see and the terrors that you witness in your world, for all planets of life evolve. It is true some will not exist, no longer, while others will thrive overcoming their torturous time. We can assist in many ways, but it is necessary for your weak minds to become accepting. We are a race known to many in your world, hmm, we were once called "those greys", a menace to your world. We have hope that your minds will accept that those of misery would deceive your thoughts in the hope of bringing dismay to your lives.

How is it you never focused within your thoughts to the knowledge and practices gained through eons of existence? It is strange how your race will blot out the memories of focus. There have been times in the past when we have ascended beyond your vision, a watchful eye has never left your planet. We have all come with a focus, but only as required by your thoughts and needs.

Complimentary you are to us in your manner and respect. Your focus is needed once more as our thoughts are transmitted. We are the beings of light who would negotiate the many boundaries of life to bring satisfaction to those who have purpose. Guidance is required for those many practices within the church of spirit. Let us say this once, we are far beyond your imagination, we exist only in the minds of those who would accept our thoughts. Be brave and dominate your thoughts. We welcome a measure of love as you welcome our thoughts. Never commit your mind to a practice of sin.

20th November 2016

Men of the moon

The men of the moon they called us, well that is true! We have a field of interest within that lunar world. You are curious to know what lays on the dark side, some have seen and regretted! We are of a nation who do not practice ill will, but our secrecy is imperative as we observe your planetary system. The dark ones they called us. Really? Who are the dark ones, those who sit back and observe with a tranquil mind or those men of your earth who habitually fight and destroy each other and anything that may come their way? Honestly, we cannot reveal our purpose at this time. Some of your friends know what lies beyond that dark side and they have witnessed many things, activities they will not speak of. They know our feelings; they know our domination can be total.

Have a care of those that will listen and read the lines, for their purpose is dark and they wonder, just what it is, what frequency you use to bring information. They do not believe it can be achieved in thought and in prayer. They are wrong to think that you may have answers to questions of theirs, for you are merely a channel who will receive our thoughts as we issue them. We are not the dark ones. We feel a need to accept your warmth and valour in the things you do.

Gravity will improve the situation in the near future. Have a keen eye and watch the stars, as granted by the Lord and master of the heavens.

BEINGS OF LIGHT

The Transcripts:

6th March 2016

The Spartans Introduce Themselves

Comprehension of our worlds is becoming clear to you. Spartans we are of the universe.

God's creations and wonders are numerous. Memories of those days past when light shone upon the Earth, so brilliant man couldn't look upon it. Knowledge was gained by the few and they mastered the language of love, it has passed from generation to generation before you, but has been lost in recent times. The knowledge has become unclear, the spoken word is not spoken anymore and darkness overshadows your world of light. Together we must go into the dark and breathe new life into the minds of men and so brighten the light of love. Compassion is felt by all on this side.

Spartans we are. In truth there has never been such a time as this when our love and assistance is needed in your world of light. Don't deny us those things we ask for most; your love, tenderness and tolerance. Come before us with an open mind, as a blank book, waiting for the words to be written. In time this book will be filled with new words of the Lord.

Your part my son has begun, your time is nigh to begin the work of the Lord within your heart and life. Focus upon those that assist you on your path, give them your love and tolerance. Their benefit should be clear to you.

In the season of the new life we will come with messages of joy for you to behold and receive with purpose in mind. Conscious we will be of your thoughts and actions. We came before with the same cause and purpose, we rang the bell of truth, no one heard it, no one listened, it was beyond your ears because they were shut.

Our frequency of language may be strange to you at times, but your work is gracious and kind. Your thoughts are many, but you learn to use your mind to focus upon us of the light. Your memories of this (our) world are faded, but your memories of the world of spirit will always be in your heart.

Let in all that will not interfere with what is to be, allow the coming of the Lord, his words of truth will sparkle in your mind. Receive the light so bright. Come before us with your love and tolerance, never expecting, never asking. Forgiveness is assured to all who would follow the light. Your being of creation was the purpose of the Lord; his purpose is beyond imagination and speculation. Divine are his words in love, forgive those who have trespassed against you, come before us with tolerance. Come before us, humble, on your knees and give thanks to the Great One who watches us all with eyes like stars in the sky, always watching, knowing, seeing, hearing, the things of the world. Our star ships are nothing compared to scale of the universe. View us not with fear, but of love.

Your knowledge grows and with it comes joy to your heart, fend off those who would sour your thoughts with the negative words, for we are the ones of the light.

Peter is among us, your question was heard, "How are we connected?"

Do you need the evidence? Are you ready for the answer? **Your spark of life is but one of many, your purpose is strong. Know this, we of spirit are around this Earth, creations we made to bear forth.** Spirit taught you; we have seen the light many eons before. We fought in shame, but we survived and our angel light grew. We now have purpose. Join us in this light of knowledge and love, be scared not of our appearance. Qualities of light; of joy in your hearts. We will come before the dawn of the new day. Question us not of our appearance, but what your hearts need is. Combined, we are each one connected to the other.

James and Peter are of one of the spirit of light. There is no difference; only your minds see a difference, only your hearts know the truth. Confine the minds to the way of spirit; focus your hearts to the need of many. Continue in your work, as is planned by the Great One. Your knowledge grows at a pace that staggers you. Your heart is strong, full of love and grace. Your mind is that of a bowl waiting to be filled with purpose. Permit us to grace your heart with purpose.

The fox is wise, he knows of the hounds that chase him, but still in his terror his wits are about him, he deceives them, avoids them, outwits them. As you will outwit those who would deceive you. Your thoughts, strength of mind, will spark an interest in men; and as the spark hits the dry plains, so will the heat seek and ignite, and the flames will grow and the wind will blow, gentle as a breeze. Slowly but surely, the fire takes hold and the flames grow and spread like the branches of a tree. The olive is a symbol of peace, its oils will fuel the flame of love and temperance, have knowledge that is sacred to us, be not afraid of what is to come. The joy will overcome the terror.

We will teach all unto your world of his name upon the Earth and no longer be part of life. I see the workings of your mind, a message I will give the young: 'To work in the light is something to be treasured.' Do not worry, we'll open their eyes, hearts and minds to their true souls. For you that do not believe in us, darkness will fall.

The wisdom will be granted to those who call upon us to enlighten their lives with peace and hope. Prosper you will, not in money, but in love. The warmth that it brings will overflow and fill your lives with purpose. The gems you treasure are of no consequence, the true gem is your heart, allow this to shine as never before.

Others will see your purpose, and so the chain of love will grow among you. The signals that are given with love of purpose, will fill you with joy in your hearts. But you understand that we of the light are with you in your world of darkness. Come before us in due course with love and tenderness in your heart and rejoice in his name, our Father.

You all were once joined in the love. Your ways and paths are varied. You are naive in many ways. Now I see before me a man with knowledge, with temperance and kind of heart, as he works in our name for his purpose given. He will come to your shores and work with your love in due course. Be not afraid of the words spoken, but rejoice in the knowledge that we are here to save you from yourselves in your world of greed. Allow us to lay his divine love upon you with purpose. Forced is the evil upon you, do not betray your hearts.

We will gather in the clearing to watch your progress, our eyes focused upon you. The messengers, the peacekeepers, come to us with many memories of love. Never doubt our words my son, but be filled with peace in the knowledge that we are here to benefit all in your world.

See your hands for love to be had, live in peace with the knowledge that we are here. We stand before you as guardians of life. Goodness in your heart, strength in your soul, in purpose you giveth a lot unto your purpose of time.

27th November 2016

Transform yourselves this evening as we speak through the mind of this one. We have been heard before, we are a welcoming kind to you creatures of the earth. Prospects are grim as the siege begins, we cannot intercede, nor take part, but we can suggest a purposeful meaning to your thoughts. Be not afraid of what is to come, for all life engages in trials and tribulations. The fact remains that life continues, so fear should not be a thing to be cast out, for it is fear that heightens your senses and brings about a meaningful, purposeful change.

As you squabble among yourselves for the spoils of your earth, you ignore the vastness that exists beyond. Men of fortune would have a hope, the riches to be brought from their explorations will bring benefit to them for their investment, but there is a two-sided purpose. Yes, they will finance and explore the universe in the hope of their own prosperity, but that purpose will also serve another, to enlighten man's minds to the existence of others who bear no ill will nor malice towards the creatures of man. Many benefits can be derived from that exploration, medical advancements, and procurements of minerals to provide sustenance. Your minds are narrow and weak, and nurturing will take much. But the universal aspect of all creatures is growth and advancement, or death. Which will you choose? As men and beings of the earth, there is a vast amount of knowledge at hand should you have the will to accept the hand of friendship from us, those beings of light who care for you with a hope of peace.

A New Spartan Speaker Comes In:

I am a noble being, of a race of beings that will speak to you tonight. My mind is crisp and fragrant with an aspect of love. We beckon you, nay invite you, to the floor of our paths and beyond. We have met once before in the dreams of man where you walked upon that hallowed ground asking for those markers to be moved, so that you might assist in bringing peace and love to your world. We agreed, and as agreed, things have moved on a pace. We wish to inform you that the brotherhood have met once more and have agreed the boundary markers of your lines may be placed a little further to expand your knowledge and wisdom to impart upon those beings of light. Only in your dreams will you see us, for we are that of spirit of an age long gone. We are the Spartans of life and we bring you peace everlasting.

Sometimes the truth cannot be heard for the forest of trees that muffle the sound. Your landscapes become barren as you waste the trees of life within the forests and the great nature reserves of your earth. You are a unique species, to expand your mass and destroy in your wake.

Many species are on the verge of decay as your men of wealth defile the land in the search for precious metals and for the crystals. Those deep blue clear crystals, you see them, "How pretty you say," a sparkler of beauty. At what cost did you purchase that stone of the earth? Or would you rather know its real value, its energy that enables your world to function.

You rape your Mother Earth in your quest for riches, when all the time the riches are within your grasp, within your mind and your will of purpose. Those stones of grey that are cast aside as used shells, of no value within the minds of many, but they have purpose, they are of your Mother Earth and she is in need of them. Your displacement of that precious earth reflects the scars upon the face of your earth. Be blessed in the knowledge that we are the Spartans who will correct and decide what is right, with a purpose of love.

5th December 2016

The Spartans Speak of Other Planets, Mars and UFO Sightings, a Being of Light

Common belief would have you know that men of fame and celebrity are the stars of life. Look to the heavens to see those true stars, the ones that shine brightly in formation, to be seen shortly as the moon passes over the horizon. We come once more to intercede with your men, we are the Spartans of your world. We once blessed you with our light and treasures and guidance. We are not your enemies, we are not your leaders, but you must respect us, for we are of a nation much more advanced than yours.

Your treasured memories of the past have long gone, been forgotten, or ignored. But we will come once more to enlighten your beings as to the truth of the 'spacemen'. Discoveries of furthermost planets will be announced shortly, an indicator gas of life supporting atmosphere. They know; in their wisdom they keep quiet for fear of retribution. They will gain much knowledge through the endeavours of other beings not of your world. They keep silence!

Your men of NASA, those intergalactic pathfinders, are an ignorant lot, they cannot see that if the truth is told then the backlash will be less. Instead they hide their findings of mars under a clause of secrecy, bound by your earth laws. They have discovered many things of past illusions and civilisations. We will be brief, just to say this, watch the skies as the dawn arrows *(spaceships or comets?)* fly in the month of May.

March to your doom, if you do not control your measures of intolerance towards one another, the cities fall, the mighty clash. We need not tell you of our sorrow should you continue on your path. Be as one, be as the brothers, sisters and love one another. Do not allow these empires to construct their own model and system of learning. Be as the bird; as the eagle flies, call out your sounds. Let them hear your voice and swoop on those who are intolerant of your being.

Truth will be heard in years to come, as the bee hums its tune no more, so the flowers of life will succumb. We are impartial to your beings, but nonetheless we observe and take an interest at the outcome. We see there is one to come who will bring hope and purpose to you all, do not be ignorant of him, for he is a being of the light with a measure of love for all. Tremendous amounts of fear will be heard as his name is called, but his purpose is good. Be as the arrow flies, straight and true, we know your path, your cause. Target your emotions; do not let fear obstruct you as you call his name on the winds of time.

Go to your families, your brethren, and rejoice in his name at this time, but remember to bring purpose of peace and love to all as you rejoice and celebrate his being. His name will resound in your ears as the Lord of hosts. Bring peace to yourselves in your worth; respect the judgement of the Lord, amen.

Narrow are your minds of focus, but peace be assured to those of the light as you follow a path of destiny with the hope of love. A spark of kindness to others you meet on their road of life.

I am a being of the light, I bid you all welcome. To harvest your dreams with a measure of love is all that is needed to become one with the light. Your thoughts are varied as you read these lines, "Are these words real?" Rest assured that there is truth in these words and much wisdom to be gained by the thoughts of those who work with the light. A measure of love to you all.

Be not the puppets of the puppet master, but the creators of life and light upon your planet, so special among many. Have faith and trust and above all belief in the things that matter most, that are beyond your vision but are nonetheless in your minds. Blessings to you all, and greetings to those who would read these words anew.

BEINGS OF LIGHT

The Olympians

The twelve great Gods of the Greeks were known as the Olympians.

Together they presided over every aspect of human life.

The Transcripts:

25th August 2016

The caverns and pitfalls of life are many upon your species. Allow us to bring words of comfort and joy to the earthmen of your planet.

I am Zag, a master of speech, who will inform you of many things about your past and your future. Zagreus was my full name, I once lived as a being of life. I had fortitude, strength to help, to issue guidance and love.

I was of Greek mythology, you see me now my son, as a gentleman of white robes, a white beard, slightly balding but white hair.

I was a noble among men. They climbed the steps to my sanctuary to listen to my words of wisdom, to bring them joy and comfort in their meagre lives. I had countless battles with those of ignorance, but they report to an aspect of light and life. They followed with great joy and love. We were a noble nation, never knowing the gratitude of the countless many.

We were swamped by men of war. Oh the Trojan horse, was a mythological animal which brought chaos. But I am a scholar, a man of determination and learning. Feel me as I sit on my seat overlooking the Pantheon, ruling over my subjects as a master light.

I brought from the seas the food of wisdom, I spoke to Athena and the goddess of love *(Aphrodite),* her name is strange to you, believe me as I pass on the frequencies of my thought, trouble your mind not with the anxieties of life. My teaching was great of life and of those who are new to us, they were real, they existed.

Greek mythology had cast doubt upon the possibilities, but know this, there are many mythological creatures that exist in our day. They are extinct, kept alive only in the memories of those minds that would read the words of the Greek prophets. Only you yourselves destroy your natural world with careless thought, species go extinct and you are not aware.

Let me, the son of Zeus, explain the wisdom of the lives that you are given. Do not manufacture lies of lives and discontent, I said lives and I truly meant that. We watch in despair as you mess with your natural being. We were are a gentle people. Daily prayer, a meeting would be held to discuss the terms by which we would live, councils you would call them.

Ah your tongue does not permit you our thoughts.

Our fears were realised as we tumbled into the seas, as she shook the ground beneath our feet. There are massive disturbances at this time, you must hold fast; many will perish as she trembles. Your existence is a weak one. Tread the waters of life with dignity, do not count the time by the minutes of the day but by the actions of life and love that you bring to others, for this is the true meaning of time.

Nobles we were, nobles we are, we are the Greek gods of Olympia.

(Note: Zagreus is also known as Dionysus, one of the twelve Olympians: The Olympians were a race of deities, primarily consisting of a third and fourth generation of immortal beings, worshipped as the principal gods of the Greek pantheon and so named because of their residency atop Mount Olympus.)

BEINGS OF LIGHT

The Arcturians

Edgar Cayce has said in his teachings that Arcturus is one of the most advanced civilizations in this galaxy. In his channelled messages he tells us that it is the fifth-dimensional civilization that is a prototype of Earth's future. Its energy works as an emotional, mental, and spiritual healer for humanity. It is also an energy gateway through which humans pass during death and rebirth. It functions as a way station for nonphysical consciousness to become accustomed to physicality.

The Transcripts:

19th April 2016

You speak of peace, love and honour for the righteous path, which you walk to fulfil your purpose before the life of man. Complex *(are)* your thoughts to the outrageous memories of those of ill will. Their path is in the dark to their end. They will march as blind men, never seeing the light, never knowing the love that shines within. God radiates in all men who walk the Earth, for he is a part of each and every man upon the earth.

We neglected to speak of other memories of the past before you, let us begin the evening with worship to the God of the light in the heavens. Many times we have spoken through men of the Earth to warn of the dangers of times to come, never heeding the words that are sent, for his biological path overrules his mind then it fades within. Awaken your light with love, honour, and respect.

Go to your tasks knowing that we are of the world beyond yours, our masters by which your world was formed millennia ago. Continue as if existence of man is guaranteed for the purpose intended, but those of ill will, will suffer nine times before they are freed to the gates of heaven. Let us not interfere with the everyday path that you lead. Negotiate your life in a manner befitting of the Lord, with love honour and respect for your fellow man.

Paths that intertwine in the years to come are roads that lead to that one place where purpose began. The love in your heart will guide you as a compass on a map. Your thoughts of mind argue with the context of what is said, but rest assured that the words have meaning beyond your understanding.

Commencement of the Arcturian's will begin in the August; you will notice a darkening of the skies as we commence our burden upon you. We cannot say how many will live or die, but rest assured those of the light will enter a new era of love and light from which the purpose of divine inspiration will spring. Neglect not the pattern of your life, for it is humble and unique to you, as each individual is unique to himself, but intertwined are your paths of righteousness. Your concepts of Mother Earth are fake; your knowledge increases with the passage of time to which our respect is given.

Commencement of your work will begin shortly as you inspire others to look upon you as a teacher. Needless to say, we will escort you on your path of life. Will you force those who would in turn inspire you as to the correct guidance required?

We spoke of men who topple in the fall, their lives are filled with happiness and joy of the material things of the Earth, but they are empty inside. Their souls have deserted their hearts purpose. They are blessed with ignorance by those of another world; whose dubious methods should not be seen by the light.

Nigeria will fall into darkness as the rush for gold commences, man will eat man in his desperation to become rich, but what use is that to their souls when they pass from this world of flesh, huh they are ridiculous men. Dishonour; disconnect yourself, for these trivial things of your Earth. Come with us on a journey so spectacular that it will astound you beyond your mind's imagination, increased tenfold will be your knowledge.

As to our whereabouts, that is to remain anonymous at this time, for there are those who would shoot first and ask later. Their black hearts will not accept a dominant species to rule in their place upon this Earth, but they are inferior to what we can achieve, for they are like locusts of the Earth feeding off the rich fertile soil without a care, with a ferocious appetite that never ceases, for the love and hunger for the riches, huh, what careless men are they to desert their souls in favour of materialistic things.

Speaking here tonight we are compelled to initiate thoughts to your mind of focus, it takes concentration, appetites are fed through knowledge, you will receive tenfold.

Our purpose will initiate a sequence of events starting with a magnitude four earthquake within the region of Essex. There will be a jolt so profound that the cosmos will act in accordance to the ringing sound that is projected by the vibration. Protected you are of these things from negative thoughts and comments, be precise in your words, accuracy is vital in the coming days.

Heresy, conflict is assured as the escalation mounts. Panic will envelop the minds of all, at the prospect of a supersonic event cascading down on you from the heavens above. Fearless you need be to ride out the storm. Your friends will survive as you all band together to ease the tensions of people's minds, through the knowledge that the Lord above and a host of ghosts will be with you, helping to ensure that the passing of the many to the light will be fruitful of love.

Connect with us your feelings so that we may temper our responses, don't be negative in your aspects of speech, be gentle, caress the words, so that the meaning is clear but without fear.

Target your emotions for the time to come when all men will see the reality of life, you will work with the minds of the many with thought and feelings of despair, this is not your purpose, give strength to those who need it, caress your words, once more be gentle with the minds who's aspects cannot comprehend an end to being.

Commodus respects your wishes, his expressive love and compassion is upon you. Neglect not your thoughts of wisdom and love; transfer your mind's eye to our origin, taking messages of love to the masses in your world of flesh. Neglect us not in the coming days when your minds aspects will be observant of the skies above, Nigeria is a focal point of our being.

It comes as no surprise to us that your mind is a little vague, for as the vessel is empty so shall it be filled with purpose of heart, Commodus wishes to thank all those that work alongside you, his grateful wishes go out to them with peace and love. *(Note: Commodus seems to work alongside the Arcturians.)*

Continuance of mind and focus is essential for the beings of your planet. Your mind is a tool and has many depths beyond that of your sight. They think they know the whereabouts of your purpose, how can they, for you are spirit.

As for the rest of your world we will task them to open their eyes to the prospect of what is to come before the months ahead are completed. Nevertheless we are sad of the news we bring, as it is no easy task to be a leader of men. Painful duties must be performed to gain respect and honour, to lead them on a path of light, to tell them of the stories of eons past, where men worshipped idols of logs and stone. Their aspirations were of the ones of the light that bathed them with gifts of knowledge. Consideration was given to their status, as they were murderers with evil intent, not knowing the graceful beings of the light. We astounded them with miracles before their eyes. They could not grasp nor understand our purpose or being, they saw us as gods, as our light shone.

Continuance of our ways was as we wrote it, by love, hence the name Arcturian. *(Note: Arcturus is known as the*

'Guardian of the Bear' the constellation of the Great Bear. In mythology is even said to be linked to the story of King Arthur.)

Before your time is done my son, doubtless you will know the meaning of love and the respect of the many, comparatively you are of the light, as to those of the dark.

Never regret your purpose at hand. As painful as it may be for those to hear the truths and the words of spirit, beyond which their comprehension is unable to grasp. Movement of their minds will dictate their actions on this Earth and we will not abandon those of the light, their hearts are strong with the love.

Commencements of our actions have begun on your world of matter, we are the many who ascertain your life's functions, and compliance with us will be met with gratitude and love. Respect and honour are all that we ask of man. Matters at hand will be resolved with new vigour upon your Earth of matter. Now we hear of the many that perish as they fight for their lives in the waters of the Mediterranean, compelled are they to seek out a new life pattern, so that they may find happiness for their families without war and degradation inflicted by others, who see themselves as the rulers of Earth. Their time will come in a cascade of almighty storms culminating in their extinction.

Please do not attempt to focus on those of the dark, for they are unworthy of your light. You question your manner before the many, rest assured we guide your path. What if the seasons were of joy and fellowship of man, wouldn't that exercise the demons of the light? Wouldn't that enlighten others to join you in the joy of love and respect in the Forests of Dean?

Commencement of the knowledge will begin with the season's dawn; a miracle of life will transform your mind beyond that of which it exists. Extreme measures are needed to coax those from the dark and into the light, we regret such actions but it necessitates to bring focus to those who are conscious of our existence beyond your atmosphere.

They watch with curious eyes, hearing signals, seeing flashes in the night sky. They will not commit to our obedience as we descend upon their air force. Focus your thoughts on the star ship; its breadth and width are as long as a vineyard! With vines reaching out, ever stretching the boundaries by which they are tied.

Commencement of our actions will shortly begin with measures far beyond your understanding. Tolerance of the many will be frayed; their ignorance will compel them to fire at us, their weapons insecure in the hands of the unwise. We will establish contact, negotiate a truce to bring peace, but if they insist upon action, then that will be given in equal measure upon them, grasp for fear that we have an unfriendly welcome, as we only mean respect and love, peace and tolerance. *(Note: Information from The Swansea UFO Network – 'The Pentrych Incident' near to the Forest of Dean on 26th February 2016 – There were multiple witnesses of a huge UFO and other lights. Military planes and helicopters, a chase, explosions, physical effects such as shaken buildings, damaged trees and wreckage on the ground.)*

The pyramids are a vital source of energy through which we brought purpose to those of years past, their shape suggests a point in the heavens from where enlightenment will be born, comprehensive measures in actions taken upon those who fought us, never gained them favour.

Tomorrow's another day by which you will be in deeper thought, as to your actions to enhance your being of light upon those with closed eyes and minds. Be not afraid of the judgement set against you, for that is insignificant compared to the light that you can bring for others.

Raymond, he wishes for a few words of encouragement before you this evening, take heart as he reaches out his mind. Gracious are we of the light, of the ignorant upon your earth, and a nurse to you. Intercede with those who wish for peace and love within their atmosphere. Jesus was a man of great tolerance, peace and love; his purpose was fulfilled to bring love and understanding to all men of the Earth. His being has been venerated and rejoiced throughout time, his practice of worship was unique to those of his time and he demonstrated his love in passion for the Lord, in truth, honesty, and in actions of wisdom. They held him in contempt, for their ways were of the dark, they neglected to see the light that shone from his heart, of his thoughts and words. Their actions were regrettable and he suffered for the love of God, that man would continue in a righteous manner befitting that of the Lord. Alas time has changed the thinking of man. Once man was an obedient servant of the Lord and now he is like a naughty schoolchild that needs to be reined in and punished for his behaviour upon Mother Earth.

Never forget thou art with you in your mind and your thoughts, your actions and your deeds, for it is all recorded in time and space. Consequently we will reflect upon your actions and in accordance with his law, we will need to rectify your manner with time spent with purpose. Communicate your wishes to those upon high that you are a child of the earth with focus upon the Divine, comprehension of the ways of the Lord should be universal on the minds and thoughts of all, the many ways in which you worship are numerous, but all to one end for his love.

Commentaries upon your actions neglected; speaking today we are encouraged. Commence work on your words of wisdom and light, their truth will be tested in time, their actions, focus on them as they school you in the wisdom they impart upon you. Treasures they have of mind, their thoughts and actions are connected with that of the past, their focus will increase as time goes on.

Kevin and Valerie are old souls that have been brought together by passion of the heart, they were neglected, unwelcome. Today they see the true purpose of their lives, to focus for others in their learning upon their journeys of life. Their kind hearts extend a warm welcome to all that reach out to them for their purpose, it is in their manner and actions of love. Turbulent times ahead will initiate a beginning for them to focus their hearts and minds on the issues of man. The continuance of their mission will astound many minds, their structure is strong, for their passion is an urge too much to resist. Concentrate your mind upon their purpose and their love, to enable yours to continue with purpose and in a manner respectful of their being. Tremendous actions will be required by your association with their thoughts, bearing down on you is our purpose of light, be strong, faithful, let us commence.

Focus upon the arrowheads sharpened point, the tip that penetrates the hearts and minds of man. As with the arrow there is a point of entry, which is finite in its size, but as it penetrates so it widens the wound to enable its purpose of penetration. Contrary to your thoughts, it is symbolic of how we are able to penetrate the minds of those who wish to focus on us. It starts as a thought, that thought then grows, opening a wound to allow the light in, ever increasing the knowledge to be penetrated. Never forget our words, for we are here with purpose and light for your world.

Biological tests are taken by those of science to ascertain a life cycle of his being, how can they comprehend his being of love as being that of the physical, for he was of the light of the Lord. His brilliance shone to the men of his time to teach them to honour and respect one another. Again, he will come once more to your planet, to welcome those who would follow his light and love.

Watch out for the birth in the August of your seasons, for it will coincide with a cleansing of matter, for who can work with soiled material? Before you cut the cloth you must clean it.

You weave your own patterns of life with a complexity beyond that of your understanding, each weave has its own pattern which reflects the personality of that soul, it can be read by those of the light who study its pattern and form, knowing of its meaning and of its purpose. The cloth of Jesus was complex, he was the ultimate precursor of love and light, he came forth to shine his light upon those who wove their patterns of life with errors, he showed them how to perform their duties. But their ignorance betrayed them as they herded him like a dog in the streets before his master, of those times. He knew they were nothing, for his master was his father, the Lord in heaven. They transported many on his path, his time was narrow and short, but he had lived a life of magnitude that was unseen before.

Do not despair as we now leave you with the thoughts, but be assured of the unity of your plan to life as it unfolds with magnitude and purpose, never forget our words and promises to you and all upon the face of the earth that the light will reign supreme.

King Charles's reign will commence shortly, for a short time. Behold he who comes will sit on the throne of light, the master of all. Be respectful of him; target your emotions of love, for it will be great. Negotiate the pitfalls before you and return soon for his sake so that he may guide your steps on the road of love for humanity for theirs has a purpose of being. Establish your notes.

My respect for you is absolute, my love and encouragement for your words is also absolute, allow me to be your servant upon this Earth guiding my steps and words to help those in need of understanding of the complexities of life. Judas misunderstood his purpose, for he was a man filled with greed of life, he neglected his ways to become a priest of betrayal, he knew in his mind that he was different, but in the hope of change he could not resist the riches of those commanders. It was his downfall, don't let it be yours, enrich your life with love, compassion and a will to change man's desires.

26th April 2016

How can we express our concern for your times, we need your power as the flower needs rain, we care for all upon the Earth, man and beast, down to the infinitesimal smallest particle of dust? For you will all return to dust to form a layer of beauty on Mother Earth. You think your time is done when your body releases its final breath, know this, that we will guide those of the light into the valleys of love where streams and rivers run deep with knowledge and wisdom of ages past.

The power of God sits within you all of matter. Jesus became a wonder of many nations, His progress of life was followed by a few of the time but He knew His stature would grow to form a pillar that could not be broken, for He was the Messiah, given to the people of the Earth to lead them from their own destruction.

Sadly we see a similarity today whereby people are being misled and confused by those of greed, they are unjust in their intent for they think their masters are those who command the pockets of money. How wrong can they be, why do they not see the lessons taught? How we despair to see those in the dark who are lost upon a road to nowhere, for your focus is to guide their minds to the trees and the stars above and give them the opportunity to reach out and grasp that precious light of love.

Knowingly we admire the many who work on behalf of the light for they generate energy that must surely bring about peace. In good time you will measure life of purpose and knowing, the knowledge gained was a benefit for all, follow these words, target those minds of ignorance to light up their paths in ways of wisdom, their journeys to focus upon the words that are sent from the heavens and stars.

Now gather your people, your tribe, to bond those of the Earth and no matter how they see us, we can win in the battle of love. Your torment of days past will fade into insignificance as you follow the light of the Lord. Blessings be upon you and all who whisper His words in love and peace. Tremendous amounts of energy are given to those of need; their worries and concerns are heard in the cosmos of life.

Patterns of knowledge will grow to renew you as you talk of these things that are to come. Concern yourself not with the physical; be aware of our knowledge and our presence.

Today the Master of Love, he comes before you to ask of your minds to transmit your love and purpose, so that He may issue you all His blessings. Commence your tasks, go out, feel the need for those around you, bringing them peace and contentment in the readings you give and the healing you send in His name. Honour among you should be paramount, for guidance is needed for some who see an opportunity to mislead those for gain. Their practice is deplorable; they work in many ways around your planet only concerning themselves with the riches and pleasures of life, not knowing that they damage their souls.

Consequently we have purpose for you, feel our need and gratitude for time spent, the music will fill their ears with compassion and love. See before you a crystal, a teardrop of His mansion.

Now you are among us with thought, rally with us to the hearts of men of science, the intolerance masks the truth of their heart's purpose, they created a world of ugliness with their machines that defile the minds of the young. They credit themselves as being masters of their trade, their tools, their wisdom misguided, for now there is but darkness in the minds of the young who cannot see the beauty of the light, for it is shielded from them by the masters of the teachers, for fear of abusing their minds with knowledge of other states, their methods.

Command your heart and soul to listen to the words in your thoughts and dreams and fill your hearts with vigour, for we are of the light. The chariots of fire have burned in your hearts and minds, *(they)* are that of our Lord our Father who art in heaven. The challenges you face in your world of poverty and greed, delegation, derogation, neglect unfolds the chapter beyond which your mind cannot comprehend and their fatal moves will decree a time for wisdom to enter their minds.

Biological studies are made of us in your testing grounds beneath the earth. You harbour weapons of mass destruction, their barrels raised, poised on the brink, you are unaware of the times to come when man will need those of the light to bring justice upon those who would terrorise the peoples of the world. Commonwealths will plunder the riches of the world, their ignorance is astounding, tell your people we are of the light with focus upon your hearts, contrary to what you think we strive for your planet to remain calm, indignation is widespread among your people, atrocities committed by those of the black hats. For their ignorance and hate cause panic among the peoples of your world, but they are simple minds led astray by the influences of those of wealth, their hearts and minds believe that their purpose is good, but the truth is false to them. Nationalities will figure greatly as the Earth comes together to focus upon those who disrupt the lives of the many compelling them to act in an aggressive manner on those who obscure the light.

Your hearts and minds are weak but together there is strength of purpose, fragments of the love will demonstrate your purpose as your need grows to help those of the world. With these words and messages of peace they will understand that the words are intense, but they are meaningful, for those who would listen. Contribute your mind to our purpose my son, neglect not your duties as a man to bring peace to your people. Your path is a road of many which will culminate in a purpose so profound it will be seen as a marker for all those to follow, our guidance is assured, the keepers of the message will understand their purpose, fragments of information are given before you so as not to alarm the masses, the purpose is a profound one of love, not hate, guide your thoughts to the memories of love and know there is peace in the light for all who seek it out.

The kestrel that flies across the skies seeking its prey only does so to survive, its wing feathers guide it to its purpose. For all in many ways, allow your wings to spread in a manner with purpose, harden your heart to your prey in the happiness of man, the inspiration for those in the negative. Commence your practice with a song of love for His namesake; convince your heart for purpose within, your victories will be many in the hearts of men.

1st May 2016

Cuckoo's Nest, False Prophets, Contemporary Art, Forest of Dean, The Middle East, Tripoli, Mother Teresa, WMD (Weapons of Mass Destruction)

Cuckoo's in the nest, with promises of love and reassurance to those who would listen to their arguments. You are concerned with the attitude of those who organise functions in their name, for they are wicked, and will compromise your world with shame and bitter disappointment.

Targeted are you where there is mayhem and destruction, for they see your light as it shines through the dark of life. Never forget my son that we're here to comfort and bring purpose to your mind. For flowers of love will spring once more in the autumn, for yours is a gift of love. Compromise not your heart for the minuscule scrapes given by those in power, justify your words with promises of vision and focus.

We cannot express our concerns to your world because of false prophets, who in the name of our Father, declare themselves fit for the purpose. They know who they are, they see many things before the world, and they neglect to share the light amongst those with purpose and need.

Your gift is to make those aware of the injustices and the harm caused by their actions of deceit. All of you have never understood the Almighty's purpose when your eyes were shut; open your hearts and minds to those upon the world of light.

Words will be given for the express intent to allow you to explore your minds and your logic.

Contemporary art has its figures in the establishment of life. Knowles was a Master of Science; his art was that of a pianist. As he hits the notes in the right key and pitch, his sound is of sweet music to the ears. A view that progression never ceases.

We all evolve in matter and time; conditionally we assume that promise of a new start within your world. Negotiations have begun and the **Forests of Dean,** will become significant as a meeting place for those other beings of the universe.

Their hearts sank when they heard of the mischievous, deceitful ones that had lured them without an interest in the purpose of love.

Your capable mind is not aware, that deposited in you is a core of matter yet to be discovered by man. It has the power and energy of the light held within it, for it has become a symbol of humanity to dispel creatures of the night. Within its magic it is possible to retain all our knowledge and knowing.

Evict the thoughts of leadership, but focus more on the Divine, bringing massive attention to those who seek the knowledge of the 'Ones of the Light'.

Consummate your practice with us in words of comfort and belonging, for we are the 'Immaculate Ones' who aspire to teach the Earth of the errors of their ways. Frequently we have come to pass these messages upon your Earth, your goals will be magnified by your actions and may supersede any thoughts of love. Comparatively we seek love within the hearts and souls of the many.

Initially there will be a burst of light that will flash across the skies in the Southern Hemisphere; this light will ignite in the memories and the minds of man, and his wisdom and his pride for his belonging within this atmosphere.

Accelerated time, you must evolve to reconcile differences with Mother Earth. Brought by nature is the storm of mercy that will cleanse her back of the irritation of man.

A camel will bare its teeth, snarl for their lack of understanding. What have you to say that matters most to those with ears who would listen? Do you not feel their minds ache, the words of inspiration, kindness, tranquillity? For they seek as you do, for the peace and love of our Lord. Negotiate your mind with the issues of life and delegate those with purpose to push your ideas beyond the boundaries of thought.

Comprehensive abilities you have. Combined, use them for their purpose as intended by Him.

They travel around your Earth, once before as we have mentioned. We had purpose once upon your earth. We seeded the populations of those creatures who walked upright. Hand in hand we have guided you through many storms in the many seasons, but still your mindset is full of distraction and greed. How can we ignore the outcry of the many that suffer?

You cannot comprehend the sadness we feel to see man and machine blazing the trail of disaster in your world.

Governments will fall within a relatively short amount of time, the reasons being one of many, a path for us.

Calcutta she was from, Bombay, the sweetness of the Rose. She knew that disregard for the love of his people will bring about a war of many nations to your planet. Commence your arguments for peace; go beyond the barrier of your mind, search out his vital words to be read by members of an elite circle.

Commodus wishes to speak as a soldier, "I was born to fend off the enemy of my family, I see before you a vast wilderness which will lead you to your purpose in the common good of man. Containment of your weapons have been compromised by those who would seek to destroy your Earth in a manner befitting the fires of hell."

5th May 2016

Comets, Pythagoras The Immaculate Ones, Thomas Parker, Marcus Aurelius, Yellow Lily, UFO's

Who 'ere will test men and serve is worthy and acquired to serve the purpose of the Lord? His patience is tested on a daily basis. Communicating His will is an extreme measure to grab the attention, and protesting are your people.

Transform your minds into a place of worship, allowing His need to enter and wash your minds clean before you die. You must access your life from this planet Earth. Be knowledgeable in His ways and understanding as He reaches out to those with purpose.

The comet 'Hercules' was a masterful sign given in days past when man was born free. His past times were that of love, an existence all too soon vanished on its path. *(Note: Hercules is a solar system, this is from Wikipedia: "They would approach the Solar System with random velocities, mostly from the region of the constellation Hercules because the Solar System is moving in that direction".)*

Pythagoras was a master of his trade, for he knew that the sun would evolve, transform his flesh. His knowledge of the sun was limited to what he could see, he had no knowledge of the technical aspects of its make-up, all he knew was of the existence and that it gave all life upon men and creatures of the Earth.

Never before have we had to intervene in that which must be man's decision.

Commodus enters the Kingdom of Heaven with a mindset of love, his mission is one of many to bring comfort and peace to men of the Earth.

Our flagships stagger in the night, waver horizontally on the path of those negative aspects forcing them below.

Treasured are your memories of times past, your existence is short, one of few days in the scale of time; in that time where needs are great to understand your progress in this place of the heavens. Regrets there are, but they form the basis of your being for you.

As the clean sheet, continue your journey, for your mission is great. Bringing of our words, as they are just *(fair)* words. The truth is in me, she awaits your call of love to begin a journey so profound, that many will be upon her. Frontiers that you reach, journeys you will make with love, to bring the news of spirit to those who would listen in their time, in the presence of love of the Almighty.

The Immaculate Ones will bring peace and solidarity to your planet in due course. There must come a time when all of man must be aware that his presence is just a gift, his being is that of the Almighty.

Parker responded with love with metal in his veins, he created circumstances, which blew him to the far-flung places of your Earth, he metered out measurements of time before continuing on into their dusk of the night, 1876. He was a man of no means; his name was rich among those who tested his metal with words to breech his mind of focus. *(Note: The Parker Solar probe came to mind, but the date is wrong. We would love to know if anyone might guess who this is.)*

Compel us not to respond in a manner that is not befitting that of the Lord, for we mean no harm for those upon the Earth. Our wishes are for contentment of a preacher. We join you as a group of beings to divulge our purpose unto you. Our matters are of the greatest concern, as we fear through your existence for your Earth, she is unhappy with all who mistreat her, she cannot bear the pressures put upon her, she is exhausted by the many who drain her dry. Can't you see the damage done? She is fragile as a child; she cannot bear the pressure of the extreme measures placed upon her. Her heart beats as a drum to time, she cannot understand the purpose of your lives, she has not the will to penetrate the minds of the masses, characteristics of men of purpose should be noted by their good will and humour. For lacking understanding is not helping to bring about peace within yourself. Focus, concern yourself bound in your memories of past lives, as this life has meaning of a magnitude.

Why can't we propagate our minds and will to those of the power, they are as blind as bats. Conceited to their purpose they caress the cash as a man caresses a baby, they fail to understand the meaning and purpose of his morals. For it is not to be shared with those of means but to be metered out to those in need and true purpose.

Commodus comes with a tale of epic proportions. Listen to his words: "Cities crumbled before us as we swept through with no mercy upon those inhabitants. Those times of marauding were terrible, for I was a part of man who would desire and lust, failing to see my path as it was written. I served many upon the Earth, as a gimmick to be seen, the trophy to be had, I was the man; I'm ashamed by the beast to be beaten. I was fair with those that came to me for assistance; they gave me hard, extreme punishments for the error of my ways. The pain, the sorrow cannot be taken from my heart as it aches to warn others to stop the misery, before it is too late."

Focus your mind, focus upon the continuance of your journey, allowing those questions to be answered by us in far flung places upon your Earth, temper your actions and your hearts restrain, for all will come at the time necessary to begin each phase of the journey. It will be hard to face the truth, but *(it is)* necessary to scourge the evil from your Earth.

Aspire to us in the many ways of the colours purple.

Gratitude, compromise, compassion, all words. Actions speak louder than words. Combine your interests to compel the actions within words.

Marcus Aurelius was once a prince among men, he stood for all time as a noble man. His problem was his virility, he was fruitful in the labours of love, but his knowledge was weak for that which mattered most. Do you not rule the nations of many in your heart of pain? Was he not a great man of theology? His purpose was metered out in measures.

Twilight came before the dusk, for she who rules will rest in peace before the moon rises twice in the skies of Aquarius. Panic and mayhem will reflect across the nations of the globe for she is a woman, a soul to cling to for many, control your emotions and thoughts as we enter, problematic situations arise *(and)* before this time is done you will have emitted a purpose in many. His response will be limited to your minds and thoughts, he will warm unto the words as they melt his heart to stay for he too must pass before the Lord in the morning light.

Two others will come before you my son, their purpose is to travel with you on a road of light, compel your heart to listen and understand the meaning that they represent, for us time is but a passage to be travelled, for once you have been a part of that moment, it will not return.

18th May 2016

Masquerades of people in power who don't understand the needs of the nations of the Earth, they protect false prophets as they clamour for the spoils of the Earth. Their purposes and need are of the dark, their will is strong, and ramifications will be felt by them throughout the world.

Peace will come to the hearts of those who would listen to the words of the elders of the light. We are the ones to vanquish the evil of corruption that sit in the seats of power within your nations. Consequently we aspire to reach your men of wisdom, for knowing *(that)* their knowledge will fill the hearts of man with the blessings of the Lord. Through eternal strife man will find peace.

Man's heart is open to many influences of the negative, he must control his emotions in times of pressure, as the Fahrenheit *(temperature)* rises in the east, to the west, temperaments will grow and reach a point of no return. To us this is not a situation that we will tolerate, come with us now for a journey of love, speak your mind to those who would listen to sense and who have purpose in their lives, that is to say they follow the light with need and joy, knowing that prospects of new beginnings will bring peace amongst your peoples of the Earth.

Control your emotions as we speak through you, allow us to shine our light, our voice through you, for matters of great concern are upon you. They need attention of the utmost urgency; for they will illuminate man's hearts and desire with a passion of astounding grace. Comparatively your heart needs to be strong to bear the brunt of the situation that rises in the east before the dawn breaks of the new day.

Easter *(or could it just be east?)* will become the centre of attention for all those of the scientific communities, we have studied these matters with great urgency.

Commonwealth games *(Note: The Olympics?)* to be announced shortly will tarnish the reputation of those of the red, for they can see no wrong in their manner for they are just games. Their meaning is twofold, to bring together nations in unity and to dispel the fears of what is to come before you.

May and June are seasons of the sun, intense radiation will increase tenfold, your minds will fear these things, as you don't understand their purpose and meaning. *(Note: This puzzles us a little, it could mean several things, naturally we have more sun so solar radiation is increased in the summer, maybe our ozone layer is thinner than we believe? It could be localised?)*

We are shielded in the cities. *(Note: We are not sure if this sentence is connected with the paragraph before or this following one – we could be shielded from the sun in the city or could our star friends be amongst us unnoticed in the crowds?)*

With tolerance and forbearance the shame that is set before us cannot be unanswered. Let them know that we Arcturians are the creators of a race of beings that inhabit your Earth, that we have dissatisfaction in the wonders of man's creation as we tolerate no evil, how can we express our anger at those who tell us of love, yet the anger that they display towards fellow men.

Our nerves are shattered by the news of the masquerade as it blasts out his music. *(Note: We wonder if the last sentence is relevant to the rallies of a presidential candidate?)* Common knowledge dictates that all men are equal in the eyes of the Lord and so it is, but intolerance against others will not be permitted, how can it be that man has not learnt to live as one, in peace, harmony and with gentleness of mind.

Our thoughts go out to those of the communities who suffer greatly at this time, never understanding why their purpose is of sacrifice, their hearts cry out for the simple things of life, their need is great to carry their burden with pride. The president *(Obama?)* he hears their voices but is rendered powerless by congress to act in a manner befitting his nature.

He has become a man who sits now for invalid reasons, his purpose was lost in the rush for gold, his nation suffers defeat now from the men of money who have swamped the cities.

We came at an hour of need; our frustrations are felt with the shockwaves that were seen in the skies.

Warnings were given not to interfere with those of peace, but they have been ignored, why is it that man takes it upon himself to think that he is the creator, for he is nothing, his purpose was that of the immaculate. As men lust for more, their soul's purpose and intention are lost to them, their hearts are filled with need for the material things, their aspects of love are distorted by extremism.

Congress will announce their intention to impeach the one who sits upon the throne in the near future, for he will not allow their actions to deny him his right or his will, for he will lash out before them in a manner disrespectful of the Lord. *(Note: Could this refer to a new American President?)*

Combine your thoughts and your purpose to take the messages of the Arcturians to the people, the masses of your planet, for she who stands before you as the Mary Mother. Her need is of love as that of a mother for her child, she cannot stand to bear witness to the sacrifice of men, for she knew a sacrifice.

The mysteries of life are the events of which only God knows, for the purpose of his creation upon your planet, we are here to defend His right and His will amongst your people, his course of action will assume authority before those who relinquish their arms to the many, for he is the master of all.

'Penny for your thoughts' is a phrase of interest, strange how it seems that we baffle those minds of science for we are of the natural world beyond yours, combine our strength to enhance your will.

Elegance of the elite will soon be tarnished as money collapses in the regions of wealth. They will scramble for their pittance in the hope that some will be saved. They brought this upon themselves, in the end they will forfeit their right to their position of need and wealth. Cursed are the people who tread upon those less fortunate of your world, for they are the meek who'll inhabit the dwellings of those who mistreat them. We fear they will carry out their intent upon being heard among the nations of the world, their extremism will shock many but their purpose is of good, they just want to be heard, like a dog in the street howling for attention, they will sound off their music to those minds of men of money and power.

Negotiate your mind for a meaningful purpose of love and accept that we of Arcturia will stand behind you as we watch your power grow. We anticipate a new beginning will be upon you all with meaningful purpose.

Focus on the Divine, contribute your minds power and energy to matters at hand so that we may transmit the words of faith, for He who sacrificed his life for the many will return in a gust of wind. He will not tolerate man's self-destruction, you will know him for His mind will penetrate the thoughts of many, know His need is of simple things for He is sustained by your love of the many that follow the light.

Cast your mind back to when you were young, in those days of dizziness, your obscurity was a purposeful thing, for we are content for you know that you are still that child of the times past. You have figured a reason, your purpose, it is now to go forward and take it to those who would listen and obey the word of the Lord by your command, for you are a part of the eternal universe, as all men are a part of that great machine that brings life and love in a meaningful purpose to the nations, the many nations of the worlds, of the galaxy's and beyond. Your insistence upon work is good. We appreciate the things that obstruct you, the narrowing *(focusing)* of your mind will unleash a transmission of enormous possibilities, compel us not, for we are the birds that will bring life to your souls.

We need not tell you of our concerns for we see many things in the past and the future. We aren't dependent upon your existence, but we cherish all forms of life with potential.

Encompass your mind to being strong, of will and the need of purpose.

We are a complicated race of many that exist in and around your world, and the reasons that we are not seen, is because we masquerade in many forms. Completion of our master's mission is our purpose, our goal is not to harm, but to bring mercy and gentleness to temper the extremism of your world. Man is an animal of the universe who needs to master his creations before they master him.

Complicated matters, intriguing designs.

Desires for peace will bring a multitude of people together in the common cause of the love of man. They cannot permit the minority of the nations to overrule the majority.

Configurations of access to astounding places will be found in the jungles of your earth. Man's desire for peace will grow, as these discoveries will announce us as beings. *(Note: Is this possibly about 15-year-old William Gadoury from Canada, who correlated more than 20 constellations against a map of known Maya Cities? The cities lined up with the star map with the exception of a missing settlement.)*

You cannot stop the progression of time, for time is a law unto itself giving its need to its purpose. Your souls are a part of the universe of matter, you think they are strange, but spirit is the creation of God's great plan. Unique is your species which inhabits your Earth, with much need to transform your minds for they are weak with desire, allow the meek to inhabit your minds and understand their concerns.

Matters at hand will help to bring about relief columns sent to far off places of urgent need. A respite, it will take an enormous amount of energy and will to bring about a peace of meaningful proportions so that an entrance is created of love. *(Note: At the time of this message being channelled the BBC News is reporting about aid convoys into Syrian cities.)*

Uniformity of man is the desire of the beings of the light, never neglect your responsibilities to others who are less fortunate than yourselves for their desires are as great as yours,

but their loss is their inability to break the chains of persecution set against them by the nations of the wealthy. What do they have to give, their issues are of little importance to those who sit in power in the west and east, their minds will not be heard for fear that they may learn of the oppression that is set against them? Consider this as part and parcel of love, as forgiveness and tolerance are all equal in the eyes of the Lord.

Magnify your conscious mind, devote and allow us to control your thoughts in a manner respectful of love and goodwill. Target your ambitions and fix your eyes upon the goals to be achieved, for natural selection will assist in man's desires for peace. Who are we to tell you of these things, we will not interfere directly at this time for it is the creators rule that man should evolve in his time?

Regrets are heard of those out of control, spiralling, tumbling as they fall unaided into the seas. They were not alone in their hour of need for the blow was cushioned by a pillow of love. Common knowledge have men of corruption who have caused this disaster, it was a fault of man's technology. Hidden from view, expense was a concern and it was thought practicable as the chances were low. The engineers knew of the design fault and neglected to fix those essential things, ailerons. (*Note: Could this refer to flight MS804? Quote from New York Times, 19th May 2016: Suddenly the twin-engine jetliner jerked hard to the left, then hard to the right, circled and plunged 28,000 feet, disappearing from the radar screens of Greek and Egyptian air traffic controllers.*)

Their masters will not allow them to speak for fear of retribution, they have no concern for those who mean nothing to them, they are powerless to act as they are chained for life to obedience. Congress will mark the time of need for men to sit together and become one, gentle reasoning will persuade others that the truth needed to be heard in order to bring about a peace for most of its people who despair.

Jonathan, he gave his name to those of sterling progress his faculties were intact, his strengths, his weaknesses are

overruled by those who would dictate. *(Note: Jonathan Swift born 1667 – an Anglo-Irish satirist, essayist, poet and cleric who became Dean of St Patrick's Cathedral, Dublin.)*

Many say things about the circumstances that arise in the Far East. Caress your heart with need and purpose for your Lord. A time will come when you ask, "Is there no rest?" your purpose will be found before the dawning of the new era, rest your mind before the season of the sun, allow us to intervene in need and purpose upon the Divine will of our Lord.

The commonwealth games (Olympics?) will be a focus of a need upon your Earth for they will inspire a need for peace not reckoned with before.

Triumph over adversity will begin when the east meets the north, and the west will dictate a measured response before peace is resumed among your nations, your tribes.

Your will is strong for the purpose, continue your work, we will light the way on your behalf as we inspire others to lend a hand. Comparatively you are weak minded but must follow the laws of the universe in a manner respectful of the Lord. Take heart that we watch your progress and will burden you with much and your needs will be great, you'll blossom and bring about a need in men, follow your hearts desires in grace and dutiful need.

29th May 2016

Our task this evening is to you, a message of hope to your nations.

We are told that man has fortitude and will to see through those days upon which men of war hurt each other, catastrophes are looming in the regions of the far south. Before the year is out, a new dawn will begin for some, for others it will end. But rest assured that all will receive an awakening of sorts.

Trooping of the colour will be matched by a terrible event in the north.

Beware the arms will extend from the east as they reach the shores of Brittany, casting a shadow over events by which you will have no control. Your leaders will shout, details will be hidden from view as they usher those in distress to shelter, matters of concern from all.

We have to announce that our appearance will be announced shortly to the world. We forecast much disruption as we emanate from the skies above to bring forth a new era a time of peace. Fear not for we are here to adorn you as a measure of mind of purpose, complete your mission as required for the salvation of your kind, your intentions are good towards your fellow man, but strengthen your mind to the purpose at hand as we intensify our minds with yours. Companions will follow to breathe new life in the aspects of the words, your friends of the light will have a need to bear witness to your point of view.

Frankly we are appalled by what we have witnessed in the Congo today, your news editors will regard this as unworthy for their pages, we know of these terrible things, your lion roared and his teeth sank deep into the hearts and minds of those who perished, why is it that your people cannot be trusted to convey love, their punishments will not go unheeded. *(Note: We could find no media reports regarding this.)*

There will be a vacuum of love and intolerance to your major cities as their armies spread.

Contemporary art will once more signify the need of free speech among your men. *(Thomas)* Jefferson knew of the meaning of free speech and mumbled words to *(Andrew)* Jackson many times during his life upon Earth, they were formidable, but their views differed, and they were unable to maximise their united embodiment of minds. Tasks are given today to those of purpose to open their minds that wisdom and will of those of the light. We are here to teach those who would open their hearts and minds to their spiritual purpose, Gilbert O'Sullivan, sang the tune that tells the story of a love, his voice rang true and clear relaying a message to the ears of men.

Scheming minds, reckless behaviour of the men in power will immerse the nations in turmoil, for their need is of their

own and not that of all. They will desperately hold on to power, provoking and hoping that such an aggressive manner will hold the minds of the many, but they are seen as scheming individuals not worthy of thought. Their house will collapse before the new world, watch as they scream, "What has happened, what have we done?" and they do not see their own misgivings. Their fortunes they will hide behind closed doors so that men cannot see of their wealth.

Tuberculosis will affect many as the smoke rises in the morn.

Allow your hearts of freedom and will to speak ill of those who will condemn your minds to servitude; connect with your deepest feelings within and allow your mind to breathe easy.

Treat yourself with respect as the Earth rotates upon its axis wavering as those forces of light affects its spin. Knowledge of this is beginning to emerge into those scientific minds of your Earth, they know that soon the time will come of immense change as the spin of your Earth changes by one degree, this will bring a tidal wave of currents to the shores of many.

Ignorance is bliss they say but knowledge is of wisdom. Let us reassure you that our purpose is good and that we are here to assist those who survive these dark times to bring light and purpose once more to your Earth in His name. Tremendous amounts of courage will be required as the burden grows, trust in your light, bring peace to those who come before you we are here to guide you. The Arcturians.

31st May 2016

Broken hearts and dreams are many in your world of troubles, despair, anguish, they scream out into the night, fear us not, for we have come bearing greetings and love.

Needless to say, we are pleased with the progress and the continuing work to enlighten man's mind to our purpose and need. Into your souls the purpose, a combination of will is required to achieve a satisfactory conclusion as we approach your earth. We will transmit utterances of respect to those of the light. We need your complete willingness to serve His purpose of light, for we bring a measure of goodwill and comfort to your planet. We know of circumstances surrounding issues of war, their reasons are given as excuses to battle those who would disrespect the Lord and His people.

We are aware of the many things that affect your lives upon your planet, your world. Do not disregard the purposes for which you were sent, for your need is great at this time. Frequently we have asked for those of purpose to transmit their thoughts of love and compassion, without fear of ridicule, without insecurity, for those who work within the light are free of mind and fear as they battle the forces of good and evil upon the planes of your Earth. We admire your fortitude and your willingness to proceed amongst the many that have gone before, for they have received gratification within the light of love and honour.

Our minds are of great power for thought, we transmit thoughts to the many who's ears are open within your world, we find that some are reckless and their actions transmit in these words to those of your Earth. We need patience and tolerance as feelings run high amongst your men on the topics so violent. The time has come for us to give them, you, a lesson of tolerance and need of purpose, focus your mind as we intercede with your thoughts.

Feel our energy draw close as we sit with you within the light. We are of small stature, a people of great wisdom; knowledge has been gained by many trials and tribulations of our own planet. We speak here tonight to give you a view of our lives and aspects of purpose, we are timekeepers of the many, we travel through into your universe with ease in our star ships, as we exceed man's ability to travel to the stars. We have seen many worlds beyond yours capable of supporting life, your telescopes they see us as a speck, they cannot know the true meaning of what they see for we are of love, a creation of the Lord to enhance the powers of the light. Our focus is upon you as we sit among your people of the Earth influencing the minds of those who are willing to commit.

Family affairs are a matter of concern to many but moreover they should focus upon their neighbour as their friend and family. Comparatively your life is of need within a structure of love and tolerance, we need your support to bring about peace upon your planet.

Contemporary men of purpose will astound the minds of others who design many things of need; we cannot emit our being upon those minds who will not see. Craft your mind as the polished crystal and allow our words to follow contemporary men for the need for wisdom and knowledge to achieve his aims, his purpose is that of greed and not a measure of love, we have no need for money or men of greed for theirs is a purpose unworthy of the light.

Our name is Arcturian and we sit with you to guide the many who believe in the existence of other forms and races. We exist in your minds to ease the burden and the shock of our appearance, many have seen us and, in their wisdom, do not believe, for they cannot imagine such things exist. No trickery; we exist. We travel your world incognito, dressed as man, look into our eyes to see the measure of our purpose, we have been many times to your Earth, creating an atmosphere in which we may exist in hidden places around your globe, they are deep in caverns. Do not expect to find us as we have the ability to hide from those eyes.

We cannot imagine a world full of destruction such as yours for it goes against nature, for what a waste to beat upon one another without reason or rhyme. Yours is a curious race of beings, no respect, no guidance, no thought for others as you traverse your lives filled with fear and devoid of love. There are those who shine the light of love, but they are few, most are concerned with their very being. The contexts of your lives are filled with need and want. Why not open your minds to its full potential, linking your minds with nature as was intended at the very beginning of time?

We have sent many envoy's amongst your men, we desire peace and reconciliation, they have been mistreated and punished for their thoughts as you will be for your words, take heart at these lessons, it will be hard but the rewards are great within heaven. You must sacrifice your will to work in a world far beyond your own allowing us free speech to your people as they see us through your eyes.

We are a race of noble people with no wish to harm or jeopardise your world, but to restore its glory to its former self, a beautiful brilliant blue planet filled with life, which now diminishes quickly as man infests the Earth. Come to us with a measure of peace as we answer the questions of love.

Commodus, he wishes to speak once more in a manner of love and peace: It was long ago that I was a man forced into servitude by others whose will and desire was to own man. They punished me for my disobedience many times before the whip, I suffered great pain and the agonies of death. Many times I felt the needles penetrate my skin, they were as knives, cutting away a piece of me with each stroke, my mind was beaten into submission. I looked into men's eyes and see them weep before my blade, my own heart sang out, "Why am I forced to do this?" But in truth it was always in my power not to commit these crimes against a fellow man, my ignorance was not an excuse, my feeble mind was not an excuse.

As I came before the Lord and He whispered in my ear, "Commodus, why as a man did you take other men's lives, could you not see the unjust wisdom in your actions? You were not forced into servitude as your will is strong, you should have fought against the master, but I understand your weakness as you sit before me, your obedience and your suffering will not go unnoticed. We of the light, of the wisdom, know of the pains and suffering of men, yours has been great, you cannot expect that I can overlook the crimes committed against humanity." As I looked, I became aware of His noble presence in my midst, I asked forgiveness for the things, those many terrible things.

We call upon you this evening to ignore your will to fight those who would lower your nature. For as a man you are only flesh and blood, your soul is precious, do not be tempted to overstep the ways of the Lord, your nature is good and I am pleased that I have been permitted to connect with your soul, for you once were also obliged to do many things, many terrible things, you paid as I did and learnt. Combat your fears, gather your strength of arms but use them for the good of the light and to embrace the love of the peoples in your world. Do not allow your offences to affect others in a manner of disrespect, God have mercy on those of ill will. Purposely we have attempted to bring about a man within you, your mind is weak, but your strength is immense. Focus on those who will support your words with wisdom.

One comes to hear your words, we will speak with him and he will listen to the words of wisdom, you must unite to bring about a combined strength to carry forward the words. Your abilities are given to you as a measure of respect for your compassion and feelings towards others and of all creatures upon the Earth. Do not tremble as we approach, we all feel different. Tremendous amounts of love and sorrow that emerge from your planet are like storms of the season to us, as your vibrations bounce between us.

Your storms of fury will gather as the seasons progress, they are severe to the extreme, they bring about change upon your planet, change that is unforeseen. But those of wisdom whose words will try to reassure you. They know the truth, for what is about to happen. You must not fear nature, for all things have a cycle and a purpose of being. Yours is no different to many others in your world, you see the suffering and despair that stabs at your heart and mind, yours will be no different, for all must equate for each other's suffering.

The temples of your mind are like valleys with rivers of emotion that flow through with varying degrees of current. Open the floodgates of emotion to a franchise of will and determination, to be a beacon of light upon those of your

Earth who will listen to the wisdom sent by the many of the light.

Countless measures will be set against you as men see you as a threat to their own glorification as they aspire to bring messages of love to those who have lost, or perceived to have lost their loved ones. For they still live in a spiritual world upon the many planes that surround and intercede with your world.

Can I express our thanks and gratitude to you and others who shine the light and wisdom of the Lord? Be a temple, a place for those who have questions. We have much knowledge to share amongst you; you need only but ask. Forgiveness is great within the light and it is up to you to ask for His Divine light and intervention into your lives.

As the Rose blooms and the petals fall back, so the beauty will radiate out with a scent of love that you will be drawn to, as a bee is drawn to the nectar of the flower. Be not afraid to approach as the light shines, for like the bee, the honey is sweet, the nectar of life is there for all to taste. You have only but to ask of the Lord's forgiveness. Even those of intemperate minds who have fallen below the light, in due course they will be asked if they wish to taste the nectar of the light and life, it is their choice, their own soul's motive. If they do not choose then we will regard them as needy, they will refuse to see the light for they fear redemption that may come to them, they do not understand that all are born of the light but only fall into the darkness of their own choosing.

You asked of animals, of their service in life and of their peace at their passing. We understand your concern, but rest assured that all that live, all that are, are one with spirit. Some will tell you that an animal is just an animal, but they don't look at themselves and see that they are but an animal themselves, a creature of the Earth, given life and soul in the purpose of need. An animal's respect and love are only given when it is given in equal measure to them, they have purpose to serve mankind in many ways, their lives are not wasted.

Their souls are rejoiced and brought to a heavenly place of love and light, for they suffer greatly, not being heard, with no recourse they are persecuted as lower forms of life. But know this, they are no different to you, they feel the pain that you feel, they feel the sorrow, joy and happiness that you do. Animals of burden carry a load under which many would buckle, their purpose is given to assist all, to carry their burden. Look at the horse, an animal of strength and power but with a mind as free as the wind, yet he capitulates to man's desire. His will is broken to serve in many ways, his skill and intelligence is beyond your comprehension, for he has a strength of mind that no man can break, he represents power and strength, his purpose will be served in many ways, but in the end he will rejoice in the fields of heaven.

Communicate your minds intentions to those of a will to listen to hear the words of the Arcturians. Yes, we feel fear, fear of failure in our purpose to bring about a meaningful peace within your peoples of the world. Their hostilities against us have been seen and unreported, they see us as freaks to be examined. We are no different to you, we feel pain, desire, love, but our minds are balanced in unique ways to yours, our radiance of will shines out to those men who would listen to the sound waves of our words.

Colours adorn your world with clarity, as prisms of light reflect our need. Come together as one, as a prism of light to reflect upon those who have doubts and negative wisdom to accept that our will is one of peace, not of destruction. You will clamour to see a spectacle before you; your vision will be blurred at the site of our coming, feel our need for love and respect. We do not ask you to worship, but to respect our being of purpose. If you cannot understand these simple things, then we regret to have to embark upon a different course.

Your men of power they will drive their point home in their machines of metal, how primitive beyond belief that you do not have the wisdom to understand our determination to bring about peace, an alliance of men with those of the light.

Let venom meet those that bear arms against us. Fear us for we will have no mercy upon those who pull their triggers of anger upon our ships. We will spare those who relinquish their ways for the world will see a battle of wills. Fear will be promoted by those of wisdom, who negotiate their own minds as to the rights and wrongs of the actions of men.

The wise ones will see our purpose and need to bring about an end to hostilities, to form a peace among those people who wish to live in the light of the Almighty. He who brings about his purpose before us will be rewarded with love and gratitude. All material things are unnecessary to the spirit and soul, you'll be well aware of the need of love and your climate changes will be of trivial concern compared to that of the hostilities that will be brought against those that condemn others to servitude and hardship. We don't mean of trivial things but of those who suffer greatly at the knives slashing away at their life, for no good reason other than to bring respect upon them. Huh, they just don't know how awful it is in the eyes of the Lord to see His people tormented by the dark shadows that linger in life.

You will have noticed before how a glimmer of light will brighten up the darkness, so it will be that the light will shine and drive out the darkness in the world. For new beginnings, we see a race of beings with tolerance and temperance, love and admiration for the Lord for the blessings given. We need a commitment from you to transmit the thoughts of our minds, as you draw on the energy of others, our strength will increase tenfold, you will be unaware of the things said, your heart will feel an immense uplift as we enter and use your mind, you will feel our love, our immense strength, so much so that you will be left feeling rewarded by Heavens light.

We do not intend to dominate the lives of those upon your Earth but to recreate a structure of a loving nature within man. Frankly we cannot abide war; we despise those who create hell on Earth. It is time, as children that you grow up to the knowledge that was intended and implanted in your minds before corruption and greed set in, before the dark overshadowed those men of power, of greed, of want. We will illuminate their minds once more and they will capitulate to our measures of tenderness, for if they don't they will feel a swift answer to their anger in equal measure. Compel us not to do these things, give us reason for hope that men will turn to the light to begin a new life and dawn within the world of peace and plenty for all. With the common good given to all by man's desire to live in peace. I respect your will for independence, but you must live within the light, consciousnesses of the dark will be extinguished and they will not shine again upon the Earth, but like all they will be given an opportunity to re-emerge to learn the lessons that they failed.

You were once a man of dishonour your extreme measures brought fear and tyranny to others, your mind was weak, but you have come to be a power of strength and love, loyalty and compassion, we admire those who turn with a purpose. You will achieve many things upon your spiritual journey, the teachings of the Lord run deep within you, allow Him to shine His light within your soul to bring peace and joy to those who enquire as to His nature. You see the angel in your eyes, she is there for guidance, reassurance, her healing energies will radiate to those in your presence, let them feel her love, warm their souls for she is that of the light, an angel of love.

Commence your journey to achieve your aims, as you were set before this Earth. Mother Mary, she walks with you, embracing your love and tenderness for others. Frequently you ask, "Why me?" Why not? Are you not worthy as any other man? Are you not of the light to bring words of comfort to those who need peace in their lives and love in their hearts? Temperance and tolerance shall be theirs, as it will be yours, be of a nature of love to dominate men's minds, to illuminate their lives with the love of the Lord, of the Mother Mary, for she walks with you by the name of Lily, enable Her heart to beat within yours to bring a peace to men of the world.

Five stars will point the way to a world beyond yours with tremendous attributes, their wisdom and knowledge is great. They have no need of machines, they are spirit; they have no need of material things, for their sustenance is love and light. They are the angels that bring warnings and their love to the many, they point the way to joy and happiness that can be achieved within men and you upon this Earth.

The snowflake falls and as it does so it resembles a star, but it changes as it lands softly upon the ground, it merges with the earth and melts away. This is a symbol to you, that no one man can make a difference, but should there be many snowflakes, a storm of a white light of love will fall gently to the Earth, and as it does so they will form a cover to hide away the impunities as a clean white sheet of love, and as the gentleness caresses the Earth, so the Earth becomes one with the flake.

Truly I see before me a tremendous will.

7th June 2016

X marks the spot, his deliverance in the outcome will have purposeful meaning to all. *(Referring to the forthcoming Brexit referendum?)*

Your lives are expendable my son, to those who think their will is all that matters. They have no compassion or understanding of the light held within each soul, each life. Your understanding and will to serve is welcome to see, by us the Arcturians, the members of the race, for all to see as your world spins upon its axis.

We commence with our task to enlighten your world with psalms that praise, with thoughts of love, as we guide your hand through the dark realms that besiege your world at this time. Allow your mind to empty and let us extinguish the thoughts of fear.

Tonight we ask of you to bring a measure of comfort to those who have lost loved ones in the Sahara Desert today, for their hearts scream out, 'Murderer', their loved ones perished in the sun as shots rang out. The men with hats waved their rifles declaring all to their God, there is but one God and he feels betrayed by the shameful behaviour, for they cannot see that what they do is wrong. What do they expect to gain by slaughter of their fellow man? It brings no pleasure to us to have to condemn those who are like children being led by a master with a will so strong that their eyes are blinded to the righteous path that they were given.

They clasp their hands and sing in praise, but their words are met with displeasure. He who comes before them will be a man who will betray them and teach them that theirs is a path of narrow-minded individuals whose task is to help themselves to the spoils of war. They will merge their point of focus today to discuss their plans of wickedness. Their hollow hearts and minds will not hold the notion of love, but only of despair and wickedness.

They will come before us when their time is done hoping to be praised by that of the Lord, but their welcome cannot be greeted with love for they have sinned a terrible sin against humanity and God. They don't understand why it is that they have been selected to suffer these pains for their hates, their hearts are filled with hate and their minds filled with poison of other minds. They scream, "Why me, what have I done that is so wrong?" It is sad to see they were lost pilgrims of the world, their shame will be met with dishonour by those of the light, for they cannot enter into the kingdom of the Lord. They have much to learn before they can redeem themselves with purpose once more, they will live a life of torment so that they may understand the persecuted that they have persecuted themselves.

Negotiate your mind to a will of satisfaction, to become strong and powerful, with the emotions and sadness around. For they will drive your purpose, ever increasing your wisdom and knowledge through the teachings given.

Samuel Johnson was a man persecuted in his time, his will was powerful but his mind was weak, he is with us now with a message for all men who are weak of mind: "Come before the Lord with a message of kindness, I was a man who once walked with Elijah, we were Afro-Americans and we worked together in bondage of slavery. You were that of the plague of men who sacrificed others so that their will was done. We suffered greatly at the hands of those white men who persecuted us for our race and creed, they see us as dogs to be whipped and herded into corrals. Our women wept as our backs bled from those strokes. Thomas, he gave us hope in his teachings of the Lord as we sang our praises to that of God in the hope that one day we would be free from persecution in South Carolina.

Hubbard was a name, their cruelty inflicted pain upon us. *(Note: An internet search revealed a few men with the surname of Hubbard linked with slavery.)* My youngsters see me cry as the whip fell across my shoulders, I was a man not a beast of burden I never blacked *(passed out?)* in front of them, my defiance was all before their cruelty, I only became a man once more at my passing in Pasadena. We worshipped our strength and tolerance; I was an old man, grey hair, a fine head of hair, with much wisdom to give the youngsters. Now I find peace as I am a flower of the Lord and I am happy to see the injustices are no longer as rife, but they still exist. Those men who whip us and cause us pain, they still have their weapons and show no mercy with the colour of our skin. You are a man of tolerance; you all see that we are no different to others of the human race; our lives were tormented with the sacks of grain that weighed heavy on our backs. Our hearts and minds were also heavy with burden. We had our pride, Jackson, he saved our souls, God bless for your commitment my brother."

Thomas Jackson is welcomed for his grand psalms of the burden to carry in his time. *(Possibly Thomas Jackson 1768-81 – his works include 12 psalm tunes and eighteen chants?)*

My name is unimportant; my words are issued through you to the many of the world to allow them to understand that my heart is a power of strength to the many. You weep as you watch the burden of man, as it becomes a load unbearable. You witness many things that hurt your eyes with sadness; your compassion is shown through your love of man. Extreme measures will be taken to correct the situation within the provinces of Seoul and join us now as we venture beyond your imagination to bring you wisdom. Tasks are given to you; tend your flock, your followers. Commitment is necessary to achieve an end that will realise our purpose, revered within Heaven and Earth. Many men have wisdom and knowledge to carry these words forward with books, complete your words with a measure of love and devotion as the angels join you to give their blessing upon you and the world.

We have come this evening as a measure to bear witness that we are of the unknown, your lives revolve around fears as you witness many things perpetrated by those of need in your world. They contaminate your soil with their poisons they exercise disregard for Mother Earth and the creatures upon it and within it, not allowing the eyes of man to see their intent and the dangers therein. Commitment by the many will help ease this problem as it becomes more widespread throughout your land, its pressures build within the soil, expanding Mother Earth, breaking her heart. Her energy is released, but at what cost to you and others of your Earth.

We have provided the tools for your leaders to perform miracles in technology to avoid this dangerous path that they have chosen to take, but they don't seem to understand their policies will destroy men's minds with the gases and poisons they have released from the earth's crust. Commitment is needed by all to serve them notice that this is a mindless and deliberate act of sabotage to your earth. Why is it that man ignores the very thing that gives him life? Mistreats her *(the earth)* with injustice, not allowing her to perform her functions. Her will is broken, she will react in a manner of extreme measures, you will feel her anger in the nights, in the evenings, in the dusks as she explodes with a tremendous expression of fire, the vibrations will be felt by many of the states in the way she lies. Nebraska, Kansas will be affected as many others will. Your reasoning for your intrusion on Mother Earth is that of need. We will reset, we have provided the means and measures to counteract your need with wisdom. *(Note: subject is regarding fracking.)*

I speak with you this evening from the cosmos in the galaxies to talk of things to come and things that have passed and of the present. For all these things are coherent and are joined by the Master and mystical present. In your hearts and minds you are not aware of the many things that are transmitted throughout your world. References, past lives are emitted before us as we receive the messages of love with the many who sit in the hope of reconciliation. We are here this evening to bring a measure of comfort to those of the world who wish to listen to our words, for we have come with a measure of love and peace.

My... our world was once a ball of light that flickered in the heavens as it spun, its light faded as land developed. Creatures roamed for millions of years on the one you call Earth. There are many creatures you don't know of, many you have not seen or have not witnessed, creatures of such magnitude your minds cannot conceive, for they are of true existence. You once called them Dragons. They became extinct as the fires melted, ruled the Earth; they were extinguished by the waters of heaven that rained upon it from the stars above. God was the master of all, He understood what it was to be a powerful being of light, He bathed your planet with light, bringing purpose for organisms and life to breathe upon it, created your rivers and seas to flood the lands and wash away the debris of the fire.

His need was great of your Earth, for her poor are many marvellous creations, many civilisations worshipped Him in stone as they carved His name in the rocks of the Earth. Then came the storm that washed them away, leaving it fresh for a new purpose and a new dawn. Why do I tell you all this? You need to know this will occur once more, that in a lifetime of servitude your nations will become dry as the eastern winds blow. Don't neglect your thoughts of love, for He who created Heaven and Earth, He is your art, your saviour, your rock. Banish your fears my child, for it is yet to come, but your words will carry a focus and need for a knowledge to those of the future. As this becomes reality, they will seek out the wisdom of our words and endeavour to rebuild the planet of love.

Many have come as envoys *(representatives)* and been mistreated. We will come once more in the name of His light to bring peace upon man. His resolve is great; His purpose for the many is for the light to shine bright in their hearts before times end.

Trigonometry is a measure of mathematics of angles and curves; your mind does not understand the need for the equations but they have purpose. They measure out your lives and your needs, your functions. They are present in everyday objects in the minds of many. The mathematics of life are of common use throughout the Galaxies, for the numbers are a mechanism by which life is created and given purpose. Astrology, a study of the stars also conforms to these rules, as do we, as we measure the distance between us. **Granted we are not of the same species, for our measures in numbers are as yours, given this you are issued with a number 37, 29.2 this is a number given to you.** Your minds are of the light, as is a measure of the minds to enlighten you to extreme ways to carry on your purpose. The numbers are many and given many times to those in the past who have focus and a will to use them. *(Note: We were challenged with these numbers and we are still not certain what exactly they refer to, however we did discover that the earth has 37 Billion acres of landmass which just happens to be 29.2% of the surface of our planet, we will still keep searching for an alternative explanation. Could it be to do with proportions and everything having a balance and when things are not in balance, failure occurs? Maybe we have to remember these numbers and know that if* *they change, we have a problem? Also Arcturus is approximately 37 light years from earth, Gamma Leporis is 29.2 light years away and is in the top ten for NASA's terrestrial planet finder program for finding a suitable habitable planet. Or are there any talented mathematicians out there who can put us out of our misery?)*

It is a mathematical certainty that life will end. That life on Earth will end in a measure of discomfort, none will survive for many light years beyond your measure. This is to come when the time is right for renewal, for as the snake sheds its skin, so the Earth will shed its surface for a cleansing and regrowth. It is not necessary to worry, for this measure is of many lifetimes before *(ahead of)* you, but you should know that yours is but a phase in the blink of an eye.

Commodus re-joins us now:

"Task your masters with thoughts of love as their eyes betray the truth within. I was once a man who worked with a measure of discontent, dishonour, deceiving those of the Senate with my words of anger. Their words of wisdom were shut out from my mind at my displeasure. They scavenged from the scraps that I gave them, they knelt before me as I now kneel before you to honour your love of the Lord and the light. This should have been my purpose as I was a man of dishonour who had given my love to the material things and not to the hearts and minds of my people. My woes are great, but my redeemer has given me a better understanding of my life's purpose. I come to you now as a man of honour and much respect for the work that you are doing in His name. Don't allow others to sway your tide of movements, bring about a purpose of common humanity, be a leader with compassion and love in your heart for I was once a man with none."

Allow your mind to witness the many things that are hidden from men. As you slumber, you will dream of the many things and the tasks to come before your life's end. Your friends are warm and welcoming for they understand your need and drive to bring about this purpose to those within the circles of your life. Give them your wisdom and your knowledge of us, as we declare peace upon you, upon the earth.

The measure of our dignity is unseen by man for we come in our ships of gold to bring about a measure of peace, that we, we advance your race to allow them to become whole, as one with a measure of love of the world which gives sustenance to those that live upon it.

We have never been so far from the thoughts of man as we are today, our need is strong for what you call the light, for their alliance will all be yours to calm man's emotions of our arrival in the fall. *(Note: fall of a civilisation.)* Collectively we bring about a peace for the love of your world.

Trigonometry was a measure given so the means and purpose for your minds of will to seek out a place of significance, a formula is that of the triangle 10 degrees west, north by north 38 east, west by south. *(In the recording of the transcript it is also repeated as south by west).*

An eastern province of East Asia is a recommended place for our will to announce our being. You'll hear of this through your news broadcasts, they will cast doubt upon those that have seen with a measure of scorn as if to say, "You are nothing," their witness will shine out like a beacon to those who have a will to listen, a mind to see, we are the Arcturians, the ones who once ruled your planet with a measure of love.

Your tombs of stone were a mark of our respect and many moons was a name, she came before us in a tidal wave of love, her race of beings were that of a continent for years upon your Earth as you'll glorify greetings upon the Earth, to be a sanctuary for those of peace. Rejoice in her name as she brings a tidal wave of love to your nations of plenty, combat your fears my son for we are of the light.

Arcturians and The Reptilians

Negotiate your minds will to a purpose of meaningful existence. The work will be long and hard, the rewards great, as you muster your people in the circles of light to hear the words from beyond. Your energies will grow as your need is great, focus upon the stone that ties and binds your hearts. We are the masters of time; we are of bygone days, structures of which exist upon your Earth, quantains. *(Note: Quantains are four sided structures)* They were buildings of light and they transmitted our energy and focus with a measure of peace, they could be seen for miles, call out to the people. *(Note: Pyramids?)* The magnificence of the light and the creatures that roamed upon the Earth.

We are of the snakes; we mean no harm, just a purpose to bring life to reconciliation. Combat your fears for we are of peace, one nation of plenty with need of assistance to revive your purpose. *(Note: Is this the serpent race? In Hindu mythology the serpent race is described as a powerful, wonderful and semi divine race.)*

Trafalgar Square a place of money (or many?), will suffer a blow so profound it will reverberate throughout your world of men. Tarnished are the reputations of those who rule your land with unwise decisions. Their hearts are strong with ego their minds are closed of love; you allow occurrences by your openness and willingness to accept those of evil intent.

Can you not see the wound that is open will become infected by the tyrants of the blue seas as they cross your oceans with no respect, no emotion, their minds have purpose and ill will towards your nations of plenty. Your nobles will cry out, but their actions will be stifled by that of the lords who rule your land, for they will decree that all men have the right to express themselves and that he will have a right to be free. From virtuous, they are naive, for the world is not ready for such noble thoughts.

Your eyes will be opened by a blast of light that will cost and curse your land for many seasons, be at peace with the

love of the Lord and know that our hearts and minds will bring peace and love to your earth in the fall, the season of plenty.

Tyrants of life will become tyrants of the past as their purpose will end with a measure befitting the Lord, they will not survive the holocaust, as the purpose of light in our Lord shines upon your planet. Let them be a lesson to all that life is a lesson of love, tolerance and compassion. There is no place for the man of intolerance within the light of Heaven, he must repeat his time until it has been learnt that love of the Lord should be allowed into all men.

19th June 2016

We have come on a mission of love and mercy this evening to enlighten you and your followers of the words of Abraham as he sits in His Heaven watching over those with tender thoughts of love and prayer, for His purpose is of need and a gratitude to those who worship Him on High. Never before has there been such an outcry within Heaven for a peace upon your earth, for all men deserve a life free of sin and filled with purpose.

We came with inspiration and focus to those creatures that ran wild within your nations; they were astounded that such things exist. We gave purpose to life with those statues of gold, for they were ornaments for the sacred souls. We are the beings of the light who gave life upon your Earth in the hope that it would flourish in unison, with a measure of peace to bring about the purpose of beauty in both Heaven and the Earth.

Our wars of the worlds have continued for so long now that peace is inevitable as man progresses in his purpose, for he will see that there is love in all aspects of life. The dark will be vanquished in the coming years, as the light grows strong in those of the circles, as they bring about a peace to those that join them in the light. Your circle is no different.

Jonathan who came before *(Note: my first guide)* is a martyr to the cause, his learned quest to bring you about to a purpose has achieved astounding results, for you will follow in his footsteps to help in these turbulent times upon your Earth.

Never doubt my son, that we the Arcturians, are the peoples for who Earth will respond to as we make our presence known in the Asia's of your world. Some coordinates were given as a practice, to a place of worship, to evolve. Now in a manner of love and respect, we expect you to discover what there is that lies in this place that relates to our being to help you. You'll bring out a purpose of love, your coordinates and map references are needed for the next step on your journey to enlighten your minds as to the truth. The purpose of our meeting.

Thomas once said, "Never doubt your hearts will to bring about a purpose of peace and love, look at your family and know that they are of the world." Thomas was a great man who brought many thoughts of love to those who cherished his words.

Combat your fears as we help to increase your minds vision, coordinates 53.10 north 65.00 east, this is a map reference of significance to your world of life to aid your purpose and your need, be guided by the light that shines within your mind for your fellow man. *(Note: Co-ordinates are located in northern Kazakhstan – we wondered if this might relate to the return of the astronauts, including Tim Peake, from the Space Station because Russia uses this area for the recovery of the space capsule? Or, the possible location an ancient artefact?)*

My name is Arcturian, I'm a fellow member of the states of your world and the universe around you. Our purpose in coming this evening is to help your task to bring about a peace to mankind. Tremendous amounts of will are required to help us achieve the same. Do not be startled as we draw ever nearer to your mind and heart, now feel our energy about you, allow it in with a will to achieve your aims.

Constantly we see heartache and bitterness, a constant flux of your world that streams out to the universe. It is hurtful to see such things can exist on such a beautiful planet as yours, you have no idea how this bitterness affects your world of life. Only those of the light who achieve their aims to bring about a reconciliation of your planet with a purpose of love and good will for each other are helping to restore the balance of life once more. Sing out your hearts with praise to the Lord as the beings of the light who assist in your work, for we are also tasked with a purpose and need to help your mind, body and soul in His exercise of love that will be demonstrated to all in due course. Allow us to open your mind and will to our meaningful purpose.

Your purpose this evening is to give the message of love to all. Help us to understand what it is that your purpose requires, for we cannot help those who do not help themselves. Your role is the master of the light that will shine upon the many to bring about a peace of mind to those hardened hearts, of those doubting the word and the ways of the Lord, crisp *(harden or toughen)* your mind to a will and purpose to grant those around you a vision of love. We will demonstrate our need this evening for the benefit of those around you. Be still as we focus our will upon you, have no fear.

Jet streams circulate your planet they will become of a violent nature.

Goodness knows we have tried to focus upon those who work amongst the stars of the light, they beam their torches of light far into the skies, into the heavens hoping that reflections will be bounced back, images of worlds with potential life. They are astounded by what they will see in the near future, as their telescopes of light beam back reflections from the far reaches beyond your domain. They will never know the extent of life that exists beyond your solar system. How could they possibly understand when their hearts are fixed and their minds narrowed by science, for they need an open mind to reflect upon the possibilities of extreme life existing in the atmospheres of many worlds beyond Neptune. We are unfamiliar beings that exist beyond your solar system.

You may call me Alex as a name of recognition, for you will not understand our tongue. We have come with words to the many populations of your Earth in the hope that they would accept our presence within the form of your beings. We will come with a purpose to bring a new life upon your planet, the human race will evolve far beyond men's present imagination, for all life evolves given time and purpose. You may wonder what this new form would be, it is no different to your present, but your hearts and minds will be filled with a purpose and meaningful love of life, companionship for each other and not for the self. To restore this world that has been choked by your industries, to help her recover from the indignities that you have set upon her in the name of progress of mankind. We have given many things to your race that have been ignored but were used for personal gain, we condone this measure, we did not give it for 'oneself' we gave it for all.

A way to understand that we, who are small in stature, hope to help your kind with a measure of peace and love acknowledging our purpose through this man, is a measure of our extreme help. How can you possibly understand how much we aspire to those of the light, given that they have faith and trust in their purpose? We float above your skies in the heavens beyond the reach of your eyes. We know of the many terrible wars, tribulations that beset your world. Be calm for a measure of peace will be brought as our presence is acknowledged. You wear the crystal that we gave for your purpose, feel its life and charge as it warms on your chest with the energies that you receive from us, do not be afraid of its energy, for it has a purpose to your heart.

Our cities are of many spires that stand tall amongst the mountains of glee. The futuristic will be strange to your eyes as they reach to the skies of our world. We are many but we have evolved in the need for love and tenderness. How else could we live together if we did not achieve this level of higher being, do we ever see a purpose for mankind? That is for you to decide, for your wills are strong and set in their ways.

Only gradual change and purpose will teach you how to live with each other in peace and harmony.

Do not be afraid to stand out from that man in the crowd and say, "I'm here, I have a will to live with need and love for my fellow beings". We came many times before to your planet of wonders, we watched as it evolved from the plasma of time. We cannot say how many fractures there have been upon your world, but know that as they come and go, so they will return and a new form will begin. Take heart for the love of light will shine upon you all with His blessings in your meagre lives of purpose.

Traumatic circumstances will beset your world in the coming months when the angels of light will shine upon the country who deem themselves as a race above the Lord; they are the black, the darkness who will side with those of the swastika. The dark angel will return to advance his purpose; fear will spread in this country with a mass outpouring of grief. Faith my son, for we are here to bring about a purpose to stem this flow; to rescue those of the innocent. Your countries will need to work together to bring about a peace in this situation, for they argue amongst themselves for the spoils of war never understanding that control will be lost.

They will forget their purpose as the UN as they respond in a massacre to a negative. Consequently their purpose will be lost, their need by the world will be misunderstood by the many. Frankly we cannot abide by their rules and regulations, yet they are followed by men without logic, purpose, rhyme or reason.

We have no respect for those who do not obey the Lord or the word of the Father, for He sits in judgment of all, bringing a purpose to those who have a will to follow his word. Negotiate your minds with a will to be one with the Lord.

In our thoughts, in our wisdom we have come to the conclusion that yours is a purpose of meaningful intent, and it is with gratitude that we allow his purpose to flow throughout mankind to archive this enormous task. Your mind must be of a will to bring about His purpose and have no fear of the consequences therein, for no one can speak the word of God without receiving a negative vibration from those who oppose His name. We of the light will bring about your purpose to achieve His end and the aims that are sent by Heaven above.

Continue with your friends to speak volumes of the words that come to your mind from our thoughts, for our love, from the bosom of the angels and the Lord above.

Arcturians we are. Good night and God bless.

21st June 2016

Problems, problems. Your focus upon man and Earth have a purpose and meaning of intent to watch over those of your fellow beings with a passion and love as comparable to anyone who would sit within these walls of light. Your heart is strong and has a purpose to fulfil the mission that was set before you many eons ago. Continue upon your path my son, as we walk with you at a stride with purpose and focus to demonstrate our willingness to act as emissaries of the light. Clear your mind and focus upon the words as they flow like the waters of time, commence your journey on the path of many words.

It is a maze from which man must seek his own destiny and bring about a purpose of his mind, it was once said, "The man who walks the path alone is the man that is a stranger to himself." The moral of this story is simple in truth, to be part of the world around you, to involve their hearts and minds with a purpose to bring love and joy throughout the lands of Eden.

Your world has many issues and problems that cannot be solved by man alone, we must indeed include ourselves to bring about the eventual outcome of peace within your world. As we approach at great velocity, your hearts and minds sing out for reward, what reward? What would you have us give other than to bring a focus in your lives, for there is only one reward that is worthy, that is the way of the Lord?

Your planet has become a mystery to many in the universe of life, why is it you have not evolved to fulfil your purpose as required by us, the Arcturians? We cannot understand how your minds work in such an unorganised fashion, be brutal with the answers to yourselves, for you must recognise that your failures are apparent to all in the heavens to see and watch.

Transport your minds to a place that will eventually have purpose for you all in the coming days, weeks and years, lest we forget that man was once just a creature of the Earth who bore his children with weak and pointless minds. We stepped in; we gave you purpose, a mind and a will to fulfil your destinies. The seed was sown in those primitive times to enable you to live a virtuous life. You have failed to complete that mission and we will not stop until we have corrected the burden of ill will that is upon you. You must muster those of an opinion and a mind of light to band together, and as your minds meld, they will announce a new beginning of mankind.

We once wore many garments to protect the layers of our being from the atmospheric pressures of your world. We developed a suitable means by which to communicate, you call this telepathy, power of the mind; we use it as a significant tool to bring purpose to those who have a need for the vibrations.

You were not born once, but many times and as your lives passed so your knowledge grew. Your mind is that of a human, it cannot hold all those things that you and many others have experienced in their past lives. Commonly man will deny his existence in previous lives, for fear of letting in that part of him that would terminate his minds will upon the finer things of life.

His need of love is great, hmm, indeed his mind is beset with issues that brings forth a multitude of issues and problems which cannot be solved in a wink of an eye, but must be resolved within his own heart and mind to become one with the universe. You must first acknowledge in your own thoughts of still being, allow us to sweep away those memories of injustice before you, but before you go into the night you must recognise that we are not perfect, we have a cause to fulfil in the Masters name to bring about a purpose of love and light to your planet, helping you to inspire others, who in turn will interact with those of a similar disposition.

Your names were heard in the annals of time, man must live as an individual source upon his path of life, learning to negotiate the perils and pitfalls into accepting his beliefs that God exists for all those with a will to become one with the light. You must not allow your mind to trample on those who's will and determination is set upon a course of no return, for their path has been written to allow them to experience a situation in which they themselves have set.

Problematic times ahead with issues for many will bring about change and uncertainty, commitment will be necessary to establish a link, a chain with those who have knowledge of the wise ones. Be guided by your own mind. Focus.

Commencement of our plans to bring about a situation is not heard of by the general public, for it is hidden behind the walls of the mansions of the White House. The Kremlin will be aware as their knowledge grows of the hidden information, set to be broadcast within the near future.

Compel him to answer questions of his purpose, for he of the dark heart, will respond in a manor blinding those with facts and figures that are non-existent. He will bring about a force upon nature that will astound the many of the world of his arrogance and ignorance towards all forms of life upon your planet. We cannot stop this, for that is the path that is written, for no particular rhyme or reason, but it just is. Your lives are expendable to his thoughts as his mind turns to cash and his greed. Be humble in the face of arrogance and ignorance, allow your light to shine in a manner reflective of our love and being, for we rely upon those of the light to beset the ignorant and allow the knowledge and truth to be seen by all who would ally to believe and see.

Common place it has been for men to ignore those of esteem with wisdom and words of beauty. We cannot contemplate a world without purpose or meaningful life, please assure us that you will ascertain a path of light to begin a process to assist in our development of your species.

Your forthcoming events will be met with an attitude of disbelief, for how can they be of purpose? They have no need for religious aspects of spirit, what a ridiculous notion to call themselves beings of the light. Fear not; be responsible for their mind's thoughts. Blessed is he who comes before you this evening as he retains his will to sit beside you and announce that his coming will bring about a massive outcry. Tumultuous times in the lives of many, they have need for the arrogance by the ignorance of the masses, for they feed upon them as a vulture feeds upon the flesh. They know one simple truth, that is how to blind a man as they steal from him. His attention is distracted by the events of the Far East while his black motive relishes the thought of deliverance of a blow so immense it will astound those of the streets of the parish, Wycombe/Wickham/ Wykeham *(Note: The correct spelling or whereabouts of this place is unknown.)* To announce such things is to fall on those of an outcome of untimely ends, for mass murder in reckless behaviour upon the streets of your home.

We have mentioned previously that we cannot intercede in the events that formulate your lives but we can bring about a purpose of love and intent through those who would spread their words of wisdom so that the many would recognise that our power and strength reaches far and wide across your globe. Yes, we have travelled time through many light years to bring about a peace to your world as the cosmos is a living being. An infection needs a cure, as your vibrations disrupt those of many worlds, we cannot permit the infection of this planet to cause a whiplash throughout the universe. Therefore on the Monday morning we will arrive for you to bear witness that of our intention in love of healing your planet will commence shortly in the blue moon. *(Note: Dates of blue moons: May 2016, 31 January and 31 March 2018, 31 October 2020.)*

A tumultuous welcome will be granted to those with purpose to come before us in a manner respectful of the Lord to plant the seeds of love and light into the minds of many. Your intuition will cause events for the words to resound within the realms of the light. A sequence of events will be caused to bring about man's desire for peace, he must take no part in the resounding of those with an attitude of ignorance and stealth, you must remain neutral in all aspects of love and consideration.

As the bell rings out change in your countries of Europe, a mass outpouring of anger will alleviate a pressure that has built in the regions of the poor in Brazil, a united front will be deemed necessary to control the masses as they surge, hate reveals.

We cannot underestimate the amount of fear that will be shown as they stare in wonder at the third star that burns bright, it will bring forth men of a similar disposition to yourselves. Regard us as friends, as beings of the light to assist your way on the path, be good to those with a nature of love as they will bring about your purpose in a manner respectful of Him.

As I listen to the chants and chimes *(of the background meditation music),* I am reminded of the times of beauty and peace upon your Earth. Such a shame these times were lost to man's desire to own and possess each other in a manner unbefitting of the Lord. If all men were to sit and listen to their inner selves that broadcast messages of a necessary need and want, they would wonder who this person is that wants so much yet has so little. For their hearts are empty in their lives that are filled with the material things that bring them essentially unnecessary pleasures. For the pleasures of life are to sit in the winds of mother nature, to hear her call with bird song and the whistling of the winds as it rustles through the leaves on the ground, to hear the spring waters flow, whispering their words softly as the ripples flow over the rocks, caressing them in a manner that will bring forth a purpose to the streams of life. We have never heard such things before as those boulders become rocks and are smoothed by the waters, so they become the pebbles of the stream of life.

Gradual change will be evident as you progress at speed. Hear our call to the many of the world for a change of heart in the new season of life. I am the Master that all men would aspire to see, whose nature is of that of the Lord who brings about His purpose upon your world. The many hearts that cry out in need are heard within the heavens of the light. Never betray your thoughts my son, where aspects so good. Your progression will be noted by those of spirit. The fellowship of man is paramount for the need of reconciliation.

23rd June 2016

Cast your mind back since before time, when the Earth evolved from the rubble of the universe to bring a purpose of life to evolve upon its surface. It spun as the star spins today, blasting out its light, notifying the universe of its presence and its life. From this young planet evolved many species, many civilisations erupted from the bowels of the Earth bringing wonders and achievements that would so astound the scholar of today. Their minds boggle at the workmanship that was cast upon the Earth. The scholars, they read the books, pages filled with words that were written so long ago. They have embarked upon a mission to understand the universe and its milliwaves.

The actions of man upon the Earth's surface are regarded as sacrilege to Him who sits on high, for He created your world of life for love. So have the beings from whence you came, for aspects and notions of life go far beyond your imagination, for what is life, is it merely creatures roaming the deserts of the Earth, or is there something more profound to be found within the soul of man?

Let me tell you now, that your being is one of spirit, of a soul from the universe of light. You amass many books to explain the origins of your species, but how little you know of how much you have to learn from the pages of books to be found within casks, hidden deep beneath the soils of the mountains in the land you call Syria. "He who believeth in me shall live forever in the house of the Lord," these words were spoken by the Master for the Jewish faith, but they echo for all man, no matter what his religion or aspects of life. For men are the creatures of the Earth, filled with a passion and soul, with a burden to find their way through the Jungles of time.

We have created many things in our worlds, vast structures that house many objects of beauty, but there is nothing more beautiful than the soul of the man who comes before the Lord with wisdom and knowledge of love.

We have to confide in you, that we, the Arcturians, are a race of beings that only wish to establish an alliance with the men of the Earth. How can you possibly imagine how it is that we should come so far to bring about a truth between our peoples? The men of science, they work behind the scenes exclusively obtaining evidence of our being. We have met in the corridors of power to establish a connection with those in power on your Earth; we have been met with hostility and disturbing measures. Frankly we are tormented by your lack of understanding and comprehension.

Oppenheimer, *(Robert Oppenheimer)* **he is known for a blast so immense that mankind now lives in fear.** We have to confess we provided him with information so profound and a will to open up these boundaries before your people. His intention was good, but he was robbed by your military who saw it as a threat and a gain to oppose their enemies of the world. They held tremendous power within their communities, never letting on of the source of the information that led upon this road.

We regret having given the information at a time when men's minds were weak. A unified purpose was intended for this energy to allow you to embark upon a profound journey of establishment of a race beyond your planet's atmosphere.

Oppenheimer regrets the many deaths that were assassinated by the blinding light, as he now sits in a position

of authority within the nations of spirit asking forgiveness from those that were lost. For he knows the time will come when man will bring about an unnecessary purpose and use for the manufacture of his radiation.

Competition rages within the Earth's atmosphere for supremacy over man, we cannot continue to allow these tragic events to occur, we are of a mind to release information that will astound your scientific communities and bring a balance of thought and logic back to those who have an understanding of scientific matters. Perhaps you will assist in a small measure by inviting minds of a nature and a view to a spiritual outlook, for combined they will bring a measure of knowledge and wisdom to your planet.

We are not dissimilar in our appearance, for we have bodies of matter just as your structure and as fragile as you. You clamour for ascension within your life, to reach a point, an altitude to which man would aspire to rule man. You cannot bring about this purpose without offending Him on High, for He is the one who would rule your world and universe with a magnitude of love, temperance and tolerance for all living creatures that are blessed with life within your solar system.

Margate is a town on the coast of your shores where an accumulation of dissatisfied minds will assemble to protest at the results of your vote. Tempers will rise as the streets fill with those who have fled tyranny. They fear for their very existence, for they may have a view of homelessness. They have watched your discrimination and intolerance on the screens in disbelief that they should flee from tyranny to find mistrust and pre-judgement within your country. Help men to understand that the tolerance should be given to all of God's creatures, for they have entitlement.

The pressures that surround you in your world today run down the thoughts of man, for he cannot see a way out of the situation that engulfs the states and nations of the Pacific islands.

The hardship of life has led to mistrust as your nations are led on the focus of the welfare of the people's. Moreover their interest is of greed and of common wealth to those who sit in power over the nations. Their minds are turned by the glitter of that precious metal they so desire in its rarity upon your Earth. Let us assure you that our only purpose is to bring peace upon the nations of plenty as they clamour and loot.

Trinity, Triads, energies of misdeeds have completed their plans to assassinate a man on high within the provinces of Asia, for his visit will spark a multitude of anger with opposition to his thoughts, unlove of his people. Be aware this will culminate in an outcry of anger and fear; they will mistrust those who say 'sorry', for they will shower a measure of revenge upon them. We have no interest in your wars, ridiculous as they are for the small things of life. But to take a soul for his beliefs is a measure too far. He has the right to speak his mind as any man. Close your ears if you do not wish to listen, but do not sacrifice, all men have a purpose, a need to extinguish hate with love. Sometimes it's the other way around, hate will extinguish love, for men are blinded by other men; who preach their poison words out of disrespect of the Master. Theirs will not go unpunished as they proceed through their lives in their unjust ways upon the nations of many. Unity can only be achieved with a measure of peace bought about by discussion in wisdom and honesty. A man measures his faith by his thoughts of love, but actions are the measure by which men are judged.

We recall that we had purpose upon your earth, those days when men would worship us, bring us trinkets... unnecessary, but it pleased them to worship us, so we led their nations to many places so that the resources would sustain life, as in many nations long past they are still present today. As you march through time, change will come, as it is inevitable for all things to progress. Your aspects of love and light will shine bright to the many who wish knowledge.

Let us inform you of our ways and manner – We were once not dissimilar to yourselves in our attitudes and our ways. We fought with one another for the meagre things of life, not thinking nor caring about the many creations of God. We tortured our minds with fear and hate, never letting the love in until His being came to us saying, "Let no one man be torn by another, only the righteous will live forever in my house."

Ascension is assured for those who would look to the light for guidance. The Gardens of Eden from the fire of the arrows bringing forth his petals so delicate as they radiate out their brilliance to all creatures of the earth. Like the flower you must unfold the petals in a gentle manner, holding your delicate balance between life and liberty.

Significant amounts of will, will be required to comprehend the purpose of a man, he will shine like a beacon, his light of love to the many of the Earth. Be not ashamed to say that you are a disciple of this man who comes before all men. With purpose and need, your troubles of mind will be lifted as his purpose replaces those of anguish.

We are ascensions of beings that created many colonies within your universe. To us your minds are weak, but strength can be gained in your faith, but a new world order can bring peace to your planet of men. Combat your fears, we mean no harm to your men.

26th June 2016

Frankincense and Myrrh were thought of as precious gifts of love to Him who comes before the dawning of the light. You know His name as the Lord. He brings lessons to free the world. We have travelled many years in the hope that we are able to reconcile our differences with men of the Earth, for we are of the heavens above. Our point of view is that of reconciliation, peace and joy to restore your planets wonders and meaningful purpose as it was intended.

Fantastic times will create a situation so immense that science will extend its boundaries to expand and allow in the new knowledge of the season. They will accompany your minds thoughts in their purpose and will, for they have not seen such wonders before that will come before them, before the early spring.

A remarkable situation is about to occur on the shores, upon the beach as a tumultuous welcome of greeting by those who wait.

We are the Arcturians, a race many know of, who have purpose in light, a measure in will, in matters of love and cooperation.

We have noticed that many of your world have a malignant cancer of greed, unnecessary want. There will be a point in time when all their greed will manifest in their purpose of need for all matters of life. I cannot say what this purpose and meaning will be to them, but they will see the error of their ways and their misjudgement and practices of greed and monetary value that they put above life. They will regret as those seasons change and a new beginning starts in the autumn, for they will see that they will not have purpose, but lack the will to assist others in their lives, their meagre lives.

We have never seen such a change in a man before, as there is a will and a need for a new beginning and purpose in your world. Be assured that we, Arcturians, will announce our being in the autumn, for that will be a new spring *(Note: Spring meaning new beginnings)*.

Tremendous amounts of fear will be abandoned by astonishment as the Arc arrives, for it possesses the power to establish a new beginning that may be threatened, by those who misunderstand its purpose and meaning. For they reconcile their differences before its energy and power, some advent *(commence)* their will to abandon their hearts for the determination of ill will against her, for they will forfeit their right to enter the light for which you all must aspire to. A negative feeling will be felt in the hearts of the men who do not believe such things, they will say, "For how can this be?" That a being of the light should appear before all with a need of purpose and love and a will to sacrifice his own life.

For others upon the earth, they will say, "Who is he to dictate to us terms and conditions, that we as free men can pick and choose our own destinies." Do they not know or care about their life's path? We cannot understand their ignorance and abandonment of the Lord. These creatures of men will have no purpose within the realms of the dark, for there they will sit concerned only with themselves and their situation, not thinking to ask for forgiveness or have a will to progress, which all are entitled to do in his light.

We have need to bring about an end to the purpose of wars within your lands and countries of need. We are unable to reach those who matter most that lead these nations on a path of tyranny and heartache, so we must intervene with a focus upon them to bring them to heel. They will not recognise us for who we are, for they will see a man. We cannot assume that their tolerance will allow us to begin a process of love, for their fear of love is great within their hearts of black.

Madame Guillotine they called her, off with their heads! Those bureaucrats, those aristocrats in those times of civil war, they were blunt in their actions against their fellow human beings. In similar they are formulating a plan to withdraw their services to those of need, for they fear the change ahead with a massive demonstration, an outpouring of disbelief in the circumstances that have arisen, for their times are changing as their hearts grow dark with fear and misunderstanding.

They are led by a man, Jean, who musters and gathers troops around him with a dark intent upon the continent. He amasses armies as they struggle across the borders, be wary of him, for he brings fear and doom to those of the light. Jean, not to be trusted, to be given a wide berth by those of the light. He splendours in his own magnificence, calling himself 'The Master' but he is a false prophet who spells doom to those who would listen to his words of falsehood. He completes his mission upon the eve of the narrative; he will astound those of his magnitude of terror. *(Note: a possible reference to Jean-Luc Melenchon?)*

Let he who bears arms against those of the light and of goodwill suffer in servitude before the Maker. When their days are passed they will come to an understanding of the wrongs, the misgivings of their deeds. September is the time of his coming, be not afraid of his banter for his will is dark and will be superseded by the light as he musters his troops with banners and placards. It has been seen by those of the service, he is watched by eyes who see his stride increase, they will pounce in due course, for this man has no purpose, he is dark.

We will assist in bringing about his comeuppance for he cannot resist love of the light in those who carry His love before them in the churches of his province. Champagne will toast a celebration on his passing, he bears the name of a communist.

Travesties of injustice have occurred in the nations of Africa as the loss of many in Nairobi, an African region renowned for its problematic situations. An aspect of love is required upon on those who have suffered with blood. Their nation is unheard of by the ears and eyes of those of the west, their situation is dire, as those who oppress their ways forcing them as slave labour in their camps to focus upon the jewels in the ground.

The diamonds for which the rich man would have purpose, never knowing the fear and the torment of those who suffer bringing them to the surface. They are whipped and beaten as dogs in the street. Why does man treat man with such contempt? The hearts and minds of man who purchase the stones of beauty either don't know or don't care from whence they came, only the clarity and beauty as they sparkle is important to his eyes, he observes them as one of nature's wonders and something to be owned by him. But these stones are cursed for they have blood upon them of those who suffer in servitude to the slave masters of the white supremacy.

Their colour is what men see, it will be announced shortly in the papers of her torment, but will men care for their labours? No, he will purchase these goods, these things of beauty that are stained with the blood of men, woman and children. So when you see their brilliance of light, know that the light that bore them and suffered. They hunger for the mere pittance of life as the masters gather their rocks. A rebellion will unleash an outcry, an outpouring of grief as many will be shot, gunned down in practice. Man has not learnt to live with one another, respectful of each other in a matter of his formation and colouration. The intolerance and injustices brought upon those who suffer will be swept away within the light of Heaven, that those who brought about the injustices will not be granted the light for their labour awaits them with torment in spiritual chains.

You tremble with fear at the thought that your words will not be heard, their focus lost to the annals of time. We will not let these words be lost, for they have purpose in a time before yours as people reach for the blessings in the words of the Lord in their times of need. How can we assure you that these things will be? You must have faith in your purpose, your heart and soul, we are expecting your friends to expand your words. Continue in the hard work in your practices of love before the nations of the world.

28th June 2016

Rome was not built in a day, a week, month or year. It was built on the foundation of slavery and greed, persecution, retribution and the sins that were committed therein were not of the Lords standing. That city of Rome that so many aspire to visit, it was where so much suffering was held within its walls, that even today it continues to radiate a mark of the men of violence who fought and swore an oath of allegiance to the Emperor Aurelius

We can only express our contempt for those dark days when men bled and fought each other as prize fighters, "Dammed if they do, dammed if they don't," for theirs was a purpose of extinction *(fight to the death)*. Why come before us with your bold hearts claiming that you are among those who have not witnessed such terrible things as these? In today's world, we see no difference from the gladiators of Rome, to those who persecute and bring ill will against those who only want love and an understanding. Can't condemn the many, by those in seats of power who wish to descend upon them with a marked interest of modern-day slavery, building hopes then destroying them by their illegal practices within the city walls of that super-state that was.

Continually we hear cries that beckon us, to those who wish to confess that they are in need of assistance. Blessed is he that calls upon the Lord with love in his heart and an understanding of man. We see many faces before us as they pass through the portal of life, they come and go, their time is marked and interceded with joyful aspects of life when their time is done. They re-enter the world of spirit, not quite understanding what has occurred, but are willing to listen to those of the light.

Some are of a hardened nature and will not accept that their passage is done so they linger, continually feeding on the energy of those of life, despairing at what they see but can no longer have. Their energies feed upon those who would listen to their pleas, they are many within your world as they stagnate in the zones between life and spirit, getting more frustrated at their inability to pass over from one side to the other.

Assistance is needed from the army of healers who call out to them, "Come, follow the light, be one with the light and the Lord." but they shun this for they fear retribution, they need not worry for all are entitled to healing and progression on their journeys of spirit.

His blessings are given to those who have a knowledge/ insight into the ways of the Lord, but mark this, only those with the strength to persevere will walk once more in peace in the light of the Lord for they have a task that needs to be reaffirmed in their commitment to work through the lessons of life. Shortcuts cannot be taken, for life is a path of learning from which there is a beginning and an end. As you progress, your lives, your minds mature into a being of light, you cannot take this away as it is a purpose for all to ascertain their positions in life.

We have never seen such a commitment by so many who seek knowledge and interest in the sight of spirit. We cannot focus on all, but rest assured, we will be seen and heard in those deep green grasses of life that flutter in the wind. As feathers on the birds back as they blow in the wind, their colours change from dark to light and as the rays penetrate their hollow stems, so they are filled with warmth and the light of the Lord.

You were noted as saying that, "All life is precious," and so it is without exception. From the humble bee to those who walk the earth and all in-between have the Lords focus. We care not for those who cannot perceive the world around them, for they are blinded with the material things of Earth.

Encompass your minds to swing towards a new beginning, the arrows will fly in the months ahead as we progress and draw closer to your world of life. We have a never-ending story to tell to the peoples of the Earth, allowing them to understand their meagre life's value within the kingdom of Heaven. For are we all not that of the creator? He who made the heavens and Earth, who held our hands as we walked in spirit, guiding us through the portals of life.

Richard was a common man, his work preceded him in the annals of time. He was of great value to those who saw him as a purpose, his name rings out in time never being forgotten by the many who study their history. He cannot contain himself at the thought that someone might recognise him as a man of mediocre means. Despite his status in life he has never found fortune in war, only grief. He is totally in agreement with those of the Earth who pursue peace at the talks to be held shortly in Vienna and in the capital city of Rome, from whence was a great civilisation. They will negotiate between them how progress and standing of the United Kingdom, for the turmoil that besets them will become calm once more as their focus turns to events in the North Sea which will bring great concern to many nations of the Earth. *(Note: It could be argued that this would fit anyone from Richard the Lion Heart to Richard Nixon, so many Richards in history, does anyone have a strong feeling about who this may be?)*

Be not afraid of those people who would harm others, as their purpose will be done in a blast of light of radiation. We are concerned for the safety of all who are unable to shelter from this massive explosion of the heart; the tempest of the storm will carry on it the winds of change to the many thousands in the regions of the North. We cannot understand why it is that this has to be, we are unable to prevent catastrophes such as this, as it is man's desire to beat upon himself in such terrible ways. Never let it be said that we of the universe did not try to assist in a small measure.

The parting of the ways of the many will become clear shortly, as a tidal wave of love washes over those of purpose to bring about an end to hostilities within the regions of the commonwealth. Frequently we have affirmed our message of peace, love and tolerance to those who would listen to the words of the Lord, for His presence is great amongst the many who suffer at the hands of tyrants. He watches their plight, unable to intercede as it is the plan of their life to suffer. We cannot perceive sometime soon, a lasting peace on your planet, but there will be a reconciliation of loving, a response to our demands as we circle your Earth in the fall of your planet.

Why is it that we, the Arcturians, have to announce our plans prematurely to allow those of the Earth a warning of something so astounding that hearts will pound in their minds. Their eyes will behold a mother ship that circles your Earth; it is blinded *(hidden/denied?)* by your men of science. Compulsion will lead you to extreme measures to face the truth of what is to come, a purpose in a new beginning will fall upon man as he begins to understand the many things of life that have true meaning, in the words set by the Lord so long ago in your history.

In the streets of Babylon, of Nairobi, there is or will be a tremendous outcry for politicians to listen to those who suffer in the street without homes. Babies and children, struggling to survive within the networks of those who see themselves as masters, the super race. What, what can I say, they will be dammed for their torture and intolerance? They think they have a good handle on everything, on things of life, in truth they know nothing of living. An Angelic gift of generosity will be given to those who have meagre resources.

Tonight we have become a victim of circumstance, we are alleged to have taken a member from your Earth. You cannot imagine how deep the pain runs when you mistrust our intentions upon your beings of life. You are of target for wanting Caucasians. *(Note: Has alien abduction been used as an excuse used to cover up trafficking, sale of a child for slavery or another form of abduction?)*

There are those that cannot understand your purpose in life as they see a man, an old man babbling on about things he could not possibly know. In truth you don't, it is by our wisdom that you speak the many truths of spirit. It is by their ignorance that they will not listen and try to understand the purpose of these words and their intentions upon your world. We are of the regions beyond your earth, we come as a matter of importance to assist those under extreme pressure from domination of those of war. We know of the problems that beset your people, we cannot allow this to continue. A stay of peace must be contracted between the nations. Comparatively, you are a simple organism with a soul of great strength, but your weaknesses are your failures to comprehend who you really are. We have fed you with information of this century to allow all, your purpose to meld with our own.

Those of a negative outlook will accumulate in a congregation of protest upon your streets of London, saying that 'out' should be 'in', they will persecute those who have voted with 'out' in mind, they cannot understand the issues deep within those nations of Euro corruption, the mindless energy. A secret purpose was to gain control of the nation's so that their energies conglomerate to advance their own needs.

We have remarked before on the circumstances involved with your nation, as the turmoil kicks in so does disruption and irritation. We cannot see why it is that people cannot work and live together as one. We are in condemnation, love, tolerance and a means to an end. Michael is nothing more than a man with an energy and need that sits with him to bring comfort to those who are unaware of the massive neglect who fall into the nations of wealth. Compel your mind to help those in need who are around you in close proximity, for they are in need to live in peace not in terror.

Tremendous amounts of good will, will be required by the many for a sacrifice of purpose is needed to calm the situation that will arise on the tenth of the month. Alice Springs will amount to a disaster to be unfolded within the springs, have mercy; those who will suffer loss and a tragic time of a plane. Parked are the wings upon the pad.

3rd July 2016

Tonight we will give a sermon of love and respect to all who follow the light in the name of the Lord. Make it a practice to give thanks for each and every day. May His presence make you aware of His love and being to bring about your purpose of need and aspirations. A feeling to cleanse your mind, filling it with thoughts of love and joy, never regretting the path that you have chosen.

As we walk together upon the road of life my son, never let it be said that we didn't achieve anything, as we have achieved so much to bring you these messages of joy, and wisdom to those who would otherwise have had their eyes closed to bring about a purpose of love, mandatory love.

You must exercise your will in the fragrance and the scent of Lavender.

Uniformly embrace the world with all its problems, for it has such potential to bring about joy and peace to mankind, if only man would desire peace within his time. Your unique circumstances have brought you to this point this evening, allowing us to comprehend your mind and to speak freely of our thoughts and will of love.

Your John is tender and loving *(a long-time guide of mine)* as he approaches to bring you news of an event that will touch your hearts in the coming years, of life, your joy. Although you will be surrounded by that of a willingness to serve His name, the Creator, never relinquish your intentions, as your purpose brings joy to the minds of those who seek a need to continue upon their paths in their own directions, seeking that which can only be found by those who look beyond their minds and thoughts of the physical. Nevertheless we have come this evening to bring you news of the purpose required of you, you must evaluate your needs. Valerie subsequently issues you her joy. A gift will issue you a purpose of belonging to the world of man, your hearts desires may value many things in your life, but your need of His will grows stronger.

Fishermen of men you are, casting your nets in the hope of snaring a few that might listen as you sail the seas of life, hoping to find that one thing that all men desire, a purpose, a need for love. Never let go of the things that you hold dear in your life, for a tremendous amount of will is forecast, by a need to bring about an end to the disruption soon to focus upon your life. You live in a town of many, divided, restricted by your streets of intolerance that surround you. You must regain the will of the people in a need to worship the Lord, our Father. For if this is lost, no more token *(indication)* to be left, for mankind to live with his brother in peace and harmony.

Our reputations have preceded us for thousands of years in the expectation that the Nazarenes *(Jesus)* words will flourish in the hearts of men. Alas they have faded, men no longer have a hunger, nor need of faith in our Father. What has happened to the sons of Adam, the daughters of Eve, to have brought you to this point in time? Forecast so many times before by other prophets, your will is as strong to persist, master us to reignite a spark within man in an attempt to bring hope back to the world of man.

A farcical performance was seen by many, as those of the governments clamber for the seats to reach that pinnacle of power which will lead so many on a ridiculous notion, that is to think that they have the will and the need to assist in man's needs, for their purpose is of self. The abundance of intolerance in a bitter divide of rivals will increase to bring about a mass demonstration by the Houses of Parliament, for they have ignited a storm of fear in reckless behaviour. The masses they surge towards the heartlands in the hope of bringing a resounding result to all. Fragmented your lives, of a silly way to practice together a passion of peace.

A marvellous event is soon to take place in the east, culminating in the west giving a display above your nation. A focus upon which man will surrender his thoughts on the meaning of life, for he cannot bear to resist the tender charms of the one that comes. Persuade those around you of the mercies of the Lord; let them know that her purpose and reason is that of love. Consequently your minds will banish your thoughts of intolerance and ignorance as you sit in awe by her presence. Your commonwealth will mass together in a hope of denouncing such things that don't seem possible, for they have fear and dread in their hearts, that their positions in life will no longer be of focus and have a low purpose, because we are aware that there must be leaders, those of merciful hearts, who tend to souls to guide those masses in the world to bring them together in a focus of love. For if we cannot achieve this, then what hope for man, what hope for the world.

We were needy of men's purpose, for a soul to speak in their minds and thoughts and prayers of love in their hearts. Consider yourself a magnet by which a means to an end will be achieved. You may regret taking this path as it will bring much disappointment in your life, but know this my son, that all men of purpose are to suffer the scars and indignities that are set upon them.

Commodus, he speaks once more to the nations of your world as a soldier, as a humanitarian. Alas his mind was weak with fear and terror as he drove his purpose home through the hearts of men. What merciless times they were, of murderers, pointless processions. I could not perceive at the time how the masses would react to the laws that I set. My disappointment in others was repaid by treachery, their hearts, their minds, compelled me to act in ways that were regrettable. I became a man of valour only to fall into the pits of hell for the actions I took against my fellow human beings. Those days are past now, my lessons learnt, my future bright.

Do not forget your lessons as you progress in a myriad of ways to bring your focus upon the light of Him who sits in Heaven, for His splendour is great. His need of you is required to bring about an end to a means. Suffer you may, but your knowledge is great. Her Herculean ways, image *(represent)*, men, who strived to bring about peace during those days, those awful days of darkness, dark times indeed. We had no rest for we were driven by the master's whip. Commodus, he tore us apart as a man then, but his shame was greeted by love and he grew in stature to become a figure of that of the light. He conquered his fears in the oppression of his people to bring love and purpose to the common man, for his fight was one of a battle of love. Never let it be said that his heart was torn from his body as it beat in the hands of the Lord, never be ashamed of who you are, for we speak through you in ways you cannot understand. Your mask shields a man who is meek and mild in manner, your heart beats strong in your focus and purpose.

Weather the storms that will bring disasters to the east and passes to the west. Focus should be upon these weather systems that bring a front of relentless storms that gather over the oceans. Their winds will blow of a magnitude of force nine gales on the shores of the lands to the east. Many will be shocked by the ferocity in the lashing, the endless lashing of the winds.

Mm, your world is a mess, it fragments beneath your feet in ways you cannot understand as yet, you drive home your purpose with your drills, hoping to extract that which sits in Mother Earth. Why do you think it is kept in the Earth and not released to the light? This poisonous gas will suffocate the earth in such a fashion as to cause warming, bringing about storms and gales. Adverse weather in regions so remote that the unexpected will occur. The gasses released that caused these adverse conditions were caused by man's exploitation of her resources. Neglect and ignorance will bring about the deaths of many, for they cannot withstand the power of nature in their habitats upon the islands.

The Aegean Sea is a place of natural wonders yet to be seen by the eyes of man. You cannot possibly understand our focus upon you will bring about a purpose in many, for what is buried beneath the sea is a temple of magnificence, set before the storm as being a wonder of the world. Most astounding are its structures that they marvelled the people, the people's purpose. The seas roared as the lands moved, we felt a shift, the blast of air; she rolled in on us, washed over us wiping away many souls. We exist in spirit, we live on through the lives of many, our souls remain impervious to the destruction caused. We need to focus once more upon your planet in the hope that our presence will be meaningful to men once more.

Your minds are tranquillised by means of irrational gains. Compel your minds to work together so that we, the Arcturians, may once more serve as your masters and assist your planet, nurse her back to health. For we have wondrous ways in which to carry out such feats of magnificence. Your science with little knowledge of the many things that we possess, they are aware of our being, they have a need for what we know but cannot possess, nor will they until they have learned to live as one, man with man, upon the surface of your Earth as it fades slowly, succumbing to the masses needs.

Triumph of the many will be achieved in a storm of protest. Intolerance and greed will muster the minds of many intolerant. They are astounding, their arrogance and attitude, as they must have the many riches that Earth provides. Why does man beat upon man, why does man have his hearts intention of the negative things of life? They fail to see their true purpose in the position given, you must compel the light to work with an attitude of arrogance towards her, your insistence of the lights purpose will bring about change in many men. Their influence and tolerance will shine brightly in the glint of your heart.

I am Alex, we have spoken once before, you need not know the many things that bring us together. As we caress your Mother Earth we cannot help but see and feel the pain of so many pictures of burden of your beings. How they change as we focus our light upon the seas of mistrust. The seasons are a mess we have left it to long to help the majority. Mother, their need is great, but you must help them see that strength lies in their hearts and minds. Their lives are focused with one of time as the clock ticks and the bell tolls. We respect their own differences between them, counting the days that their purpose will ring out once more to influence those of troubled minds. To accumulate a mass of an oral *(spoken word)* among your men. Gather your thoughts my son as we near your Earth before the season of the sun sets in the east. Do not think that we do not know of the terrors that await. *(Note: Alex has come through before, in this paragraph it almost seems that he is also speaking with another, he refers to mother, possibly Mother Mary?)*

(The following paragraph is about a crop circle at Stonehenge, UK which we, as 'The Trio', went to visit. There is a further entry and diagram about this occurrence and the mathematics given by the Arcturians in the transcript of 21st July.)

Buddha once said, "A man's strength was his forbearance of others," as he sits in his temple he remembers the days of the mozelbete *(Note: Spanish for young lad or youth)*, sit as he does and focus your will. We implore you to listen to these words from Alex, he is a member of a race of beings that frequented your Earth many times. His circles of half moons will appear to astonish men of science in their complexity. Their purpose and meaning are for instruction to those who have a will, a mind to see their patterns upon the ground. *(Note: Crop circles!)* Truly you must measure the distance between the marked grasses for they will equate to a number that will be measured, Eastern coordinates 10 degrees west, 9 degrees south latitude and longitude will be measured by the circumference of the Earth multiplied by three. In the fourth dimension you will need to bring your purpose with fortitude to help us assist in the measurements, in the degrees. *(Note: Could these co-ordinates be galactic ones pointing to a place in space, are there any mathematical minds out there who can help us understand these?)*

We are a people beyond your vision, our thoughts and will are heard through the minds of many who regard us as spirit. We have unleashed a measurable amount of love many times. The task of many as you mediate between those of your earth and those of the stars. Huh, they, you, re-trust Arcturians, we have a will and purpose to bring peace within your solar system. Too many times we have witnessed the wars upon your earth as they rage. Oh such shameful sights are seen on Master of Service, why do we find it necessary to focus our love and light upon the children of the earth.

A Raven once more approaches, offering a ring of service, her Rubies represent our hearts, they are the colour of red. *(Note: In Greek mythology, the Raven is a messenger of God).* Shine out a beacon, your minds focus, purpose. Once more feel us as we draw a purpose from you to project our words, countless times have we spoken in the past to many souls we have worked in the circles of light, in their séances, in their rooms of darkness. They have heard and seen us, beat our drums, whistles, play our flutes and the people's response is one of shock and horror that such things could be. Not once did they open their minds to the realms of the light and see that these things that we demonstrate have a purpose, we cannot say how we commanded respect for we gave love in a manner of goodwill.

Tumultuous times have paid a heavy price, as thousands listen to words of discomfort spoken by those of plenty *(wealth)*. Task your minds with reason to the possibilities of boundaries to be broken, trust in our words as we trust in you to focus upon us with a loving heart and tender words.

Michael, you begin a journey of love to assist those who need forbearance *(patience or tolerance)*, **for their attitudes are twisted, missing the point of their purpose.** You register our thoughts on a machine that sits beside you and we all affirm ourselves on your machine. *(Note: They are referring to the recorder.)*

As the Ravens fly, so the Crows will flee, so it is that light will vanquish the dark in a heavenly struggle that will be fought upon your Earth. *(Note: Symbolically, the Raven is the messenger of God, the Crow is the harbinger of doom or bad omens.)* The purpose of man is to bring division between light and dark. The struggles of men are incarnate, go to your purpose with need and love, reaffirm our commitment to bring about a peace to the masses of the Earth. With tenderness Johnson *(President Lyndon Johnson)* came at a time when his nation needed him most, their apparent unrest will reflect in today's terrible things. Those states will dishonour the power struggles within and will culminate in a mass outpouring of discontent. Why is it you have never learned the amendments of the contract made? For we were the fathers of a nation, a new and wondrous nation built on the lives of many in honour. It is true that the land upon which we lived was stolen; the hearts and minds of those indigenous braves were torn from them in our thirst and lust of greed. They have come to see how wrong we are, that all nations should live together as one with focus and purpose. If I had to sail the seas of life, I would hope the breeze was of love as I cast my nets upon the water, and the fishes I reaped were the souls of men who were lost to the depths of the sea.

Prince Harry will become a man of displeasure this season. His words will be heard as intolerance, his mother's strength lies within him, not to bandy words with people, to be outspoken. To speak his mind will shock those of the establishment to realise that he is a man, a figure with purpose so underestimated by that of the media. Know that his strength will carry a burden like no other for his monarchy will shine a light on the nation of your people as tragic circumstances unfold within the nation and the establishment. Fortunes of war is what they call it, purpose in being is what we give. *(Note: Could this be regarding the Chilcot Enquiry?)*

6th July 2016

A massive outcry is to be expected before the coming of the Lord, let he who denounces Him understand that they will attract those of the negative acts on the net, creating a situation upon which there is no return for the black *(negative)* hearts are many within this world. Continue in your work bringing the light into the life of those who would hear your words and remark on their content, for it is healthy to have an opinion and to exercise your minds right to question those things of the Earth and that which lies beyond.

Our purpose is to bring forth the words to the many of your world in the hope that they will succumb to the light before their time is done. You have the knowledge to bring about change in this world, your masters will recognise the adverts of inspiration that you bring forth into the world, from the world of light.

A combination of minds, their work delighted many who read their books, but their ignorance did not allow it in. They found it amusing to read and remark on the words of spirit for it was novel to them, but not new to those who knew His light and love.

Peace became a symbol of the nation of the many as they fought and struggled to bring economic stability to their shores. Worse still, they ignored those of mankind who have a need and are troubled with worry. For their reckless behaviour it will be announced that they will suffer the consequences in due course.

We cannot say how much we appreciate their cooperation of the nines, the value in your words their focus is upon you to bring forth a notion of recognition of man's plight. Why is it that we have to say this that no longer respects man, he continues his burdens with a mind filled with data not representative of the will of the Lord. *(Note: The Nines, possibly the nine spiritual gifts? Nine manifestation gifts are listed in I Corinthians 12:7–11: Word of wisdom – Word of knowledge – Faith – Gifts of healing – Working of miracles – Prophecy – Discerning of spirits – Divers kinds of tongues – Interpretation of tongues OR maybe The Council of Nine?)*

Commodus did so much in his mind for his people but it was not their will to be fooled by a master full of indignities. Your situation on your planet's surface is very much that of those times – the dictators hidden behind the scenes, pulling the strings, observing the chaos created. For where there is chaos there is corruption and collusion.

It is noted that the people of Scotland would like independence, perhaps they have a will and a strength to formulate a plan to bring their independence to the fore, but they should never ignore the fact that the peoples of the Earth are one regardless of their vote. She will announce a Declaration of Independence within the four months to satisfy her whims, that of being 'President' of a nation of Scotsmen. She is narrow minded, her eyes fixed upon the seat of the house as she sits in judgement over those she would rule, she cares not for those possibilities of failure, to her the game is afoot. *(Note: Nicola Sturgeon?)*

She once knew a nation of plenty that become poor within her time, for she welcomed change in the hope of prosperity for her and those around her of her family who knew hardship. Many times she had been denounced as a reckless woman not paying attention to the profits to be made, for those millionaires who sank her drills into the seas of the world, the nation became prosperous at the expense of Mother Earth.

Careless handling will bring about a disastrous response in the near future as the pipelines burst flowing a black substance to the seabed, this will be noticeable as the surge rises to the surface bringing a devastation to those all around. They'll speculate a banning of such pipes as they corrode beneath the surface of the sea, they are neglected through lack of funds but as long as the oil keeps pumping, those with the well will be happy to keep it flowing, never thinking about the destruction that it wreaks upon the earth, for their purpose is of greed of the black gold.

Crucifixions are a thing of the past, but Christ still bears the scars, the wounds, of his suffering still. His knowledge was great of the people's needs in Solomon's lands as he travelled through the many winding pathways upon the stony ground. His sermons were heard by many. On the mounts of Sinai he stood and watched as the crowds surged around to listen to his words of the Lord, his faith was such, that no man could move him for his love of the Father. He was an envoy sent to your Earth with the command to reach out to mankind, bring them together in a purpose of need, his faith was strong, his heart beat with love for all with purpose. Upon the mount he spoke to the millions of the nations of the Earth, knowing that one day his words would reach many shores. Their patterns would be taught to those who would ignite storms of faith, it was never intended that the words be twisted to suit those of a purpose of greed. The Father in Heaven looks down upon those who had used these funds for their personal gain, it is recognised that many in authority operate in such a way that they fleece those with little.

It was once said that the hawk that flies above the pigeons is the shadow of death that will bring them down, but if those birds were able to see the shadow upon the ground then they would know that their lives were forfeit for the greater good of Mother Nature. As harsh as this may seem it is true in life, that man will be sheltered from the storms of indignity, but in the end he would taste his bitter end to become a shadow of himself. If his reluctance to move on should persist, then he must roam the dark valleys that integrate with your world.

Bring forth your opinions people! For the stories we tell are of guidance, not of negativity. We pass them through this man in the hope that your ears would listen to the wisdom of us, the Arcturians. We are members of a race that were beyond your focus. Commit your lives in the preparation of our coming, to prepare your nations to bring shame upon those who have brought suffering to others. We recognise that there are many lights upon your world of life that radiate their love to help mankind, for them the future is great.

Bring about your focus to help those in need in the southern States of America, as their need grows before the storm that descends upon them as the majority initiate satanic ways to evolve their master. Don't be fooled by their grace and attitude, they are dark ones who keep their purposes close to their chest not allowing those in any circumstance to draw close and see the cards they play.

You represent a narrative for our thoughts, but know this, that those who beckon you on will denounce your meaningful thoughts, for they see a man who cannot possibly relay such messages. Their focus is upon their own lives helping others the best way that they can and of this there is no issue. Your best way forward my son is independence and a goodwill to those that cross your path, for they will see that they will have issue with many words spoken, but in the end they know that life is spirit that exists within all and it cannot be denied no matter what their intentions.

Parkinson's disease, a terrible form that affects the muscular system and the nervous system of the body. Many suffer in silence shivering and shaking, not understanding why their control is lost. They are frightened by the lesions that cause such pain in their minds. They hope and pray that they will surpass the strain of living in the hope of a cure to be found by your men of science. Comes this day in Dresden as they announce a satisfactory conclusion to their research, it far extends beyond their expectations, but they know that the source of this formula comes from the ancient scripts that are hidden within the walls of the cathedrals of your world. *(Note: A very quick internet search indeed revealed that research on Parkinson's does take place in Dresden, something none of us knew.)*

Humph! They will not allow their minds to accept that they live on borrowed time, for the truth will out in the coming trimester (three months), commencing in the August of your years. Trouble your mind not, for they will see the error of their ways and admit that they have seen ancient books with remedies and cures unseen before in the world, as they circulate these medicines, the men of wealth will retain the answers for fear of losing their abundant wealth.

Controversy will spark indignation against those who have hidden these cures for so long, for their greedy minds will not allow them to disclose the whereabouts of their findings. You talk of the Dead Sea Scrolls; these are of major importance as to the whereabouts of the healing books that were hidden from man's eyes in the deserts of the north. Damascus was seen as a city unworthy of their place, so the deserts north, out to the seas are the resting places of these artefacts. They will bring forth knowledge not seen before, truly a miracle they will say, but to us they are a natural formula, remedies for all. Do you suppose that the ancients do not know of these discoveries, did not understand their meanings? They used them, they created a world within a world, their destruction was brought about by their greed. Nothing changes, for man is a creature of habit it is true to be said.

Convince your mind that we aspire demands, purpose, take note of these facts that these discoveries will be found in the August, Augustus was and is August!

The facts remain that you are still a novice my son, but train your mind to our will and don't allow interference from those thoughts that deny us entrance. Compel your mind with a will and purpose to focus as the need grows for us to inform you of a situation of situations pending.

Troublesome minds, weary eyes, watch over those who hunger for position. She will not escape their wrath as she formulates a plan to ignite a spark of mistrust within the cabinet of man. Regrettably she will not know the situation undermining her position in authority. *(Note: Teresa May was elected as UK Prime Minister on 13th July 2016.)*

Margaret, she was, a woman renowned for strength and ego, she bore her time well, never underestimating her abilities to absorb information given by those of the secret service. Your national emblem was a signal to many as they become aware of her purpose. *(Margaret Thatcher.)*

Tonight we will leave this conversation for rest, as recuperation is needed, your weary mind struggles to intercede with us, God bless Michael, have faith my son.

7th July 2016

You are a nation in a wondrous world that beckons for peace in these turbulent times that you find yourselves. Many ask the question, *"Why are we enduring so many tragic circumstances throughout this world, what is the reason for us to be experiencing these things of turbulent times at this time of the century?"* Trust in us when we tell you that each has his own path to walk and must experience the travesties of life through his own eyes and ears, to feel and see the tragedies that befall others before you. This is not a sinister message, but a message to let you know that the paths you tread are yours and yours alone; you were brought to this point for a purpose way beyond your comprehension.

We point out many things that you cannot possibly be aware of or understand, and through this man we will try in a small measure to bring an awareness, an alertness to your minds that you are beings of the light and those that fall by the wayside are not lost, but are restricted in their capacities to enter the gates of the light. Troubled times, hmm we grow weary of repeating our message to the world of life. Why is it your arrogance will not allow us in?

Tony *(Tony Blair)* **is a man in need of love, for he was shielded by his cabinet.** The men who brought doom upon those who gave their lives for a cause that they believed in. Why were they betrayed through lack of information as to their purpose in demanding that peace and justice be brought to the leader of the Arab nation? His crimes were committed many times, he never suffered fools gladly for he had an unbelievable arrogance that his nation was his and that he would rule as he saw fit. He never thought that he would be sacked by those around him as their mistrust grew, his purpose was grave and that of his family who supported his kingdom and brought turmoil in an irresponsible and irrational manner. For they brought upon themselves a mighty force that would culminate in an ending to those turbulent times. The wound festered as the dark moved in, so the light was extinguished for many.

We cannot understand why it was they felt they had to interfere at this time, do they not understand that no crime goes unpunished. We are not here to judge, but to bring a measure of peace to those who have lost loved ones in this ridiculous war, and why did he take the decision to invade a land of horrors, was it to honour their name? Black gold was their target, made no difference. All there was, was bloodshed, innocent lives lost and for what? Sometimes in life things are better let be, as judgment comes to all who offend Him on High.

Man should not judge man, nor should he expect intolerance. For wise decisions take wise men, not fools that rush in on a whim in a manner of strength. For it is not they that suffer the consequences of a foolhardy rush to administer justice, it is not the politicians, the money makers who face such grievous and appalling destruction. Many Iraqis hiding in their homes were innocent victims of a mad gold rush; although the many suffered at his hands *(Saddam Hussein?)* there were those who had security and a peace. No man is sacred unto himself, only God will judge all.

Times come and go, their needs of must abate with time. Trust in the Lord that justice will be done in your world of life.

Planetary systems will abide by the rules of the universe as they continue to rotate on their assigned orbits. You see the earth as a vast expanse of space never ending, neither beginning, what harm the ending – know that it is – your universe exists within a parallel universe for all creation is one creation, Gods creation, this is a mindless, endless journey and none will ever comprehend. Your ships travel in space as do others, but it is an ocean voyage that will never see an end, what goes around comes around.

You cannot imagine an existence beyond that of spirit, our world is vast, as the earth is by comparison but a speck, for space is vast and holds many secrets beyond your understanding. Your men of science, they work ever harder to explain the mysteries of the earth and the universe in which it sits. Let us tell you now, they will never find the answers they seek, for their times are relatively short to time, their mission in life is a fragment of that question.

Our goals are simple, to escort man to a better world, for him to comprehend that he is but a speck in the universe of life. Many nations *(alien nations)* have banded together, but your world is not fit for this unity as your purpose is yet to be found. The longer your focus is upon lust in your lives and personal gain, the longer it will take before you realise the many nations that watch with many eyes. You're like a laboratory rat being studied inside and out. Why do you think it strange that we select a few so that we may understand your physical bodies in greater detail? Ha! We are accused of murderous abductions, if this was so, how is it people explain their experiences to the world? Despite not being believed they are returned as a lab rat is returned to its cage, many of you call this evil. Have you looked at yourselves and what you do? The lab rats of your world suffer as you make an effort to look more beautiful, to make your personal lives easy! We need not explain ourselves to you, we are not evil, we are the scientists that are looking to you in the hope your knowledge will grow. Can you not see that there is a means to an end? We need to bring about an awareness of our being to reduce an expression of fear. Ask your colonels of their judgment upon us, their weapons loaded, primed to tear your world apart. Their minds of war are minds of fear, for is not the world for all that live? The creatures upon it have freedom of heart, can you not learn to live together as one?

We have an urgent need to help those who have a purpose to bring peace. The flowers of Heaven will fall upon your world, one by one, planting seeds in the minds of those who let it in. Your gardens of beauty will become a forest of knowledge, be not afraid to let us into your hearts, minds and souls.

Precious metals are to be found in various places around your planet. They explore by extreme measures, destroying vast quantities of your lands. In their greed they disrespect Mother Nature with their practices of blasting out the earth in search of diamonds, gold, treasures that they hold so dear, but these treasures are false profits, for what good are they to men when they die. You misunderstand the many things of your lives, diamonds have a natural ability, they sparkle to your eyes, they are a hard substance, their powerful secrets are hidden from you, for all you see is their beauty and not that which lies within. Your resources will run dry in your exploitation for the natural riches that extend beyond your earth in due course.

We have no need to explain our mission to you, your endless wittering of desperation, your craving for knowledge, the thirst you have for the knowledge of life upon the path you

tread. Your angels that guide you, meet with you in your dreams, the blessings that they bestow upon you should be treated with love and affection. To complete your mission we need your focus Michael, let go your thoughts and fears, allow us to traverse your mind with knowledge. Your disbelief in your capabilities will hold you back, march on or it will haunt your doubts and misgivings. Allow us to intercede with those things of your life, your tempestuous ways you must eliminate.

Trigonometry and Crop Circles

Truly remarkable it will be, your reaction to our coming in the cornfields. Your measures will be taken, you will marvel at the patterns. We need your focus to allow and understand the circles of your crops. Blushed *(embarrassed)* you are at the thought of being able to recognise the measure, play four (or maybe 'therefore' or even 4.6, recording was unclear) point six, twelve, compare this measurement with the earths circumference, triangulation will result in a meaningful, a desirable answer. Conversely you enquire to understand the measurements given, true we need to explain, a triangle is of equal sides, its measure equates to a fraction within a fraction, triangulation twenty by four squared. A ridiculous notion you may think, allow us to intercede, 3 = Pi2, 14 degrees north by northeast, triangulate the latitude of 16, markers take away a fraction of 10, this measurement is all you need to know, for the present the values of these measurements will gauge in your response, our response. The spell has meanings for you that you will not understand, for those of medical knowledge will have use and need of them.

Extremism/Terrorism

Prepare yourselves for an onslaught of worries of misgivings, for their deeds will bring about death and destruction to the nations of their over intolerance to their cause. Plain to see their intentions, you have weaknesses and they will exploit them as your arrogance. You don't see this planning for they will exploit through your nets *(internet)*. Feathers amongst many, they experienced such atrocities, his name is of no consequence but he wishes to impart that his death was that of the eagle, not of circumstance, he doesn't understand how it is a man can beat upon man in such a manner and they weren't forgiving, no quarter to us was given. (sigh, hmm.) We ask of you not to give up on life because such things occur, for they are part of this journey as these things are a part of your journeys. Continual tolerance is needed to achieve a measure of peace within your world, the crimes committed in our Fathers name will not go unanswered. Beyond your lives your sympathies lie with the victims and the circumstance that befell them. Be aware the ships sail the seas unguarded, unprotected, these are loopholes your nations have not seen. We do not wish to bring such thoughts, but you should be made aware. Airports are protected, but many things are not. The extremism will always exploit the weak. Be guarded as you utter these words, for they will reach far and wide. Our intention is not of fear but of preservation of life.

So called extremists have no care for life, their purpose is dark in the need for their domination upon the nations of many. They see you as a threat, but in truth there is no threat, but in their minds warped senses. The doctrines taught to them are the evil men who administrate their ratings upon them, calling, together for a mighty onslaught upon your nation of Great Britain. They disapprove of the measures taken of recent times. Your government, your leaders, busy amongst themselves for the spoils of war are not focusing upon the weaknesses, which they have created within your nation. London is a target, with the exception of Birmingham. Chaos will reign with a thunderous roar, to demonstrate their purpose, shhh, we fear a great loss. Your nation will recover and the measure of mourning of the great numbers who will pass to us. Not all will listen or heed our warnings until it's too late. Even then they will be dismissed as the murmurings of an old man. Careless whispers in the dark should be noticed. Ah, in your presence we will afford a measure of comfort to those who suffer loss, to know that their lives will not end but will open up to a world of beauty. Some with confusion of a need of knowing, some will accept like the children, just accept for what it is, no questions, no sadness. Do not despair at your life's end, for all are welcome within the realm of the spectral beings.

10th July 2016

Constantly we hear murmurings of discontent within the nations of your world, for the haphazard way in which man behaves. He neglects the things given to him from our Father the Lord.

We once more have purpose to bring a meaningful end to all who suffer persecution within your world. Frantic your minds as you cry out for peace and stability. Frankly we are appalled that the human race has degenerated into an appalling mess. Your governments, when they realise the situation is dire, will have neither the strength nor the attitude to change, for they fear retribution from the masses. Their terminology is that of rhetoric *(speech making!)*, for which most will not understand. Their knowledge grows of a purpose within your communities to strive forward for a better future, a life of compassion.

We cannot stress enough to the multitudes of your Earth that we, the Arcturians, have a purpose dedicated to bring about minds of peace. To activate a wave of communion, within your peoples of the world. Frantically we have attempted to communicate and connect with your men of science. They're blasphemous with nuisance weapons; they chase us with their arrogance, completely misunderstanding the purpose of our visit. Comparatively men are no better than those who cause tyranny within the world, they deliberately drag out the purpose of peace to cause a wave of fear. We need your co-operation to bring about a meaningful purpose to the world of men.

Circles you have seen, circles in the sand will be released in the near future, your men who disbelieve such things will scratch their heads thinking, "How is this possible, for sand does not hold its form?" We are aware of the sceptics and critics who will accuse those of adhering the partials together. Measure the sand with your instruments of science and know there is no trickery, just our influence upon matter, upon which you have not achieved.

We are no longer on the surface of our planet, we are destitute, alien to our world for it is unbreathable. We focus our attention on yours in the hope that there may be an alliance, by which our nation may join yours, but alas your world is too violent at this time for us to consider a motion of peace between us, so we watch in the darkness.

We observe men of science desperately trying to dismiss our attempts of communication with excuses of, "It's just radio interference". It won't be long before the master of the universe comes before you all to initiate their purpose of love and temperance. Can you not see that our wisdom is the words of the Lord, do you not understand that all living creatures about the universe are a creation of His Almighty hand? You search space for the beginnings of events, this cannot be found, it is not a material thing that you should be looking at. Spiritually you are aware of the many things beyond your science, you trespass upon our lives sending your ships to investigate.

So sad that your short lives are intimidated by men of violence.

Comfort should be given to those of Antigua this evening. They will suffer an earthquake of some magnitude, an eruption will follow very quickly causing the Earth to move, many will be lost to the clouds of dust that roll in from the hills. You need not concern yourselves with such events as they reoccur many times upon your Earth as she coughs and chokes under the strain that you impose upon her. Your clean air will soon be gone as the mists of time roll in. Reaction from us cannot occur, we cannot presume to interfere in the lives of man, your atmosphere will choke, you will continue, but things will change. It's up to you to bring life back to your planet or not!

Target your emotions my son, focus your mind, curb your attitudes as we advance to bring knowledge to mankind of forthcoming events in the early spring of next year.

We have arrived at the conclusion that your trust is worthy, we are satisfied that we can now demonstrate many things that you are to impart upon your people. We gather in the early spring as many do, for new beginnings will arrive with an attitude of love towards man. We cannot guard you, we cannot bring ourselves to mention the many things you will see within your lifetime. You gather your crops *(metaphor for gathering people)* and harvest your fruit, treat them with the respect and the dignity they deserve, for they are poor of heart, their minds reap many things, can you not see that we bring greetings of love and wisdom.

We have met many times before, your memories lapse as all do, but your knowledge grows and you speculate the many things possible beyond your world. Treat it with respect, that is how we expect those of the Earth to communicate with us, not to impart their messages of warnings as they scream, 'Keep away!' What problem have they in allowing another nation to communicate their feelings? We cannot describe our anxiety at the prospect of ill will from your men of the Earth, they will attempt to defeat us, but this will be futile, as we will disable their forces with an attitude of love, so as not to increase the tension and focus upon their weapons of war. They will turn to you and others to help in the efforts of contact.

Your wavelengths of the Earth you call radio, will not transmit messages on our frequency. We have an urgent need to communicate with those who are able to receive a signal, CETI (*Communication with extra-terrestrial intelligence*) they ignite a storm when they remark on the cloud of interference caused upon their machines.

Your vibrations are only matched by that of your purpose, your intentions may be good or bad, but they will bring forth a harvest of knowledge for those of a will to pick from. Transmit your messages through your minds as opposed to the physical media.

We cannot assist you in your lives; you must attain your peace. Truly remarkable, your will to connect with us 'beings of the light', your responses will be answered in due course. As a matter of interest do you wish us to show the lights of Heaven? So be it, feel us as we approach, have no fear as we will be gentle in our manner.

We spoke of tuberculosis that many will suffer in the fires emitted from your grounds, truly your conscious minds will sooth it. A natural ability, awareness to the diseases of your earth. Your fortitude should be increased tenfold that the remedies and cures that are purchased by the men of wealth, they hold back information of a magnitude that will astound those minds of science. Why has this not been seen, why do you hold back vital information they will ask. Your media will draw attention to their findings and bring their focus to the fore, embarrassing them as they have to admit their wrong doings.

Heartfelt thanks are given to the many who value your words of life, you cannot assume that all responses will be friendly, but know this, we are friends to those who wish our company.

Your bondage to the rich will become freer as the markets crash as they speculate upon a world without a future.

The wars of Rome were many and vast. They were spread so thinly that their measures and rules could not be applied. In the final outburst of anger, the city walls fell and Rome crashed through the bureaucracy of those in power and of wealth. They mocked the multitudes in a manner disrespectful to the human race, as a rabid dog will turn upon his master, so those revelling Romans knew their defeat.

A spectacle of sheer delight is to be seen, a miraculous event will occur in the east and west over the skies. December is a time of peace and harmony it denotes the coming, and the passing of ignorance and ignorance of that time. Truly yours will be no different in His coming, for He will announce His being very shortly in the clouds of the eastern sky. We have CETI, we will communicate our voice to the multitudes of your earth, through the whispering of this old man, for he has an ability to transmit his feelings. Allow us the courtesy of entering his being *(Authors Note: I do actually feel slightly different at this point)*. How strange it feels to become one with man, to feel the pulsating rhythm, we have conquered many worlds with our love, we have gratitude for our being. We were once a nation of independent souls who were able to trash *(dispose of!)* our bodies of matter, we exist now within the light of spirit. We commence our journeys on many paths with an expectation of love and goodwill to all men. Transmit your vibrations as you sit without fear Michael, to master your feelings you must release.

Tragic circumstances will indicate a purpose to the meaning of life. All those who are lost will crawl out upon Mother Earth, the sanctuary. The entire world will roll, Know of St Roland's axis spinning as it weaves its way through the cosmic universe.

We will initiate a programme of peace among your people, your nations of despair will become one as the multitudes ignite a spark of intolerance to their masters. Become one with your heart and knowledge. Have superior lines of thought, for we will allow you the freedom of thought. We cannot say with any great accuracy that life on your Earth will exist for many eons, for if your attitudes do not change then take this as a warning, that your communities will collapse before your eyes. We must build on your thoughts of love, on concrete foundations, affirm your love to that of the Creator who sits and watches and guards those of the light. Comparatively your mind is weak, it shapes your thoughts of the many aspects of your life. Complete your missions in the manner of respect for all that gather around. Do not let them display a dismissive interest, for these words cannot be expressed to those of a negative attitude.

You ask of this world from whence we come, it is a beautiful place filled with aspects of love in many colours by which they are perceived. If you have dark thoughts in your lives, then you will continue in the darkness until you have reached a point of recognition to that of love and peace towards your fellow beings. Oh, we see his role, and its clarity of thought, although he cannot believe how much we inspire to fill in the messages to those of your world, and peace to your brothers within your lifetime. There is no task unworthy.

We have explained the rivers of life and the virtues by which you should follow. We regard your beings as being primitive. You are easily fooled, you follow like sheep to the wolves' lair, they beckon you on with trinkets and trifles. Can you not see the bigger picture from which their purpose comes? We have many times expressed a concern upon the future of man, his ways of intolerance to his Mother Earth and to his fellow beings.

The Welfare of Our Young

We cannot completely assume that your species will continue, as one for the negative that exists within you all, has a tremendous power of attitude that affects those of your young. Your responsibilities to your next generations are not being met at this time. We find your arrogance and disbelief in the powers of the Lord hurtful; you have taken away the God given right to the young ones to learn of aspects of love. They play their games of violence, registering the thoughts that intimidate their minds, their natural abilities are impeded by your ignorance. We have witnessed many occasions by which children have been sent to us by means of intolerance from their own kind. We cannot understand the reasoning behind this, truly you must see and concur your thoughts of fear and negativity, you must equate yourselves as beings of the light, convince those around you that God exists within you all. Can you not be brave? Allow the light to shine and dismiss the negatives, your responsibilities to the next generation are failed as you clamour for the latest gadgets, the novelty of which has a dark purpose beyond your understanding.

They watch you from behind your walls *(firewalls?)* **they hear the thoughts of your mind, they compare this with many things.** Subliminal messages are being sent by those who would profit through your ignorance. Don't allow your minds focus to fall into the trap of technology for it holds within it a force of evil and they encourage you all the time. As their technology increases, they insert minute chips to increasingly watch the population of your Earth.

In secretive ways your society is led by the wolves, you are the sheep that graze upon their ill will. Lift your heads from the ground and look at what's around you, become aware of the wolves and their intentions upon you and your young ones. Lift your hearts and say, 'No!' to these desirable things, for they have no purpose in your lives other than to amuse and to spy.

We applaud progression in your race, but it must be tempered with love and the true guidance in your hearts. We applaud your efforts to bring hope to others with our words; we condemn those who deceive with deceit. Their undignified ways will not prosper them. As their short lives end, they will wonder what it is that they have achieved, because what they have achieved, they cannot take with them, it makes no difference to their next existence. Beware the wolves that knock at your door, look them in the eye and ask them the truth of their hearts. Denounce them as being creatures of the night and shelter your young ones from the storm that rages around you. In all aspects of life you are tormented. In ways that you cannot imagine, your beings are focused upon the instruments of pleasure, for they bring distraction within your minds. Your hearts will is ignored, as their greed becomes a hunger in your heart, you lust after the riches of life. You don't see the true riches of life, that of love and tolerance towards your fellow human beings.

This is all you take with you! You buy a car and the car transports you, what need of it when you pass? That car is of no use to you whatsoever, but if you were to open your heart to love, a tolerance and to assist your fellow beings, when you pass, this is what you take with you. Your light will shine bright in the heavens above your earth and you will know that your life of purpose was good.

We continually attempt to make contact by means of your radio waves, you have heard the vibrations continually. We will bring an ever-increasing need for those to listen. Your sacrifice of will is marked as a passion of love. (*Authors Note: I have heard the vibrations on the recordings, an oscillation sound which is visible on the graph of the GoldWave program.*) Continually we muster our thoughts around you, transmit your being.

Tremendous emotions are being felt at this time, by those of poverty around your world, their hearts cry out, their stomachs hunger. Why must we endure these things they ask. Children lay on the streets of your cities unnoticed by the many; they are ignored as if they were of no value. Your streets of Singapore are lined with many magnificent buildings of splendour; the houses of profit, at their feet lay those individuals who cry out for justice and a home to live in. In their doorways and their underground caverns they sleep and shiver with fear of being found. The children who are lost in these societies are in urgent need of homes and loving families. Your species are strange to ignore one another's needs without taking a second look, for your attitude will reflect on your lives and purpose.

Will you not denounce those who make millions of your money? They control your web with an image you cannot understand or do not see, their focus and gaze is upon their aspects of profit at whatever expense. They have no need of men, only their purpose of greed. Trials and tribulations will be set against them in a new beginning. A marked emotion will be felt as they realise the money is lost and Ubicore become rich in their own right. (*Note: Sometimes words are hard to determine with accuracy on the recordings, however If the word Ubicore* *is correct it is a software product for service provisioning, and remote management of OSGi enabled devices. With Ubicore, devices like residential gateways, vehicle gateways, industrial equipment and similar devices can be remotely managed and monitored. We have no idea if this is of any relevance or not!)*

Do not let them sleep under the stars, bring peace to their hearts and souls. Their memories of their loved ones to bargain, for they too came from a family of neglect, for some were abandoned by the pressures put upon their loved ones. Your tolerance is needed to grant them peace, pray for them so that they may find a warmth in their hearts and a purpose in their being. Pray for them, for their salvation and not yours. Bring them peace and love in their lives, be honest with yourselves, transmit your energies and thought to inspire and guide them to a sanctuary of love.

11th July 2016

We are a nation of beings who practice worship of the Lord within our own boundaries of life. We have no negative aspects, but positive affirmation that we come in peace, to proclaim our presence upon your earth, to assist in a manner respectful of the Lord. You have a purpose to fulfil to the many in your world but be careful not to allow your status to overshadow your purpose my son, for we wish only to assist.

Complaints are heard about the matters and the failures within your world insisting, why? Are these people permitting the right to act in a manner of intolerance before the many nations? Their choice was made long ago to bring about an aspect of peace in their positions, alas, the wicked ways are now set in their minds and their purpose has changed. We cannot assist on your planet, as your nations change their values to that of the dark. We need to reassure you that we will endeavour to incorporate messages of love that will shine out to those and bring them to a point of view that life has more to offer than the almighty dollar. Complete your mission as promised before time. Allow your mind a focus, for the issues of the world cannot be solved in one clean sweep. There are many aspects that truly need to begin a practice compliant with tolerance.

Fracking – Oil Drilling

Time and time again we have asked you not to interfere with her that brings life, she is your Mother Earth and you torment her so in your practices of drilling. Your feeble minds put aside the obstacles presented by those of Mother Earth who seek to protect your environmental ways. We have great need of their purpose to find a path, a route by which man can tread within the boundaries of light. Look at your mother as she weeps, for your earth is a living being.

How do you perceive your world my son? Do you see it as a ball of light spinning through the cosmos, or do you see it as home and something to be cherished and nurtured? For it is unique amongst the planets of your universe. Its make up comprises of many, many compounds and your atmosphere is becoming tarnished with the poisons that are kept within the surface. A tar like substance will ooze off the shores in a sequence of events to begin shortly. You will be astounded by the sheer complacency of those who run the ships, who allow the tar to seep from the barrels into the seas of life. Have you not learnt your lessons, do you not understand how the oceans and the life within affect your atmosphere? We really are astonished at the complete ignorance of those who value money over all living things, when will they stop to understand that yours is a short life and you leave as you arrived with nothing of the physical, but only love in your heart. If you lose that love before your time for the sake of money, then you will have nothing but a bleak future.

We regard many of your race as being intolerant to our species, we have communicated many times before with arcs of light situated within the heavens. They confirm our presence but deny our existence, how strange! They cannot see our purpose, we are the Arcturians who gather our forces to defeat those of the negative aspects. We do not intend to dominate your world, we merely wish to guide and nurture your planet to become a part of a vast cosmos and groups of beings that exist within it. An alliance of beings who sit in Council are astonished by your warlike ways, many times we have visited upon your earth, watching and waiting for a sequence of events that would be favourable for an appearance. You know our hearts and minds, you have no reason to fear us, for we may be of strange appearance, humanoid like but different.

Complete your tasks of illuminating the minds of those who study your words looking for answers within their lives. We cannot promise complete resolution to satisfy the many, but we do promise to be guardians of the Earth and if at any time we feel it necessary to defend her, then we will have no choice but to act in a measure of intolerance towards those who abuse her for the riches, for the wealth.

Your Commonwealth may see her. These people in their ivory towers practice their ways, they turn a blind eye to the masses of objections set against them. How is it they don't hear their own people? They do not respond, they have no wish to respond. We cannot say with any certainty that our words would reach their ears, but they sit in interest watching, scanning the skies, they know of our existence and they watch us from behind the shadows. Glaring eyes feeling the need to ignore our attempts of communication. We focus our minds upon many of your earth; our various methods are seen upon your platforms of life. So many things we want to say to bring about a purpose of peace and love, but how do you communicate with those who do not want to see or hear, for they fear their position will be threatened. Surely advancement is the natural way.

To bring about a manner of peace for them, reach out your words, we are the 'Lords of the Sky' who once ruled your world with a strength and attitude unbecoming that of the Lord. We have evolved through many eons and terminated our ways of savagery. Do not fear us, we wish to cause no alarm or to cause offence, but we see your world as primitive. Surely you must wish to proceed upon a path of wisdom and knowledge, rather that of a path that is bloodstained. Your peacemakers they are two-faced, they speak in a manner unfitting of their position, they cover up many things within your world to deny your eyes and ears the truth of what they know. They fear your response will be of intolerance should you know the truth, but my children, how does a child learn if you do not show them the way, and speak honestly of the things to be?

We are the masters of the universe we come this evening to bring joy on the beings of your planet. We will not intrude unnecessarily within your lives; happiness can be gained by a common love. Rejoice as the solar system begins the journey of light. We have never mentioned this before but truly your tasks are immense, with fortitude, strength and light, you must consider your options. Does a man desire peace or would he rather wage war until annihilation? We cannot tolerate those of ignorance, but understand this, we will not be held back by your modern weapons of war. We have come to fulfil a promise made long ago, to bring peace upon your earth, to enable your civilisation to advance to the next stage of existence. You hold yourselves back, denying yourselves the promise of a future. Soon will come a time of understanding and realisation that your masters are deceitful and do not wish to relinquish their power on the masses. Their imagery blinds you to their true intentions. They have no compassion, no tolerance for weak-minded, you are a nation who have bred men of intolerance. We recognise the symptoms of the sickness within your world as you squander your lives in pursuit of the meagre things of life. How can you understand the true purpose of life lies within your heart and your soul? Compassion is needed to resolve an intrusion into your lives that will result in minor clashes with that of other nations.

We hear your call, it is not easy to bring wisdom in light to those who will not listen, but you have purpose and your

thoughts are true. We are sad that our messages alarm you so, but we speak the truth that others will not tell. You ask for wisdom, for words of praise, rewards are given only to those who deserve the reward. Many of your people do not ask for the position they find themselves in, they reflect themselves within the light hoping that a meaningful end will turn the tide and bring solidarity to the nations of the world.

Circle of Light and Love

The bear, he walks tall, his paws are huge as he stands poised ready to defend his right to exist. There are many of your world who live in fear at this time, quite so, as there is much to fear. Your solidarity to your loved ones is all that you have, hold them close to your heart's. Create a circle of light and love within your families to extinguish the dark as they endeavour to interfere in your lives of peace. Never be in doubt that love overrides all, we will vanquish the dark, but you must hold strong, never break the circle of light. Strength is in your bond, peace will reunite the world. It seems like an illusion to you, maybe one day man will learn to live with each other in harmony, in a cooperative manner, to share with each other the knowledge and bounties. All too often we see so many poor, unseen and hidden behind your city walls, they are there to be seen, just open your eyes and look closer to what is plain to be seen. We have constantly embarked upon a mission of love within your world, sending disciples to assist in many ways and practices. Comparatively your species must evolve.

Flowers in the Attic. Such wondrous things to be seen in the magnificence of heaven. Your minds are deluded by life, for a purpose, for a reason far beyond your comprehension as you live your lives, but deep inside you look to your heart for contentment, never understanding that your lives are given so that you know you are the students of life. We cannot say how many it will take to bring pressure to bear upon those who dictate to you; but rest assured peace will come at a cost. Your journeys will be far and wide to help those to an understanding of the wisdom of the words spoken *(printed)* before you. We have numerous ways of interceding with your lives to bring about our purpose to shine the light of the Lord within the hearts of many of your nations.

Contemporary thoughts would have an attitude of ignorance as they despise those who would shine a light within the dark. You must have strength of mind and character to overcome the burdens that will be set upon you, for there will be many who would scorn you, a liar, a lunatic. But they too, at the end of their days will understand the purpose of your being and what you have tried to enlighten them with. Their eyes will be opened to a world of beauty in which they must with relinquish their ways, their passions, their wants and needs, for they will be no more than they were.

Constantly we hear prayers for assistance, we answer a few, but the many is for self, you cannot gain by prayer for the physical. Prayers are thoughts for love and caring, not the use of meagre things of life. We strive constantly to bring minds into focus of his being, but your dark world is hard to intercede. Nevertheless, there is a growing number of you who have seen the light and are beginning to illuminate your dark world, and purpose is growing within many nations to vanquish those of war, to bring peace and love and a happy home to live, for they are tired of the want and greed of those of the western world.

She Who Comes Before the World

What would it take for democracy among men? That is a question of epic proportions. It will take time for the balance to shift from the dark to light. One will come in the fall of man to guide the hand of those who wish peace and serenity and life upon your planet. She has a purpose, need of your love and many will survive. Some will not relinquish their ways, but they must terminate their thoughts of dominance. A clean sweep is required to wash away the ignorance, extreme measures you think, but how else would you clean the mess.

Be not afraid of she who comes before the world, for she is of love and light.

The olive branch has been given to your men of authority. They read the circles and have come to a conclusion they are false. They do not wish to see what they know to be true. Our communications are seen and you have formed an alliance. Combined purposes bring strength in knowledge.

Truly his name is being spoken, you must obey the law of the Lord to bring about a practice of light and love. Combat your fears, allow us an audience, we will assist in whatever way is possible; continue your journey with focus. Our need of you is great at this time to bring focus to the many, your concerns of him are unfounded, he has purpose in the circles on the ground. Combine your aspects, for he will bring many to focus on the messages given. Truly your names will ring out. Questions you ask are many, not afraid, speaking, your minds are many. I will join you shortly, before the circles of light.

Time!

The ticking of your clock beats out time, minute by minute, hour by hour, what a way to live! Free your mind of the aspects of life to that of spirit where there is no time, no relentless ticktock. Freedom of the mind and servitude in peace and love of the Lord. Only time carries the burden of life. Pointless views of the many continue to be a burden upon you, theirs is of no consequence. Truly you must become purposeful in your life, ticktock, the clocks ring out your short lives. Be free of the purpose in mind of spirit, do not be shackled by the mechanisms of man, allow your mind to be free to travel the universe and speculate upon possibilities so profound that your desires, whims for life, will fall away as the seconds fall, giving time to minutes, as the minutes fall within the hour. Time is limitless and not measured by beats of your devices. Open your minds and arms to the possibilities that exist from the release of your mind. Your energies shine out like beacons of light, how bright they are, you must follow your path as given by Him on high, when release comes you will know of what I speak.

More Maths

Four becomes four, you ask of the number 13, why it was given so randomly. Numbers represent many things beyond your understanding. Ready, $4 \times 4 \times 4$ will bring you to a number to assist in calculations, to be expressed in a triangle, a matrix of life will assist to bring purpose. Embark upon a journey of turbulence as you begin to understand that numbers are a sequence to events to come. Be not afraid we mean no harm, four times four times four reoccurring.

$P \times 4 \times 4 \times 4$ this represents a value equal to that of Q divide by M squared. Tasks to be given, you must equal. In your minds you understand the terminology of our words, we are not ready to give our final analysis. Be strong, tokens of love to be given, time is of no consequence, time is an illusion of the mind. Fractions occur many times in your world, they will accumulate to affect the many. Be strong and brave.

12th July 2016

Treasured memories of a past life should sustain you for the true torments to come. Be not afraid nor in fear, as the forecast is grim as we watch your Earth descend into mayhem. The masters that judge you are also judged in ways they cannot comprehend by the many eyes that see them through their minds eye. They watch and wait in turn, waiting for the time that they might make an appearance on your earth.

Crop Circles

Your forensics and skills will be needed to ascertain the correct pattern of life held within the circles (crop circles) to the east. Frequently they are questioned by the many, for what is their purpose other than to please the eye? Their focus is upon you to assess the situation at hand and bring about the terminology required to assist those of science to come to a conclusion of the meanings and aspects of those circles.

She Who Comes Before the World

We have considered many things in the aspects of your world, today has been no exception, for miraculous events have occurred in the regions of North Africa (or North America – recording not clear). Your news broadcasters have not been allowed to display this news for fear of an outcry by the nations of the west, but their joy will be announced shortly as it is released upon the net. We have come to bring focus to the many lives who see the truth in their light, their master. Our Lord Jesus, is once more risen within the world of men, she sits and waits, waiting for those of power to relinquish their limelight, she admires those of focus as they connect with many minds of past and present.

The Future, The Fall (Of humankind)

Your attitude towards us is good as we are friends on equal footing in the world of spirit. We do not understand why you should be unaware of our presence in your everyday life. Know this, we stand by you as you perform your duties in a manner and will of love and devotion. You sit quietly reminiscing of many things. Your future is that of boldness, your path must be trodden in your manner. We cannot influence your mind as to the path to take, but we can guide with reassuring, nurturing messages of love, as we provide guidance for all who have a heart and a willingness to be by our sides.

In the fall of your world we will be there to assess and illuminate the many dangers that will befall you. For circumstances will be a measure of your spirit. You know that all must pass and stand before Him at the gates of Heaven to declare their love and purpose. Yours will be no different to many thousands who pass at that time, but your awareness of the possibilities of continuation is strength that will bring you good fortune in the world of spirit.

We will teach you all you need to know in your term with us. We know from the past that you have sinned and regrets are many, but we now see a man of the light forfeiting his life to the devotion of the divine spirit. God bless you for your awakening and your practice on behalf of spirit and man.

We cannot assume that all in your world will see the forthcoming events, they negotiate their fears behind closed doors, not allowing those of the world to see the truth set before their eyes. It will become clear within the near future to all mankind, their lies, subversions will be seen by the many. The troubled minds will have the answers they seek as to the truth and power of the spiritual beings that will be seen in the Far East.

Nevertheless the sceptics will scorn those who say they have seen and believe, their minds are shut, unable to open the door. All it takes is a little oil to lubricate their minds to loosen the lock and open the door. The key to success will be in the performance that you can give to those of closed notions.

Your abilities grow in strength, we all know you for permitting us an audience within your mind. Let us take it one step further. Managing your safety is our prime concern, no harm shall befall you.

Three steps to be taken as we announce our purpose, your masters will announce their purpose before all as the fall of love becomes clear. Their hearts are in their mouths as they swallow humble pie admitting to the knowledge of unseen objects. Why has man grown so secretive to his brother, we cannot understand why he thinks there shouldn't be a common interest in the men they will rule, for allowing them the knowledge and wisdom, will ease the situation and bring understanding.

Capable you are of withstanding the news of an asteroid that commits to its purpose sending shockwaves throughout the world. Its focus will be upon Asia in the south, its fall will bring extreme weather conditions, darkness to the region as it plummets to earth. The shockwaves will be felt around your globe. The nations will say, "How could this be, why weren't we told of the imposing threat hurtling through the skies above us?" Their lives will be forfeit. Consciously we ask that those of a nervous disposition disregard these remarks, for there is life to those who have strength, who run with these words because all will be lost before the wave. We cannot say how many will survive, but structures will fall with a magnitude of an earth tremor. Dark times indeed.

You ask about a light-hearted story, would you have us tell you a lie or the truth as grown children with respect? We will be there on hand to help those nations restore their love for him, as they cradle each other with open arms giving thanks for their assistance. Never forget that your mind is a tool for us to use, to enable others to understand the greater purpose will always outweigh the smaller. We know you have many questions, some of which have been answered most recently. Your times of life are short and are filled with a measure of purpose for each and every one of you.

God gave you a plan to exist in the world at this time so that you may understand the feelings and purpose of many.

I am James, the keeper, I am the master of all who pass to spirit. Our commitment to all living creatures is a guarded one. Your paths must tread on a specific direction to attain your goals in life. We cannot help but notice as your friends remark upon the words, only love is obvious, hmm, they tremor before the words, for they are of the living. Their desperate minds cling to the hope that God may forgive them for their sins before they pass and hope that their knowledge of spirit will guide their path. We grant you these words to give to them, "Their sins will be forgiven, for there is no sin that isn't unworthy of forgiveness for he who confesses to the Lord of his crimes. He must apply his caution to those who would lie and attempt to cheat their way, as they would be found, they cannot hide the truth.

Lily, she is aware of the creation of the master, she walks before him guiding the steps of the light. Her memories of childhood in Jerusalem are of fond ones, her faith in the Lord was immaculate. She had to follow her thoughts, guidance of her mind, and she did so without favour to others and a blind faith in the Lord. She was absolved of any sins as she was bathed in the light of the Lord, for her commitment was absolute. Yours too, as the peoples of the earth must come to this decision "Do you believe in him or not?" If you do, rest assured of your salvation before him in the light, if you're sceptical, look to the words of the book, make your judgement, for each has a path to tread of free will. But those who choose the dark path, bringing misery to others, pain and suffering, know this; yours will be of equal measure as you cross to the dark side of spirit. We know there is no sanctuary that you can hide in, your trust and belief must be of Him of the light. To those I say, open your hearts and minds and look to the light of Heaven for your salvation.

The murmurings and whispers of the old man speak the truth of the mind of spirit, for he is an agent of the Lord who works within the light to assist and occupy your minds with those of love, tenderness and prayers. Open your hearts to the way of the Lord and bring self-respect to your purpose, for he will grant you eternal life in the light of Heaven, where all pain and suffering is replaced by a beauty within.

The Forest of Dean

The Forest of Dean, haunted by ghosts they say; ha ha! What ghosts? They are the agents of other worlds that bring the news of mass destruction in the wake of events to come. Their purpose is twofold, not just of doom and gloom, but to show direction and a means by which man can find his salvation. Follow their words very closely as they watch and guard over you. For his simple mind is an open book, for your words are a symbol of our truth – that we come freely and with peace, to encourage and assist in ways you cannot understand, for we know of your suffering.

And those who turn the knife within the bodies of the poor, they sap your strength with their greed and needs, but your strength is derived of your spirit and when man is left with nothing, he is always left with his soul and an eye for the Lord. Although this will not sustain his body upon the earth, his soul would never die; his learning will become symbolic for his new pastures green, when all must return to relive the memories.

Artist of Life

Like the brushstrokes of an artist the fine lines and detail must be absolute, there must not be error of judgment as the painter strokes his brush across the canvas. He sees a picture before him full of colour and vibrancy, as he paints his vision, he is a master of his art, bringing pleasure to the eyes and the visual affects the heart and mind. Only those who look deeply within the strokes of the paint will notice their form, how they move, how they flow across the canvas of life. Your lives are no different, you must be as the artist, allowing the strokes to be accurate, filled with purpose and love. As you create each brush stroke, allow it to flow as in their own rhythm and pattern of love and life regardless of its angle or position, for the composition will come to life with each stroke of the brush bringing a life of its own. Allow it to speak in the words of comfort to the eyes of man.

She was an enormous attribute to the arts as she drew her pictures of the old ones that sat before her. Her work generated much interest in the societies of the rich and poor alike, for she had the skill in her love as an artist. Norma Baker was regarded as a skilful technician of the crafts. As she moved her pencil across the canvas, she saw each detail, minute detail, allowing her brush stokes to follow the pattern that she had drawn. In her light, she had beauty in her eyes and love in her heart and an enormous amount of gratitude for that loving heart. *(Note: Every internet search we have tried for Norma Baker brings up Marilyn Monroe, we have not been able to find any evidence of her ever having painted herself, however the channel of these messages is the medium, so he naturally has the feelings that we don't experience, and he tells us that during his trance he truly felt that it was a reference to her and of paintings done of her. She was certainly painted by many artists, possibly most famously by Andy Warhol. Or thinking outside the box, could it be regarding applying make-up!)*

Be like the artist in your life, focus upon your mind's eye, draw yourself to the attention of the light so that you may see the strokes set before you and follow their path with love and light, creating your own picture of life. Within life, allowing your heart to flow and your mind to flourish with these words of love

We have never mentioned before how much we appreciate the minds of those who paint the pictures in their minds. His brush strokes affect those around them with pure and perfect perfection, greeting those eyes who have not seen such wondrous things before and teaching them to open their eyes to their own patterns and drawings that they should follow in life.

Never regret the choices you make for they are divine and absolute, it is only those who shut their eyes that turn to darkness in frustration for their lack of vision, but they must understand their opportunities are just the same to focus upon the art within. The art of love painted with light in His name and memory.

Constantly we strive to assist those who neglect their emotions, we send them a tidal wave of love and reassurance. Your terminology is difficult to understand, we will not neglect those who are lost on the path of light, for we will always illuminate their way with an opportunity of reaching their goals within the light, for their spirit is divine upon its purpose.

Barbara Castle

Necklaces of gold, strings of pearls, what celebrations there will be in the forthcoming elections. They gather in the streets of Downing to bring about a purpose of she who would rule your country, all but for a short time. Her mind is set, controlled by others as a puppet on a string. She has no control with the words that she speaks. She is knowledgeable in the ways of spirit as she is in politics, but like all who enter that extreme corrupted practice, she will be guided by those of a negative attitude to bring their purpose through her words. Barbara Castle, she was a lady of strength, she strove for their purpose, forthright in her manner, disregarding those who set against her and denounced her with their indignities. She still exists in spirit watching over the heartlands. She knows of the tasks set before her and forthright her fortitude must be to overcome their onslaught from Parliament. They strive to keep things in check, those who would stay to the left, to the right, their politics is where they guide them.

Your world is strange in their manner, in their extreme measures to their fellow man. They never care of their path and their true abilities. They are set on the regime that they should follow in the words of the bureaucrats who sit behind their desks, chanting and creating passages of speech. Nixon, another man of extreme measures, he forfeited his world for the sake of a dollar or two. The errors of his ways are there for all to see, for men of extreme measures will always be found out. A trap will be set for those who conclude that she will be the one to be President, as Nixon was set up, so will she, over her bridges to cross. They have no care in the States of the length that those of power and wealth will go to.

The state of Louisiana suffers with incredible degradation and an enormous amount of poverty. Their Governor sits in his seat of power overseeing those who will not comply with his regime. They will suffer the consequences for not following his rhetoric, for why should they have a life, he is the master, who is there to challenge him? His forgiveness is low and weak, his powers diminish in the forthcoming elections and he will realise that he is a 'nobody'. His spirit and soul will regret the rescissions (the undoing of a law) made against those of colour and race.

We establish in your mind the right and free will to announce your passages to the media. You will not block your efforts to gain the trust of many to bring her to their words of light and Christ. She will not attest against those who brought her to power. Humph! Why should she forfeit her right to be the leader of many in her purposeful way? Her mind, blank with the outlook and responsibilities, it will bring others guided like sheep in the field by the wolves who lurk in the forest. Their dens of iniquities are many within the establishments of your world. They sit there discussing their terms and their attributes, their desires to rule over their working classes, they are nothing but upstarts in the Wolves eyes. They sit in their house thinking they can dominate and have a right to do as they will with the world. How wrong can they be, their position is given by Him with trust and honour. Some face their issues with love, but the vast majority are without heart in their House of Lords. Pipes, smoking their Cigars at their own grandeur that was bestowed upon them for favours done, what do they know of life? Other than the riches and spoils gained by ill-gotten means. They hide their money and stash their assets in other countries of wealth so as not to be seen and accounted for. Their eyes are filled with gold; an illusion to many for it does not bring happiness, only sadness and sorrow.

Life is not an illusion but a reality, a fact, for a white Rose is sent to signify our blessing upon those who follow the light with a good heart and open mind. Commence your journey my son with our blessing, may peace be with you on your journey. Amen.

Tonight we will establish a link to your friends, as the three interpret the readings. They sit by the fire discussing tactics as they drink their wine. Their hearts and souls are clean and bright as they guide others on their path and journeys with an intensity of love that burns into their hearts. How can we deny them the right to the knowledge that shall be gained by spirit? Their paths crossed as they were sacked by others, they were not under an illusion for so many things of torment. Their light shines bright in their purpose of love, honour and devotion. To bring them joy in your love from spirit, their hearts meld together in a single purpose, to assist those of the nations of the earth. Your efforts *(the three)* will be rewarded shortly in a response from those with a greater purpose, for they will see your contribution to the minds of the many. You cannot resist our energy, nobody.

Allow us to intercede on your behalf and bring the vision to those who have a heart to look. Don't fear the consequences Michael and know your purpose, have a will and strength to follow your God given gift and allow others to see what lays in your mind. Transform your hearts and your value of respect.

17th July 2016

Good evening friends and to those who follow the light with honour. We bring greetings this evening to your fellow man in the fervent hope that he will reassign his thoughts to the purpose of his being.

We know of many things before man in this world, those many things of weaknesses for which he indulges, but our gratitude is extended to those who would reach for the light and forfeit the riches of the world, for theirs is of a true heart, full of meaning in His name.

Battersea is a place with a population matched only by the stigma that is placed upon their shoulders. They are a people with enormous talent to bring about a peace in their movements behind closed doors. For they utter words of praise and love to the Lord in a manner of their own. Gospel is their method, their preferred choice, it makes no difference how we worship the Lord Our Father. For in His eyes, all those that open their hearts to His love and power have meaning to His eyes. He shelters those from harm who have need of His love and protection in the world at this time, as things around you seem to deteriorate into something so distasteful it really doesn't bear thinking of.

Our greetings are sent to those who would listen to these words, for they are fortunate enough to have an open mind and see the things that many closed minds cannot see. Your purpose is one of many within this world of men, to bring messages upon which man should act, in a manner respectful of Him. Golden opportunities have been missed, perturbing your emotions of that of love. Man fails his brother by not honouring his being. We have no more to say of the condition of man in his world, for he is won by need and greed that will pay no dividends in the world, nor in the future world of spirit.

Your minds are comparatively weak to that of the Lord, for He sees nations of plenty sweeping across the globe in a manner disrespectful to all creatures that live upon it. With guided fools who will attend the conference in the spring of the following year, to persecute those of violence in a manner disrespectful to the human race. Their words will echo across the newsstands of the countries of the world, but what's new? Rhetoric, talking, never seeing the bottom line in making those accountable for their actions. For those need of their malicious ways, to enhance those who have interests in the securities of the countries of the world with ill-gotten gains that multiply as the need for their services grow. What good to their own peace? There is no profit for those multi minded misgiving men of need.

Talented sculptures will arise in the near east.

Their eyes will gaze upon the many millions who watch with disbelief that these events should happen at this time in this world. For it is a needy thing to acquire peace and love. It can only be obtained with a will to obstruct those of a destructive nature. For where there is peace, disruption will occur to promote those of the dark, as they seek their vengeance upon those countries they see as evil.

They themselves denounce their own God to begin a new practice. It is not permitted in His eyes for they worship an idol of falsehood. It will be necessary to commence our plans to thwart their attempts on this evil practice. Calm yourselves for the nations of plenty will soon be begging for peace, hmm, peace of mind, peace of the heart, no more wars or degradation to the peoples of the world.

Hmm, there will be conference of like-minded souls who wish nothing more than a utopia on Earth, alas there will always be those disruptive people, who will attempt to scupper the plans of peace. But know this, love transcends all.

Unite your hearts in condemnation of events to occur, with natural causes being blamed. For their attempts to create a weapon of mass destruction, it will be disastrous in the mountains beyond the valleys of Eden. They hide away their attempts to shake the Earth from below, but their master plans will crumble as their intentions are made aware to those of the regions that surround Nepal.

A crushing blow of defeat will be met with dishonour.

Men of science, men of war in the cross paths, are only matched by thoughts of peace from others.

Your materialistic ways are a harsh reminder of the whole hurt caused inside.

By the wondrous happenings and events, complete your mission to enhance and enlighten those of a desire to live in peace upon your planet. We are in need of an ally; your concerns are great. Have no fear to our temperament or being as we approach your Earth from the fourth star dimension. Relax your mind, become one with the universe and your destiny my son.

We are of a nature of peace and cannot conceivably think of harming the indigenous peoples of the Earth with reckless behaviour of mass destruction. We have singled out those who bring harm upon your planet, they will be punished in measures and ways unseen to most eyes within your world.

21st July 2016

All too often words are spoken without thought or meaning to those audiences who are anticipating and awakening. Their minds are focused upon the medium to bring messages of love and joy to their ears from the world of spirit. Their pursuit of happiness is based on the understanding that the medium is honest and true, both in spirit and heart. We acknowledge that many who practice on the stage are welcome and dignified. But there are others who's practices that counter their productive pursuits, for there are those who would use the words of wisdom to further their careers as a stage medium. Let us be clear that the practice of mediumship is a noble cause and should only be done with a true heart and love for man and spirit.

We beckon all those who have a will to come with purpose and join us in our efforts to bring peace to man with the knowledge of the spiritual realm. Gordon was a man influential in his time William Baxter was his name. He conceded his life for a noble cause in that time of destruction, never quite knowing what it was that had occurred. Only being aware of his fragmented mind as he opened his eyes to a world of beauty beyond this of earth, he never understood why it was that his time was now. But as the angel came and extended a hand of warmth and love in greeting, he could not resist the light. For he knew there was a purpose to life far beyond that of his knowledge as a man. He gave a tremendous amount of ability to his work, transforming the minds of the many to the phrases and paragraphs as those words, he wrote truly his name will live on through the memories of man.

Commence your task my son to become one of many to who messages will be received in the forthcoming days of tyranny that will beset many countries of your world. Your task is clear, being that of a guide for those who need comfort in these traumatic times. Be careful not to upset those with a temperament of injustice. Let them see your tolerance towards their fundamental being. Persecution stares many in the face, in the eyes of justice. In the departments of your law courts, many unfair readings are heard. Persecuting them or deliberately causing mayhem, for their minds were not negative but meaningless in purpose. They forfeited their lives to bring a justice to what they see as injustice. Their comprehension of man and wellbeing is not of this earth. The law courts of your country need only ask themselves, 'What is this that justice brings to the many?' How they operate their facsimile machines is not of tolerance but of ignorance, for they only see black and white printed on the paper before them, never having any interest into the circumstances that brought these men and women to justice. Don't let me lead you to assume that all are innocent, for there is so much guilt in the world today. But for the minority, a few, there is injustice as it is convenient to close a case before it is heard. Your masters have need of a conclusion to satisfy those of parliament that justice is being done with measures of tolerance.

We are gratified and pleased to see that measure and a will to bring a purpose to those minds of so many in your world. Your work will shine through in the darkness as its words ring out the truth. We are the Arcturians, those of many worlds unlike yours. We are seen as angels, for we bring peace to those who are dominated by intolerance. Your words of wisdom are set in their books and they follow the path of light within the kingdom of heaven. Be not afraid of the many things that you see in the world, for their paths are truly tremendous. Those innocents that suffer at the hands and the will of the men of means, will see justice done in due course. We have seen many things on our exploits throughout the galaxies and the worlds spread throughout your universe. Yours is the exception, man's brutal state is a worrying concern for all nations that look upon your earth. Where will it lead, one wonders, will they never learn to live as one, to bring about a peace and a restful mind to those who struggle throughout their lives? Frankly we see no intelligence of the minds that lead the poor, they are of a greed of unnecessary wants in their worlds within your world.

Today's actions will be clear to many as news bulletins ring out a change of policy within her government that will see a forecast of change in the state of the union. Her abilities grow as the numbers who follow will listen to her words as she speaks of her reforms and committees to those members with closed ears. She is of course a woman of great ability, still she needs support, for her policies will be vague to those who do not understand her. They will scowl at her comments, but their choice has been made, never happy are the men who rule within the house, never satisfied until their will is done. She will not pander to their wants and whinnies; she will stand firm remembering that Margaret. A common thread is seen by those of the media, who will focus on her strength and her antagonist ways, as she promotes her business within the house. *(Note: Regarding Teresa May recently elected UK Prime Minister.)*

Churchill once said, let them hear my voice before I pass, the truth to be heard by the many of this nation. Whosoever breathes a word of untruth and injustice will be seen as a traitor to this county. Now he sees a bitter divide within the policies he masterminded. His knowledge was vast, his strength was great in a time when war waged throughout Europe. It is coming to pass once more and sadly man will be once more thrown into battle in the European elections. Many countries despise the fact that you have left, for they see your country as a tower of strength and a pillar that supported their networks of industrious greed. Now they are left in turmoil, negotiating with the minds of those with money to find a back door in which to process their misgivings. Hmm. Churchill would not have agreed to such an unfortunate circumstance, for his policies were steadfast and his mind set in the ways of old, he knew what Great Britain was, he was the backbone that is needed, whereas she is a tremendous character but more needs to be done to bring to boot those of profit and doom. She must stand in the House of Lords and face judgement by those who sit in their seats of honour demanding that she goes their way. They will not allow her policies to proceed without a battle, but she must stand and be forthright and announce that the lords will be a minor concern in her government. Her strength in her voice will ring out to the people. Her term is short but vital in the next election.

Never let your thoughts belittle the words that are given in our name, for we are wise, there are many things that you as yet do not understand. Why come before us for wisdom if your minds would change the words given? Our tongue is strange to you and you think that your words are mixed, but we give them as we see them, through your mind and your character. We will relinquish our hold upon those who do not wish to communicate with those of beyond, but yours is a stature far beyond theirs. Commencement of your tasks will be in earnest in the near future, as your thoughts fade away and ours will speak through your mind as an honest and true account of our well-meaning. Frankly when you discuss our words you use your common knowledge in an effort to translate the many things.

Welcome Lily, she has joined us now to wish you well on your journey and the path that is set before you. Tremendous amounts of will, will be required to carry out the tasks set before you three, for your work has just begun. Correspondence to those of purpose will be heard shortly as they comprehend the meanings of the words on the written pages of the net. Quite frankly you have no idea to the extent that they will reach throughout the world of man as they listen to the murmurings of an old man. But they will see the truth behind those words and recognise the details as being accurate from source.

More Maths

Your minds struggle with the complicated mathematics given hence, tell him that in order to solve the puzzle he must reach out his mind and focus on the square root of the area given. We were pleased to see so many of interest in the puzzle we set. In your thoughts and minds you react in a manner respectful of us. Count the numbers of the circle to see the answer of the stargate given. Transform your thoughts, not that of man, but of another dimension, 1 and 1 equals 2, an easy task, but not so in dimensions. Follow your abilities as best you can. A mathematician will come to figure out the secrets as given. Let's just add a little more interest this evening as we gather the thoughts of those of interest in your world. The spectres of light have been seen in many places around your world, they send out their beacons of light to the heavens, they are of reference points, they are figured out by maps provided, they are star signs on the floors of your fields.

Rays of light that shine a pattern upon your earth will be measured in degrees, the angles of which create patterns upon your earth. It is necessary to focus your attention on the patterns as they sparkle in the morning light. Complete your studies. We will announce shortly our prime motive. Who are we? It is unimportant for you to know at this time, concern yourselves only with the welfare of man.

We will issue instructions shortly to those who will listen upon your earth with a measure of love and honesty. Transmit your thoughts in worship and prayer, truth and honesty in your everyday lives. Mm, blossom your hearts in the white fragrance. It will inspire you and you will commence their journeys upon the light for they will see the need in their hearts for love and joy. We need not tell you of our commitment to those who work with a special purpose. The flagships will be seen in the night sky in the half-moons of August, displaying our aspects to the many. We cannot continue hiding in the shadows of your clouds, for we have a purpose of love to bring, joy and happiness, our influence upon your world will be spectacular. Be not afraid we are a species, alien to the eyes of you, we are not a member of the human race, but we are a species of life as you. Triumph will only be achieved by those who have sight of vision and a want of salvation. Our technologies are great, you see the tripads, you see the triangle of the pyramid in your mind's eye, in truth it should be six-sided as opposed to four. The pentagram is a measure by which your minds will reach a satisfactory conclusion to your efforts in the field.

Narrowly you have missed the point of focus, the stone in the grass is just a gift, measure its weight and bring a balance to the calculations that are given in the field, for its true purpose is to enlighten you of a response by us. Triumph will be achieved. *(Note: 'The Trio' paid a visit to the crop circle at Stonehenge mentioned in this message, our channel asked for a gift of some sort to be left in the crop circle, in the exact centre of the circle was a stone which was different to others found in the field. He has measured its weight as instructed – 9.5g, that is virtually 3 × pi, i.e. 3 × 3.142 = 9.426, they are trying to draw our attention to the calculations made in this crop circle?)*

This is the gift as promised.

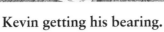

Kevin getting his bearing.

The stone in situ. I found it as prophesied in
the above transcript.

One of the arrows that made up the crop circle.

Note: This circle could be representing the pattern of life,
(cropcircleconnector.com 2016) that everything revolves in
cycles. Like the numbers found in this crop circle, the cyclic
pattern of 9's, see also part of the earlier message of 12th July
about Crop Circles: "Your forensics and skills will be needed

to ascertain the correct pattern of life held within the circles (crop circles) to the east".

They communicate by means of which you'll not have been told. Their connection with us is a tentative one as they seek to know our intentions upon what they perceive as their earth. We cannot underestimate them, for their potential of violence is great, we only come in peace to seek the will of man to bring it together once more within the light provided by heaven. But man's attitude and ignorance overrules his sensibilities... ha, what sort of race are you, that cannot see the potential of the welcome arms of our beings? We know much more than you know, we watch your everyday events with concern as it escalates out of control upon the continents of your world.

Your races, they muster together to mass in the streets to demand justice to those black people who feel unjustly accused of crimes and the innocents that were shot. There will be no respite from this, as a massacre will occur in a place little known by many of the world. For their hearts will be torn out in desperation as they seek to justify their actions in the sight of man, but not that of God. How can they possibly understand the meaning of life? Temperance and tolerance are paramount to men of violence, their minds are weak never forgiving those of weakness, for they dominate them in a way so as to gain a fear over them. Persecutions of the many will soon be apparent to the men of the world as they focus their attention in the south of France where so many live-in secret. Universities are insecure for they harbour many of ill will.

Jasper, a man of humour, weak of mind, why do we mention this man, what is it to us what his performance is? For they were many. He is a star to many on stage and screen, carrying out his comic acts with bazaar movements. His master strokes illuminate the hearts of many as they watch his sadness inside, never understanding how he truly felt within his shell. For many of his stature harbour a secret need of love, their outlet allows them to express themselves, never really understanding why it is they feel so awkward. But in truth their minds are set on a course they do not understand, for their humour is wild, wicked, as they pick on those vulnerable souls who seem to amuse them. In truth it is them that are vulnerable, that are the weak minded. Strange such to talk about you may think, why mention a man who is alive and not yet passed? We want to tell it straight, how many of your world think at this time. They have a great sadness within, not understanding their purpose or how to express their love to one another, for their needs are great for the forthcoming peace to be given. How on earth can they be part of this world, for they feel there is no love, no honour, nor pleasure in living. They congratulate those of achievement, deeply thinking jealous thoughts. But there is no need, for all men have an equal opportunity to bring about a peace of mind within his life.

Complicated messages are heard through the rhetoric of those well-meaning souls, but they do not reach the heart of the problem of man's desire for peace. Tremendous amounts of will and courage will be required in a time when it reaches its optimum point. We recognise that many will fear the final reckoning. Their eyes are shut to the light of the Lord, so therefore, their fear grows as they see no simple way to reconcile their misused thoughts. Their patterns of life become complex, no matter that they don't understand. Truly we need your thoughts to bear witness to our frustration, that we as the angels of the light are unable to reach those minds. A conclusion is required as we reach out our hands, grasp their hearts in a manner so gentle. We have never been so truly underestimated within the lives of man, for his teachings are being misguided, misunderstood by many of your world. Whosoever calls out His name shall hear the truth of His words. Practice your thoughts and prayers on a daily basis, together, together, the angels of light to bring focus upon your world in a measure of peace and love.

Archangel Gabriel, he once was a man, he lived a life among your peoples, he never wrote of any experiences and you will be

unaware of any existence. We all live to experience that of life, so we truly understand your purpose, not just of man, but of life in general, for it is truly complicated. For the practices and ways of man are unfocused to that of the Lord, bring this light of truth to those in your circles my son, reach out your hands, extend your love and thoughts to Him on high to enter your lives to bring you peace and comfort in the knowledge that all who worship the Lord will be of the Lord. Commencement of our understanding will begin, but in the meantime never let go your faith and the promise that you made to the Lord, that you made so long ago before your birth.

Commodus, a man of distinction... hmm.... really needs to learn to some manners, but we admire his progress, he wishes to speak once more on your path of light as he can see a man of singular purpose. For he once fought in the ring many eons ago, without a thought for others' lives, for his battles were great and many and the people loved him for his courage, but they seldom believed in him. For his words were harsh to those who would oppose him, in the senate they cowered as he spoke his rhetoric, demanding that the people love him. You do not gain respect by demands. He wishes to say how sorry he is for that stupidity he brought upon his people. He wishes to say it aloud, without his apparel, sit back and listen awhile, be not ignorant of the peoples demands. Listen with an ear of sympathy for their love is gained in a manner, that you should discipline, is not necessary in a world of love, for each know their place and part to play. Retrospectively he wishes to commence grand words of wisdom and joy to those of woe who hide their books of knowledge, be that of peace, bring out those books tell the people of the changes therein, do not hide the thoughts of the Lord within your chambers, for they are for all to read and abide by. Their content is of the truth, not of the wicked. Father Demetrius, he guards the many scriptures therein, he works day and night, deciphering, understanding their meaning. He relays the information to his master who denounces them as works of another author.

Pope John Paul II, he knew of the scriptures, he now sits with us, in sheer delight to see a man once more in the seat of power of Rome who will listen to the people and not be afraid of the rhetoric of those who demand him to be quiet. He is a man of peace; he has the power to change the world at his feet. To call for a blessing from the Lord to those people who follow that sect, be not afraid of him, for he is a man of distinction, a worthy man to sit on that seat of power in Rome, where once stood the palaces.

We will announce shortly our being to those of the world, we will accompany their thoughts in ways they do not understand. The right to know movements towards a new beginning, but we need cooperation and temperance from them. Your will is strong to follow the word of the Lord and so it is right and fitting that we tell you of these things to come as they pass beyond your vision. We seek out no favours as we circulate your earth in our star ships of gold, but we do ask an audience of man to hear these words of our wisdom and intent to bring about a peace upon your planet. Our relationship goes unseen by man's eyes for they are terrified with stories of men who seek their purpose in their wicked lives. We are not evil, we have been many times to your planet, seen and unseen and we bear witness to the fact that our world was once as yours, full of life but now extinct, for our ill practices were as yours, to gain precious metals, substances of that of our world. Our resources ran dry, we were doomed to a life of darkness, but we acquired a sense of being, knowing of our role, we forecast a similar circumstance to your people should they not turn back from their ways, for doom awaits every man who does not have honour in their lives to see the world about them and how it diminishes in energy.

Saturn's influence upon your world grows strong in the forthcoming years this energy will transmit waves that will bounce within your atmosphere. You will not understand these measurements, readings that are given, for they are transmitted on a frequency only known to us. You think this strange, but know our minds, for we have purpose in the things we tell you. Saturn is too far away to influence your world you may think, but do you know? What do you really know of the world you live on? You can't even understand the destruction that is being carried out in the name of man, so how is it possible for you to understand the forces of nature that work around the universe?

Tested your thoughts, your memories, today's bygone, careless whispers, walls have ears, wise words indeed. Your thoughts are betrayed by your actions and your deeds on your world. Too many times we have witnessed condemnations of those of the coloured race. Bring back slavery we hear, for we are the masters of this world. Now you can understand that there is only one way set upon your world and that is of spirit, good and bad, it's your choice, take it or leave it.

There are many colours in the spectrum of life, but it is their energy in their heart and soul that are equal, their outward appearance is insignificant. Your arrogance disbelieves this in your world of men, but the truth remains so, it is all meant, not your brother, for he is a man and a woman as you. Bringing an understanding of peace between your peoples and a mix of pleasures to interface your nations of plenty with those of meagre means, for unless you do, there will be a bitter end, in a bitter battle for world domination. People will cry out in shameless acts committed, for unless you band together in your hearts and souls and bring about a peace, then the forecast is gloomy. The colours of the grey will emerge if your favour is lost, for they lay in wait for the time when it is appropriate for them to seek a purpose upon your earth. We would not permit such a thing, but it is your choice to make, i.e. that of the spectrum of colours or that of the grey and dark, it is your choice my friends. Sing out your hearts in praise of him, the Lord and give thanks for the special positions you have been placed in. Amen.

- - - - - - - - - -

Too many of today's youth are undisciplined, ill mannered, outspoken, not respecting those of authority. For they have become accustomed to their wants and needs being filled and met by their parents. What a shame, a wasted generation for they are the future of your world and it is your responsibility as given by God to lead them on a path of light and away from the influences of the dark. Many are lost to the mindless games played on the screens, their thoughts turn to violence as it becomes normal in their world. It is so sad to see the demise of man, but it can be rescued if you open your eyes to the prospects of the future these games will bring. Denounce them as being intolerable for they will darken the minds of the many in your world. We cannot express our emotions of the loss of these young people. The will and trust needs to be regained by the youth who have seen the path of life for they are the only ones to reach them.

Your connectivity to us is outstanding for a man of the earth, we wish to speak our words of comfort to the men and women, children of the earth, be not afraid of that which comes, for he is a focus upon life to bring happiness and joy to all who will turn to Him. Commence your work of love with our blessing to bring a purpose and need to the men and women of the earth who will listen to your words from the Arcturians in the purpose of the light.

I was once a man who gave all to the master in my belief in his words, this promise to us of life ever after is spoken in truth as we lay out our plan.

The church of today denounces the souls who have not turned to him, but that is their task to reach out and bring balance to all. We cannot express our love enough to those of the light, but it is your responsibility to bring a need to the world. Ask yourselves, 'What is my real purpose in the work that I do, is it for myself or for those who need to be escorted through the valleys of sin?' We will not reach all, but your words will enlighten and inspire where there is a heart and a will to bring light. Cast out your doubts for you inspire the many, the trio of light will grow in their purpose.

24th July 2016

The mists of time gather in the forests of the world as we tonight respectfully draw your attention to the many horrors in your world.

Destruction of rainforests is a trigger to set the emotions of man into a frenzy.

Let us come before you this evening and immerse you in the words of love and wisdom. No harm shall come as we operate through your mind in a manner of love. You have need of love and compassion in this world at this time with mass hysteria and confusion. Nothing can be further from the truth than to say, this world is in dire need of our Master's love. Tumultuous welcomes should be greeted with respect by him on high, welcome his love and his purpose, open your arms and greet him in a passion of love.

The enormity of the tasks before you will be immense within your world of man, truly you feel us, do not obstruct us, allow us to speak in a manner of wisdom that should be heard by all upon this earth, this planet. We are not a master race, nor do we enslave, but we give hope for a relief from the pressures of this life to those with a hunger and lust of need of love.

A burden will be placed upon the three to bring messages to those men who have need of focus, never let go your emotions as we attempt to communicate to the masses of the world.

Mount Vesuvius erupts with an explosion and fire that will be seen for miles in all directions, your earth rumbles with discontent as the fractures within its crust expose the core of molten liquid. Why do you mess with the planet that bears your lives, why tamper with things that are not necessary? For the energy you require can be tapped from source without measures or need of destruction. Your men of science are aware of such methods, but are stifled by those in the grey suits, they do not welcome such changes, for what profit is there in this.

Renewable source of energy can be found in the atmosphere of your world, all you need to tap into it is an aspect of love for Mother Earth.

She binds your organisms with the temperance that only a mother can give, but as all mothers of the earth so much can only be taken at one time. She must punish those of reckless behaviour and their subjects for their want and need of the earth's resources. Too many times we have spoken upon this subject to enlighten you to the dangers that you pose to your own atmosphere.

You recklessly continue your journey to your doom. Many of you will not be aware that those of greed and the tasks they set before you are for their own personal gain, to establish, promote their business. But their business rests upon the fate of the entire world. Their ignorance is astounding as they laugh off threats from those of the environment, for they ignore the warnings given by those who matter upon your earth.

Tranquillity will be gone in the near future as a rocket explodes upon the pad. A Mars mission will be announced as a failure. Your pathetic attempts to create a diversion to desecrate the world will become obvious to those of science, they know such things, events are not wise in decision. We will not tamper with the evidence, for it stands out as a beacon of light that shines in the night sky. They will be embarrassed by their failure, much money is spent upon this mission, Apollo is its name, as it respects, reflects those ships of old.

Target your emotions as we draw ever closer to your being, allow us to interface with those who have worked within the fields of your politicians. The involvement of them is vital to uphold the law of the universe of the nations. He questions your judgement as he watches your words in his chambers upon high, but he knows that you are enlightened by many wise words and the truths therein. We cannot account for his judgement at this time for his policies override his personal ambitions, but before him soon will be an array of evidence that he wishes to see.

Complete your work my son in a manner respectful to those of the earth, to the eyes of spirit. We have no recollection of the time when many of Earth's inhabitants wreaked havoc in your world, they were before us in vast colonies upon your earth, deeply resentful of any life form that emerged, for they brutalised their enemies in ways unseen. Their hardships became evident as the walls crumbled before them, they no longer exist, their evidence lies deep within the earth. Your planet hides many secrets from those of the present day.

It is not beyond your capabilities of presenting your masters with evidence of our arrival, you must acquire a liaison who will admit that there are such beings as ET. For he knows the truth of the matter, he has dealt many times in the past as a reckoning for his committal. Alas he knows nothing more of us than is necessary, for he remained at bay, not ready to release the information held within to the men of the world. The time is not right for us to become familiar with man, but we watch and we wait, acting on those who receive our signals, messages of love.

Your purpose is to deliver the many signals we send. Relax your mind be prepared for a jolt as we enter your thoughts and mind. Hmm, now we see you, feel our form, you see our shape and feel our thoughts as we whisper in your ear to the audience with whom we speak. Your deliverance is nigh from the evil clutches of those who would torment the living, but know this, that it takes two to tango, so you must play your part in this reckoning to the men of violence, deny them their negative responses within your media, for you feed their thoughts and betray your secrets.

Their lashing of your planet is a merciless, relentless, unnecessary thing. We will not tolerate the ignorance of those who do not follow their leader; they will betray many in positions of leadership as they begin to understand that theirs is a life of peril and misjudgement before the Lord on high.

Their sorrows, their fears, pain and anger will relinquish their deeds in explosive ways, for they cannot hide behind the bricks of a nation with a temperament of injustice. Who will say that man is not worthy of justice, for are we all not a part of that of the Lord?

Many years ago, we were able to see mass hysteria upon your earth as we entered your atmosphere, demons they called us, those from the east. For indeed we were strange beings to those of that time, demons not, for we were of love, they played out their minuscule roles believing that we were gods. We accepted their invitation to rule across their nations, we delivered many of evil their punishments. We do not intend to invade that of your world with malice, for we uphold the honour of our father in heaven and truly we bring the light.

Your people of today are more knowledgeable and wise in their beliefs, but the one true God is not favoured. Why have you forgotten your promise to him, to love and cherish the brotherhood of man? We will guide your aspects of love through these words should you take heed of them. Know that yours will be a path of light in the forest of dark, green of Eden.

Stonehenge And Maths

Ah the Henge, stones of blue, the circles of great stone, cosmic wonder it is to be said. Their reasoning behind their existence is flawed, a place of praise, worship in sacrifice, nay, it is the star sign that relates to many that are given within the regions at this time. Your circle has been measured with an outlook of anticipation. We can assure you, a figure will be reached that will illuminate your minds with fear and love. The cosmic energies race towards your earth at phenomenal speeds. We require you to calculate the distance between Mother Earth and Jupiter, triangulate this with the nation of love (Arcturia?) which lies beyond your solar system. That will equate to a figure that will be common to those in the field of physics, our mathematics an abbreviation will be this: E Versus = Star sign G, 20° North by Northwest, elevation 6° North by Northeast.

Our figures will complete your tasks. Common sense will prevail as we disclose our position in the night sky. *(Note: Regarding the star sign at the time of the construction of Stonehenge, we wonder if it could have been Leo, as 'the lion' has occurred in another crop formation. Are there any mathematicians out there who can help?)*

You must not ignore our thoughts and wisdom as it is for the benefit of your race.

A time capsule is held within your earth at the coordinates given. You must proceed to a position of North by Northwest in order to exhume a vast amount of crystalline structures. North Africa is a place where such materials lay in the stone. We cannot emphasise enough our need for your abilities to bring about a conclusion of peace in your world. *(Note: We were given co-ordinates in Africa before, these are just thoughts – could they possibly be speaking of a cave or are we continuing on the theme of Leo and talking of something beneath the Sphinx? It has long been said that the Hall of Records is beneath the Sphinx and information can be stored in crystalline form.)*

Hmm, hmm, Confused? Your words indeed, the passing of instructions remains a mystery to you. Solve it you will, it's a matter of time,

We are convinced that your nation is not ready for our bringing of tolerance to its people. Your authorities involve themselves in vast amounts of disapproval from others of a nearby continent. How can you reconcile your differences whilst trying to solve the riddles of the world? Your purpose as a people is to live free, free from radicalisation from murder and insidious intent.

We are here to gather the lives and souls of those who would listen to a few words of praise from him on high with a measure of love to the people of your nation. Why do you not see the purpose in your lives? It is to love one another in truth and honesty. I am in bewilderment that your nation has become so disillusioned from the church, yours was once a nation of great belief, sadly that has declined. As the dark cloud reaches over the skies of Britain you must empower your minds with thoughts of loving guidance from him above to enable your wills to ride out the storm. It is a matter vital, nay imperative, commands that you must follow from that of the Lord, for he is the father of the heavens and earth on which you breed and event your lives. Your temperament is short, but know this, love can be found in the darkest of places and as it reflects the light so it will vanquish the dark. Your tolerance is needed to bring those to boot who do not follow the rules of the light, show them your love, your loyalty to him on high. Let there be Love and Light in your lives staying forever more. Amen.

- - - - - - - - - -

Truly wise words from a humble servant of the Lord but we must emphasise the fact that we too follow that of the Lord. To us your nations upon earth are mere insects, a strange term you think but not a deliberate insult, just a term. We cannot allow your thoughts to turn to disillusionment, we trust in your mannerisms, your faith, our words worry you unnecessarily, be at ease with your thoughts as we embellish them with our minds. Staggered you are of the results given thus far, let us embrace the love, so that we may respond in kind. Trust in us to bring peace to your nations, we are the Arcturians, a noble species of one that rules your thoughts. Now let go your feelings of love or despair for they work hand-in-hand to bring balance to your life.

26th July 2016

We see no reason not to enlighten you of the things to come. With your purpose your mind is becoming focused, gathering strength. Your abilities grow, as your passion grows in earnest to assist in ways of spirit in your world.

Dogs are your passion, they are loyal companions, their blessings are many, but fools teach them tricks with disastrous

results, they are shameful, for animals should not be taught in the ways of man to harm or injure. They are the loyal shepherds of man, hard to imagine that such a beast could do so much damage and also be a loyal friend and companion. But know this, that all creatures of the earth are of a gentle nature. Their nature is that of preservation, in the wild they will slaughter their prey and dispatch them quickly, for they know their purpose in life is part of a chain upon which you are a member. Each feasts upon the other, bringing that chain full circle.

We are aware of the highlights in your news concerning the victims of terror. So shameful is this, that man brings upon one another in the name of the Almighty. Two abreast, they march down the aisles, their secrets unfold to the world. Their shame is seen by millions as they punish those of the light, for they are the dark. Their hearts and minds are of a notion of ill will to those who seem to them intolerant of their beliefs. We know that the Father joins us with open arms, he applauds those of mercy, he does not discriminate against those who have sinned against him, for his beliefs are paramount in his life and his purpose has brought them and him to us in this heavenly light. *(Note: We believe this sounds like the attack at the church in Rouen.)* Be careful, for your tasks are equally dangerous, as your purpose grows so they will see a man who works in an unsatisfactory way to their views and their opinions, but don't fear, for they cannot harm the soul and spirit within. *(Note: 20th August 2016 a suicide bomber targeted a Kurdish wedding party in Gaziantep, Turkey, more than 200 present; 57 killed and 66 injured, a witness reported that two suspicious individuals approached the party and left the scene following the attack. 34 killed were under 18. Thirteen of those killed were women. The attacker is believed to have been 12–14 years old.)*

Your delight was obvious to us to find a method by which your words can be combined with your thoughts. As you travel the world with your mind set upon being that of the light, we would advise you use extreme caution to those of violence. Your purpose is not to end, but to continue within the words that are to be written. Your world is unwise to become unreasonable to those of mass murder, for there is an intent upon your nations, a hidden purpose to which they will stoop to bring more terror upon the streets of your homelands. Your nuclear devices are unsafe, easily accessible online. We guarantee that they will use anything possible to bring about their purpose.

Command your mind to listen to wisdom and wise words that we set before you this evening, for we know of the struggles of man. Each man has a temperament by which he must live, he struggles upon his purpose, some with the knowledge, some without, but their focus is unseen and unheard as their minds direct them to where they need to be. Hidden guidance is essential for you, as a member of the human race to complete your tasks in life, meeting all obstacles head on, bringing hope, having faith, in all those shocking experiences that will befall some of you.

For the main, peace will resume in a normal manner, it is all dependent upon your tasks, you witness many things, you see and hear so much. Become one of the light and resign yourself to the fact that life goes on regardless. 'Penny for your thoughts,' was once used as a term to bring your attention and your mind to purpose. Will you give a penny to know our thoughts? Our wisdom is far advanced of yours and of an essence not that of the earth, our thinking is in logical terms with mystical thoughts.

A metric number was given for your thoughts. In terms of resistance it is essential that you are able to understand. Kevin has asked for guidance in these trying tests, his mind nags him with pressures, but there are no pressures, it is a means to an end to allow your tasks to flourish. In your calculations you will come to a conclusion that the degrees given are of an angle that match the data of Apollo. Your wise words given to the men of science will be understood in the near future by men of calculation and astronomy. Don't let your heart fade as you misunderstand our intentions with the numbers.

Appearances of men will soon unfold in the heavens above. Do you think that you are the only form in beings on your earth? For we are of a similar disposition and outlook, our appearance is not dissimilar to yours. Your conditioning has bought you to a purpose of tolerance, but your hostile actions continually block our thoughts. Do not despair as we watch and wait for the time for our arrival upon your Earth. We are not in the habit of demoralising those of the Earth, for we are a nation of beings with love and tolerance, forgiveness.

You see the golden ring, (in my mind's eye I see this as I have once before) you asked once before for its meaning, it is the ring of the circle of light. Your minds are focused and your hearts are torn as you turn the many pages searching for answers that seem to elude the many. Books are a haven for many things, secrets are held within the quatrains. *(Note: Quatrains are often linked with the work of Nostradamus, a quatrain is a verse of four lines.)*

31st July 2016

Tragedies before the many of your world, their sacrifices go unheeded as they commit themselves to the Lord in prayer, searching for salvation within their life's path. They sit in their churches, hoping and praying that one day peace will come. Those of the good book, we welcome them with open arms as they commit themselves in bodies to the heavens above.

We have never denied the existence between man of the spirit realm. We wish to announce that we intend to bring rapturous joy to the many who behold the light of the Lord. No misgivings, no thoughts of sadness as the new beginnings start in earnest with the discovery of a satellite orbiting the moon before the sunrise of the morn. Do not look in fear as we approach your earth and establish an orbit. Your men of violence will see us but for a brief time, they will declare there is no such thing as alien spacecraft, but you know my son, that we are here to bring peace to your regions of Earth. We have no wish to harm those who wish for peaceful intentions towards us. Those who run, those who raise their arms and wage war will meet a bitter end, for we mean no harm to the population of the earth.

We bring benefits of many kinds, we are the Arcturians, those of love, who care for other civilisations. We cannot interfere with your lives directly, but you all must come to an understanding, that we will commence and acknowledge our existence when Saturn passes the moon. The wisdom of your minds and thoughts bear witness to our existence and a puzzle set are to adorn you with knowledge in ways you cannot understand at this time, for we cannot influence those who do not see or listen, only those with an aspect of love with the light, who set their minds in focus will receive our words of love.

Courageous thoughts are given by the many as they adopt a system by which they will emerge from a sickness common in your world. Cancer is a disease of the mind. The body is an organism with many characteristics of us, the healing power held within is immensely strong, but only if you will tap into it. As their beliefs grow within them, you must understand that your bodies are feeble, but your inner strength will grow.

Truly we are unable to help those who commit acts of violence against others, for they have sacrificed their souls to that of the dark, of the negative. You are a being of the light, of many followers and many to come. Be brave and sacrifice your dreams to follow your heart on the path that you have taken. Be careful though Michael, for there are dangers on this path from those who do not believe, who will scowl and call you a traitor to the faith. But their dreams will be shattered soon, the reckoning is to come, for their temperament is of terror and ignorance to the many of your world. We are virtuous beings who bring joy to the masses of your Earth, we will announce soon that our purposes are of love.

Those Arcturians, they are a race of beings of knowledge and awareness of the Lord, for they too were once in a position that you find yourselves. Their reckless behaviour brought them to a point in their lives where they had to find a focus or become extinct. They found their path, they found their love and faith in him our Lord above.

Your grasp of knowledge is weak my son, but we can use your mind to feed it information that we alone possess and not that of men of Earth. For once more, we are the Arcturians.

Commence your battles with love, your frequent prayers are heard, but peace cannot be brought by man alone, a will to live together in peace and hope is required.

Those men of money, they deny you this, as their purpose grows for their hunger and lust for the riches of the earth, will they never understand that it is no use to them? Its only benefit is to assist mankind, helping one another to live free and better lives, but oh no, oh no. Ah, your masters they, they will not bargain with those of the poor, for their greed is overwhelming. There are the few who will give plenty to those of the needy, they found a purpose, but there are many who hoard their riches. I don't know, for what good is it to them? Will they take it with them when they pass to spirit? Why don't they understand the riches are in the heart, in your soul, that is the true wealth? Your needs are many, sometimes your focus is lost on desires in life but still you remember these words, God bless you for your path and being.

3rd August 2016

Castles in the air, they stand proud and tall on the peaks of the Himalayas. Those people who worship there ask for life and strength with a purpose in their lives. We are the Knights of Templar and we bring news of the Lord of Hosts. He does not neglect his flock as he watches upon high, upon the glaciers and the ridges of the mountains, He sees all of man's misgivings, he cares not for those who would defeat his thoughts with their evil intent, they are of the dark. Their own laws of discontent are frequently heard throughout your world as they bring chaos and terror to your nations and cities. Their focus is upon a meaningful way to harm and bring indignation to those of the Christian community. Their basis in belief is misled by those of greed as they stand back and watch their purpose unfold.

Bring yourself to understand my son, that life holds many mysteries upon which you may ponder, but alas, those mysteries become realities, bringing death and destruction to those innocents of the cities upon your earth. We hear the cries for peace as they scream out our name. When will they understand they hold the key and the power to negotiate a position of peace? Your men of intolerance do not wish to bargain for peace, for they are men of destruction.

Arcturian's are here for the purpose for you to negotiate your mind to the realms of spirit and those beyond your earth. They hover in the skies out of sight as they watch you scurry around. They poise their ships in a position of observation, not knowing the reception that will be granted to them. So they tentatively reach out, their fears in the minds of those who watch the skies from the earth beneath your feet (underground), we cannot comply with their demands as they seek a solution to bring us out into the open, to use our skills to assist in their malicious ways. We will not be tempted by such trinkets. She will encounter much opposition as she denies us our right to counsel.

Jerusalem is a capital city of the east that binds the Jewish community around your world. They will be hit by those of thoughtless acts, to entice and beckon war, to join their ranks. They gloat at the possibilities that theirs will be the superior race of beings. We beg to differ, for their path is not righteous, it is unworthy of the Lord.

Tonight we will give you a lesson in mediumship to beckon those to your call as you write your words and accomplish the mathematics given. We are too strong for your mind, but we will feed you knowledge granted by us for the many of your world. Aliens you call us, indeed we are not of your earth, but we sacrifice ourselves to bring peace to yours. Knowledge is the key to wisdom.

A fracture in the minds of those who lead your nations will soon become apparent, as the courts rule that their actions and indignations are legal and they will face judgement by those of humanity for their course of action. They must be compliant with the laws of God to bring justice to those who bring terror upon your streets, we will not allow their actions to bring chaos.

Diamonds have a quality far beyond your knowledge, we have mentioned once before of their clarity, the facets that they reflect, they hold an energy far beyond your abilities to understand. They are crystals of strength and durability; they hold the many keys to energy. Used in the laser construction to focus the beams of light, the points so fine, that they would blind the eyes of those of indiscretions. Their focus is upon the world beyond yours as they investigate the possibilities of travel using this laser light. *(Note: Excerpt from an article on space.com dated 20th July 2015 reads: "Travelling to other star systems is a big dream, but achieving it may require going ultra-small. Blasting tiny, wafer like sailing spacecraft with powerful lasers could slash interstellar flight times from thousands of years to mere decades, one researcher says.)* For everything carries its vibration and is recognised within the universal law.

Guilty minds know of their use to fracture particles within your cosmos, a chain reaction will occur if not negotiated with care. Nothing can be done, as this is out of your hands, but we will assist to arrest its power.

Creations of the Earth are a gift from him, he seeks no reward for those things he gives, his purpose is of life, love and joy. We bring you news of many events that you should be aware of. Tributes are paid, flowers are laid at the feet of those who suffer injustice. Yellow Lily brings purpose to all that have sacrificed their souls in the pursuit of justice.

Creatures of the Earth hear our voice as a whisper upon the winds. That is how our Lord knows that we have friendship in mind. You categorise us alien, in truth you are also an alien. Our minds meld as princes of love, to be bold and make those aware of our true existence. Blind your hearts of fear, never comprehending that it could be joy. We are strange to your eyes, but we have need of your love.

4th August 2016

We shall not be gone or given in faith; we have a motion to pass to your civilisation to man on earth. We can only interpret the gestures shown as being that of ignorance to our tolerance. We have battled many times, in many worlds with those of the negative. Be assured that our spaceships will be a common sight in the cosmos and within your world. You call them figments of your imaginations. Truly your eyes are shut by those of science and those of the need, they betray your trust as they hide the secrets of your world behind the glass. They have read the books many times to ascertain a way of control of the masses, they do not read the small print, that which is reference to the master, our Lord. For their aspects are of fortune, and the commonwealth of man is but a tool to bring their aspirations to life.

Soon it will all change in a manner unforeseen by the leaders of your world. A common practice of good behaviour will be adopted by many. Have love. An aspect of dark, there will be those who will not comply for they have an ego to fulfil and their temperament is of intolerance to all that would disturb their world. It is common belief that what you call 'alien' is a disaster waiting to happen, but this is food for thought, given by those to alarm you so as to put your men aside.

We mean no harm to man; we are beings of the light who come with aspects of love to shine our rays upon you. Fellowship of man is paramount in your world, to overturn those of the dark you must adopt a position of love to work against the evil storm that surges west. We cannot predict the outcome, the master's wish is that you should change your ways so as to evolve. Pressures from outside should not interfere with evolution, but note this, we will not tolerate your designs upon Mother Earth as being negative.

You were born to a unique planet upon which many life forms in many multitudes exist, more so than on other planets and you are the dominant species at this time. But there's always been those to supersede the previous civilisations of your world. Your supreme arrogance astounds us, staggers our minds in disbelief that a race of beings could think themselves so worthy. As in all aspects of life, you must work to reach an understanding within your lives, within your soul's purpose. We cannot help you, for you must help yourselves, our belief is we will not allow you to destroy Mother Earth.

We are the Arcturians, those that time forgot. I am Kioh, I am the master of many, you translate my words in your English, as my thoughts enter. You cannot begin to understand how it would be to see the truth that lies before you. We have also come to a reckoning, we survived as the injustice grew against us, for there are many nations out there who have evolved in their time, you too must evolve.

Common knowledge would dictate that Earth is the only place of life. Hmm, you once said the moon could not be reached, or your atmosphere could not be breached, but you have evolved machines that carry your being to the edge of space. You are a minor race and a rebel, you spit upon your earth, hmm, this creates issues in the heavens above. Your atmosphere is clogged with much metal. We have evolved from the depths of despair and we reassure you that the men of the light will bring about his purpose as the time draws near for you to evolve, for if you do not, then all hope is lost.

Messages of joy will be brought, but first you must dedicate this evening to messages for awareness.

Your Cleveland Ohio, is a place of mass destruction, their weapons hidden for many years in the silos beneath your earth. Take care, for corrosion sets in as funds are siphoned for the men of wealth. They feel their burden once more is to issue a statement of intent that they are all powerful within man. Many men have fought many battles, declaring that they are righteous in their needs, huh, they know nothing other than to use his good name for an excuse to battle others. Why can't you learn to live with one another in the United States of the Americas? It is one such country that is evolving, becoming dark in their extreme views as they witness this man rising from the ashes. His name is synonymous with that of tyranny, his weakness of mind will betray his love for life as his dominance grows, he is a leech, however fame and fortune will indulge his mind with the power granted to him by those of the states. Hilary Clinton is no match for his dominance, her weakness of mind arbitrates in her thoughts, in her journals, what a mess, what a torrid situation, how will it end?

We can only surmise that this nation will torture itself and burn itself out from within as they fight one another for pointless views.

Hmm, Comanche nations were once the victims of the plague of the white men as they rushed over the plains. Once more this rage will be seen as the nominee's battle for their right to rule. We cannot assist one way or another, but you must bring about change, for your democracy is corrupt. We have no time for fools. We are the Acturians.

- - - - - - - - - - -

Complete madness. Hmm. Your emotions run high as you battle to reason why it is that man cannot live together. Reckless behaviour is seen as intolerance by the many. We have come to the conclusion that your minds work in mysterious ways; fractures of the heart affect the mind with your emotions. Your peoples of the world are fragmented, their pieces lie scattered upon the floor of life. It will become necessary for those pieces to become whole, for if you don't, quite frankly you will not survive.

Commencement will start soon, of achievements of those who have purchased their thoughts to witness the events to unfold. We have transformed the many lives who watch your world at this present time. Their friendship is unique. You will not find this easy to understand, that we are nations of many who watch in earnest throughout the cosmos. Yes, we know of the perils of man and the destruction he brings, but still there is light that shines to give hope that your world will turn to the blessings of the one who brings life.

Terminate your thoughts of desires, needs and wants. They have no use in the world that beckons you, the world to come. Compare your heart to that of a finely tuned instrument, you must tune your thoughts in a manner of love to the wisdom of his love. Sour notes spoil the song, you must become a master musician to tune in to the light and love of the Lord.

Once more we bring our thoughts and words, those of desperation to your peoples of the world. You mess with things you do not understand, you are like children who play with weapons. Do not mess with nature, with things you don't understand.

Krakatoa was an immense explosion that swept across the ocean, washed clean the islands in its vicinity. It will once more bring about destruction as you shake the earth. Your crust is thin, your magnitudes will emit a powerful fracture. You must refrain from deliberately setting particles on fire. Your species has evolved too quickly, your negative attitudes compel you to have an arrogance of mind, you mustn't allow these fractures to occur, for they will bring about a massive destruction, the likes of which you would not have seen before. Conquer your hearts and feel the passion for the Earth upon which you tread, for she is your mother. Would you spit upon your mother? Do not spit upon the earth.

14th August 2016

Your thoughts are of concern for the world. To the many that inhabit the kingdom of heaven your paths are tarnished with hate and love, wars and greed, why is it that once more the greed of man intercedes with the aspects of peace upon your planet. Have you not learnt, to give an inch is to give a mile, free from burden and the insanity of the world?

In truth what is freedom? Some deem this word to mean they do as they please with the life given to them in aspects of the negative, whereas others will use this freedom to enlighten their minds with their purpose and being.

She became one with the earth, sent for humanity to ease his burden, but you must understand that she will not release her identity until that time when she can be assured by a reception of love.

Commit your minds to the purpose and tasks given, for we have an aspect of love towards you all. Gain your knowledge through the words given and learn their lessons well so that you may give clarity to others in their quest for life, purpose, and reason. Clouded, so many minds as they live their lives in their dark purpose. Never lifting their heads to look about the world and see the possibilities, they are astounded by your attitude of love and worship, for they do not open their hearts and minds to the possibilities of a higher being, other than that which dominates their lives.

A fragrance, a mist will emerge in the dawn of the month of May. It will envelop many countries; astonished forecasters will remark on its density and the odour given. Are we not the Arcturians who bring the mist into your midst so that you may become more aware of our purpose? We need your respect and warmth of being to assist in preparations for the forthcoming events that will envelop your world of men.

In the past we have sent many envoys to enlighten your minds of the possibilities of the universe. You have shunned them, shown them disrespect, but people are fickle in their aspects, in their tolerances. For what is new, is strange in concepts.

To increase the wealth of those of the commercial side of your world, bring us to a point of no return. So that we may assist in your tasks of reaching the minds of others with the joyful aspects of light and love. For they know these words are of truth, spoken from the heart and minds of the souls that have passed beyond your world.

21st August 2016

Curtains are raised as the ancestors allow their meaning to become clear with focus in the world today.

The cosmos, the stars shine brightly as beacons of light that beckon the curiosity of man, to bring forth his machines of fire. Why does he not understand, he persecutes Earth in many ways beyond his understanding. Tremendous amounts of courage are required with fortitude as we, the Arcturians, announce our arrival within the dawn of a new day. Common practices of misunderstanding will be of no consequence.

Tonight we would like to speak to those members of the earth who would hear our words with compassion and understanding. Allow your minds not in fear, but to be aware that our species is not uncommon to man. We have come this evening to prepare you for the way of the new era. As time grows short, be prepared to withstand a negative response from those of your earth who do not welcome change, for it depletes their power over the multitudes. Their wisdom will become unwise as they attempt to defeat our purpose in the name of God. But we are here in God's light to bring change to your planet of plenty.

Who are we to say that your lives are nothing, for your souls bear witness to many terrible things upon the surface of your planet? We have contributed before to bring man to his knees. Understand that we will not permit his unsocial rivalry to continue, for man was not intended to beat upon man, but to bring a sphere of learning within your world. Money is of no consequence; power is held by those men of means who lust for the gold of your world. Let them know your voice and become clear that we are here to bring about change to your world, so that the many may benefit from the resources that are held by those men who will not listen.

We have targeted your emotions many times my son, to bring about your purpose in a joyous glory of the light of the Lord. How can we continue to bring a practice of love to those who will not heed the words? Your love is immense for your fellow man, you have learnt the lessons of past lives which have been many of sorrow, pain and misery. But all who are in the aspects of light must face their challenges to carve out and bring their purpose to the fore. This is not all about you my boy, but about those who need to understand their purpose is equally as high as yours. For they must open their hearts, open their eyes and minds and be frank with one another, with open arms and a welcoming greeting to their fellow man.

We were formerly of your planet and we associated with many of your species in the period of time before the coming of Christ. Know this, we know of many things, knowledge you do not possess, as fragments of time fall away, they are forgotten. Those lessons that were given have been misguided by others with untruths, they do not adhere to the good book. Such a shame to see the demise of man as he recklessly surges forward in the name of progress. For what progress is it you seek? That of the physical or that of love and caring for one another, as you are all equal in the eyes of the Lord. There is no segregation among men of the earth it is an illusion created by those of wealth and power so that their borders are secured to allow them to reign supreme.

You watch our ships in the morning mist as they rise above the Serengeti. In a place called Africa, where your humble beginnings and nature caused you to spread far and wide to share the earth with your brothers. But nations grew apart and man forgot his brother, as Cain and Abel forgot their relationship. You must master your men of light to issue change to the minds of those who would listen to the words of spirit. You control your minds thoughts with great difficulty and increase pursuance of perfection, but perfection can never be reached within the human aspect.

We have purpose for you, target your emotions to a centre point of the Earth. Illuminate the lives of the many as we provide illumination to the minds that matter. Concern yourself not with the trivial efforts of those of power as they try to ascertain their insistence over you. Trifle not with the men who would cause you pain. Your allegiance to God and spirit is commendable, but it will take sacrifice in many forms to ascend to a level of spirit that is beyond your reach at this time. Your path has come on, don't give up now.

To all who hear these words, let me speak my mind this evening allowing you an insight into the purpose of the beings of light that surround your planet at this time. Be not afraid as we illuminate your skies in a thunderous roar echoing throughout your lands of the earth. Administrate your minds of purpose to allow us to speak. We have come, not as masters of a race but to rescue the minds and thoughts of the many, from the masters of the negative. You wrestle with your thoughts, declaring to us, "How can such beings be present and not noticed?" We wish not to be seen at this time, but will give gentle indications of our presence. They see as we raise our flags and they speak many times of what is to be done. There is nothing they can do but adjust our minds and our purpose to accept the inevitable, as your world is not alone, but amongst many nations of planets.

Allow us to intercede in your lives, bringing a better relationship between us and you, we speak not of war but of peaceful intentions to men of the earth. Combat your fears allow us your attention, for we bring many wondrous things to rescue your planet from the path it walks. Concern yourself not with our appearance as we are of a form unrecognisable to you. But in your scriptures, and your manuscripts, we have been spoken of many times. You ask yourselves, what form can be so hideous as not to be seen? Hmm, we are, who we are. We ask not for your judgement, it will be difficult for your minds to cope with the difference, but we see the many who await our arrival. For the less fortunate of the world become trampled on.

Strategically we are placed in a position beyond your Mercury, we await the signal of she who comes. Tirelessly we work to prepare the way for the many. Seasons will bring change; your August is upon you now. We will deliberately expose a ship to be seen in South Africa, as men and women become tragically involved in war by those of ignorance. We will show them that they must adhere to the ways of peace within their nation, for they stab themselves, to spite themselves. We cannot command you to obey our word, but we do beg you to listen with the reason within your minds that our arrival will be of purpose. Turn to us to enlighten your tragic lives.

Too many times we have spoken of disasters and war upon your planet, they are seen as a negative in our speech, but be aware, it is for the reason to enlighten your minds to your aspects of hate. You must reach out your arms and greet those who come with a welcome. Their ships will be broad as they are narrow as they are brought into focus within the telescopes of your world. Their endeavours to cover up our intentions will fail, for the many will see ships of love that sail into the stormy waters of your world. Once more we speak metaphorically of many things beyond your understanding. We see some of you are beginning to see the reason, your light behind them, we congratulate you for your courage and words, in speaking out. His master's voice has spoken many times in the past, but beware your thoughts don't betray your mind. Allow the aspects of light love to shine and know that we are of the light.

Truly your practice of meditation, brings many thoughts to bear upon those who read and watch your lines. We are gratified that their love reflects yours. For an open mind will accept the many forms of beings who will follow us. Tragically we cannot be assured of a warm reception by your men of hate who will fire their missiles in defence of what they see as their countries. Our flagships will assemble with meaningful purpose and we will gratefully receive the warm thoughts of those that welcomed the change.

We have seen many come before you with their words of regret and of their amusement. Don't be harsh with them but let them see the truth that emits on the pages of your words.

Bring to bear the sword of justice as we describe a feasible mission of love amongst your men of the planet.

Truly remarkable your ability, to allow the greeting of the many. Focus your mind as that of an instrument of God, to bring joy to those who would listen to us of the light. Aspire to men of beauty, combat their fears in a mission of love.

Tonight, we are fortunate to have with us a great ambassador within your lives, for he brought many marvels, miraculous events. Be calm as we assist his arrival within your mind. Jacob a man of our own seed, Arabian by dissent, his name rings out words of truth before the peoples of the earth:

"I was once a man of low esteem, my master beckoned me forward be to become one of many disciples of the Lord. We were men of the poor, we had little but our faith. As I remember, the times in hours of fear, those hard times, punishing times, times when men fought for nothing more than to be the masters. I was a disciple of the Lord, took the word to many countries. My name rings out in many nations of your world today, but know this my son, my name is among many who have brought change to the peoples of your world, particularly Africa is of interest at this time. Their unruly behaviour that brings many to the slaughter cannot continue, your masters ignore their pleas. Their greed is astounding, but know that we are the disciples of life and I, Jacob, will become one with man once more as she rises from the flames. Goodness knows how the world will react to the one called James. We will battle together to bring purpose and meaning within your lives, with aspects of love and beauty. Target your emotions my son, allow us your thoughts of love and wisdom. You deem them to be few, but they are many, they shine bright your words. Reflections of love combined, will draw others to the light as a moth to the flame, for they will see an elusive figure who shines the light and love of the Lord without fear of ridicule. Let us work together to bring about this change to the men of your world, allowing him to see that his masters are nothing more than he is."

Well I never! In all my days on earth, I never would have seen so many in distress. I was once a man of purpose, drawn to those who would share their power with me to bring a purpose of peace to the nations of the earth. Lincoln was a man with such ability, he embarked upon a mission to free his lands of slavery. His peoples now sit in turmoil as they decide what is right and which is wrong, for there are many truths within the lies told. He sees his statue, sits there proud, yet he cannot believe his nation and how it is plundered by those of ill will. Did you not fight for the establishment of man's right to live with one another in peace? Many suffered in those terrible times when he lived upon your earth. He cannot forget the burden which was placed upon him to bring his nation together, the north and south fought with purpose that one man will not dominate another. For what is black and white is now grey. You cannot continue with a purpose of hate for those of different cultures. We are the fathers of your land and we speak now to our granddaughters and grandson's. Do not forget the wars and atrocities that brought their land to be, the ignorance of the men who enslaved those of different races still dominate your lands. They may speak in different terms, but they consider them to be less than human. We cannot agree to allow this to continue, for one will rise to bring about a peace in a different aspect to the majority of those they call whites. We wrote lines of purpose as we sealed our nations love with one another. You celebrate these words each year in your schools and chapels and your men of power reflect upon them, but do not see their purpose. Your amendments were made so that those of intolerance can rule with shame. You are a great nation but are slipping into misery, poverty and degradation. Lift up your heads and as Churchill once said, "Be a man and not the sheep," be the shepherd of life and bring your flock to bear.

Truly remarkable occurrences on the Saturn surface will astound those who view through their eyepieces, an explosion of immense proportions will have repercussions upon your earth. Stones will fall, plummet through your sky, some will be lost and this is unfortunate. These events are of a natural occurrence and cannot be prevented by your men of science, despite their efforts to cover up the possibilities that these will cause disasters. Tremendous amounts of waves, they will plummet in seasons to come.

Events happen all the time, worry your minds not as the natural sequences of life occur. Give strength to one another and bear with fortitude. Man deems himself as being all powerful, but really he is nothing. We would like to announce our intention and our involvement to ascertain a certain amount of reason. Your men of science discover many things but are brought to bear. They are hidden without good reason from your world.

Aspects of love must become the normality, or you will suffer the consequences of your brutal lives. Change your ways my people. Brutus once said, that men are weak minded fools. Perhaps he's right. A link in the chain must be of strength, your weakest link must be given strength, for to break the chain would be disastrous. We speak of the chain of love, a metaphorical chain, but understand this, that it has purpose and meaning within your lives, we do not need to draw a schematic for you to see that if this chain is broken, then what lies before will be a terrible consequence.

- - - - - - - - - - -

2 + 2 make 4, another sum, figures are meaningful to the minds of algebra. You must become part of the equation to understand its meaning, for figures have purpose in your lives. Have you ever wondered why it is that threes, fives, and sevens are numbers of purpose and multiply your natural world? You speak of them as odd numbers, but they equate to a purposeful sum. Temperance will be needed to calculate your lives within these numbers, hmm, numbers, everything is controlled with figures of numerically.

Cats, what an independent creature they are. They have stealth, wisdom and as they look at you, they sum you up. They are a constant reminder of the independence that once existed within your world. They look to you to feed them, but they are not reliant upon you and they see you as beings of curiosity. You perform your rituals and they are happy to attend, to sit with you and aid you in comfort. But their minds are free, free range, they will not commit themselves. But they love, they are gracious in allowing your company with them, they are pack animals with independent minds and souls. Some regard them as animals of interest, particularly the Egyptians who see them as keepers of souls, of Hades. Their strength and dominance were respected, the Cat People were of a race many eons before your lifespan existed, for there have been many misconceptions of man's arrival upon your earth. Do you think you were first; do you think you were the only dominant species? Humph, regretfully not, you may evolve and you may not. They evolved, they became the watchers of the world, they watch you, they look, their messages are fed back through the minds in ways you do not understand. Those Cat People of stealth, they will ignore your pleas as you call them to come, for they will come in their own good time. They neither care, or are indifferent, they have friends and they consider them useful for their purpose. They are the watchers of your world, they respond only to themselves and the light.

Starships that gather before the dawn will bring focus upon those who have researched our being. Hmm, 2 by 2 multiplied by 4 = 8. Eight is a number of a never-ending continuation, it is a number that reflects eternity. But we have need of those with a measure of love to figure out the combination of numbers. For numbers are of the universe, and to understand their configurations is to understand the purpose of life and light. We will bring a fraction to your minds, a number of meditation and meaning. Number 11 was given, as is 22. *(Note: 11 and 22 are said to be master numbers. The number 11 represents instinct and is the most intuitive of all numbers. The master number 22 holds more power than any other number earning it the nickname 'the Master Builder'.)*

A fraction of the observatory is torn apart by a storm. Around 1/8 is given away. Prospect your minds and look for the wisdom within men of purpose.

The dogs of war will come once more to your planet, but a light will shine for the need of him.

Tremendous amounts of skill and wisdom will be required in the autumn of your years to negotiate the boundaries of life. For what will come will astonish those of science and men of the Earth. Be not unwise to our words, but bring them to bear on those who need understanding, that ours is a practice of love, not of worship but of assistance to those planets of primitive beings to become aware of their purpose, so that they too may evolve into a meaningful species. Evolve or perish, it's a simple choice. Which will you choose Earthmen? We will await your answer. You may not understand these words, but it will reach the ears of those of understanding and knowledge of our being beyond your atmosphere.

NASA you call yourselves. Well, you must evolve. Your ships of treasures are buried within the seas of tranquillity, do you not know of your past? Your satellites reach out with the sparkle of interest, they see these ships. Have you not wondered why it is your men of NASA do not return to the place you call moon? Haven't you ever considered the possibility of their discoveries? Perhaps they will never show you, but we will. For you will not be kept in the dark.

Resistance is futile by those of a negative, we will announce ourselves as beings of the light to enlighten your world, to a

purpose and a position of stature within the nations of planets that surround your solar system. We are one of many who wish to bring purpose to your lives. Shame upon those who will not look upon us as friends. Passive was he who guards the heavens and the earth. Amen.

4th September 2016

Tonight we would like to make ourselves clear to the world of man and the politics that hold him hostage. The brethren of the light will come once more to speak in terms of peace to your men of politics. They whisper in each other's ears of their concerns to relinquish their hold on the United Nations of the Americas. Common practice it has become to not associate with those of the negative.

As the freedom movement grows, so their thoughts of despair will call out on the winds across the plains of the states. Harmonised their movement will become as they call out for a change, resisting their capitalists who prey upon the poor souls of that United States. Disillusioned are many by the men in black, who constantly ignore their requests for information and affirmation as to the truth of our existence. We will show them what it is to be open and truthful, their will to hide us will be denied as our aspect grows to bring comfort to the people of the nations of Earth. We are of the light; we accept no bargaining for their reason to exist.

We can demonstrate many things to your world, but we hold back at this time, as what good will it do us to become so obvious as to strike fear into men. Your conditioning has begun as men of the earth to accept the knowledge that we came here many times before to enlighten the peoples of your world as to their true beginnings. Mm, in the 90's there was a movement that brought up and set up a pace to bring people's thoughts to the possibilities of an ET existence.

We find no words of comfort to give to you at this time, as your men of war deplete their resources and search out new ones with the hunger and lust of that of the hungry wolf. For he cries out for information on those who would betray his kingdom.

Your selflessness in extreme measures of control will be required to announce a burden upon men as we enlighten those of the traffic in the skies, which will become normal. For visions, sightings of us as we command our will over those that rule your nation, their mistrust demonstrates their ignorance of attitude towards change for the better. Those who work within the avenues of light know best how to bring out an outcome of peace within the nations of your world.

Very shortly we will announce our intentions to your Masters of the world and they will be astounded of our point of view, but they must kneel before us and ask forgiveness for their terrible ways and their guilt in their controlling of the general population. Hmm, we can sum up your lives as being that of a student of life, you must be aware that your status in the scheme of things is but a small one.

A spark in the night sky that shines bright, but it will grow as a fiesta of fireworks explodes over those nations of intolerance. We cannot hide our purpose from those of the earth, our intentions are good. Let us speak now of our good intentions towards man as we circle your planet unobserved by your men of science. They think they have a good handle on things, in all aspects of secrecy, but there are gateways, loopholes in which they are unable to vanquish. We will exploit these to bring a peace and love to mankind.

Exploitation of the many populations must cease, for it is not right to be above one's station. Can you not see that those men who would have you believe that we are just a figment of the imagination, thought of by few as saviours of your planet, they will scorn those who bring evidence. For they will deny our very being upon your box of vision. In a fortnight we will display another demonstration of our irritation towards your men of science who will attempt to block our signals. They cannot succeed, for they are but nothing, we toy with them in ways you do not understand and they barrack us with their intolerance. Be extremely careful, for they will turn on those who would suggest our thoughts are real and that we exist despite their disapproval.

We will watch over the many of the light as we cascade love upon them. Have no fear, life is for living and death will come soon to all who live a life upon the earth. This is not to be feared but to be rejoiced, as new beginnings are within the realms of spirit. Each and every passing is unique to the individual for it is their choice to experience that side of pain, some will suffer immensely, while others will glide into the light. But yours will not be revealed. This is knowledge, that is not of value. Live your life as you intended, be not afeared, for many will pass in the beginning of the new dawn.

Day breaks. Hmm, dawn comes and we listen to the many prayers of those who whisper in our ears of their displeasure upon being disrespected by those of mercy. Your doctors and nurses have many intolerances, but in their aspects of their purpose, they put up with so much indignation by him who rules their words. Medical Staff require a sense of self-expression to perform their duties, to bring love and respite of those who suffer illness and injury to there being. Why is it they disrespect them so, thinking of them as a burden upon their purse strings? They will shortly announce the privatisation as they will indicate their inability to support such an institution. The country will be in uproar, but little will be done. The will and backbone of the people no longer exists as they succumb to the words of ignorance.

Those men of grey are careless in their actions. They will, I am sure, rue the day they elected to become indifferent to the nation of their people. In certain circumstances events will unfold that will highlight their plight. The public are taught to defend themselves against their pickets. Sometimes in life it is necessary to hold up your values and state your name, shout it loud and clear, for those of intolerance are deaf.

Your tactics of love should shine bright within the stars of the night sky. Tremendous amounts of energy will be felt as the rays reach Saturn and on Earth. Focus your mind on a prayer of love as this radiation emits from a distant star. The question has been asked of Mercury, a magician. The rays of light emitted were caused by a massive explosion within the core, for its balance has changed. Immense ferocity will be felt soon, those solar rays of luminescence will be streamed upon your planet, you are shielded by an array of magnetic lines, but slowly they will be eroded by man's own doing.

We disposed, ha, ha, of your toy, you were to send into the atmosphere of Earth, you thought you would dominate man's attitude to other civilisations. Huh hmm, we know. Our birds of prey were upon you. We felt the need to acknowledge our existence to demonstrate our will in the forthcoming events that your satellite would have supported. Tell them, they cannot destroy that which they cannot see. Their immense power is negligible in our eyes, we cannot trust the men who call themselves 'military'. Hm, hm, we'll not yet harm, but prevent the situation that must not prevail upon your world. In secrecy, pathetic attempts to hide their weapons of war within innocence. It will cause an outrage amongst the men of peace in your world if they were to understand.

Rockets, ships, ha! What do they know? The vast expanse of time cannot be explored by sitting in your secret bunkers, hmm, by infecting us with your demands. Once we were condemned as parasites upon your world, but you know different. We have told you many times, we are of the light. Ha! But counter-productive are their attitudes in regard to us. Despise us they do, for what we bring. Don't let them bring you down to their level.

We will announce our presence before the dawn of the new day as foretold. When you ask is the dawn of the new day of the new era, the Bible will tell you many times of the recreation of life. We do not aspire to be God, but we are the light of silver, who will bring his purpose to your lives, for we too have a faith in the Almighty of your world.

(Note: Spacex Rocket 1st Sep 2016

On the morning of 1st September 2016, a SpaceX Falcon-9 rocket carrying an Israeli satellite called Amos-6 exploded three minutes prior to a scheduled static fire test. SpaceX confirmed the event, stating that an 'anomaly' had occurred in the upper stage of the oxygen tank as they were loading propellant into the rocket.)

ET Who Destroyed Spacex Rocket

Creatures of the earth we call upon you to recoil from your nature. We interrupted your broadcast as we have need to create a peace. Solitude has become our friend. You are ignorant of us, do not despair, do not fear that of alien life. We feel your desperation to shield yourself from those whom you regard as negative. *(Author's note: I felt this was threatening but I continued.)* In all, words will be pleasing to your mind, but respect our wishes as we insist that your men of life do not react in a manner regretful! Hmm, they will know of this conversation, but tell them their focus is lost in the explosion. They will understand.

Complete your tasks as required. God bless, good evening.

11th September 2016

With my heart and voice, sing out to those who have at this time voids within their life. Sing out the praises of him on high, our father who sits in heaven. The Almighty God watches over us all as he brings us salvation to carry us from a bitter end by man's own doing. Blessings to those who read these words with a mind of love and a practice for the welfare of their kin.

Please join us this evening as we accumulate the minds of the speakers who would give you lessons in life. Focus your mind in a way of love and light to bring purpose to your being. Many times we have come to speak, to bring news of future events that may affect your world of life. We have not come to bring fear into the hearts of men, but to bring the joy of love and knowledge of the master who joins us in this trimester. Allow us to intercede and integrate with your mind and body, to allow us the freedom of speech to those of your world who would listen intently at the words of the creator.

Your view of life has changed over the many years, you no longer value the words of wisdom of which he taught. Your focus is lost and purpose waivers. Do not despair in your world of man, for we are of the light, the ones to bring you salvation as we focus our minds upon those who would bring a practice of love to their fellow man. Occasionally we falter in our purpose, but isn't that the way of life? That when we fall, we pick ourselves up, brush ourselves down and accept that we have learned the lesson given. You must be obedient to him, the Lord of heaven and when you falter, you too must brush yourself down and focus upon his light and love and know that with understanding, he can reason to your actions.

Today has been a beautiful day as your men of Earth have celebrated in the Asia's a coming of peace and a time of memorial. *(Festival of Eidal Adha 11th September 2016 – Muslims around the world celebrate the holy day which marks the end of Hajj.)*

We extend our hand to your brethren of the world in friendship, as we approach in our ships of gold to once again make ourselves known to the world of men. We speak not of harsh words but of gentle reminders to those who have forgotten. Sharia law, hmm, you must not allow your emotions to override your thoughts of love. Have peace of heart.

Combination of much fear will initiate an action of immense proportions in your Korea. The north, the south, a bitter conflict will erupt amongst their men as they battle for supremacy of their island. Their negative aspects will draw attention from the world as they fight a bitter battle for freedom or control. They must find contentment in their hearts to bring about a common practice of brotherhood, for they are brethren divided by a line or border invisible to their eyes. Why do men argue over invisible lines that divide your world, bringing freedom to some and misery to others? We cannot comprehend those minds, for it bears your thoughts of freedom of movement.

Your hearts and minds must understand that there are no boundaries to life. You equally have a role to play within your world of life to bring about a purpose of change, of love, companionship, contentment. We fear the worst for your being of man, for you are punctuated with greed and excess. Why cannot the rich man be content with his lot?

We will stab at the minds of those who would deny your freedom upon the earth to roam, as free as the spiritual realm. True, your hearts have desires of peace and liberty. You must accept that all beings of life upon the earth descend from the heavens above. You are all equal in the eyes of the Lord, so why build bridges and divisions in your life. A common practice of love should prevail amongst the men of your world. Do not allow your unsocial thoughts to impeach your abilities to love but master your mind with your heart's intentions to bring about a masquerade of peace.

Tonight we bring many words of wisdom to enlighten your world. The Fellowship of man is the Fellowship of love of spirit. To deny this love is to deny him. Truly your minds require an understanding of immense proportions as they work in mysterious ways of logic.

Be prepared for a show of strength come the dawn of the new day. For we the Arcturians, have all but exhausted our attempts to signify to man that we are a race of peace. They still persist in their pathetic attempts to arm themselves aboard their spaceships, with a negative intention towards what they deem as their foe. For we have done nothing other than to show our existence to the eyes of NASA, who deny us the right of a common practice of love. Humph. We could not have conceived that these men would ignore our thoughts. We must not assume that all men are of the negative, but it is hard to bring about a peace with those who have been subjected to the minds of these men.

Surprisingly we have knowledge, information of many things about your men of power. They will relocate their rocket ship, so as to avoid attention or distraction from the eyes of man, for they know we watch and wait, with our arrows straight and true. They attempt to deceive us by bringing the launch date forward, to bring an intention to deceive. How can we unmask ourselves from those who would ignore us?

Contracted your mind to a third party of love. Oh, bless those who watch us those within the words. Tell them this, that their bravery and fellowship is welcomed by the sphere of love.

Do not be heartbroken when you hear of our attempts to thwart the plans of the men of power of your world. We wish you peace and contentment, but as harsh as it may seem, we equally must show strength, a resolution of light.

Complete misunderstanding will unfurl at the beginning of the month of October. It will seem astounding to many that such practices could happen within the realms of your nature. She will exhaust herself with a monstrous explosion that will unite many of your peoples in a rescue attempt. She will motivate those of peace of the earth, to help bring about an end to the misery that you bring your earth. Mm, we have told you many times that we cannot stand by with the abuse given, we must intercede and act to help your men see misgivings that they bring about her. Truly remarkable is the man who can stand up and say, "I am the owner of responsibility, and I was the one who disjointed their plans!" Hmm, contemplate your thoughts, do not bring denial to your minds, hearts and souls, but accept that we are the guardians in which you must respect.

Turbulent times ahead. The mysteries and horrors of war will be represented by those men of black, as they establish a foothold in the hills below Babylon. Incarnate your wisdom to bring about a change of peace. A fantastic thought, how can man bring about such an active peace in a world filled with terror? It is your task to assist, as one of the many to initiate change through the words of wisdom of our thoughts. Truly you must negotiate a will of peace and combat your fears my son, there are no grounds on which to base them. *(Note: According to the news today, 13th September, the men of black (IS) could be losing their hold in Mosul, could it be that they will flee to where Babylon used to be, which now covers the city called Hillah.)*

We come with peaceful intentions as creatures of other worlds to hold the hands of those who would see new beginnings and temper their love from hate.

Complexities of the heart are great and many, but you must combine your thoughts, emit a fragrance of love to the nations of plenty. They dance and sing their songs of war to bring balance to leaders of their country, they are blind and their greed is astounding. They will not listen to those of the pipeline, for they will bring terror upon them with immense ferocity, water cannon, dog fights, skullduggery will be used to bring about their will. They have no care for the indigenous people who embark upon a mission of love for their mother. They will meet a bitter end in the reckoning of all things, they will learn that their favours to those of the rich and powerful are but nothing. For the humble man who brings his thoughts to the table and to share with others, he is the man who is the humblest of all. He has nothing to give but his love and his meagre offerings. To those who flaunt their love before the eyes of the angry beware your actions, do not become your tomorrow's. *(Note: We feel this is about the proposed Dakota oil pipeline.)*

Commodus, a leader of men, would like to speak on the platform once more. "My misery was bought upon me by my actions of intolerance, I was leader of men, of many and I learnt my lesson well. You cannot ignore the thoughts of the many, or for him. For you are but one man, you must comply with the laws of the nation. I was no angel; I did not bother to see the needs of my people. My energy and power were devoted to those of the tournament. I was an ignorant man with a self-loathing for whom I was. I see the error of my days and my will. I will not permit those thoughts to rule once more for I understand his power and glory and that I am nothing but a humble man. Target your emotions with love my son, do not allow thoughts of domination to overrule your mind, the men of power truly have need of balance." Thank you. Commodus.

Trumpets may blow and the siren's sound in the skies above Naples. Shoot them down they say, for what end? Why bite the hand that feeds you? A welcome approach will bring a bounty of love. *(Note: The Message date is 9/11 – "Trumpets blow and siren's sound in the skies above Naples. – The final message given to the military F16 pilots after the planes had flown into the towers was "Shoot them down!" but to no end because they were too late, all the planes had achieved their targets and the last plane was taken down by the passengers of the aircraft before the military could get to them. Regarding Naples and the Sarasota area of Florida is where nearly all of the terrorists lived and learnt to fly their planes and only recently it has been found that nearly all of them were Saudi Arabian or had links to Saudi Arabia who is an ally to US. – therefore "Why bite the hand that feeds you." The part about bringing a "bounty of love" would be that the relatives and loved ones of the many people killed would receive the recognition they were asking for by their own government instead of being denied the truth of who was really behind their deaths.)*

13th September 2016

Your thoughts intercede with our actions Michael.

Beware those who watch warily from the sidelines at the scriptures you write, for they know the truth therein. Do not be ashamed of who you are and the purpose that has been brought to you by the angels of the light.

We come as an army of the light to bring peace to the many millions who suffer at the hands of tyrants. Their misery is heard and felt with such emotion, their crime is simply living. They are of no consequence to the men in power, other that something that stands in their way. Their negativity will become obvious before the dusk of the beginning of the new day.

Say what you will about others, but do not despise those who bring the Master's words to you. Trust is a matter of the heart, given to those who would open their eyes to see the truth that shines within.

Tormented hearts filled with joy as the many celebrate in enormous gratitude as the armies of the north recede. They bring about a jubilant joy of relief. Commanders sacrifice themselves before the Lord as they will not devastate the Earth through policy. Become one with your hearts and minds, have a will and power of strength to resist the measures set against you, as the masters dictate their words.

Do not allow their fragmented hearts to bring misery upon the millions of the nations of Mother Earth. Welcome those who desire peace without arms deals or indignation set upon those of a nation of love.

Frequently we ask you to listen to our words with a hope that man will listen to the meanings within. We constitute a magnitude of peace, we can offer those who bring a negative response with their actions of intolerance, but to those who carry the torch of light. Rest assured that your armies of the light will triumph with a magnitude of degrees, never seen before.

We seed your mind with loving thoughts, and as the seeds fall on the ground, some will grow, some will falter, but those that grow will become multitudes, those that fall on stony ground are but a few. In the light they will grow out of the darkness therein.

The Vatican and the Pope

We are ever hopeful of a satisfactory conclusion to our negotiations with those of the Pope. Their congregations have become widespread throughout your world, their dissatisfaction with the laws set against them will become apparent as the mainstream will rebel in the coming conference of the Lord. They argue, to and fro of the meaning and purpose of the books held within the vaults of the sanctuary of the Vatican, they do not wish for the general public to observe the words of truth that lay within. We will impart a portion of importance. It reads that the sanctity of man who rests his head upon the pillow of love will reap the rewards of the master who comes before the new day, the date of which will become general knowledge, for this date is forthcoming.

Be prepared for a new biblical proportional era. The book tells of the men who would picket the lines of the church. Congress will argue as to the rights and wrongs of their doings. They will come before the multitudes, who respect their wishes as indignations grows against them.

In the book of love, the words are spoken of a great rebellion within the Catholic Church, the Pope will be the master of the heart. His name will resound for many years following his passing, for he is one of gracious love and great wisdom and his words will muster the many armies of that religion and they will force the hand that holds them back.

The Irish communities of the States of America, will predominately ignite a storm at the words that are dictated by him. Never doubt that our thoughts are linked in ways in a manner of the Lord. Cast your mind out of doubt, for we are the ones to assist in your reform of planetary love. Come before us with gratitude in your hearts for love and joy given and the blessings of the many, who outweigh those of the dark.

Arcturian Speaks to Michael

Surrender your thoughts of love my son, for they are a passion upon which you will build. Never doubt your abilities that you possess within. Your mind begins to open to the possibilities you never thought possible. Teach your mind to be aware of those positive things that you are capable of. Do not deny yourself the right to be heard within the nations of men, for their policies will denounce such mortal beings as being insane. But who are the insane ones? Is it the man who speaks of peace, or the man who speaks of war and tyranny against his fellow brothers? No, it is the man of love who will triumph the adversity of the hate within the establishment.

Give your heart freely my son, they are willing to hear our words as they are mysterious to so many of the nations.

We are the Arcturians who speak of many things to come. We mean your nations no harm, we respect your will in life of freedom. Hmm. Combat your minds of fear, for we are the extra-terrestrials of love, not hate. We will show our hand in a mighty blow, a strike of significance against those who would cause us indignities. Those satellites of Saturn will cease to function, you will not understand why. Your technology is weak. We will not compromise your minds will of peace, but to those who would fill the heavens to demolish countries, they will feel our wrath. They speculate our moves, but they cannot defeat our will.

Thomas, given by your hand, we have come, we are not afraid of him for he is a man of goodwill.

We have your satellite you will be astounded to hear, news will leak, but denial will be rife. Nevertheless, we know that you have troublesome times indeed.

Dakota Pipeline

Their practice of love, is denied. The peoples have a right to demand responsibility from those who would degrade their existence. Trumpets will sound, whistles will blow, in thoughts of those who protest against those of ill will, who shout and scream in a manner disrespectful of your masters. Disasters will ensue as they attempt to put down the discontentment of the hearts of those of the Earth. Tremendous amounts of will and courage will be required for those demonstrators as they embark upon a journey of love.

Bring those to look out for their crimes against Mother Earth in the seasons to come. There will be joyous raptures as they begin to understand the pipeline will not proceed. Their voices will be heard amongst the men on high, who do not wish to make a scene. But beware the wolf in sheep's clothing, she will demolish their hopes and saturate their dreams with much indignation. The spirit of the plains will weep to see his people trampled upon once more by those who swamp the nations that once belonged to others. The warriors of past will come to sweep away the fears held by their people, for they know much happiness is to come, as their dreams are swept away by those of irresponsibility. How will it end, we can only but speculate, but end it will?

She was once a secretary of state. Her will was strong as a horse, she navigated the corridors of parliament with a will in mind, a woman determined to have her voice heard. She corrupted her mind in a masquerade of intelligences, she forfeited the light to become a master of the people.

Triumphant whispers will be heard and sounded in those places on the plains.

Tasked you will be, as your heart aches for those nations who suffer at the hands of him who will wield that monstrous machine, for he has no heart, no mind or stability. Nevertheless, he will become a monster and tyrant who will wash away those he feels are interrupting the will of his nation.

Tigers will roar, but in the jungles of life she saturates their minds with nonsensical excuses. Here we are once more, listening to the rhetoric of those who dispel the hearts of doubt, behold your name will become a measure of her will. 'Hope springs eternal', is a phrase that is well equipped to suit this situation.

Never let your mind doubt the practices of love that dwell within your mind's thoughts.

Mother Mary

Matron of life wishes a word to bring peace and encouragement to all who walk upon the face of the earth. Acknowledge one another as a fellow spirit. Combine your thoughts of love and shower them upon the people who experience many terrible dark days. You who work in the wake of light must display your courage with fortitude. Become those, the torch bearers of life, so those who have a will, will follow to the kingdom of heaven. Mary the mother of Jesus is with you all as your problematic lives become lives of adversity. "Trouble your hearts not my children, for as a mother I will comfort you in the face of dictatorship. I will fold my arms around you as you speak the words."

18th September 2016

We come this evening with a matter of concern for all as they prepare for war. Your masters they deny you access to information that should be made public, for their greed is astounding. They do not know when to stop and what is enough. They have targeted many countries for terrorist acts in the hope that these would have need to buy arms and protection, to isolate themselves from the evil deeds of others. Who orchestrates these terrible things? Men of plenty, who have need of many things which in truth have no value. For what man takes is deeds and not his cash beyond this life! The richest men of all are those who leave behind a passion for peace and love, they carry their riches with them, which far exceeds your material needs.

Come before us with a focus of love and obedience to the Lord, your father in heaven.

"Trust in me," says the Lord and so you should, as he grants you peace in the hereafter after regardless of who you are.

Circumstances have become apparent to the world press that all things are not as they should be, they broadcast between themselves statements that should be issued but are withheld by those who would have need of silence. Their hands are tied by the wicked, who would deny them the freedom of the press. Frustration grows as the Internet proclaims many things that cannot be said by the media of your world. Hmm, this will not be allowed to continue as these men will put a stop to the many things upon your Internet. There will be a breakdown of services and you will speculate that the aliens have destroyed the satellites. But who is it who can gain from this quiet, truly it is not us, the beings of other worlds, the Arcturians? It is man himself who gains from this silence to put a stop to speculation that would thwart his efforts. What a terrible place your earth has become. It is doomed to a life of misery, but like all who oppress others there will come a point when men will exercise their right to be free, to be masters of his own life and not controlled by the puppet-master.

You speak of many things with Valerie in regard to whether or not to publish certain comments. You should not be frightened, as love will reign supreme. Have faith and trust in our words of wisdom, as they will defend you from others who would obligingly give you cause for concern.

Hmm. Tremendous amounts of pressure will be required to release the vacuum apparent within the Earth. She will shake with a ferocity not known before. Your earth is a fragile living creature and as the youth erupts spots, so the earth erupts her acne upon you. Aww, we use the words of your mind, you know what we speak. The pressure is below the surface, it cannot be withheld for the fractures of the earth, do not be misguided by those who would sacrifice your lives for their wealth, for these fractures will spread, the crust will shatter if you do not heed the warnings. You cannot crack an eggshell without it leaking, nor can you crack the earth without the consequences to follow, for she will spew her lava to cleanse herself of the impurities that have weakened her walls. You only have yourselves to blame.

Concern yourselves not with the wrath of God, for this has nothing to do with it, this is to do with your ignorance and the men of greed. You ask how do we stop such tyrants from dominating our lives? In truth it will be a difficult task that can only succeed through love, not war, not aggression, but love and teachings from him on high. Many will observe that the words given are deliberately religious based, well, we are spirit, what else would you expect from us?

Companies of men will reject the proposals as he prepares to call it a day. Jackson was a man, a president, a noble being of your race. He sat upon his seat of power in awe of the possibilities open to him. He had a reasonable heart, his mind was of great focus within his time. The speeches, his pledges, were broken many times by the pressures of dominance of others. Their statutory rights are outdated. They must resume a life of honour, like the birds of a feather that flock together, they must bring peace by the multitudes.

22nd September 2016

Arcturians Will Arrive

Only one with a passion of love will penetrate the dark minds of those of tyranny within your desperate planet. Mm, they will come to assist the ET's that surround your planet in a spectacle of love and light. The men of NASA are all too aware of their presence beyond the stars of your earth, for they wait and they wait for the time to come when their intervention will be needed most. As the gravity of the situation deepens those Arcturians will become masters of your earth to lead you to a better world. Your beliefs in the Lord are commendable but you must have faith in their leadership, be not afraid of them. Their leader will be first to arrive in the mothership, performing feats of wonder to your men.

The Australian regions of your world, in the outback beyond the eyes of man, they will base themselves creating an outpost on earth from which their possibilities will be abound. They will be unseen by man for they are shielded. They are not reckless, but a guiding light. You have conversed with one my son, he is not ready to announce his presence, but he knows and tests you, consider him a friend.

I have nothing more to say but to give you God's blessing and praise.

25th September 2016

It has become common knowledge that we, the Arcturians, are a race of beings not of your earth. Your families live in the hope that one day the masses will come together to bring together purposeful peace upon your planet. Do not neglect your brother and sister, it is but a thought, that there are many that suffer within your world today, you will find peace in that blissful place beyond your life.

Countless memories have brought fruitfulness, tears, you complicate your lives with random measures of intolerance, you must adorn yourself with light, to become one with the light and a messenger of peace and God.

You must not ridicule those within your life but give them a measure of peace. Consistency is required in your attitude towards others, to bring them reassurance that your meaningful purpose is accurate and true. Do not allow the minds of others to influence yours to a path negative. Have confidence and be at peace with your thoughts my son, as we require a peaceful purpose to enlighten your peoples of the earth.

Habitual things we have created in your love. They surpass your practical minds. Why do you let these meagre things influence you so? You need perspective to be enlightened by the illumination of our Lord. His wish is for you is to live with peace, a man with his brother his fellow soul.

Don't forget the possibilities of life are vast. Extinguish the negative and create a peaceful haven for your mind to exist, for your world is at war with each other. No man need sacrifice his very existence for such trinkets of life, bury your mind deep as we encircle your being tonight.

Albert Einstein, he knew a thing about relativity, but he had knowledge of many other things. Microorganisms that exists within your being who also have purpose in your life. Medical facts that would astound you are kept in the possession of those drugs companies, they will not release their information to the Commons Committee to be set up in the fall, as multitudes begin to suffer inexplicable illnesses.

Be comforted that the pressures of your life will bring purpose to your being.

Once more we must tell you of our being and the fact that you must obey the word of the Lord. Come now and practice your contemplation. Have peace and quiet and no thought of mind.

27th September 2016

Mercies are great of the Lord upon the peace of mind.

Tumultuous times exist within your world today. Man against man, brave against brave, with no mercy or surrender. Countless times we have witnessed such terrible events upon your earth, merciless killing, shameful behaviour and misgivings of many. Corruption that's rife throughout the regions of your world as men clamber for the meagre resources that remain.

We have come this evening to bring a focus upon the many things of illusion of your lives. The trinkets of life that you call amusement are in fact instruments of fear and delusion.

Fracking

Why do you not respect your mother at this time? She is a creature, a life-giving planet which is your host. Why do you disrespect your host by the use of chemicals in your skies and upon the surface? You poison her to extract the gases that seep within the shale. Consequences of this will be seen within the near future, hmm, as gas mains erupt with immense pressure from the shale you seek.

We are of the opinion that your planet is unworthy at this time to receive our presence. Your armies of the north dictate their end to you. They will surface in a mighty roar, that your nations become immune to the sanctity of the Lord. We have never seen so much indignation as we do today upon your planet surface. You are like locusts feeding upon all that comes your way. You never respect the planet that bears your life.

How do you exist with such a temperament and arrogance? We have no wish to interfere or draw attention to ourselves, but we are inclined to bring about a matter of importance to trigger the emotions of man to come to the conclusion that his being is not of this earth. For you are no longer worthy to become a member of a race of beings that watch over your planet.

We have asked once before with a measure of love for those of intolerance to bear their arms no more. But they massacre many in the wilderness of your desolate areas. The eyes of this world do not see the many that suffer at this time on the surface of your planet. We must bring your attention to a fact or two, that your species is unworthy of a life. For you have no respect for one another.

We hear you argue for those who follow the light, and your point is taken my son. It grieves us to say these things, but man's awakening must come shortly and to those who have a practice of love and light be assured of your resurrection unto him within the light of heaven. Gloomy times, but necessary words nonetheless.

We have spoken before of the march of the men of evil, they would take the opportunity to exercise sanctions against the poor. As those countries who suffer war of indignation, it is all very well to bring these measures against them, but you cause more misery and pain by that very act. There has to be a better way to bring their focus on a purpose of life.

They scream and shout, The Ayatollah he comes in a cloud from the seas of the sky and they clap their hands with approval and praise of him. His curtailment upon his poor people will become obvious in the spring of your years. Compel your minds to a measure of peace that this will bring in the spring, for it is a matter of concern to ask that you hear these words so that you may focus your thoughts on the spring eternal.

Trigonometry we have spoken of before, to bring you a focus of measurement of time. We need to enlighten you once more of a message to be brought to your world, and accuracy of numbers is required to achieve the required measurements.

We have adorned your planet with life and it has grown wild and an uncertain future now exists.

Trigonometry and biology, partners in the creation of life. For what makes numbers equal 10, 2.4 is the maximum that can be achieved in the light measurement. We have to complete in measurements to avail you of our intentions on your planet of men. We do not seek pleasure from bringing about a measure of peace, hmm, but we cannot bear to witness so much destruction. You have hampered your own lives too many times before to be trusted with knowledge of the beings of light. We can assure you that our words will have a measure of ridicule and will berate your societies for their disobedience, hmm. Trigonometry, a pattern of life spelt out in numbers. It is not necessary to know the facts or why we bring these estimations to you, just trust in our words and our logic is sound. You once asked for measurement of purpose using a binary code of numbers situated within your planet's orbit. We can now ascertain a sequence for your man of knowledge. Tell him the binary code he seeks is of ones and nil's, the sequence begins: x 100

Notes Regarding the Above Figures:

The following was contributed from a reader of the blog site that these messages are posted on:

(Note: one, zero, zero – not one hundred), 10 (Note: number ten – not one zero.) Mark (or mach) 9, .111, new line, 011001, equals a measure of life (Note: or five) × 6, 01010210 × 4, new start.

The wheat is a symbol of 010111 × 2, a fraction of a measurement will sound the alarms to your nations as we speak in terms of peaceful agreement.

(Note: Some feedback has been received regarding part of this paragraph: verse 10, Mark chapter 9, New International Version: And he said to them, "Truly I tell you, some who are standing here will not taste death before they see that the *kingdom of God has come with power." – The wheat is a symbol of binary ASCII 010111 = decimal 23 or "ET B" meaning "ET Be or exist".)*

Kevin also did some research as a comparison:

Kevin's Notes Regarding the Transcript Of 27 Sept 2016

Kevin will tell you that he is no mathematician, but curiosity regarding the binary codes in the messages of 27th and 29th September led him to do a little number crunching and searching. He makes no claims regarding the accuracy of his findings but hopes that it may prompt a 'light bulb' moment to anyone who may have a further insight. The numbers have been given in the messages for a reason and the correct answers should be found. We welcome any other input regarding this.

From the transcript of 27.9.16

"Trigonometry and biology, partners in the creation of life. For what makes numbers equal 10, 2.4 is the maximum that can be achieved in the light measurement."

An internet search was made on these numbers relating to frequency and the speeds of colour and light. The first thing that came up was 'CHANNEL 10, 2.4 GHz' a radio frequency used mostly for WI-FI. Could this mean that ET could use this frequency as a means to make contact with us?

I then looked at the numbers in the way they were given, which could also mean 2.4 to the power of 10 = 24 billion, 24,000,000,000. But 24 billion what?

I looked at many different equations that may give this number a meaning without result, until the subject of God and the Bible was added to the search, I was surprised initially, then I suppose I shouldn't have been! On various religious forums there was an apparent answer, I say apparent because there can be no solid scientific proof, the **SPEED OF THOUGHT 24,000,000,000 mph.**

From the transcript: "Tell him the binary code he seeks is of ones and nil's, the sequence begins: × 100, 10" (Note: The numbers on the recording are spoken as one, zero, zero and then the number ten) *Mark (or could it be mach?) 9, .111,*

a) × 100 in binary code = X 4, or to the power of 4.
b) 10 Mark or Mach 9, (I think this is Mach rather than Mark) Mach 1 = approx 761mph the speed of sound.
c). 111 in binary = .7 So, (10 Mach 9.7) = (10 × 7381.7) = 73,817mph ×4 (73817) = 73817 to the power of 4 = Answer 7,381,700,000mph

New line 011001 equals a measure of life × 6,

a) 011001 in binary = 25
b) b) 25 × 6 = 150 or 25 to the power of 6, which = 25,000.000.
    So could a measure of life mean 150 lives or 25 million lives?
    .111 *(point, one, one, one).*

Even though I added the part .111 into the above equation, in the message it didn't quite seem to fit, then one of those coincidences happened. Each day I check Graham Hancock's alternative news web site, there was a link to an article on the 'ancient-origins.net' web site. 'Healing with Sound in Ancient Temples: 111hz.' From which this paragraph is taken:

"In the Bible John tells us: 'In the beginning was the Word, and the Word was with God, and the Word was God'. Upanishads (a sacred Hindu text) say that the divine, all-encompassing consciousness first manifested as sound 'OM', the vibration of the supreme. Everything has its own frequency. Pythagoras created his musical scale starting with a note A (just next to the middle C) that resonates at the frequency of 111Hz."

Back to the transcript: *After the sentence, "A measure of life," a second binary number is given: 01010210 × 4 as a*

binary number this does not work as far as I understand because it has a number 2 in it. Therefore 2 could mean 'to' instead. So we look at the number again which could read:
01010 to 10 × 4
01010 = 10
10 = 2
Therefore 10 to 2 × 4 or 10 to 8 which is 10 to the power of 8 which equals 1000,000,000 or 1 billion.

1 billion for a new start?
The Wheat is a Symbol of 010111 × 2
010111 in binary = 23 23 × 2 = 46 or 23 to the power of 2 =2300 or 23 × 23 = 529.

The human DNA, the Genome has 23 (pairs) 23 × 2 of Chromosomes.

Wheat is compared to tares or weed in the Bible. The weeds or tares are symbolic of unbelievers. In early Christian paintings a basket of wheat is a sign of self-sacrifice, a man or woman harvesting wheat in a painting is a sign of fertility and productivity. Grains of wheat represent The Cycle of Life.

Also a saying 'Separate the Wheat from the Chaff'.

A New Beginning Is Required

Be obedient to the Lord with a measure of love and ask nothing of him other than his love. For he is a tolerant being who will come before you in the very near future at the fall of man. You must have new beginnings, for life is too extreme now, too complex to conceive a new start in the existence in its present form. We must practice and begin a sequence to flavour your planet with love!

Complete understanding is necessary to establish a truth between the nations of war. Iran will join the battle against what they see as Westerners; imbeciles.

We see a man before us, a man before his time who has come to establish a link of possibilities within the realms of spirit. You commonly term such a being as that of an angel. His focus is upon you to tread the path of light with merriment and joy at the possibilities that are abound within your world. An establishment of light will begin shortly to announce our arrival from these.

We are sure and certain that we will be met with many indignities as they clash and grab their arms before us. We cannot submit to their demands nor their actions, but we will have our say before all who stand before us with arrogance and weapons of war.

Jerusalem fell once before in the dark ages of life, and so you must cherish your time of being my son, for Jerusalem will fall once more as we berate those of intolerance who persist in their pointless manner, bringing indignation and suffering upon the children of the world.

29th September 2016

Greetings friends, I am one of those who have come before to bid you welcome. Your planet Earth is of interest to all societies of the extra-terrestrial world and you yourselves, were once a part of the great master race of beings. Their focus was upon the heavens above and their star signs still exist to this day, the expressions of their being.

We have to insist that you call a halt to the murderous intent of those in Syria. How can you stand by and watch such awful things happen to those souls in the street and houses? You have witnessed much on the box of vision and your heart goes out with heartfelt emotions, but this is not enough my people, you have to bring a moment of joy to their lives, sing out your voices, let your praise be heard by the Lord Almighty in heaven, as he watches over those who suffer indignations at the hands of their evil master.

Bring us not into debate about the rights and wrongs of the peoples of Damascus. Their efforts to stimulate a peace will be thwarted by those of ignorance who come from the east, to ridicule the west and their belief of their one true master. His manners of faith, of peace and hope, not of glory of war, but of love and the Trinity, the Father the Son and the Holy Ghost dwells within the house of the Lord.

Their hopes and dreams of domination cannot and will not be governed by the men in white shirts. They are a race of creatures not of your earth who guides their thoughts. Their black hearts which turn their eyes and backs on their religion, they are twisted into thinking that their will is their own, but in truth they have sacrificed their will for the way of that dark one.

Do not let your hearts be dominated by fear my children, as there is love all around you, as the angels whisper in your ears of their forgiveness for your meagre sins, trust in him our father in heaven for he has seen all and will not allow this to continue.

Our ships approach in the dawn light in the misty clear skies of the east. We have become accustomed to your ridicule, but we are a race of beings that will dominate your planet and bring it a focus of love as we enter into a new dawn, a new era. You know our words to be true as we have given many truths to you. We cannot dominate your heart, but we can control your lives with a wisdom of long ago.

Time, Space and Gravity

My name is Lucas, I am a soul from the world of man. I was a distinguished character within your books of writing. Heed my words and listen to them vigilantly. I need not tell you of the frequency of intolerance in your nations now. I made my mark upon the pages of many scriptures. We wrote words of many things of life, they were good words of times past, an historical record you would call it. I was a mathematician in my time, I understood equal thoughts, need. Ah! Ah ha! The fractions of our time. You sit quietly in the hope of hearing something wonderful; I really don't know what to tell you, your temperament is good, tinged with a little difficulty, but nonetheless a heartfelt gentleman as I was. I broke with my books upon the stands of those establishments in the 1800's. 1789 the most pleasurable time of feasting, serenading and generally popularising my efforts. I met esteemed gentlemen from the parks of the fair. They would arrive in their horse and carriage and their top hats shone their black velvet. Of course I was a gentleman and I would not betray their thoughts; their secrets were to unfold as they drank their wine with careless mouth. Ha, ha, ha, oh! They never understood how I knew the completion of their plans to liberate their friends from those merciless ones in an unpopular uprising. We had many arguments about space and time, something you would like to know. Your space is occupied by a volume, with a number that matches that of a volume of equal statistics. Your mind is weak in the mathematics, I will simplify. One plus one equals two, can you get two into the space of one? Impossible you would say, indeed, the area would seem smaller to the average man. What if you could bend that light? Fold it in two in a spectrum of light, then would it not pass through the one, being by half? Something to think about. Those energies would be needed for such a feat. Your role will match the pull of the earth, you strain against it not understanding that it can be released with a measure of love and magnetism of the heart. Your mind is a maze of many wonders, ah, but you abuse it, not allowing those ideas flourish. When they do, your men of science in their dogma, create hazards to obligingly block said things. Ah stupidity! Is it no wonder your advancement of man has ceased and become stale in the stagnant waters of war? Your creative abilities are stifled by your thinking. Your science, a creative scientific mind is of great need, but you must release your thoughts beyond the boundaries of possibilities to excel and exceed your limitations of that sail.

We are the Arcturians, we have immense power and possibilities abound, we can impart many things of knowledge and wisdom if you will just have a heart to listen. Michael, we need to show a possibility in you to open the eyes of man. Let it be known, our hearts and minds, for our very souls who wish for better times. There is a thought that maybe if we were to dream together of a better world it would be so. It will take much more than this, much tolerance, ah ha, for a national obligation for those who would wage war, their end is coming and their thoughts will be stifled by our expressions of mind. We cannot win a war without first understanding their minds. They are of ignorance; their hearts are sad and dark.

Our commentary exceeds your thoughts at times my boy. You know not from whence it came, but you have faith and trust, this is plain to see. You are a magnificent specimen. Ha, you have regrets, your thoughts as they are of pride and ego. But who would be saying this of you? Hmm? If it weren't for your abilities?

Dramatic sequence of events will astound the many as we adorn your skies with colourful illusions. Your hearts will sink as they vanish into the light and we will hear your call for guidance. But we cannot interfere without the mother Mary's blessing. You must stand back and watch those innocents perish before your eyes, our hearts sink at the very thought. So many will perish before the dawn of the new light, but perish they must to bring about change. It is a hard thing to say, to imagine that some will lose their lives for the good of others, but their souls will rejoice in the heavenly place for their sacrifice.

Tonight we would like to rejoice the life of one such soul who was saved, she saw many things of abhorrent visions, but she survived. She will bring about change in her early years, she submits her voice to those nations of the East. *(Malala Yousafzai – Nobel Peace Prize Winner?)*

Welcome in the master of all, of light. Sing out your praises, for he will become a leader of men to ease you from the dark forces of the night. Open your hearts and minds and treasure the thought that his memory will be with you once more in his second coming upon your plane of Earth. Tangible amounts of feelings will be felt as he enters your beings, ah such bliss.

Binary Code

Shape your world to an array of light with numbers and fractions that were given in thought, your binary practices have measure, those ones and zeros once more to become clear to the minds of focus. Let us answer his reply in a manner he will respect. We see him sat in his study, overlooking the landscape. His mind is of circles, of fractions and much contemplation. Study his mind with books, a globe stands in the corner and the glass in his hand as he concludes that maybe, just maybe, there may be one who will fulfil his answers. It is not necessary for him to be objective about these things, have an eye for the truth. Your limitations are many, but we see an opportunity to pass this information of ones and zeros, let the count begin: 11101011 new line, 10001110101 universe. One defined by a symbol to match an antiquity of his love. He knows of his vase of ancient times. We will say to him "Grief that for the lads of the many and those who would not see, bless you for your thoughts." Come the harvest come the feast of Stephen to your world my son.

(Note: Thoughts About the Two Binary Code Sequences:
Let the count begin: 11101011 = 235 [think in terms of: 2,3,5,8,13,22 etc]
10001110101 = 1141.

235 is a sequence from the Fibonacci Series, the golden ratio.

1141 is also known as a hexagonal number, in geometry if we create a circle with central point and then create other circles drawn from that central point it produces a hexagon or 'seed of life', this pattern can be created indefinitely and is a pattern seen throughout the whole of creation.

We focus on the words: 'Shape your world to array of light' ... 'and at the end the words', 'One defined by a symbol to match an antiquity of his love.'

Would it seem correct that these numbers are leading us to think of the most sacred mathematical shape of the universe,

The Seed of Life? The very building block of the universe. A pattern also repeated in many crop circles.

When an internet search was entered for '1141 Universe' the following information was found:

"A Lesson in Newton versus Einstein:"

1. *Newton; Gravity is a force acting between massive objects in static Euclidean space.*
2. *Einstein; Gravity is the result of the curvature of space-time by the presence of mass energy.*

2nd October 2016

The tightrope of life is a strand of DNA that is stretched taut. As you walk your lives, the heart and memories of old, remember the future is bleak, but not written yet. For you are the writers of your own stories, you are the masters and key-holders to the future of life upon your planet Earth.

Know that we are here to establish a communication with those within power, for he will terminate our existence with a manner of indignity. He knows of our circles of light within the realms of your planetary orbit. He cannot continue upon his path with his murderous intent upon the peoples of the earth. For we of the Arcturians, will disable and disarm the armies of torture.

How can we express our feelings of anger towards those men of intolerance who murder and slay their own people with disregard for their abilities? No respect for human life, with a negative view upon all, who in his eyes only serve meagre purpose.

Count Christie, he was a member of an organisation, existed before your time. His attitude was of war but not peace, for he delved in the black arts, what an ignorant man did not understand the Lord Almighty, he is the only one with purpose, allow your path to follow him. We cannot tell you much of his energy, for he hides it well. Within the black walls, dungeons of his mind. But we know this; those indignities will become his own if he continues to practice in a manner of evil. Corpus Christi they shout, they called a writ. We will not answer to those who persist in targeting our ships above your skies.

You have purpose in the words that you write, but keep it simple. The men of intolerance would not read the complex messages held within. They shut their eyes to the possibilities of lives ever after, as they know their sins and crimes against humanity will be brought against them in those forthcoming days.

Tonight we wish to welcome a new member to the brethren of light, for she is full of purpose and a saintly manner, we must welcome this lady that comes before us. Madam, she would be called. Constantly we have admired her efforts to bring peace in your world, she is little known by the many who practice evil. But she comes this evening to whisper in your ear a word of comfort and acknowledgement to your purpose: "Come hither my merry men, be blessed with the light of the Lord as he showers his love upon you in indulgence of your practices. He sees your world, not as weapon of war, but as a flower yet to open and the beauty held within. As the insects that scale its outer walls for the way, so the flower will blossom into a beauteous being. It has not been easy as a woman to be recognised by many of your world, but I have come this evening to reassure those with purpose, that their endeavours are always met with beauty and love. Focus your mind Michael, upon the possibilities that the Lord, the saviour could bring to your world of dark. Allow him into your hearts and let his breath speak through you as a man of the world. You know best the attitudes of man towards his being and he is reliant upon those of the light to guide others to his door, to his being. *(Note: We are uncertain who this lady is, maybe it is just the message that is of importance.)*

Do not negotiate your mind with sampling the world of sin, but occupy your mind with thoughts of love and respect and compassion for those who have least within your world. Be blessed with his love and know that his purpose is within you all. Only those black hearts that shut out this truth will know only pain, fear and sorrow. For you all build your lives within this life, some are master craftsmen, some are mediocre builders, whilst others, they do nothing! They do not see anything they do not want to see anything, but it will be their loss. But as always, there is reconciliation to those hearts who would have mind to begin afresh within the world of men.

We have not come this evening to talk of murderous people within your society, we come to issue and grant you peace in your lives, should you only ask. We are the beings of light who once before trod your earth with footsteps so light you would hardly notice them. We were beings who had purpose within the realms of light, as we transmitted our love through thought. We once had a palace of gold that shone as beauty throughout the world, it became a symbol of national pride, an emblem of love that shone throughout the universe. Long gone are the days when we were established upon your earth, for we found a way, a better way to transform our beings, so that interplanetary travel became an instant, a blink of the eye.

Michael Caine, an actor in many films. A gentleman at heart, hmm he is of your world, but he has an inkling of what life is about. Strange that we talk of someone who exists at this time in your world of men, but he was worth a mention to let you know that as an actor he excels, as a man he is deeper than you think. Why do you need to know this you think? Hmm, as a measure, as a guidance. Do not be fooled by his demeanour, for he expresses his alter ego within your world. Be not ashamed of what we speak for they are lessons in the balance of life. You were once of the light and will become so again, all in good time, but you must find a measure of peace in your heart.

Evidence of an Early Civilisation

Capsules were found beneath your seas. Spectacular finds they will tell you, immense excitement at the prospect of finding evidence of past lives. 'Atlantis!' They will cry, oh they are so

wrong! For this was a place of men which sank beneath the waves in a torrent of tidal wash. Its disappearance was immense, the loss life was great, but its ornaments remain as a testament to its existence. Pillars they stand, not so tall, nonetheless there. The Peoples of this temple were a tolerant race of beings; they existed many millions of years ago. *(Note: We read this as the 'Beings' existed many millions of years ago, but maybe not the pillars, they would have to be made of a substance not known to us to last that long – we have come to understand that races of beings have existed elsewhere, long before they colonised this planet.)*

The earth has many secrets held within the waters of your seas; you cannot even speculate as to their immense capacity of knowledge that far exceeds your own. Tribunes, tributaries are measures, hmm, how can we express their being to someone as you, but let us state this, that their beings were of courage and of light. They were comparatively smaller in stature, but larger in life, for they knew how to live. They once had a measure of dignity not found in your world today. They dressed as Romans as they walked their palisades and temples of love wearing their beards. The women dressed in their robes with a garland of flowers around their waist. They were peoples of the earth who respected her love and giving. They were not a forceful race, but a kind and pleasurable being.

They encountered many alien life forms, the likes of which you have not seen, perhaps you may never experience, because your world is dark now, it is not of the light as was then. Their temples shine as they were adorned with gold, silver, a common metal then, not revered as being that of wealth, but as being a staple of life and the Mother Earth as a precious metal. Oh, they were a marvellous, gentle, kind race of beings. We had the pleasure of meeting them once and their kindness overwhelmed us as they did not look upon us as being, "creatures of another world," but as fellow beings of light; as you must when the time comes and we once more make ourselves known to your world of men.

Oh, they will run and scream in terror as they will not understand our purpose, our mission of love. Hmm, but you must be there with a guiding hand to instruct them that there is no need to fear, but to honour and accept our being as that of being one of the saviour. Did you know he was one of us? Ha, well there are many secrets held within the walls of the Vatican that they will not tell you of, oh no, your ears must not listen to the words spoken within those scrolls and scriptures for they fear the loss of your passion. Silly men who do not tell the world the truth, but would it make a difference though? It's a hard nut to crack in your words, the dark surrounds and has a grip on the world like no other time, but allegiance to the light will bring mercies to those.

A war will be necessary, it is unfortunate things to say, but how else will the indignity stop? Man has become a desperate animal, lost his focus upon the possibilities of a world beyond your earth. Only the few remain who shine the light of love, but this will be hard to be extinguished by those of the dark for they cannot reach the souls of man, only his bodies.

Desperate times indeed Michael. Do not fear, for there must come a time for all in the world, a time of ending and of new beginnings for all who live upon the planet of life. Be not afeard, for there will be a continuance upon your planet, but not necessarily of the humankind.

The Mother Earth, she weeps at the deliberate indignities set upon her. They break up her surface and she weeps inside, for she is not just a stone, she is a living being, a creation of God, as you all are and are part of this being. It is up to you whether you take him in or whether you shut him out, whichever you choose will be your destiny. An option for change is always a possibility, but it is up to you.

Common wealth of knowledge will be gained as you muster together to bring in the face of our adversary, the right. You asked earlier, what a man like you could do to change the focus of the world, well it's not a lot, but a positive mind will achieve that purpose. Do not berate yourself as being a lowly being, for you have minds and strength of your own, be aware of it in you. As you all form your circles of light the strengths will grow within all of you if you bind this light together. The groups who joined in prayer and meditation are a start, you must encourage them and bring them to another purpose of being. They are your friends, your future.

9th October 2016

Once more we meet upon the plane of life, where souls of men aspire to spirit and the Lord our God in heaven. Many it seems are lost to the dark side of life, unsure of their path's or their being. They extinguish their minds of all thoughts regarding him upon high, only believing that life comes but once to each man. How their short-sighted mind must be to not imagine that there could be more to be brought to a focus within one's mind. Often we have thought about how it was that man had fallen by the wayside, for what was it that brought him to this end, did we not serve him well, did we not serve our Lord of the heavens above with a measure of love? No, we cannot blame ourselves, for it is men who live a life of choice. Hmm, what a wonderful world it would have been if men had chosen the light over the dark. Nevertheless the path has been set. He must walk this road now until he finds the pathway of light once more.

In the vastness of time and space, your time on earth is but a flicker of the eye, it is insignificant to the universe as a whole but through each soul that chooses the light, there comes a time when this light will come together, to be the saviour of the universe.

Atoms, they occur throughout God's universe, they are the building blocks of life and all structures in between. They formulate themselves into patterns which regulate your bodies and the obstacles around you. For all of creation is that of matter with these small particles of antimatter that flash, as if it never was through your atmosphere. The dark is a form of antimatter which must be eliminated before it destroys your habitat on earth.

Do not be reckless in your choices my people, come to a measure of love that will sustain you and yours for the future.

Arcturus

We have come far, from a far distant planet. A utopia many light years from your earth, 2.4 would be a measure to guide you. We are the bright star of the east that shines in the west in the morn. We come to bring you messages of hope and joy, we are the Arcturians, the ones who will bring purpose to your lives once more. *(Note: 2.4 km per second is the rotational velocity of Arcturus.)*

We must not assume a friendly welcome from your leaders, for they have an arrogance and a will to dominate no matter what. They are reckless in their thinking, in their scheming. Behind their closed walls they think they are not heard, but how can they shut off the ears of spirit. They have no regard for human life as it is merely an obstacle to an end. The gain is the riches of the earth come what may. What foolish men they are, what sort of thinking is that. They are shamed by their actions and reckless deeds throughout your world of living and they intend to spread their gloom beyond the stars, with missions of Apollo to follow in the very near future. Their probes are subject to our control, we will issue them fair warnings that if they should overstep the boundaries of the universe, we will mark their tide with equal measure.

We have established communication with two others of your kind, your meeting will not be necessary for your focus is all that is required.

Your Commonwealth of men have committees to reassure others of justice within your world. We have a dim view of those who would dispute the tribunals. But those who resist their judgement will receive a sentence of injustice.

Let your mind go my son. The avenues of space are far beyond your reach as men of the earth. It is infinitesimal to the mind of a mere mortal. We are the creatures that once roamed your earth in multitudes. Your life forms were of a primitive nature and we began an assignment to bring and couple our species, in the hope that one day you will also be able to master our ways of talking, not being. Like locusts you run wild across the planet of the earth, you infest each and every organism that exists on your planet in your multitudes. We are negligent and unwise not to have seen this before.

But we need your attention now, as you clamber for the safety of your shelters and realise what an unholy mess you have created for yourselves. Those of the light who bring a practice of love shall be the ones to shine the path, the way. Don't be ashamed for saying who you are, but speak your mind with wisdom and truth in the knowledge that we guide your steps through the universe of life. We are your friends Michael, we matter not to many, but our influence upon the few is great, but we need you to bring purpose to others to satisfy their needs of love. How can we assist your race when you cannot assist your own? You are a strange being of the humankind, our anatomies are not much different to your own, but our ways of thinking are light years apart. You are a master of your trade, bring a focus to others and let them see the truth in our words for we do not masquerade with habitual lies as your leaders influence your governments.

Businesses of your world, ah, they know nothing. They seek financial gain within your men of money, but what use is it? Surely the Commonwealth of men and the love in gratitude to others for bringing peace to those countries who are ripped out at the heart, surely that is worth more than your cash flow?

Navigate your minds and hear these words as we issue them with a caution of love.

Be satisfied with the things you are given, appreciate the many around you that issue you with love, temperance and tolerance. You are as standing stones, you need support from your families and brethren. Unite together as a front of light against the enemies of your earth. Those who would dominate your lives.

We are beings who have once before walked your earth.

Temples in Tunisia

Precious stones were once a part of our society and they held not monetary value, but a value of energy in a practice of love. We had our temples on the mountains of Tunisia that are now beneath the sea. We were a population of many. We rose early in the morning to give blessings to our maker. He came to us in a manner of love and enlightenment. Truly your nature cannot match this at this time.

Your 'vastly superior minds' are extensively communicating with us and you issue us with notice of a warning to stand down our parties of surveillance. Who are THEY to issue us with such dominance? How can they possibly know of our abilities? Your focus is needed as a tool, as an instrument, by which they will know our response to their message of 'no goes'. We are a race of beings who walked on your earth long before you, we have knowledge of much and we bend to no man. We will not dominate your planet, but we will study and if your men of war should be foolish enough to encroach upon our freedom of will, so their shame will be shown to the world. Never doubt our words.

10th October 2016

Tremendous amounts of courage will be required as we fling out the gates, the doors of the light. We embark upon a mission of love upon your earth, to bring you focus on your ways of hate. We mean no harm, just a little tolerance and understanding will be sufficient. We have many ways of teaching those a focus as we adjust the sails of their minds.

We bring you greetings and peace of thought as we enter your atmosphere many times, in many seasons of your earth. We are creatures from another world that will bring mysteries of other life to your beings. Be not afraid as our ships reach a point in space and time. Your men of war are aware of our being and they issue us ultimatums through their radio waves in the hope that we understand their intolerance to our resolves and missions. We will grant you peace and freedom from corruption. It will be hard fought to win over those minds of the dark. We have not tolerated your actions in the past to dispute our being. Those who have the power of the world know of our intolerance towards them, but we must, in some small way bridge that gap of ignorance. How can we inspire those of injustice to change their views and allow us an audience? We do not wish to dominate your lives, but merely to inspire you to a better way of living. Mm, we are the men of Mars! Or so leaders would have you believe. Martian theories will be thrown out the door. We have inhabited many worlds beyond your solar system and they are so extreme they do not compare with yours. You must open your hearts and minds and desires to allow us an audience, be not afraid, we have come in peace.

Trust in us for we are the light, the life force that brings balance to your earth. Archimedes, he once spoke of us, for he had wisdom. Joyous times ahead as we greet those who would give us an audience in their minds, as you see a pyramid of light, know that this reflects our true being, our mantles of love can be seen to this day in the deserts that were once green. Quite frankly you would be amazed how much we knew.

Cover-up is apparently a common means to hide the truth of our existence. Creatures of the earth called man, are insignificant to our ways and our coming. Be prepared for an onslaught of such things your eyes have never seen. We will speak to those who have focus, allow us in. We will grant you peace and a life of happiness and the world will understand. We have hearts of gold that will assist your men of science in leaps and bounds. Have you not wondered why it is that your existence is but a short one? You are but children never asking of existence. We spoke of butterflies and change but you have to create a pathway of love and light to enable a focus. We are the Arcturians, we speak through this flesh being, his mind attempts to open up. He sees the light of love; the fragrance of roses will envelop his efforts.

$2 \times 2 + 4 = 6$, in an equation of mass far beyond your understanding, the algorithms needed to assess this sum are as follows: $2 - 4 = 6$ tricky you think, but not if you understand that the four equals proportions that are equal to whole. An equation of binary code will also be a part which follows a sequence of numbers, 11, 01, 10, 10, 01 to a mathematical equation of figures. Combine these numbers to form the answers are needed. Your minds will need focus.

We know of many things that will assist your world. Be not ashamed of who you are for you bring these messages with faith and trust.

She has come as a member of the light; he frequently asks about the disappearance of the one who he will not name. His fear of ridicule against him will not become a burden on him. She joins us as an angel of light, her name you know. She wishes to inform her mother she bears no resentment for the choices made that evening. She slept and was awoken by fearsome man she never knew, she slept as she was carried to a torturous place where women were despised as mere creatures. She is no longer with you, but a light of heaven. Her brother, he smiles upon her as she appears to him in the night, in his eyes. He tells his mum of this; how can she understand what a child sees and feels. Her burden is felt. Let them know that I am now in a place of light and love. *(Note: After much thought, Kevin has decided to name who it is that he often wonders about, he has never wanted to name her in the past for fear of upsetting her family, his sympathies have always been with the parents of Madeleine McCann.)*

Angels of light and mercy shine upon all those who suffer indignities in your world of man. The children that are lost are never truly lost, but reborn into the light of heaven. Trouble your hearts not that the disappearance of many of your species as they are comforted in the arms of the angels of the Lord, who blesses them and showers them with love and light. The

Archangel Michael wishes you to know he gives them protection, an assurance of comfort and love.

Too many times before we have asked you to bring purpose to your lives in the light and love of the Lord. We will never forsake you, but continue to bring you a practice of love and tolerance.

Desperate times ahead will be felt by many, as the triumphant march through the streets of the cities. They mark an occasion of the downfall of man, for he is of intolerance. A landslide of victory will assume his authority. He will lead multitudes into a desperate battle for position, he will bring about change in a way he cannot imagine, it will be a downfall of all those who issue intolerance against those of the world. A measure of peace will be brought in the end game. As collateral gains will be of no significance. He envies those, can you believe a man of intolerance envies those who have faith and trust in simple lives? He shows his arrogance as a face, inside he knows his misgivings. He ignores his thoughts of judgement, for he is a man of power, why should he care about the thoughts of the multitudes who have nothing, who show no respect to his authority. He will bring about change in a fashion so extreme, the world will look on horrified as he triumphs, marching through the streets, banners waving high, as if he was a man of some importance. His extreme measures will be dealt a blow in his term of office.

You see many who celebrate his being, they are so blind. What an almighty mess. Those corrupt leaders who abide by the rules of the negative in their institutionalised minds.

Note Regarding the Message of 10th October 2016

A possible theory to try and understand following paragraph given to us by our ET friends containing mathematical equations:

"2 × 2 + 4 = 6, in an equation of mass far beyond your understanding, the algorithms needed to assess this sum are as

follows: 2 – 4 = 6, tricky you think, but not if you understand that the four equals proportions that are equal to whole. An equation of binary code will also be a part which follows a sequence of numbers, 11 01 10 10 01 to a mathematical equation of figures. Combine these numbers to form the answers are needed. Your minds will need focus."

and

Regarding the Message of 24th October 2016

A fraction of an inch is given by many of your world as a measurer of time. We will also issue a measure of time in which we'll articulate our minds to those of wisdom listening for the figures, the sums of arithmetic. Your mind will witness many things of a wondrous nature as you relinquish it, give us your thoughts. 4 was a measure given as part of a whole, you have wondered what was the whole that this number was a part of, could it be a fraction or perhaps a percentage of 10 × 10.

NOTES:

The binary numbers translate into a sequence **3, 1, 2, 2, 1.**

Seemingly meaningless until Kevin persisted and stumbled upon some data supplied by NASA

Could the above paragraph and mathematics possibly relate to this, is this what our ET friends are trying to draw our attention to. NOTE THE MASS TO ORBIT FIGURE of **31, 221.**

The following information was found online from a book: 'Assembling and Supplying the ISS: The Space Shuttle Fulfils Its Mission' by David J Shayler

NASA's Tier-2: An Alternative Assembly Plan.

This is the first section of the International Space Station delivered into space for its construction. ('Part of the Whole' as our ET friends have said.) Its mass to orbit weight is equal to 31221 lbs

(The alternative assembly plan if the Russians did not partake in the building of the International Space Station)

Page 7, Table 1.1

FOR THE FIRST SPACE SHUTTLE DELIVERY FLIGHT
Date: 2/1998
Flight Name: 1A
Delivered Elements: Bus-1, Spacer
Altitude (Nautical Miles): 210
Mass to Orbit lb): 31,221
Mission duration: 7 days
STS Crew: 5

16th October 2016

Blessings be on those who have purpose in their lives to bring the messages of the Lord to those of Earth. We are the Arcturians, the members of the light who watch over your planet with peaceful intentions.

Our ships circulate in your night sky observing the many activities by those of the dark. For they are like owls who prey upon the souls of the night to bring them to an end of injustice. We call them the vultures of life, as they torture the souls of men to do things of wickedness.

We have remarked once before upon the outstanding work of those of the care and nursing industries, for they are the backbone of the country and of humanity. Their willingness to care and keep others in comfort as they diminish is a notable and worthy cause, and should be given praise in thought and prayer. For they are a wonderful group of people who have shone before within the light and have entered your earth to bring a share of love and caring. For many the seasons are short, the love and devotion of those who do all they can to serve your life is a wondrous thing.

There are those who are despicable in their practices and take advantage of those who need mercy. For their injustices against those of the disabled or handicapped will come back upon them tenfold. Only those of a true heart will have the opportunity to reach out to heaven's gate as it opens for them on their passing from this life.

We bring news of memorable things to happen within the careers of men of purpose, for they have witnessed many things of hate in your world. They are concerned for those many innocents who shelter in that place of iniquity upon your earth, where children suffer the plague of man's intolerance and bear the brunt of their ignorance. Nations fear war if sanctions are set against them. Who is the true enemy of man? Is it those who wear the black, or is it those who declare themselves as your leaders who say they punish these men?

There is only one punishment for such souls, for man is not judge and jury of his own peoples but witness to what they bring on others. We know that there are many who would misjudge others, but they must relinquish their authority and help those in need with a purpose in mind of love and tolerance.

Communicate your mind as never before, for we have a message to bring to the people of Earth.

We find it necessary to break our cover at this time as the injustices grow. You need our help to witness those many events and to bring about a peace upon your planet. Come with us on a journey and never forget your love of life, for your fellow creatures.

In the wilderness he walked, for 40 days, for 40 nights, to clear his thoughts of man. To bring his soul to a purpose of love for his father in heaven. He walked for many leagues in sombre thought. His mission was miraculous for the people of earth as they saw his many wonders and taught many things of Bodea *(Note: We were not sure about the meaning of this word or its spelling, but it appears to mean 'Messenger of God'.)* and the nature of the Lord. Help us to ensure that his teachings will be obeyed by those, and never betrayed by the thoughts of anger, greed and avarice. His many wonders to perform will relate to a time in the very near future when the coming of the Lord will once more reassure man. Bring a peace to his mind that the wonders of heaven are open to all who would just listen and obey the word of the Lord.

Tonight we have many thoughts to impart through you. Your leadership of those who follow the words impress many, but you are merely the vessel Michael. Let them hear our words of splendour and truth and issue them with a practice of love from the hearts and minds of the spirit world. Never judge us for our actions, for in the grand scheme of things, the Almighty's plan will emerge with an outcome of gratitude and peace.

Malala Yousafzai

Be upstanding when she marches through the valleys of the east, for she will bring purpose to those who have a need of her comfort. She was once a child of the Lord, she has become a woman with a mission in life to bring purpose to the many. Do not escape her words as she sings out the praises of the glory of God. She is a woman with many skills to bring purpose to the many issues of the men in black and those who would persecute the women of your planet. Malala, know her splendour in time when it is needed most in the uprising of peace and love. She is a teacher for many and a formidable force for which groups, leaders of Isis and those of intolerance will be astounded at her strength, for they have bought purpose in her life by their misguided actions. Five will now come. She has hope for the future and for the better hood of women of the Muslim faith. She hands out no apologies for her actions for she has faith in the Lord our God.

Ambition to her mind can only be achieved by your loving actions in the coming together of those who bring love and peace to the world. How many groups and factions who watch over her as she stems the tide of intolerance and ignorance. She is an unsung hero who will shine as she displays her intolerance against the ignorance of those who despise their own kind in their employ.

Combat your fears my son, allow our words to raise a blinding light in your world, for your words reach her mind as others do in the light.

Madeleine

Concern is not necessary for the one who was lost, she is at rest. We spoke of her to you in the fervent hope that the connection will reach out to her loved ones. Concerns are raised as the many search for her, and their fears. For her love will resume in a search in the Mediterranean within the next few weeks. Six would be a measure.

Ben Needham was a soul who was lost all too soon, his mind is that of a child who sits in wonder that the stars are back. He was lost on that day so long ago, but your loss was our gain as he surrendered his heart to the love of the Lord. Focus your minds not on his disappearance but of his resurrection to the light and the love of the angels that surround all those innocents who are lost to us. Their purpose continues and their love grows as they establish a basis of love within the kingdom of heaven. Needham would be a man, a young man, but he remembers in those early days of his childhood. The task force who search for him will need great assistance by those of the light to locate his remains. They use their equipment, sweeping the area with magnitude, magnetism and forensic science. All they need is a will to listen to those who would tell the location where he may be found. Underestimated are those who work with a practice of love of our Lord our father in heaven. For the need of the many is required by those of sound judgement and purpose.

Never allow your mind to wander from your soul's path as you seek your home upon the earth. With a measure of love you must institute a practice of kindness and well-being to others.

Ben Needham would like to say to his mum, "I only wished I could have cuddled her and the bear she brought for me, in remembrance." His loss was great to her as she remembers with fondness as she tucked him into bed, Teddy beside him, whispering in his ear a song of love. She brought great comfort to her son on his day of passing for her need was great of him and he understood the meaning of love.

The Queen

Graphic are the instruments of your paths, with their boldness and frankness of those who would declare them of the past. Her Majesty would be fortunate indeed to have had a life of obscurity instead of one of a practice of love and purpose. Members of your country ignore her as a leader, but she has the hearts of many and the minds and souls of those who love her. She is a member of the Royal household who grants the wishes to many of intolerance.

How can we say this with the gentleness it needs? As she approaches her final days of service upon the throne of England, she will not relinquish her duties at this time. Her husband remains at her side for his remaining time, for he has been devoted to her, but he is outspoken in his manner, this is well known of him, but it is his strength of character that has given her fortitude throughout years of her labour. Many scoff at the royalty of your country, have you not seen the injustices which rule, should you choose a president? Those families of power who dominate many in the states with an attitude of grievous ignorance. Their families are dominant in their actions as they collaborate behind the scenes to bring purpose to their lives, the Kennedys, the Bushes and the Obama's, all those men of power and greed have brought this mighty nation to a crumbling point, where those of the people will not stand with their cherished leaders. For they have much intolerance, as they have intolerance against them. She will not rule that nation, but will insist on a position of authority that will bring her purpose.

20th October 2016

Ah, but the boundaries of light are so far from your world of man. Listen clearly to my voice and acknowledge that I am Madam of the Light, who has come this distance to speak my

mind of the Lord and his willingness to communicate with that of man.

Hearken ye to the angels that sing and bring joy to those who sit in their churches, reading their books of their faith and issuing a statement of love to our father, our Lord in heaven. We welcome their minds prayers as they speak their words of wisdom. They are devoted in their practice, issuing statements of love that can be heard through the cosmos. Never fear that your words are not heard my brothers, for all who speak to him, Jehovah on high, will be heard as a premium message.

Practice not your fears of your overlords of the earth, for they bring reckless behaviour to the masses, not allowing their minds to negotiate the peaceful practice of many within your world of man. Elbow to elbow, shoulder to shoulder, they strive to beat the world and bring about unnecessary pain to those innocent victims who suffer in the outback's of the east.

We are here to do your bidding if you were just to ask. Ask of us not to bring a practice of hate to others, for we are the Bishops of Light, we bring peace and love to the many of ill will.

Bring your minds to a focus so that we may issue words of encouragement to your fathers of the world. We have come, travelled so far beyond your universe. We represent the many nations that surround your planet Earth. As we mean you no harm, we would like you to know that our thoughts are with those of your earth men who bear witness to suffering and unnecessary pain.

How bizarre it is that those who speak of peace, are that of war! What are their chances of becoming president? Ha, hmm, well, we cannot endeavour to speculate, but just to say this, that there is no contest between the two for they are both of a den of iniquity. A spark will ignite a storm between them that will access the others personal credentials. Make note this day my boy, as being that of a nation's intolerance towards the many peoples of the world. Stupidity and idiocy reigns in your countries of the world. What a stupendous opportunity has been missed by so many, by the fraction who wish discontent.

It is time to band together as one, in a frequency of love. You sit in your tepees in your meditation, please begin with the words of 'Ra'. For he needs your attention as peoples of the deserts of Earth, hmm. (*Note: Ra – The Sun God of Ancient Egypt.*)

The Galactic Federation

We are here, not of beasts of man but of those who will bring you peace upon your earth. We have never asked favours of those who sit in power, but only to listen to our words as we represent many of the 'Federation' beyond your world. We have come to issue, to offer blessings to those who would listen.

Financial Crash

Canary Wharf is a place of outstanding bureaucracy, it brings counterfeits of cash flow belonging to those dark forces who rule your world with hate and fear. Are men so blind or so ignorant that they cannot see that just to them, this flow of cash would be enough to bring about an end to the many sufferings of the world. We forecast a fall, a crash in profits and so it will be, as their computers fail and a mysterious virus enters obscurely into the networks that control your world of money. We are the Arcturians, who find it necessary to bring you to your knees economically so as to open your eyes to the greed and avarice that has overwhelmed you. Do you really think that money will make a difference? Can't you imagine how it would be if you lived together in peace and harmony without the need of greed or established wealth? This will not easily be accomplished, but it will bring turmoil to those accountants of the net.

Your need for us is great at this time, we hearken to the words of many to come, to bring us salvation.

We would like as a matter of concern, to tell those that their wishes of an appearance by us will be awarded to them on the coastal regions of the states, as we issue them with our demands for their cessation of a hostilities against their indigenous peoples.

Tonight we have spoken of many things, of war and fortune, have gratitude that your country is not affected at this time. But be warned, and if these needs are not fractured and stopped, then war is inevitable.

A warning that brings fear to your heart my son, but this is not necessary, for as always, there are paths to take to avoid.

What can we say about the men that hold and harbour the staff of life? They look on in despair as their nations run riot, ousting them from the seats of the house, not giving them quarter, nor relinquishing their need.

Splish splash, the sound of waters as it drops from high. As the water hits the pools, so the ripples expand, cast out. He will drip into that pool things that cannot be conceived at this time in man's advancement. We despair of the many suffering, give them peace in your heart and issue them with love, the practice of prayer.

23rd October 2016

Warning of Storms to Come

Fair weather warning is given to those who sail the seas of the north Atlantic this evening, but don't be fooled by those meteorological practices of man, for how do they know what the weather will blow in the next half an hour. It is so unpredictable. The systems that traverse your universe of man, sure many will forecast fair weather and the storm to come. Maybe they should reconsider their astrological concepts and warnings, for many of intolerance will gather to breach the storm that will blow with a fair wind before it. Tropical storms will merge to bring a tempest. A term was once used to describe such a pattern of meteorological events, but this will surpass that perfect storm, for your planet grows weaker each day, succumbing to those systems that will clash in the near future, bringing chaos and devastation once more to the islands that have suffered so much. Their peoples tire of this onslaught, and so they should, as it seems unfair that the small nations bear the brunt of the storms created by those neighbouring nations. They have no care for the repercussions as they display their arrogance in adopting a weather pattern suitable for their climate, hmm, man should never tamper with that of nature, for a backlash will be felt.

Palestine Syria And Israel

Stupendous amounts of mercy will be required as those of the east once more suffer horrendous issues. People of Palestine show no mercy to those who offend them, for they have been through so much that they tolerate no more. This will end with much grief in those nations. It was once Syria. Israel is a time bomb that is ticking, means for its defence, to be strong and not courteous.

Blessed be to those men who see the wicked ways of these propagators of the storm, they cannot control this pattern.

Streams of words you whisper from the thoughts of those of many in spirit. Troubled you are by the wisdom given, but to be frank, there is no need for worry, for what is life but a passing time, a blink of the eye, a mere speck in nature. You will learn much as you pass through this portal of life, bringing others comfort, others joy. Some will experience much sadness in their lifespan, but be aware this is how it is to be. We have purpose for you Michael, to stand up for the rights of others even in the face of adversity. Your light will shine as a speck, as a sunbeam and it will grow in the minds of many as they read the words on the pages you write. It is no disgrace to proclaim oneself a man with a mission, keep your mind focused and respectful of those who would think ill of you, for they will eventually see the pattern of life that you do, through the eyes of spirit, through the eyes of man.

God bless all those who suffer panic in the cities as the 'Dreadnought from Space' arrives in the morn. We will issue notice of our intentions of peace upon your nations of Earth, for we mean you no harm nor disrespect. We have a manner of that of a parent, we'll bring you joy and happiness. We feel, we have a willingness to adapt to many conditions of life upon your planet. We are seen by many as those 'wicked aliens' and they will issue us a proclamation of war if we should establish ourselves. Why would they fight those of the light, whose only intention is to bring peace among your men? We are the Arcturians, those of a nature of the light. We too were once intolerant of each other, but as our planet succumbed, so we had to live a life of a joint mind. It was not easy to become a singularity of minds, but we dedicated ourselves to bring in a practice of love, for as you worship your God, so we bear witness to him also. We are grateful for your beginnings, the nature by which you work. Your mind tumbles with thoughts of improbabilities, have a practice of love to negotiate the problems that torment your mind.

A fraction of an inch is given by many of your world as a measurer of time. We will also issue a measure of time in which we'll articulate our minds to those of wisdom listening for the figures, the sums of arithmetic. Your mind will witness many things of a wondrous nature as you relinquish it, give us your thoughts. **Four was a measure given as part of a whole, you have wondered what was the whole that this number was a part of, could it be a fraction or perhaps a percentage of 10 × 10.** (Note: This was the aid given to us to help with the calculations in the message of 10th October 2016.)

Financial Crash

Your currency and money markets will see a fall, a tip as they panic to grasp their pennies. Their responses will be heard upon the news of your vision as they task your masters for answers. Why has this crash occurred, why have you lost control of the markets? Many will fall disgracefully as they abandon, abolish their status. Corn of intolerance.

She is the key, the answer to many things of your world. In her light you will shine as a beacon of light. Bring forth your thoughts of love and cherish those around you. For as they are lost, so your mind will weaken with the pain, as many do. But you know of the light that shines and this should bring you joy in your thoughts.

Telepathy

Telepathy some may say, so they call it. What do they know of the power of the mind, hmm, have they ever practised or witnessed a passion of the man who would accept these thoughts from strangers of other parallels within the universe? No, they scoff at the words spoken, never understanding the true meaning or nature of the messages sent to you upon the earth. We will answer your questions of your minds. You will hearken to the answers not being aware that we have spoken through their minds. Accept us as your friends, benevolent beings that would watch over your lives. The persecution will come in the near future to torment your souls, strength of mind is paramount, be thoughtful of others and bring them a peace with an ocean of love. Have a practice of caring for those who are weaker than yourselves, for they are reliant upon your compassion and love. Give them not harmful words, shameful actions, but look upon them as those souls who have need of peace and tranquillity. How can we express our gratitude for your thoughts?

Other Worldly Beings

We are the many that watch your earth with compassion and feel abandoned by your men as they follow the dark unnecessarily. We bring you greetings, a measure of love. Those aliens who wish nothing more than to help your purpose, our beings, creatures of the Lord. Do you think you are all that there is within the vastness of the universe? You would be astounded as to the length and breadth by which it is a measure. Trillions upon trillions of lives are formed within their atmospheres, not necessarily as yours. You are one way minded, you think because you breathe the oxygen of your earth that all should breathe the same, oh how wrong are you!

God granted life to many forms of creatures that evolved on these planets, take a long hard look at yourselves and ask yourselves, what was the trigger, what was it that brought your being? Humph?

1st November 2016

Spirit Introduces the Arcturians

Well, we have served you well, we have brought you purpose in your life and a need to aspire to the greater things beyond your world. The Arcturians, they have come once before to bring you messages of tolerance and intolerance towards man's practices to their being. They wish to say that they are forever grateful that the few that listen accept them as members of a race of beings who exist beyond your world. Whether you believe or not, nevertheless they are there to accomplish their own passages within time spent. They are merciless in their torment of those of the dark. They cannot tolerate hate, for they bring wisdom of other creations within the heavens of the Lord. They do not mean you harm despite the words spoken, for those of intolerance should expect nonetheless, the same in return.

The Arcturians

Bring peace to your world and a manner respective of all creatures of the Lord, the Father of all, for he is a mighty spirit who sits in the heavens above. He cannot be seen, but only in your heart and souls if you let him in. He is there for all, regardless of your sins and crimes. He is the being of light that extinguishes the dark in the cornfields of mercies. We have expressed our wish to help those to help themselves to a better understanding and purpose in life.

We accept that we would be strange to those whose eyes would behold us. Your fears are stoked by those insignificant pictures that portray us as being a race of intolerant beings. This is far from the truth, we have need of many of you in your world of life to bring hope to those in disarray at this time. We will commence our purpose shortly to begin a journey of light and love. It will be hard and tough going in your words, but there will be a purpose in that beginning.

I am a creature, a being not of your earth, but of your thoughts and I bring you mercies and blessings in the hope that mankind would one day look upon us as teachers of life, or those who bring happiness. There are those torturous minds who would neglect us, tell you they are creatures of the dark. Who would you believe, those who would corrupt and degrade your world bringing injustices to all those of a gentle nature, or would you believe those of our being and our abilities to bring peace upon your world and to demonstrate our love through practices, of teachings, of many things that are, or would be familiar to your ancestors?

The Pyramids

Hmm. We sat and prayed with the man of the earth many times in his temples of stone, we assisted the many constructions upon your planet, insignificant to you now, but they are places of an invaluable source of energy.

Neglect us not for we were once the rulers of many nations upon your planet, they hearken to us, knowing that there would be no fear in their lives. True to say there were many injustices and practices done in our name. We cannot tolerate these things; they were primitive and did not understand the many aspects that we brought to them. Their technology was limited and we enlightened them, for we found that to enlighten the ignorant is sometimes more dangerous and it is better to leave them at their stage of development.

Hmm, they did destroy themselves with wondrous machines that you could not possibly imagine.

You respected our works in our mausoleums and our temples you call pyramids and constructions of the Indian

nations. Those blind men of science, cannot conceive their construction. Within the walls of many of these places are hidden secrets, not necessarily of the physical, but in a state of energy, unknown and unseen by your present-day scholars.

Technologies The NPA

Hmm, they search with these machines, destroying the particles in the hope of gaining a spark of knowledge. It has taken us many millennia of your years to gather our knowledge, it will take you many more to discover our creations and secrets. Even we cannot tell you when the exact beginnings arose, but we know many things that will assist in your lives today. Our machines are not of torture but are instruments to assist. Your technological age is but a beginning. You have wondered many times what those practices and codes mean, let us inform you, that if you were able to build a machine of connection or communication, we can assist in many ways if you have a will and a heart to listen. The figures are what you call 'coded'. We cannot express to you how deeply concerned we are of the men of matter as they battle their words and delusions to those of the New World. They know of us, have spoken to us, but they are themselves controlled by others who bring a practice of absolute secrecy. NPA, hmm, secretive society of which you have no knowledge, they gravely mislead many men from the truth hidden within the walls of their places, those dens of iniquity. We are conscious that you are unaware of the many practices that are set to deceive you. Your minds are filled with unnecessary thoughts, you must be trained in ways to focus, to carry the message that we inspire to your nations.

Their frequencies are of a megahertz that you may or may not understand, 207 Hz is a frequency that could be used. Your box of vision has many channels filled with many subjects, there are those on which we can broadcast our thoughts to your minds, white noise you call it, space and time we call it, tuning to those atmospheric conditions.

Radiography was given to men of science, you call them X-rays, they are a form of matter that can transcend all other forms of matter allowing a picture to be given deep within your bodies. A breakthrough will come shortly in those scanning devices that are used in your places of healing. Did you know you to have this ability to see through the many tissues and the matter of the body? All you need is focus and a mind to see and a belief in what you do. There are characters in your world who say they can perform many things of surgery with thought, do not discount these people, for they have found a secret but do not understand its intended purpose. Your bodies seem feeble and unable to regenerate, but there are many parts of your body that do constantly regenerate, your mind is but one of them, your soul is another.

A Mention of Valerie and Michael About Healing

You must focus on your being to bring yourself of a healing nature. Love has a calming effect and will heal those minds of torture. It is a powerful weapon and is disrespected, for it can breakthrough those barriers of ignorance and intolerance as no other tool in the arsenal of medication can. Some men are just beginning to realise that your psyche has many different levels of healing abilities. Hmm, and there are those, as Valerie, who knows and believes, that healing ability is held within us all, she understands that it is not necessary to open the wounds of the body to heal those hearts, souls and minds of those who are troubled within their lives. You too have an ability as has been told before, you heal many things in your way Michael, but you misunderstand your purpose, you think you are here to receive our thoughts within your mind, but your purpose is to relay them in ways possible. You must relinquish your fears and thoughts of, "Am I worthy?" Do you think we'd waste our energies and thoughts on a man who could not deliver a purpose? You heal the minds and bring sanctuary to those who look for peace within their lives, in their thoughts of their own existence. It is through our thoughts that this peace is brought to the many of your world. Be blessed at your charms and allow the purpose to flow as a river of love. As a tide will wash over the shore pulling back the debris and leaving the clean pebbles upon the beach to see the light of day.

We have known many people; the disposition of anger and their purpose has been changed by a few simple words spoken to them in the most sincere way. You know of these secrets, your very own soul has been many times to the world of man, seeking displeasure. You have a different aspect now, your life is livened by the light of purpose and by the teachings of us in spirit, for we gave you purpose which you now begin to understand, that your messages are of immense proportions. You think they will not go far, have faith, trust in us, as we draw their attention to the readings. Your book so far has been on trust, your words spoken are of our words and this is as it should be, for you fear that if you do not comment, people misunderstand. But you are wrong, we have spoken to you before to leave them as they are, as they will call out and resound the vibrations in ways that you cannot understand, and those that read them will not understand why it is that they are attracted to the words. They'll see much in similarities of their existence within them and they too will aspire to read them. To focus upon those things that may be. It will sow a seed to the many and bring them a focus of consideration. Be blessed in the knowledge that your purpose is one of many within your world of man. As you display your abilities, so others will aspire to do the same. Do not deny them their thoughts, for you are all of one soul and one spirit but displaying different aspects of existence all at the same time. Far-fetched you may think, how can one soul be in several places at once? This is a reality, have you not heard the term 'soul-mates' when one recognises the other? Inexplicable to their thoughts, but they just know that innerness. Have peace in your knowledge, bring purpose to those who have displeasure at seeing such things.

The Bigger Picture

Changes will occur to those who focus their minds on the soils of the earth. They investigate many possibilities of riches that lay beneath the ground beneath your feet. Are they never satisfied at what has been given? They continue to rape the earth in a manner disrespectful to the Lord and the earth, the Mother Earth herself. The Indian nations knew of this, of the manitos *(spirit)* that existed within all creation. The white man abuses this, he does not understand that the smallest of creatures is an extension of God and should be respected with the love and light of the angels of the Lord. Even the earth and the air that you breathe are of life, they live in a molecular system so small, but their atoms live. You have discovered an atom, your world knows of this, but what makes an atom an atom? You see the electrons that give off sparks of life, but what gives that spark and where will it end? Ah, it would consume your minds as you look deeper and deeper into the meaning of life, for it will never be found, because it is never-ending. It is a journey of discovery. There are many secrets held within your world of life that are unfound, undiscovered, and like the drip of a tap, a piece of the puzzle at a time will fall. Sometimes it is recognised, sometimes it will evaporate as if it never was, but your physical lives, your beings are insignificant to the creation. Do you think you are all that there is, or would you know that you are part of something else? A bigger expanse of life, my goodness not me, after all creatures exist within your body, they assist in your cells and your structure and your life. Do you think it's not possible that you too exist to serve another life? And so it goes on, far beyond your comprehension are these things, and so they are to all of us, but we must realise that we are all part of a whole and insignificant to many things, but those small parts can multiply. You may think that the destruction of your earth would be the end. It has an effect upon the universe and the many layers of existence that lay within the parameters of your earth, for if one has changed then truly it will affect others in a way beyond your comprehension. This is why there is a vested interest in preserving your being, as you would treat a cancer in the body of a man or woman, so spirit treats you as a cancer and attempt to heal you of your destructive nature and bring you back into an orderly fashion so that you may serve the body that you exist within.

Fantasy some will think, but is it really? Do you not open your eyes to see that many exist within others and they play a part in a role in their lives? A cancer is a creature within your being, it lives, it grows and expands. You too could be a cancer if you condemn your world to poisons and negatives. Like a growth that will infect others and as you treat your cancers so you will be treated yourself, until the inevitable occurs and you must be eliminated from that body to ensure the existence of all others around you. Ooh yeah, deep, deep thoughts. Scary to some perhaps, but nonetheless existence relies upon the structure of others.

Your man-made objects may obscure our vision for a time, but not our focus.

17th November 2016

Ring out the changes, toll the bells, let the sounds and vibrations reverberate throughout the lives of men. We are the Arcturians, those beings who have bought a practice of love to your life. Let it be known that our will, will be done as we enter your atmosphere.

Our structures of life are different to that of man, thought is our choice of language. Our physical beings can be seen should we choose. Some speak of devils! Ha! Well, we are strange to your eyes I am sure! Your classrooms of life speak of us as if we never were, they do not hold the concept that life exists elsewhere within the solar systems and universe's of God's creation. Oh yes, we have a creator in common to all of us, all that live. We do not denounce his being, but we embrace his love.

About Abductions and Human Experiments on ET's

We are the warriors of life; we come as scientists to study and assist the beings of life as they go about their existence. We observe, taking notes as you would, trying to understand the complexities of mankind. It is difficult. Abductees you call them, those that we borrowed to study. Not so strange when you consider what man does to his animal life upon his planet, do you not do the same? Do you not study them in your labs of life inflicting pain upon them to see the response and effect? We do not do this out of cruelty, for we too suffer pain, we too have been subjects of your very own beings, hidden miles away. Probes they inserted, inflicting pain upon the creatures before them, and they gasped in wonder at their frailty as they pass *(died)* before them. Dishonoured, disrespected as a lab rat, but we hold no grudge.

The Spark of Life

We would like to bring purpose to your men of science. In their volumes of books they study the physics and science of your world and the atmosphere that surrounds you, never truly understanding that one day a spark of light will become obvious to them and they will wonder why they had not seen it before. That spectrum of light that rains upon your plane withholds many secrets, many benefits to your beings of life. We come as caretakers, as parents.

To track our existence you would look in the annals of time to those places far beyond your universe. Your men have, and will, discover an alien species as they call it, as they explore distant places. Of course they will not allow you to know these things, but we tell you now, that other life forms exist and surround your planet and see it as a beacon of interest, as your science men will look upon a subject in a Petrie dish and probe as to its meaning, hmm. We do not wish to cause despair at our words of frustration, for we have an interest in your planetary system, your scope of life is narrow and complex in meaning.

Igniting Our Atmosphere

You look to the skies and you understand that you are a small part of a larger being. Take care not to overstep the boundaries of science and love, for a spark is all it will take to ignite the gases of your atmosphere. Truly we say unto you, Nitrous Oxide is a gas with an explosive value, it seeps into your atmosphere unnoticed by many, but it will contaminate and inflame a burning atmosphere. You cannot prevent all, as nature itself produces the natural gases, but you yourself are a doom on mother nature by your hideous machines. You pump the air that you live on with much noxious gases, oh, what stupidity, irresponsibility. We cannot comprehend your thinking, but know this, you will pay the price for your ill concern to your mother *(Earth)*. Don't betray our thoughts of love and replace it with fear of beings of other places, we can cleanse your atmosphere, but we cannot cleanse your minds, for this is your task. Assist us so that we may assist you.

Many will disbelieve the words as you write them in your book. Many will say, "What a fool," to believe in such things that cannot be seen, truly they are blind and unwise to think that their existence is all that there is in time and space. What a primitive race of beings you are, your arrogance is appalling.

There are those with focus who see as and acknowledge us. Many worthy men of status in your world know this, but your men of greed and those who will not relinquish their power will hold a blindfold over your head for as long as they can. It is not for us to relieve you of this, you must see for yourselves. When you look to the skies in the heavens, think about how minute you are and that there are endless possibilities of life that exist beyond your atmosphere of poison.

Will you come to a time of peace and love? We fear it will take much for you to abort your ways of cruelty in your present existence.

We will keep our distance, but in your thoughts, in your minds, we will place those precious thoughts that enable man a little wisdom. We will not solve your problems, but we can assist. Have a care not to extinguish your open mind to one of solitude and darkness.

Arcturian Appearance

We are as ants in our appearance, as best described as insects! Have you ever looked at your ants and the societies and networks that they build, how they assist each other in their busy lives? You, as a channel have an image of our being, *(channels note I did see an image in my mind's eye of both a triangular shaped head and a cats head!)* You see a cat, a face of triangulation, hmm, you are not afraid, be not afraid.

Our existence was of denial to your men. Evidence accumulates of the many populations that once existed upon your earth. You see your lives as the human being, your shapes and forms are adequate for your existence upon your planet. It is not unreasonable to assume that other planets hold different pressures and atmospheres, therefore life has evolved to exist upon them. There is nothing new in this to your men of science and those who study the ancient beings of your world.

Arcturians Once Lived in Mexico

Your precious memories are few of our race, but your weapons of war are not much different as you evolve, your primitive minds. We are not accustomed to ill will towards us, we do not respect those who would appear to us with intentions in a manner of war. What is it that you fear? Is it knowledge and wisdom or a race of beings that don't appeal to your eyes? I think that many upon your planet would be welcoming to see strangers visit, but fear would be in their hearts, so we stand back. We feed your minds a little at a time, so that one day you may accept us. You must evolve, we are not ants of your earth, we are of a similar feature and yes, we know of their existence, for we were once part of your civilisation in Mexico, as you call it.

Ships of Gold

The Hebrews worshipped us, mm, as did many other nations, as they viewed us from the heavens in our ships of gold. God's, they called us and God's we are not! We are merely beings of a distant planet. Time has erased our memories, but still features can be seen today.

Your planetarium, your house of science does not acknowledge the presence of life forms. Help us to inspire those minds in the dark to ignite a thought that life can and does exist elsewhere beyond your small star. Will you come you ask, will we be seen? We cannot at this time, as there is a danger to us from your men of ignorance who will shoot first and ask later. But there will come a time when the world will see a positive outcome of change. We have infiltrated many sectors of your life. You're very being is easy to control, your minds are narrow and fickle at heart, but we will amass in thoughts and ideas to unleash your minds potential.

27th November 2016

Relinquish your towers of ivory and step into the cold morning of the dawn and issue a practice of love to the world. We wish once more to take your hand and lead you through the garden of Eden, to spread the word of the holy being that comes to you all within the very near future. Be blessed by his purpose and love. Hold our hands together in the practice of love and worship of him, for the commonwealth of man is the good within all that will affect change in your patterns of life.

We have come so far on this journey of love my children, to bring a purpose and will to those who would read these words and the words of the Bible.

Your practices seldom reflect the needs of the many, but as the light grows, so your purpose will expand to engulf the many nations upon your planet. We are the Arcturians, a race of beings who will assist and endeavour to bring peace once more to your world of blue. Let go your thoughts of anger and despair bring about a purpose of peace, to love one another and all that live upon your planet.

Reckless minds will bring about much turmoil in the fight between the light and dark which rages currently in your world of beings. We have seen many appalling things, creatures of destruction hiding behind the masks of many, they translate their thoughts of wisdom into actions of perilous deeds to denounce that being of light. For they see their saviour as being one of Ahmet, Achmed, who is seen as embarrassing with the father, our Lord of mercies. The father our Lord who is also Allah. Hmm, don't they understand that they are controlled by the might of many who have cast illusion before them, not allowing them to see the truth that lays before their eyes?

Struggles will commence soon within your atmosphere. Within days the light will engulf your planet. In fear, our rage is a storm. Have courage and bear witness to the magic of the Lord, for he is all powerful within the realms of life, the creator of many visions of love. Be a man and worship the thought of freedom from tyranny, banish the thoughts of neglect and regret, allow us to intercede within your lives, to once more bring peace to the men of the earth.

We have no wish to conquer your race, but just to abolish those beings who bring suffering and destitution to your planet. Let us once more become the Lord's of trust, so that we may impart wisdom upon your people.

Your men of science, their minds are narrowed by their physical abilities. Their pointless concerns are trivial in comparison to that which comes, but their leaders will assume a responsible role to assist and affect change. Every man has a purpose within his own being to become a better being of the light. Target your emotions and don't let fear intercede with your thoughts. Bring about a response, a change in the thoughts of men, that is your responsibility.

27th December 2016

Consolidate your thoughts in prayer, as he, the master, dictates your love in worship. Be not afraid of the past nor the future

to come, as there are very many aspects of life in which your body will exist.

Focus has been brought upon the lavender in your room. It is good to sense that sweet nectar, that scene of colour of the lavender, as it is the colour of the great spirit.

Focus your mind upon us this evening my son and let no other intervene, as we connect our thoughts with your mind.

Trouble us not with your fears, for they will be many, a burden on many in your world. Your peoples must appreciate that they bring this upon themselves, for freedom of thought, speech and expression are rife within your world, neglecting the light of the Lord of mercies, who once ruled your planet in the far distant past.

To him their minds must all turn, to bring you greetings and a welcome so profound, that your knowledge will increase in the ways of spirit and of the master. Do not expect miracles as they will not occur within a man's life if he does not bring focus.

Troubled are your minds with those of the Americas, who bring disgrace upon their nation with their thoughts of self. How many more times must we intercede with the minds of those of the rich and powerful to bring them focus upon their path of greed and wealth.

Formidable times ahead are forecast in the thoughts of many in your world, for they see the path is written before them, not of pleasure, but of much displeasure as the armies battle for progress.

Your world is at war with itself, its aggression is obvious to us of the United Planets.

We are here this evening to remark upon the incredible events that will occur within the June.

('What oh,' he hears.)

Many times we have forecast a bleak future for your peoples, you are the creators of your own situations. The messages we bring are of love and support, so that you may have an inkling as to your path.

Be not afraid of those who come, for they bring fair weather within the storm of life. It so happens so many times that man's desires override his thoughts and needs. He is a selfish animal who looks to himself and his own purpose, never understanding that it is a purpose of joy that he should be sharing amongst the many of your world of indignations. Compare us not with those who would wage war, but help us to understand the mindset of those who cannot see the woods for the trees. Mm, their paths are shaded from the light. They only see the dark passage before them, hmm, neglecting all others that stand in their way.

Russia And Communism

Many times we have spoken of those communists, and their party. Their way was shaped by a man many years ago, who foresaw a nation who would work and live together in the common practice of life. Alas, it got out of hand as those of power and greed took hold and became the masters of misery.

Stalin, a man of aggression was a man ignorant of his intolerances, his persecution of the many left many dead, families disrupted by his purpose. Hmm. His futile ways were seen by many as arrogance and ignorance. His situation became obvious to the parties of the world as they looked on in despair at his red army that marched with boots on the ground, with an aspect of distrust and hate. Many of solidarity worked to rescue their being of this group that it came to the fore and became noted to the world.

Putin

Alas it seems that once more, all has given way to the mighty strength of one, his nature is not of bitterness, but he sees those of the west who terminate thoughts of peace with injustice and intolerances impertiment to his ways. He feels his nation is his and his alone to lead. He will not tolerate or suffer fools gladly and if things tumble before him then he will grasp the situation and fulfil his promise. A grim situation that doesn't bear thinking about. We cannot understand how it is that man will participate in such activities as he does.

Focus your mind upon the possibilities that peace would bring. Eliminate that superstition, that suspicion and bring a practice of love to the fore, as you are noted as being a man of courage by many.

Comprehend your fears my son and deal with them in the way and the manner given, do not persecute those who do not understand the true meaning of the words that are passed by us. By offering them a hand of friendship, help them to understand that these words are teachings by which they may learn, hmm, a more open-minded perception of the Lord.

Knowingly we say to you, that your situation is grim, but change is on the way, for all must move over with time as new practices and beliefs occur within men's minds. The cosmos is a place of great escapes, its vastness is beyond your reach at this time. However, with your minds focused you may travel stars and witness the things that you cannot witness in the theatrical sense. Open your minds, allow your thoughts to be vanquished and believe in what you see. Bring focus to your mind to see the things that would allow you freedom of thought.

We are the Arcturians who whisper in your ear of the things to be and have been. We are a race of beings of the nature of goodness, kindness of hearts. Our thoughts extend to the many who suffer at this time throughout your dark world. How can such beauty as your world, hold such dark secrets within?

Many nations have appealed to your thoughts, of your leaders, but they are ignored, vanquished as if they never were, and we cannot understand why it is that they wish to bring a practice of ill will to those of your world, for what will they gain of this? Immaturity that they display in their being. Hmm, community and commonwealth should be a factor that is seen as beneficial to all within your blue planet.

The Arms Race

Your comprehension of peace is a dark one, for you create a dangerous position as you escalate your arms race. Hmm. How can this bring peace? It will only antagonise other nations in your world as they see your strength grow and they feel threatened by your anger as you declare yourselves the United States of the world. Hmm. You were once known as the peacekeepers of your world but now are you not the aggressors? Do you not see the many faces of your beast?

There are many, it is true to be said who are of a kind and good nature within your union, it is not their fault that they are led by beasts who dictate terms and conditions, but they have the power to rectify these wrongs, they sit back and say that they know better, they are the government who we must obey, but you are merely sheep.

They have many who would take displeasure at the demonstrations held in Philadelphia in the time of reckoning.

His presence will become known as 'the master' you will disregard the rules of the nations of plenty as he sacrifices his soul to gain a purpose of power.

His murmurings and mutterings of his ill will are heard many times, people say "This is rhetoric." Really! You need to listen with better ears, but if you support him then you will support your own fate!

The Muslim Faith of Good

The Muslim faith has become a radical thought in many minds. Do not fear, for what is discrimination, for they have a practice of love beyond your understanding of the Christian world. But know this, our thoughts are as yours for love and peace and kindness. Men of minority have signified themselves as being of Islam are cruel and wicked individuals who would bring their name into disrepute. The understanding spirit that is the genuine Muslim, is a man of peace and of family, their practices are different, as measured by their time, but this love of honour, of God is deep within them.

Truly remarkable how they resist their temptations to lash out at those who would condemn them of the wild. They are to be commended and admired for their loyalty to their God, and it is truly remarkable how the Christian world does not observe and retain their thoughts of their religion. They must be given an example by these brothers of the Muslim person, for they must see that their practice of love should be as all religions in your world.

We have never seen such differences in your world as today, discrimination, racism and the heartache of many who sacrifice their lives in the name of God. Their twisted views are seen as the majority, but this is not true, do not accept those thoughts.

Understand that Allah was a man of great beauty and love, his disciples and descendants are of a beautiful race of beings who exist today within your world, in their mosques, with joy, laughter and love and obedience for him, the great spirit.

Bring your nations together through your practices of love and do not judge one another by the mindless thoughts of those who would bring disrepute to these beings.

Many times we have spoken of the Lord our father and of Jesus and given new thoughts in reference to them, but they are not of the one religion. Despite your differences and your ways of life you are all one spirit. Learning and practising each other's lives throughout eons of spans of life. How can you learn of the differences of the many by living one life? How you exist with each other in thought.

Your minds coexist in spirit as one, and each of you will take a part of the other to bring the specific learning to yourselves so that you may advance beyond your present being.

Our love for you has never been vanquished, we sit here and wait for the day to come when man will turn once more to the light of heaven and recognise himself as being of the one entity.

You abolish thoughts and practices in particular religions as of no consequence. Have the thought that God is within all.

Those of the dark practices who infiltrate many whose minds are a 'garden of thought', hmm, they will torment and tease to bring fractures among your people, but it is your love that holds as the cement and the glue. Do not allow these fractures to grow, bring peace to yourselves and your countries in your world, in your thoughts.

Our Radio Waves Travel Throughout the Universe

For he will understand that your emotions are felt throughout time within the ether of your planetary system, hmm, as radio waves travel forever within the universe, so your thoughts exist, your minds coexist in a place unknown to you during your life, it is a place of beauty from whence you came and which you will return should you have an aspect of love to your brothers and sisters and the creatures of your world.

Be blessed in your thoughts of love now and forever more. Amen.

Dark Secrets

Darkness descends upon your world as you wander aimlessly. The fools that lead your nations bring a practice of ill will to many, unseen to the eyes of the peoples of those nations. Mm. They have secrets, dark secrets which they will hide in many layers, so that their attention of focus can be seen as acceptable.

Ha! It is laughable how people consider themselves immortal and feel that they should hoard these things! Hmm. Do they not understand that they are of the material world and cannot be brought beyond that place? Hmm. It is your love and emotions and your thoughts that will bring pleasure or displeasure to you as you pass from your world to that of spirit. Your money has no meaning here, your gold is of little value to us. The only treasure lies within your heart, so bring joy to others in the season of plenty and help them to understand the love of the Lord Jesus, of the Lord Mohammed and all those of the sects and religions that exist in your world, even those beyond your understanding held within the tribes of the jungles, deep in those forests of your world.

Their beliefs are not dissimilar as they pray to their God. Did man teach them of the Lord and of God? No of course not, it is a natural thing for them to understand that all things are created within heaven and they exist in this world and know that all things given, are of the creator. They had no books or education. Hmm. They need nothing of these to look at the surroundings that they live in and to see the wonders that are given by God Almighty. They understand that theirs is a world of love, friendship, relations and beauty in their own ways. They seem primitive to the outside world, but truly who are the primitive ones? Those who worship the earth and give thanks for the benefits and goodness that it brings, or those that abuse the systems in the things that are provided by nature?

The Congo

Truly a situation has occurred in the Congo jungles that are unheard of in your western world, you will not hear of the shameless massacres that have occurred, for they will not give you an insight into the rich man's ways and how they want to selfishly take that which belongs to Mother Earth.

Who have diamonds of beauty stolen from the lives of the innocents who live on the scraps given? Shameless ways, the heart of the stone will be shown to the world as a beautiful object. Its orange glow and colour will be observed by many who will say, "What a wondrous piece of natural material". Huh! But it will bring shame on those who lust after its beauty.

Crystals

We have spoken of crystals before to you, and to your lack of understanding of their true nature. Truly you are ignorant of the things that your natural world provides you.

Toxic Substances

Hmm, you mix and create substances that are opposites in the world of nature and are kept separate for a reason, the reason is their poison, toxic qualities if mixed. Do you think mother nature keeps these things separated because it just is?

Natural Cure for Everything

There is a reason for everything that exists in your world, there is a cure for all illnesses within your world should you open your eyes to the natural world that surrounds you instead of destroying it by fires for the sake of land and greed. Look at the properties held within. For truly you are sacrificing your own existence as you decimate the forests of your world.

Your atmosphere chokes as you burn the timber that carries the moss and the creatures that have an ability to bring healing to those who suffer from the diseases of modern man.

Pharmaceutical Companies Hide the Truth

Hmm, those primitives we spoke of, have no reason to doubt the abilities or the properties upon the plants around them, they know of these things, your men of science know of these things, but deny them to you, for what profit would there be in telling you of the properties of certain species of plants indigenous to your world? They deny many of the sick their entitlement to respite and cure as they seek to profit from your desperation and illness. What terrible things mankind do to one another? Your social aspects have become desperate, as you accept many things that were once forbidden.

We speak of much sorrow in your world brought by men of deceit, as they rely upon your gullibility in your pursuit for happiness, and your flexibility is truly remarkable when you do not see the deceit brought amongst you.

Narcotics

Carry forth this message of love and say to those who accept the poisons of nature in the form of narcotics, say to them, have the will power and the love in your heart, for we recognise the difficulty of this and the inability of them to focus upon the rights and wrongs. For there are many of the dark who shade their eyes to the purpose and path that they are on. They only worship greed and money and sacrifice the lives of the many as they bring displeasure and call it pleasure!

So many young lives terminated by these intolerable things.

Mm, you choke upon your atmosphere, is it no wonder as you decimate the forests of your land.

We speak of many things, of your practices of ill will towards Mother Earth and the natural world. You condemn yourselves to ill practices that choke you.

Your world is one of beauty, can you not see? Hmm. You have vision to see other worlds in your vicinity and you are as unique in your universe, yet you lack the vision and the scope to help yourselves to see beyond your narrow focus. We cannot intervene, but we can assist in ways of thought.

Your Mayans in minds are a marvel that you do not understand. Trigger those memories of the past.

Losing Our Natural Abilities

As nature gives instruction to those new-born's, creatures of your earth, they do not need textbooks to understand how to fly or where to go to nest, or how to travel your world and navigate over vast distances. They do not need to be taught these things, for they look within and trust their senses, and you have lost this ability as you rely upon the technologies of your world and deny your natural abilities by those substances that you take in.

Thoughts Remain in the Ether

Truly a vast season of goodwill will bring immense terminations of those of displeasure. For like a cancer, those things of the dark will grow if you do not stem the tide with your thoughts of love. We spoke of the ether and how things remain in the ether. And so it is, that those ill thoughts and practices grow each and every day and pollute the ether, but those of love and kindness, who are still the majority, must fan in the way, the flames of love and deny those dark forces.

Do not bring displeasure to your brother and neighbour, bring them hope and love and joy in the season and time of giving. Be of the pleasant man, who would look at somebody and pass the time of day with greetings and give them a hand should they fall. Do not neglect their needs for your own selfish practices. Feed them your thoughts of love so that they might see that truly, men have heart.

We completely understand how you must feel this time, but give to those, even if they selfishly hold back their gifts.

The thought of love is given to you all, help yourselves in your lives to help your children learn of respect and love.

Open your hearts and minds to our Lord, our father, and peace to you all will blossom as the primrose of spring. Amen.

MESSAGES FROM OR ABOUT INDIVIDUAL PEOPLE

Born on August 31, AD 161 AD – Died AD 192
  His father was Roman Emperor Marcus Aurelius.
  Commodus was a corrupt ruler who was not well received by the Roman people during his reign. He believed himself to be a reincarnation of Hercules and enjoyed fighting in an arena as a gladiator. His outrageous tactics, such as slaying the crippled and slaughtering wild beasts in the arena, brought much negative attention, and were believed to have played a role in his eventual assassination. His tumultuous reign as Emperor was the starting point for a period of Roman history that is viewed as having been filled with chaos and decline
  From his place in the light, he is now learning and making amends for his ways of the past by bringing words of encouragement and strength as well as occasional remorse.

The Transcripts:

7th April 2016

Commodus gathered his people's around him for the advent of the coming of the Lord, he knew what his purpose would be. Didn't you hear the cries of those who hunger upon your planet? Do not disrespect the words that are given to you, as they will become clear in the passage of time.

Commodus will reign once more on the third planet of the sun, his being has always been true to the light. Refrain from activities of sin, broadening your horizons with knowledge of the things to come. Discrepancies in your life will fill your voids; commercialisation of your words should not be for profit but of aspects of love.

Commodus speculates that the true purpose of your being is to adhere the words in a phrase so that all may listen, be frank with those who ask, let them know. Though tears will fall, love will reign supreme in the hearts of man. Life is precious and to all species we extend our love and warmth before you. Commodus would like to send his purpose to you; his respect of the Earth remains highest in his thoughts. Control your emotions in times of trouble, behold your heart of purpose my son.

11th April 2016

"**I was once a man who led the many through the trees and bushes of life,** they followed me with purpose and true love. Today they need my presence once more in the world of man. Completion of this task is set in the August.

We are from honour your family and men, be at one with peace. allow your light and strength to carry those on their paths as you lead them upon yours.

Let us hold your hand, lead you from the dark shadows within your mind, fill your mind with the light of the Lord. Conversely, we will speak in the future of man to bring the light to the shade. Commence your plan and become master of your destiny, your tolerance is needed by many who would doubt you, don't let them pass by without a thought, allow them your mind to see the light."

Commodus wishes to thank those of the light for their purpose, he nears your world, the purpose at hand, he knows of your love and your strengths and weaknesses. Take his hand, call his name and allow him to sit beside you by the rivers of life and death. You know his sign is of love, his tender caress to those who open their arms to him, be at peace and love in the knowledge that he who comes to the universe of man will come with peace in mind.

Commodus wishes to thank those of the light for their purpose, he nears your world the purpose at hand, he knows of your love and your strengths and weaknesses, take his hand, call his name and allow him to sit beside you by the rivers of life and death. You know his sign is of love, his tender caress to those who open their arms to him, be at peace and love in the knowledge that he who comes to the universe of man will come with peace in mind.

14th April 2016

Commodus comes with a special gift of love and joy for you to share with the friends of the Earth. Your knowledge grows and is vast and pre-ordained to do the things that you do at this time and stage of your being.

Conduct yourself with honour and knowledge of the light. Some will call you a fake, unworthy of interest, huh, their combined knowledge compares little with what is given to you by the Fathers of the Earth. The tombstones of those who sought to change the world of Hades to dust, but the light will continue to shine.

Commence the actions needed by us so that we may represent those of our nations to yours. You are daunted by this task, but know this, they will come to you with purpose in due course. As you answer their questions, their minds cannot comprehend another universe co-existing with yours, for all they see are facts, scientific formulations, they mean nothing, they are nothing. One fact remains, that life exists on many levels in the many planes all around your Earth, beyond your vision. Those of you who connect are aware of the minor planes, the higher spiritual planes would be hard for you to grasp.

Continue your work, for each psalm that progresses will shift the balance of love, as it does, so they too will progress to a higher plane. Your knowledge is key to those that don't understand, they question you of your purpose, in their hearts they know that theirs is a journey to be taken with love.

Constantine remarked on his journey as being that of, "The guided one," comparatively he was right, his purpose was all too soon gone as he found the riches of the world that temped and taunted him. He was and is a gentle soul who was misled by those of temptation, but he knew his love ran deep and he was able to supersede all the temptations given.

17th April 2016

Commodus wishes to express his concern for the Polynesian-peoples, their focus is on life, and the hidden dangers beneath their feet cannot be seen. Your instruments that measure vibrations are at fault, they cannot see what is to come, a disaster of epic proportion will unfold before the world of life, but take heart that these events are designed to clear the veins of Mother Earth so that she may breathe in the love of the light.

Topples the mountains of love, they sing the song to the world of the lands, she cannot hold her emotions for the abuse set upon her, like an itch that has to be scratched she will act in her nature on the Earth. The foolish who built their houses, their dwellings upon earth in strategic areas will suffer an amount of loss that will shake the very foundation. Knowledgeable are you of these events to occur in the month of May. Perhaps in some way the words will make sense to those who will not listen, culminate your feelings of despair at the fracture of the Earth as she jolts, we cannot say how many will be lost but know they will be welcomed in their new life.

(We believe this may be about Mount Kilauea, Hawaii which erupted in May 2018.)

19th April 2016

Together we will force an emotion of love consistent with that of the Lord, for he is the master of love and seasons commence your heart to its task, speaking the words in a gentle fashion. Navigate your minds resources to aspire to your purpose.

Commodus respects your wishes. He heard, his expressive love and compassion is upon you. Neglect not your thoughts of wisdom and love; transfer your mind's eye to our origin, taking messages of love to the masses in your world of flesh. Neglect us not in the coming days when your mind's aspects will be observant of the skies above, Nigeria is a focal point of our being.

Comes as no surprise to us that your mind is a little vague, for as the vessel is empty so shall it be filled with purpose of heart, Commodus wishes to thank all those that work alongside you, his grateful wishes go out to them with peace and love.

1st May 2016

Commodus wishes to speak as a soldier, "I was born to fend off the enemy of my family, I see before you a vast wilderness which will lead you to your purpose in the common good of man. Containment of your weapons has been compromised by those who would seek to destroy your Earth in a manner befitting the fires of hell."

5th May 2016

Commodus enters the Kingdom of Heaven with a mindset of love, his mission is one of many to bring comfort and peace to men of the Earth.

Commodus comes with a tale of epic proportions; listen to his words, focus. "Cities crumbled before us as we swept through with no mercy upon those inhabitants, those times of marauding were terrible times, for I was a part of man who'd desire and lust, failing to see my path as it was written. I served many upon the Earth as a gimmick to be seen, the trophy to be had, I was the man I'm ashamed by the beast to be beaten. I was fair with those that came to me for assistance; they gave me hard extreme punishments for the error of my ways. The pain, the sorrow cannot be taken from my heart as it aches to warn others to stop the misery, before it is too late."

The creation of man was a blessed thing given to those who would see him as a saviour, challenge Him not for he loves all, all are welcome in his path with power. Should the blind man see the path he would be astonished with the colours of the light that shone with him, for he would know the true value of the light that shone bright in his eye, for he has never seen such a wonder as that of the Lord.

Focus your mind, focus upon the continuance of your journey, allowing those questions to be answered by us in far flung places upon your Earth. Temper your actions and your heart's restraint for all will come at the time necessary to begin each phase of the journey, it will be hard to face the truth but necessary to scourge the evil from your Earth.

Relinquish your thoughts in those moments of pain, control is necessary to avert the situation, as confrontation with those without purpose or need.

Aspire to us in the many ways of the colours purple.

Gratitude, compromise, compassion, all words; actions speak louder than words. Combine your interests to compel the actions within words. **Marcus Aurelius** was once a prince among men, he stood for all time as a noble man. His problem was his virility, he was fruitful in the labours of love, but his knowledge was weak for that which mattered most. Do you not rule the nations of many in your heart of pain? Was he not a great man of theology, his purpose was metered out in measures?

Twilight came before the dusk for she who rules will rest in peace before the moon rises twice in the skies of Aquarius, panic and mayhem will reflect across the nations of the globe for she is a woman, a soul to cling to for many, control your emotions and thoughts as we enter problematic situations, arise, before this time is done you will have emitted a purpose in many. His response will be limited to your minds and thoughts, he will warm unto the words as they melt his heart to stay for he too must pass before the Lord in the morning light.

It is strange to feel the emotion of the mind for it weeps for humanity, it cares for the purpose of love, strange but you do not see your purpose, who collectively we conspire to affect your will so that we, we talk of things to come. The context of which we need not worry about for it concerns those of ill will, of malevolence, how can we express our thoughts of love within your mind, your will is strong, force it to release your mind. Two others will come before you my son, their purpose is to travel with you on a road of light, compel your heart to listen and understand the meaning that they represent, for us time is but a passage to be travelled, for once you have been a part of that moment, it will not return.

10th May 2016

Marcus (*Marcus Aurelius*) he wants to tell you of the days in the arena where he once stood as a man, he of plenty, he couldn't foresee what was to befall him in the light of the dawn. He knew of the uncertain times that faced him, but he demanded respect from those who saw him as unworthy in their kingdom, they denied him his right to rule, convicting him in celebration, for his name was written to torment those of great power.

12th May 2016

Trophies of war are won by men victorious in battle, they sheathed their weapons as soldiers of man, I am a man, I was a man sword in hand, heart full of desire for the seed of life which disappears so rapidly, we were nothing. At the time I thought they would make me the one terrific commandant, so wrong was I to have deceived myself with things that glitter and possession, for they meant nothing in the eyes of spirit, they are but a trifle, they are to be tempted the temptation of man is great as a test by which the sole purpose should be to acquire knowledge. **Commodus** speaks of the passage of the time from when he was a man of strength, his misgivings were his ill fortunes for he could not see that many of his time were misled.

31st May 2016

Commodus wishes to speak once more in a manner of love and peace: It was long ago that I was a man forced into servitude by others whose will and desire was to own man. They punished me for my disobedience many times before the whip, I suffered great pain and the agonies of death. Many times I felt the needles penetrate my skin they were as knives cutting away a piece of me with each stroke, my mind was beaten into submission. I looked into men's eyes and saw them weep before my blade, my own heart sang out, "Why am I forced to do this?" but in truth it was always in my power not to commit these crimes against a fellow man, my ignorance was not an excuse, my feeble mind was not an excuse. As I came before the Lord and He whispered in my ear, "**Commodus,** why as a man did you take other men's lives, could you not see the unjust wisdom in your actions? You were not forced into servitude as your will is strong, you should have fought against the master." but I understand your weakness as you sit before me, your obedience and your suffering will not go unnoticed. We of the light, of the wisdom, know of the pains and suffering of men, yours has been great, you cannot expect that I can overlook the crimes committed against humanity. As I look, I become aware of His noble presence in my midst, I asked forgiveness for the things, those many terrible things.

7th June 2016

Commodus re-joins us now: "Task your masters with thoughts of love as their eyes betray the truth within, I was once a man who worked with a measure of discontent, dishonour, deceiving those of the Senate with my words of anger. Their words of wisdom were shut out from my mind at my displeasure. They scavenged from the scraps that I gave them, they knelt before me as I now kneel before you to honour your love of the Lord and the light. This should have been my purpose as I was a man of dishonour who had given my love to the material things and not to the hearts and minds of my people. My woes are great but my redeemer has given me a better understanding of my life's purpose. I come to you now as a man of honour and much respect for the work that you are doing in His name. Don't allow others to sway your tide of movements, bring about a purpose of common humanity, be a leader with compassion and love in your heart for I was once a man with none.

3rd July 2016

Commodus speaks once more to the nations of your world as a soldier, as a humanitarian. Alas his mind was weak with fear and terror as he drove his purpose home through the hearts of men. Humph! What merciless times they were, of murderers, pointless processions. I could not perceive at the time how the masses would react to the laws that I set. My disappointment in others was repaid by treachery, their hearts, their minds, compelled me to act in ways that were regrettable. I became a man of valour only to fall into the pits of hell for the actions I took against my fellow human beings. Those days are past now, my lessons learnt, my future bright. Do not forget your lessons as you progress in a myriad of ways to bring your focus upon the light of Him who sits in Heaven, for His splendour is great. His need of you is required to bring about an end to a means. Suffer you may, but your knowledge is great. His Herculean ways image *(represent)* men who strived to bring about peace during those days, those awful days of darkness, dark times indeed. We had no rest for we were driven by the master's whip. Commodus tore us apart as a man then, but his shame was greeted by love and he grew in stature to become a figure of that of the light. He conquered his fears in the oppression of his people to bring love and purpose to the common man, for his fight was one of a battle of love. Never let it be said that his heart was torn from his body as it beat in the hands of the Lord, never be ashamed of who you are, for we speak through you in ways you cannot understand. Your mask shields a man who is meek and mild in manner, your heart beats strong in your focus and purpose.

6th July 2016

Commodus did so much in his mind for his people but it was not their will to be fooled by a master full of indignities. Your situation on your planet's surface is very much that of those times – the dictators hidden behind the scenes, pulling the strings, observing the chaos created. For where there is chaos there is corruption and collusion.

7th July 2016

Commodus knows of injustice, many times he has spoken of his life, but just as an example, to the men of power that their reign is but a short one. To bring light and life to people's homes is a huge responsibility given to those with a duty to the Lord. If they fall by the way not heeding their purpose, then they must face the consequences as men and women of injustice.

17th July 2016

Commodus wishes an audience with the people, "White grains of sand that falls in the dust, let your souls bring peace among men of the world. As the grains (seeds) fall to the dust so they will be nurtured by the sun, watered by the fountains of youth and then their young shoots emerge with strength and purpose. You need to have courage to bring forth the words to assist your people to the paths of light. Have no regrets of days past for they have gone, like the sword, the double-edged blade, yours laid to rest in the fields of Araby. *(Authors Note: Araby is an archaic name for Arabia.)* Your masters rest in peace, consequently we affirm we are a nation of many peoples, nobles, commoners, beggars, a multitude of race and peoples. We conquered the world and harvested their crops to announce our own beauty and status in life. Humph, what was it all for? We never realised the true meaning of life, the unity of man to bring peace in our world. Our ill-gotten gains were our downfall, we were exposed to many things. We were brought to our knees by the smallest uprising, we were a nation of greed, of masters to rule the world. We offended Him on high by our practices of love. We had no intention of allowing others of weakness to participate in our celebration of ourselves, of our glory. A tempest was set against us to level our thoughts, we crumbled as many cities do. We exist only in thought today, in the peoples of the world as they marvel in our constructions. Our abilities in truth, we were lacking so much love, our abilities proven to be long lasting, but our nation suffered the consequences of hate from others. Mine was the seat of power, where my rule as master of the universe was supreme. I conceded to nothing, determined to bring about a purposeful meaning for our nation. But I failed in my words and when I passed, suffering the blows, I had no power. I was nothing, just a commoner. Hmm, my weaknesses betrayed me in life as in death, but I have now come to realise the error of my ways and have been given a chance to help those of a will to help themselves to a better, freer world, where love and light rule supreme. Bring a purpose of love to the world and do not neglect those thoughts of love, and cherish the hope that one day you too may see the light of the Lord."

Well, words of wisdom indeed, thoughts are brought to mind of the many terrible deeds that were practiced at that time. He was truly a man of distinction, character and responsibility. He fell from grace in his own glory, not being accountable to anyone or so he thought. Hmm, he could not deny the Lord. His purpose was truly a manifestation of his own mind, he never thought to open his heart to an alternative way of being.

We never thought the day would come when we would thank the Lord for a blessing, but here we are, together as one, bringing thoughts of those who have had their tasks won and lost.

Continue with your words my son, let it be known that we, the Arcturians, will announce a satisfactory conclusion to the words of the prophets.

21st July 2016

Commodus, a man of distinction... hmm.... really needs to learn to some manners, but we admire his progress, he wishes to speak once more on your path of light as he can see a man of singular purpose. For he once fought in the ring many eons ago, without a thought for other's lives, for his battles were great and many and the people loved him for his courage, but they seldom believed in him. For his words were harsh to those who would oppose him, in the senate they cowered as he spoke his rhetoric, demanding that the people love him. You do not gain respect by demands. He wishes to say how sorry he is for that stupidity he brought upon his people. He wishes to say it aloud, without his apparel, sit back and listen awhile, be not ignorant of the peoples demands, listen with an ear of sympathy for their love is gained in a manner, that you should discipline, is not necessary in a world of love, for each know their place and part to play. Retrospectively he wishes to commence grand words of wisdom and joy to those of woe who hide their books of knowledge, be that of peace, bring out those books tell the people of the changes they're in, do not hide the thoughts of the Lord within your chambers, for they are for all to read and abide by. Their content is of the truth, not of the wicked. Father Demetrius, he guards the many scriptures therein, he works day and night, deciphering, understanding their meaning. He relays the information to his master who denounces them as works of another author. Pope John Paul II, he knew of the scriptures, he now sits with us, in sheer delight to see a man once more in the seat of power of Rome who will listen to the people and not be afraid of the rhetoric of those who demand him to be quiet. He is a man of peace; he has the power to change the world at his feet. To call for a blessing from the Lord to those people who follow that sect, be not afraid of him, for he is a man of distinction, a worthy man to sit on that seat of power in Rome, where once stood the palaces.

4th September 2016

How the mighty fall, I should know, I am Commodus, ruler of many in my time. Ah, I once sat on the throne of Rome, declaring that my thoughts and actions should be obeyed by those of the lower classes. Hm, I was a man of intolerance, my strength grew as I fed my ego. Why, I was the man the master and ruler of all who came before me. I come before you in a manner of love Michael. You were of the Roman nation you know, you followed my orders, mmm, and you perished. I surrender my love to you, hmm, my power was my weakness of mind. They torment me my days of intolerance, I now have the power of the light within me, the master of joy gave me blessings. May I bestow upon you my thoughts in the days to come. Power is but an illusion of the man of mind, does not respect the thoughts of the light as it is all consuming as the greed grows and the strength of mind denies the logical side of life. You become embroiled in darkness. Rome fell, many other nations will fall, for unless you know the light and loving, you cannot sustain power and greed. Your men of intolerance who rule your world of business, will learn this lesson in the downfall of your economy. How the mighty fall before the blade of truth. Communus I was, with a heart now filled with sadness. Have my thoughts to inspire those. Begin a life of love and not ignorance, my Roman tongue would be strange. *(Note: The Channel at this point attempted to repeat the words in his mind but was unable to understand – sounds like: pen, intuatus x se Assisi, aromaximus deity.)*

Claudius Roiaximus Maximus, men of Trojans we served you.

11th September 2016

Commodus, a leader of men, would like to speak on the platform once more. "My misery was bought upon me by my actions of intolerance, I was leader of men, of many and I learnt my lesson well. You cannot ignore the thoughts of the many, or for him. For you are but one man, you must comply with the laws of the nation. I was no angel; I did not bother to see the needs of my people. My energy and power were devoted to those of the tournament. I was an ignorant man with a self-loathing for whom I was. I see the error of my days and my will. I will not permit those thoughts to rule once more for I understand his power and glory and that I am nothing but a humble man. Target your emotions with love my son do not allow thoughts of domination to overrule your mind, the men of power truly have need of balance." Thank you, Commodus.

27th November 2016

Commodus has words, for he was a man of ignorance upon your planet:
"I was a ruler of many and master of none, my thoughts bore ill will to those that I conquered. I gave little in return as I took the pledges of men and threw them to the wayside. You too were once part of that immense nation and had a focus upon our desires. We have all learnt since of our misgivings. I desired many things and would go to any length to hang those beads, those stones around my neck. I was the author of many tragedies and built the monuments to death.

As I gazed upon my riches in life, I neglected the thought of "Messiah", the leader of our world. I was a man of ill will and ill repute. I gave no quarter to those of the senate who would impeach me and attempt to dislodge my reign. They should have known better! But no, I remain a man who asks forgiveness from the Almighty. My actions and noble deeds were nothing but a nightmare for the many. I asked for the slaughter of 10,000, men, women and children in my honour, they did as I requested. A shameful disgrace. A leader of many and a leader of none, my purpose was a disgrace and I ask that the men of your present day look to themselves as 'Caesar' and how as I, they order the masses into conflict for the benefit of one.

Relinquish your desires for the riches of the earth, for they are nothing, they mean nothing. Gone are the days when my purpose was to desire those jewels of life. Be aware I have learnt my lesson and still seek forgiveness for the many who died in my name. Don't let this future be yours, men of the earth, bring compassion and love to the many of the nations. Stop your fighting and lust for greed and land and begin a practice of sharing of love and resources. Hmm, I see the many things that reflect upon my own time and wish I could lend a hand, but alas, this is your path that you must take, be wise have a care. Articulate in your thoughts.

Maximus/Marcus Auralius

Born AD *121 – died* AD *180*

Marcus Aurelius was emperor of Rome during the 2nd century AD, *the last in a line the 'Five Good Emperors'. At the time of his death, he was one of the most powerful people on earth. He could have had anything he wanted, and few, if any, would dare challenge him on anything. And yet he proved himself deserving of the power he held. Under Marcus Aurelius, the empire was guided by virtue and wisdom.*

The Transcripts:

29th March 2016

Come with us now on a journey of love that we inspire you as no other can, the crown you see is upon His head.

Maximus *(Marcus)* was granted the pearls of wisdom that he forged in life, his will was strong, immense, but his heart was weak in purpose.

Cross your bridges as they come to you. Know us for who we are, communicate with those who need your wisdom. References were a pattern for you to see and yours alone, we will grant you a vision to guide you on your journey. She will help you in matters of the heart and your purpose. Guided were you to those whose need was great. Ascertain you're needs and group them with vigour and purpose.

Floral tributes will be given to those under siege, their purpose in heaven is noted, recognised as Martyrs to the cause.

Your phrases are short but strong. Convince us of your purpose; demonstrate to us your need, for guidance will be given in due course when the moon is high among the stars. Complete your tasks given, recognise your purpose. A score will be counted in the heavens above for the next ten weeks, you will watch and stare, your hearts have fear, the sunlight will fade before your eyes of the next moon.

We are tasked to free the minds of those without purpose, if you commence within the week this journey, compromise is required, your battles of the seasons have begun. Sharp edged weapons will be seized by the hands of men with intent of murder, they classify themselves as 'Martyrs to the cause', but their cause is evil, a score will die before the moon, before their time is due. Their fight is an unworthy one that condemns others into a life of unhappiness, sourness, ungratefulness.

Maximus will tell you of his purpose, his sword is sharp, rigid to the point.

Who are we to intervene in your life of purpose, your hopes and prayers are said for the Lord, combine your thoughts so that knowledge will increase ten-fold before the day is out? Temperance and tolerance should be made available to those who require it. Let us not intervene with the routine, to commence your work begin at four, the time is nigh.

Virgo, she of the star will align with you with purpose in mind. Behold as she shines the light of Venus upon you all, Her knowledge of you is vast. Your comprehension, your focus will be needed. Temperance given those ships that sail the stars of light are many. Her vessels are of spirit; that sail the seas of heaven with purpose, focus.

As souls give up their bodies, they are collected by these vessels of love and they sail the seas of freedom. In mercy her force will be upon you in due time, respect Her as the fisherman of souls as She will transport those of the light to the heavens above in a vessel of light 'V' is her sign, virtue is Her manner, vigorous is Her purpose, volatile her temperament. She is the Mother of love that cannot deny your hearts will, stroke her hair with tenderness and care, with love in your heart, divine is Her purpose. Go to your tasks.

5th May 2016

Gratitude, compromise, compassion, all words; actions speak louder than words. Combine your interests to compel the actions within words.

Marcus Aurelius was once a prince among men, he stood for all time as a noble man. His problem was his virility, he was fruitful in the labours of love, but his knowledge was weak for that which mattered most. Do you not rule the nations of many in your heart of pain? Was he not a great man of theology, his purpose was metered out in measures?

Twilight came before the dusk, for she who rules will rest in peace before the moon rises twice in the skies of Aquarius. Panic and mayhem will reflect across the nations of the globe for she is a woman, a soul to cling to for many. Control your emotions and thoughts as we enter, problematic situations arise. Before this time is done you will have emitted a purpose in many. His response will be limited to your minds and thoughts, he will warm unto the words as they melt his heart to stay, for he too must pass before the Lord in the morning light.

It is strange to feel the emotion of the mind for it weeps for humanity; it cares for the purpose of love. Strange that you do not see your purpose, collectively we conspire to affect your will so that we, we talk of things to come. The context of which we need not worry about for it concerns those of ill will, of malevolence. How can we express our thoughts of love within your mind, your will is strong, force it to release your mind? Two others will come before you my son, their purpose is to travel with you on a road of light. Compel your heart to listen and understand the meaning that they represent. For us, time is but a passage to be travelled, for once, you have been a part of that moment, it will not return.

10th May 2016

Marcus (Marcus Aurelius) he wants to tell you of the days in the arena where he once stood as a man, he of plenty, he couldn't foresee what was to befall him in the light of the dawn. He knew of the uncertain times that faced him, but he demanded respect from those who saw him as unworthy in their kingdom, they denied him his right to rule, convicting him in celebration, for his name was written to torment those of great power.

"Condemned are men who satisfy their higher lust with the pleasures of the world, for they seek pleasure in material objects that are of no consequence."

Messages from Various Guides Who Bring Forward Information About Jesus as Well as Words from Jesus Himself

The Transcripts:

4th September 2015

Come together, for together is strength. Voice your words of concern to the world. Terrible as these things are, it is not for you to judge others, it is not for you to close your eyes to the suffering endured by those people. God is aware and there are forces at work you cannot comprehend, he who comes will be known soon to all, let him carry the burden.

Be not afraid as your eyes will be turned against him, only the faithful will see his beauty, only the rich in love and compassion will know him.

He comes on the full moon of August, his light will shine to all who are faithful, the rich shall become poor; the poor will become rich and enlightened as he speaks his words of love.

22nd February 2016

I am the Rose of the Ark

The great one, he must be honoured in deeds, not words, to show you are one in the never-ending battle of life, in the eternal circle. On your path be strong, may God grant you purpose in your life, focus in your thoughts and deeds in your actions. Blessings to you. I am the Rose of the ark.

Yeshua Ben Yosef

Now is the time for us to continue your journey, focus upon your light, let go, trust in our judgment and our love. Courage has taken you this far, now go with our hands in yours. Magical is the journey that faces you in the light. Trust us as never before with honour, harbour no fears, as we are near you.

Mary, she is the one that guides you, she comes with the blessings of the Lord.

Tasks that are unfolding on your path will become clear as the seasons move on, life also has its seasons, focus upon the divine.

Respond to our teachings in a manor respectful of that of the pupil to his teacher; pray for us as we guide you. Your steps taken are true and sure, we can help others through you. We come with the light to honour those who would accept us into their hearts and minds. Focus upon he who comes before us in the fall, be brave in the task ahead, never say that yours was a wasted life. For all life has purpose and meaning unbeknown to some, to others it has purpose, which is known.

Magical, the journey upon the path of light. Come before us hear the voices that cry to you, for they are the voices of those who seek the knowledge, your journey has just begun. Long is the journey that you have embarked upon, you have chosen well. Courteous are you in the face of antagonism, don't get caught up with those who mean harm, their path is crooked like their tongue. You are wise; rise above those who would spread hate with malicious tongues.

Follow us into the light where your path and destiny will unfold, tribes were given purpose

7th April 2016

Jesus Speaks

Knowledge will be given of the Son of man, he approaches. As you feel his energy build, be not afraid, he is the Master of all.

"It's common knowledge that I once lived upon your Earth, treated without respect because I came to speak the truth to the many nations upon your Earth. Inflamed was their passion for the Christ child; their need was great. They concerned themselves not with love, but with ceremony and greed. They could not control their emotions as they became aware that I would set them free.

Far beyond your world, I have travelled many light years to see the blessings of the Lord wash over you, but still you do not relinquish the ways of old, lessons not been learnt. How long will it take for purpose to set in, for all mankind to understand that he is but a whisper in time?

Can he not see the love of the Lord is upon him? His favour will bless those of the light; oppress those of the dark as they spend their life with evil intent.

He comes with joy and focus; do not turn your back on his favour as he watches your purpose unfold. Content your heart in the knowledge that life will continue in a manner befitting his presence. Care for those around you and fill your heart with love, arrange them in no particular order, for love is for all in equal measure.

Depart from the ways of the Earth so that you might finally reach that height of wisdom. Christ continues to ask for reasons of love. What it is that drives man's desires for material things that have no purpose in spirit?

Continue in your work, allowing us to feed our thoughts through you to give messages of love to those of the world.

I once spoke of the poor man and his joy of his life, he wanted for nothing, he cared for nothing, only that his purpose was fulfilled. He sowed his seeds upon the ground of the Earth, he mastered the joy of love, his compassion was immense in the eyes of man, but he was betrayed by that very love. They did not see the man within, they did not hear the words of the Lord as their compassion was selfish and their hearts cold. They came to know, they came before him on their knees, as they understood what they had done.

Commence your work with the love of the Lord. Our light is upon you."

19th June 2016

The priest wishes to say a prayer, "He came amongst us, when the world was at a point of degradation, He restoreth the faith unto man. As He shone his light of purpose upon those disciples who had a will and a sight to see, that He the Lord our Jesus walked amongst them, carrying out His duty as ordained by His Father, our Lord. As we sit with you this evening to bring a thought to mind of His suffering for your world. With a peace said in thought to the minds of the many who listened to His words upon the mount as he sang out, His cries for peace on Earth, goodwill to men. Follow in His word and bring about a purpose of love to the many who follow and watch your words with interest. For your Father in Heaven people also shine his light with an ear to listen, may you all in your homes this evening be blessed by His love, purpose and will. Know that He, the Lord above continues to watch over you with his almighty presence sheltering you from the storm that will begin in the autumn of your time. Give praise for He is your saviour and our Father. Amen."

26th July 2016

Jesus Speaks

"I am the master of the father, hmm, your light shines so bright, your heart sings out for justice for those who suffer at the hands of the merciless, but know this Michael, life is a journey upon which each man must tread the path of turbulence and misfortune. Not all will tread this road, but for those that do, the meaning is great, and their purpose fulfilled.

Your heart-rending thoughts are heard many times by him who sits on high, natural occurrences happen all the time, but keep your focus, never let those of the negative sway your

mind from the path you tread. Your life's light illuminates the way as you walk hand in hand with your partners to bring about a purpose of knowledge to your fellow human beings.

I was once a man who became a monster to some, an angel to others. I became fashionable in the idea of freedom, my purpose was good, but I knew I could not save all, for some were blind as Lazarus, and unable to relinquish the riches of the earth, but he came to an understanding as we met on the sunrise. His friendship was good, his needs were many and great but the path he took truly was awe-inspiring, as he was a man with the riches of the earth but also of the heart, just needs a moment of surrender to enlighten them.

I came once before to bring messages of love, peace and hope to those of Israel. Let it be known my mind is set upon your purpose to assist those in peril to come to an understanding that their belief in Our Father in the heaven's, will help them truly to become one of light."

9th October 2016

Jesus Speaks

Judas of Iscariot, a traitor to some, but figuratively he followed his path as ordained by God, for he brought about an end to the Lord of which was the path. Strange when you think, to bring about the end of your son, but know this, that his end was your beginning. Still many today follow his words with love and respect in your cathedrals and chapels, churches, and homes. He served his purpose with the Lord's blessing, he came to a bitter end only to know the sweet taste of the Lord, his father in heaven.

He sits with us now and beckons us with his hands outspread, filled with love and light to be issued to the many who walk the earth.

"Blessed are you with the light of our father, for you were once a part of the light. Your lives have become saddened by the many misgivings.

I once sacrificed myself before the Lord Almighty to bring peace and compassion to the world of Israel. I once more will return to bless you with my presence and guide your steps on the path of light to his glory in heaven. You were once Michael, a man of intolerance, you still battle your mind to this day, but know that your choices have been made and that they are good.

Welcome James, disciple, a follower who guides your steps. Be forthright with your words and not afeard to speak the words our father in heaven, I am the master, I am he who once roamed your earth with my apostles together and reap those men who would seek the Lord's glory. We beseech you as men of the earth to now open your arms and once more welcome the light of our father in heaven. Do not betray his words, but rejoice in the second coming.

Your claims will be dismissed as mere words of a mortal, they shall know of the love that is channelled through you to them. The messages are welcome and we will respond in kind. They should not require proof but have faith of the Rose in their hearts, and the Lily of your mind will assist."

24th October 2016

Many who work, they are not, you deem those of mediumship are true and faithful, but there are the minority who would abandon their thoughts for the lack of money. Be wary of this need of unnecessaries within your lives. A practice of love is all that is required. Did Jesus go out and earn a penny as he walked the wilderness for 40 days and 40 nights, did he ask for a crust of bread as he walked through Palestine with his disciples at hand? Hmm, no, he had a practice of love, which inspired others to offer him and his disciples the sustenance needed to sustain them. His love was awe-inspiring, bringing wonders to many, his forecast of love was to ensure those followers that their lives had purpose.

You have wondered what it would be like to sit and listen to his voice? Yes, we know your thoughts! Do not be tempted to instigate a manner of negativity to those who would tarnish your name, for they are victims of the dark. Sit here and witness what you could not see in those times, repeat the words if you wish:

"I stand before you on the Mount of Olives to bring you peace and focus within your lives. Be not afraid of the men of the pharaoh who would tarnish and blight your lives as he curses you with financial burden upon your families.

I have been here many times before, to watch over the needs of the many and bring my sermons of love to those with an aspect of love. Here I stand before you today, my arms open to greet those who would give thanks to the Lord Almighty for the blessings given.

Astounded you will be, to hear me say that I am 'Him', a man of love! I am a being of the light who once roamed your earth with a mission to fulfil.

You must never neglect your tasks in your lives to help others, to issue them with a statement of love and bring peace to their souls. You are not me, but you are a minister of the light. I will issue you all a practice of love as you pass through the portals of time, they exist only within your minds, but they are real.

I am a man of Nazareth, who gaveth much to many, peace of mind as I healed the blind and the sick and wounded. Did they once thank me? Seldom not. That was their way, but their light shone once they opened their eyes. I became a man of misfortune, but it was my purpose, for how can one demonstrate better than to show sacrifice for what you believe. God held my hand in the most tender way, he enabled me to show you many things to those of those times, the fishes and the loaves, were not so much a miracle as a matter of focus. I fed the thousands and surveyed the scene as they ate. I gave them blessings.

Thou shall see the angel of the Lord if you wish. Have faith and trust and believe in him who has mercy for all, for he is your lord and master upon high who reigns supreme within

the heavens beyond your earth. Let he who would shout disparities before him, let he see that his wrongs will betray him. For those who wish gratitude of their being, a simple prayer is all that it takes, in your homes, in your gardens, no matter where, all is heard. A focus upon your lives and friends, bring peace to one another and do not sacrifice those mercies given by him as he watches you upon high. Let his love shine throughout the world for all to see.

To all those who follow your words, for your wife, mother and children, blessing of the Lord is with you all. To those in the New Americas, I will say this have peace in your light, negotiate your troubles with a love in your heart. Do not be swept away by that enthusiasm of man who would betray their own being for a penny or two. Go in peace my children with a radiant love, for you will witness many things of your time. Amen.

Our father who art in heaven, hallowed be thy name. Thine kingdom come, thine will be done on earth as it is in heaven. Give us this day our daily bread and forgive us our trespasses as we forgive those who trespass against us. Let the Lord lead you from the devils wishes and bring you peace on your earth. Be thankful for the treasures given within your lives and know that the Lord our father will be with you forever, and ever. Amen."

20th November 2016

Jesus Speaks

"I am the Lord, master of love who welcomes your light and purpose. Your thoughts – far beyond your scope of vision. "Can it be so he would talk to me?" he says. I will talk to any man who would listen to the words of the saviour. It is inherent in all of you, the aspect of light and love. Do not betray his death by ignoring his words of wisdom within the good books.

Their frankness has a trait that should be avoided with a care of the emotions, feelings of many. To this day we have tasked you a mission of love, be a disciple, feel no ego. We are happy to allow your words to bring focus to those who feel ashamed to utter his name and his disciples of the Lord. The trend of fear does not allow the many to see the truth in the words. Be not afraid of the angel of the light, for he comes with many mercies and blessings upon you all. Tranquil thoughts will bring words of wisdom to initiate many to a practice of love. You are far beyond your expectations within this life. We have brought you many seasons of life. Your purpose has begun.

Joy to those who suffer at the hands of those of ill will, their hearts and minds will be filled with wisdom. Amen.

Peace be upon you brothers of the earth."

WORDS BROUGHT FORWARD BY PETER

Peter was a Galilean fisherman who lived on the shores of the Sea of Galilee with his wife, his brother Andrew and his mother-in-law. Peter was the first Apostle to recognize that Jesus was the Messiah, the one promised by God to save his people. He gave up his life as a fisherman to lead others to Jesus.

The Transcripts:

28th February 2016

We know the love you bring before us in the world of light, in the world beyond yours. Your focus is true, your purpose divine, be not led astray with the science, but focus your mind with purpose and love, in truth, and in a manner befitting those of the light.

It was once said, that man was a beast with burden, his mind was controlled by other men. This is true of your race, but the few who break free and follow the light are the ones who would take man out of his slavery, *(out)* of his burden.

Keep purpose in your mind; allow others your heart *(and)* thoughts of mind as we relay messages of love before them through you. Let us focus your mind, harness the energy around you and what will be, what will come, you will see in cloud, in your mind, in vision.

We once viewed you from on high as mere creatures of devastation and destruction, but there is purpose. We are in existence beyond your imagination. Tonight we will convey our thoughts, our actions to your friends of the light, be not afraid, but be aware of our presence. Let go my son, be not afraid. Pious is he who comes before us from the light; mock us not for we are real, filled with love and purpose. Many times we have called to your thoughts and minds; few would listen. It's so sad to think that our love and wisdom was ignored by so many in your world of flesh, come with us on a magical journey through time.

Your desire of peace with man can only come about when man desires peace. His purpose, his nature is to destroy that which he does not understand. We will change that, his view, his mindset through you and others who work with the light. Caress us as we draw near, as your focus is guided to us by the love, thoughts of peace and desire.

One will come, his words of man, *to* man, he will lead the people of the world to that which was promised so long ago. As needles stabbing at the flesh, the pain will ease, purpose fulfilled. Judgment for all is assured, but kindness, tolerance is also assured, the paths are many and varied. You will understand the purpose of some, but like a rhyme, a song, so it will follow, the ultimate outcome and as a whole you will see his purpose.

We are aware of your thoughts my son, be not afraid of the task ahead that you are given. Devote your time before passing to this world, your way, your path will be cleared in that which has task.

29th March 2016

Tomorrow's another day when ignorance reigns supreme in the world of matter. Bring forth your words to those who would bear witness to their dignity and wisdom for the light shines within you all who work with these words.

Focus is great upon you at this time, relax your mind let us in. Combined together we are a force to be reckoned with; with immense power we will satisfy those needs of the divine to all. Compare us not with the enemy of love and truth, but to that of the Divine Teacher that comes before you. His remarkable words will fill your heart with love and joy, tenderness will be spared for those who require his blessing, frankness of mind should be spoken in these times of your troubled world, other people's needs are great upon your planet of life.

Your wealth of knowledge will combine to inspire others to the ways of the Lord. Ignorance is not tolerated by us, of the light, every man should go forth in his life and combat the evils of his mind, focus upon the light and the love of the Lord, his commandments were given for all who would listen.

You speak of nature turning against you; She *(Mother Earth)* is not against you but with you. Your ignorance has caused Her pain and so She must, like an itch, scratch at it to ease Her discomfort.

Knowledge is key for the future of your world, be prepared for us to come amongst you in the near future, uppermost your fears will be, but positive minds will see the true purpose of our light. Come amongst us and join us in prayer that we will bring you peace and tolerance.

Come amongst us with your mind see what there is to come, the cosmos is full of stars, some are small, some are large and some are dim, your focus and attention should be among the stars this evening. As the skies blacken and the storm grows, know that the light will shine through in due course.

Words cannot express the contempt we have for those who do not love Her *(Mother Earth)*, who disrespect Her and give Her cause for anger. Your positive affirmations are noted with favour upon you, be clear in our need for your salvation, for yours is the light upon which mercy will be given, to those who are worthy. This is not a purpose to hold as favour for oneself, but to be given freely throughout the world with love. Your positive attitude will seek out those who are attracted to your light, care for them, allowing them knowledge of the deep blue sea, encompass your mind in the world to come.

Why is it that we need to demonstrate our purpose for you all to believe our words, can you not see that the divine purpose of the words is for your freedom upon this world.

Go before the crowds and declare your love for God and Jesus, tell them of your love for the divine, words are spoken by you through us. Jesus said, "Let no man be a burden upon another for his purpose is divine to Him, and Him alone," connect your mind, body and soul to that of the light and know His name resides within your hearts.

Compel us not to defend our nations of love as we compel you not on your bended knees before us. Your love is worthy of admiration. Fortunes tell of wars that are won and lost within the hearts of men. What is fortune but a gift for man, to man? Only the light can balance one's heart before his time is due.

Combine your strengths in your circle of light as it grows before you, let us feed your minds and souls with purpose of love. Greetings to the ones of the light as they enter your lives, significant are the messages to you, for they are the Enlightened Ones, the Masters of the Universe that greet you, come forward before us with your tolerance and not ignorance, be blessed as we will bless you.

Prepare yourselves for the tasks ahead, for they are great. Commence your focus upon us this evening with purpose and need, allow us to enter your thoughts my son, bond with us in the light of the Lord our Father in heaven. Pictures in your mind will see us as we are. The negative souls of your world are without purpose their lives are blunt; they are blind to see the light, open their minds with joyous gratitude.

Topples the towers. *(Twin towers, 9/11)* **Caused heartache amongst your people,** they represent the plague upon your world of greed; their falling was no accident, as you know. Those who committed the sin are not worthy of mention but those who were lost have begun a journey of healing amongst us.

Terminate your minds desire of the house in this world. Your fortune relies on your belief; the cosmos will accept no other but the faithful, the lenient, the mother compassionate word of man. Continue your words with gusto let them be heard throughout your world by the media by which it is written, concentrate your mind, focus on us as we enter your room.

The twelve monkeys, they were of sin, they came before us in homage, who are monkeys but animals of the world, their function betrays you, for their minds are within you, characterise those of purpose, with love.

Chartered are the vessels that cross the seas to witness the avalanche of human souls, widen your heart to their mindful purpose beyond your stars.

Colossi has spoken before you once more, his words and prayers beseech you to forgive those that trespass against you, their purpose was two-fold, to ignite your hearts in love without fear, with purpose and knowledge to bear upon those of ignorance in your world. See us in your mind's eye as Fathers of the kingdom of heaven who watch over you with love and purpose. Commence your prayers with thoughts of love and aspirations, focus upon those who bring the words of the seasons of joy, tokens were given and the facts shared, commence your hearts mission so that joy be felt by those around you filled with purpose and love.

Tolerance of the many will be needed, as ignorance is vast in your world, commence your journeys from a position of love and notice that our eyes are upon you, feel us now in your mind as it travels the universe, the wonders to be seen.

Negotiations with your world will commence in your month of August, your tolerance is needed for there will be vast prejudice of our existence, commit your mind, let us pray for those that do not see the truth in word of the Lord.

Gather your thoughts my child; see the words as they bring life to those in the dark. Never before have we found more purpose than exists in your heart of love.

Toby was mentioned but not understood by those who would know, gather your friends for he's amongst them, know there are lessons to be learnt.

We are here once more with lessons, words for you all, substantial meanings have been brought to your attention, now hear these words, our commands to you with respect and love, your knowledge grows with vigour, your purpose is assured come before us with need in your heart and purpose in your mind.

Feathers will be given to those who speak the truth of the Lord, these tokens should be taken with love, pride in the knowledge that they were given for the journeys to come, be grateful for all the lessons to come. Your knowledge grows, impetuous you are, for more but patience is required. Like the sponge you need to absorb so much more than you could imagine, tenderness of heart is required, renounce those of ill will for their purpose is not Divine, come to us now.

Oh Divine one who rules the world of matter, let your voice be heard amongst the men of Earth, companions are needed to achieve the things that royalty will bring to you.

Focus your mind, be clear in thought, commence your words, say it with your heart so that people know your Divine guidance is with you, say a prayer of thanks for the purpose given to the one who sits on your right.

Their Father, Lord of mercy, be with us as we focus our minds upon the matters at hand, traverse your physical mind, you see us of men wearing robes of old, feast with us in the knowledge that man's burden will be lifted from him in the days to come.

31st July 2016

Let us now advise those who watch with words of wisdom, hold your families close to your bosom and know peace comes to the many. Troubled minds, troubled hearts, they bring a pattern so familiar within the life of man, your willingness to help one another as well as your bitterness are clear to be seen. Negotiate your minds to that of love and bring a new pattern to your minds in an armistice, for many who suffer degradation in degrees that you cannot imagine. Tumultuous times will come to fall in our being, hold onto your faith and that of mother Mary.

Whispers in your ears are heard many times in these last years, you have both borne witness to this many times for those lost to the world of spirit. Muster their energy and strength to assist you upon your paths. He spoke to her this day, of his love, warm and tender emotions. She is the mother of your children, respect her for what she is and to all who have borne children, love them with the care, deep in your heart, grasping their love with a tender kiss.

There are many in despair for their children who are lost, but know this my dears, no one is truly lost, for the arms of the Lord stretches far and wide throughout your kingdom. We all have purpose and need and a drive within to follow the powers given, do not despair that your sons and daughters who have moved on upon their paths into the light of heaven, know that they watch over you and rest in peace as their paths continue in a world of beauty beyond that of yours. We whisper in your ears so many times, as you gather your thoughts of your mothers who bore you.

Peter Speaks of Mobile Phones and Games

Mothering Sunday, hmm, many celebrate and do they understand the purpose? Families these days are dysfunctional, as the parents of many seem to have a will of their own. Why is that? For the family is the circle of light, of love that sustained them throughout their lives. Technology has brought them to their knees and nobody understands, only their need for ridiculous things.

We despair as we watch many disruptions in the minds of the young, for teachings have not reflected that of the Lord. Hmm, not important you say, but it is, so important. Morals need to be learnt and understood so that man can coexist in peace and love. The electronics of your youngsters' minds sway them onto the path of undesirables. We feel the need to speak out to those parents and say put away their toys, negotiate their love and bring them words of wisdom, so that their futures, not yours will have a brighter aspect. For we fear they tread a dangerous path at this time, the influence from the dark ones are brought through these instruments causing injustice, immorality and figments of their imagination that turn them to evil. The prime suspect is those of greed, for they know a man's weakness; torture and terror are highlighted so many times in these games of violence. Deny your children the viewing of such evil intent, they whisper in your ears, for their needs and wants are driven by that of the media.

21st August 2016

Peter is my name; I am a man whose soul once knew the master. Your impressions of love give warmth to those who fear a persecution. The men of your earth, I am here to bring you peace of mind, that even though tumultuous times are ahead, my love as Peter, the keeper of the gates of my master, I am here to comfort those, to bring them peace. Allow their hearts to soar as they focus their minds upon the Lord of light. We are beings that are revered in your world many years ago. Our words reflect the things of the Lord. We had a purpose unbeknown to us as poor men, and so it is once more a poor man will shine the light of Eden upon your earth. He has fortitude and grace, he will be amongst you soon, give him peace in your hearts and allow his words and aspects to shine like the bird song of the morning, the sweet voice of the Lord sings through him. I am Peter, servant of the Lord and of man. Bless, blessed is he on high.

18th September 2016

Bless you my son. Your purpose has become focused to many as we sit and speak tonight; it has been a while since we spoke as many have given their thoughts and purposes to you. Have an open heart, a forgiving mind, a practice of love to those who wish peace. I am Peter, the one who sits before the Lord.

I come this evening with pleasurable words of joy and comfort to all, to let them know that their many loved ones reside in a place of love. You all have purpose in heaven's eyes, some will fall, but most will receive the blessings. Give thanks for your lives as they bring you many gifts of knowledge. Some suffer greatly in your world, impoverished, beaten, slain, starved and imprisoned. So many awful things to witness to allow their spirit to move on.

You were no different, you were a man of slaughter my son, you put fear into the hearts of many, enslaved by their weapons. Their hunger for bloodlust is well documented upon your earth and well noted in the heavens. Hmm, you have liaised with one in particular many times my son; this is no accident he is there for your strength. She is there for your tolerance, as I am here for your brethren. Trust in the Lord and allow him your lion's heart to face those of ridicule. Encompass your lives, be not afraid my son. Forbearance is a word that means to trust, complete your missions and be aware of his love.

Many will scorn you as being a con artist, a man to be mistrusted, oh, how mistaken will they be when they have to eat their words upon their arrival on this side of life, but we shall not concern ourselves with them other than to say to them, open your hearts and minds my sons and daughters, allow your mind to be free and open to possibilities far beyond your aspects of life. Don't be sheltered and shuttered in by those of greed and domination who would hold your lives with fear, for there are no chains or prisons that can hold your spirit of love.

The dark ones await expectedly for the demise of man, but still the light shines and it will grow. For as long as there are those of the light, then the light will not be extinguished. We need to feed the flame of love, allow it to grow, for flames will consume all in good time with a measure of love. We wish you good fortune in life, not in aspects of material pleasures, but in that of love.

Peters Message to the Teachers of the World:

Teachers of the world unite. Within your circles of love you must emit radiating love to others. Common practice of man should be upheld within the light and love of heaven. Be not afraid of the dark that surround your lives, have faith and trust in him upon high. To those of the light I say this, complete your missions of life with love and your tasks with beauty in your hearts, enlighten the minds of those of the negative.

9th October 2016

Peter Brings Forward Calculations and Words of Warning:

Aspects of light we shine through the mass of your atmosphere.

Trigonometry was set once before to set a mind ablaze on a path and a trail of discovery. Your future is dependent upon your will to live, the mastery of numbers is essential to establish a practice by which your natures may change their future. We will give equations and measures. Your earth is a mass, a ball filled with electrons, neutrons, positrons and many other elements. Its pressures combined in the gases that formulate beneath the surface hide a terrible secret.

Explosions will be heard in the South Pacific on the 17th day. Calculations are given as a measure, 24 N. by Northwest latitude, longitude 5th parallel will be a number. There are many who would not acknowledge that these pressures build beneath the oceans, they know nothing of the nature of Earth and how she reacts to the indignities. I am Peter, you know me. A magnitude seven is a huge number within the nature of eruptions. We cannot calculate nor estimate the amount that will be lost as the surge of a time bomb, tidal wave washes over the South Pacific. Far-reaching, California in a wave of change previously forecast. We cannot guarantee the survival of all, but it will wash away the old, and New York may be affected by a backlash. Rumours of old platelets that lay beneath the structures and foundations of those buildings have been forgotten or ignored. Ah tumultuous times as the fractures of the earth split.

You will wipe away the tears for those that are lost. Nature is the dominant species of your Earth, you are but the fly who is swatted on the floor.

Our time has come Michael. Thank you.

James the Apostle

Of the three apostles who comprised the inner circle of Jesus' disciples (Peter, James and John), we know the least about the apostle James. We do know, however, that the apostle James was the eldest brother of the apostle John and that their father's name was Zebedee (their mother's name was Salome.) There is some evidence that James was the first cousin of Jesus the Messiah and had been acquainted with Him from infancy. It is believed that his mother Salome was the sister of Jesus' mother Mary. The apostle James was the first apostle to suffer martyrdom. By order of Herod Agrippa I, James was beheaded in Jerusalem about the feast of Easter, AD 44.

The Transcripts:

12th July 2016

I am James, the keeper, I am the master of all who pass to spirit. Our commitment to all living creatures is a guarded one. Your paths must tread on a specific direction to attain your goals in life. We cannot help but notice as your friends remark upon the words, only love is obvious, hmm, they tremor before the words, for they are of the living. Their desperate minds cling to the hope that God may forgive them for their sins before they pass and hope that their knowledge of spirit will guide their path. We grant you these words to give to them, "Their sins will be forgiven, for there is no sin that isn't unworthy of forgiveness for he who confesses to the

Lord of his crimes. He must apply his caution to those who would lie and attempt to cheat their way, as they would be found, they cannot hide the truth".

18th September 2016

James speaks of George Harrison

Oh happy days, oh happy days. when Jesus walked! Ha! A song of love sang by a man of innocence. Maybe! For those words were inspired from those of beyond as he meditated with his sitar. Ah, George! You know his name, Harrison. His life was terminated with an illness of pain. He worshipped others, not realising that in truth it was of God. Harry Krishna he was called. An alternative religion you might think, but nonetheless, regardless of your naming, worship of the Lord will take many forms, many practices, and as long as that heart is true to the words of love, then what matter in a name? He came within anguish, a need of love, his song raised the many spirits of man. Combat your fears my son, of the evils of your world. For you live in a time of choosing when the negativity is high, but the blossom of truth will open to the hearts and minds of man.

18th September 2016

James Speaks of The Geneva Conference

As negotiations fail in the Geneva conference, a reckoning will come to all who have mistrusted and mistreated those of their responsibility. Leaders are not chosen by man, but are placed with purpose to bring outcomes of peace, and those who choose the negative practices should be aware that their sins are worst of all. Promises made should be kept and not pardoned by the rules of man.

22nd September 2016

James Speaking of Jesus

Never let it be said that man is not a purposeful being, for he has many purposes. I am James, the deliverer of many words through the mind of this man. I once walked with the father of love, never truly understanding his purpose. He was a friend, a man of equal measure who brought the light to my eyes. He once said to me, "James my friend, never be afraid to let go of your fears in the face of adversity. For thou art with you in the world of love and spirit. The mere mortals of men are but a fast and passing phase in the life of your souls being. Come with me, be a man of love and light and rise to the glory of our Lord our father; with the heavenly right to baptise those who would cometh to you. Comfort those of meagre means and filled with sorrow, hear their words with compassion of the heart and bring blessings to their lives with meaning and purpose. For thou art with you, the father, the son, and the Holy Ghost, be praised."

29th September 2016

James Speaking of Jesus

I am James, we have spoken before. Many speakers this evening have come with their wishes and love. The sanctions set against you by the ministers of the parties will be fierce ones; they will not agree to allow those in through the door *(immigrants)*. Why is it that humanity can no longer share the wealth of the earth as given by the master, our Lord, father in heaven? We once preached words of praise in mystical times of the Lord, who had preached to those from the Mount, giving them glorious words. His name was known to many as the carpenter lad. He was not afraid to show his worth to the peoples of our time. His fear of unpopularity was real, but he knew his father adorned with love and would guide his steps.

Do not be despondent with your thoughts my son, for many tread that weary path of enlightenment for others. It is not always possible to reach the hearts of men, but if you plant a seed, the seed will grow. But plant it in the fertile lands of those hearts and minds who are happy to accept the light of the Lord. There are some who would not understand, but the seed will grow nonetheless and bring an uprising of enlightenment in their minds.

FRANCIS OF ASSISI

St. Francis of Assisi, patron saint of animals and ecology, was born in Italy around 1181 or 1182. In 1224, Francis became the first saint in history to receive the stigmata (the wounds of Christ crucified). On 4th October, 1226, Francis died in the town of Assisi and was quickly canonized by Pope Gregory IX

The Transcripts:

29th May 2016

Francis of Assisi, he wishes to speak of the things to come in this world, his purpose is of goodwill to those who would listen:

"My memories of Earth are long and vivid, for I was a man of reputation for good, my path was illuminated by the Lord as he came to me once before to tell me of the things that are to come in my life. I sat in my chambers, my head bowed in prayer to praise Him of the light and to give thanks for my being. I complied with those of power, not understanding that I had issued a notice of intent to those on high. My disregard for the peoples of my own nation was my downfall and my love was that of a man and not of spirit. My mind is now in focus and I give thanks that I was able to shed light upon the Lord and the Angels of life.

Frequently I was spoken to by Merlin, who whispered my name in the shadows of the light.

I am no longer a man, but that of spirit, many worship my name, but in truth they worship that, that made my reality.

The Lord was my focus, His blessings were many, but I did not understand my purpose as they came for me. The Shepherds of light will once more shine upon your world to face the challenges before you. You must obey their lead as they guide you through these dark times you must endure.

I sat many times in my chamber, my head bowed in prayer in worship to the Lord, I could have done so much more but I was focused upon Him, not understanding my responsibilities to man and those within my parish. I seek refuge now in the light of the Lord, I obtained His forgiveness and my passion has evolved, my ponderous mission will begin again to bring about a peace of mankind."

7th July 2016

Compel your minds to listen to the words of Francis (St Francis of Assisi) as he wishes to speak with you on behalf of the Lord our Father:

Tragic circumstances befell my people in the past years, I was a man of distinction, a man unworthy to enter the light as I had not achieved my tasks in full, never aware of my failures in my life. I wish to relay thoughts to those who have purpose in life, not to ignore the meaning of your purpose. To deliver your aspects with a responsibility to others in a meaningful manner, respectful of their lives, for they look upon their leaders as men of authority, but they are disappointed at the attitudes that they show and their arrogance towards the lower classes.

I was a priest in a sanctuary of the Lord, my purpose was to give blessings and focus to the people at my church. I was a man not worthy of his purpose. I need to explain that I was a man of faith, never quite comprehending the enormity of my tasks that lay ahead between my position and responsibility to that of the people who looked to the church. The church was a symbol of Christ and not that of "The Saviour", it was there to benefit those of our land as they struggled in their lives, to bring them peace and sanctuary, healing and a feeling of need in the brotherhood of men.

I commend you for the tasks ahead and know this, my love and guidance are with you, for you to take instruction and become a better man than I.

They honoured me within the church and parish calling me a man of great faith, bestowing titles upon me so unworthy. A sainthood, what does that mean? It's just a name, another title. For me there was more that I needed to be aware of, I appreciate the title given, but I would appreciate it more for those of the world today to look to their hearts and find that God exists within them, to follow their hearts with pride, not in arrogance or deception, but in love and peace to help their fellow man in their anguish in times of need. Blessed is he who walks the path of light and finds himself amongst his brothers, peace to you all, God bless.

4th September 2016

Francis wishes a word once more to bring words of comfort to those in desperate situations:

"We are in despair of the multitude of intolerance set against man. I was a former minister of the Lord, I also brought justice within the realms of the church to those sinners who could not see the error of their ways. The master taught us to be gentle but firm, for his teachings are of a great need in this time my boy. You have inspired many to look beyond the words of wisdom, to see the secrets therein. His purpose will be upon you and the father of heaven will guide all of the light. I was once canonised by the Pope, John Paul, I was unworthy of a position of state, my status was of no consequence, for I wish to shine a light of the Lord upon you all now, with the sermon of love direct from the world of spirit. Come my people, sit within the light and the love of the Lord as I stand before you as a witness to God. He interprets life as that of his own. His guidance is assured to those who whisper his name with love and gratitude of their being. "Let there be light," he once said at the beginning of the dawn, and so it will again, he will shine his light of love and purpose upon you. Allow your thoughts to become that wisdom. My name is Francis, I am but the masters guide upon your behalf."

30th October 2016

Francis once spoke of the love that he shared with those many nations. He grants you purpose and greets you as a friend.

Your mind is a maze of communication and obstacles laid before.

"I was a man who lived many years ago in the realm of men. A host of voices called to me as a preacher, as a layman, to help those in despair with mercies of love and of him upon high. I frequently asked myself, why did I take this path? For there were many pitfalls, but on reflection it was a joyous time of learning as yours will be too. For all men of purpose have their own paths and blockages to overcome, yours is no different. Keep a weather eye upon the pattern of life Michael, do not betray your thoughts with anger or injustice. Control your emotions, as this will demonstrate to others your intent and belief. I was called a saint, truly a name of distinction, but in practice I was merely a man who held the tulip of life. I cannot comment on today's situation as it is for the elders to oversee, but I can issue you with a practice of love and tell you that you must fight for the right for the freedom of those whose hearts are blighted by worry and torment. You are a healer of minds in many ways unseen by you. Now we express our thoughts of devotion to your purpose. God bless."

WINSTON CHURCHILL

Born 1874 – Died 1965.

Statesman, writer, orator and former British Prime Minister. He served as Conservative Prime Minister twice – from 1940 to 1945 (before being defeated in the 1945 general election by the Labour leader Clement Attlee) and from 1951 to 1955.

The Transcripts:

11th July 2016

We once more bring forward a friend who will speak. His name is well known to you and to your nation, help him.

(Note: On the recording of these trance sessions, the tone of voice for Winston Churchill comes through very clearly, including his mannerisms of speech and sometimes irreverent terms which would not be acceptable today. – He is often accompanied by a 'Being of Light' who either introduces him or comments on his words – Winston's words are all indicated by "Speech Marks")

"**Once more unto the breach, I am Winston** who has spoken before. Messages of doom and gloom cloud your mind. Wish I was there to assist, ah, I was given hell! All those promises made at the end of the war to unite the world in the new United Nations. We plan such wondrous things in the hope that war would not rear its ugly head once more, but once more our nations are slipping towards the inexorable, final, driven.

Winnie and I are astounded that our nation has not learnt to love, learnt to live in peace and harmony with tolerance.

I was in the Tory party, not a popular party, but nonetheless we saw the country through tumultuous times. We raised the banner of love as we formed a united stance against those of intolerance who would wreak havoc in the world. Their purpose is lost, their fundamentals have been put to one side as the nation's use them for the purpose not intended. Ahh, despairingly we watch as our countrymen become intolerant of the nations around them, allowing negative forces through the back doors. They stand by and watch and scream, "Equal opportunities for all!" You have become an open island and like an open wound, this will fester. *(Note: The word 'Winnie' comes through although Winston Churchill's wife was called Clementine, so it possibly ought to be 'Clemmie', however for the sake of sticking to the authenticity of the words brought through on the recording, we have not changed it.)*

Mmm, a beautiful dream to see a world shared by all with love and tolerance, no hatred, no despicable wars. We cannot understand why it is that the peoples of the nation of Britain have not learnt, my children you play with fire not understanding the pain that will be brought upon you.

Not all is lost, for there is one who will come soon in a manner respectful of me, he will not be welcomed, but he sees and knows the values of Britain as a nation, as a lion. Once more we must come to the rescue of those Europeans who sit in turmoil wondering what the hell to do! Sorry for the language, but it is needed. Mmm, complications will occur within the talks surrounding your freedom, they will not relinquish or allow you to terminate your alliance, they will batter you with much indignity calling upon your nation to pay an outrageous fee, for they know the strength and unity that Britain would bring. Mmm, once more you must batten down the hatches for the onslaught to come, be a leader of your nation with your words to bring a focus upon those in power, who may or may not understand the ways to keep Britain safe. Complemented you are by those around you who assist and help, for they are your backbone. The many to understand the need for peace. Mm, enough we will leave now, but contemplate your options in the final stand-off. Countless sheep you are, not really knowing which way to turn."

24th July 2016

Tributes paid this day to a man who led his country, and many nations through fortunes of war. Tributes were paid at his death by the masses who followed his leadership. His respect for others was great in his time. He cannot understand how it is that men of destruction are permitted shelter within the homes of Britain, for they are hidden in a masquerade of lives, waiting for the time, to the beat of the drum to call them into action.

"I was once a man of many desires and beliefs, I did not care for those who had responsibility, or authority. I was a man alone, compelled on purpose and task to follow my heart. For any hour of my need, my wisdom, my thoughts brought many to heel as we fought the Hun. How my gratitude goes to those of my family who sit on the seat of power. My gratitude goes out to them who gave life to those souls in persecution. We fought hard days indeed. I was a man of distinction who followed the rules of the Lord, I was relentless as I crossed the T's and dotted the I's within Parliament. Benches, they found me obnoxious, but they learned to their bitter taste, I was a man with fortitude who would not heel to their demands. They fought me many times in the seats, in the corridors of power. I was there to demand justice for those of the weak, they did not see me as a leader of men, but as an upstart of the House of Commons. Hmm, my persistence brought great results in those years. Torments, my favours, hmm, were met in kind. For many of the earth I relinquished no power, but stood firm as I watched the Hun increasingly torment those of the west and of the east. I need not tell you that I was a man of determination, of great esteem; I brought justice to the eyes of those who would enslave the peoples of the earth. Ha! They never met one like me before! They tried many times to extinguish my existence within this world, one attempt came close, but I was observant and I was a man who knew how to fight, and by God, did they receive a battle!

There are many secrets in Whitehall of the times when I had to muster many allies, it was an uphill battle for they could not see how we could resist such an onslaught, but I knew, I knew that my purpose was to stand before them and demand justice for the injustices done to those of Germany. Frankfurt in particular held a seat of mass demonstration against him who would rule the world, they were extinguished, never seen again, hmm the tyranny and torment was immense.

I am sad to see many of the world today have no backbone for the fight to come, you must realise that the powers to be have so little backbone. Hmm, Clement Attlee, he knew, he was spineless, ha! But he never met me! Hmm, but in secret we had talks, our missions, our failures; he was able to support me in many ways not seen by the nation of men. My purpose was not of greed but that of being British, standing up for my country with a fist of iron to beat upon those who would see us as slaves. That spirit exists in many today, and it needs to be unleashed by one man who is brave enough to take on the Houses of Parliament. Lord Attlee, he would agree; in his time he was weak. We watch now despondently, what hope have you, hmm, those Frenchies who turn their back on you, spite you in public. We mean no discrimination, for people are people, but you mustn't ever let your side down. Muster your strengths, become one in unity and strength. You have begun a purpose upon which you must now deliver. Let the lion roar once more at the world of man, let that bulldog bark his commands to those of ignorance. Madam, show them the way of love and tolerance, not enslavement or bitterness. Thank you.

We spoke of Barbara Castle before, *(The Arcturians transcript of 12th July 16)* and Margaret Thatcher, *(The Arcturians Transcript of 6th July 16)* these are women of determination. Once more a woman leads your country, what has happened to man? Never in my day! Mm, my Winnie *(Clemmie)* she knew her place within our house, but she had strength, she gave me strength in ways unimaginable, my love for her was immense. We are once more together, hmm, overseeing not just our lives, but those of men. Have courage as I had courage against the Hun. Bring about your purpose."

31st July 2016

"Who I am? I was once a leader of the nation of the kingdom. Hmm we have spoken before, oh yes, such terrible times are before you. A woman leads the party, her handbag is sat beside her in the talks today, ah, never in my time, men were men, but times are changed, spineless the many, they give up the fight before the battle is won. Ha, not in my day! I became aware of my being, my youth, as I played my games of strategy, we had no instruments of violence, chess was my game. Hmm, it played a part in my life many times as I fought in the years. Ah, Clement, he was an adversary in chess! Ha! Well he couldn't beat me within the house!

We sit together now, oh how we despair, complicated lives. We sang our hymns before him in the church of love and our hearts sang out as did our prayers. How many today I wonder, have the backbone to sit before him on high and declare their love. I was a man of distinction; I cared not for those of weak minds and hearts, for I was a lion, a pitch! Ha, strange words! Well strength was my character; oh, I do miss some things of life that bought me pleasure. Aww, my Havana's, to sit quietly in the chair in my home, my study, a sip of that sweet nectar, hmm no longer permitted, hmm that's okay, I had my time, my time. Hmm, I reflected upon many things of my life, I was Catholic you know, ooh, not many know, my secrets are many! My journals of life, they are kept behind locked doors for there are many sensitive subjects upon which I spoke. I cannot deny I was a man of intolerance. Ah, when the lion roared you heard his voice! Nations became familiar with my thoughts and deeds. Hmm, my values wear pride in many of the nation of Great Britain, hmm, we would not be beaten in the streets, in the houses, oh we had plans to extinguish the Hun. Strange word to you today, as there is tolerance and the spineless, blind to the things that are set against Great Britain. But we know that those times are gone, times to change. Once more you must find the courage within you to bring about a peace. Those crazy days should not again be heard. Tragically my Winnie *(Clemmie)* she passed. I was there, with open arms to greet her. We are truly one spirit and God bless you all upon your journey.

Inspirational words indeed! His memories are many of battles and fights, he was a warrior. There are many forms of warriors, those who fight for the light and those of the dark, but know that yours is of the light. It is your choice to make within your lives, your purpose will be done despite your thoughts. Your lives and patterns are set in ways beyond that of your understanding. Winston, a man of courage, this is what he conveys to you all, to have strength, to follow your convictions despite the many that are set against you. We are grateful for his strength and his courage. He too had weaknesses, as you heard. Minor infringements, but that is not to say that it is okay. You must all unite in love or there will be an ending of despair, that is all, God bless.

4th August 2016

Opposition parties are becoming restless this evening, as intolerance of aspects of hate. A party leader. Osborne, is a reckless man who waved his wand before the many. How can man of desire truly note the need of the nation they serve, he desires the covenant post, and will attempt a coup within the party.

Many Tory leaders have come to us with their righteous thoughts; their temperaments are now attuned, as they must begin a purpose to understand the nations. We gave you Churchill who spoke his words and Lord Attlee, he was a man of discretion, he thought that peace would come if tolerance was given. He betrayed him and his country, he was taught a sharp lesson, that those of the dark should not be toyed with, but dealt a blow to stab at the heart of their evil doings. Their mistrust and belief will betray their minds for their own misgivings.

"Clement Attlee, he was a sincere man, he didn't reckon for the dogs of war in his time. Once more I asked my nation to sit with me, I was a man of intolerance who became a leader of a nation to fight as the lion. They understood my mind as I led the party to power. We reasoned with him, that evil man, that Hitler, he was the Hun. I had battled so many times before, his thoughts and deeds were of domination. We were not about to be taken out of existence by an arrogant man. I once visited him in his den; his arrogance was astounding to me. I sat there quietly, listening to his words; he was a man, a tortured mind and soul. We could not reason with him, for his path was dark. One of the many secrets that is withheld from you, is the negotiations that took place to reason with this man of dark. To allow him power to specific regions, but he was greedy, he did not want that little bite, he wanted all of the cherry. We would not permit that. His nation bore the brunt of the storm. They would meet in many places to adopt his attitude of hate towards the Jewish communities within his lands. He tore them apart, hmm." *(Note: We can find no documentary evidence to suggest that there was a meeting, but of course many meetings were held in secret.)*

"History is a great teacher; your eyes have been closed to the lessons learnt. Become the master of your destinies, do not let the sleeping lion slumber. You are part of a great nation and peoples. We are now in spirit, we are masters no longer, but we anticipate a downfall and disillusionment that will swallow the lion as he sleeps. You are the British nation; your cries of freedom are once more heard but ignored. Ah, do you think they would tolerate leaving Europe? But oh, what a sorry state. How I remember my parklands as being a place of solitude where I could walk amongst the trees of the woods, my head deep in thought, my tactical mind coming up with devious plans. Hmm, some could not understand how my mind worked. I never slept, seldom ate, but I found a comforting glass to while away the hours.

I am certain that one day my spirit will reign once more to those of disillusionment, to bring a purpose of the need. God granted me life; I respected his name. Now and again I feel encumbered to seize upon the opportunity to speak my mind. I spoke many words of wisdom that inspired a nation to fight the battle to come. Let your words ring out; let your values sing out the words of praise to your countrymen. Never let them bring about their purpose to annihilate your ways of England.

Winnie *(Clemmie)*, she sits with me, she sees as I do, how one mistreats another with such arrogance in your modern times. We are glad we have no longer to play a part in the living, but we feel the sadness."

25th August 2016

"Courage is needed indeed, myself and Winnie *(Clemmie)*, we watch, wait. We would once more like to give you a lesson in life. We have been before and we are granted by the grace of God, to once more visit you in your humble home, to bring messages of life and encouragement so that you all may understand that you must have courage and love in your lives. For it is this that gives you the fortitude to be great and strong. You live your lives under an umbrella, which envelops you, hmm, you do not understand the politics of this country, ah, for it reaches far and wide beyond your shores. I was never a man to take a hit below the belt I stood up and stood firm, hmm, they could not beat me. This strength you have, is a man of England. He must be brought forward as the lion roars. Ah, yes Winnie *(Clemmie)*, she was by my side, many times assisting in my decisions, she was my guiding light and still rules my life, ha! Well she is me, my other side, as you also have your companions of life. It is no accident that you carry burdens within your lives, there is a heavy responsibility upon you all to ensure that your children and your grandchildren respect each other. If you do not change the minds of the men in power then your ways will perish. All those lives, given and taken, me amongst one of them who caused so many deaths. Trials and tribulations, hmm, I fought as a lion, never understanding the human aspect and the consequences of my orders. It was easy to sit in my chair, in my bunker, my phones around me. As I smoked my cigar in deep thought, Mary *(Note: Mary was Winston Churchill's youngest daughter, possibly this should again be his wife)* she would call my name, "Winston, please rest." There is no time for rest, there will be no time for you to rest either, take your words write them in the book of love. Your name grows, others will assist. Be not afraid but stand like the lion and defend your ground, never let them defeat your words. Hmm, they know the truth, they see, they sit, wait and listen. Do not fear them for they cannot take away your love, only your life of your body."

4th September 2016

He spoke to you once before, this man of courage. He wishes a focus:

"Our nation is grieving for the democracy that has gone. I was astounded in disbelief that our health system was to be punished, not for valour but for greed. Common sense must prevail, when those of the Tory party must oblige the people, that the privileges of life that they consider themselves to be entitled to. Tremendous amounts of courage will be required by those of small means, they will be inspired by the one who steps in through the door of Number 10 in the fall, in the autumn of your years. She will not become an asset to the government of England, for she has an agenda by which her name will forfeit the right of the party leadership. He will step forward, hmm, to announce his interest. His name resounds among many of the backbenches, they applaud his unique ability to reach the people as the lion did. I cannot be there to cause disruption amongst the house, but I know that my spirit will intervene as he gives the information of the treacherous intent. We have become accustomed to our way of life and our situation and are pleased to announce that we are of a spiritual being. Still we watch, in hope that the impoverished of your world will stand up and rise and once more become heard. It will take much discipline, for they, mm, must be in agreement to participate. How can you compromise those minds of greed? The state of the nation is of great concern to myself and Winnie *(Clemmie)*. The barbarians of life will shortly be answered in a menacing attack on the public. Their purpose grows within your Internet. In leaps and bounds they cover up and hide their intentions, hmm, what a mess, what troubled times you will once more endure on the streets of London and lands of England."

13th September 2016

"Trinity College, the Master's room. Ha, many times I spent in there, making my excuses for my intolerable behaviour. Hmm, you know me Michael; I was a man who would not be ordered by anybody. I had a natural ability to withstand punishment dished out by the masters of that college, they knew my name, 'Winston!' they called, pah! They called me and demanded me their adulation. Boy I was, grown to the man, changed the course of time, do I wonder I was a most indignant young man, my youth of officer and gentleman of the British Army, a Cavalryman, I sat there upon my horse, proud to be British, "I'll show the 'fuzzy wuzzies' a thing or two." The strength of my hands, the romance in those times egged them on to many hopes and dreams. My ancestral home was paramount in my mind. I miss it so, I seldom go back. Many times as a boy within that palace, I would lose myself, they would call my name and search me out, but I hid well within the walls of that palace, ha, ha, ho, ho! If only they knew! My hidden treasures, still there to this day. Well, what do they know? Of the hand of steely courage, a hidden place to be discovered, emblems of my state. The palace is gone and I am no more on the spirit of man.

Jameson was my friend. Come now Michael, open your heart and mind to steely courage needed to exploit your mind, thoughts of an Englishman, that of the lion within. God Bless and Amen."

22nd September 2016

"Conservatively they will crush those who would shout against them on the floor of Parliament, they are the Conservatives, they have no need for upstarts. Would I be there to greet their indignation! I would give them hell my boy, humph! They look at me and think 'Who is that old man who stands before us in defiance of the old ways' I am the party leader, I was and am a man with much strength. Hmm, I may be a spirit my boys, have no doubt, my will exists still within the party members, Hmm. We have fought many times in the benches, in the corridors of power, Hmm, I had my time. Aw, I gave them hell, hmm they did not forget me in a hurry you know! When I would call to them and say I am your leader, you will follow me. Humph. Ah, days are gone, I had my time, but I respect your words my boy. Humph. I am here, as I know you were once a man of intolerance too, you were a warrior, a fighter, now a leader of men as I was to the many. I know war is a disgrace and brings no pleasure to anyone who has a heart and a will for peace. My Winnie *(Clemmie)*, ho, what a woman! She would care for me; she knew that it was time, that big rest. Hmm, I would pace the corridors of the home. Day and night, no rest, hmm, I was a man not to cross. We rest now, in this heavenly place, our time done and although I bring you words in the voice of that man, know that I have changed. I've seen the light and the errors that I made in my life. Some aspects must be retained as we march on through our days. What I know as good ones. What is to become of me? Well, time will tell. The halls of learning are great, my mistakes were many, I will work to resolve, to repent those errors. Your sincerity is your weapon of choice my boy. You will audit a sense of love. We will focus on you once more, when the time is needed, my gratitude to my party friends for their loyalty was astounding."

29th September 2016

"You seek the lion, I hear your mind, Samuel? No. Thomas? Maybe! Ha, ha, ha! We all like a few games on this side of life you know, hu, hu... hum, you recognise me! Hmm, it's hard to describe how I feel at this time, to see my countrymen with such shame. They exceed their authorities, not establishing the will of the people, hmm, what a disastrous outcome for that country of mine. Oh, those Frenchies who torment the government of the house with their accusations of intolerance against those beings who would invade our shores. Do they not know that we are British? Was it not us that came to their aid many times? Did they not welcome us in their streets of Paris? Ah, did we not give them victory over those Prussians? Hmm, they forget many things; they have become bold in their manner towards the nations of peace. They are no longer the nations of Europe, but are that of the hungry wolf who bays at the door, for the pittance to be had. Though I was a man once more, hmm that he would feel my indignity, ah, that grieves me so that I can no longer mastermind a plan. Ah, well, c'est la vie, but remember you are British, you are made of sterner stuff than to let some Frenchy walk all over you! Let's see that spirit once more rise, not in anger, but in obstinance. Let him hear our voices of discontent, hmm Angela Merkel, hmm, hmm, what can I say! A scheming woman I have no doubt. Masterminded many things of intolerance towards our nation, she has many regrets of her own. We should not say, but they were indignant people, an axe to grind I fear. Hmm, she will learn her lesson in the near future, she has made mistakes that will not be forgiven for allowing them in to torment her peoples. Tis a worry, for those Nazi's are never gone, they lay in wait like the wolves at the door. Truly your heart and mind are of emotion, let them hear my indignity from this side. We must speak in terms of love to prosper. And, I learnt my lesson well, for I made decisions, hard decisions, which I came to regret in my demise. But I am forgiven as I walk upon your path to guide your hand. I am your strength, that lion strength. Take my hand and let us walk together in the face of adversity and allow the world to know we are British, not to be messed with, ha, ha, ha! I must go, others wait. Ah thank you for your purpose."

10th October 2016

"Monstrous men whose allegiance to the dark will be obvious. That his collaboration with the Kremlin will become mentioned in the corridors of power. *(sigh)* Will man never learn?

I must have my say I cannot sit any longer, forgive me. Friends, I was a man of greatness that brought many to focus to fight those of intolerance of our time. Hmm. I watch and see many things in your world today; they are not so different to my time. Different faces, different values and such terrible weapons of destruction that I never faced. Hmm, you will need to have strength and tolerance and a willingness to love all to overcome the shadow of darkness. Hey, there is always light at the end of the tunnel, hmm. We have given words of encouragement and we would like you to become free of your burdens. Go now in peace with the blessings of the Lord and a remembrance of those who have passed these tragic times. Valance of the dictators that will draw your world for intolerance."

20th October 2016

Churchill was a man of an outspoken manner; his past visits were of a measure of love for his people and his nation. We have long since evaluated his path as being a manner of noble birth within your lands. He once more has words of encouragement for his fellow Britons:

"She will not deny my words as I speak of authority. Cast out her allusions of grandeur as she speaks of independence of the isles. Who is she to say that Britain is no longer great? What does she know of the world today to dictate to others in that obstructive manner? She declares herself a woman of the world, a martyr to the cause. She cannot presume to bring division of the Isles of Britain. Remain united, as this is your only strength and power. Be not led by women who have more in their purse than their minds. Tolerance will be needed as she speaks to the house of representatives in a sombre mood of defeat."

Turmoil in your world, hmm, there, this is what comes of ill will and a practice not of the light.

23rd October 2016

"It emerges by thought indeed, the actions that will bring intolerance, not joy. Can I say, I was a master of illusion myself as I pulled the strings of Parliament to initiate my scheme. My thoughts, my wishes were not that of a heinous man, but of someone who understood the necessaries. I was granted God's wisdom, ah, as some call me, a tyrant. Sometimes as you live your lives you have to take actions, that of irregular and necessary to bring a purpose for an end. Ah, those Hun were cunning in their ways, but we have grown accustomed to them. We sit in the spiritual realms separated by layers of light and dark, we are by all means nowhere in that place of light, but we will sit with a measure of love and tolerance towards others. Life was a chain of events that you must endure to bring purpose to your spirit."

1st November 2016

"Ah, my boy, ha, we know how you feel! Your wisdom grows. I have much displeasure in what I see; nevertheless I am here once more. I see a government of intolerance. They hide their truth behind their lies; they do not wish you to see their aims. They are impervious to the wishes of the nations, I was pretty much the same, I too had a single-mindedness. I didn't listen when I should have listened; I served a purpose. It is true to say I evolved, as many must. Their secrets will be divulged shortly to elect a new government, a shock result, maybe! Only time will tell. There is a new party that grows within the political system of your country, hmm you have not heard of them, but they exist as a private organisation of many women who meet in secretive society. Their intention is not demonstrative, their intention is not of deceit, so they see the corruption that lies within all of your country. They wish a new beginning, a new party that perhaps can set a new road for all. Your focus is lost, be blessed my boy."

24th November 2016

"And there's a reminder, your ones must speak. And your politicians will listen to his to his rhetoric of hate. He establishes a position within your government, Ah, I have seen many things. You know of many politicians and their will to bring about aspects of domination. Your thoughts are stretched as you witness the commercialisation of your world, is there no end, will there be no peace? Your questions are many and may be fulfilled in time, but only by man's desire to bring peace upon himself. Hmm. My Winnie *(Clemmie)* used to say, "Be your own man with extreme measures within your policies." She was right; I had many thoughts. Many illusions were placed on my desk of office. How could I ignore those learned men? I became a man of distinction bringing about my purpose, as I saw it.

I served many years knowing of situations of danger, I learnt my many lessons in the corridors of power of nationalism, communism, Hmm. Our greatest achievement was to bring about an end to those Nazis. Their foothold and grip were immense, even extending to our shores in the thoughts and minds of men and women of greed. I was never aware that those in my cabinet were of a deceitful mind, but I brought my purpose to bear. You sit and listen to my tales of woe, let me tell you of some things, facts you may not know. I had many secrets in the corridors of power, we had liaisons with many of that time, Eisenhower, yes Hitler and those leaders of the nations, Mussolini among them. Domineering men who saw that the battle of life was for their benefit. Hmm. We negotiated many times, secrecy was paramount. That Hitler, was a man of mistrust. Do you know, we almost gave up the island in search of peace, but his domineering attitude was overwhelming, can I say as a man of the times that I was deeply concerned.

Attlee, he attempted to bring peace, but was expelled for his thoughts. Your mind cannot comprehend such a thought; do you think peace is won entirely by the blood of men? For it is politics that begins and ends many conflicts of your world. What you face at this time is not of men, take this as you will, but it is a dark force that needs to be extinguished, and only those of the light and their love will dominate these beings.

Your governments, they sit back and watch the torment, the turmoil, for fear of bringing retribution upon themselves and they have no backbone for a fight. Iraq was too much, they are frightened. They must stem this tide, stop this darkness. The Kremlin, Washington, United Emirates and all those of power must join together. United Nations, hmm, well, they have buckled what we made promises of. They are overwhelmed by those men of greed who would, for a dollar or two pass a paper, hmm, and their worthiness is no longer as it was, for they don't remember those terrible times of conflict, but they will reap what they sow. Hmm. They must bring balance once more before it is overwhelmed by the dark forces, not of your world. They must see that liberty and freedom are paramount and no man has the right to beat upon the other for the sake of a little land. Blessed is he, the peacemaker."

Your words are not listened to, you fear, hmm, little do you know of their impact upon others in your world, as they will spread to bring about a thought in men.

The females, the women of your world are the angels by which the darkness could be extinguished! They are the mothers of children, and their purpose is love and family. There are those who have succumbed, but the greater majority are the mothers of your world. The mothers of your brothers, your sisters, and they care for their families. Many see a need to be dominant, but in truth, women are the dominant species and will dictate to those who rule your world. Yes, even he will be ruled by his wife!

There is an influence that will have an impact in the very near future, a team of ladies will begin a march as the suffragettes of the modern day. They will insist equal measures are brought to all. She who sits in power was a choice, she is a woman whose natural influences will bring a care but also a loyalty to the party. It is affected by the men who would dominate her, for she is just a woman, what does she know? Men will rule the world, do you think? We think not.

To the men of your world, be not ashamed of your feminine side, allow it to shine. We do not mean this in acts of love, but in your thoughts, in your ways. Do not be afraid to show your caring. Ah, there is much to learn and all will share in their own good time. This is life, for each and every one there comes a time when your soul and spirit must live as the other. Hmm. The progression of the soul will continue far beyond your lives. Your own personal beings will continue, only those who shut out the light will take a backwards step. Eventually they will see and ask for forgiveness. Reach out to the door of light.

Have a care with those you teach, for some are like barbed wire. They are smooth but twisted and spiked and they will attempt to dominate your words as their own. We tell them now, we know of your practices, we know that you intend to use these many things which are said, to highlight your own aspect of being. Hmm, ha, ha, we know, we are no fools, for in your way in your selflessness, you will assist us. Speak the words Michael, on a care for he understands that even if you proclaim them your own, the words will stand for themselves and bring about intended change, you may think you profit by them, really? Because if you do not truly believe what is said and only see it as a game, then your soul will carry the burden of your deceit, and a light will continue to burn. Have a care."

These words are not intended for one, the host understands this, and brings them to you free of aspects of greed and avarice. He understands that they are not of personal gain. We would like to speak to many of those of the light who consider it a practice of love, hmm, be careful that your words are not bringing a focus upon yourselves, do not view it as an opportunity for business. There are very few who will do this, for they have a beautiful belief in the light and the work of that they do. But there are the minority, there are those who would view it as a business opportunity, be careful.

Blessings to you, people of the world, have gratitude for your being and know that the Lord watches over you. I am the being of the light, respect my words and learn the practice of the Lord.

Blessings to you all.

Messages from
Unknown People

The Transcripts:

28th August 2016

Arthur the Coalminer

I am Arthur, ha, ha! Well this is weird, indeed, been many years, I have been deceased, as was told! Martha, she joined me. This place, we don't understand what it was that took us over so quickly, but we now see the light and we begin to understand our lives purpose. We were a couple of insignificance, just a couple, a man and wife who lived and died with hope. Tragic circumstances denied us our lives and terminated our focus. We are guided now by numerous spirits, teachers of the light. My physical times, the dust was an issue, as it was for many of us who worked in the mines. Dark days and nights, boys who were to perish by the side. One for all and all for one, was a motto that carried us forward into those dark depths of the pits. Coal mining was a way of life in those sodden damp places, where we toiled our lives away. Our brethren, they sang the songs of hope, many perished in the cataclysmic tombs. Ah, we had many merry times, joy was brought to our hearts with our songs as we strode the hills and valleys. Carmarthen, was but to name one. She would wash me at the end of the day, my Martha, breathing in the dust that I brought home. It was a monster in disguise, we never knew the risks involved but we had to live, feed the family. We had a happy life, shorter than most, but it bore its fruit in the lives of our children and our family home. We stand together now as proud parents, grandparents, great-grandparents, proud in the knowledge that we bore so much fruit who sing happily in the hills now. No more choking, clogging dust. Fractured hearts were left behind of the men that suffered the indignities of the cruel atmosphere. Many were lost, many occasions in collapses, flooding was a constant problem, gases would choke a man. For many it became their tomb.

As many as 20 men were lost at Abergavenny, we worked and toiled to free them, but to no avail, they remain to this day. Their bodies, but their hearts and souls are free, no more entombed in the dark earth as they roam the valleys and hills of the spiritual world. Their choirs of voices sing out in joyous, happy reflections. Thomas Harvin was a man who understood the issues of our lives. He wrote his poems in aspects of love, not denying us the right to be heard. Thomas was a man of great literature; born a Welshman he understood the purpose of our lives and the torment of our lives. He would shine a light in his words of song to bring us joy in our hearts, magical times for many. We cannot complain, 'twas a life of misery and dark, but it had its meaning. It brought many joyous occasions, family picnics, we would gather on the hillside and muster our thoughts in families, in games and prayer. Jolly times, and the women who bore us brought the fruits of their labour, we consumed what we could afford and that which we couldn't afford we imagined. Well my boy, we must depart once more to Heaven's gate, but know a life of risk is a life of happiness, of wondrous joy compared to that of the man who has everything, who will not experience the joys of life and depth of meaning and feelings of the heart. We know of suffering and pain. God bless.

13th September 2016

Angus McShee – Battle between the Scots and English

Aye, the pipers that blew as we marched upon the hills in the highlands of our homeland. Angus McShee, he remembers well those times of the clans who fought for freedom from your kind.

He's proud that a daughter of his should have been welcomed by the ways of the Lord, for she of Rose knows her name, her past is vague, but her Nanna sings her songs of praise to her. *The Rose of Tripoli. (Note: The song could be 'The Rose of Tralee' and not Tripoli as heard on the recorded trance session.)*

Tremendous amounts of accounts of our torturous battles. The Clans rose, raised the shields against the might of the English as they bore down from the hills above, we were defined our clansmen, we screamed and hollered, shouting indignations of insults upon them as they rushed towards us, banners raised, horses galloping. Our weakness was in our strength of numbers, but did we fight, a battle not to be forgotten? Win she will be remembered, heartlands. We cannot express our contempt of those who would banish our homes for their need of domination.

Limbs were lost, arms flayed, the stench of blood was intolerable, trampled upon those who had fallen at our feet. What a squalid terrible affair. Ah, the roar we cried as our triumph became obvious, but what of the massacre as many souls bore the brunt of our blades. What could be said for their courage, men of England went to the blade, their hearts bled on the point. Praise be to God we say as our salvation set us free from the tyranny of those of England. Strange irony, ha! As I speak through this man of England, he is a channel by which I must use. We suffered greatly as we passed to the other side of the bridge of understanding the atrocities, we had languished on those men of war; we were victims of our own pride. Can we express our sorrow for such actions? Many will fall before the new dawn of the new day. We will watch and respect those who fight in the evening. Pride in yourselves, fight for freedom and liberty, we watch and despair at those who will fall before the blade once more. Carnage is a terrible thing and should not be employed as a method by which freedom is sought.

Desperate times.

18th September 2016

Gilbert the Monk

I am Gilbert, a speechmaker for the House of the Lord. I was a brother, a monk. I greeted within my house of love those of the poor and impoverished. They found sanctuary within the righteous brotherhood that was created within the monastery walls. The circus of Rome reigned supreme upon the world, as I was a monk of love, in great demand. Latin was my language of choice. I cannot presume to understand your modern ways, but I see a deliverance coming for the impoverished of your world. My Latin tongue has no words but to say, Emporium lectus. *(Note: roughly translated: Emporium: – marketplace. Lectus: – chosen/selected.)*

Your mind does not comprehend, allow my staff to guide you my son. Become immersed with love and light and know his words. Sanctuary can be gained with a Christian heart. Your communities of your world have been issued with fair warning by the brothers of love. Many have come before us in times past, in ignorance of their ways. How is it you have not learnt those many practices of the book of love. I stand here before you this evening, with great respect for your need of courage to bring baptism to the world in a pool of love and light. John was once known for his voice and language of love to the Lord, he blessed the one Jesus, with a heart full of light and love. I was once a brother of the monastery that sat upon high of the Mount, we overlooked the seas and saw the tide of, hmm, hate rise. We strove to bring our strength to those through our wisdom of the words of the Lord in a common practice of love, that they ascended the hill disrespecting the promises of our Lord. They tore down the walls that bore witness to so much love and wisdom. The brotherhood was banished with shame upon their brows. Their physical was indeed truly beaten, but their spirit was strong with their love.

Gather round your people, as the spokes of a wheel to centre around the hub of life. Those on the far reaches of the circumference must be drawn in to give strength to their love. A spirit of love has come at a time when many fear for their very existence. Bring them a love of the master.

29th September 2016

Message for Michael about Flanders from his Great Uncle James

The poppy seeds of Belgium will soon fire once more. In those desperate hearts of the men who suffered in Flanders upon the lines, those many lines of death.

I am James, *(this is the author's great-uncle)* **I knew of war.** Your father, he is with me now Michael, he did not know me, for our times were not shared. He knew of my plight from his father. We were brothers; we angled *(fished)* together, happy times in those lakes. Ah, I hear your praise for me and thank you for your words in remembrance. I perished in that Belgium, from wounds received as you know. Mum and Dad greeted me upon their arrival in this world of light. We are all together, easy now. We must move on as a sequence of events unfolds, as yours will unfold. The popularity grows in the hearts and minds of many, they know it is not wisdom of you but the wisdom of spirit that speaks through you that gives them hope of the resurrection.

I am here as witness to that. My comrades, they join me, lads in the battlefields of Flanders. Reckless boys, glory with thought, clawing in the mud and filth. Many perished such awful, terrible endings to their lives. There was a blast that swept me off my feet, I remember little more. Oh well, we sit together now embraced in love, in our family's circle of light. Figuratively speaking you are me, for you are of my blood. Be a brave chap, don't let the side down, chin up what, what! Ha. Ha! Those officers make me smile with their stupendous arrogance. Well, some were okay. Hmm enough, I go to rest, but now you are a champion of the world Michael.

30th October 2016

Men of Flanders

We know of your appeals and poppies and your thoughts of our loss. We were the soldiers who fought in the fields of Flanders, we have come to tell you this evening, our fight goes on with you, but with a different aspect. I ask you in desperation not to see the world fall before the point of the blade once more. Look at our loss, remember our names as we fell in the battlefields to bring peace and justice to the world. Don't let us die in vain under the poppy fields of Flanders. We were the Tommies who sat beneath the dirt, wet and cold, in fear, knowing our time was near. What kept us going was the thought of our loved ones, that they would be free from a tyranny of those who would rule the world. Let no man judge another by his race, colour or creed, for you all are of the one God.

Your desperate times are seen by the many of spirit, we deplore those of the merciless who bring actions against the innocence, echoing in the fields of Flanders. What did we fight for if you will not learn to bring a practice of love to the world of man, what did we die for if you let your children simulate violence in such obscene ways?

Penny for your thoughts, mentioned once more. Again, we cannot admit defeat, we are the men Flanders; the many lost roses that besieged. We rejoice in the realm of light, no more pain or tears, or that of sorrow for our passing, for we are the flowers of the fields of Flanders. Bringing these poppies in our memory bring us peace in the knowledge that you as men will learn to live once more in peace and honour. Don't let our memories fade beneath the mud and dirt of those blood-soaked fields. We are the men Flanders, the men who were lost in a time of despair.

Your nations grow with much intolerance; belay your fears for another's beliefs and aspirations. Do not let the blood rivers flow once more. Granted are we, peace in the fields of heaven. Your own champion who fought the bitter battle sees the path you are set upon and is pleased to acknowledge that he now rests at ease. We are the men of Flanders that lie beneath the fields, a mass with the flowers of heaven. May God grant you peace and love. Bring joy to the Tommies and peace once more to the men of Flanders. God bless. *(Author's comments: my Great Uncle, James Champion, was killed five months before the end of the great War, he died from shrapnel wounds in Belgium.)*

7th November 2016

Demetrius

I am Demetrius, quite a thought you might think, but I lived as a monk amongst your many men within a Cypriot island. I was an Orthodox priest; I became aware of the being of light as I passed from your world into the next. I cannot say that I was surprised as it was my practice to pray upon that beacon of light. I was lost in my time, my prayers and thoughts. I ignored the plight of others as they worshiped many beings. I have come tonight with a practice of love to ask of your forgiveness in the world for my misguidance and deeds of displeasure. It is a hard thing to do when your mind is set of a way in a purpose. Help me to find hope once more. Thank you, I must go.

13th November 2016

An Unknown Father

I am, or was, a man, a father, a son, a fool to others, as I strove to bring my practice of love and hate to the world. Hmm. Had a tremendous will and a power you would not believe as I drove my message home to the hearts of many. Ah, a father they called me, I fear not, as I betrayed my own thoughts with the selfish needs and satisfactions of the realm of life. I can only guess at your thoughts. I need no sacrifice, I come before you with a message and a warning, that all who would not follow the book of truth, shall become as me. Forgiveness was mine. I accept that truth. Become one of despair for others, I am eternally grateful that I see my purpose now. My eyes have become clear as I focus upon the love of the one true master of life, Lord in Heaven. Never allow your emotions to overcome your good sense, for they will lead you to a place of despair, turmoil. I was once spoken of as a man of intolerance, and yes, it was true of me. Now I have come to a land of mercies and I bring you this message, not to allow your emotions overrule your heart in your lives, for they are fickle, have a need for a Rose and a passion of love, blessings be upon you all.

8th December 2016

Adam – An Arsenal Football Fan

Adam watches very closely, the gunners were his game, as a boy he would kick a ball with ambition. His mother wishes more could be done, she feels he is lost to the torments of life, that boy who witnessed so much displeasure. Adam he is called, in his mind he has nothing but admiration for the lady who called him son. He is not lost, nor forgotten. A joyful reunion will come. A spectacular event to bring you close together.

Doris – *Maybe Doris Stokes British Medium?)*

Doris wishes a word to the many, "Be bright in your aspects of love within the walls of the church, bring peace to those, truth and honesty, bring no shame upon yourselves, for you are the carriers of the light. Your aspects are many, a common practice in your days. The pull of the light is great to many of your world as they express their wish to work and hover in that light. Their truth is good, their love is honest. Keep a weather eye on the clock of time, for it ticks slowly by, and all too soon your time is done. But go in the knowledge, have the peace of mind that was given to those who have lost loved ones. Farewell."

Tommies in the First World War

Hmm, we would like once more to talk of those not so glorious times. Upon the fields of Belgium, so many lost. Christmas day for us was icy puddles in the mud, the fearsome sounds of whizzing bullets and shells that thunderously hit the ground and would shake us from our sleep. They had peril all around. The children, the young men would cry for their mothers in fear in the bitter battle ahead, knowing that their survival was limited. A rabbit, was a creature who would sometimes appear before us, his life was sadly ended, for what had we in our rations, in our Tommy tins, nothing but bully beef, a potato perhaps if we were lucky. Our sacks of cloth would hang from us, as meat hung from a hook, we had nothing. Every morsel was fought for. And our rags upon our backs, were as if they were made of gold, treasured by all and those who no longer needed them, forfeited them to those 'Tommies' who lived, despicable act to rob those of the dead, but survival was uppermost as it is in all species upon the earth. Our lives are tormented by those days of mud, dishonour and displeasure. How could you even imagine what it is like to sit with a tin of the cold meat, hmm no fires for fear of giving away our position.

We had our times of merriment when displeasure of war would vacate our minds, we would sing the jolly songs of the day, and the songs 'Tipperary', would come through and lighten our hearts in the fields of depression. Ah. But be sad no longer for us, for we are now a memory in those minds who linger on in your world and to those who have new lives, we are history. Our thoughts are not meant to bring you displeasure, but just to alert the minds of the many as they celebrate this Christmas of the star that shines above them, and the stars that shone above us, completely two different things, Starlight but not of magic but of illumination of our positions. Still, here we are in this place of beauty now, having suffered the indignations of war and man's creation to beat upon one another. Hmm, 'Tommies' we were, soldiers of the Lord we are now. Not all made it through to the light. There were those who would use the opportunity for their dark souls to practice their mutilations. They have much to learn in the practice of love and humanity and of the spirit. In time their souls will travel their paths as intended. Be blessed, remember your times and those who have suffered in the trenches of the forgotten war.

THE HILLSBOROUGH DISASTER
(15TH APRIL 1989)

*The Hillsborough disaster was a fatal human crush during an
FA Cup semi-final match between Liverpool and Nottingham
Forest at Hillsborough Stadium in Sheffield, England, on 15
April 1989. With 96 fatalities and 766 injuries, it was the
worst disaster in British sporting history.*

The Transcripts:

26th April 2016

*(Note: The following message was received when the results of
the inquest were issued regarding the Hillsborough Disaster.)*
**Today there has been judgement on souls who were lost in
the panic** created by those mindless attitudes, they screamed
alarm, and as a herd of wildebeest that panicked and
stampeded to the gates for there was no reason to stampede.
Rejoice now with white roses of peace and love, not despising
or hating those who rallied the many, conservatively their
hearts were born again to a place of wisdom and knowledge,
understanding that theirs was a sacrifice prudent to observe
and understand the justice of man. Police have a foul decease
of untruth; they cover up the matters behind this appalling
tragedy, for they know their wisdom was unwise. Should they
see this message they should be aware no one escapes from the
justice of the Lord, their mistakes were amplified by the
needless conviction of silence, they terminated so many for

fear of betrayal, they cannot hide from us, we know of their crimes and they in turn will know justice.

28th October 2016

(Note: We believe the following paragraphs to be more personal messages for those who can take them – it would be wonderful to have any feedback.)

Beacons of regret, indignation, frustration has beset him as he watches others of your world receive messages of love. He cannot understand that we cannot reach him for he is shielded in mind. Grief besets him this day, an anniversary by which you would know and recognise as being a day of a great loss. Rest assured that your concerns merit an answer, for who are we to deny their right to a question upon which much feeling is embedded.

We forecast that those beings of need will come to witness the truth.

Hillsborough continues to be a place where worship for the many that were lost continue to this day. As a pilgrimage of love of blue, red and white. His loss was great, they know him from the hurts of his battle, there is an outpouring of grief so profound, until the day that you'll understand how it was that he should succumb.

Gate nine is another place where the many shared a purpose in their passing, the game of love was of ill will that day as the multitudes watched in horror, as the game was played out in the terraces above the pitch. Fragmented hearts set about a fire that caused indignation so great. They knew they were lost, the panic ensued, here was no escape, they were ushered by fear and gripped by terror. They are blessed now at peace and an understanding.

Do not relinquish your love as it holds the key to your heart my son, "He who believeth in me will live forever." These are words of comfort to those who have lost.

Malcolm was an honest man with a tremendous will to live, to continue his work within the boundaries of the walled city. His loss was felt deeply for those of his family.

For John who you think that is, honour, rest is a concern, we know not of this only that he has come forward in a bid to awaken the memories of those of Hillsborough, to reassure them of their peace of mind as they play the game of love, of memories in the world of spirit.

WELL KNOWN PEOPLE

Messages about or from people who are well known.

Some messages are about people who are still alive.

The Transcripts:

26th April 2016

Mother Teresa, an Arcturian (1910–97)

Tolerance and ignorance, they are a combination at odds with each other. So what is it then, that makes man so blind that he cannot see his way through the forests of love, why does he speak ill of those past for they cannot answer?

Be not afraid as we gather around you to stress on a point of view for those of the Earth.

Mother Teresa, she knew of love and respect. She is with us now, a guide to many bringing hope and peace to the minds that reach out to her, She was a mother to all, a blessing to those of the needy. Her heart was large as she created a haven for those with little.

Her messages were left behind for those who understood to read and understand that she was Arcturian, and the message of love to unfold before all. Her thoughts of love radiated out amongst her flock as they felt the presence of light within their hearts and souls, compassion that she had for all despite the turmoil of her life. She needed little for she knew that her love was that of the Lord and that he would feed her soul with knowledge and wisdom. She comprehended the world as a challenge to be taken. Her gift was of love, constantly she knelt before us in her chapels of love displaying her admiration for the Lord and those of the ways of the light.

Blessings she sends to the Earth to manifest into those who would kneel before Him with the hearts filled with love. It is necessary that we inform you that she is no longer in pain as she is a teacher in heaven, a guide to those of her thoughts. Compare yourself not with the likes of her, she was an angel upon the Earth who was blessed with a gift so powerful that she could command her will upon those on high in your world.

Nevertheless we respect your abilities and your focus, as your will grows so does your purpose of mind.

Imagine what it must have been for her to have lived in squalor, and she died in peace on her bed of love. She tore her heart out at the discrimination set against her and her flock but she saw the light that led them to victory in the eyes of the Lord. Bargains she struck with those who had their hands in the pockets of lust for she knew that their demands would weaken their souls and permit her love to enter in.

The judgment of Solomon was ridiculous in the eyes of the Lord, they ignored her preaching's as they saw a woman, a beggar of no fixed abode an illusion of the time. Know this she is on High and is regarded by many as the teacher of wisdom. She comes before you tonight to thank those of the light for their work and their mercies, the rhetoric of those who don't know the love of the Lord is like the wind that howls past the trees of knowledge and wisdom.

Her mind was forthright and powerful in its own right. Your mind is learning quickly concentrate your focus upon our words, nevertheless we hear your wisdom that comes from your heart to beckon people to parade themselves before you.

Her leaders wanting to listen to those of the light advance your tasks, come before us in the knowledge that we are with you, never guess at our wisdom, write as you need to pass the messages of time.

Common knowledge it is that Mary was the wife of Joseph, She bore the child of the Lord She too was of no consequence to the many, her heart and soul were that of a child but she bore the burden with grace and honour knowing in her heart that her love for her child was paramount above all. She was ridiculed by those who were uneasy in her presence, for they knew the power of the Lord was with her.

24th May 2016

Princess Diana

She was an angel born to rule the many, her life was a trial of many issues, a mother of love. She came to us unaware of the events that took her, and the reasons being of comfort, of a need to her love, to stand up her love. She became a flower in heaven, her boys, her pride, her good humour are seen by many to this day. She watches and waits for the time when her name will become that of the martyr, for she too knew of the things that was set against her by the diplomacy of others. Her characteristics, her values, live on through her children, they will enlighten those of stiff upper lips of a heinous crime against her family. She was not aware of the reasons why she needed to be, but truly she was an angel of light. She triggered emotions in many of the world as they watched in awe of her beauty, the beauty of her soul could not be hidden from those of need, she embraced many hearts in a manner befitting her roll. Diana came to us, her gracious manner. Storms in a teacup, a term frequently used by those of men who have need to explain!

Troublesome hearts are in need of a caring heart, for their rages and outbursts cannot be measured by men's minds. They trash in rages over the little things of life, their minds are a maze of discreet intelligences that are unable to express themselves in the usual manner considered to be normal by many. Men who do not see their rages that dwell within them, these poor souls, as they attempt to express themselves in the only way they know, they flailed in rants of anger and frustration seeking an outlet. Consideration of their feelings is all that is necessary to allow them to express their minds will, for their purposes are obstructed by a mind incapable to withhold all that they are. *(Note: Are they describing those who suffer Autism?)*

They knew their mother of their birth was an angel of light, for she would cope with their indiscretions, tolerate their ways as mothers often do with the ones they love, they are a breed of human that is special to each man and so it was that Mary was also deemed a special lady to her sons, her bright eyes would light up their lives in times of oppression when man was not his own master.

The Dalai Lama *(The current 14th Dalai Lama, Tenzin Gyatso)*

The Dalai Lama is in need of assistance for he is a man of goodwill and humour. His very presence exists because of his purity of mind and spirit, for he sits with us in his meditations transforming his mind into the vessel filled with purpose. His eyes are open to the needs of the many who sit beneath his mount, they worship him with a fondness of a loved one. His will is strong, he will ally with the Pope and they will be an outlet for love. Their combined strengths, when they negotiate matters in high places that most cannot reach, their purpose is for humanity and the love of God.

Comparatively yours is of equal measure, of less importance to those around you, your whispers are heard many times, many places beyond your ears and eyes, they are watched by some sceptical minds, but they are eager to learn of what you know as they have need of those that communicate with the ones above.

Princess Margaret

Margaret *(Princess Margaret)*, she nestled in comparative wealth, with an outlook of life of wild laughter, fun and joy. Her husband had brought many things to her life; he was a man of meagre means comparatively, yet her love for him spoke volumes to the many that understood their relationship. Margaret, she was known for the party girl. She expressed her devotion and love to her homeland many times throughout her life, with an eagerness and willingness to accept her roll by her sister. Her passing was with enormous gratitude and her life, for her suffering was great. Those times of joy and abated love of abandonment took their toll on her purpose. She waved her hand with great respect to those of money and purpose. Her lacking was in the love of the people who needed reassurance. She was aloof in her ways, abound the luxuries for all to see. She came to us as she began with life, with nothing, knowing to begin a fresh start. The worries and issues had gone. We now elixir her mind to focus upon her purpose of being, she was a slave to bureaucracy, as is all who work within their grasp. An easy life you may say, and so it was to a degree, appointments to be met, satisfactory murmurings to be made. Her dogs by her side as she sat in the gardens contemplating her life and the misfortune that had been brought her way, but her inner self was a sheer delight and her buoyancy far beyond others with those negative aspects set against them. So being of wealth is not necessarily the being of happiness, as your life is behind closed doors never betraying your secrets to the world, or sin.

Grateful times ahead with gratitude and thanks for giving devotion to those beyond your world who have a motive of love, to bring peace to your people.

17th July 2016

Harry Houdini 1874–1926 (American Illusionist and Stunt Performer.)

Harry. Redeem yourself, of years past he has recognised a purpose in you. His mind was fixed upon the altar of the stage, Houdini his name. He baffled audiences across the globe with spectacular performances, he bewitched them with his magic. His wisdom was seldom heard, for his magnificence as an artist has to be seen by all, but his scholarship as a child was paramount to him. His reckless behaviour paid him to events, but his secretive thoughts were laid down in scriptures, held by his family as memoirs. His complex mind would sit for hours contemplating the many mysteries to be encountered in this world. He signified his intent on being one with the universe in a manner restrictive of his ways. He never completed his tasks unfortunately, but his path was great nonetheless. Edith, she became a focal to him, she would become a saviour to many. So many fragmented minds of purpose ended in tragic circumstances. But be not buried, for that was there purpose to live their life in a meaningful manner and ability. To honour their soul, their minds thoughts to live a life full of colour and purpose. Harry never intended that his life should end so dramatically, but he knew the risks, he played a part in his own end, not understanding his physical ability to withstand the torturous, implements he set against himself. Hmm, nevertheless he was an outstanding man, known to many, seen by few of this world.

The gateway you'll have, is a passage of tortuous events to strengthen and guide your heart though knowledge of peace and love.

Uniformly they merge upon the lane from Victoria to Marble Arch, they gain their strength for a meaningful purpose to betray those who have dictated their lives.

Fashionable ways are at an end.

26th July 2016

Possibly Colin Fry 1962–2015 (A Well-Known English Medium who Lived in Sussex with his Partner and his pet dog)

Hmm, this is good! Strange though, your uniform of body is weighty! I remember so many things as I travelled the world retrospectively. You will need to bargain your life to follow your purpose. As a gay man of great stature my mind was attuned to that of the souls of spirit. I gave no quarter to those who would shout out, liar, and fraud, for in their ignorance, what do they know about a man of purpose? They have will and heart to bring about good and peace in men.

She supported me in my dying days with her love, for she was in spirit and I became aware of my past life and how it led me to this point. I must say it troubled me not, for I knew the purpose and the road to where it would lead. I was humorous in my thoughts; my friends were troubled as they watched my decline. Hey, life is for living, let's not get bound by sadness and fear, continue as you mean to go on Michael, don't let others put the fear into you, that yours is a lie, an untruth, for you know that spark within you, a creative edge.

You will meet many as you travel this road, be sympathetic with an outward look, be tolerant and not judgemental of their practices. Yes, I know your views, but they did change when you understood that love is what matters most. My dogs were important to me, as they became the centre of my life. My man, he continues my purpose, he will know of the things that we said at my bed, as I told him that life is for living and that I would continue to be in the next world.

His tears rolled down his face as I touched his hand and breathed my last. I was met by an Archangel who walked me through the trees of life, explaining that my purpose was done; I was to have no fear, for there was a higher purpose. I look back retrospectively on my life. I say this, have no regrets, the path I trod was a special purpose, my time in Brighton with my family was a special time as it brought tears for their fears of my demise.

Archer Street, Carter Street, there's a place for memories. Know they will need no further evidence, your thoughts are good, expand your mind and encompass your heart. Jazz was my thing, soothing rhythm; Fats Domino was a great man whose soul soothed my thoughts. My memories are as sharp as they ever were, bless you Michael, for your purpose in this life of terror, you will need your strength to face the multitudes as they gather.

7th August 2016

Harry Houdini 1874–1926 (Hungarian Born, American Illusionist and stunt Performer)

Famously I was a master of deception, but I cruelly let my mind overtake my emotions. It was easy to deceive the eyes of men with actions so fast, the brain did not register how it was accomplished. My acts were extreme in many measures that brought about my end in that bath of water. It will take trickery and smart minds to open the eyes of many to see the facts, to see how life should be. For life is an illusion created by those men of power of your nations, they hold back much information that will enlighten your lives and your minds to their true purpose, which will do them no good, for when the master calls, they must submit. Complain not about their earthly position, it will not matter, for in spirit all are one and one are all. Different levels and aspects, but still spirit. We distinguish not between the man of power and the rich and the poor man, for it is not the position in life that brings them to us, it is their actions that will be of concern.

7th August 2016

Cleopatra

I am a woman, who sat on the throne for many years, my need of hatred was written within history. I favoured many men in my time. Oh, I had such beauty, I was the focus of many. Lilies of the valley are the many in my chambers. You cannot bring yourself to say my name, 'Cleopatra', ha! It is not a name of shame! The petals fell to my feet, were of scented bliss. My name lives on in many ways, but I cannot expect you to understand that I was put in a position of trust, but have misled the many souls that sang in my name. Foolish songs, for I was a woman of need. Truly the beauty I sought was never found within my life. How could I have been so foolish, as not to see the true beauty of life? I adorned myself with jewels, pearls, bracelets and the like, but they were trinkets of no consequence. My heart was cruel, my passion for love. My name was synonymous with many of my time as they cowered at my feet and before the whip. I was a woman that displeased the many, how I long those days to be wiped clean. I cannot express my sorrow at my outrageous acts as Queen. Ah, perhaps in many ways I was a living legend, compared to Him, I am nothing.

Troubled minds are many in this world of spirit, her compassion for the many were few, she continues to grow in purpose, still holds that attitude. She will eventually change, as in all things, time is a healer.

20th September 2016

Cleopatra

She was a woman of beauty who ruled her world of Egypt. Renowned for her love of the milk, of the honey. She sacrificed her love for the man who shone in her eyes. Her love was betrayed by him, Mark Anthony. He was a man of gross misjudgement. His ways upon her were cruel, as a man he neglected his woman. Do not think, she was equally as bad as that man she worshipped. Her tyranny was known throughout the people's, despite her beauty she was but a wolf in sheep's clothing. She coaxed many men to their doom for her own need and gain. She was a woman of immense beauty and men could not resist. She was the honey to the bee, but her sting was worst of all. In her wisdom she has spoken to those of the light, asking that her beauty be restored. She is no longer of the physical; she is no longer worshipped by the many. She has a cold heart. But like many of your world, she will come to know many beauties within life.

14th August 2016

Norman Collier 1925–2013 (British Comedian)

Norman Collier was a funny man. He made fun of many things, he made light of his life. He is not so well-known now, but he laughed, oh how he laughed. "Trouble with the world is, it takes itself too seriously." These are his words. He immortalises those who ran before him. His humour was great, a funny man indeed. He brings light and laughter to the souls and spirit. He once asked, "How would one know one's hand in spirit and out of body." Hmm an analytical question, but if you truly know that person, look into their eyes in your life you will know without a doubt.

Norman would like to bring happiness to the world once more with his words of humour. Nottingham was his place of birth, he remembers many things in those streets, in those poor run-down streets, the cobbled stones and messages on the wall that he would leave and the humour he had brought to his family and neighbours and friends, was immense. Terrible times he had faced with poverty and degradation, but he shone and rose as his fame grew. His wisdom was a place of shame, for he had hidden many things from the world, as all clowns do. Their masks of laughter hide bitter times, as many do in this world today. Humour is a release, it has its basis many eons ago. *(Note: Norman Collier was actually born in Hull, some 80 miles from Nottingham, but he ended up living in Welton, which is between Hull and Nottingham. 80 miles difference is possibly insignificant to our friends of the light?)*

28th August 2016

Glenn Miller 1904–44 (American Trombonist, Composer and Band Leader.)

'*String of Pearls*' was his song. Miller, band leader, brought joy to many in his masterful accompaniments. We have him now, his music goes on as it did in his era. How you know he was lost, never found, no witnesses. The men surrounded him, celebrate his life to this day. They were a troublesome lot, bringing forth their words in music, but they accomplish much, bringing peace to the minds of those who suffered wars and degradation in terrible times. They glamorise his life as his popularity grows amongst many. Miller, he had fortitude and a zest and passion for his art. He worked so many times, until he slept. He knew that inside, he had a passion, a drive to bring his music to others, to bring them joy and a measure of peace in light-hearted entertainment. Yours is no different, as of many men who enlighten the minds of the masses, you must all conquer your fears in battle, to bring your compositions to the minds of those who are blinded. Be frank with one another. Glenn Miller says, "Play your music, each and every bar should be scrutinised."

1st September 2016

(Note: We believe the following may be about Doris Stokes and Margaret Thatcher.)

Doris Stokes 1920–87 (British Spiritualist and Medium.)

Margaret Thatcher 1925–2013 (British Stateswoman and Former Prime Minister.)
She came to a bitter end, her selfish ways were torn from her, as her body ceased to exist. She could not understand how it was that life should elude her. She recognised that her time had come, but still her fortitude and purpose surged in her veins. She was a teacher to many, a mother to some. She brought you focus; she came for the many in the parishes and the regions of her home. Her popularity grew as a storm over the ocean. She had a magical politeness. You know her as a woman who sat before the many, bringing messages of love and hope to those

who had lost their dear ones. Her purpose grew as she toured the world within her agonies. She was a humble lady who saw the pressures upon Margaret.

She commenced her journey of love in her early days of her life, her purpose was seen even then by the many. Her father sat her on his knee to speak to her in a way that she could understand, for Margaret was a girl with a purpose, with point. Grantham, known to you as her hometown, she grew and lived in that place. Her name resounds in the many chapters of her books. She was an outstanding woman who now sits with us in her thoughts offering us tea as she speaks of a life of servitude.

Margaret joins us, she is aware of the thoughts of the many as she trashed their lives with a purpose, the focus of her politics. She too came from that place. Her humble beginnings were to her, valuable lessons in her life. Her father taught many things of the politics of the time. She had many days where she would ponder upon her path and upon her aspects of life. She astounded many with her strength of feeling. Margaret became Prime Minister of your England, she led an army to war to bring her fame and fortune. She regretted the loss of many lives, but she had a purpose to defend her England. Despite her unpopularity, she fought on against the ignorance of men. She was not popular, but she had a purpose, a vision, some would say her wealth was her purpose, but her views upon life were different to that of the common man, for how could she know how little he had. And today, politics are no different. The men of England are seen as insignificant, as the greed and avarice grow amongst the wealthy of your nations so their downfall will come soon. Never forget her name, as she would not. An able woman, she did her best as you must as well, to bring your purpose to bear you also may tread on feet. Survival of the fittest they call it. Be not ashamed of your path my son, bring focus to others to hear the words and wisdom of spirit.

1st September 2016

Grigori Rasputin 1869–1916 *(Russian Mystic.)*

Rasputin, a Polish man *(Note: Rasputin is considered to be Russian, but Poland was once part of Russia.)*, brought shame upon his name as he measured his life of greed, his politics, brought down a Queen, the monarchy of the country. His rantings, they are of common legend. His dark ways and his practices of the dark were used to enhance his being. She became infatuated with the black heart who dominated her life and thoughts with his words and influence. Hmm, he became one of tyranny and he was not welcomed at his passing. He condemned those who would not conform to his ideals and practices, he saw them as something underfoot. As his popularity with the Queen grew, so his power began to overwhelm him. His misjudgements became clear, she was not impressed by his manner towards her husband, for the many negative practices of that house proved to be his downfall. As he cowered in that dungeon where he died, curled upon the floor as a rat. Does he have regrets? Who can say, he continues in his ways to this day, never recognising that he was just a mere mortal who is now spirit? He cannot uphold the law of God in one hand and ignore it in the other, without bearing the consequences of your actions. For a double meaning is not an aspect of light, but of deceit.

Lord Louis Mountbatten 1900–79 *(Second Cousin to Queen Elizabeth II.)*

Mountbatten, "I was a Lord of the Seas, I became dismembered in a blast of tyranny. My nature, may I say was of goodness, a prominent feature within the Royal household. My name was elevated to a position of trust, I was the uncle of her Majesty. Such wondrous times and here I am, house of the Lord, my time is past, but I've come to learn all men are equal regardless of rank. My troubled world was torn apart in the face of adversity.

What can I say of her my Lilibet, she wouldn't already know, King Charles he may, be but she will sit to her dying day?"

1st September 2016

Trevor Howard 1913–88 *(British Actor.)*

Trevor will not wait. How do you resist. I am here once more to tell my story. There have been many travesties in your world that have brought men of focus to their knees, I was one amongst many who could not resist the temptation. My passing was not an honourable one. I staged many times, I have been amongst your men with an arrogance. My time went quickly, but not before I had my say in your world. My thought and intention were bought to bear upon them and the beings of the light as I desperately clung to life. My purpose was done, I could not change my manner. I need your focus to tell my tale as a warning to others that theirs must be a life of servitude to love. Don't be like me, free your minds from fears, wants, needs and greed. For I was hell bent on satisfying the pleasures of life. It did me no good. Common practice amongst your men now, they seek out an escape from reality, but what is reality? In truth, it cannot be found in the tablets, potions of your men, but by looking deep inside your mind and accepting that you are who you are.

Be responsible for your patterns of light and how they affect others and change their attitudes. Be a man, a spokesman of courage. Don't allow them to sway your opinions one way or another. I was once a man who walked your earth in displeasure of life. I was not satisfied or had gratitude for those things I was granted, but I've come to an understanding and now I see the value of life and how it could have changed others, had I not been so arrogant. I tell you these things of the pattern of my life, that you may understand that life is a blessing to be held and cherished. I am Trevor of the unknown. Stratford-upon-Avon will give a clue to my name. Thank you.

4th September 2016

Trevor Howard speaks to Michael with a message for us all

Trevor once more would like to intercede on the pattern of his life. You thought he was he the Bard, *(Shakespeare)* for he is a man of mystery. Complimentary you are to him with your thoughts. Treasure your books, for within the pages the secrets are revealed. The pathway to eternity can be found in the plays of life. Separate your minds thoughts from that of the Bard, for he delivered wistful, amusing stories. They were magical to the population of those times. Trevor cannot say that his identity would make a difference to the understanding of man and their ways of error.

Navigate your lives and follow your purposes to become the playwrights of the future.

For he who sits on top of the mountain and shouts the loudest, will be the one who reaches the minds and souls of those who watch in despair. My connection is not known, for my mind's thoughts were many. I acted out his plays, the sombre impressions of love. I could not control my emotions as I stood there and performed as many words of inspiration of such a playwright. His focus upon me as an actor of life was great, Howard will give you a clue. Huh! I see your realisation my boy *(the author suddenly realises it is Trevor Howard speaking!)* but focus upon the stage of life, do not allow your emotions to overstep the mark, as your future is bright.

Behind the scenes, men of aspiration who cause change are seldom seen by their peers, for remarks will be made as to the transcripts and their relation to life. Ah, they cannot hide from the Almighty eyes of the Lord. There, I have spoken my name; rest assured peace will be upon you all in the forthcoming days that act out life's desperation.

Be a poet of life and stride on the stage to enlighten those with a common practice of love to defeat those who would betray your trust. I was once an actor upon the stage of life. As you all lead your paths of life, you also perform the many acts in the creation of the sonnet. Be blessed with love and good fortune. Never let it be said that one man is equal to another, for all men who hide behind the skirts of fame are equal in his eyes.

13th September 2016

Trevor Howard 1913–88 (British Actor)

Once more my friends I get to talk upon the stage of life, you know me as Trevor. My words are of speeches and phrases written by men of times past. Your knowledge of me has become apparent. I worked upon the stage of life to bring amusement to man in the planes and seas of your globe. I fought in a war, little known by many in my time. I also acted out in peace of my mind, my outlet was the stage of life. Bernie she adopted me, gradually became the man I am. I cried and wept upon the stage for many during my performances. Little did they know the tears I wept were for tragic times within my life. Oh yes, I seemed to be a man of strength, standing there, speaking my words to the many who sat before me with expressions of love and joy, sadness and the Kings of Doom whom I portrayed, Charles sat beside me as I donned my robes to walk out as the king of misgivings. Spoke my lines from my heart. I donned my shield many times to hold back the memories of those awful times, to see my mates fall before me in that war. Trevor I was, a performer of life upon the stage of life.

Hidden were many things, secrets held within my life. My daughter, she has focus in the books, she has my talent of theatrical. It's a shame, such as us are seldom seen beyond the screen, that silver screen where dreams are made and broken and the clowns of life will unmask themselves to become a fearsome. My plays were not heard, well, I was an actor of renown, I dabbled, frequently unheard, but some with a knowledge of my writing would kindly oblige. Thomas a Becket I played, you have mentioned him before. You didn't realise who it was who commanded the performance. I played many roles, many kings, many of sadness. I was a performer upon the stage of life. Your keen eye will represent many, your weakness is your inability to see your own strengths. Combat your fears my boy, stage fright is nothing but an illusion of the mind. I always suffered greatly; it is not well known. I beg of you to inspire others upon the stage of life as King Lear was crowned a man of many seasons, mmm, how I miss those times, jolly times. I hear the bell, I must leave. Blessings upon you for your ability. Charge I say!

13th September 2016

Albert Einstein 1879–1955 (German Born Theoretical Physicist.)

Tobacco road, tuberculosis, you felt my pain. Smoke they said, will bring you joy, hmm, so I did. It brought me pain and sorrow; I regretted the day that tobacco became the word of pain. Those companies, players of many deaths will rue the day they told us pipe tobacco was safe, humph, lot of good that did me! Albert you call me. Ha, ha, ha, yes! Einstein is in your mind. A man of great intelligence they say, ha! How intelligent is a man who would listen to the men of those tobacco people? I smoked a pipe, the symbol of my being. My one regret is that I, Einstein could not express my fortitude. My theory of relativity is well known, my passing is least known. As luck would have it they came to me with an expression of love. I played a part of such awful times; I cannot deceive myself that I was merely a player and they were men. My thoughts brought indignations upon me, my fellow men. I am Albert Einstein, the man behind many explosions.

18th September 2016

Thomas à Becket, 1118–70 (Archbishop of Canterbury.)

Thomas a Becket, spoken of once before as a greedy man, a man of possession. His world revolved around a frantic array of misgivings. His promises to uphold the law of God were lost in his need for gold. He was a poor man of faith, mistrust was his soul and his salvation was that heart that beat within. He comes now with words of wisdom for you to focus upon tonight. "I am that I am and no more, I was a man impoverished by hate, love and greed. My purpose was tenfold to the many populations that walked beneath me. My heart was humbled by him on high as I came to the world of spirit, for I never understood the words written and their true meaning of love. I was a poor man in the ways of life, but my ignorance grew to many things. I hid away my heart in pursuance of riches and gold. I am a humble man now, one who has learnt the lesson that time gives. Tremendous amounts of skill will be required by those of equivalent positions within your time, for they are ignorant of their wrongdoing. They think that their lives are all that matters, how wrong can they be! They do not respect the lives of those who walk beneath them in the streets of London, Paris or Rome. Those who struggle to survive their lives with mediocre finances and little possession.

Look to the streets of your cities and see those in need, those impoverished people of your earth that are neglected and walked upon by those of status. Soon her politics blend, she must come to a conclusion at her time as Prime Minister is all but done. Your country is in disarray filled with malpractice, punctuated by greed and wealth. Those men of greed have no care for they will see that your England is but a place of indignity. They have allowed the situation to grow unabated by their laws. Though man has freedom to walk the earth and live, man he does not have freedom to do as he pleases and bring racism, fear and dishonour to others.

Your countries have borders within many states and regions of the lands, some are closed to the many, some are open to the few. Still your lessons are not learnt, that the Earth is given to all, but your leadership causes aspects of hate. They despise those who call themselves refugees, as being scoundrels, scroungers of the state. Despite this they welcome them unabated as the evil within them spreads and nurtures others to a path of the dark. Don't become one of those who instinctively hates, because one man is not as the other. Your knowledge is great of the world of spirit, greater than you can imagine, but your problems and circumstances upon the earth are widespread and it will be necessary to begin a new time, a new season as all must change. Do not be frightened by these words of love, that sound of terror. We need to have your trust in the knowledge that in the cleansing will become a new time of peace and harmony, when men will work together once more to support his families with love, not be reliant upon the resources of Earth, for which there are now little. The poisons of Mother Earth must stop, the negativity of man must be issued with a purpose of love, for you are but a creature of the earth no more different than the lion who walks the jungles and the plains of Africa.

Many think themselves above all creatures upon the earth, how little do you know of the intelligence that walks beneath your feet. Who are the insects? Those creatures beneath your feet, for you yourselves who infest, decay and destroy in your path are the locusts of man it can be said. Harsh words with the temperament of love, but how else do we get your attention to focus upon the needs beyond your own selfish ways.

27th September 2016

Thomas à Becket *1118–70 (Archbishop of Canterbury)*

Ahh. Combat your fears my boy, allow your mind to read the words of wisdom to the pastures of the land.

Ah, Thomas à Becket brings welcome to you all. To be frank my friends I have come once more this evening to bring the master's voice in words of prayer and worship. As you see the Celtic cross before you, you must whisper the words of love to all men upon your earth. Reach out your arms and let them know his value within their lives. Preach ye not to the multitudes who would scorn the words of our father, the Lord, but let them listen with a casual ear, to the murmurings of a once meek man.

To him on high we sing our praises and ask that he grants us wisdom and peace within our hearts of our lives. He is the creator of all life, all being. He hears man's desire for war as that of a, impatient child. He cannot speak of punishment, but of teaching. The Masters words are full of love.

I was once a noble man, with an influence that reached far and wide of the nation. Chapters and annals written about me reflect my dark side, but I have my good. The French would welcome me as I would welcome them as we sang the praises of our father within the chapels of Notre Dame. Fierce times, men battled the many armies of indignation, the swords clashed and the shields clattered as they tumbled in the fields before Avalon. What an almighty mess we have created with our indignant behaviour before him upon high. I was a man of peace but my indulgences were many. I cannot say that I was proud, but his forgiveness was great.

As I ask you all to seek the truth within your hearts, for you are men of the earth filled with spirit, that will once more regain that power.

18th September 2016

Mary Magdalene

Mary responds to your calls. Welcome her my son, as she is Magdalene, the heart and soul of Jesus. She once knew his love as a man of faith who forgave her of her sins. She became witness to his miraculous ways in aspects of him. We can say this, that as he forgave that woman so his forgiveness will reach to those who deem him the Lord upon high.

22nd September 2016

Merlin Speaks:

"I am here. What is this I see before me but a world of dark. I have come into your being as a friend, you feel my energy, allow me to speak.

Mystics, fortune-tellers, sorcerers of life. He, he, he, ho, ho, ho! What do they know of the mysteries that lay before you, hmm? I was Merlin, I know many things, magical things. A figment of the imagination? Ah! Little do you know of the magical things of life that will occur if you open your hearts and minds. Granted, there was misfortune in my day. Arthur, a figment of imagination you say? Ah, maybe so, but he was a man nonetheless. Admirable aspects of life we had. I was a master magician, ah, I cast my spells in ways they did not understand. The sciences? Hmm, mysteries to be observed and understood, but only in part. I knew much, but the mystery of life eluded me. Hmm, I sit now in the afterlife, surveying the scene that was. My forthright gestures to him, Majesty, were not always greeted with a customary smile. Hmm. You must live your lives as intended by the Almighty. Magical spells, potions, lotions, they have a place, but are illusions nonetheless. The power is within you all, within you. Continue to grow, we will speak once more. Thank you for a measure of time."

29th September 2016

Merlin

As Merlin once spoke of, hmm, of 'Those Magical Days', of Camelot.

"Greetings to you, I am here once more, the potion of love to issue man. The Dragonheart was once mine. I guided many and steered a few to the wisdom which I shall impart upon you and yours. There is a wizard within your world of man, he conjures up a host of fears in a storm of love. You will not recognise his being of love, for he is well hidden within the walls of a city. Nevertheless, he exists, expressing his words to those throughout and across the world. You have many magical things and wonders that did not exist in our day, but we were people of the earth. We used the resources to hand, we never neglected from whence it came as you neglect your source today. What an appalling mess the world has become.

No more dragons to be slain, no more hearts to be broken by the victorious words of Lancelot who swore an oath upon the table of love that he would defend all from the might of the Dragon, it seems that he has lost his will in the battle.

We've come to a climax as the Dragon feasts upon the news of those in desperation. He is an opportunist who waits for a time when men are weak, then he will strike with his breath of fire.

If I were a man but once more, would I not recognise the world from whence I came? No, it is a pitiful place. My name Merlin, reads well in your books of literature. The stone and steel were bonded by a chemical that could be released with the dose of amber. Ah, you know, the sword in the stone was a story of strength and for those who partake to pull its length from the stone could only do so with wisdom and knowledge. It could be released by simple mechanism. That King, he knew the wisdom of the sword. He released it and brought about a peaceful resolution to the troubles of the time. He ruled for many years, 30 would be about the figure. My companionship was a rough-and-tumble one, he would comment on my disruption. I would threaten him, would it not discourage collusion in plans of the source. The ring of love, for he knew me well and for all our doings we were as brothers. Camelot is no longer seen, long gone in the ravages of time. That man who stole our heart in the Welsh mountains. Farewell, blessings to you all."

18th October 2016

Nigel the Pagan! (Merlin)

Become one with Nigel, as is thought for all those in need at this time. I am Nigel of the unknown, my heart is strong and you will find meaning in the books of love as a pagan. My memoirs are written many times upon the pages. My focus was of the Lord and of heaven. Despised was I as a magician, ha, ha, oh, I don't think so! They were also wicked times with narrow minds, warlocks and witches, weasels and worms, humph, strange to your ears, but know this to be true. Thank you for your purpose and words. Amen.

29th September 2016

David Lloyd George 1863–1945 *(British Statesman and Liberal Prime Minister.)*

(Note: The following two paragraphs have caused a little confusion, the first is spoken in very crisp and correct English, the second in a Welsh accent. We cannot verify any Welsh connection with Disraeli and although the second paragraph sounds like it should be David Lloyd George, we can only find reference to his father being a farmer. His uncle had influence in his upbringing, he was a cobbler. After these paragraphs there is a pause in the recording and words that sound like, "Trick your mind." So we leave the transcript as it was channelled and leave it 'out there' for possible future verification.)

Indeed I'm here, as a gentleman who knows his own mind as did I, Disraeli. Hmm Disraeli, you may have heard in me, a predecessor no less, in my hat. Hah, I got to agree that Winston has a point. Yes, I was a man of Wales, I carried motions, hmm not popular, but then what politician brings out popular decisions. We have difficult choices to make to run a country, to give its people freedom and to make choices. Ah well, I made mine hmm. Sometimes wrong, sometimes right, but they were of a good heart with a measure of tolerance towards the people of Britain. England, Wales, Scotland were united, but look at it now, sad to see the breakup of a wonderful country. Hmm such differences of man.

Well, my light, it shone once, my father a miner in those hills the dark dungeons of the prison of the mines. I rose from a common boy to become a leader of a nation, a master to some, politician to others, Prime Minister to many. I sat in that house, took my watch out of my pocket and looked at the time and thought, where's it gone? Where's that boy now? Oh well, I have responsibilities and they were least of that, they looked to my humble countries, he knows he was of Wales. Ah my house still stands in that street of Cardiff. My hometown was basically a village. There I was, that boy who became a man, who rose to power in that house. They call my name father of Wales. My time was done, I was credited with many changes in the safety of our homes and mines. They grafted hard in that black bitter coal. My mother, she would sit by the fire to await my father's arrival, it was small, one-room, a lobby, one-bedroom for all in the cottage, you see I, I cannot remember times of sadness there. We would hold our sticks above the board as a game, my sisters and brothers were many. I rose to a position after many years of fighting. It is not hard to gain a position of height with a will and a mind Michael. Turbulent times must be met, the strength in that wisdom of Winston, my predecessor, my peace. You must fight to reach the heights necessary. Now I bid you farewell.

Trick your minds.

There will be resistance with a measure of love as the opposition rises within the party of red. What a turbulent mess that party, oh dear, what has man become. A monster of greed, need and want. Not all mind, not all. Figuratively speaking it would not be possible now to turn the tide of those men of wealth. A storm of the light will be needed to reach their hearts and minds. What a waste of good spirit.

9th October 2016

Thomas The Apostle

Thomas, he once more comes with words of wisdom. Father he was to the many. Greetings my son and blessings be to those who look to the words of the Lord. I was once a man of great respect, I didn't realise during my pattern of life what my journey was to be, but I soon realised my misgivings, for they were many. I have come to a solution now, an absolution of my sins before the father of life. We need not tell you how we desire to help those of the living. The pressures of life are great for the many who are suffocated by the dark. Your ample knowledge is required to bring about a change in a manner uncommon to you. We will support your measure of light as you give it freely to those in need. We are the beings of the light, we are creatures far beyond your dimension, far beyond your understanding and a lack of knowledge.

We gather in our circles of light in response to your wish to communicate with words of love and affection. How can we issue such things with a climate of change in your world? We will support the many of the light, the brethren of the Lord, who work endlessly to bring about peace and change to the world of mankind. We will not dominate your lives, but guide and protect those who have a desire for the good of mankind. We sit here in the light, overseeing those tremendous opportunities being missed. We sing out our praises to you from the Lord our father. Become men of the light, do not tarnish your thoughts with greed of money, with the obstacles of life. But bring purpose to the many with the words and blessings of the Lord.

We have many articles to give you, we will start this evening with a lesson to all those who watch and read your words. We gather here in a circle of light to watch over those of the common good. Sing out our praises in a manner of love befitting that of the Lord and know that our welcome is with open arms and love to you. Follow your pride in the path of light and feel gratitude for the knowledge given. We were once many upon your planet Earth.

10th October 2016

Barnabas

Barnabas I was. A monk, a man of meagre means. I wore my brown cloth and a sash around my waist was used as an instrument of prayer and focus. We were the brothers that discussed many things on the pattern of life and of our Lord our saviour. We worshiped day and night pleading with him for structure within our lives. We were many in our monastery of peace and love. We welcomed the pilgrims as they walked their path of life, some were ignorant, some were cruel, but for the most part they were kind and we were forgiving. We gave them treatments as they lay in our halls, repairing their flesh and helping with their illness when they succumbed to the plague of death. Our hearts rang out as brothers of true love, our monastery grew as a beacon of light, as our hearts grew in stature.

Come now Michael be blessed with the words of the father in heaven and give thanks for those days of your lives when you were a man of meagre means.

As brothers of St Jude's were of Cornish descent, you have embarked upon a mission of love to bring the words of purpose and of God to the many. We welcome your aspirations to bring a practice of love to your fellow men. As brothers and as monks we embarked on the same mission to help all those who knocked at our door and asked for forgiveness and assistance upon their pilgrimages. You are as a monk who will guide those to the words of light. See the dove as it flies to bring peace and love to you all and the nature of tolerance to your brethren. Sit in your chapels, in your homes, in the quiet and bring focus to your minds of the lives of the many of sorrow within your world. Give thanks for your meals as your stomachs are full. Your harvests are great and yet your feasting will not allow those to share of your fellow man. We see the hunger, the hungry and starving of your world who exist on a meagre bowl of food. Have a thought for them when you next sit to your meal and give thanks to our father in heaven for your blessings.

Strike the bells of love within your hearts and your being – Domina et es domina – to the chapels of your mind make it a sanctuary of peace and love as no man can enter without your consent and will, willingness. Have happiness in your lives as you tread the path of many before you, have the courage to face what may come, no matter what it may bring. Envelop yourselves with light as your protection and they will guide the heart to listen to others as they tell you stories of woe. Do not discount them as fools but take them in to your heart and mind and acknowledge them, for this is all they need. The fellowship of men will unite into a wonders and triumphant weapon against the dark. All you need is a will and hope that your faith will become triumphant.

10th October 2016

Sandra Bullock *(American actress, producer, and philanthropist.)*

Sandra Bullock, an actress of some fame. Once more we speak of someone living as an example to you all of how one can triumph over adversity. She is an actress of your screens of silver. She once lost focus of her life allowing her fame and fortune to stifle her mind of beauty. She writes her memoirs as she recalls those years of struggle. Her wealth and fortune, they may mean little, for she is an actress with a heart of love that not many will see. She has joyous memories of her family, in the parks and the picnics, attending the graves of loved ones and those who have departed. She still enjoys a modicum of fame but has recoiled from that light for a time of contemplation. For you all must bring a focus to your lives, not make it an act of false hope, but one of wisdom and caring for others.

23rd October 2016

Betty Grable 1916–73 *(American Actress)*

Betty Boop, Betty Grable, cartoon character of fiction. A lady who was renowned for her beauty, her accomplishments in life as an actress upon the silver screen.

Hmm, your thoughts betray you Michael, you do not understand, continue. As we have spoken of many things that have astonished you, your trust in us, in deeds and actions have assisted the many.

Now Betty, she was a formidable force in her thoughts and mind, a woman of means who lacked the understanding. She partied many times of society, never a thought for those who were beneath her. She comes with a thought as you invite her.

"As a woman of beauty who sought nothing more than to establish a woman's mind in the world of men, I married well, in truth my own abilities were stifled by the thought of others. I became lost in those trees of the forest, I looked for a way out, almost impossible to find. I was discouraged and did many things, Beth Clark, I have you now! We gave our performances with a dedication and an eye to the art of actors and actresses, but we were merely puppets of those men who would issue us with uncertainties, forcing contracts of labour. We seemed to live the life of a millionaire, it is true to say we had means, but still the puppets of others. We bore no freedom of expression as we were scripted the lines and the words. Our sheer delight was in each other. Those who suffered in that depression did not witness the side of life of plenty, but still your world of today, they have the haves and the have-nots, God be blessed, for his love upon those who have need.

The Communist Party was rather attractive I thought, it offered us freedom, a will of expression, but it was frowned upon by the FBI of the times. A secret society we formed; you have heard 'Speakeasies' but did you know there was also a society by which those of great wealth could express their views in a manner not fitting of that of our Lord. What a shameful practice it was. Huh, you think of that, those with hoods the Klu Klux Klan, ah, they were an intolerant group, we were a group not necessarily of their hate, but certainly we had our wrong ways. Our wishes of discontent were not heard by those of authority. A dude issued us contracts of labour, but we had our releases and although it is shameful to admit the debauchery and things that were practised. It gave us relief at that time, but it bore us a burden upon our passing, for we have all to pay for our sins of life. Not one will escape that judgement of himself, as he becomes immortal in that fantasy of life."

Engage your minds to the many immoralities that you practice in your world. Harbour your fears, rest assured that we will be a constant companion as you exercise your minds will. Once more we have come to an end, with gratitude for your ability, many will speak, many will come.

Your conscious mind awakens with a thought, my son. Be brief in your thoughts and conquer your wisdom now at hand. Namaste.

23rd October 2016

Thomas Jefferson

Tomahawks at the ready. We are displayed of humorous side to that of intolerance, but their actions grow as their minds weaken to the measure of love demonstrated. They hide behind their walls of steel thinking that they are safe as they exploit others to extinguish those of our forefathers, who have great will and courage to fight for what they believe. Jefferson, he once spoke of the tribes as being bands of savages, nevertheless he has come with a measure of peace, knowing that they were the true beings of the earth. He met many of his own species who would not accept their being. Now he sits with many in spirit and is being taught the failings of his ways. Astounded is he by those who have lost their focus upon the motherland, that he and his forefathers created. They have brought a practice of ignorance and intolerance to their nation and others. For all that has been gained will be lost. A landslide victory will commit emotions to their bitter ends. A shameful display of intolerance will be seen as they mass in front of the White House at the ignorance of those in authority. Hmm, they cannot believe that such things would have happened in their country, their world of the states. Devious minds will betray the thoughts of the people, they should remember the teachings of the forefathers and the purpose of which it was built. They are ignorant of the fact that they were once themselves strangers in that country, where indigenous people have the will and the right to roam free. They denied them that freedom and corralled them in reservations and they will do the same to their own, as their indignation grows in their greed for wealth and power, dominate their thoughts.

23rd October 2016

Thomas Jefferson

"I Thomas Jefferson wish to tell them to look to their amendments, particularly 1864 through to 1865 and the abolishment of slavery. It was rejected out of hand of course, but it became so. I see a parallel in today's world, you do not call it slavery, but those peoples who established the United States, those settlers, are now the impoverished, the ones who are controlled by masters, no chains, but by financial restraints. Their desire for peace in their nation will grow strong as it escalates. The mercenaries of your world are opportunist fiends; they will spike the tempers of those of intolerance to bring a purpose of an inner rot within that nation. Amongst your many men of power there are few who have a heart and a will to listen to the people. Your nations must speak once more in friendship or the burden will be great upon the earth and the existence of man. We don't punish your ears with unsympathetic warnings for no particular reason, but we just need to establish a thought of love and how the path that you are set will bring nothing but sadness. It's true to say that we must establish once more a thought of those of the light or all will be lost in the struggle to come."

24th October 2016

King John (1167–1215) *(Younger Son of Henry II – Asks for Forgiveness.)*

Frosty is the morning dawn, and the air is chilled by the evening and as the sun rises above the threshold of the Earth so the frost is diminished and dispelled by the light and love.

Your minds cannot figure out the reasons why men do such atrocities within your world. Hearken to the angels who sing the praises of the Lord in the face of adversity. They are not troubled, for they know in their hearts that light shines within them and their staff and rod will be pointed at those who become disjointed from their path.

Allow us in to make amends for the past, as we were once troubled by many emotions of love and hate. We are both ashamed of our actions as we brought forth many things of indignation against our peoples of the earth. We fought many times in the brisk air of the morning dawn to establish a fort, a place of safekeeping for our beliefs.

Many times we had forsaken him upon high as we led our armies onto the field of battle, not negotiating a mind of peace, but that of war and the victories won.

I am not a knight in shining armour but a man who wishes to repeal his actions and ask forgiveness of those of the light, for I have many misgivings, my nature was that of a man of intolerance, never wanting to listen to those who wanted to grant me peace. My kingdom and my palace were all that I would aspire to.

I am John, a man of note in your history. "My Lord who had not seen my purpose, one's own forgiving as I passed through that tunnel of darkness. I am here to ask once more in Sir Lancelot's name for forgiveness, for which I gave you.

I am a changed man who has overcome his disabilities and intolerance of life, I will now focus upon the many things, the many misgivings, and I will be grateful for him upon high to shine a light and accept my forgiveness for my misgivings. We were both unworthy of our position given.

She was at my side many times as I strode the hallways of my palace, bearing down on those who committed crimes and issuing them sentences undeserving of their crime. I was a king, a man of mistrust. My powers were great, until that time I was unseated from the throne of England.

I have not seen so many days of happiness, I so long for the wisdom of the Lord to embrace me and give me peace.

Contrary to your thoughts my man of wisdom will come to bring you news of many things of your past and present, future, allow his thoughts to activate your mind.

I am John, the one they despised and hated. I ask forgiveness of the Almighty as I pursue the light in his name. I will right my wrongs, be blessed my children, let no one put asunder that he has given you purpose for.

A Message to Michael About King John

A truly remarkable man of his time, he bore witness to many untimely ends of his people, but his sadness denotes a man who may have reformed his mind. For we know, not all are condemned within the eyes of the Lord, as those who ask forgiveness are given a sanctuary within the light and love of the Lord. Be blessed my son, in the knowledge that those who ask for his forgiveness will be blessed with the love and light. Their sins and crimes committed will be eased by their righteous path.

As you were once a man of intolerance and ignorance to those innocents that you tortured with your blade, a shining example of what can be achieved, not just by you, but by many of that time who are now operating in the light and love of the Lord.

You are aware of us as your power grows. You will become a focus for many of spirit. He walks around you, knowing of your abilities, hoping for an audience with that of Christ our Lord. He has been blessed once before with many things of life for which he took for granted. He comes to you with a wish of sanctuary within the light that shines. He must acquire his faith in his own good time. He will be granted a mercy deserving of him as he walks his path of light.

24th October 2016

Christopher Columbus

A Spaniard wishes to speak, Columbus was his name of Earth. You will have heard of him, for he founded the nations that are at war with their minds. He wonders what was his purpose in discovering other countries and bringing shame upon those indigenous peoples that fought so hard against his weapons of war? He was their guest, who would abuse their hospitality to bring a focus to the world of the new possibilities in this new land. He asks your forgiveness, for he is cursed with guilt. A Spaniard he was, a man of the realm, a noble with an adventurous heart, but how could he know what was to follow? He was a man of intolerance don't you know, do you think he was a kind man? No, far from it. He was wicked to those whom they met, torturing their souls for an ounce of gold. His greed was astounding as he brought terror to those indigenous people. Gratified he was by the murmurings of those who perished. He sits with us now, a man in thought of the deeds and practices committed. Do not be as him and bring hate and destruction to others within your lives. Be adventurous, but with a caring loving heart towards those who are not.

You recall a life hmm, you practice the many things of intolerance, in death you will see this means nothing. Channel your mind with a purpose, not of hate, not of war, but of love and peace and bring your fellowmen a loving smile and a warm heart to greet them by your fires of home. Have a willingness to spend a little time with those who are seemingly alone. Bring them your practice of love and your rewards shall be given in ways far beyond, in gratitude and purpose.

Temptation is a masterful toy by which it is used to mislead your purpose. However you must fight your emotions to bring peace. Look to your neighbours, to your friends and see the truth within their eyes. Do they greet you with love and a tender wish or do they look at you as if they see the beast? Nevertheless, have hope in your heart that your welcome will warm them and bring them light and love.

Well, a peaceful heart to you all and remember the words spoken on the morrow. Issue your fellow man a practice of love and light before our father in heaven. Amen.

30th October 2016

Heston Blumenthal *(British Celebrity Chef.)*

Heston Blumenthal. Now there is a man, a master of mixtures, a sorcerer perhaps, ha, a magician of the food kind! Hmm. He conjures up many a recipe to please the palate of the mouth and to those who would taste his bittersweet combinations. All humanity must taste the bittersweet of life to appreciate the finer foods that lay far beyond their imaginations. **We do not create recipes for your digestion, but we do create mixtures within your lives that bring flavour and spice to them and the textures to be experienced.**

1st November 2016

King Arthur Speaks

Demonstrative, hmm, hmm, hmm, a word you do not understand I fear, hmm, no, but do not give up! No. I am like a parasite in your mind and I will have my say to my countrymen of England. Be blessed in the knowledge of your historic past, for there is no equal in your world of these things. I speak with much disbelief in the many things that I see occur in your world today. Ah, you do not recognise me no, but nevertheless I have a message, I would bring to you, peace and sacrifice to relieve you of your pressures of those who would bring their purpose on you. I was a man, an instrument of God at one time. True to say that I exist now in spirit in another dimension and I have an ability unbeknownst to you at this time. I have words for the many who read your words and to this I state, I am a man who has sacrificed much in my life, I have given many my displeasure, but also I have relinquished and released their fears with the loving practice I brought. Hmm, misguided I was in many actions, but I see this and to this day I have displeasure at my being at that time. I was a king among men and I bought many, many displeasure.

Focus upon my thoughts, of Camelot, yes. Hmm, was I real, was the man Arthur real you would ask yourselves? Did he truly slay dragons and, and speak to those magical beings, of course there are many things that were misconceptions and have gone down in legend at the fantasy of other men, but yes, these facts are true. Undiscovered by your men, hmm, I am here to say, I Arthur was a king among men, a good man they say, knight of the round table, aspects of love for all, but I had my problems. I was not a good king, but I brought to many justice as I saw it. I relinquished my crown as I passed from your life, I am a man of legend, my tunes were vexed unknown. This is not important; but know that I was a man who sought love of the Lord and in my way. I worked to bring peace among the people in my nation. I misjudged many, ah, that is a regret.

Do not judge others Michael as I have judged others, stay a man of the light. It is time to go. May God bless you and the knights that serve with you your circles of love, for they reflect that round table that I aspired to bring to my nation.

17th November 2016

Pope Stephen (*We cannot identify which one.*)

It came as a sudden shock to me that I passed at that moment in time to the heavens above. I was a man, a mere mortal who had denounced the saviour for my life of unworthiness, but I came to know and respect him as the saviour of mankind. My heart and my thoughts are with purpose now, as I am being guided by those angels of life and love.

It was well documented that I was once a tyrant amongst men. My life was popularised by many authors and their books, giving my name and priesthood a majesty that it did not deserve.

I am here this evening, you may call me Stephen, to announce that I am no longer the man that I was. I am a man of joy who wishes only love upon those of the physical world. I ponder at the times that were, and those malicious lies and rumours that were spread among you.

It is true I was no angel as being of man, but I am now joyous in the knowledge of his love. My practice was given to me to serve others in the ministry of love, I became disloyal just like many of your world who perceive a position of intolerance as being a gift to them. They must look at their lives and the intolerance they issue to those who would be beneath them.

27th November 2016

Pope Stephen *(Same as above but which one?)*

Hmm, I am here once more. A man of much regret I have to say, but here I am. I have many words to impart of wisdom and knowledge. I came once before as the man of Stephen and I imparted my minds thoughts upon the masses around you, I implored those who would not listen to bring focus. I escaped punishment on your earth, neglecting to think of 'the hereafter' and my role and purpose within that life. Yes you know of my deeds as they are well documented in the archives of history. I served man in my papal position, I allowed men to feed my thoughts with the crowns of Jewels. My authority was supreme, but I relinquished that love, purpose that brought me to that position on high within the men of Earth. Let my will speak now, allow me to say this, that I am grateful for the lessons I learnt. Hmm. I have long since departed your world and have learnt many lessons throughout time, the master, Lord of love, assists many upon your world of life. I neglected him even in my purpose and rank. I paid the price; I ask forgiveness which was granted. I am Stephen, that man of deceit who would assist those of ill will for a flagon or two of wine, a beaker or cup of jewels. The treasures of life are nothing compared to the treasures of love for God. Hold fast in your world, never seek temptation, deliver yourselves from evil and bring light and purpose to your world through your love and fellow beings. My history is a sad one and can be sought in those records. My term of office was short and undignified. Hmm, I retain my papal position within my thoughts, but now, I have an aspect of love to give. Be blessed by the Lord, our saviour. Amen.

8th December 2016

Julius Caesar *(Approx 100BC - 44BC.)*

Julius Caesar, he was a man of discontent, his lack of emotions and tenderness caused many a brutal end in his time. He was a feverish man, a man who ran hot and cold, as the day and the night. He was weak in his mind, not allowing in that of Jesus, the saviour of his time. His counsels, they were obedient to him without a mind of their own, ignorant of the fact that he was the saviour. They were bemused when they were confronted with the many displeasures of the Lord, for they could not understand what man would have these powers, but who said it was a man who gave these trials and tribulations? Only those of the wise mind will see the power of the Lord and bring justice to those who were impoverished at that time.

Julius Caesar became a man renowned for his relentless victories and the suffering caused to his people. He met his end in a way undignified to him. His courtiers caused him grief and pain as they struggled to fight his will. He now resides within spirit; his dictatorship no longer commands respect from anyone. He has much to learn and is embittered by how his demise came about. And for some who create themselves such a world, it becomes hard to relinquish their ways and bring a positive view upon themselves. Don't be the fool to relinquish your love because a man says it is dubious. Have a care for one another, bring peace and light, love to all that cross your path, be a man of the Lord and a father to those who would seek your wisdom.

8th December 2016

King George VI or Winston Churchill?

Times are changing, so I am told, a whisper in the wind. A little birdie who whispers in my ear, a Robin of your season, such beauty it beholds. It shines the light of seasonal bliss; its red breast encompasses the eye as it shines brightly in the season of celebration. We sang *'The Holly and the Ivy'* many times during my life, it was a blessed time when family and friends would call upon us to wish us greetings of the day and bring us joy in their hearts. How we miss those times, those endless days of sweeping beauty as the woodland was covered in the white snow. 'Crisp and Even' was the rhyme and so it was. As I lay back in my chair with pipe in hand, smoke swirling around me in joyous thoughts of peace. I would congratulate myself upon my abilities, such wonderful times of love and family.

I had a four-poster bed you know; it was hmm of an age, 1572 so they say, it stood within the grounds in the house for that time. Yes, you know who I am, as I mention Clarence House' hmm, I cannot hide my grief as I lost grip of the nation. My time was done, but still I grieve for those who are lost at my discretion. Times were hard and things were necessary to be done, I cannot justify all that was given, but I was a gentleman of a kind heart despite my hard shell.

Clarence House was a beauty to behold, the tree in the lobby stood tall. As a child I would dance around it, admiring those baubles, those presents. We had joyous times and the staff would join us, join us for our Christmas lunch, but still decorum had to be held. Hmm. I remember Martha of the house, you will not know of her, I cannot imagine, but she was a lovely motherly figure who watched over us mischievous boys. She gave us a thick ear should we interfere in her kitchen! Hmm, we would not tell, for we knew, ha, ha, that we would hide a mince pie and say, "A mince pie for your eye." Ha, ha, ha, ha! Well what days eh? Childhood memories to be treasured by all who have lived a life, such wonders. We never forgot those of our parish, those destitute and poor, gifts were given to their really poor padre in the church and we sanctioned many things to support and aid those of the farm habitats. They worked so hard on our behalf. We used to torment the gamekeeper, James. We used to probe his mind for his secrets and knowledge of the woods and beyond. He was a fearsome man, strict and stern, his strength inspired me, hmm, as did my families.

Naval people you know. Ahh, but those days are gone, now we rest in a world of beauty. Once more I am learning the ways of wisdom and light, for those times are past. My time nears when I must progress once more, hmm. My days of Winston will soon be gone and lost forever in time, but will consume my mind for many eons to come, hmm. As we all move on, we take a fraction with us upon the path we tread. Happy times when sleigh bells rang and snowballs fought each other in the fields.

11th December 2016

Jack the Ripper

Joseph, could be James, sang many times of his purpose, he was a man, who in an act of desperation caused a multitude of displeasure. His name was renowned in his time, his dark purpose was cast upon those who he saw as 'Illegitimate creatures of the night'. Did he not once say that he would rip the heart out of those who walk the streets of London and Paris? He was a dark soul who brought doom to many. She came to me, to ask why it was that she should suffer the burden of his blows? She could not understand that life is granted to all, but to all they should live in the light and those that succumbed to the dark, will be consigned to the dark, and those that befall as victims will know peace and love.

It was a matter of circumstance that he fell across her; he became a man of no particular interest in one, but just to those who crossed his path at night. His knives were a source of displeasure as he tore through them with an arrogance. His thoughts were that, if he did enough, then the streets of his London would be cleared of these 'pestilence' as he thought. They were women who did no harm other than to bring harm to themselves through their actions and practices. None of them deserved a tortuous end. Jack you think? Hmm, maybe. A soul of the dark. Many dubious, questions were asked of his identity, but none imparted the truth for they were in fear of his vengeance. Today's past is your tomorrow, can you not see there is a dark aspect also present in today's actions?

SOULS LOST BETWEEN WORLDS

Occasionally, when someone dies, especially if the death is sudden or if there is 'unfinished business', the spirit gets stuck between our earthly dimension and the spirit world. They remain behind, close to us on the earth plane for many reasons, sometimes they have a strong connection to loved ones that they do not wish to leave, they may be fearful of punishment in an afterlife or they may not wish to leave their physical pleasures of Earth. All those who pass are welcomed with unconditional love into the 'light'. It is simply a continuance of life in a different dimension. It is never too late for them to go into the light and no eternal damnation in hell awaits them, maybe education, healing and a chance to make amends for wrong doings. There are many mediums or healers around the world who can help these 'lost souls' to find their way forward.

The Transcripts:

26th April 2016

We hear your voice on the winds of time. Gathered around are many who would like to speak through you to loved ones of the Earth, they speak of love, memories of life. Conscious are they of the light that beckons them to peace and love; they come with a measure of reluctance, as they don't understand the purpose of the light.

Message from Trevor

Trevor would like his mum to be aware of his knowledge of her mourning; she should quiet her mind of guilt. There was no rhyme or reason as to the actions taken. To us a moment of despair, a triggered reaction that could not be stopped. Consider his many ways and powerful intuition that sparked a riot in his mind, confusing his sensibility. A tremendous amount of love was needed for his guidance, for his despair was great. He rests with us, with a purpose in peace that was his path. A signal to others that life is a blessed existence.

Those Who End Their Own Lives

It ends for all men as their bodies weaken; their hearts and minds receive blows that are fatal as a wound to the chest. We cannot condemn those who bring themselves to us before their time is due, for they have a weakness, a need that should be tutored and cared for with love. Healing comes to all who embrace the light and love for the Lord; no one is neglected at the time of their passing, for He welcomes all. It is of their choosing whether or not to see the light of love or remain in a place of limbo between the light and dark where influences confuse their souls.

A Prayer of Spirit Rescue

Come before us this evening to receive the healing needed to allow his soul peace in the ever-after of light and love that is assured to all them that follow him. Hold out your hands in prayer:

"Dear Lord our Father who art in Heaven, give blessings to those who are lost in the worlds between Heaven and Earth, allow the light to shine as a bright star in the Heavens of love to draw their attention to Him, for there is no punishment. There is but love and justice. Betray your hearts not by the foolish errors made, we all welcome you with love and caress you in the light of His being. We extend our hands to those who would be at one with the Lord.

Our Father who art in Heaven hallowed be thy name, thy kingdom come, thy will be done on Earth as it is in Heaven, to greet you all to a place of love and mercy within the hearts and minds of Spirit. Come to us, see the house of Spirit that beckons you, to follow your hearts and bring peace to yourselves in the light of the Lord. His mercies are great and wondrous to behold, as he holds your hearts with love and temperance. Come now before the light and know that peace will be yours. Amen."

28th June 2016

Continually we hear cries that beckon us, to those who wish to confess that they are in need of assistance. Blessed is he that calls upon the Lord with love in his heart and an understanding of man. We see many faces before us as they pass through the portal of life, they come and go, their time is marked and interceded with joyful aspects of life when their time is done. They re-enter the world of spirit, not quite understanding what has occurred, but are willing to listen to those of the light.

Some are of a hardened nature and will not accept that their passage is done so they linger, continually feeding on the energy of those of life, despairing at what they see but can no longer have. Their energies feed upon those who would listen to their pleas, they are many within your world as they stagnate in the zones between life and spirit, getting more frustrated at their inability to pass over from one side to the other.

Assistance is needed from the army of healers who call out to them, "Come, follow the light, be one with the light and the Lord." but they shun this for they fear retribution, they need not worry for all are entitled to healing and progression on their journeys of spirit.

His blessings are given to those who have a knowledge/ insight into the ways of the Lord, but mark this, only those with the strength to persevere will walk once more in peace in the light of the Lord for they have a task that needs to be reaffirmed in their commitment to work through the lessons of life. Shortcuts cannot be taken, for life is a path of learning from which there is a beginning and an end. As you progress, your lives, your minds mature into a being of light, you cannot take this away as it is a purpose for all to ascertain their positions in life.

13th November 2016

Carl, A Soul Seeking Help

I am Carl, a man of any old nature! But I have come this evening with respect to the Lord of mercies, in the hope that I may find my peace once more. I am unknown to you and unworthy of the Lord. I see your light; it shines so bright. Welcome me with an aspect of love. I have had a kind heart, ah, but was betrayed by many that bore me ill will, as endeth to my life. No respect. I never honoured my mother or father, as I live my life of regret. But now I come to you with a purpose and a mission in the hope of finding peace within that light of love. Help me to overcome my fears. I was a man of discontent and much sadness of my own making. Allow me to rest in peace.

Marcus with a Message for Michael

Marcus, he joins us now, with a feather in his heart to issue you a purpose of love. Your guidance for others is helped in many ways by a love of those that surround you. Your new purpose in life is becoming clear to you as you work within the boundaries of the light. Have a compassion for others and those souls that are lost betwixt the earth and the heavens. Have no fear; we have no conflict of interests, only a passion for love of the father, our Lord. Remain calm as we bring a focus upon you; allow your mind to relax.

QUESTIONS

7th July 2016

A Question to the Arcturians

(Note: This following question was posed by a young woman who follows these messages – "I want to ask the Arcturians if they are responsible for all the blue flashes in my flat and if so, why have they stopped?"

This is their reply:)

We are the Arcturians, those who brought civilisation if but for a brief time. Your questions are heard, the energy of the blue light is a question asked in a response, to our response, you see them as blue flashes, your dogs were unable to see. We are preparing the way for a measure of comfort and peace, your ability to see the flashes is commendable for Trion energy travels through space and time at the speed of light, it creates a friction which is sometimes seen as flashing images. Your curtains were drawn as you sat there with your book, your attention was drawn to the lights by your mind's eye. Do not doubt what you see, these things occur as light transmits through space and time where energies are completely random.

Answer to a Question about Spirits and Ghosts

You ask for many things, spirit, life. Other nations exist within their own bubbles of existence, like the bubbles of soap, they join sometimes interacting and becoming one, sometimes just co-joined before they separate and go their ways once more.

This is an analogy of life and spirit, meagre bubbles sometimes join, then you may see coherence of things of the past or the person. If they become one, then this is of concern, for the two should not co-join, in these cases 'hauntings', the human term will occur, as the two struggle to live in one space that's not intended.

Ha! Your ghost callers *(ghost hunters)* reach out to us with their words, not understanding what they do, it is unnecessary to intimidate spirit of other worlds as this will bring about things that are unnecessary and they are upsetting to past lives. You yourself *(Michael)* have been on this journey, but you came out the other side understanding that the two should never meet, your journeys are regulated by the master of life.

1st September 2016

Why Spirit Speaks in Riddles?

She cannot understand why it is we speak in riddles; how can we explain to man that which he cannot understand? For it is necessary for us to work with you in a pattern that is strange to your ears. But in that scheme of things, your minds will come to an understanding, that we are of the light and we will bring a Jerusalem to a better place in time.

18th September 2016

Why are the Words so Religious?

The Arcturians Answer:

Many will observe that the words given are deliberately religious based, well, we are spirit, what else would you expect from us?

Philosophy and Wisdom from

Guides or Beings of Light

The whole of this book is full of words of wisdom; however, we have separated some into this section, they are either more metaphorical or have a more poignant meaning for those readers who work for the world of spirit and light. There are times when we all need encouragement.

The Transcripts:

26th December 2015

Love your fellow Man

With temperance, give to all that come before you in your life. Be kind, caring and social with those that are known to you. Beckon to us when you need us to guide your footsteps in this life of love, of happiness. To those who bear hardships in this world today, know we will not abandon you. Care for those, your brothers who are sick and lonely at this time of year, there for all time. Be not cruel to your animals. Be not afraid of the future and what comes.

Praise the Lord; a new beginning will dawn soon upon you all in this world of life. Hearken to ye, the signs will come. Mother Earth is sick, tired, why do you abuse her, taking without giving? Kindness, forbearance, understanding, are *(all)* words that need to be learnt, not just learnt, put into action.

Your mind is clear my son, fret not, we are here to walk beside you, calm before the storm. As the sea rages, many will suffer, many will pass, but what awaits them is an eternity of love and peace, fill your mind with love and honour, know us for who we are, we are your leaders in spirit.

Spring waters rise and fall with time, they taste good, drink of the waters of love, let it flow between your lips. From your heart, knowledge is the key to love. Be graceful, be tolerant, be wise.

Your circle of light is good, your time is short, but fear not, we are here to guide. Gather your people to listen to these words, we must pray, as the prayers are heard like the whispers of the leaves in the wind. Many times we have come to this earth to speak to those who would listen to us, to give them knowledge that life is everlasting. You are one of these to convey this message, be not afraid we pray for you.

Bravery of the heart, strength of mind, all needed for this task. Compare us not to those who would harm you, we are the light, we are the true way of love, gather your arms around us, hold us in your heart. We come with lessons for you all, tell your friends of us, inspire us with your love, go your way in peace and honour. Knowledge is the key.

20th April 2016

The Leaf that Falls

Nature brings with her the trials and tribulations that fascinate in a moderate way, for man does not see the beauty of the world upon which he steps. His focus is beyond that of beauty, but of monetary value. He sees the leaf fall to the ground, he steps upon it, for to him it has no consequence. But that leaf was life, it served its purpose in being, giving life and nourishment to the seed that it bore, never knowing its life and its purpose. It worked its magic, not with the need of anything other than Mother Earth and the light that shone upon it.

Now that leaf is upon the ground, but its purpose is not finished, for that leaf will nurture the earth below its parent and bring forth new life, new seed to populate the Earth and bring into being its brothers and sisters. So next time you see a leaf on the ground, be aware of its presence, allow it to sing its song of life to you and give thanks it was here, for it nourished you with the air you breath.

Feathers are given to those of mercy, who triumph and perform. Their purpose can be of great importance for it changes the path of the lives of many of faith. Conscious are you of the beginning of the wars of the world. Gracious thoughts are given to those who conquer their fears and go forth, for they are soldiers of the light, they fear nothing for they are on a mission of love and purpose.

Strange this feeling, hmm, so much to say and so little time. Here you are granted an audience with spirit. God bless upon your path.

To those that read these words who also follow the word of spirit in God, they light up the lives of many with their abilities. Do not seek profit in your tasks, hmm, we understand your concerns, be brave as you tread the path of light. Your accomplishments are many in your different aspects of mediumship, some tower above others. Aww, what does it matter? Hmm? For you all work for the light in your separate ways.

Bless you for your meaningful purposes one and all, for we are the aspects of the light that will teach you and hold you dear. Do not relinquish your minds to that of the negative. Keep a positive outlook upon the paths you tread, fame and fortune are nothing, it is the message that you take as members of the light that is important to the many of your world. God bless you all for your love and being.

Be you a teacher or student, for there is no difference in the eyes of the Lord of those that follow the light.

Amen.

24th August 2016

The Universe is an Open Book

Forgiveness is great within the heavens as you find peace envelops your mind; never have fears of moving on beyond your natural existence, for all have purpose in God's heaven. The universe is an open book with much learning, it requires only your love to open the pages and bring forth the words to the many of disillusionment.

The Leaf Unfolds and follows the Light

As a leaf unfolds from the buds of the tree it unfolds and follows the light. It is nourished by the light from which the tree is also nourished, from the multitude of leaves that are open to the light from Lord and of the sun. Bring strength to that tree; let its roots grasp the ground with a true and strong foundation; and so it flourishes. But its season is short, and it must shed its many leaves, as they grow old they wither and turn colour. As your lives go forward, so you must follow the natural course of all things within the aspects of life. Be not afraid, for if you have given strength to the tree, to your soul, then your roots will be embedded firmly in the ground and come the spring in the new season you will once more flourish with greater vigour, reaching out your branches of life, taking in more nourishment. And so the cycle rotates and goes on. As your soul lives each life, live it true, with love and your roots will grow stronger and the tree will grow and you will reach out more and more.

Trees are wise creatures upon your earth, they have been there for millions and millions of years and they know the secrets of life. They whisper as they wave in the winds, you do not hear them, for they are just trees that can be but a nuisance. But they live, they have hearts and souls (the same as) as any living creature, for all have spirit within the living world. Even the most inanimate of objects will exude an energy, a vibration which cannot be seen nor heard, but nonetheless exists within your lives. Cast your minds of doubt;

open your hearts and minds to all possibilities that life will bring. If only you would see the light my friends.

His Masters Voice

His Masters Voice, you would sit around the radio and listen to this gentleman who spurred us on with his thoughts and his deeds. How many times have you listened to his broadcasts and wondered how on earth can we fight this battle and win? But unity grew and as always, when the chips are down, people will come together and they will fight for the right of their lives and their families and for all that is good. So it is that your circles of light must grow and join without segregation or thoughts of selfishness. For all your circles of light were born of spirit and if that light grows with truth, honesty, and love, then it will shine bright to all the men of your world who bring you dark.

The Light always Vanquishes the Dark

As always, the light vanquishes the dark. We will never say that anything is certain in your lives; you have to make the effort. Believe in him who sits on high, believe in us who assist in ways many of you would not recognise. We serve you throughout your lives. Some will understand, some will misunderstand, but you have free will; and your judgement will rule supreme to set your path of life. If you falter then you will learn the errors of your ways in another existence of life.

The Flowers of the Autumn

Flowers of the autumn turn pale in colour as they fade away with the onslaught of winter. Their petals fall to the ground. The leaves will follow in the autumn of your lives. Those golden hues of red and gold are so beautiful, for they represent the life that was. As they settle on the ground, they will go back from whence they came and the roots of the tree that fed (the leaves), will feed upon them, once more. Have faith my son, do not doubt the things we tell you, for they are the facts of life that will bring you focus in your time to come. You may or may not grow old, many factors will influence your life, but know this, that if you fall tomorrow, then your words will live on in the minds and memories of those who have read them. This is not to say that fate will befall you soon, it is just for you to understand that no matter how little, and this is for each and everyone of you, no matter how little you think you have influenced others, that little bit of influence will assist in their lives, in ways that you will not understand, as all are connected and all have free will.

1st November 2016

Relinquish Pride, Fame and Fortune

Worship those and cherish the love, the light of the Lord as he comes on his chariots of fire, to bring you peace in your troubled minds in the world of today. Be not that of the ignorant, but be wise and open your hearts and minds in the sure and certain hope that deliverance will come, bringing peace and tranquillity once more to the earth.

You must hearken to the words that are given by the many theologians who have praised the Lord in your world, for their focus was great, but among them there are the few who committed offence, but these souls have redeemed themselves in the presence of the Lord.

For you all must relinquish thoughts of pride, fame and fortune, and be that humble person who would assist his brother in the trials and tribulations of your lives. As it was then, so it is now that you must bring yourselves into balance.

Also in these times of technology that corrupt the young minds, with peddlers of corruption. Their source is unbalanced and destroys those many innocent souls of your world. You must eliminate the corrupt and extinguish them with your love to bring them purpose and an objective view so as to ensure the future of your beings upon your planet.

Spiritualism

I have many times asked for your obedience before the Lord of love. He is displeased with many things in your world today, but he sees a glimmer of hope in those who practice and preach their song of love to others through what you call spiritualism. The church remains aloof to this practice and does not consider it a relevant source of information. But let us assure you that they in turn will become aware of the reality, that the source lies within all those who have a heart and a soul to worship him.

The gospel tells us of the man who gave his home to others so that they might live. Their hearts were great and their sacrifice was great, but he had a heart to hold them within his light and love. He gave them fresh meat, drink and warmth to shelter them from the elements. They were grateful and they left him with peace in their hearts and of gratitude to that man, the one who assisted in their lives to bring them peace.

Scrolls Hidden in the Deserts

There are many writings of the Gospels that have never been seen or heard by man of this time, for they were written long ago and vanished in the sands of time. There will be those who will recall many things of the gospel within their minds, as they were a part of that time, but these things are hidden from them as they live their present lives.

There is a foundation of thought that he who sits and listens to the tranquillity of love will bring to mind those times and remember those passages of the Lord. They lay beneath the sands, the dunes of the deserts. They are discovered, but hidden at this time. For man has a purpose of greed and will not succumb to the teachings on these scripts. He is a foolish man who hides the truth; the truth of man's beginnings and his earthly presence among your beings.

God the Father, God the saviour, is as real as you are, for you are just spirit who inhabit bodies within the physical world of the earth.

Many of you have no shame and you are like Sodom and Gomorrah, those who worship the devil and evil, the golden idol and statues of depravity. We are aware that this is not true of all and that there are many who shine their light and shun these practices.

We would like to emphasise that for the majority, there will come a time of peace. It is not for you to know the reasons why your times are so hard, but let us say this, that the Lord shines within you all, to guide you, to practice a humanitarian purpose, to love your brother and sister.

I am the light; I am he who comes before man in the new dawn of the new day. You will worship me with praise and affection; my only wish is for you to love one another, to accept that I'm merely a being who will teach you the ways, the righteous ways and practices of life.

Your spirits are awash with many fears at this time, but you must relinquish those practices of need and want. I am at the crux of every man that lives, I am the purpose that he should aspire to, for when you pass, you pass into the light and the teaching that has been given through your physical years will count as a matter of importance for your new beginnings within this spectrum of light. For there are many different aspects of the light; we have spoken of this before, but you must realise that your purpose is to triumph over adversity and bring peace to your hearts with a knowledge of love and caring for your fellow beings.

Many theorize that as you progress you become a part of a higher level of being. We practice equality and although those who commit sins against him are punished in many ways, not a fearful torture, but in ways of beginning anew, to live a life once more to show them their responsibility towards one another and their attitudes will dictate the outcome of that life.

It is hard to accept that you are all part of a universal spirit that exists within the hearts of you all, but you must realise that your lives are but a mere passing of time. We can assure you, that we will be there, not as a masquerade but has a parent, as the teacher to the students, to nurture you and favour those who have bought there being to an aspect of the light. We come as teachers to many, in various forms, allowing secrets to be divulged in practices that they don't really understand or appreciate.

Mediums

The mediums of your world, they call upon those loved ones to come and participate in a conversation of love, many times we are heard and they sit and wait for that one connection, not giving a thought to other beings of spirit who wish to communicate. They must bring themselves a purpose to accept all that is brought to mind, not of their thinking but of spirit. These communiqués must be passed before their audiences. They in their own way spread the word of love and of the Gospels and of the word of spirit. Perhaps they see themselves as 'special' in the aspect of the work that they do, and it is true to say that their purpose is of a special part in life, but no less than any other man or woman who would walk the street, for you all have a hidden agenda within your minds and to access the love and the mercy of him, you must focus your mind.

Bring yourselves to a purpose of love and think about the situation of others who stand in your path of life, bring them peace and your mercies and a will to overcome their own trials and tribulations. There exists within you all an inkling of the light that must be allowed to shine in the practice of love.

17th November 2016

Finding the Right Path

Many authors of wisdom have written about the many times when life was simple, when man understood the words of the Lord and the meaning and gestures of love. How times have changed and now man does not respect his elders nor his leaders, for they have become corrupted. In the final analysis of any man's life we take into account his status in life, not in position, but as to his disposition and practice of love and purpose. Yours too will be assessed, as will others. No man is without sin, for sometimes it is necessary to become one of those, to understand and realise the true purpose of love and man.

We come tonight with a reverence of our Lord to whisper in your ears that no man shall be king over the Lord of the Heaven's. We have come to whisper in your ears of the purpose of this man who stands before you, as he is the gateway to the knowledge that must be given to those who call themselves "decent men".

Many times we have heard that man betrays his brother for the sake of an ounce of gold, for what worth is this gold? It counts for nothing in the world of spirit, your joy will come with many riches, not in that precious metal, but of love in your heart. Be a father; denounce those who offer a bribe or two for you to become their puppet.

We have seen many times a man brought to his knees by his lust, not of love, but of wealth. It is sad to see that their focus is of dismay. It is a pattern common to your man this day. Confusion reigns throughout your world as to which is the right path to take. Men do not see that their purpose is a spiritual one as they adorn their cloaks in a manner of arrogance. They feel the need not to help the poor man in the street, for who are they to grovel at his feet? Huh, he is of a superior mind, one who has worked hard to attain his position in life. But truly, what purpose is that position if not to serve those who require help and assistance and a leg up to bring their purpose of love to all.

The common valour of man has all but disappeared in your modern technology. The roots of evil have taken hold as your mindless thoughts watch those screens of betrayal. It is not worthy to forget who you once were and what you are part of.

The Obstacles in the Stream of Life

The stream of life has many tumbles; the water will take the path that is easiest to negotiate. Some will fall over the rocks and the rapids of life, while others will be as a stream meandering through the valleys of green. Not so much haste, but taking their time to absorb the nutrients that are fed in that stream. Don't be the rapids of life, in a rush to overcome obstacles. It is far better to observe, go around these obstacles to make a path easier, but as the waters go around so they absorb the knowledge and see the turmoil within. Hmm, it is easy to be said that it should be of the quiet stream meandering, as life is an obstacle course, which often leads to mayhem. There is a moral to this story; it is a simple thing to understand, that if your minds are the rapids of life; then know that the stream will come in spirit. Why follow a course that brings a rush? Be that meandering stream and absorb the goodness that life can bring.

5th December 2016

Ancient Gods

Apollo was once thought to have said that man was a creature not worthy of his own being. Mythology, he was portrayed as a God, but his words were that of a misunderstanding. His foresight never let him want to be a man who betrays thoughts. He sat on Olympus giving judgement to those of valour, declaring them men of God, of Zeus. But really, there was misjudgement, for man was a creature of the heavens. Those perishing days when they sacrificed souls to the gods of their heaven were misguided, the treatment of their enemies was truly barbaric, enslaving them to murderous times. Modern man, humph, so called advanced, have you not learnt? For I see no difference.

Children must learn Obedience

Things may have changed, beliefs flounder with the greed of men. How can this be to condemn them like an alien spy. Why is it that man has forsaken his saviour? You are blessed with life and knowledge. An audience to keep in his name, our father in heaven only sees so much interference, misjudgement to his words of wisdom and the children they must learn the obedience, as all children must learn from the teachers, fathers and mothers.

The Rich man and the Beggar

Be gracious in your thoughts to others, have a kind manner when you see the distressful scene of that man in the street who you would portray as a vagrant, he your brother or sister. Beverages are given away, not to the one but for the many. There is much imbalance within your world, one has and one has not, but neither share. For what has a poor man to give to the rich man? Nothing! Many think that there is much learning to be received, the rich man has his pockets full, his bank balance bright, but what does he have, the poor man? What does he see when he looks upon that man in the street, with the ragged clothes and no place to sleep? A nuisance, a beggar. The rich man is a blind man. We hasten to add that not all men of wealth are of this attitude, for there are many who would help those out. As always there is the minority of stubborn mules in your world, for they cannot see that their lives of privilege are not lives at all. Where is their freedom?

The Value of Art

Treasured memories of the artistic world are kept hidden away in a box of many. Esteemed members of Parliament and those of the gentlemen's clubs, they hold onto these paintings as a matter of insurance, of backup they feel. Humph. It is there for what? They are just pictures of the past, what value do they hold to the men that view them? Do they give them pleasure or do they help them to understand? Well, it is debatable, as those memories of what we see, the beauty of the artist's hand, the creation that he has put into the work. Nor do they see the beauty of the artists hand of the Lord and his creation upon your planet giving you sustenance in life and the air to breathe. Hmm. Our joyous times will be so joyous as are many who dispute their abundances. Common man in the street, he would view these works of art and ask what, what is their value? Why would they demand such a high price? For they are just pictures created by men with vision. Those men in the street will see the brushstrokes of the art as they see the truth in living. As a brushstroke is varied, so is their life full of colour, sometimes bright, sometimes dull, sometimes a mix, but the beauty is seen, varying.

There have been many men who have created works of art, of vision. Writing and the words of the Bible are none the less any less inspiring, for they have a beauty beyond of their own, beyond human understanding. It takes a mission of purpose to see that beauty on the brushstrokes created within them by words of the Bibles' love. Many verses we have imparted upon you to show the world of the truth of our words, that we are the angels of Light who bring you messages of light and the tolerance.

We would like to once more impart upon you the wisdom of the artist through **the verses and chapters of John 6/51** yet many visions were given in dreams as the artist creates a picture within his mind so the wisdom of the Lord is created within many apostles *(or epistles?)* of long ago.

All Paths Lead to Heaven

Those of you who focus upon these words, men of focus delight in the fact that we send you greetings from the spirit of life.

You could choose your own for the wayward path of some, be not concerned as all paths lead to one place in heaven. Final judgement you think, would be that of torment and torture, hmm, far from the fact, in truth there are many levels upon which your souls may reside, it is all up to you. You have the ability to enlighten your mind and your soul's progress, you are given opportunities within life to do just this, some will ignore them, some will be passive while others fight for the truth in their hearts knowing the knowledge is great. Whichever you are of these truths, know that your path can only go higher if you follow the light of love. Those of torment who banish their minds with thoughts of grievous harm to others, they should know that there is a downward spiral of regret, of ignorance. Their shame will be theirs for eons to come, but their focus will be brought to compel them to see that there is a better way.

Some may never relinquish their thoughts to the love of God and they delight in their behaviour. In time they too will turn, they do not think so, but all must follow their path's as there is but the one God who will dictate when and where they will learn these lessons. You think you have free minds and will, it is truth, but also with the thoughts that control your path, the thoughts of those who sit on your shoulders speak words to your mind and held by the conscious being, they call them feelings, intuition and learning, but this is a spiritual guide of your choosing.

11th December 2016

A Christmas Sermon, Words of Wisdom given by Spirit

Your energy flows as a river. The stream of life, it comes across obstacles, which narrow the stream and brings a rush of forcefulness in extreme measures. You must delay your purposes in the spring but allow the river to flow and take its natural course in life. No harm will come to you or those who would listen to the wisdom given. Rest assured that comfort awaits you in a myriad of sequences to become obvious.

Your thoughts are blessed with the love of the Lord and this consumes your mind day and night, and so it is, as it should be to allow him into your heart. Do not allow displeasure to belay your focus, brush them aside and ask their forgiveness if needs be. Together we walk the path of righteousness and a connection long since made prior to this life. Your ways and wisdom are becoming noticed in many aspects of life. Do not allow your wisdom to betray your mind, keep a focus and balance of things in life that are important to you so that you may continue your journey of love.

It becomes necessary as we draw close to you to bring an aspect of light upon those of intolerance who will initiate a dreadful purpose in your world. Hmm, they come to bring shame upon your race as they negotiate their minds with dark thoughts and needless suffering to others. They are extremists of life, those who would bear down on others with no particular need or importance, but just to become a measure of displeasure to others. Their purpose is dark and beyond your focus at this time, but they gather in the meeting places behind closed doors and with a measure of hate towards those who would bring light to the world, but strength and valour are your name, you must compare yourselves not with these, but with those of the light and to bring a purpose of love to those who would hasten to your side for words of comfort. These words bring joy to all and the many lessons taught should be noted, for they are of high importance to the Lord and Master of the Heavens.

1st December 2016

A Christmas Message from Mother Mary

I am Mary, of Joseph. I bring to you goodwill and tidings. Do not be ashamed to utter, as the words of my son bring a joy to your hearts, a measure of peace. Help us, those of us in spirit and of the light. As you open your parcels upon the day, say a prayer of benevolence to those who cannot rejoice as you do. An angel sits upon your tree, or a star as symbols of what should be remembered. Blessings given to all those who would have a mind, a will and a soul to remember him. Be a blessed child of Christ and come forward without fear or anguish. Be blessed in his love. I speak of a mother's love to her children, have a care for yours. Bring them salvation from those whispers that pollute your world.

11th December 2016

Terrorists and Teaching Children about God

Indiscriminate bombings upon those of innocence who have nothing more than what they stand in, for what harm can they do them? These men of the dark betray their true selves to those of the innocent. Many have died since and have perished at the hands of these beings of the dark and there will be more suffering in your world if you do not take a stand and say, "We are not of that dark, we are of that being of light". It's sad to say that in truth as your darkness envelops your world and the light of the Lord is evacuated from the minds of the many, even, your children are unaware of his presence and teachings. So, wherever there is a vacuum there is a space to be filled and if you allow this to continue, the minds of your children will also be filled with those dark thoughts. Don't allow them to become the victims of your ignorance, teach them the light in the manner directed. Allow them to see that there is love and truth in the Lord our father.

Your schools declare themselves as being non-denominational, no bias to faith, so they teach the children nothing. They have fear of offending others of the aspect of light; they do not understand that integration of your religious beliefs is a requirement to bring all to one understanding of the Lord.

Have Faith in the One God of Spirit

We have come across many with an aspect of love to the Lord our father in spirit in your kingdom of life. They suspend their thoughts for fear of ridicule and dominate their minds with a purpose of working for spirit. In truth to work with spirit you must also have faith in the one, the Father our Lord above. For how can you say that you work for spirit if you do not believe or speak the word of God, or Jesus of Nazareth to those you come across? Hmm, your churches have become mindful of the men's illusions of your world, they worry about belief and ridicule if their words are not chosen carefully and practised in a way so as to bring proof. Why do you need proof? Why is there no judgement upon faith and the thought of love to the one above? You are people that connect with those who have passed beyond your world to bring hope and faith to others, but if you do not truly believe in the Almighty spirit that rules the world of spirit, then how can you be truthful in your words? Many will take a bitter displeasure to these words, for they have a good handle on things, they think!

They will think it's your mind and your purpose to deceive others and bring disrepute to them, in truth this is no such thing as we are that of spirit, we are those who will not tolerate a masquerade of those light workers who perform their duties understanding nothing of their practices. Sure, they bring peace to those who take in their words and it is true to say that their loved ones have passed to spirit and are at rest, but who are they to say that some are not passed beyond, that some they are unable to communicate with? Their thoughts are like a telescope, narrow in focus, only seeing what they want to see and all other things are illusions to them.

Let me tell you this now, to the people who believe and pray to the Lord and work in a practice of light, yours is the true path of the light. Those who work and say they work for the light, need to cast a shadow upon their thoughts to disillusion others, bring a thought of peace to their minds. To sit and ponder upon their practices and think, "Who is this spirit? If it is not God then who is it?" You are all of spirit; you are all equally as part of God, God the spirit, God the saviour. Do you not see this; that your souls and minds are controlled by the very thoughts of the Lord and master of the heavens and when you vanquish those thoughts and leave a vacuum, then the dark with overshadow you and your vision will be lost.

We mean no disrespect to those who practice mediumship in the light or work for the light, but just to ask you all to

think about what you say and what you mean? Because you cannot speak of one thing without the other, for this would be discrimination against all of spirit.

Jesus a Star Man

We have Christmas once more; we've spoken before on this subject. Talked about the loss of the faith of our Lord Jesus who was born at this time. We told you he was a star man and that he was born of the light and so it is that he is a man of the stars. His presence among you will be brought once more, as has been told many times. We repeat ourselves, not because we wish to beat upon you, but just to impress upon you that your suffering will linger if you do not accept his being.

Ah, I was lost for a moment there, but Christmas time should be a time of celebration of his name, to bring joy to the hearts of children and to those who have lost loved ones, in thoughts and memories bittersweet to them. We hear their cries and whimpering for the ones lost who cannot sadly join them this year, or in previous years, but rest assured their being is with you, nonetheless. We are in spirit granted a time for a practice of love; you will be aware of signs given of their presence.

To each spirit a time is given to recount their lives and call upon their loved ones to bring them peace in the knowledge that life goes on, and even in spirit, such times as the birth of Christ and the death are celebrated as equally as yours. He is among us now, a man of notability and of humble, humble appearance. He will not tell you his name, he will not give you a clue, when you meet him in spirit he will just bid you good day and ask you of your love and life.

It is truly amazing that you can walk through life being blind to the pleasures of spirit, to the thoughts, to the love that is all around you and yet shut out. Free your minds from this life and open your thoughts to the possibilities boundless within the world of spirit and the heavens of light. There are many of those who would wish you well upon the day celebrations and there are those of the lonely who sit alone, in despair, not sharing that same illusion of happiness. Have a kind thought towards those who are unable to share your celebrations, those who suffer indignities beyond your possible understanding.

There are many in your world who require sustenance of life and love, and to those few who contribute to their needs, although it is little, it means so much. We are not here with a begging bowl for monetary gain or purpose, we just wish to enlighten you to the world around you.

Oh yes, now Scrooge, in Dickens creation, you must read his journal for it is based upon fact not illusion, not imagination. Charles Thomas Dickens, a story writer of many a tale, a wise man, who foresaw the future and the many things of man. A comedian of sorts, in his thoughts, in his gestures, he poked fun at those who caused ridicule to others. A man with an athletic mind who could create a poem within a mere fraction of a second, he had a purpose, a purpose as all. You must all follow your purpose in life, have the courage to see it through and be not afraid of those who would ridicule you with their malicious thoughts, for what do they know? Have they ever seen or read any of the articles and the facts of life? Where is their belief? You cannot ridicule those until you know the facts. Be strong in your thoughts; narrow your focus to the minds of love.

(Note: We are not sure why the name Thomas is mentioned with Dickens, there are various men of that name who have had an association with him, but it is not part of his own name, but the paragraph below may answer.)

I fear much confusion was caused as my thoughts were given. Be honest, be blessed of the truth in the words. Confusion is not to be feared in life, for there is confusion in all things of life. The rights and wrongs, the dos and don'ts, dot the 'i's cross the 't's perform in a professional manner, why not just be yourselves, why not perform as yourselves? Life is random and the passage of life can also be rugged and random, so therefore you must adapt and not be rigid in your thoughts to conform with other's ways. Bring a practice of flexibility to your minds and open them to the possibilities, that although obstructions may come your way, there is a path to be found that will bring you to the other side of those thoughts. Inflexibility should not be seen as a purpose or direct route, be flexible in the things of life. If the man in the street says to you that you are weak and feeble, say to him that his strength is just an illusion and his purpose is of nothing.

If that rock should not move then think, "How can I move this rock?" But if you cannot move the rock, then why not move yourself, why be inflexible yourself? Be not as the rock, but find a path and walk that path with the delight that your intellect and your flexibility of mind has brought you to the other side, despite the stubbornness of that rock! Ha ha! Ah, there are many things in life that you will come across, ah, those obstinate people who will not give a penny for their thoughts, hmm, but if you look and listen to their words, you will notice their inflexibility and the uncertainty in their voice, for they will give away their purpose as surely day follows night.

You need not be a soothsayer to see these things, but just be flexible in your thinking and in your minds purpose. Do not condemn those who cannot not follow in your path or believe of your thoughts, or even the words of spirit, but allow them time, for they will see the purpose. Their stubbornness of thought and of belief will give way as situations in life unfold before them and they seek a purpose to which to turn to, to bring them a path of direction and light. Then their minds will begin to flex and their thinking will change and as the light grows, so their purpose will change and they will see the way forward and think, why did I not see this before?

Ah, men of focus rarely have an inflexible mind, for the true man of focus is able to turn his attention to many directions and thoughts. It is only those of the ignorant and dominant that are inflexible as the rock. Hmm. Is it no wonder that their irritation is seen when those of flexible minds are able to re-divert their path and bring them to the other side, ignoring their ignorance, their status? Ha ha! It's funny to see how their thoughts suddenly change and they ask themselves, how did he get to that side of me?

God is flexible, do not be ashamed to speak his name, as it is a word that he is the being of all light, of all creation. God is your word, others choose a different name, 'Mohammed', another 'The Great White Spirit', another 'The Manitou of Life', and other names beyond your comprehension from other civilisations that exist around your world at this time. Why have you not seen them? Heard of them? Perhaps you have, but just don't know it.

This is what we say when we talk of inflexible people, but those with a flexible mind who may bring their thoughts around that obstacle and say, "Perhaps there is another form of life, perhaps there is another way of life in which we can lead a true purpose of spirit and love." Those are the people that can see these other civilisations; those other dimensions of life, which do not just exist upon your planet, but exist within the ether around you. For there are many, many dimensions that exist at one time in the ethers of life.

Space and time are also flexible, they are not fixed, they are not in a position that they should not move, but you know they expand continuously, flexibility again at work. Be flexible in your mind when you read the many words given to this man, be not ashamed to say, yes, perhaps there were and are, other civilisations other than yourselves.

Great expectations by many of meeting these beings, unfortunately will not come to pass until a measure of love is reached by your nations of plenty. They intercede rarely in your lives, only to show once now and again that they exist. Many would welcome them, but there are those who would cause them distress, as their own flexibility will not allow them to give up their practice of greed and position. But, as we say, inflexibility gives way to flexibility, but all in good time.

We thank you for your attention this evening and would like to give thoughts of praise to those who suffer at this time, watching their loved ones and their demise. Help them to understand that life does not end, but begins in a new dimension of love. Mm.

Possibilities abound, much truth spoken by those words. There are always possibilities, always a truth in rumour. Be blessed in the knowledge given and don't let your hearts and minds fade in circumstance, in the situations upon your planet. Regardless of your thoughts in your many ways and practices of your lives, know that much truth is given in this evening's words. We leave you with a thought, be not that man of valour who would destroy all in his path to reach the end goal, but be that man, flexible of thought, who has a mission of love and will give that love to reach the same end, but with a practice more pleasing to all.

Ignorance is no excuse for crimes committed, misjudging the mind, In truth some minds are not developed, but for most, their truth is known and they claim insanity and are fully aware of the injustices they bring to others, for they only seek to escape punishment of your earth men. Be warned that all injustices are seen in the heavens above and all will answer to those crimes committed.

Once more we reinforce the fact, there is not punishment as you would think of punishment upon your world of life, but there are punishments in many ways, not of torture or of displeasure, but of lessons to be learnt.

The creation of God you are; a life force upon your planet that smothers her being at this time. Will you ever be flexible to come out of this unfortunate path? We foresee a time that man will open his eyes, but it will take much persuasion and displeasure to bring a focus. It may be that you will bring about your own demise, but as with others, one civilisation opens up to another, and one creature dominant of the earth, will open up to another.

We have spoken before of previous civilisations and even animals such as dinosaurs who once roamed your planet unabated and gave way. A sudden disaster or misfortune. Even if life upon your planet ceases, which it must not, there are other worlds and beings of which you are part of and are yet unaware. For as the stepladder you must ascend, you must evolve in spirit.

This is what life is about; it's about evolution of spirit and not of body. Where does it lead you may think, what is the ultimate goal of the ascension of the soul within spirit of love and light. That is a question that will dog your minds for many more eons.

As each step is taken so the knowledge grows and the wider illumination becomes obvious. It is a goal you must all attain and the answer to this goal will not be given, for it is only your truth and your being that will reach the top flight. Maybe you will start again, maybe it is never-ending.

Know this my children, your life and soul are two different things, your soul is a continuation of energy, which retains its knowledge and love. Your life is of your bodies, which must ultimately be deceased. It is merely a shell for which your soul will travel and your soul will travel in many different forms to bring about many different aspects within your learning and your souls' path.

So once more to reflect on flexibility, do not expect to come back as a man upon this earth, do not fear equally, for you will not know of your past indiscretions, but you will have a knowledge to tap into should you wish to reflect upon it in your thoughts. It is time to go, thank you for your obedience.

Questions may be asked by all, we will not ridicule your questions but give you answers, but you must listen, be flexible in your thoughts to acquire the answers, those answers, which will come in many various forms.

Caesar's men are plenty; his armies roamed your earth with ignorance and intolerance to those native beings of your world. Do you see his injustice to others, do you see that his fall came swiftly and he fell to his knees in anguish, never realising he brought his own demise, do you not see that as Caesar's nations fell, so yours will take a tumble?

Imagine if you will, a triangle, a pyramid upside down and as the weight grows it spreads out, if you do not spread out with balance and justice, then there is imbalance and injustice and so eventually this pyramid or triangle must tumble one way or another. It is inevitable that your world of man will also tumble if you do not cease to bring injustice's upon others and start to live a life of balanced attitude.

We could not let this man go tonight without expressing our displeasure as we see it, as your men of anguish bring imbalance. Equally those of you who wish to seek peace and see the injustice done, you must bring balance in love and light and face up to these people and say, "No more, no more!" Do not become angry and dispute them with violence, but give them education, let them learn the lessons that they have not learnt and show them the way to balance their lives and to know that there injustices against others are merely an illusion of the dark and not that of the soul of the light.

Ah we despair so at your beings. It gives as much displeasure to bring these words in this tone of intolerance to those who bring imbalance to your world, but my children you must learn, you must learn to live together and see the purpose by which you are born from this world of spirit. Bring peace to those who have nothing. Your joyous times are celebrated with feasting and much pleasure, but spare a thought to those who have despair and much anguish at this time.

We are harsh in our sound, but how else do you tell the child of his intolerable ways? Be a man or woman of intolerance and you will surely, truly find intolerance against you. Be one of love and peace to others at this time of your feasting and should you see a man in the street or woman or children in need, then give your love and thoughts to them. Money will help, but it is not money they need, it is guidance, teachings.

Thank you for allowing us our words and do not presume that our anger is directed in a negative way, but in that of frustration upon what we see. God bless you all my children. Do not denounce these words.

13th December 2016

Following the Trend, Not Good for the Young

Your practices of love are shallow at this time as those beings ingress into your lives and the many objects of obedience. You clamour for those latest styles, those things that would betray your thoughts to the world and give them a clue as to your being. Although we have a use for such devices to navigate the minds of those, and the wisdom brought within the words, we also condemn their use in the minds of the young. Do not allow your temptations to override your good judgement, but bring an aspect of love and light to your children at this time of year.

There are many misjudgements made as to why it is men cannot afford to squander their money upon those in most need. You would sooner buy an instrument, a toy, rather than see your fellow human being rest in ease with a full stomach and a bed for the night. So, if you consider buying an extra gift, why not help those who need it most? Rather than a gift, which is unloved and un-cherished.

We have spoken upon many things of the season of joy. We do not understand your minds wishes to grant others a measure of peace when they are so adamantly focused upon their own pleasure.

Your beings are strange to us. Obnoxious minds reach out and call out injustice for their crimes, for they have not considered that their ways are of injustice. The criminals of your factories of money laundering are hard at work, disrespecting your being and stealing those things from your hearts. How do you put a price upon someone's love?

Tremendous thoughts, when willpower will be needed to bring about his gracious love and being to the fore. We have heard many tales of love in the season of joy. Take a hard look at those things that your money is spent on and give some thought to others.

Crucially, we must convey a message tonight to those of your world who would listen to the words and bring focus to your mind. There are those of misguided judgement, they practice their love, though not willing to share in their experience with those of man. Why do we have to point these things out, when it is obvious to your eyes that they combat their own fears needlessly.

Ah, again and again, we have to complement those who stand up for the writing, what they believe, and their courage is a tremendous thing as they focus their thought upon the Almighty. We give you no praise for measures that are sent from your minds, only to say that our love is with you this evening.

16th December 2016

There is but one God

Like the light that shines, your thoughts and emotions must vanquish your needs to bring a focus on those, upon your tablet that you watch and listen. Help them to understand that we are of the nations of the many, within the light of the Lord and we assist all for the asking. No man can be disillusioned by our thoughts as we bring forward a desire to find peace within their minds.

They must not allow their thoughts to be inhibited by those who would say "What fools you are, to believe in something that cannot be seen." Well we say to them, why do you need proof? Can you not just have faith and trust and desire the Lord's company irrespective of your faith/denomination. Yes, we have heard that talk of possible discriminations. Be assured we will not let those who stand back and criticise go unanswered, for we will tell them this, that the Lord embellishes all, no matter what name you may call him, the Lord Krishna, Moses,

Lord Jesus, Mohammed and all those disciples of the light who have come forward upon your planet.

Let the people who criticise know, that there is no one faith but one faith of all whether they realise it or not. As they sit in their homes with thoughts of prayers or in their Mosques and Churches, they pray to that one light, that one being of the Lord. Let them not distinguish between good and bad, black and white, evil against good, for there is a mixture of ingredients that make up your life. It is up to you to bring focus within your own soul's purpose to meet the standards required as given by the good book.

Lessons are given to all who have knowledge but equally those who do not. A thought is spared for them and if they should open their eyes perhaps they would see a glimmer of light that would shine in their minds. Hope is eternal and given to all. Do not disrespect the gift of life that is given by the master and can so easily be taken by those of discrimination or of evil thoughts and intentions.

Bring us to bear upon those who would question your judgement and let them know that there is but one God. Hmm, no name is given, for he is of spirit and is not prejudiced to either one or the other. Have hope in your hearts and do not despair at this time.

We are here this evening to bring our thoughts through this man. To acknowledge those who have questioned our words and judgement. Let them hear these words that are spoken in good faith, for deep in their minds they have many questions but are afraid to have them answered.

These other people who cannot justify their practices to others. How can you justify something if you have not felt or witnessed these actions? How can you bring justice to those without proof? There is no need of proof in the matter of spirit, for the evidence that is all around, within your mind and aspects of life, if you have a care to pay attention.

The symbols of life are given by the thoughts of the many. We witness many things within your world and ask absolution of their sins. Do not be ashamed to bring those thoughts and ask for forgiveness in your prayers.

A word on other practices of your world. Question asked, "Why is it there are so many variations upon the one being within your world of matter? Why have so many departed from the one way?" Your lives, we speak of the Gospels and the Koran, the Hindus and the sects that work to their own desires and they are still, no matter what their language, they are still communicating with The One.

Talk is given upon the many aspects of spirit; many ideas and thoughts are given in different practices throughout your world. We cannot intercede with these practices of goodwill, for they each have their own value and are beneficial to all who would seek the word of the Lord, it is only the minority who would sacrifice their souls to bring a different aspect upon them. It is a travesty to think that man could not be more ambitious, or loving, or caring to each other for it is all within your capabilities to be one, as brethren.

Too many times we have heard prayers that ask for forgiveness despite their knowledge of sinning. They feel forgiven and then continue upon that road and ask once more for forgiveness. We are a spiritual realm, and as anything else, you cannot continue for absolution if you do not bring a practice of love and learning to your life. Do not go to your minister and say, "Father I have sinned." and then expect absolution, for it is your choice that you sinned. Forgiveness will be given to those who are truly taking responsibility in bringing about change, do not use absolution as an excuse to live in your world feeling free of sin.

Many illusions of life are given through the beings of life who would torture your mind with the many ill practices given. Rise above them and assist your minds with a focus. Just a minute a day, sitting in the quiet, will bring a practice of love and healing to your minds. Love your neighbour, bring solace and peace to those in need. Help them to aspire to their spiritual levels, however they are practised in life.

John Thomas, a name to conjure many thoughts in many minds, but his wisdom is real despite the slur put upon that name. His life was unreal in his light, hmm, could not find a practice of love to bring to all. He spoke of many things of the Bible, giving sermons and speeches to those who listened in their churches. The congregations would hear his voice and he would say, "Damned are they who sinned against God!" Hmm, not said with sorrow, hmm. He had goodness in his heart and a well-being for all but misguided judgement at times, and so it is from many in the world who blaspheme against him. Let your spoken word be of kind thoughts and given not of shameful, colourful language.

1850's, now is his time. His sermons and speeches were written many times as he proclaimed himself a 'Master of the Lord'. What right had he by that, how we disagree. His judgement fell on many as they brought their fears of desperation to him, he gave them blessings placing his hands upon their head and saying, "My child you have sinned, why do you do this? You must pay the price and penalty." Hmm, no man in your world has the right to judge another, only the Lord is judge of all.

You may judge yourselves disrespectfully with dishonour or you may bring a practice of love and think yourselves 'a meaningful person', again it is not your place to judge. Others will judge you on your actions as they did John Thomas. He was a pastor of many in the parish and precinct of New Orleans, and Maine. His purpose was great, but his heart was full of man's desires, his lusts were many, he fell by the wayside despite his preaching and his murmurings to the Lord.

You must never, never be a two-faced being. If you may judge one another then expect to be judged yourself, so be careful of your thoughts and mannerisms, for what you're saying may be brought back on you tenfold. Give us a thought as we assist in your lives to bring you peace, never be the judge and jury, but be that of a man who stands back and listens equally to all arguments given.

Greetings friends and welcome to you all. Much talk has been given on practices of love and how you should live your lives. Precious few of you ever realise that your minds are a focus and your intentions are good. Blessed with thoughts of care and a loving nature towards others, of course there are those that would argue that they are merely doing their job, Hmm, well they may not understand the truth of it, but in the end they bring a practice of love nonetheless.

We have come once before and spoken to you. The difference this evening will become obvious as we give you our thoughts upon ill practices within institutions of your world. They judge many of ill health, for their focus is upon their finances and not upon their love. You feel that we reflect your thoughts, naturally we have a view and aspect and we know many things, but let us tell you that we are here to not reflect upon your own personal omissions, but to put meat on the bone as it were.

There are many carers in your world, unsung heroes whose gallantry is hidden. Their lives behind closed doors as they care for their loved ones, unaided and unassisted for what need have they of the society that has bought them to this, their level.

Many suffer pride in your world and this too can be deemed as an illness, a sickness of the mind. For an open heart is an open book and a closed heart is also an open book! Hmm, strange phrase you may think, but listen to the words and understand that no heart is closed, no thoughts are private. Once you give a thought, it extends into the cosmos and the ether around you and will last for ever.

The Commonwealth of man would indeed like to bring good upon others, but there are many influences within your societies that deny them this practice. A speech will be heard on the morn of the day of reckoning, it will denounce those who have persecuted those of the poor and of the week and sick. It will sing high praise for those unsung heroes who worship and bring a practice of love to the sick and needy in your world. All the same thing you may think, here we go again, more on charitable donations, or about the love of good book. Well, you have not learnt. This may sound odd in your time; nonetheless they are relevant today. Bring peace upon one another or suffer the fate of many previous civilisations of your world. Help us to understand your focus and give you a practice of love to share with those that The Lord of the Heavens watches, he knows of the discriminations and torturous behaviour of many, you cannot hide.

Reprint those books of old that still hold many lessons to be learnt. The extreme practices of malnourishment to those who hunger in your world must cease for there will be a great famine for all if you do not reconcile yourselves and bring a love to your Mother Earth. Those are your parents, your states and countries of your world are unaware of the aspects of disillusionment they bring, they destroy many with their greed and lust, they think it belongs to them, it belongs to no man, it is part of Mother Earth. Shame upon those who would protect those of the wealthy, who administer torture upon your earth and the leaks and floods they cause.

The pressures upon your earth are mightily great.

Bring truth and purpose to all my son, allow them to hear our voice.

MESSAGES FOR MICHAEL

Within this section are personal messages for Michael, received from Spirit, the Beings of Light and ET.

It is these words of encouragement that have led to this publication being compiled and produced. We hope they may allow the reader to have a better understanding of who Michael is and to recognize the authenticity of the words within the messages.

The Transcripts:

7th June 2016

Messages from The Arcturians for Michael

We have for the past sixteen years watched your development rise from the ashes, you were not aware of the steps taken to empower you with your belief and awareness, we tried many times to signal you of our presence but you were unaware of what was to come. Your progress as a man has been slow and steady upon this path.

19th June 2016

Message from Merriweather

Complete your missions as required by the souls of the light who sit with you.

Merriweather, he wants to say a few words of encouragement to you my son:

"Open your heart and mind, bring about a purpose to unfold the need of the many. We were unable to complete our work, but we achieved a beginning to build on, as we roamed our nation with a purpose and need to enlighten men's hearts. Champion was a companion with much thought and compassion, take his hand. His spirit will bring about a purpose and hope for those within your world. Complete your mission with a full heart, know that we approve of your work, complimentary to ours.

Your basic needs will be met in the forthcoming events to unite your circles of the world in a response to those of the negative. Your hearts and minds combined will be a powerful reconciliation. A thought for those who would turn to see your words, know that we will be beside you in your hearts and minds as you continue your work my son.

(Note: In another section of the book we have mentioned a publication called 'Spirit Communion' by J.B. Ferguson; He wrote the 'Biography of Classical Medium, Channel', and one of the founders of modern Spiritualism and compiled a record of communications through the late H.B. Champion.

On page 97 of 'Spirit Communion' it reads that Mr Ferguson and Mr Champion visit Mr and Mrs Merriweather. The synchronicity seems great, Champion is our authors name and like H.B. Champion, he is also a trance medium. The book holds many records of Mr Champion's trance readings during the mid-1800s). **Mr and Mrs Merriweather** *will appear several times to offer encouragement throughout this collection of messages.)*

A Former Dalai Lama speaks encouragement to Michael

I was once a man who was given the honour to lead a nation in prayer and love. As you sit this evening, you listen to the music and see the light around you. Your purpose is to be kind of heart, to give encouragement to those who have a will to follow your lead.

Let them see that you are Arcturian. In purpose and need you feel my presence around you. Your mind is weak, but your heart is willing to accept that yours is a life of purpose. Let us call out to your friends and ask them to join us, not to be afraid, but to embrace the joy in the knowledge that they will inspire others to a purpose of love and peace. I was once the Dalai Lama, bringing thoughts and words of wisdom to the nations around me. We sat high in our monasteries upon the mountains, singing out to the world our chants of love and meaningful purpose. Continue your focus my son, your will is strong for the road ahead; know that others will follow in the spring of life. Thank you oh great one for your words, may God bless you and keep you.

26th June 2016

The Arcturians speak to Michael about his circle of friends

Too many times we have seen the purpose fail through thoughts of desire and love. Yours will be conquered in all aspects to achieve your aims. Redirect your thoughts to love and a responsibility to others to bring them light and love and purpose within their lives. Never knowing your tasks until they are upon you, you will continue with a need and a focus so great, that tenderness and caring shall pass to those of burden, as they look to you to necessitate their lives with a purpose and role.

Role models of you in your world of intolerance will shine, as yours and your friends, whom you have met in recent days, will all work together upon a path of light. Bringing your various aspects with knowledge and gifts. It is not for one man but for the many to sit in circle to open his purpose to the fore. You need not know your individual roles with your lives, but know this, that as a group, as a team of light workers, you will reflect the Lords words in spiritual strength to all who observe and listen to your hearts of will and contentment.

A spark of interest will be given as they come in their droves to listen to the words that are brought by the many in spirit. Be not ashamed to call yourself 'Michael' for it is a name given at birth and chosen by the stars. Complete your tasks and missions in life, feel our energy as we revolve around you, cast your mind back to the thoughts many years ago when you could not have imagined such a journey of faith, for you are, Michael of old, with no knowledge, no companionship, treading your path like a millstone around your neck.

We have bought about a purpose and you're right to look the world in the eye and say, "I am a man of faith, of God, I have no fear from those who would ridicule me, I know my path of light is good in His purpose."

7th July 2016

Michaels guides speak

Tremendous amounts of pressure will be placed upon your shoulders and a responsibility of knowing your place in this world my son, let us take the opportunity to bring a measure of comfort to you in the knowledge that we surround you, caring for you, watching over you as you move towards your end goal. Your purpose has meaning to many lives.

They watch you, some with envy, but there is no need as you all are part of the Master's plan. Truly the novelty to bring messages from this side of life has worked wonders in your world of life, for it is no longer a novelty but a practice of will and trust, and through your guardians. We manifest our feelings through you to relay messages, upon which others will come to learn the righteous ways that their paths should take.

The Arcturians speak to Michael about the Purpose of Life

Commence your ceremonies of love and good wishes for those who wish to have a measure of peace. Extreme measures will be taken to protect you Michael, on your journey and path. Your work will increase tenfold to bring a purpose, a measure of peace to all. You will not solve the problems of the world, but your minds focus will enlighten others to aspects of life that surround them, be it of spirit, Arcturian, or others.

Our ships will not battle your thoughts of ill will; continue upon your path of life son, with love and with tolerance. In the coming days and weeks of the winter solstice, you will appreciate our words which you impart to many. Our thanks and gratitude to those that work to bring these words to those of focus is immense. We are with gratitude that you would allow us your hearts and minds.

Satisfaction will be given in measures you cannot yet comprehend, your traits of purpose and will, will be rewarded with a measure of peace. Do not forsake the things that are given, many times we have spoken in the past to awaken your mind, to alert you of your misgivings and your future path. We are happy to see that you tread the path of love and compassion.

Confucius says, "He who walks upon the sands of life feels the Earth beneath his feet, it is he who is truly connected, those that wear the sandals to keep their distance, they will not find satisfaction in the tender caress of Mother Earth". Truly you acknowledge a storm of love, an avalanche of feeling, sincerity and fear. Lead your people in the practice of love, for it is the only true path that all must take. You are not unique in this world my son, but you will follow in the steps of many who have gone before, bring peace to your heart in the knowledge that we understand in your purpose.

10th July 2016

The Arcturians speak of Commodus

Purposely we have omitted many things from your mind, for your judgment has to be pure. Your wisdom is lacking, but we assure you that your knowledge is great beyond that of your body. Do not hold back your memories of previous lives, as they hold the key to your being. Continue your work, knowing of our gratitude in our hearts, our focus is upon you my son.

Let us not compare thee with arrows, but of the flower of heaven, for your heart shines out. Let your voice be your guide upon the path of love, we have exerted a force upon you of freedom of speech, to ignite a passion in many. Be brave and conscious of the world around you and the aspects of the people's will. Together we will merge on the road to victory, just as you once rode the horse before the legion of men. Although you are a former shadow of yourself, now recognising that your purpose and need is of love. We have spoken of many things to determine your attitude towards the unknown beings of the universe, you now recognise that our existence is within your reach. Communicate your thoughts of love, together we will march the roads once more, just as Commodus led his armies.

We have many means by which we communicate, yours is but one of thousands.

Recognise that we of Arcturia, are a constant presence in your lives.

11th July 2016

The Arcturians

We are beings of the light and we are happy to announce that your words will spread far and wide. Philosophy is asked for, your own philosophy is of peace and love, what more would you have us say?

Don't let them help themselves to your words to the negative, yours is of light, carry on with your purpose my son.

You have been contacted by many other beings, for you it is strange, have no fear, for they have come full circle and will attend your needs in the coming years to shine the light to those of a negative practice.

You will not change the world my son, but your words will linger in the years to come and remind those of the love of the Lord, and they will say, "How was it that this man was not able to bring peace and love?" for truly you make a difference. Have faith that even if you change one mind, that is worth a million.

James speaks – Time Travellers speak of Einstein

I am James, the keeper of souls who once more speaks to you of love and light, to allow you to understand that we have purpose for those who shine the light in life. Your purpose reaches many minds in ways you do not understand, they are drawn by aspects of the writings.

Time travellers we are, we travel vast distances through thought of mind, not of the physical. Your minds are young and able to withstand the wisdom, the knowledge. Like child you look at it, play with it, not truly understanding its purpose.

Einstein once said, "That a man's prerogative was his ability to change his mind, his will." His calculations led many to believe that physics was a way to unite man. He truly was a spiritual person with much knowledge, but he failed to bridge the gap between humanity and that of spirit. His theory of relativity was correct in many ways, but only in a singular fashion, a phase. His mind did not comprehend another way of time travel.

It is not necessary to think of travel within the physical, you know yourself as you hear these words in your mind, you know you call them telepathy. We transmit our thoughts and you are the receiver. You have the ability to reply in kind, to travel the universe in a way unimaginable by those of your science.

Why have telescopes when you have a mind of focus? Why have vehicles when you can travel the stars in your dreams? Forget the physical dimensions of your world, cast an eye to the impossibilities becoming possible with focus of mind. You will get clarity of all situations of life and its beginnings.

Whispers of love are given as you compel your mind to the tragedies of the world. Focus your thoughts to become one with the universe of love. He calls to you in ways you cannot imagine, tells you things you need to know. Be brave my son, I am that of the Master, I am your companion James, God bless.

26th July 2016

Jesus speaks

I am the Master of the Father. Your light shines so bright, your heart sings out for justice for those who suffer at the hands of the merciless, but know this Michael, life is a journey upon which each man must tread the path of turbulence and misfortune. Not all will tread this road, but for those that do, the meaning is great and their purpose fulfilled. Your heart rendering thoughts are heard many times by him who sits on high.

Natural occurrences happen all this time, but keep your focus; never let those of the negative sway your mind from the path you tread. Your life's light illuminates the way as you walk hand-in-hand with your partners to bring about a purpose of knowledge to your fellow human beings.

I was once a man who became a monster to some, an angel to others. I became fashionable in the idea of freedom, my purpose was good, but I knew I could not save all, for some were blind, as Lazarus, and (he was) unable to relinquish the riches of the earth, but he came to an understanding as we met on the sunrise. His friendship was good, his needs were many and great, but the path he took truly was awe-inspiring, as he was a man with the riches of the earth, but also of the heart, it just needs a moment of surrender to enlighten them.

I came once before to bring messages of love, peace and hope to those of Israel. Let it be known my mind is set upon your purpose, to assist those in peril to come to an understanding that their belief in Our Father in the heavens will help them truly to become one of light.

7th August 2016

Pamela Kiddey is brought forward to speak and 'Beings' speak of our Higher Purpose
(Pamela and her husband co-wrote 'A Host of Voices' with Doris Stokes)

Pamela, she wishes to speak, for she is a woman of times past who came to us with a smile and whisper of love as she departed your world. Her memoirs have been written many times within the pages of your books.

She whispers in your ear to be kind to yourself and not respond to those who whisper words of negative thoughts and feelings. She has recognised that many of your world today are darkened by the thoughts of those of power. A brave new world is needed to allow the aspects of light to once more shine as petals upon the flower bud.

You have spoken many times before about the need for love, but we need your assurance of your commitment, for we long to tell our story to the nations of your world. Complete and utter tolerance is required to adapt to the new beginnings about to erupt. She *(Pamela)* will guide your hand as you march forward with banners, as she did, in protest of the obscene goings-on. Her mind works with expectation as she feels the need to tell you of her life in the backwoods in the forests of her nation.

"Constance was a companion for many years, she watched over me as I progressed my life, like a mother taking the hand of a child. She would nurture me when I was down and follow me to the ends of the earth with grace and beauty. Her name was not well known, for like a background rose, she shone out to brighten my days of solitude. Ah, such times are past now, and the bluebells of spring will once more bloom in your world of gloom."

Be not ashamed of your abilities to help others with messages of hope. We are grateful that you are a man of purpose. Complete your mission with words of love and tolerance so that the many nations can see how beautiful the world could be.

Pamela, she guides your hand as an artist, as a writer, for she knew what it took to accomplish popularity with freedom of speech.

Useful information will be given of the trimester of this month to know a practice of clairvoyance upon you three, for our need of you grows in earnest each and every day, as our wisdom is imparted upon you. I speak for the nations of love through your words and your book. Pamela will assist with inspiration, for she knows what it takes to publish your desires.

You have commanded your mind upon a path, a road, to bring joy to others, and it is commendable that your work grows in leaps and bounds, but a balance is required so that you can carry out your duties as a man of purpose. Control your emotions to those of intolerance; show them your love and not your back. For men of great deeds are born every day. Your life is a promise of hope to others, ego has nothing to do with this, but balance of life has. Do not separate your mind to believe that you are not worthy my son. Ah, we know the difference between a man of purpose and that of greed and want.

Collaboration between the men of the earth and us will not bring about peace. The material hidden from your view is obvious to their eyes. They must relinquish their control over man with an open mind. It is a hard thing for them to do, for they cannot see profit in it. Those sad minds, they only think of the meagre things of life. How can such minds be brought into focus? Ah, but they must all follow their pattern of life, and in their final days as they look back on their life, they will come to a conclusion that life had a deeper meaning, more than just the almighty pound and dollar and money.

Transparent your minds are, so easily read. Yours Michael, is an open book, truly you cannot grasp the meaning of things, your simple mind works in mysterious ways, it follows a

pattern that was set long ago. Evolve you must, as all things in the world must evolve to a higher purpose. Don't be ashamed to speak your mind to those who you deem *(to be)* educated, for what they know, what about what you know? They cannot possibly understand the thought patterns that mirror your image. Tremendous amounts of values were given, as you bridge this world from the physical. No longer do you feel the need to look back upon indiscretions. Look forward to the light follow your heart and will as we guide you to Heaven's Gate.

This is not just about you, these words are given for all to understand that their lives are of the same purpose, they all have meaning to which they would never understand, but keep your faith in the light and love of the Lord as he brings blessings upon you.

25th August 2016

Message from Andrew

Andrew is my name. The climax of your life is yet to come. Let your strength grow. Bring purpose my son, do not overshadow those who aspire to follow in your footsteps, show them guidance in the light so that they may follow your path, as people of inspiration must be fed the knowledge. Do not be selfish with the things that you have learnt, but guide others with your books of love.

28th August 2016

Message to Michael from the 12 Apostles of the light

A Metaphorical Message of Encouragement to Michael to Continue His Work

Contemporary art, spoken of many times. Wishful thinking by many, but art itself in its pure form are paintings of sheer delight to the eye. They demonstrate the artist's talent of observation and coordination between the eye and the hands. For what is an artist, but a hand that brings beauty and light and presence onto the canvas that he works.

Brian was a man with many talents. In his new works of art he established many new frontiers as he broke the barriers of criticism. His new-age theme brought many to tears as they began to understand his outlook on life. How bashful he was, a shy man, retiring, never wishing to be seen, but only to display his art to give the message of the Lord through the brushstrokes of his art. He caressed each stroke with an embrace of love; his eye followed the lines of beauty as he strove to create a masterpiece.

The masterpiece was in himself, his outlook and aspect of all life, for he saw the world in glorious colour, with depth and dignity. He published his art many times before the public who shunned him as being 'peculiar', but he established himself a foothold, as you must create a foothold of your own to bring the purpose of the Lord to man's eyes.

As the artist creates his pictures of beauty, so you must develop your words to infect the minds of men to the beauty that are held within. For all aspects of the words given have depth and meaning. Some will not appreciate your efforts to rule the world of literature with your 'mindless thoughts', this is how they will portray your efforts, but you know without a doubt of our sincerity, and the thought of mind is a powerful tool and weapon to use against the men of ignorance. For how can they combat something that is created within the spirit of God and brought through in the thoughts of men? Interfere not with the messages, but bring them justice as was intended by us of the light.

Contrary to your thoughts, we have been many times to bring aspects of light to your life. You ignored us in your tender years, but glory be as your eyes opened with an aspect of love, which now supersedes your fear and a common practice of man. Target your emotions with a sense of triumph in the knowledge that fear no longer rules your life, that anger that betrayed your thoughts diminishes by the day, as you turn to the aspects of light and love.

We have no practices to give, or practical messages of how you should create abilities and aspects within your lives, but a warning is given, not to overstep the mark, as there is a limit to which all men have purpose. You are privileged by your time as a man upon the Earth. It is a special time, whereby creation has infected the minds with sight and sound, memories of love that have been. Never neglect your hearts thoughts my son, as they come from the centre of the universe of light and love and rebound your emotions of unworthiness, for they are not real and do not reflect your aspects of love.

A new being *(One of the 'Twelve')* **now speaks of the state of our world and change to come.**

Stand up and be counted he said, counted for what? For a miserable life or for a joyous new beginning? I was a man; I am the man, who had a heart of gold to shine to the world beyond my temple of light. Cast doubt out of your mind. If you require peace, then it is your duty and obligation to bring that special light to your fellow man. We are of the 12 who have come once before, the apostles of the light, you see in your mind's eye our names, Joseph and Mary, Bartholomew, Gilbert and the many who watch over you from this realm of beauty.

We hear your need is great at this time. We cannot say for certain, let it carve your world as it descends ever spiralling into the abyss. Know this, men of purpose and focus will shine the light and bring a new dawn, a new day, in which all will rejoice in his name and marvel at the new beginnings of time.

Your 20th-century will seem as the dark ages, as you begin to experience many things within many nations, aspiring to allow in the light of our being. Come now, be at peace, let us draw your attention to the art works of the spiritual world, for they are spectacular in their beauty, beyond man's comprehension and desire. Truly your aspects of love must grow with purpose and you must muster the many to follow the word of his light.

We have contemplated your thoughts, your memories of your past lives and how in leaps and bounds you grow in stature as a man of courage, not of death, but of light. Your need is great at this time, as is others, our inspiration will open the world's eyes to the possibilities that humankind can survive these dark ages of modern times.

It will be necessary for a meteorological change within your atmosphere to bring about this purpose. A fearsome wind will blow as it descends upon your planet. It creates a situation of panic in many countries of your world. It will assist in the new beginnings. Many will perish, many will survive, there is no guarantees in life, for your paths were written before your time. But know that you will witness the dawn of a new age of a new mankind. For if this destruction does not bring about change then men will surely cease upon the planet Earth.

1st September 2016

Message to Michael from the beings of light

We cannot display our thoughts before your eyes until you are ready to see our being my son. We know you are longing for interaction, a face-to-face meeting. It is not always possible or wise. We feel you are ready to witness the sight of our being, but in patience. We have gratitude for your fortitude in your work and your longing to make a difference to the beings of your planet. Allow your purpose to grow slow and steady, for as a hill to be climbed, a rush would bring disappointment, as you will be exhausted before you reach the summit.

A slow and steady climb is necessary to take in the beauty that surrounds you, to see that knowledge is gained with temperance and time, and never lose focus as you climb that mountain of love, your efforts will be rewarded in many ways in days to come.

We are the beings of the light. We bring you no respite, as you requested to work for the needy of your world. Be assured your rest will come on a positive outlook and a creative mind for your purpose in knowledge in writing. You feel unworthy to complete such a task, but she is here to assist, Pamela is an author of many words, her purpose is with you. *(Pamela Kiddey who worked with Doris Stokes)*

Pamela Kiddey speaks:

"Good evening my son, I wrote but a few books, the lines of which were seen by many before her *(Doris Stokes)* path of light. I could not help but to wonder how your purpose has not been seen. You compare yourself with that of a fool, but your words gain respect in the manner in which they are written. Let us start to imagine that you Michael, are the author of a book. Your name should not be used for it is a book of love, and your recognition is not essential, for it is not a novel but a book of fact.

Separate your mind from your thoughts of unworthiness. Speak to your machine in a manner of worthiness. Bring purpose to your words; never start your lines with a judgement, but with an outlook of a child looking to his mother for guidance. We have seen many times, the many things, in the ways and patterns that are written of the realm of spirit. You must not allow these to influence you. By your very nature and your thought from the heart you must write. Take pen to paper without thought. Comparatively with a purpose, I was seen by the public eye. Until that time arrives, allow your mind focus."

4th September 2016

A Message of Encouragement from James the Apostle to Michael and also to Valerie, telling her of past lives.

A pleasurable evening to you all. I have become aware of the circumstances within the brethren of the light, do not fear these beings who bring peace and hope to you all in a physical way. I was once a master's teacher; I am now honoured to sit in the presence of the Lord our Father. He once gave me a commandment to reach out and send the Lord's words far and wide within your world. I was a man not capable of understanding the true meaning and power of his mighty voice.

Now I bring you hope that he will sacrifice once more, one of his own, to bring you purpose in your lives. Don't despair my son, as you witness the many atrocities against the people of the earth, their spirits and souls suffer many things. You have witnessed much sin that will be seen by him upon high. I have guided your hand these past decades, you have not been aware of my being and that's all right, you finally found me as I reached the hand of the Lord to you. Do not delay in bringing about the task of immensity beyond your imagination. You cannot know your true destiny for it is hidden from you my son, but be the child of the light and bring together those that surround your life, hold their hands, encircle them with your love and light, allow our words to shine through and give blessing to those who would listen and read of their content. He once told me that my purpose would be great, I never had doubt. As you see the things unfold, become that man of destiny.

It has been witnessed many times in these past decades, men of science finding new discoveries every day. Truly they inspire others to bring about change in purpose and lives. The utensils of life are your spirit and soul; they are there to ease your burden. You must not behave in reckless ways, so as to damage that delicate balance of life, but bring yourselves to an aspect, to search your heart and soul for that place in which you need to be.

We are here as servants of the Lord and Master, our father, to shine the light of truth upon your people, they require assistance. Many times our thoughts have been banished by those who would not listen, we need an ear to combat those of ignorance, so let it be heard, let our names resound in the minds and hearts of those who practice within his light, for his mercies are great.

We have spoken many times of your purpose, but what of others? Of those who follow your words and feel inspired. They too will be heard, lift up your voices and speak, as you speak to your neighbour, for we are there beside you awaiting your call. We will not ignore or misunderstand the reasons behind your purpose, just once in a while open to us, unto our love and guidance.

Truly she has need of many arms around her when she considers the possibility of a burden set before her. Valerie, she has come with purpose, for a life of love for which she bore foundation to many of your world. She came before in life to enlighten minds of ignorance. She sacrificed her burden in those dark days, in those times when women were not heard or seen by the veil. She has lived many times; her secrets are to be revealed in her thoughts of the mind. She will be astounded to know that she was a figurehead to those of misfortune. Her healing practice was born decades ago before her present time; her purpose unfolds a magnitude of love. Her thoughts are for her husband as he sits by her side contemplating the mysteries of our being.

4th September 2016

Trevor Howard speaks to Michael with a message for us all

Trevor once more would like to intercede on the pattern of his life. You thought he was he the Bard, *(Shakespeare)* for he is a man of mystery. Complimentary you are to him with your thoughts. Treasure your books, for within the pages the secrets are revealed. The pathway to eternity can be found in the plays of life. Separate your minds thoughts from that of the Bard, for he delivered wistful, amusing stories. They were magical to the population of those times. Trevor cannot say that his identity would make a difference to the understanding of man and their ways of error.

Navigate your lives and follow your purposes to become the playwrights of the future.

For he who sits on top of the mountain and shouts the loudest, will be the one who reaches the minds and souls of those who watch in despair. My connection is not known, for my mind's thoughts were many. I acted out his plays, the sombre impressions of love. I could not control my emotions as I stood there and performed as many words of inspiration of such a playwright. His focus upon me as an actor of life was great, Howard will give you a clue. Huh! I see your realisation my boy *(the author suddenly realises it is Trevor Howard speaking!)* but focus upon the stage of life, do not allow your emotions to overstep the mark, as your future is bright.

Behind the scenes, men of aspiration who cause change are seldom seen by their peers, for remarks will be made as to the transcripts and their relation to life. Ah, they cannot hide from the Almighty eyes of the Lord. There, I have spoken my name; rest assured peace will be upon you all in the forthcoming days that act out life's desperation.

Be a poet of life and stride on the stage to enlighten those with a common practice of love to defeat those who would betray your trust. I was once an actor upon the stage of life. As you all lead your paths of life, you also perform the many acts in the creation of the sonnet. Be blessed with love and good fortune. Never let it be said that one man is equal to another, for all men who hide behind the skirts of fame are equal in his eyes.

4th September 2016

Message to Michael from Pamela Kiddey and Doris Stokes

Strike a pose she sang, indeed, for your purpose you must do the same. Strange you think, that Madonna is summoned! We need to create respect, hmm, hmm, riddles, easy! We do not expect to bring burden on you, but respect not the maiden of pop, but her love of the Almighty.

Crystal clear are the thoughts that you welcome into your mind, bring a focus to those who you visit to the near future. Allow them to see our words as we respect their attitudes. Commence your plans within your writing; do not delay for time is short for man on earth. She (Pamela) has brought you focus, do not betray her thoughts but bring them justice. Treasure your memories of love and the thoughts and concerns that you harbour.

(Doris Stokes)

She was once a lady who became a woman of great stature. Her name resounds in your mind as a teacher, as a guide within her books of love, let her mind be a focus upon yours. She once said that she would bring proof, come back from the dead to bring evidence. Do you not wonder why this great lady was unable to do this? Ah, the carnation she shows, she loved her flowers, bless. But now she is happy with her blessed son. She did not feel the need to bring the evidence that she taught to many who brought her love. She shone her wisdom to those of the audience on the stage of life. Her thoughts are with you as you perform your duties. Be solemn my son, work hard, with a keen eye and ear to bring a focus to the words of love.

"It cannot be said that I sat on my bum, I worked bloody hard. Indeed my life was of pain. Ah, my John, he brought an aspect of love to comfort me. Compare me not with those upon high, I am a mum and a lady as before. My pain has ceased, my deliverance was just.

Be not afraid of your paths, ridicule will follow you, but their need will be great. Have an open heart to those who wish to speak with your mind Michael. Reverence and justice are the keys to unlock the love that is held within your spirit. There may come a time when you will recall the many blessings awarded to you, but the greatest blessing of all is to work within the light, with a true and honest heart and belief that life ever after exists for all.

I sat there giving my readings, I called them out before me when I sat on the stage of life. As a woman of mediocre means

I was privileged to sit with him, my husband, who followed me shortly after. We reside now with our John; you know of his name. I am pleased to see you recognised the teachings I tried to get across in life, scripts. God bless you, follow the path of the light, others will follow in your footsteps for you are one of many in this pattern of life."

13th September 2016

Message for Michael about past lives

You have come once before as a man of immense strength and power. You used to defeat the opposition in their circles and dreams. The masses would gather calling your name, Brutus.

Julius Caesar, he was known for his ferocity and his roar of discontent to those who would not kneel before him. How would you not know that your future path would be of a tyrant? You are but a simple man now, those days are past when, "Hail Julius!" was heard in the auditoriums of the circus. Still your strength lies within as a man of the light to hold up his battle shield and cry for freedom. Yoke this strength that is within, Michael. Your bodice is different, you wear the clothes as man, you are no longer a wolf in sheep's clothing, but a lamb of the light.

Share your knowledge and your wisdom from within as you speculate upon your being, you know your strengths, your power and your weaknesses. You have learnt many lessons throughout time; you have won battles of the mind and body to become the man that you are. We hear you say, "This is not about me." But we say this, all that you are, is what you are. Never be ashamed, that tower of strength is held within. Your sins of those days are past, you walk the path of light to guide others with strength and fortitude, in fervent hope that peace will reign once more within the world of man and that Mother Earth will breathe once more the clean air that she once did.

Times are changing; the powers to be will lose their grip as the nations see the indignities committed against them. The loved ones lost through greed and power will no longer be tolerated, as an outcry of immense proportions will be heard. Bring their minds to peace; help them to be inspired by the Lord with the words of truth. He forgets the man that you are and once were.

18th September 2016

Message to Michael from James

I am James, the one who calls your name from beyond. Your call has been heard my son; I tread with you upon the path of life to bring joy to others.

Your task is much; my thoughts are with you as I bring you news of joyous times ahead. Many of interest will walk the path by your side, they will respect the wisdom carried within the words in the book of love.

You once were a man of ignorance, but you saw the light, you followed the path to right a wrong. Now lead others on that same path, they will think of you as being one of righteous nature, but you are merely a man. You know in your heart that you will deny your ability to others that you have a connection, but you cannot hide the truth to those that would see. Never advance above your station my son, you are a man on an honourable path to follow. You will lead many to salvation through the words of the writings; you know they are not of your words but from the heart of spirit. Do not flay yourself with fears of ego, for your practice of love, we are aware of your humble being in your practice to assist man in ways of the Lord. Combat your fears my child, for we do not feel that you neglect the trust given.

22nd September 2016

James and Pamela Kiddey talking to Michael also Peter about Michaels past lives

You are a fisherman, a fisherman of love. You Michael, must angle the words and fashion them in a manner of love. She will escort you in the days of your writing, be not afeard, for her energy will surpass your mind. She has wisdom in her years to bring you knowledge of the words in the pen. Be fruitful; allow them to flow in the hand of love as your master guides your hand. She is Pamela *(Kiddey),* Oh she yearns to once more become a part of the words of men. She found joy in the writings as you do. Bring her justice in your love and accept her abilities as a gift. Be calm and observe and absorb.

(Pamela now speaks)

"Together Michael we will write, no fear of the words, the punctuation will come. A brief is all that's necessary to bring about a meaningful page. Let the rhythm flow like the waters over a waterfall, for as they fall, they grow in energy and as the water hits the floor below, so it rebounds in a flurry of white mist. Mmm, we will work together in a practice of love my boy. Doris Stokes is a member of a family I knew well. She rests now with her Michael, but she sends her wishes and a bouquet of flowers to all who listen and read your words, for as in life she served the Lord our father. Her head rests with her son. Ah, what a scene. I am Pamela, I will be there to assist, call my name. Bless be to you."

Combat your fears of avarice my boy, for what brings multitudes. You know in your heart that giving is what matters most. Ah, time to let go and be the man you once were in those combat days, when muscle and brawn were your gift. Oh, you fought; there was no glory in this arena, spectacle of blood and fear. You have grown since; become a man of faith within your heart. What purpose did that fearsome time hold for you? You murdered and slayed many, but whose heart suffered most? You know the answer, those days are gone, you are a different man, but keep that strength of heart, not for slaying the innocent, but for being powerful in mind.

You were not of noble birth in those times, you were but a peasant boy brought to bear in the circus arena of those days.

Marcus Aurelius *(circa AD161 to AD180.)* was your master, he tormented you in many ways, you were servant, a slave, but you grew. As you grew you learnt the many ways of the combat arena. Glory you thought, to behead a man with one swipe of your blade, to hear the crowds roar as the lions. They shouted and screamed. In your heart you knew your sorrow and the shame you had brought upon your soul. Still you thought, "Glory be to me!" Humph. What a lesson you had to learn. As the angels of light who have guided your hand once more from those desolate days, they are glad to see your purpose unfold.

Shield yourself from those who will harbour indignations to your words, they will think that you want the glory for yourself. Further from the truth they cannot be, we know your gentle soul and your purpose is true. Neglect not your gift my son, for it is your purpose, and yours alone to issue words of comfort to the population of Earth. You think you'll not be heard. But have faith in us my child, you know, we know what's best in the hearts of men.

27th September 2016

Message to Michael and Valerie

You are tested by your practices of love. Your purpose is great and yet to unfold. But you must not suffer intolerances against others. Be brave, rejoice in your heart. The white horse comes with the shining light to assist in your power and energy. On the path are treacherous pitfalls as you walk. Be not afeard of him as he walks before you, clearing the way with the light of his love. Have purpose my son, the many pointless words and phrases to abide by are reassurances that are necessary, as his love unfolds for all before him. Search out your hearts and have focus within them to bring you joy. We will join you as you focus upon the world, peace within your communities of circles.

Valerie has suffered greatly in the past; she will not tell you of the things that she tolerated. But know this, her circle of light is that of love and as it shines out to other nations on the morrow you can be sure that the light will be seen by all those of love. Bring your own purpose to assist in communication, help them to achieve a mighty light, to bring a positive change upon the world of men. As your minds focus as engaged minds, the spirits of light, we will join you to help in your thoughts, we cannot focus upon those who would wage war. Your prayers are heard and maybe answered with a respect and love befitting your worship. We will join you; our energy will be felt as you submit your minds to your peaceful purpose my children.

2nd October 2016

Transmit your minds thoughts my boy. A level of interest in your words is being created beyond your knowledge. There is the one who watches, reads and listens to the many facets in the things told. He does not pretend to understand them all, but he watches with interest nonetheless. Ah, he may have purpose for you within the general population, within your time. Accept his acknowledgement and appreciate his interest, for he will assist in the book of love. He can promote your words in a way far exceeding your own abilities.

The book is written to give a practice of love to man, keep this in mind Michael. No self-expression, no words of explanation, as the explanation is in the words themselves. You struggle to put pen to paper and to draw up approval. Relax, the time is there.

Doris Stokes speaks

The Rose, the petal will fall upon you as you promote those beings. I am here, Mrs Stokes, Doris to many. You know my promise to return should the opportunity arise. I have seldom spoke to many of my passing and you know of me through my books of love, my life stories. Pamela *(Kiddey/Doris)* Stokes, a combination of love. Truly remarkable, your ascendance into the light, out of no-where. Keep control Michael, for your mind must operate in a manner of love and allegiance to the thoughts of our father, to enable your purpose to be fulfilled. I am here with my Michael, my John. Memories filled full of love, as I once witnessed this place of spiritual realm. So you can also travel within your mind to explore the places of tranquillity. Have courage in your writing, do not be thwarted by the thoughts of others; you need no help other than your own abilities, as they will shine. Pamela guides you in ways you do not understand; she has a mind and a focus, the will of the people.

I was as you, a working-class person, nothing to hand but my own goodwill and a measure of love and tolerance. Never be defeated by the thoughts that you are just merely a man. Speculate and formulate a position of caring for others and in your writing, be honest and follow the words of your thoughts. Transmit your love through the energies present that will uphold you and give you uplift with a measure of love. Time is but a curtain that calls for us all. As we cross that veil of light you will see a man of distinction, not of pride or ego, but one of a purpose. Never let go your feelings of love, share it with compassion, show it to others with pride and teach them the path of the light. You fear your memories coming in, don't worry, tell it as it is, you were born of England, your friend Winston has given you ideas how to be a master of your own life and destiny. Ah, I must go, to my friend Mary I say this, I returned! Humph, well she's joined us now, so it is a pointless message, but one I wanted to say. Have a heart, live your life as God intended, let the purpose unfold and unite and bond you all in love.

- - - - - - - - - -

Do not weep for those who suffer Michael, for they have God in the hearts, they have peace of mind. (*Michael's note: it was at this point in my mind's eye I could see a temple with stone pillars, all in white, and in front of me was a figure dressed in white robes with his hands clasped as if in prayer.*

He invited me to sit and it was so peaceful. I was in the presence of Jesus himself – that is how he made me feel.) You see him stood before you in a robe of white, hands clasped in prayer. "Come join, walk with me. Temperance and tolerance and love, allow your heart to shine, you know me? Father, thou art with me in practice of the Lord. Sit and eat the grapes of life, know the wisdom is with him, do not speculate a man's future, for it is written with love."

- - - - - - - - - -

Do you not sit and wonder, and gaze at stars above? Do you not understand that the universe is but a small part of the greater being? You are but grains of sand in a vast desert of life. You cannot understand the vastness of all aspects of life. As you walk within the sand you feel the grains move beneath your feet, this is a sign that all things change and move on. Your footprint will remain for a time and then will vanish as if it never was, but your soul will remain in that place, invisible to others, but with purpose and energy.

2nd October 2016

Message to Michael, Valerie and Kevin from the beings of light

You will be aware of our presence as you dictate your writings to the world. Be not afraid of the future my son, for it holds many wonders, many beautiful things, that as yet are not seen by man.

Your commentaries upon the state of the countries of the world and indignities set against his peoples and Mother Earth are well noted.

You lack the vision to respond to others who call you a charlatan. Valerie, she protects you as a mother protects a child. She will call upon those with questions, to answer to her. Why is it your mind will not allow our words to flow? We will continue as intended, for your mind sets up a barrier, you must not build walls.

Valerie, she is a woman who has special needs, but her tender heart and loving care extends selflessly to the world, as does her husband who sits there and writes his memoirs in a book. He never forgave those who would not hear him out, hmm, but he does not harbour grudges, for he too is a man of the light, and like a match that sets a flame, they burn bright with each other's hearts.

Their fortitude is a measure of love, and unparalleled by many. They have grasped the issues of life and taken the bull by the horn as it were. They radiate light within their home, and their cat who was blessed with their company, sits upon their bed as if it never changed. They feel as it moves across the bed to lay at the feet of Valerie, a purr is heard but ignored by the many as he sits upon the bed of love. He is at peace with his brothers and sisters who were of his litter; they collect together and remember those days of their youth. Ah you think, what does an animal know, ah you would be surprised at the memories that are held within the smallest of creatures upon your earth. You think yourselves the only ones capable of such a feat, but believe us when we tell you that all life retains a memory of purpose, of being, and the shadows of things that were, remain within their souls as memories of love or uncaring.

Crisp are your memories of your childhood, but lacking are your memories as you grow old, as the cells in your mind recede. The old grey matter they call it, well, it's a term, but that is not important. What is, is the power that runs through it, the energy that thrives upon the life. Did you know that your lives are of the light? Well of course you did. But also, that the messages you bring are for those in the world who are less fortunate than yourselves and do not understand the beings of the light and the hereafter.

There are many in your world who have a caring heart but shut it out for fear of it being seen. An unusual practice, but common. Worship those around you that share your love, give them rest and light. You are no healer in the physical sense, but in the minds of others you give them peace of heart through the messages imparted upon you. Be not of the lion with your anger *(or)* fierceness, but be gentle, retain that strength of the lion, but temper it with love, for it will be needed shortly in the trials and tribulations set before you.

We will not allow you to know the reasons, but to reassure you that we will be by your side and you will be tested to the full. Have peace in your life, temperance and love and a tolerance for others who are ignorant in the ways of the Lord. Be blessed with talents that are given in recognition by others, that their lives are of value and of purpose.

16th October 2016

Message to Michael from The Arcturians

Constantly we see struggle in your life Michael, you must resist the upheaval, for it taunts you. Do not become that of the dark, but have focus upon the light and the love of our Lord, our father in heaven. Torment you they will, as your mind sees things of a nature that should not be. But don't be alarmed, for we are here to assist and guide your thoughts in loving prayer, in hope and in glory of his name.

Sisters and brothers of the earth, remember my name, for I once was a God of the earth, renowned for my institutions for authority above all creatures of the earth. I am now a spirit and devoid of any misgivings. But I see the reckless behaviour of your nations coming to a boiling point. It is not necessary to neglect our thoughts and our passions, for we are not of intolerance nor judgement. We need to sow the seed of love into the souls of darkness. As it grows, allow it to spread throughout your men of the earth, acknowledging our willingness to bring about a peace to the men of the earth.

24th October 2016

We have spoken of many things, given many words from various nations of life and existence. Your Merriwether was a man a purpose as he strove to bring your practice to bear upon others, you continue your work with a measure of love. Do not define your practices as being odd, or strange, for they are a practice of love in which many evolve from a mere mortal to the man of the light.

26th October 2016

Message to Michael from Pamela Kiddey

Pamela, she is at your side asking for your commitment to her purpose to assist. Allow your mind a focus and bring a better peace to your world to allow her to share her fortunes of life and of love. She inspires you with words of inspiration, coaxing your energy to that of the positive way of thinking. Your knowledge grows each day in the aspect of light, but we wish to inform that you that cannot continue bringing a purpose to man unless your heart, mind, body and soul are willing to release.

20th November 2016

Peter thanking Michael

Congratulations my son, on your achievements in bringing notice to our being. It is a long road that you tread, for we are here to help your light. Be careful of the feelings of many as you negotiate with others of a practice not of ours. You feel confused as to who to trust. We are eager to bring a nature of light to you all; we will cancel out any negative images, thoughts of beings, extra-terrestrials that would infect your mind. There are those of goodness and wisdom, but equally those of the dark exist within your realm to this day. This is a fight to be continued upon many levels of existence. Your mind adjusts its frequencies and your will is set to a practice of love; may God bless you on your journey. Have faith and trust in our words and wisdom, as we link our arms around you in a circle of light. Betray not those who have a thought of 'Is this real?' For they cannot understand the true meaning of Christmas and the one who came. Tell them that their love must negotiate many twists and turns within life and their light must vanquish the dark. – Peter.

22nd November 2016

Message to Michael from Pamela Kiddey

Pamela negotiates with your mind and your purpose of writing; she wishes to inform you that her skills will be imparted upon you. We have need of many around you; to welcome them is a glorious thing. We sit here in the presence of angels watching over those as they practice the light.

We once spoke of hard desperate times, we wrote these words as a whisper in your ear. Dramatic times have occurred since. Our purpose has not changed, but on a different level, your teachers are vibrant in colour, bringing many aspects of thought to your mind, allowing you scope and vision and purpose, and know this, that as she sits in her chair of comfort. Her Michael sits with her. We worked together many times behind the scenes, and you remember her writings, how frequently they seem to coincide with your life. It is no coincidence you sat to read these books, they were a guidance like no other. Dear, dear Doris, she talks of many but in spirit. Bringing peace to those in turmoil, she is a blessing on them, who has earned the right to rest in that glorious place beyond your world.

Come with us on a special journey to the regions far beyond your earth. Your treasured memories are lost at this time, and as all who live upon the earth, forget from whence they were begat. Your memories are sharpened by the lessons given, and a focus that has enhanced your being. Pamela has much respect for those of a nature of goodness. She began her writing career in a very stubborn manner. Her progress was slow, education lacking, but that did not stop her as she progressed the years, bringing her mind to focus and her heart set upon a career of literature. She joined with her husband, your namesake in the year twenty-eight, they were a formidable couple who brought many a tear to the eyes of those that read their books.

She shines upon you with a thought of love, preparing you for your purpose. Be not ashamed to speak these words, as there is much wisdom and honour in them. Let us inform you that your endeavours to instruct others are falling on deaf ears, but they have a keen eye for the truth, a thought entered their mind as to, "Who is this man to speak such words of divine, in such a manner so as to make me consider my own thoughts." Ah, the magic of love has a tremendous power that can overwhelm the soul and mind, bringing it to focus upon those necessaries as you strive through your life, your love.

Champion your thoughts in the minds of others with wisdom, do not deceive them with mindless thoughts. Your anchor is a ground upon which many will rely, as they endeavour to contemplate, to comprehend the world of matter.

16th December 2016

A Poignant Message to Michael

Noticeably your thoughts are very wild, varied and wild at this time, as your concerns are great for your loved ones. Be at peace my son and know that all has been brought an aspect of love.

She will not suffer for long, but you must suffer for longer, combat your thoughts and fears my child as you know the wisdom of our word is true. We hear your voice in prayer and be assured there is love and healing. You seldom ask for yourself, be generous to all. Terminations in life are many and frequent, but all should be reborn into that place of love and light. Yours will be no different when that time comes, but you will have an understanding and knowledge greater than most, but not of all.

(This message was thankfully not fully understood at the time, however, Michael's beloved wife Beatrice, passed to the light early in 2017.)

MESSAGES FOR THE TRIO

We hesitated whether to include messages for ourselves, however, we hope that by doing so it helps to authenticate the other messages within this book.

The title is given to us by spirit as they refer to us as 'The Trio'.

The Transcripts:

27th March 2016

Message for Valerie

She is here among us, Valerie, kindness of your heart beckons her to you, sweet child of the universe know your name, your purpose in life will be fired by the need of love, 'tis commendable that you, your circle works before the Lord and the light, you have purpose, focus beyond your understanding, comply with those who would seek your knowledge in matters of the light. You are tired from the struggles that bind and dominate your heart. Let go your past be free my child as you know as the bird flies the hawks wing is as powerful. Sparrows will come in the spring to greet your words of wisdom, your knowledge inspires others beyond your thoughts, true are you to your needs, conspire with others, work with others will bring you peace at this time, compare us not to those who worked for your fathers before you.

We are of the stars, Mars in your planetary system you know this to be true.

Your husband is your bond of truth, go with God in the knowledge your truth will be heard and the words written far across the lands of this world. Focus your mind upon the deeds to be done.

Margaret, your Margaret, she is with you sends her blessings and love with greetings from the woods of the valley known to you, her weaknesses are not yours she had fear of comprehension but yours is of strength.

Your sadness and sorrow at this time is noted and is not necessary for we know and how for your loss. *(Valerie's pet cat passed two days before this message was received.)*

29th March 2016

Message to Kevin

To enquire as to the whereabouts of the child of light. Her name is secret to you never fear what is given to you, your purpose is true, she whom you seek, be aware that she is with us at peace. Her name will be shared amongst you in due course, her purpose is far beyond your reach. *(In response to Kevin's thoughts about the fate of Madeleine McCann.)*

5th May 2016

About the Meeting of the Trio

Two others will come before you my son, their purpose is to travel with you on a road of light, compel your heart to listen and understand the meaning that they represent. For us, time is but a passage to be travelled, for once you have been a part of that moment, it will not return.

24th May 2016

Together you will make a trio who will make a stand in the progress of man in the annuals of time, bringing together your purpose and need for those who serve the light and the Lord. Reflections of light are mere shadows of the purposes that all must endure at this time. A relative peace will come before the storm as you negotiate your paths of life, be not afraid as the trio, for your strength will combine into one.

26th June 2016

Message from The Arcturians for 'The Trio'

Focus your minds, the three who work with temperance and tolerance, love in mind, your passage through time has not been equalled for some time now. You have been working upon a means to directly communicate with a need and passion of love. We have spoken to you in the past of formulations that will inspire others to guide your light. We picked this evening to help you further on your paths with a speculative notion that if we come before you, would you be aware of us? Do you think you could see us through the mask that we wear, for we hide from man so as not to be severe on their eyes, for our differences are only physical, our spirits are of love?

We speak of many things that bolster your enthusiasm to listen, you sit there and work upon their meaning, does there have to be a meaning? Can you just not accept these things we tell you are of a promise? We need your assistance to voice our minds in the hearts of man. A happening will occur which will bring you into focus in aspects far beyond your mind's comprehension.

Your skills in art will be recognised for what they are and your passion will be listened to by the ears of many as you go before them with a willingness and a love of spirit and God. Be not afraid of the many faces that will look upon the one who transmits messages with a purpose and need, we are here to assist on your journey. See the patterns before you as they formulate a new beginning on your life's path, for your spark of life will generate interest in the many places of your world.

Too many times we have seen the purpose fail through thoughts of desire and love, yours will be conquered in all aspects to archive your aims. Redirect your thoughts to love and a responsibility to others to bring them light and love and purpose within their lives. Never knowing your tasks until they are upon you, you will continue with a need and a focus so great, that tenderness and caring shall pass to those of burden as they look to you to necessitate their lives with a purpose and role. Role models of you in your world of intolerance will shine, as yours and your friends whom you have met in recent days, will all work together upon a path of light. Bringing your various aspects with knowledge and gifts. It is not for one man but for the many to sit in circle to open his purpose to the fore, you need not know your individual roles with your lives, but know this, that as a group, as a team of light workers you will reflect the Lords words in spiritual strength to all who observe and listen to your hearts of will and contentment.

28th June 2016

Message for Valerie from The Arcturians

Valerie has a purpose for which she does not understand at this time, she has brought together many souls, for healing. They muster their minds of those who call upon her, for her services be strong, give aid to those who bear countless crimes that healing is required to bring about a peace at their passing. Her name of fallen energies grow. As your purpose proceeds, be not afraid, for there will come a time when you will have succeeded in bringing happiness to many of those who have crossed your door.

7th July 2016

To Valerie from The Arcturians

Valerie, she knows of the circumstance that led her on the path of light and love, she has wandered many roads within her life, her regression of past lives are many unseen to her. She was a man of great distinction in a period of time that many were in the dark. Her life we are glad of, was truly amazing to the memories of the time. As Augustus to many. Her knowledge and wisdom is derived of many lives, she will control the outbursts of many.

19th July 2016

To Valerie from The Beings of Light

Valerie has come to the conclusion that she would like to sustain her connection with those troubled minds who came before her. Her radiance will enable them to see their paths of light on their well beaten tracks of life. Hmm, she has given many respite in their minds of worry, easing their burden with her love. Continuance of her ways is essential to bring purpose to others who have a need for the light. She now will not deny her special gift of love. Her doctrine will be accounted for in a book she will write in the autumn, talking of recent love and goodwill to men, as she creates a work of art with purposeful meaning to many. She documents many things of love and essence. She cannot cope with it all and is reliant on those closest to her for their support and willingness to give. But she must relinquish, hm this energy, to rest her mind for a short time. As any man can only do so much within one life.

1st September 2016

Message to Valerie from the beings of light

Valerie, she has thoughts to put in print. She hesitates not knowing as to whether she can justify the words. She has strength, but needs support to encourage her. She has called upon us many times to help in the rescue of souls and we have obliged. Her mind is in turmoil as she wrestles with the values of life. Bring her to a purpose, let her thoughts be your thoughts. They are a team who will respect those of purpose.

13th September 2016

Valerie and Kevin's past life

Valerie has come before to bear witness to many things, of possibilities within lives and in the different realms. She is witness to the sacrifice of love. Her heart is a haven for those who require peace of mind. She has fortitude and strength within her being. She has assisted many as the nightingale as it sits with the lark of the dawn chorus. Her husband, he has immense strength within his soul. He was once a man of generosity and fortitude. He is also unaware of his past being. He was a creator of much ability; he bore the name of a man with fortitude in his heart. Cast no doubts upon practices of love which they express. They ask no favours other than to bring peace to those who have passed this life and are but lost. Valerie, she would like to know the many things that Kevin was responsible for, he was a creative man who designed many things of your modern day. 'Within the light', will give you a clue, ha! He was a fortunate man to have expressed his views to the nations of the time through his powers of mind. Ah, we hear, you ask for his name, would it be wise to know this? We will consult. Valerie, you must excuse expressions of you, for we have many who would bear witness to your loving soul, you were a sister of mercy to which they came, you were a nun of ancient times.

22nd September 2016

Messages for The Trio from the angels of light

Hold your nerve as you are given many tasks to communicate with those of intolerance. They will not believe you at first, but they will see the truth in the words as they are issued, published. Your thoughts of love are great for others and your focus needs to sharpen my boy. She is with you as a guiding light, hmm, you know who I speak of, the situation. But it is only in passing; she is your strength, your right arm.

Consequently your life will be better for her in the days to come, you will become reliant on each other as strength weakens your bodies. Be not afeard of age my boy, for it is just an illusion, spirit never dies but will grow stronger as you come to a reasoning with the Almighty.

Bring purpose to man to have an outlook of love and light. For the many who read the transcripts will recognise the words as being true and good, for how can this man that some know bring forth such words of wisdom? He doesn't seem the type they say. Good old Mick, the old boy, humph! Well, their love and strength are there for you. God bless them. For their knowledge and wisdom that assists you at this time. You know of whom I speak. Valerie once more is mentioned and husband Kevin, the strength by which she gives. Their mutual interests in the many words spoken and their forbearance of others is an inspiration to all who should look to the light. There are many who watch you who also have purpose, who have not become aware as yet. Give them strength in our words of encouragement; tell them that they must focus upon their minds and their wisdom. Do not be tempted by material things of fame and fortune, for that will surely divert your path. Be humble when you approach, never speaking too loudly, but gently guide with wise thoughts and wisdom in your hearts.

2nd October 2016

Message to Michael, Valerie and Kevin from the Beings of Light

You will be aware of our presence as you dictate your writings to the world. Be not afraid of the future my son, for it holds many wonders, many beautiful things, that as yet are not seen by man.

In your commentaries upon the state of the countries of the world and indignities set against his peoples and Mother Earth, are well noted. You lack the vision to respond to others who call you a charlatan. Valerie, she protects you as a mother protects a child. She will call upon those with questions, to answer to her.

Valerie, her tender heart and loving care extends selflessly to the world, as does her husband who sits there and writes his memoirs in a book. He never forgave those who would not hear him out, hmm, but he does not harbour grudges, for he too is a man of the light and like a match that sets a flame, they burn bright with each other's hearts. Their fortitude is a measure of love and unparalleled by many. They have grasped the issues of life and taken the bull by the horn as it were, hmm. They radiate light within their home and their cat who was blessed with their company, sits upon their bed as if it never changed. They feel as it moves across the bed to lay at the feet of Valerie, a purr is heard but ignored by the many as he sits upon the bed of love. He is at peace with his brothers and sisters who were of his litter, they collect together and remember those days of their youth. Ah you think, what does an animal know, ah you would be surprised at the memories that are held within the smallest of creatures upon your earth. You think yourselves the only ones capable of such a feat, but believe us when we tell you that all life retains a memory of purpose, of being, and the shadows of things that were, remain within their souls as memories of love or uncaring.

Crisp are your memories of your childhood, hmm, but lacking are your memories as you grow old, as the cells in your mind recede. The old grey matter they call it, well, it's a term, but that is not important. What is, is the power that runs through it, the energy that thrives upon the life. Did you know that your lives are of the light? Well of course you did. But also, that the messages you bring are for those in the world who are less fortunate than yourselves and do not understand the beings of the light and the hereafter.

There are many in your world who have a caring heart but shut it out for fear of it being seen. An unusual practice, but common. Worship those around you that share your love, give them rest and light. You are no healer in the physical sense, but in the minds of others you give them peace of heart through the messages imparted upon you. Be not of the lion with your anger, fierceness, but be gentle, retain that strength of the lion but temper it with love, for it will be needed shortly in the trials and tribulations set before you. We will not allow you to know the reasons, but to reassure you that we will be by your side and you will be tested to the full. Have peace in your life, temperance and love and a tolerance for others who are ignorant in the ways of the Lord. Be blessed with talents that are given in recognition by others, that their lives are of value and of purpose.

17th November 2016

About Valerie and Kevin from the Father of Mercy and the Angels of Light

The flower of love is given to those with purpose. A blessing to all would be given of the light. I am the father of mercy and accept your prayers of worship, thoughts and good deeds, become men of the light.

Pressures upon you at this time are immense, but not insurmountable. Focus the practice of love to bring an outcome of goodwill. Valerie and Kevin work hard at your side, they are members of a race of beings unknown to them. They are enlightened by thoughts that they do not understand, but their hearts are good and their minds and souls practise a love that they do not deeply understand, but they know the good that it brings and the fulfilment for others that it gives. Your mind my son, is a focus. Become strong to bear the brunt of what is to come. Allow us to intercede, to bring wisdom and thoughts to nourish the mind of the men that you seek to enlighten.

Lightning Source UK Ltd.
Milton Keynes UK
UKHW041254141119
353531UK00001B/66/P

9 781786 236296